ROUTLEDGE HANDBOOK ON MIDDLE EAST SECURITY

Routledge Handbook on Middle East Security provides the first comprehensive look at Middle East security issues that includes both traditional and emerging security threats.

Taking a broad perspective on security, the volume offers both analysis grounded in the 'hard' military and state security discourse but also delves into the 'soft' aspects of security employing a human security perspective. As such the volume addresses imminent challenges to security, such as the ones relating directly to the war in Syria, but also the long-term challenges. The traditional security problems, which are deep-seated, are at risk of being exacerbated also by a lack of focus on emerging vulnerabilities in the region. While taking as a point of departure the prevalent security discourse, the volume also goes beyond the traditional focus on military or state security and considers non-traditional security challenges.

This book provides a state-of-the-art review of research on the key challenges for security in the Middle East; it will be a key resource for students and scholars interested in Security Studies, International Relations, Political Science and Middle Eastern Studies.

Anders Jägerskog (PhD) is Senior Water Resources Management Specialist at the Global Water Practice at the World Bank. His work focuses mainly on the Middle East and North Africa region. He is also Associate Professor (Docent) in Peace and Development Research, School of Global Studies, University of Gothenburg, Sweden. He is frequently consulted in national and international media on global water, conflict and security issues in the Africa and MENA region.

Michael Schulz (PhD) is Associate Professor in Peace and Development Research, University of Gothenburg, Sweden. He has published over 100 scientific articles, book chapters, debate articles and reports, and in particular extensively on issues in the Middle East and North Africa region, dealing with security, civil resistance, democracy and state building, conflicts, and regionalism.

Ashok Swain is a Professor of Peace and Conflict Research, UNESCO Chair of International Water Cooperation, and the Director of the Research School of International Water Cooperation at Uppsala University, Sweden. He received his PhD from the Jawaharlal Nehru University, New Delhi in 1991, and since then he has been teaching at Uppsala University. He has written extensively on new security challenges, water sharing issues, environment, conflict and peace, and democratic development issues.

ROUTLEDGE HANDBOOK ON MIDDLE EAST SECURITY

*Edited by Anders Jägerskog,
Michael Schulz and Ashok Swain*

LONDON AND NEW YORK

First published 2019
by Routledge
2 Park Square, Milton Park, Abingdon, Oxon OX14 4RN

and by Routledge
52 Vanderbilt Avenue, New York, NY 10017

Routledge is an imprint of the Taylor & Francis Group, an informa business

© 2019 selection and editorial matter, Anders Jägerskog, Michael Schulz and Ashok Swain, individual chapters, the contributors

The right of Anders Jägerskog, Michael Schulz and Ashok Swain to be identified as the authors of the editorial material, and of the authors for their individual chapters, has been asserted in accordance with sections 77 and 78 of the Copyright, Designs and Patents Act 1988.

All rights reserved. No part of this book may be reprinted or reproduced or utilised in any form or by any electronic, mechanical, or other means, now known or hereafter invented, including photocopying and recording, or in any information storage or retrieval system, without permission in writing from the publishers.

Trademark notice: Product or corporate names may be trademarks or registered trademarks, and are used only for identification and explanation without intent to infringe.

British Library Cataloguing-in-Publication Data
A catalogue record for this book is available from the British Library

Library of Congress Cataloging-in-Publication Data
Names: Jägerskog, Anders, editor. | Schulz, Michael, 1960– editor. | Swain, Ashok, editor.
Title: Routledge handbook on Middle East security / [edited by] Anders Jägerskog, Michael Schulz and Ashok Swain.
Other titles: Handbook on Middle East security
Description: Milton Park, Abingdon, Oxon ; New York, NY : Routledge, 2019. | Includes bibliographical references and index. |
Identifiers: LCCN 2018048135 (print) | LCCN 2018051153 (ebook) | ISBN 9781315180113 (Ebook) | ISBN 9781351718370 (Adobe Reader) | ISBN 9781351718363 (Epub) | ISBN 9781351718356 (Mobipocket) | ISBN 9781138749894 | ISBN 9781138749894(hardback) | ISBN 9781315180113(ebook)
Subjects: LCSH: National security–Middle East. | Middle East–Politics and government–21st century. | Middle East–Foreign relations–21st century. | Human security–Middle East.
Classification: LCC UA832 (ebook) | LCC UA832 .R68 2019 (print) | DDC 355/.033056–dc23
LC record available at https://lccn.loc.gov/2018048135

ISBN: 978-1-138-74989-4 (hbk)
ISBN: 978-1-315-18011-3 (ebk)

Typeset in Bembo
by Newgen Publishing UK

Printed and bound in Great Britain by
TJ International Ltd, Padstow, Cornwall

CONTENTS

List of figures	*xii*
List of tables	*xiii*
Notes on contributors	*xiv*

PART I
Global contemporary security trends and the Middle East   **1**

1   Perspectives on Middle East security: An introduction   3
Anders Jägerskog, Michael Schulz and Ashok Swain

The absence of security in the Middle East	3
Previous research on Middle East security	4
Brief history of the Middle East security context	5
New and emerging security threats in the Middle East	8
The Middle East and regional security complex theory	9
Structure of the book	11
References	14

2   Shifts in the global political and economic landscape and consequences
for the Middle East and North Africa   16
Alexander Atarodi

Global trends	16
The Middle East and North Africa	19
Global power shift and implications for the region	23
Final words	29
References	31

Contents

3	Conflicts in the Middle East and North Africa: An attempt at reframing	33
	Joost R. Hiltermann	

Introduction: Writing about conflict in MENA	33
Of lineages and earthquakes	34
Cluster I: The post-Ottoman order/disorder	35
Cluster II: The Arab–Israeli conflict	36
Cluster III: The 1979 Islamic Revolution: The rise of Shia Iran	38
Cluster IV: The 1979 siege of Mecca: Sunni radicalization	39
Cluster V: The 2011 Arab uprisings	40
External intervention as compounding factor	41
Intersecting trajectories	45
What does it all mean?	47
An afterthought	48
Appendix: An attempt at a typology of MENA conflicts of the past 50 years	48
References	50

4	US Middle East policy	53
	Stephen Zunes	

The evolution of US policy	53
Subsequent events	56
Nuclear non-proliferation	60
Israel	62
Conclusion	64
References	64

5	External intervention in the Gulf	66
	Matteo Legrenzi and Fred H. Lawson	

Introduction	66
Emergence of US dominance in the Gulf	66
Zenith of US predominance	68
Deterioration of US predominance	72
External rivals gain strength in the Gulf	75
Conclusion	77
References	77

6	The security implications of the Israeli–Palestinian conflict	80
	Michael Schulz	

The Israeli–Palestinian conflict	80
Brief historical overview of changing conflict dynamics	81
The Israeli–Palestinian security complex	82

Contents

	Personal and State security implications of the IPSC	84
	The security implications for sub-complexes of the IPSC	86
	The IPSC's security implications for the Middle East	90
	The global IPSC security implications	92
	Conclusion	93
	References	93

7 The future of Iraq's security — 96
Ibrahim Al-Marashi

Introduction	96
Conceptualizing Iraq's security	97
Iraq's hard security dilemmas	97
Dealing with ISIS remnants	100
Human security dilemmas	102
Conclusion	108
References	108

8 Security and Syria: From "the security state" to the source of multiple insecurities — 111
Philippe Droz-Vincent

Introduction	111
Syria as the archetypical insecure state in the Middle East	112
The 2011 uprising and the crushing of the demand for human security	118
Syria as a new regional and international security problem: A return to the classical security ritual?	123
References	125

9 Humanitarian aid to a Middle East in crisis — 127
Roger Hearn

Introduction	127
Aid and conflict	128
A brief history of humanitarian assistance in the Middle East	129
The Syria crisis	130
Facing the future: Aid and conflict in the Middle East	135
References	138

10 Peacebuilding in the Middle East — 141
Karin Aggestam and Lisa Strömbom

Introduction	141
Peacebuilding in theory and practice	142
Security sector reform in Tunisia	145
Environmental peacebuilding in Israel–Palestine	146

Contents

Women and institution building in Iraq	148
Youth and peacebuilding in Lebanon	149
Conclusion	150
References	151

PART II
Energy, resource issues and climate change as security issues in the Middle East
155

11 The water-energy-food nexus in the MENA region: Securities of the future 157
Martin Keulertz and Tony Allan

Introduction	157
The water security challenge in the MENA region	157
The "big water" challenge	158
The "small water" supply chain	159
The "big water" supply chain	160
Farmers and "big water"/"food-water"	160
Population growth in the food bowls: Another key risk factor to "big water"	160
A sober look at the agricultural potential of the MENA region	161
"Big water"/"food water" security threats	161
Alternatives to managing the "big water" supply chain	164
Lessons from the WEF nexus: Pursuing what is possible	164
Conclusions	165
References	166

12 The multidimensional aspect of water security in the Middle East and North Africa 168
Neda A. Zawahri

Introduction	168
Water scarcity	168
Transboundary water	170
Multidimensional water security	171
Building adaptive capacity	177
References	179

13 Food security in the Middle East 182
Hussein A. Amery

Introduction and overview	182
Eating more meat	185
Political stability and food security	186
Food refugees	190

Contents

Transnational threats to food security	191
Water mismanagement as a threat to food security	192
Foreign agricultural investments	193
Less food waste, fewer food imports	194
Conclusion	195
References	196

14 Climate-related security risks in the Middle East — 199
Dan Smith and Florian Krampe

Introduction	199
The Middle East region	200
Egypt: The transnational dimensions of climate-related security risks	201
Syria: The politics of climate-related security risks	203
Yemen: Tomorrow today?	205
Conclusion	207
References	208

15 The Nile and the Middle East: Interlinkages between two regional security complexes and their hydropolitical dynamics — 211
Ana Elisa Cascão, Rawia Tawfik and Mark Zeitoun

Introduction	211
Theoretical framework	212
Recent hydropolitical developments in the Nile Basin	214
Role of external partners in the Nile hydropolitical dynamics	216
2007/2008: Gulf countries in search of new land	218
Turkey as a strategic partner in the Nile Basin	222
Importance of Red Sea dynamics in the Nile hydropolitics	225
Conclusion	229
References	230

16 Water and security in the Middle East: Opportunities and challenges for water diplomacy — 234
Martina Klimes and Elizabeth A. Yaari

Introduction	234
Water, security and water diplomacy	235
Multi-track water diplomacy	236
Water diplomacy entry points: Lower Jordan River and Euphrates and Tigris	239
Linking the tracks: Prevailing challenges and emerging opportunities for water diplomacy	243
Conclusion	247
Acknowledgments	247
References	248

Contents

PART III
**Migration, political economy, democratization, identity and
gender issues and security in the Middle East**   **251**

17 Large-scale population migration and insecurity in the Middle East   253
    Ashok Swain and Jonathan Hall

    Population migration and the Middle East   253
    Middle East, labor migration and remittances   254
    The Middle East: The region of and for refugees   255
    Migration contributing to further insecurity in the region   259
    References   260

18 Security and political economy in the Middle East   261
    Raymond Hinnebusch

    Introduction   261
    Imperialism and resistance: Economic dependency as a security issue   261
    Oil and regional security   265
    The rentier state and security   268
    Oil wars and global intervention   271
    Conclusion   274
    References   274

19 The governance deficit in the Middle East region   276
    Michelle Pace

    Introduction   276
    Trust and the social contract in the Middle East and North Africa   277
    Trust and human security   279
    What is the nature of mistrust in Middle East societies?   280
    Consensus-building as a way forward to good governance?
       The case of Tunisia   281
    Conclusion: Rethinking the governance deficit in the Middle East   283
    References   283

20 The halting process of democratization in the Arab world: Current
    challenges and future prospects   286
    Hamdy A. Hassan and Hassanein T. Ali

    Introduction   286
    Political and democratic developments after the Arab Spring:
       An overview   287
    Significant challenges to democratization in the Arab world   291
    The democratization process and regional security: Issues and
       challenges   297

Contents

Conclusion: Future prospects for democratization and security
in the Arab world | 299
References | 300

21 Democracy and security in the post-Arab Spring Middle East | 303
    Rex Brynen

Introduction | 303
Authoritarian persistence and democratic change in the Middle East | 304
Regional (in)security and (dis)order | 307
Trends and trajectories | 311
Theoretical implications | 312
References | 313

22 Sunni–Shi'a relations and the Iran–Saudi security dynamic | 316
    Simon Mabon and Nic Coombs

Introduction | 316
The religious and the political | 317
Theological reflections | 318
Islamic narratives and political action | 319
A geopolitical approach | 322
The Arab uprisings and regional fragmentation | 324
Concluding remarks | 326
References | 327

23 Muslim women and (in)security: A Palestinian paradox | 328
    Maria Holt

Introduction | 328
Double standards | 330
Theorizing gender and conflict | 331
Islam/Islamism: A contributor to conflict | 333
Palestinian women and (the lack of) international intervention | 335
Conclusion | 336
References | 336

Index | *338*

FIGURES

2.1	Share of the world economy in 2000 and 2016 (GDP in PPP current prices)	18
2.2	Military expenditure (billion USD current prices) and as share of GDP (%)	25
2.3	Oil production and consumption in China and the US	26
2.4	Import of oil (mbd) from Saudi Arabia between 1990 and 2015	27
11.1	Water per capita in the Middle East and North Africa region	158
11.2	Population growth – in thousands – in the Euphrates and Tigris Basin countries	162
11.3	Population growth – in thousands – in the Arab Nile riparian countries	162
11.4	Population growth – in thousands – in the Jordan River Basin countries	163
13.1	Population of Egypt, Iran and Turkey (in millions)	185
13.2	Arable land per capita in Egypt, Iran and Turkey	185
13.3	Beef consumption in Iran (kilograms per capita)	186
13.4	Beef consumption in Egypt (kilograms per capita)	187
13.5	Beef consumption in Turkey (kilograms per capita)	187
16.1	Linking the water diplomacy tracks	244

TABLES

2.1	Key statistics for regional actors in the Middle East (all figures are for 2016)	22
6.1	The preferred solution to the Israeli–Palestinian conflict according to the Palestinians in the West Bank and Gaza Strip	86
11.1	Principal farming systems of the Arab countries	161
13.1	Climate change impacts on farming systems of the Middle East and North Africa region	183
13.2	Percentage of consumer expenditures on food, alcoholic beverages and tobacco that were consumed at home, by selected countries, 2011	188
13.3	Overall ranking of food security in the Middle East	189
15.1	Investors/shareholders in key Sudan projects	219

NOTES ON CONTRIBUTORS

Karin Aggestam is Professor of Political Science and holds the Samuel Pufendorf endowed chair at Lund University. She is also visiting research professor at Monash University and honorary professor at University of Queensland, Australia. Karin is the former director of Peace and Conflict Studies at Lund University and presently lead author for the International Panel on Social Progress and co-editor of the Routledge book series *Law, Conflict and International Relations*. Her interdisciplinary research interests include diplomacy, negotiation, gender, foreign policy analysis, peacebuilding, and the Middle East. She has published nine books and contributed to several Handbooks on Diplomacy, Conflict Resolution, Women, Peace, Security, Middle East Security, Environmental Peacebuilding and Political Psychology. Her articles have appeared in international journals, such as *Millennium, Ethics and International Affairs, Third World Quarterly, Hydrological Sciences, Peacebuilding, International Environment Agreement* and many others.

Hassanein T. Ali (PhD) is a Professor of Political Science at Zayed University. His research interests include: Gulf affairs, civil society, democratization, political violence, terrorism and Islamic movements in the Arab world. He has authored and edited tens of books, book chapters and journal articles in both Arabic and English. His list of publications includes: *Political Violence in the Arab Political Systems, The Political System and the Muslim Brotherhood in Egypt, The State and Development in Egypt, The Culture of Political Violence in the Arab World, Political Reform in the GCC States, Civil Society and Democratic Development in Egypt, Civil Society in the GCC States, Civil Society in the UAE, New Trends in Studying Arab Political Systems,* and *Terrorist Jihadist Organizations and Social Media.*

J.A. [Tony] Allan is a Professor at King's College London and SOAS London. He specializes in the analysis of water resources in semi-arid regions and on the role of global systems in ameliorating local and regional water deficits. In his early career he was concerned with hydrological and environmental issues but gradually turned his attention to the social and political when it became evident that environmental science could not explain why people manage water as they do. He pointed out that the water-short economies achieve water and food security not on the basis of their own water endowments but by importing water intensive food commodities. He identified the concept of virtual water. He provides advice to governments and agencies especially in the Middle East on water policy and water policy reform. His analysis of the critical situation of the water resources of the Middle East is set out in *The Middle East Water Question: Hydropolitics and the Global Economy* (2001). His most recent book is *Virtual Water: Tackling the Threat to the Planet's Most Precious Resource* (2011). In 2008 he was awarded the Stockholm Water Prize in recognition of his contribution to water science and water policy. He is a corresponding member of the Academy of Sciences of Spain. In 2013 he was awarded the international Environmentalist Award of the Florence based Fondazione Bardini e Peyron and the Prince Albert of Monaco Water Prize.

Ibrahim Al-Marashi is Associate Professor of Middle East history at California State University San Marcos (CSUSM). He obtained his doctorate in Modern History at University of Oxford, completing a thesis on the Iraqi invasion of Kuwait. His research focuses on 20th century Iraqi history, particularly regime resilience, civil–military relations, and state-sponsored violence during the Ba'athist-era from 1968 to 2003. He is co-author of *Iraq's Armed Forces: An Analytical History* (Routledge, 2008), and *The Modern History of Iraq*, with Phebe Marr (Routledge, 2016), and *A Concise History of the Middle East* (Routledge, 2018).

Hussein A. Amery (PhD) is a Professor and Director of the Humanities, Arts and Social Sciences Division (HASS) at the Colorado School of Mines. Dr Amery had also served as Associate Provost and Dean of Undergraduate Studies and Faculty. His academic expertise is in water and food security in the Middle East, with a focus on the Arab Gulf states. He also specializes in Islamic perspectives on water management, and in transboundary water politics especially along the Litani, Jordan, Tigris and Euphrates rivers. He recently published a book titled *Arab Water Security: Threats and Opportunities in the Gulf States* (Cambridge University Press, 2015). His earlier book is called *Water in the Middle East: A Geography of Peace* (Texas University Press, with A. T. Wolf). His academic contributions were recognized by his selection (2005) as Fellow by the International Water Resources Association. Dr Amery had been a consultant to US government agencies, International Development and Research Center (Canada), and to American water engineering firms.

Alexander Atarodi has a master's in Economic Geography from the School of Economics in Gothenburg. Alexander is currently doing his PhD on a part-time basis at the School of Economics in Gothenburg. The subject is "Regional Economic Integration in the Middle East and North Africa". Alexander has been doing research on the political development and security in the MENA region. Alexander has had various positions at government offices of Sweden (foreign ministry and the prime minister's office) working on strategic trends affecting Sweden. Alexander is currently based at the Sweden International Cooperation Agency (Sida), implementing the government's strategy for the Middle East and North Africa.

Rex Brynen is Professor of Political Science at McGill University, and Nonresident Senior Fellow at the Atlantic Council. He is author, coauthor, or editor of 11 books on various aspects of Middle East politics and security, including *Beyond the Arab Spring: Authoritarianism and Democratization in the Arab World* (2012). He is also editor of the conflict simulation website PAXsims (www.paxsims.org).

Ana Elisa Cascão (PhD) is an independent consultant/researcher working in the field of transboundary water management and cooperation. She holds a PhD in Geography on the 'Political Economy of water resources management and allocation in the Eastern Nile Basin' (King's College London, UK). For the past decade, Ana has been involved in several projects

Notes on contributors

(Applied Research, Capacity Building, Advisory Services) in transboundary river basins in the Eastern and Southern Africa regions, namely as a Programme Manager at the Stockholm International Water Institute (SIWI) from 2010 to 2017. She is the author of several academic publications. Her latest co-authored book is entitled *The Grand Ethiopian Renaissance Dam and the Nile Basin: Implications for Transboundary Water Cooperation* (2017). She is currently working on a journal's Special Issue entitled *Water Security in the Nile Basin: Understanding and expanding the solution space* (forthcoming 2019).

Nic Coombs is a former member of HM Diplomatic Service with over 30 years' experience principally working in or on the Middle East. He graduated from Cambridge in 1984 in English; the Foreign and Commonwealth Office (FCO) then sent him to be trained in Arabic at the School of Oriental and African Studies (SOAS), London and then in Cairo for final examinations. He has served in Amman and twice in Riyadh. His second tour of Riyadh was as Counsellor Political 2000–2003 and he was instrumental in the opening of the Counter Terrorism dialogue with the Saudis in the aftermath of the Twin Towers attacks in New York. Nic has a particular interest in Saudi Arabia, Salafism and sectarianism in regional politics. Nic is currently a Teaching Fellow in Lancaster University's Politics, Philosophy and Religion Department focusing on the Politics and International Relations of the Middle East and specifically bringing "practitioner" experience of the region to bear on the topics being studied.

Philippe Droz-Vincent is Professor of Political Science and International Relations at Sciences-Po Grenoble in France. He also teaches at Sciences-Po Lille and is an invited professor at Université Libre de Bruxelles (ULB). His articles include, "Authoritarianism, Revolutions, Armies and Arab Regime Transitions", *The International Spectator* (June 2011), "From Fighting Formal Wars to Maintaining Civil Peace?" *International Journal of Middle East Studies* (August 2011), "*A Return of Armies to the Forefront of Arab Politics?*" Istituto Affari Internazionali (Rome) Working Paper 11/21, July 2011; "Prospects for Democratic Control of the Armed Forces? Comparative Insights and Lessons for the Arab World in Transition", *Armed Forces & Society* (March 2013), "State of Barbary (Take Two): From the Arab Spring to the Return of Violence in Syria", *The Middle East Journal* (Winter 2013–2014); and "*The military in the Arab World, from authoritarian regimes to transitional settings and new regimes in the making*", Working Paper, Middle East Institute, National University of Singapore, 2015. He has published numerous chapters in collective works, "The Military Amidst Uprisings and Transitions in the Arab World" in Fawaz Gerges, ed., *The New Middle East, Protest and Revolution in the Arab World* (Cambridge University Press, 2014); "Libya's Tentative State Rebuilding: Militias' 'Moral Economy', Violence, and Financing (In)Security" in Grawert, Elke and Zeinab Abul-Magd (eds), *Businessmen in Arms. How the Military and Other Armed Groups Profit in the MENA Region* (Lanham: Rowman & Littlefield, 2016); "The military and transitions in the Arab World" in T Roeder and R Grote, dir, *Constitutionalism in the Arab World* (Oxford University Press, 2016); "The Syrian Military and the 2011 uprising", in Albrecht, Croissant and Lawson (eds), *Military Engagement in Mobilizing Societies* (Philadelphia, University of Pennsylvania Press, 2016).

Jonathan Hall (PhD 2013) is a Researcher in the Department of Peace and Conflict Research, Uppsala University. Hall uses lab-in-the-field experiments and surveys to examine the impact of war and displacement on individuals' political psychology. His most recent research examines the psychological effects of war exposure and its consequences for cooperation across sectarian lines among refugees from the wars in Syria and Iraq currently residing in Turkey. Hall's work has appeared in top-ranking journals such as *Political Psychology*, *Journal of Conflict Resolution*, and *European Journal of International Relations*.

Hamdy A. Hassan (PhD) is a Professor and Acting Dean, College of Humanities and Social Science, Zayed University. Professor Hassan served as an elect Vice President of the African Association of Political Science (AAPS), based in Pretoria, South Africa. He is the founder and director of the Centre for African Future Studies, Cairo, since 1996. From 1999 to 2000 he served as a Director of the UNISCO Human Rights Chair located in Jordan. His research focuses on the democratization and development in Africa and the Arab world. He has published many books and articles in both Arabic and English including: (2017) *Post- "Daesh"? The Making of a Mobile Caliphate State in the African Sahel, Cairo, Egypt* (Al-Ahram Center for Political and Strategic Studies) and (2016) "Islamic State and The Transformation of Islamic Discourse in the Middle East". *Journal of Middle Eastern and Islamic Studies (in Asia)*, 10 (4), 1–19.

Roger Hearn (PhD) has held senior leadership positions in the United Nations and with a number of INGOs in a range of conflict-affected countries including Syria, the occupied Palestinian territories, East Timor and Mozambique. As Regional Director for the Middle East and Eurasia with Save the Children, Dr Hearn oversaw humanitarian operations in 19 countries, including a half billion dollar Syria Regional Response. Dr Hearn was also Country Director for UNRWA Syria, the largest humanitarian agency operating in the country before and during the early stages of the conflict. He has previously worked as Regional Director for CARE International. Dr Hearn has an interest in peacekeeping, having worked for UNTAET in East Timor and completed his Doctorate research on peacekeeping in Southern Africa. Dr Hearn is currently lecturing in disaster management in Copenhagen and is International Program Director for Save the Children Denmark.

Joost R. Hiltermann is Program Director, Middle East and North Africa, at the International Crisis Group, an independent NGO dedicated to preventing deadly conflict, for which he has worked in various capacities since 2002. Before that, he was Executive Director of the Arms Division of Human Rights Watch (1994–2002) and database coordinator and research coordinator at the Palestinian human rights organization Al-Haq in Ramallah (1985–1990). He holds a PhD in Sociology from the University of California, Santa Cruz and is author of *A Poisonous Affair: America, Iraq, and the Gassing of Halabja* (Cambridge, 2007), and *Behind the Intifada: Labor and Women's Movements in the Occupied Territories* (Princeton, 1991). He has been a frequent contributor to *The New York Review of Books*, *The London Review of Books*, *The New York Times*, *Foreign Affairs*, *Foreign Policy*, *The Atlantic*, *Middle East Report*, and other publications.

Raymond Hinnebusch is Professor of International Relations and Middle East Politics at the University of St Andrews and Director of the Centre for Syrian Studies. He is the author of *The International Relations of the Middle East* (Manchester, 2015); *Syria: Revolution From Above* (Routledge, 2000); *Authoritarian Power and State Formation in Ba'thist Syria* (Westview Press, 1990); *Peasant and Bureaucracy in Ba'thist Syria* (Westview Press, 1989); and *Egyptian Politics under Sadat* (Cambridge, 1985).

Maria Holt is a Reader in Middle East Politics in the Department of Politics and International Relations, University of Westminster. Her research interests include Palestinian refugee women in Lebanon; women and Islamic resistance in the Arab world; women, violence and conflict in the Middle East; and the Arab–Israeli conflict. Recent publications include 'Everyday Practices

Notes on contributors

of Sacrifice: A Case Study of Palestinian Women', *Gender and Research*, 19:1, 2018, *Women and Conflict in the Middle East: Palestinian Refugees and the Response to Violence* (London: I B Tauris, 2014), *Women, Islam, and Resistance in the Arab world* (with Haifaa Jawad) (Boulder: Lynne Rienner, 2013), and 'Resistance narratives: Palestinian women, Islam and insecurity', in *Genocidal Nightmares: Narratives of Insecurity and the Logic of Mass Atrocities*, edited by Abdelwahab El-Affendi (London: Bloomsbury, 2015).

Anders Jägerskog (PhD) is Senior Water Resources Management Specialist at the Global Water Practice at the World Bank. His work focuses on the Middle East and North Africa region. Previously he was Counsellor for regional water resources in the MENA region at the Swedish Embassy in Amman, Jordan; Director, Knowledge Services, at the Stockholm International Water Institute (SIWI) where he headed the Transboundary Water Management Unit and was work area leader for applied research. He managed the UNDP Shared Waters Partnership which facilitates and promotes dialogue and cooperation on transboundary water resources. He is Associate Professor (Docent) in Peace and Development Research, School of Global Studies, University of Gothenburg, Sweden, where his work focuses on global water issues. He worked for Swedish Ministry for Foreign Affairs; at the Embassy of Sweden, Nairobi; and at Stockholm International Peace Research Institute (SIPRI). In 2003 he finished his PhD on the water negotiations in the Jordan River Basin at the Department of Water and Environmental Studies at the Linköping University, Sweden. He has published over 100 scientific articles, book chapters, debate articles and reports on global water issues. The views expressed by Jägerskog are his own and do not represent the views of the World Bank Group.

Martin Keulertz (PhD) is Assistant Professor and Chair of the Food Security Programme at the American University of Beirut. He previously worked as a post-doctoral research fellow at Purdue University (USA) and Humboldt University Berlin (Germany). He obtained his PhD at King's College London (UK) in 2013 with a thesis on foreign direct investment in Sudanese agriculture by Jordan and Qatar. Martin's research interests center on the water-food-energy nexus with a particular focus on the Arab world, North America and sub-Saharan Africa. Moreover, he has published on the global political economy of water and food. He is an associate editor of the journal *Food Security* (Springer Link) and editor of the *Handbook of Water, Food and Society* (OUP, 2017).

Martina Klimes (PhD) has over 10 years of experience working with dialogue facilitation, conflict resolution, political and security analysis, including practical work in the field and informal diplomacy processes. Her main research focus is on peace processes, incentives and third party involvement in peace negotiation. Martina's book *Using Carrots to Bring Peace? Negotiation and Third Party Involvement* (2016) focuses primarily on the effectiveness of aid conditionality and other external tools that third parties – from states and regional organizations to NGOs – bring to the table in peace negotiations. In her current position as an Advisor for Water and Peace at the Stockholm International Water Institute (SIWI), Martina is advising on SIWI's activities in the Euphrates and Tigris region and other transboundary basins affected by armed conflicts. Martina holds a PhD in International Relations from Charles University in Prague.

Florian Krampe (PhD) is a political scientist working at the Stockholm International Peace Research Institute (SIPRI) where he works on climate security and sustaining peace. Krampe specializes in international relations, peace and conflict research, and international security. His primary academic interest is the foundations of peace and security, especially the processes of building peace after armed conflict. Currently, he focuses on climate security and the post-conflict management of natural resources with a specific interest in the ecological foundations for a socially, economically and politically resilient peace. Dr Krampe is an Affiliated Researcher at the Research School for International Water Cooperation at the Department of Peace and Conflict Research at Uppsala University.

Fred H. Lawson is Visiting Professor of National Security Affairs at the Naval Postgraduate School. In 1992–1993, he was Fulbright lecturer in international relations at the University of Aleppo, and during the spring of 2001 Fulbright lecturer in political science at Aden University. He is the author of *Global Security Watch Syria* (Praeger, 2013) and *Constructing International Relations in the Arab World* (Stanford University Press, 2006), and the editor of *Comparative Regionalism* (Ashgate, 2009).

Matteo Legrenzi teaches international relations at Ca' Foscari University of Venice. He holds a DPhil in International Relations and an MPhil in Modern Middle Eastern Studies from St Antony's College, Oxford. He studied Arabic at the American University in Cairo. He served as President of the Italian Association for Middle Eastern Studies (SeSaMO) and is a member of International Advisory Council of the World Congress for Middle East Studies (WOCMES). Before returning to Venice, his hometown, he taught in Oxford, Ottawa and Seoul winning the Capital Educators' Award in 2009 in Canada. He deals with international relations and comparative government of the Middle East, in particular the political economy, regionalism and security of the Arab monarchies of the Gulf.

Simon Mabon (PhD) is Senior Lecturer in International Relations at Lancaster University where he is also Director of the Richardson Institute. He is the author of a range of books and articles on the contemporary Middle East, including *Saudi Arabia and Iran: Soft Power Rivalry in the Middle East* (London: I.B. Tauris, 2013) and has published in journals such as *Middle East Policy, British Journal of Middle East Studies, Politics Religion and Ideology, Third World Quarterly, Studies in Conflict and Terrorism* and others. In 2016–17 he served as academic advisor to the House of Lords International Relations Committee inquiry into Britain's relations with the Middle East. He regularly appears on international news outlets including the BBC, CNN, CNBC, Sky, Al Jazeera, and France 24. He tweets at @drmabon.

Michelle Pace is Professor (MSO) at the Department of Social Sciences and Business, Roskilde University and Honorary Professor at the University of Birmingham, School of Government and Society, College of Social Sciences, UK. She has published widely on European Union – Mediterranean/Middle East and North Africa affairs including her piece published in the journal *Political Psychology* (11 December 2017) entitled 'Trauma, Emotions and Memory in World Politics: The Case of the European Union's Foreign Policy in the Middle East Conflict'. She also works in the area of migration studies where she has been Principal Investigator on a large FACE (http://face-programme.dk/index.html) grant project on Syrian refugee minors in Denmark and Lebanon and is now the Danish partner lead on an H2020 EU project SIRIUS (Skills and Integration of Migrants, Refugees and Asylum Applicants in European Labour Markets). Her edited volume *Syrian Refugee Children in the Middle East and Europe* was published by Routledge in March 2018 and her latest book, *The Palestinian Authority in the West Bank*, will be published in January 2019.

Notes on contributors

Michael Schulz (PhD) is Associate Professor in Peace and Development Research at the University of Gothenburg, Sweden. He has published extensively on various issues in the Middle East (resistance, democracy and state building, conflicts, and regionalism). The most recent publications are 2017, 'How resistance encourages resistance: theorising the nexus between power, organized resistance and "everyday resistance",' in *Political Power*, Vol 10(1), pp. 40–54, and 2016 'Defining and Categorization "Resistance",' in *Alternatives: Global, Local, Political*, Vol 41(3), pp. 137–153 (both articles with co-authors: Mona Lilja, Mikael Baaz, and Stellan Vinthagen). Other articles are 2015, 'EU and Hamas,' in *Security Dialogues*, Vol 6(1–2), pp. 79–102, and 'A longue durée approach to the role of civil society in the uprisings against authoritarianism in the Arab world', in *Journal of Civil Society*, 2015.

Dan Smith is Director of the Stockholm International Peace Research Institute (SIPRI). His career encompasses both scholarship and practice on peacebuilding and security issues. From 2003 to 2015, he was the Secretary General of International Alert, the peacebuilding organization, and before that (1993–2001) he was Director of the International Peace Research Institute, Oslo. He chaired the UN Peacebuilding Fund Advisory Group in 2010–11. His current research focuses on the relationship between climate and security, on the Middle East and on global trends in conflict, peace and security. He has authored atlases of world politics and of peace and security in the Middle East and blogs on international politics at www. dansmithsblog.com.

Lisa Strömbom is Associate Professor and Vice Head of the Department of Political Science at Lund University, Sweden. She teaches International Relations, Conflict Resolution, Identity Politics and Research Methods. She has published on identities in conflict, conflict resolution and grassroots peacebuilding in national and local contexts in journals such as the *European Journal of International Relations*, *Mediterranean Politics*, *Third World Quarterly*, *Space and Polity* and *Peacebuilding*. She is the author of the monograph *Israeli Identity, Thick Recognition and Conflict Transformation* (Palgrave Macmillan, 2013), and co-editor of the book *Divided Cities: Governing Diversity* (Nordic Academic Press, 2015).

Ashok Swain is a Professor of Peace and Conflict Research, UNESCO Chair of International Water Cooperation, and the Director of Research School of International Water Cooperation at Uppsala University, Sweden. He received his PhD from the Jawaharlal Nehru University, New Delhi in 1991, and since then he has been teaching at the Uppsala University. He has been a MacArthur Fellow at the University of Chicago, visiting fellow at UN Research Institute for Social Development, Geneva; and visiting professor at University Witwatersrand, University of Science, Malaysia, University of British Columbia, University of Maryland, Stanford University, McGill University, Tufts University and University of Natural Sciences and Life Sciences, Vienna. He has written extensively on new security challenges, water sharing issues, environment, conflict and peace, and democratic development issues. He has worked as a consultant on environment and development issues for various UN agencies, OSCE, NATO, EU, IISS, Arab League, Oxfam, Governments of Sweden, Netherlands, UK and Singapore.

Rawia Tawfik (D.Phil) is an Assistant Professor at the Faculty of Economics and Political Science at Cairo University and a former researcher at the German Development Institute/ Deutsches Institut für Entwicklungspolitik (DIE) in Bonn. She holds a Doctor of Philosophy in Politics from the University of Oxford. She was a visiting research fellow at the South African Institute of International Affairs (2003) and the Africa Institute of South Africa (2009–2010).

Her post-doctoral research focuses on hydropolitics in the Nile basin. She has a number of published research papers, book chapters and journal articles on Nile hydropolitics, regional integration in Africa, and Egypt's foreign policy towards Africa. Her articles on these issues appeared in *Water Policy*, *Water International* and *African Studies*.

Elizabeth A. Yaari has over 10 years of experience managing regional informal and formal environmental peacebuilding, water diplomacy, water governance, and capacity building processes in conflict and post-conflict environments. Elizabeth has extensive experience supporting engagement and leadership of a broad spectrum of stakeholders including government representatives, diplomats, development partners, local authorities, civil society, faith-based communities and academia. In her current position at the Stockholm International Water Institute (SIWI), Elizabeth serves as a Senior Programme Manager in the Transboundary Water Management Department managing transboundary activities in Central Asia, the Lower Jordan basin, and select African basins. In addition, Elizabeth serves as SIWI's Gender Equality Focal Point.

Neda A. Zawahri (PhD) is an Associate Professor and Director of the Master of Arts in Global Interactions in the Department of Political science. Her research interests focus on water security, transboundary water resource management, and adaptation to climate change. She examines how access to fresh water is related to individual, national, and regional security, and how water and hydrological infrastructure can be used as weapons. Dr Zawahri has conducted extensive field research in the Middle East and South Asia to also examine the management of transboundary river basins, such as the Euphrates, Indus, Jordan and Tigris, at the domestic and basin levels. Through empirical analysis, she also examines factors influencing the formation, design and effectiveness of treaties governing the world's transboundary water resources. As climate change continues to impact transboundary basins, she has researched the role of river basin commissions in adapting to increasing climatic variability. Dr Zawahri received her PhD in Foreign Affairs from the University of Virginia in 2004. Since arriving at Cleveland State University in 2004, she has published over 20 book chapters and articles in top journals in international relations and environmental politics, and she co-edited three special issues in top journals. Her work appears in *International Studies Quarterly*, *Journal of Peace Research*, *Global Environmental Politics*, *International Environmental Agreements*, *Security Dialogue*, and *Development and Change*.

Mark Zeitoun (PhD) is co-founder of the Water Security Research Centre, and Professor of Water Security and Policy at the School of International Development, University of East Anglia. His research follows three streams: a) development of theory and case-based research on international transboundary water management; b) examination of the influence of armed conflict on water and other essential urban services; and c) water security and management in development, post-conflict and conflict contexts. This stems from his work as a humanitarian-aid water engineer, and advisor on water security policy and transboundary water negotiations throughout the Middle East and Africa. He has a BEng in civil engineering and an MSc in environmental engineering from McGill University, and a PhD in human geography from King's College London.

Stephen Zunes is a Professor of Politics and International Studies at the University of San Francisco, where he serves as coordinator of the program in Middle Eastern Studies. Professor Zunes serves as a senior policy analyst for the Foreign Policy in Focus project of the Institute

Notes on contributors

for Policy Studies, an associate editor of *Peace Review*, and a contributing editor of *Tikkun*. He is the principal editor of *Nonviolent Social Movements* (Blackwell Publishers, 1999), the author of *Tinderbox: U.S. Middle East Policy and the Roots of Terrorism* (Common Courage Press, 2003) and co-author (with Jacob Mundy) of *Western Sahara: War, Nationalism and Conflict Irresolution* (Syracuse University Press, 2010.) He received his PhD at Cornell University and has served received research fellowships from the US Institute of Peace and the National Endowment for the Humanities. He has also served as a research associate for the Center for Global, International and Regional Studies at the University of California-Santa Cruz and a visiting professor at Universitat Jaume I in Spain and the University of Otago in New Zealand. In 2002, he won recognition from the Peace and Justice Studies Association as their first Peace Scholar of the Year.

PART I

Global contemporary security trends and the Middle East

1

PERSPECTIVES ON MIDDLE EAST SECURITY

An introduction

Anders Jägerskog, Michael Schulz and Ashok Swain[1]

The absence of security in the Middle East

The Middle East has been and still is a place burdened with armed conflicts and human sufferings. Some of the worst imaginable cruelties of humankind have taken place in these armed conflicts and many horrific images have been visualized via both traditional and new social media. As such, the Middle East is a geopolitically and economically significant region and has been of concern for many empires and great powers since the beginning of human civilization. Since the modern era, and the dramatic increasing importance of the oil resource for industrialization, the region has been of momentous national security importance for many states in the world. The Middle East therefore, and in combination with many local reasons, has been a highly securitized region. The long-existing security threats are played out in several different spaces. There are serious internal conflicts within countries, there are conflicts between countries and there are non-traditional actors threatening security in the region. The violent conflicts often have deep historical roots, are related to sectarian divisions, are rooted in an uneven distribution of resources and are affected by power asymmetries in addition to the problematic great power involvement in the region. Added to that, the resource situation where there is too much of some resources (notably oil and natural gas) and far too little of others (notably water and arable land) creates further potential for unhealthy competition and conflict. Furthermore, in today's globalized world, the challenges that plague the region have, and will continue to have, repercussions far beyond the borders of the region.

How can we understand and explain why the Middle East is plagued by so many conflicts and security challenges? Further, how can we relate, as well as apply, security theorizing in order to better understand these many security issues that have become such demanding challenges for the Middle East states and societies? We argue that we have to relate to the Middle East as a sub-system of its own within the globalizing world, which as Bassam Tibi said '...though integrated into the international system, is a regional subsystem with its own dynamic of conflict' (1998: 4). This is not to say that the Middle East as a sub-system does not have its own often intertwined regionally, as well as globally, complex internal security issues. We will argue below that one way of systematically analyzing security challenges in the Middle East is to make in-depth analysis of single security issues. This operational way is not novel per se (see Buzan, 1991, Buzan et al., 1998); however, to date there has not been a comprehensive volume providing an extensive overview of the many prevalent security issues in the Middle East. This handbook aims to rectify that by proving a state-of-the-art review of research on the key challenges for security in the Middle East. With a broad understanding of security, the handbook includes several dimensions of security. These security dimensions include classical Westphalia security logics linked to the military and state security sectors and spaces, as well as the "soft" aspects of security, including the various human security aspects, thereby also taking into account non-traditional security challenges. Lack of social capital, voice, poor governance, food security, and water scarcity are all challenges that are set to increase in importance over the years to come. As such the handbook will address *imminent challenges* to security, such as the ones relating directly to the armed conflict in Syria, but also discuss the long-term *vulnerabilities*, such as energy crisis, food and water scarcity and large-scale population migration-related security challenges, and how they relate to the overarching security discourse in the region.

We argue that the traditional security problems, which are deep-seated, are at the risk of being exacerbated also by a lack of focus on underlying vulnerabilities in the region. As several of those vulnerabilities are not of an imminent nature but rather of an incremental nature they are often harder to take note of and understand. In the region, where there is a plethora of more recent and imminent security challenges such as Yemen, Syria and Libya. Therefore it has, understandably, been hard to rise above the acute challenges to look at longer-term trends but this must also be a priority (Swain and Jägerskog, 2016).

Previous research on Middle East security

This is not the place to go through the immense number of studies that have used a security approach while analyzing security issues prevalent in the Middle East. First, there is no space to do so and, second, we are more interested in finding out how various studies have applied a regional approach in relation to what has been analyzed from a security perspective. Furthermore, very few are analyzing the "new" and emerging security issues such as energy, food, water and migration (Swain and Jägerskog, 2016). Despite the huge amount of security related studies, surprisingly, relatively few studies have taken a regional approach on analyzing the securitization of key issues of the Middle East (Fawcett, 2016; Buzan et al., 1998, 2003; Tibi, 1998, 1993; Feldman and Toukan, 1997). The so-called Copenhagen school have, with their regional security complex analysis, developed a framework for how regions can serve as a unit of analysis. Unsurprisingly, most studies apply a traditional security concept, often linked to realist, or neo-realist axiomatic assumptions (Gause III, 2017; Fawcett, 2016; Halliday, 2005), although important exceptions exist (see Bilgin, 2004, 2005). Also, some books have analyzed single security issues. The Arab–Israeli–Palestinian conflict(s) has been the one conflict that has been extensively analyzed, but rarely from an overarching regional theoretical framework (Swain and Jägerskog, 2016; Lindholm Schulz and Schulz, 2000, Laanatza et al., 2001; Tibi, 1998, 1993). Conflicts in the Middle East have also been analyzed and related to the regional system (Hinchcliffe and Milton-Edwards, 2008; Swain et al., 2009). Other examples of regional analysis are the US role in the Middle East (Little, 2008), issues linked to the political economy of the region (Richards et al., 2013), the Arab uprising against authoritarian regimes (Peters, 2012, Dalacoura, 2011), or the oil resource issue from a regional cooperative perspective (Mason and Mor, 2009). We also have a whole set of studies that apply the so-called New Regionalism approach when analyzing the Middle East sub-system (Harders and Legrenzi, 2008; Lindholm Schulz and Schulz, 2001; Fawcett and Hurrell, 1995). However, although occasionally including security aspects, these studies mainly have regionalization (i.e. regional integration) as the focus. The Middle East is usually described as being among the least regionalized regions in the global system, therefore also dominated by regimes of realist and state sovereignty driven discourses. In terms of new and emerging security issues, such as water, energy, food, climate and migration, studies that analyze the issue areas have been conducted, rarely from a purely security studies perspective but rather from a peacebuilding or environmental perspective (Jägerskog, 2003; Swain and Jägerskog, 2016). Although on occasion these studies include security-related aspects it has rarely entered the mainstream of the security discourse in the region. Traditional security studies have paid scarce attention to the underlying vulnerabilities, which can develop over time into security threats, and therefore they are in need of increased attention and focus. In sum, we have a rather dispersed set of studies that discuss security matters but less commonly from a regional sub-system perspective.

Hence, this handbook aims at filling this gap by compiling and analyzing contemporary key security issues within the Middle East region, as well as emerging issues, that are linked to risks and vulnerabilities and that often are linked to systemic/structural dimensions of the region and the global system. Further, the handbook will make use of both traditional and non-traditional security theorizing when analyzing the various issues. Security in brief, often seen as threats to survival, does beg the question of *whose* security we have in focus. The answer implies that we cannot merely stick to focusing on interstate relations, and states' survival, since the state is not the same as its many institutions, and certainly not the same as its citizens (as well as non-citizens) living in a particular part of the society of that state. A broader security definition, going beyond the traditional perspectives, is at the core of this handbook on Middle East security.

Brief history of the Middle East security context

This handbook will focus on contemporary security-related issues; however, a brief note on the modern history of the Middle East needs first to be addressed; both traditional and non-traditional issues. Some of the contemporary issues that will be addressed in the chapters of the handbook will relate to the historical background to them, but we need to contextualize the historical background to the contemporary security situation of the region. The modern history of the Middle East in brief can be divided into several time periods. First, we have the 1920s–1930s when new states were established in the post-Ottoman Empire collapse after World War I. Second, we have the post-World War II period until the end of the 1960s, in which many Arab states struggled to establish independence from the colonial powers, and pan-Arabism had its heyday. It was also a time in which the Cold War between the two super powers, the USA and USSR, had its impact on the region.

From the 1970s until the 1990s several changes followed, in which many states worked to consolidate and began to open up their economies to the global system. Internally, mainly Islamist opposition groups in the Arab world began to challenge the regimes, and several internal armed conflicts, often between different ethnic and religious groups and the state, broke out. In many ways, and with Syria as the exception, the USA came to be the dominant power in the region, also causing a great deal of resistance. The Iranian Revolution of 1978–79 was such a challenge, and changed the future relations between Shia and Sunni Muslims, as well as the security relations between primarily the conservative Gulf Cooperation Council (GCC) states and Iran. In the 1990s, and also after 9/11 in 2001, we have seen external influences, with direct military interventions, increased. It began with Iraq in 1991, as a reaction to ruler Saddam Hussein's invasion of Kuwait in 1990, and was followed up with the US-led coalition that, with limited international backing, intervened in the country, when the Baath regime was overthrown in 2003. The popular uprising during the so-called Arab Spring in 2011 has also profoundly affected the security situation, and the recent armed conflicts (i.e. in Iraq, Yemen and Syria) have thrown the region into new future uncertainties.

The more traditional security issues related to the many past armed conflicts between and within states in the region have repercussions for the many contemporary security-related issues. The "new" and emerging security issues have been downplayed and neglected partly since the traditional conflicts and security issues have obscured the focus on these new emerging issues. Further various actors, including governments, international actors as well as researchers, have been preoccupied with the imminent issues thus not focusing on how these new vulnerabilities have incrementally grown over time (Swain and Jägerskog, 2016). Many of them are related to the post-Ottoman Empire period in which the colonial powers, specifically France and the United Kingdom, redrew the political map of the Middle East, and new states were established. The Middle East went through a state-building process, often with repressive tools, security apparatus (*mukhabarat*) that controlled its own populations rather than protecting the state and its citizens from foreign influence. The newly established states have been directly linked with many external players since their foundation in the 1920s and 1930s. In a similar vein, as in large parts of Africa, in the post-World War II period most of the Middle East countries gained their independence from colonial influence. This liberation process also included the formation of the League of Arab States (LAS) in 1945. LAS members considered the map of the Middle East as an artificial colonial creation that only temporary existed until a pan-Arab state was established. The second issue was related to historical Palestine, in which the LAS saw the gradual vanishing of Arab control over Palestine, and the increasingly influential Jewish Zionists as a great security threat. With the establishment of Israel in 1948, and the following Palestinian refugee problem, LAS had a common agenda to unite forces against Israel. With time, it turned out that the pan-Arab idea was superseded by the single Arab states' independence priorities. Despite Egypt's and Syria's attempt to take the first merging step of forming the Arab Union in 1958, it turned out that particular national interests were stronger than the pan-Arab sentiments and the union collapsed in 1961. Pan-Arabism lost its attraction, at least at the leadership levels, and particularly after the disastrous defeat of the Arab countries in the 1967 war against Israel, when the weak unity within the LAS members became more evident. This Israeli military victory brought down further the hope of the region to recover Arab glory. Egypt, Syria and Jordan suffered heavily militarily and economically and the Jordanian West Bank, the Egyptian Sinai Peninsula and Gaza Strip, and the Syrian Golan Heights came all under Israeli control. In the 1973 war, Egypt and Syria aimed at restoring the humiliating loss of the 1967 war, and with the surprise attack against Israel had initial military success. While Israel could, however, reverse the initial military loss, the outcome became a political success for the Arab states. However, the war also showed that the superpowers' rivalry nearly led to a Third World War, in a similar way as during the Cuban Missile Crisis in 1962.

In 1974, the Arab League recognized the Palestine Liberation Organization (PLO) as the sole representative of the Palestinian people. Thanks to American mediation, Egypt left its Arab allies in the cold and made a peace deal with Israel in 1978. This development brought a huge power asymmetry between Israel and its adversaries in the region. Further, signs of rifts and enmity between Arab states became obvious, for example Syria and Iraq, who were ruled by the other major pan-Arab branch, the Baathist ideology, became bitter rivals and worked to undermine each other. In Lebanon, which used to be seen as the Switzerland of the Middle East, there was civil war between 1975 and 1991, with many regional actors involved, all competing for influence.

Another war that heavily impacted the overall security situation in the region was that between Iran and Iraq that began in 1980 and lasted until 1988. This war diverted the region's

Perspectives on Middle East security

attention from the Palestinian issue as Iran was gaining advantage (Farhang, 1993). The Iranian Revolution brought the Shia Islamic cleric Ayatollah Khomeini to power and marked a dramatic shift in political life in Iran. The change in Iran was a concern for external actors, primarily the US and the Europeans, but also for the Sunni- dominated states in the Arab world. The Sunni states were wary of an export of Islamic fundamentalism to their societies. At the same time, many Arab states, in particular Saudi Arabia and Egypt, feared a militarily strong Iraq under the leadership of Saddam Hussein. Hence, external parties' effort was mainly to ensure that neither Iran nor Iraq would win the war and thereby strengthen their regional position. After a loss of more than a million lives, the end of the Iran–Iraq War began with a cease-fire in 1988. As the war between Iran and Iraq was ending the first *intifada* began in 1987 in the Israeli occupied territories, which brought back the attention of the region to the Palestinian issue.

When the Cold War ended an opportunity to further peace negotiations in the Middle East was opening in which the United States used its influence in the region to bring all the relevant parties to the Palestinian conflict (Israel, Syria, Lebanon and Jordanian-Palestinian representation) to the negotiating table in Madrid in 1991. The process resulted in several important understandings and subsequently led to the historic Declaration of Principle (DOP) of September 13, 1993, in which the parties not only recognized each other but also committed themselves to solve the conflict by political means. The DOP identified a number of key issues such as borders and the status of Jerusalem to be negotiated in final status negotiations which were supposed to be concluded in five years. Still, even 25 years later the final negotiations are yet to take place and the hope of achieving a comprehensive solution to the Arab–Israeli conflict has gradually yielded to disillusionment. The US attempt to solve the final status issues in a meeting at the Camp David summit concluded on 25 July 2000 without achieving any substantial agreement, although the key issues were discussed formally at this level for the first time. The beginning of the second *intifada* in September 2000 brought a stalemate to the Peace Process, despite continued US negotiation attempts, such as in Taba 2001, Annapolis 2008, and the shuttle diplomatic efforts by US Secretary of State, John Kerry, in 2014.

Some economic and political reforms, aiming to give space for establishment of some democratic mechanisms, were launched by the authoritarian regimes in the region in the late 1980s and early 1990s. The political economy and the repressive state mechanism witnessed growth in GDP, accompanied by broader developmental changes over the last decades and especially since the *infitah* policies; that is, the economic liberalization of the Arab states, in the late 1980s. However, the high level of corruption and uneven distribution of resources have led to marginalization of many people. Coupled with economic liberalization policies that aimed to create a better macroeconomic situation, this created economic difficulties for many, especially in terms of unemployment, and widened the gap between the poor and the wealthy elites.

Since the mid-1990s, the EU has been consistently calling for democracy and respect for human rights as essential requirements of its partnership and cooperation. Simultaneously, the US has also been encouraging the states in the region to introduce political reforms. However, after 9/11 in 2001, regimes in the region, not least Egypt and Jordan, started arguing that the reform might pave the way for Islamic radicals to capture power. After the failure to establish security and new functional institutions in a post-Saddam Iraq, and due to international criticism of the invasion, the United States and its allies are reluctant to undertake military action for regime change, but they have increased financial and political support to strengthen democratic developments in the region.

The effects of the 9/11 attacks were dramatic for the security in the region. The focus on the Middle East peace process was shifted as a result of the military intervention in Iraq in 2003. The aftermath of the military intervention led to a number of challenges reverberating in Iraq as well as in the region. In large parts of the region the military intervention was seen as not being legitimate and resistance in Iraq was strong (Little, 2008; Diamond, 2005; Romano et al., 2013) The presence of foreign fighters, particularly from Saudi Arabia and Syria (Ranstorp, 2008), created further complications for the international community. Iraq has continued to be plagued by insecurity and internal challenges.

The events that started to unravel through the Arab Spring that started 2010 had significant consequences for the region. In Tunisia and in Egypt it led to regime change while in other countries in the region it led to smaller changes in openness and democratic developments and yet in others it led to violent conflict and war (Syria and Libya). The implications of the Arab Spring in terms of security are addressed in this volume in a number of chapters, some being devoted fully to the consequences and repercussions that the Arab Spring brought to the region and beyond.

The events that followed the Arab Spring in the region, with the ensuing violent conflict and wars primarily in Syria but also in Libya and Yemen, have changed the security context in a number of ways, besides leading to tremendous loss of development opportunities and human suffering. First, the more immediate threat to the state has yet again come to the forefront and efforts to preserve the states' integrity and authority are as present as ever. Second, the uprisings have also created the space for non-state actors to gain influence and legitimacy, most notably by Daesh/ISIS primarily in the case of Syria and Iraq but also beyond. Third, it has reinforced old power struggles and the quest for regional dominance. The engagement by regional actors, partly through support to proxy actors, unsurprisingly yet again elevates the pre-eminence of how the region focuses on the immediate threats to security in the traditional sense: through military means.

New and emerging security threats in the Middle East

This handbook builds upon the understanding that the traditional security studies approach, which is geared more towards hard security factors, is too limited to grasp the current security challenges and even more importantly the future ones. Security threats in the Middle East are no longer confined to traditional state and military aspects but need to account also for areas that have traditionally been treated more as development issues (Swain and Jägerskog, 2016). The new and emerging security threats – which are aspects of human security – include areas such as climate change, water and food security as well as migration. These threats are under-lying vulnerabilities that build over time. Furthermore, they are often of a regional and/or global nature, thus creating regional security challenges as opposed to internal threats to the state. In a situation of water scarcity in the region the transboundary aspects come to the fore. As most of the water is shared between countries, scarcity of such a necessity becomes a threat that is shared between countries; they can choose to compete or cooperate in the quest to over-come the challenge.

The regional dynamics outlined below in relation to regional security complexes provides a backdrop against which security at multiple levels can be understood (Schulz, 1995). This handbook features a number of chapters focusing on the more long-term security challenges to the region which will continue to increase in magnitude over the coming decades. Given the highlighting of these new and emerging threats we need to start asking questions that go beyond the traditional ones. Who are the actors who affect the new security aspects? And what are the main concerns guiding these actors? While the state will still be central, it will be important to understand other actors. While the more imminent and traditional security threats are central concerns in the region today, there is reason to address these broader aspects in greater depth now. In this respect, the security-development nexus becomes important as the concerns that are new – from a security perspective – are areas that traditionally development actors have been immersed in. The international system and regional organizations are now recognizing these aspects as central to their work.

The Middle East represents a perfect place for better understanding the development of the security concept as it is evolving. The region is plagued by traditional security threats such as ongoing violent conflicts in which military actors and means primarily protect interests. The region is facing natural resource scarcity (land and water) with, for example, strong challenges emerging from climate change, water scarcity, and lack of arable land for the growing of food. Simultaneously, if the threats are recognized, this necessitates a different set of responses involving regional cooperation and coordination as well as internal reforms within countries to better address the softer security challenges they are faced with. The traditional means to address the challenges will not suffice and will need a broader suite of tools and policy responses. This will require also stronger understanding of regional security aspects and how they are interwoven with each other at sub-regional level(s).

The Middle East and regional security complex theory

The Middle East as defined in this handbook includes all the North African states – Morocco, Algeria, Tunisia, Libya and Egypt – as well as the Arab states of Iraq, Jordan, Lebanon and Syria, and the Arab-peninsula states, as well as Iran, Israel and Turkey. The Arab world could be divided into three overarching sub-regions, the Maghreb, or western countries (Morocco, Algeria, Tunisia and to some extent Libya), the Mashreq, or eastern countries (Jordan, Iraq, Syria, Lebanon, the West Bank/Gaza) and the Gulf countries (Saudi Arabia, Kuwait, Bahrain, Qatar, United Arab Emirates, Oman, Yemen). This definition needs a justification, as well as explanation of why certain criteria have been applied to define the region. Buzan and his colleagues (Buzan, 1983, 1991; Buzan and Waever, 1998), have developed the regional security complex theorizing, and this study will apply this framework to Middle East security.

The security complex theory approach

Security is here seen as a relational term, and a regional security complex is defined as a distinguishable system of states united by geographical proximity. Analytically, "security" will be understood in relation to security threats. These threats bind different actors together in a web of interrelations. The intensity and quality of these webs of patterns of interaction between actors decide if they are part of a system. As Buzan writes "[t]he regional security complex is normally conceived of as an interstate system defined in terms of the *patterns of amity and enmity* substantially confined within some geographical area" (Buzan, 1983: 7). This is, however, not to say that security issues are solely linked to states. On the contrary, many different actors are involved, although it could be argued that various security *issues* among states *link the states national security concerns* together. The Middle East could also be seen as a regional security complex full of other *sets* of security complexes, or sub-complexes, which all have their own security issue that connects various actors together in inextricably entangled relations, and around a specific security issue. For example, the rivers Euphrates and Tigris form the security issue for the three "user" states and are thereby in focus from a security perspective. This could be seen as a *hydropolitical security complex,* and is including those states that are geographically part "owners" and technically "users" of the rivers and, further, as a consequence, consider the rivers as one of the major national security issues. Turkey, Syria and Iraq compose in this way a security complex, or, rather, form the Euphrates and Tigris hydropolitical security complex (Schulz, 1995).

The Israeli–Palestinian conflict could be seen as another example of a sub-regional system in which two competing national movements struggling over historical Palestine bind several actors together in system. This involves Israel and the Palestinians (represented by PLO/PA/Hamas) as well as the states of Egypt, Jordan, Syria and Lebanon. These states have all been involved directly in wars with Israel, and had historically, or still have parts of their territories occupied by Israel (Schulz, 1989)

Two examples from the Middle East that can be seen as regional formal formations, the Arab Maghreb Union (AMU) and the Gulf Cooperation Council (GCC) link several states together. The AMU was formed in 1989 with the aim to create a customs union, mainly in order to counterbalance their dependence on the European Community (Aliboni, 1997: 218). The idea with the AMU was to be an area with open borders for free movement of goods, services, capital and persons, as well as cultural cooperation. The AMU includes Algeria, Libya, Mauritania, Morocco and Tunisia, which all have trade with the EU. However, the AMU has not really managed to integrate to the extent envisioned, and many internal security-related tensions exist within the AMU sub-system (Verdier-Chouchane et al., 2016)

The GCC, which was established in 1981, could be seen as "integration as a response to crisis" (Starkey, 1996: 145). The Iranian Revolution of 1978–79 was seen as a serious security threat for Bahrain, Kuwait, Oman, Qatar, Saudi Arabia and the United Arab Emirates, and the formation of the GCC was a security response. The armed conflicts of the Iran–Iraq War of 1980–1988, the Gulf War of 1990–91, and when the US-led alliance invasion of Iraq came in 2003, followed by a crumpling security situation in Iraq, have pushed the GCC members to constant crisis responses. The current armed conflict in Yemen could be seen as a continuation of this security cooperation.

Each of the sub-systems that can be identified in the region have interrelations with other sub-security complexes within the Middle Eastern region with other security issues at focus, which in turn creates new analytical complexes. These vertical and horizontal relations to other complexes also often have links to the global system. The vertical relations relate to such security issues that can be related to a higher structural level, for instance great power rivalry. The formation and the nature of the complexes are constantly changing, and the security issues also alter over time, which in turn can transform the sets of complexes in the Middle Eastern region. Roberson explains the constantly changing complex formation in the following way:

> Because these states (in the Middle East) are new, the pattern of their relationships is in an early stage of development. A prominent feature of the developing Middle East state system is a constant pattern of realignment, which has thus far prevented the rise of a hegemonic power. This feature underlines the supreme difficulty in establishing regional security, a feature within which the Arab statesmen move and breathe.
>
> *(Roberson in Buzan and Rizvi, 1986: 160–161)*

When analyzing the various security threats and issues it becomes of interest to search for external and internal sources of change, which at best might lead to a resolved and mature security complex:

> Security communities might be seen in one sense as resolved or matured security complexes in which basic conflicts and fears have been worked out, resulting in an oasis of relatively mature anarchy within the more fractious field of the international anarchy as a whole.
>
> *(Buzan, 1983 115)*

Perspectives on Middle East security

Hence, it becomes an empirical issue to analyze to what extent the security complex with its particular security issue(s) has been resolved, and if not, what factors explain its continuous stalemate(s). This volume intends to investigate a whole range of security issues that link different actors together in a web of patterns of enmity/amity. Each chapter will focus on a particular security issue, show how it has become securitized, and how the dynamics of the conflict or vulnerability has changed over time.

Structure of the book

The outline of the book follows a sector division related to the security issues that are in focus. We have seven security sectors that are in focus. These are armed conflicts; energy and resources (water, food, oil); migration; democratization; political economy; climate; and gender issues. We could assume that the many serious armed conflicts are security issues interconnected with military and state security issues. However, a too narrow focus on these aspects is not enough. Emerging security issues are also needed for a comprehensive understanding of security in future. In this volume, in **Part I**, we have nine chapters that deal with armed conflicts; however, several of them also include the human security aspects in the analysis. By doing so, we better are equipped to understand the challenges and potentials of a long-term process of change from armed conflict to a human security-oriented situation leading at best to a sustainable and durable peace in the region.

After this introductory chapter, we begin with a chapter by Alexander Atarodi, who analyzes the global contemporary security trends, and what implications they have for the Middle East. The chapter discusses how the changing and evolving shifts affect regional security as well as playing into contemporary conflicts in the region.

Chapter 3, by Joost R. Hiltermann, gives an overview of the armed conflict situation in the Middle East. Hiltermann offers a new way of analyzing Middle East armed conflicts through five distinct conflict "clusters", each with its unique genealogy, as mediated by external interventions. Hiltermann shows that each cluster of conflict is set off by a political "earthquake" that generates rolling tremors and new fissures and unleashes secondary struggles.

Chapter 4, by Stephen Zunes, gives an overview of the US policy in the Middle East and argues that, despite the end of the Cold War and the Arab Spring, US security policy in the Middle East has changed little despite its poor record for advancing the interests of the United States or the well-being of the peoples of the region. It has further emboldened extremists and weakened moderate voices, resulting in a more anarchic international order which makes legitimate counter-terrorism efforts all the more difficult.

Chapter 5, by Matteo Legrenzi and Fred Lawson, gives an overview of the external great powers policy in the Middle East. It argues that though American predominance in the Gulf has certainly deteriorated in recent years, there is still uncertainty whether the Chinese commercial and economic role will translate into an active security role and whether Russia will be able to successfully play an active role. The chapter also argues that the European countries have been failing to play a unified role in their efforts to engage in the region, particularly in the Gulf.

Michael Schulz shows in Chapter 6 what the security implications linked to the Israeli–Palestinian conflict are, and what they imply for the core parties to the conflict, the Middle East region, as well as for the rest of the world. The chapter argues that the Israeli–Palestinian conflict is a global peace and security concern and can be seen as a key for overarching conflict transformation in the region. A solution, which all core parties could live with, should have positive ramifications for other sub-complexes in the Middle East and beyond.

In Chapter 7, Ibrahim Al Marashi analyzes the challenging security situation in Iraq. The chapter makes an inquiry of Iraq's future security and shows that the Iraqi State faces daunting challenges in this post-conflict scenario. The relations between the Iraqi Government and sub-state actors and their way to deal with security issues, not least the hard core military security issues related to the numerous militias and para-military actors, will decide what direction Iraq will take. Al Marashi argues that one Achilles' heel for Iraq's future security is that no sustainable strategy has been articulated by the Iraqi political elite to deal with human security issues, ranging from internally displaced peoples to employment and environmental crises.

In Chapter 8, Philippe Droz-Vincent convincingly shows how the Syrian globalized civil war has expanded from an unarmed mass mobilized activity to a globalized armed conflict, which causes the greatest security concerns of contemporary times. External state powers, such as Iran, Israel, Russia, Turkey and the USA, but also rebel groups, such as ISIS, are directly involved in fighting inside Syrian territory. The involvement of many external actors has complicated and expanded the conflict from an initial regime change issue to a regional and global security concern.

Chapter 9, by Roger Hearn, gives an overview of the humanitarian assistance and how it interacts with broader security issues in the Middle East. The chapter zooms in on the challenges that the humanitarian actors face in a securitized region like the Middle East. The Syrian conflict is used as an illustrative case in point and the chapter discusses the need for reform of the humanitarian sector in a region that may face continued instability for decades to come.

Finally, after the "hard" armed conflict security issues are presented, Karin Aggestam's and Lisa Strömbom's Chapter 10 discusses the practices and theories of peacebuilding attempts made in the Middle East. The four cases, security sector reform in Tunisia, the Israeli–Palestinian peace process, Iraqi women's participation in peacebuilding, and youth's role in peacebuilding attempts in Lebanon, show what the potentials are for conflict transformation in the region.

In **Part II** of the volume we have six chapters that deal with energy and resource issues, as well as matters linked to climate change. In Chapter 11, by Martin Keulertz and Tony Allan, we get an overview of the water and food situation in the region with focus on the interlinkages between the areas and how they need to be understood together in the larger political economy context of the region.

In Chapter 12, Neda A. Zawahri gives a specific overview of the many challenging water issues of the Middle East. The chapter discusses various ways in which water scarcity affects different aspects of security in the region. Through discussing the multidimensional aspect of water security, the chapter proposes means to build adaptive capacity to address the challenges, which can contribute to avert domestic and regional instability.

In Chapter 13, Hussein A. Amery gives a specific overview of the food situation in the Middle East. Amery notes that the issue of food security is a top national priority in most of the countries and that it thereby becomes an issue of wider security implications as well. The chapter discusses food security in the region and the reliance on imported food to the region which creates a level of uncertainty as it is related to global trade flows, which can be affected by political and trade developments elsewhere. The chapter concludes with a range of policy measures, including decreasing food waste, that would lead to improved food security for the region.

In Chapter 14 Dan Smith and Florian Krampe show that the conflict and security impacts of climate and environmental change are spatially and temporally different among different countries in the Middle East. They argue that climate change is only a part of the picture in conflict escalation and other significant factors are its immediate impact on communities, the response to it and the decisions made by government, communities, individuals, the private sector, armed militias, and regional organizations among others.

In Chapter 15, Ana Elisa Cascão, Rawia Tawfik and Mark Zeitoun in their case study of the Nile River basin show how the region is nowadays not just a geopolitical sphere of influence, but it is also becoming a main stage of competition and conflict between powerful Middle East countries such as Saudi Arabia, UAE, Qatar, Turkey, Iran, Israel and Egypt. These new actors are contributing to changes in the balance of power between the Nile Basin countries, and accordingly partially eroding Egypt's hydro-hegemonic control and leadership position in the Nile.

Finally, in Chapter 16, Martina Klimes and Elizabeth A. Yaari make an analysis of the potential of water diplomacy. The chapter proposes a definition of multi-track water diplomacy and identifies key entry points and linkages within and between informal and formal water dialogue platforms to improve water diplomacy in the transboundary river basins of the Middle East. Authors argue that increased linkages between stakeholders can create improved opportunities for dialogue on water issues resulting in increased water security.

In **Part III** of the volume we have seven chapters that deal with migration, political economy, democratization, identity and gender issues.

In Chapter 17, Ashok Swain and Jonathan Hall analyze the interrelation between migration and conflict. The Middle East region has more than its share of violent conflicts and human migration. Due to globalization, climate change, economic crisis and violent conflict in the region, large migration flows will continue for the foreseeable future. The authors argue that these migrants are likely to get more actively involved as parties in ongoing conflicts.

In Chapter 18 Raymond Hinnebusch discusses the political economy challenges of the Middle East. The chapter argues that political economy constituted the deep structure that underlies both security threats and order in the region. Taking a historical perspective, the chapter analyzes the emergence of the rentier states and the influence of oil revenues as the underlying factor for the security structure that has emerged in the region, including militarization and external intervention.

In Chapter 19 Michelle Pace addresses the challenges of ineffective relationships between Middle Eastern governments and their respective populations. In spite of the vast amount of research on governance issues in the Middle East, no work to date has been carried out on the possible contribution of human security and trust-building in the region's governments–citizens relations. This chapter attempts to fill this gap and aims at unearthing new understandings of the region's nature of governance and pertinent challenges to it.

In Chapter 20, Hamdy Hassan and Hassanein T. Ali discuss the relation between development and democratization in the Middle East. The chapter discusses the Arab Spring and its consequences for the region from a democracy perspective. While discussing the region it also puts a particular focus on the case of Tunisia as an example of where the Arab Spring led to significant changes. It argues that the democracy process has come to a halt in the region as states have been prioritizing development as well as security.

In Chapter 21, Rex Brynen analyzes the challenging security issues that followed in the footsteps of the popular uprisings in the so-called Arab Spring in the Middle East. The failed transitions in Libya, Syria and Yemen ended up with civil wars. Some rather changed one authoritarian system to a new form of it. Brynen explores the consequences of the aftermath of the uprisings in the Middle East, resulting in regional disorder, often followed by international interventions, as well as fostering logics of ethnic and sectarian geopolitics.

Simon Mabon and Nic Coombs discuss the complex Sunni–Shia relations in the Middle East in Chapter 22. The chapter outlines proxy conflicts across the Middle East as a consequence of the differences between Saudi Arabia and Iran, driven by the instrumentalized use of religion. However, the authors caution against overstating the role of religion in conflicts in the region as religion plays a prominent role within political rivalries, but only as a contributing factor.

Maria Holt discusses the gender aspects in the Middle East in Chapter 23, and in particular focuses on the experiences of the Palestinian women in the Occupied Territories and the Diaspora. Holt explores questions of protection and empowerment, and analyzes how women cope with constant existence of violence and persistent insecurity in their surroundings. She shows that women have had little choice but to rely on personal resilience and ingenuity within an environment of communal solidarity. This is done first by recourse to Islamic activism; second, by their willingness to engage in acts of resistance against what they consider to be oppressive systems or regimes; and, third, by their refusal to internalize an identity solely defined by victimization. In other words, women have evolved their own strategies for survival.

Note

1 Contact details: Anders Jägerskog, Senior Water Resources Management Specialist, World Bank; email: ajagerskog@worldbank.org; Michael Schulz, Associate Professor, School of Global Studies, University of Gothenburg, e-mail; michael.schulz@globalstudies.gu.se.

The views expressed by Jägerskog are his own and do not necessarily reflect the views of the World Bank. Neither are the views of any of the other chapters Jägerskog's nor do they reflect the views of the World Bank.

References

Aliboni, R., 1997, "Change and Continuity in Western Policies towards the Middle East", in Guazzone, L. (ed.), *The Middle East in Global Change*, Basingstoke: Macmillan, pp. 216–236.

Ben-Zvi, A., 1986, *The American Approach to Superpower Collaboration in the Middle East 1973–1986*, Jerusalem: The Jerusalem Post Press.

Bilgin, P., 2004, "'Whose the Middle East?' Geopolitical Inventions and Practices of Security", *International Relations* 18(1), pp. 24–41.

Bilgin, P., 2005, *Regional Security in the Middle East. A Critical Perspective*, New York: RoutledgeCurzon.

Buzan, B., 1983, *People, States and Fear: The National Security Problem in International Relations*, 1st edn, Brighton: Wheatsheaf Books.

Buzan, B., 1991, *People, States and Fear: The National Security Problem in International Relations*, 2nd edn, Brighton: Wheatsheaf Books.

Buzan, B. and O. Waever, 2003, *Regions and Powers: The Structure of International Security*, Cambridge: Cambridge University Press.

Buzan, B., and G. Rizvi, 1986, *South Asian Insecurity and the Great Powers*, Basingstoke: Macmillan.

Buzan, B., O. Waever, and J. de Wilde, 1998, *Security: A New Framework for Analysis*, Boulder and London: Lynne Rienner Publishers.

Dalacoura, K., 2011, "The 2011 Uprisings in the Arab Middle East: Political Change and Geopolitical Implications", *International Affairs* 88(1), pp. 63–79.

Diamond, L., 2005, "Building Democracy After Conflict: Lessons from Iraq", *Journal of Democracy* 16(1), pp. 9–23.

Fawcett, L. (ed.), 2016, *International Relations of the Middle East*, 4th edition, Oxford: Oxford University Press.

Fawcett, L. and A. Hurrell (eds.), 1995, *Regionalism in World Politics*, Oxford: Oxford University Press.

Feldman, S. and A. Toukan, 1997, *Bridging the Gap: A Future Security Architecture for the Middle East*, New York: Carnegie Corporation.

Gause III, F.G., 2017, "Ideologies, Alignments, and Underbalancing in the New Middle East Cold War", *Political Science & Politics*, 50(3), pp. 672–675.

Halliday, F., 2005, *The Middle East in International Relations: Power, Politics, and Ideology*, Cambridge: Cambridge University Press.

Harders, C. and M. Legrenzi, 2008, *Beyond Regionalism? Regional Cooperation, Regionalism and Regionalization in the Middle East*, Aldershot: Ashgate.

Hinchcliffe, P. and B. Milton-Edwards, 2008, *Conflict in the Middle East since 1945*, 3rd edition, London & New York: Routledge.

Jägerskog, A., 2003, *Why States Cooperate over Shared Water: The Water Negotiations in the Jordan River Basin*. Department of Water and Environmental Studies, University of Linköping.

Jönsson, C., 1984, *Superpower*, London: Frances Pinter.

Laanatza, M., H. Lindholm Schulz, and M. Schulz, 2001, "The Middle East", in Schulz, M., F. Söderbaum and J. Öjendal (eds.), *Regionalization in the Post-Cold Era: A Comparative Perspective on Forms, Actors, and Processes*, London: Zed Books, pp. 42–60.

Lindholm Schulz, H. and M. Schulz, 2000, "Israel, Palestine and Jordan—Triangle of Peace or Conflict?", in Hettne, B., A. Inotai, and O. Sunkel (eds.), *The New Regionalism and the Future of Security and Development*, Vol. III: The *New Regionalism Series*. London: Macmillan Press/United Nations University/WIDER.

Little, D., 2008, *American Orientalism. United States and the Middle East since 1945*, 3rd edition, Chapel Hill: The University of North Carolina Press.

Mason, M. and A. Mor (eds.), 2009, *Renewable Energy in the Middle East: Enhancing Security through Regional Cooperation*, Dordrecht: Springer.

Peters, J. (ed.), 2012, *The EU and the Arab Spring: Promoting Democracy and Human Rights in the Middle East*, Lanham: Lexington Books.

Ranstorp, M., 2008, *Perspectives on Terrorism: What Will It Look Like 2018 and Beyond?* Stockholm: National Defence College.

Richards, A., J. Waterbury, M. Cammett, and I. Diwan, 2013, *A Political Economy of the Middle East*, Boulder, CO: Westview Press.

Romano, D., B. Calfano, and R. Phelps, 2013, "Successful and Less Successful Interventions: Stabilizing Iraq and Afghanistan", *International Studies Perspectives*, doi: 10.1111/insp.12067

Schulz, M., 1989, "The Palestinian-Israeli Security Complex: Inconciliatory Positions or Regional Cooperation?" in Ohlsson, L. (ed.), *Case Studies of Regional Conflicts and Conflict Resolution*, Gothenburg: Padrigu Papers.

Schulz, M., 1995, "A Hydropolitical Security Complex: The Case of Euphrates-Tigris", in Ohlsson, L. (ed.), *Water Resources: the Politics of Conflict,* London: Zed Books, pp. 91–122.

Schulz, M., F. Söderbaum and J. Öjendal (eds.), 2001, *Regionalization in the Post-Cold Era: A Comparative Perspective on Forms, Actors, and Processes,* London: Zed Books.

Starkey, B., 1996, "Post-Cold War Security in the GCC Region: Change and Continuity and Change in the 1990s", in Ahrari, M.E. (ed.), *Change and Continuity in the Middle East. Conflict Resolution and Prospects for Peace*, London: Palgrave Macmillan, pp. 143–163.

Swain, A. and A. Jägerskog, 2016, *Emerging Security Threats in the Middle East: The Impact of Climate Change and Globalization*, Lanham: Rowman and Littlefield Publishers.

Swain, A., J. Öjendal and M. Schulz, 2009. *Security in the Middle East: Increasingly Multidimensional and Challenging,* A Study Commissioned by the Strategic Perspective Project within the Swedish Armed Forces Headquarters, Stockholm.

Tibi, B., 1993, *Conflict and War in the Middle East: 1967–1991*, 2nd edition, Basingstoke: Macmillan.

Tibi, B., 1998, *Conflict and War in the Middle East: From Interstate War to New Security*, 2nd edition, Basingstoke: Palgrave Macmillan.

Verdier-Chouchane, A., M. Sami Ben Ali and C. Karagueuzian, 2016, "Trade Diversification and Intra-regional Trade in North Africa", in Ben Ali, M.S. (ed.), *Economic Development in the Middle East and North Africa*, Basingstoke: Springer, pp. 173–195.

2

SHIFTS IN THE GLOBAL POLITICAL AND ECONOMIC LANDSCAPE AND CONSEQUENCES FOR THE MIDDLE EAST AND NORTH AFRICA

Alexander Atarodi

Global trends

The world today is going through major and rapid changes. Unprecedented technological progress and globalization has improved the standard of living. An expansion of global trade and global investment has led to economic growth and moved several countries from low-income to middle-income status. The progress of the past decades is historic, lifting a billion people out of poverty, mainly in China but also in other parts of Asia. The rising number of middle class people has led to more people having access to proper health care and education. At the same time the world of today is also going through turbulent times. Parallel to the economic growth and expansion within global trade some countries and people are left behind. Global inequality is on the rise both in developed countries and in developing economies. Living standards have deteriorated in regions and states which are mired in conflict and war. The poor are increasingly concentrated in fragile states where at the same time violence is on the increase (National Intelligence Council, 2012).

No other region can exemplify this as well as the Middle East and North Africa. The region has been affected by several parallel ongoing conflicts driving millions of people from their home countries. The Middle East and North Africa is also the region that is the least integrated in the global economy, making work opportunities for women and young people scarce. According to a report from the UN (UNDP, 2016), the younger generation in the Middle East and North Africa are suffering from high unemployment and a bleak future. To be a young Arab in the Middle East today is associated with more disadvantaged conditions and being more vulnerable to violence than at any other time in recent history. Arabs are exposed to violence and upheavals in a way that no other large single-language group has ever been. Though the Arab region contains just 5% of the world's population, it has 17% of the global conflicts, 45% of all terrorist attacks and 57.5% of the worldwide total of displaced people. The region has also become a place where the regional and global powers are fighting to enhance their geostrategic

Global political and economic landscape

positions and increase their own national benefits. The Middle East and North Africa is thus a region caught in the middle of ongoing global trends affecting the life of millions of people (UNDP, 2016).

The aim of this short chapter is not to describe the global trends in detail, but to highlight some of the consequences of the major global political and economic shifts that have been taking place in the last 20 years. These ongoing shifts are having profound consequences not only for the people of the Middle East and North Africa, but also for how the states are positioning themselves in the rapidly changing global political and economic environment – especially in times of rapid international change and flare-ups in security policy trouble spots. During these circumstances, it is easy to be blinded by political immediacy and urgency. At the same time, at this point the need to take a long-term view is of the greatest importance, likewise the attempt to understand the more structural processes. The picture that arises by studying these processes is one that shows a profound and rapid change in people's lives around the world but nonetheless a persistence of inequality, discrimination and exclusion. The global integration of people and markets is deeper than ever, while advances in technology and science are changing our lives more rapidly than we can comprehend. In this world of rapid change, there are both opportunities and challenges.

These trends have implications for all of us; for individuals, for companies and for states. On a broader level, traditional public institutions and global governance structures seem to be out of step with emerging needs and systemic challenges (Strategic Analysis, 2014). The ongoing Syria crisis is one example of the lack of adequate global instruments to tackle one of the major challenges in our modern history. Major political, economic and security shifts during the last 20 years make it difficult for the states to unilaterally protect their economic, environmental, political, health or other interests. However, there is a lack of political will to participate in management of these problems. This is partly due to the fact that collective action has become more difficult (see for instance the handling of the Syria crisis by the United Nations) as the world has become more complex. With the emergence of new regional and global actors, the political landscape has also changed and with it the pursuit of international norms and values and the ways international organizations do business (Strategic Analysis, 2014).

One of the major reasons behind these changes is the rapid transformation in the world economy and the trading patterns. The global economy and the global trading patterns have shifted from West to East and North to South. In 2017 China was the largest economy (based on Purchasing Power Parity) in the world and its trade is the largest among all the nations. Global economy has more than tripled since 2000, with emerging economies driving growth for the past five years. China and India represent 25% of the global economy of today compared with 9% in 1950. Even more dramatic is the fact that the combined economies of the EU, US and Japan is decreasing from 51.5% in 2000 to 36.6% of the world total GDP in 2016; see Figure 2.1 on share of world GDP (Eurostat, 2017).

Many of the global trends (trade, economics, technology, education, etc.) indicate that we are in the midst of a genuinely geostrategic change. The US and Europe are losing ground in relative terms. China, and to an extent India and the rest of Asia, are becoming increasingly influential. In a globalized world where economies and security interests are increasingly intertwined, one party's unrest, emissions or actions rapidly have consequences for others. This in turn, means that relative leverage of the major powers (US, China, EU, Russia) has been altered by shifts in political and economic power. Some powers (China and India) have now emerged, while others are still emerging. How is the Middle East and North Africa being influenced by the transformation of the global political landscape and the global economic shifts?

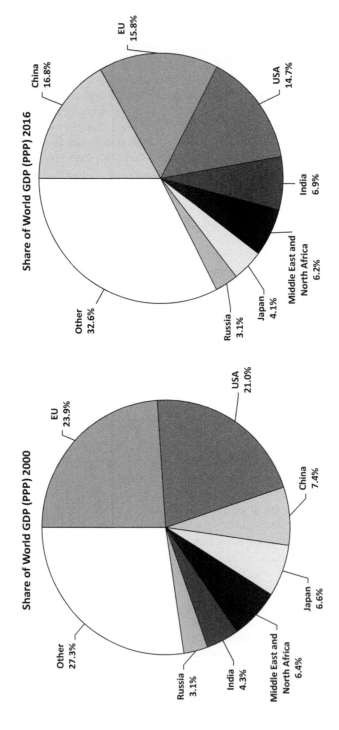

Figure 2.1 Share of the world economy in 2000 and 2016 (GDP in PPP current prices)
Source: IMF (2017)

The Middle East and North Africa

Short- and long-term challenges

One of the greatest challenges in the history of the region has been the great (political) game in which regional and global actors interact and influence regional political and economic development. The rivalry between the global powers such as the USA and the former Soviet Union contributed to the dynamics of politics and economics in the Middle East and North Africa region until 1990. The region became the extension of the Cold War between these two superpowers for decades. The impacts of this period have had profound consequences for the region, both short term and long term (Richards and Waterbury, 1990). One of the consequences is prolonged political instability, wars between the countries and internal conflicts within the countries of the region. Peace and stability in the region can only be secured when it takes root in the everyday lives of the people. This will happen if peace can bring economic integration and increased interdependence among the countries of the region resulting in economic development for people of the region (Fischer et al., 1994).

Arab states have made substantial progress in human development over the past four decades. Life expectancy has increased, mortality rates for children under five years of age have fallen by about two-thirds, adult literacy has increased sharply, especially women's literacy, reflecting very large increases in gross educational enrollment, including that of girls. Having said that, countries in the Middle East and North Africa have been suffering from lack of good governance for decades, not being able to respond to the demands and rights of the people. Authoritarian regimes have been busy benefiting a small group of elites, oppressing people of the region and refusing to provide necessary political, economic and social reforms. Consequently, quantitative improvements in health and education have not yet reached all citizens, and the expansion of services has not been matched by needed qualitative improvements of people's lives. The region also falls short of joining the global information society and economy as a complete partner, and to tackle the human and economic scourge of joblessness, which afflicts Arab countries as a group more seriously than any other developing region. And it clearly outlines the challenges for Arab states in terms of strengthening the personal freedom of people and boosting broad-based citizen participation in political and economic affairs (UNDP, 2002).

It is clear that much still needs to be done in order to provide current and future generations with the political voice, social choices and economic opportunities. Partly the lack of these elements led to the Arab Springs. However, six years after the Arab Spring, the Middle East region is still suffering from multiple crises and one of the most profound transformations in its history. In fact, many of the current political and economic challenges facing the region today have their causes in policies implemented long before the start of the Arab Spring or even before 9/11. The consequences of a lack of inadequate political and economic reforms are currently visible with high unemployment, especially among the young generation. The region is marked by political instability and human suffering on a huge scale, particularly in Syria but also in other parts of the region. Consequently, the region is likely to be characterized by fragile economic growth, reduced investments, long-term instability and political conflicts. The Arab nation-state system is under attack by the threatened disintegration of some states, such as Syria, Yemen, Libya and even Iraq. Continued civil wars in Syria and Iraq are likely to reinforce the hope by many Kurds for greater autonomy over a larger territory (Khouri, 2017).

The pattern of uneven development in the Middle East and North Africa (MENA) region is likely to continue: the oil-producing Gulf countries offer the greatest opportunities for the young population as well as for talented people from other countries; thus the gap between them and the rest of the region increases. Low energy prices have had both positive and negative effects on the countries of the region. For energy-poor countries low energy prices has meant lower costs for energy imports as well as opportunities to phase out subsidies for fossil fuels. The reverse is true for the energy-rich countries which have suffered from reduced export revenues, rising budget deficit and dwindling foreign reserves. The long-term effects will depend entirely on how persistent the low energy prices will be. The economically stable oil producing countries continue, however, to take regional leadership, while dealing with growing demands for democracy, equality and freedom in their countries (UNDP, 2016).

The demographic development is one of the most significant challenges (and opportunities) in the region. A rapidly growing population means increased pressure on state authorities and their abilities and capacities to provide basic services to all. A large young population should be an asset but is likely to be a destabilizing force since the prospects in the labor markets are so bleak. Population growth also means a growing need for energy, and the domestic consumption of energy has been growing in recent years. In 2015, Saudi Arabia was the world's fifth largest consumer of oil after the US, China, Japan and India. Its oil consumption is larger than the combined consumption of Germany and France. According to the OECD, the MENA region's energy demand will increase by 3% annually until 2030, twice as much as the global increase. Along with an inefficient use of energy and government subsidies, the increase in domestic energy consumption will lead to both increased emissions of carbon dioxide and reduced oil exports in the long term (Al-Tamimi, 2014).

Climate sensitivity

The MENA region is very sensitive to climate change which, among other things, affects access to water and food. Food security is already a major problem in the region where a large proportion of food is being imported from other regions. This is mainly due to a lack of arable land and water for food production within the country or region. The richer countries in the region can solve this partly through seawater desalination even though this is an energy-intensive and environmentally unfriendly process. An additional aspect of the water shortage is the fact that most of the available water in the region is found in cross-border areas. Conflicts over water, which are often linked to other regional conflicts, are common. Cooperation on transboundary rivers such as the River Jordan and the Euphrates and Tigris is a necessity in the future. Furthermore, the relatively high population growth and urbanization have exerted greater pressure on the already scarce water resources. Most essential in this regard, in the long term, is the issue of water management for sustainable development and stability in the Middle East and North Africa (World Bank, 2017).

Weak economic integration

Regional economic integration is one of the most important dilemmas in the MENA region. That means that the governments, stakeholders and societies are sometimes in cooperation with each other and sometimes at odds which has impacts on the development of the region's countries (Milton-Edwards and Hinchcliffe, 2007). Undiversified economies and limited mutual trade slow regional integration. Despite common language, religion and culture between the various Arab countries, the degree of regional integration is low in comparison with other regions.[1] According to the World Trade Organization (WTO) the intra-regional trade among the Arab states was only 8.6% of their total trade in 2015. This compares poorly with the corresponding regional trade in the EU (59%) and the Association of Southeast Asian Nations (ASEAN) (22%).

Global political and economic landscape

The lack of a diversified economic base makes trade between countries limited. As a result, it is a common trend that the largest trading partners of each country in the region are China, the EU or the US. Besides, oil and gas rich countries are competing for access to external markets for their export of natural resources (WTO, 2017).

Another major problem is the lack of a harmonized system to deal with standard procedures in line with WTO in order to facilitate trade with regional countries. Consequently, the local markets are closed from external competition making the local companies less competitive and less integrated in the global value chain. On top of these economic issues, lack of political trust and relatively high non-tariff barriers hamper harmonization of economic activities. The economic outlook is therefore bleak in many parts of the MENA region (Rouis and Tabor, 2013).

Regional power struggle and competition[2]

The security situation in the Middle East has deteriorated, with the rising threat of terrorist groups, failing states, ensuing wars and geopolitical rivalries. The US role in the region has been and remains crucial, not the least in regards to the protection of Israel, the fight against terrorism and economic interests. However, after two costly wars in the region the United States is hesitant to take leadership in many of the serious regional conflicts. Additionally, the financial crisis in 2008 put pressure on the level of national debt both in the US but also among the European countries. This led to the realization that not even the US is capable of managing the global security challenges on its own. This creates a power vacuum in the MENA region, a development that some of the regional big powers take advantage of.

The conflicts in Syria, Iraq and Yemen have exposed an already existing political gap between Iran and Saudi Arabia in the battle for regional hegemony (Weidokal, 2016). Although there are different views on whether Turkey is a part of the Middle East or not, the country plays a crucial role in shaping the security development of the region. Turkey has also been active in its foreign policy in order to gain regional access to protect its own national interests. Turkey, once the star of nations in getting the right balance in politics and religion, is struggling to find its footing due to multiple conflicts in and around the country. Turkey is also keen on making sure that the aspirations of Kurds in Iraq and Syria to create a pan Kurdish state do not spill over to its Kurdish minority population. Turkey seems to be the regional superpower that could affect regional trends, but the country has been weakened by both the external and internal developments (Gardner, 2017).

On one hand, the Syrian civil war has put pressure on the Turkish ability to manage conflict in its close geographical proximity, not least when millions of Syrian refugees have come to Turkey. On the other hand, Ankara's position has weakened due to domestic developments and the internal power struggle against the Gulen movement. Turkey's worsening relations with the West (the US and EU) also plays an important role in pushing Turkey away from the Western countries into further cooperation with Russia. Whether this is just a tactical or a profound strategic shift in Turkey's foreign policy remains to be seen. What is clear is that Turkey has lost the political and economic momentum the country had before the Arab Spring. Today, Turkey is at a critical juncture because of the civil war in Syria, its internal development and the changing global order. Since President Erdoğan has lost favor with Washington and Brussels over his domestic crackdown and foreign adventures, his fortunes are now partly depending on the relations with Moscow on issues related to energy and regional security (Foreign Affairs, 2016).

All the key regional players have differing interests in Syria. Assad wants his country back, whole and entire. Turkey wants a border "safe zone" under its control, principally to curb

Table 2.1 Key statistics for regional actors in the Middle East (all figures are for 2016)

	Population (in millions)	The size of economy (billion USD PPP)	The size of total trade (billion USD)	Military expenditure (billion USD)
Turkey	78	1589	342	14.8
Iran	79	1455	106	12.7
Saudi Arabia	31	1988	314	63.7

Source: SIPRI 2017, IMF 2017, UN Population Statistics, 2017, WTO 2017

autonomy aspirations among the Syrian Kurds. For their part, the Kurds want to be free of Damascus's oppression and some would like to join forces with the self-governing Kurdish regional administration in northern Iraq, a prospect Ankara views as an existential threat, given its own large, disaffected Kurdish population (*The Guardian*, 2017).

One of the most interesting political trends in the coming years is likely to be that Iran is about to enter a new phase in its foreign policy after the nuclear agreement with the Western countries. It is possible that this will open new possibilities for regional cooperation. It also lays the foundation for an intensified competition for regional hegemony (see Table 2.1 for the regional power balance). Iran has many advantages – an educated population, good industrial base, low birth rates and significant IT capabilities, which could all contribute to making the country competitive, at least on the regional arena. A stronger Iran is likely to be looked upon in both a positive and negative way by its neighbors. An assertive Iran that gives higher priority to economic modernization and regional security development will strengthen Tehran's regional capacity. The lifting of the sanctions also opens the large internal market for Western companies. Attracting foreign direct investments in infrastructure and energy sectors will boost economic growth. The much-needed investment particularly in the energy sector will also increase Iran's capacity to export more oil and even gas in the future, strengthening the financial resources and increasing the military capabilities (Katzman, 2017).

Historically, Saudi Arabia has played an important role in Middle East politics, often through other regional states and behind the scenes through the country's vast economic and financial means. However, since the eruption of the Arab Spring, Saudi Arabia has moved towards center stage of the Middle Eastern political and security development. The ongoing conflicts in the region in light of the Arab Spring have shaped the country's foreign and security policy to become more forceful and inclined towards the use of military power beyond its borders. The factors shaping Saudi Arabia's more assertive foreign policy are twofold. First, internal developments mainly due to the structural changes within the kingdom, the issue with the minority Shia Muslims and the lower oil prices that have put pressure on the economy with a substantial budget deficit. However, second, the external factors are equally important in shaping Saudi Arabia's policy towards the region. A driving force behind Saudi Arabia's assertive behavior is the regional rivalry with and perceived threat from Iran. Riyadh sees Iran as a fierce regional competitor and a main rival in many of the regional conflicts such as Syria, Iraq and Yemen. The House of Saud perceives its security under threat both from within and from without its borders. The overarching external threat that looms large in Saudi Arabian security is Iran's perceived aggressiveness, regional ambitions and interference in the affairs of other states. The perceived threat from Iran is accompanied by supposed threats from al-Qaeda and Daesh (Bergenwall, 2016).

Global power shift and implications for the region

During the 21st century, political, military and economic shifts have accelerated. The redistribution of power will continue with emerging powers filling the power gaps. In the Middle East, this development causes regional tension between Turkey, Saudi Arabia and Iran affecting and prolonging some of the serious conflicts in the region. But the redistribution of power is also creating new opportunities for Russia and China.

Russia and rising influence in the MENA region

Not since the Soviet Union was expelled from Egypt in 1972, has the Russian/Soviet Union presence in the Middle East and North Africa been as strong as today, More than 25 years after the collapse of the Soviet Union. There are certainly many reasons why we are witnessing the change in Russian behavior and its foreign policy. Russia seems to have chosen a path of confrontation with the West and NATO – aiming at replacing Western-style democratic governments with populist or nationalist ones (Trenin, 2016).

Partly due to the recent US foreign policy ambiguity towards the Middle East, Russia is experiencing a renaissance in the region. Since the Russian military involvement in the Syrian crisis, Moscow has been able to demonstrate its military capabilities. Russia has been launching attacks against the opposition in Syria from its bases inside Syria, from a base in Iran, as well as missile launches from the Caspian Sea and from the eastern parts of the Mediterranean. These are clear indications of Russian assertiveness, not only in the Russian backyard but also in relatively faraway places. Moving into the political vacuum created by the US, the Russian President Vladimir Putin now stands poised to make major geopolitical advances into areas that his predecessors desired. The recent trends in the region, especially after the Arab Spring, point to the fact that Russia's influence is rising while the US is waning (ABC News, 2016).

The Russian strategic approach is that the country wants a new global security structure, including the Middle East and North Africa. In the Middle East, there are countries that also want to be a part of this new global order/structure. That is partly why the regional interests of Iran are in line with the Russian ambitions to change the power structure in the region. Russia's behavior is also governed by the country's domestic order rather than the laws of international relations. These external and internal factors are shaping Russian policy towards the Middle East (*The Economist*, 2017).

The US has historically been able to demonstrate its global power, providing a security umbrella for the countries of the Middle East and North Africa. The US has been able to maintain its military capabilities (and political influence) in the region without any major challenges. Slowly but surely, Washington's freedom of action is being restricted. When Russia is flexing its military and political muscles, it will ultimately lead to regional countries recalculating their relations with Moscow, at least in a short-term perspective (*The Economist*, 2017).

The question is whether these trends are temporary and limited only to the Syrian crisis, or if they appear to represent a more permanent shift in the geostrategic realities of the Middle East. There are factors in favor of a permanent shift. One of these factors is that the Russian military bases in Syria will most likely remain in place in the years to come. The result of this will then be that the Russian military (Russian fighters or S-400 surface-to-air missile system) will be capable of striking a wide range of regional targets. US and allied forces will be confronted with an area denial, anti-access challenge on NATO's southern flank that they have not faced for decades. Consequently, the regional states will have to take into account the Russian power projection and the far-reaching impact on their own decision-making (Foreign Policy, 2016).

On the other hand, there are economic indicators that point to long-term challenges for Russia. The Russian economy has been shrinking recently, partly due to sanctions, lower oil prices and lower demand for Russian oil and gas, especially from the European countries. The Russian economy is not as diversified as the Chinese economy, and its dependency on raw material (accounts for large parts of the Russian exports) makes Russia vulnerable to fluctuations in global energy prices. Put simply, the Russian economy does not produce attractive and competitive products that the rest of the world wants to buy with the exception of oil, gas and arms. Thus, the long-term economic and military constraints will be difficult to overcome and consequently the Russian aims will be rather limited – Russia will probably have difficulties in becoming a new security hegemon in the Middle East and North Africa region. Despite Russia's recent political strength in the Middle East, Russia is a country in structural decline, see Figure 2.2 for Russian's military expenditure in comparison with the US and China (*The Economist*, 2017).

China: A new global player in the MENA region

The US has been the dominant power in the Middle East since World War II. China, however, is a new major player in the region and China's interest in the region started to grow during the 1990s. Historically, the Middle East has been viewed by Chinese leadership as a less significant region for China as Beijing has been paying more attention to its immediate neighborhood in the East and South China Sea. China is therefore not as familiar with Middle East affairs as other major foreign stakeholders, namely the USA and Europe. China's approach to the Middle East has also been influenced by its non-intervention policy, for example China cares less about the internal development in the Middle Eastern countries in questions related to disputed areas, ethnic issues and human rights abuses (Feng, 2015).

China's interest in the region is, however, on the rise. The One Belt One Road initiative (OBOR), proposed by Chinese President Xi Jinping in 2013, aims at further promotion of international economic cooperation against the backdrop of tendencies against globalization. As China strengthens relations with its Middle Eastern partners, it hopes that the OBOR will form the backbone of future trade arrangements. China views the Middle East region as a critical partner in the OBOR initiative (Wang, 2017).

Why is China interested in the Middle East?

The Middle East has now become a central point for Chinese foreign policy in line with China's growing political, economic and military capabilities. China has become the largest economy in the world (based on PPP) and the largest trading nation. China's rapid economic growth has led to a rising energy demand. At the beginning of the 1990s, China was a net exporter of oil. The rapid increase in energy demand driven by high economic growth transformed China and the country became a net importer of oil; see Figure 2.3 for China's production and consumption of oil. Today China has become the second largest consumer of oil. Although the US is still the world's largest oil consumer, the shale oil revolution has made the country less dependent on import of oil than before. According to statistics from EIA (US Energy Information Administration) the US is producing more than 4 million barrels of oil per day from oil shale production since 2008 (RAND, 2016).

Global trends in energy consumption have made China more dependent on import of oil from the Middle East and other countries; see Figure 2.4 for the rise in China's import of oil from Saudi Arabia. Countries like Saudi Arabia and Iran have come to play an important

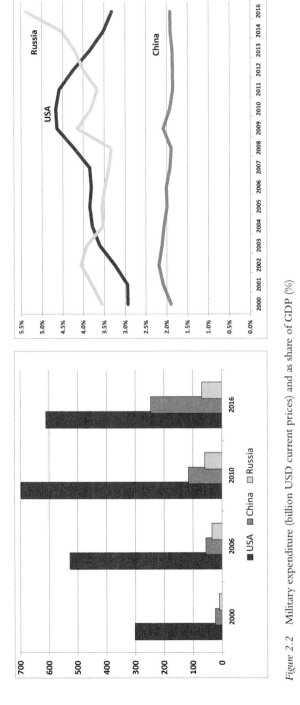

Figure 2.2 Military expenditure (billion USD current prices) and as share of GDP (%)
Source: SIPRI Military Expenditure 2017

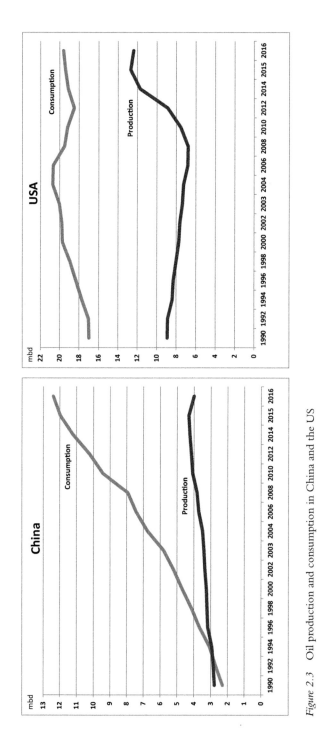

Figure 2.3 Oil production and consumption in China and the US
Source: US Energy Information Administration, 2017; BP World Energy Review 2017 and International Energy Agency, 2017

Global political and economic landscape

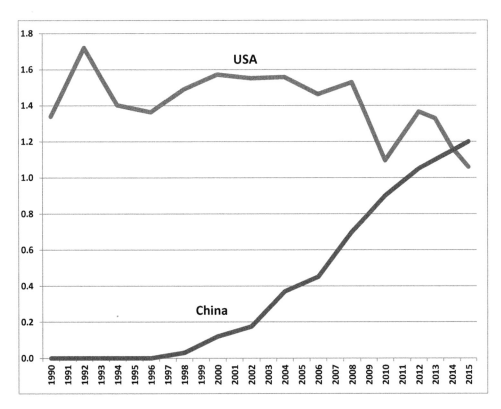

Figure 2.4 Import of oil (mbd) from Saudi Arabia between 1990 and 2015
Source: US Energy Information Administration, 2017

role in China's diversification of energy needs. Based on these facts, it seems that China's primary interest in the Middle East, at least for now, is based on securing its substantial energy needs. The Middle East has about two-third of the world's oil, mostly in the Persian Gulf. Saudi Arabia alone has about one-quarter of all the oil on the planet. Oil reserves are a form of economic rent – the difference between the market price and the cost of production (Cammett et al., 2015). At the end of 2016, half of China's need for imported oil came from the Middle East and North Africa, mainly from Saudi Arabia, Iran and Iraq (International Energy Agency, 2017).

China is also the reason behind the major shift in global trade pattern. In 2000, European countries were the largest trading partners to Iran. In 2015, China was the largest export market for Iran and the second largest import market after United Arab Emirates. China's share of Iran's total trade was 22%. The same pattern can be seen between China and other countries in the Middle East. China has become the main export destination for the GCC countries (Gulf Council Cooperation). In 2015, China was closing the gap with the EU to become the largest trading partner to GCC countries (EUs total share was 16.6% while China held 14.9%). China is also Saudi Arabia's largest export market consisting of 15% of the Kingdom's export in 2015. China has taken over the US as the largest importer of Saudi oil, a shift that took place during 2015 which is a sign of the growing importance of China to Saudi Arabia and vice versa. Thus, China emerged as the Middle East's dominant trading partner (Karasik, 2014).

The US rebalances to the Pacific and China to the MENA region

Growing energy dependency as well as economic and trade incentives are paving the way for a Chinese rebalancing of its political and security interests in the Middle East. Recent discussions in the Chinese foreign policy community reflect increasing interest in looking to the West. The shift towards the Middle East may be in part an attempt to check and balance Western actions in this region (Hindy, 2017).

In a way, China is rebalancing its foreign policy towards the Middle East, in the same way as the US is rebalancing its interests towards the Pacific region. Whether the Chinese move is a reaction to the US rebalancing to Asia Pacific or if it is simply because the Middle East is becoming more important to China from a geostrategic perspective, is open to discussion. Until recently, China has been a regional power especially assertive in its back yards of East Asia and Southeast Asia. The growing importance of the Middle East also broadens Chinese foreign policy (RAND, 2016).

Traditionally, the US has been a key guarantor of the security in the Middle East and via its military supremacy the US has secured the trading routes from the Middle East to Asia. With the growing Chinese interest, the US and China might be able to cooperate in securing the trading routes maintaining both political and economic stability in a fragile region. However, there is also a risk of competition when China is extending its sphere of influence via Central Asia to the Middle East. In order to have a long-term footing and strategic depth, China needs to have good relations with Iran and Saudi Arabia – the two most important countries in the Middle East. China wants to have solid and good relations with these nations without being involved in regional tension. However, China is also aware of the tension between these two regional powers (RAND, 2016).

Iran and Saudi Arabia have different political departing points. China's interest in Iran builds on the fact that Iran, as a regional power, has been challenging the US policy in the region since the Iranian Revolution. In that sense Iran is one of the few countries outside the global US network of allies. As we have seen in the recent turmoil in the Middle East region, Iran has the capacity and political determination to challenge the US policy towards the Middle East in various ways and places, like in Iraq, Syria and Yemen. In a possible Chinese standoff with the US in Asia, it is more possible that Iran could be a strategic partner to China than to the US. This does not mean that China is interested in a conflict with the US. In fact, China has been happy to maintain a cooperative approach to the US and the global institutions that the Western countries have created since World War II. Consequently, China has been careful not to upset the US while China is deepening its relations with Iran (Hsu, 2016).

China's relations with Saudi Arabia are different in this regard. Saudi Arabia has been a key player and ally to the US in the Middle East but still has been able to maintain close relations with Beijing. But Saudi Arabia has been drifting away from the US in light of the Arab Spring. The Saudis have been disappointed by the US handling of the major regional conflicts in the Middle East and North Africa, particularly the US handling of Egypt's Hosni Mubarak. This pushed Saudi Arabia to become more assertive as a regional actor and consequently it was Saudi Arabia who intervened (military intervention) in Bahrain in 2011 to save the ruling family (*The Atlantic*, 2015).

Saudi Arabia therefore is keen on deepening its political and economic relations with China. Saudis see China as a global actor capable of playing an important role in the region. Saudi Arabia is willing to work with China to promote global and regional security defined by the Saudis (*Foreign Policy*, 2017).

Final words

A global angle

The current global economic and political systems were created as a reaction against the disasters of the first half of the 20th century. That was in turn, caused by the unprecedented economic progress of the 19th century. On a global level, a new set of institutions like the International Monetary Fund, the World Bank and the World Trade Organization were created. Geopolitically, the post-war era ended with the dissolution of the Soviet Union in 1991 after having experienced a devastating economic crisis. Today, the Western countries are experiencing geopolitical and economic difficulties, not least after the financial crisis in 2008 which resulted in higher state debt. At the same time, the uncertainty about America's role in the world creates new opportunities for China and Russia. Both Moscow and Beijing are increasingly assertive. In parallel to this, there are openings for regional countries to be more assertive in the Middle East and North Africa.

Consequently, we seem to be at the end of an economic as well as a geopolitical period where Western dominance on the global arena is in decline. It remains to be seen what this new era will mean in terms of geopolitics. What is clear is that in this new world order China will play a bigger role in sustaining the global order. The USA, still the most powerful country on the planet, is facing the same dilemma as the UK did almost 100 years ago; imperial overstretch threatens America as it did the UK. The ability and, more recently, willingness of America to act as global policeman has been eroded. Will the US counterbalance Iran, the terrorists of Islamic State in the Middle East, deal with a nationalist Russian regime and an assertive China? It seems clear that other powers think it cannot. They are pushing to see whether America will react, in the Middle East, Ukraine and South China Sea.

What about Russia and its future role and capabilities in shaping the geopolitical development of the 21st century? Russia wants to be seen as a great power again at the expense of the US and the US-led world order. Russia wants to be free from Western values and pursue its own ideology and influence. Russia wants to be respected (not neglected or underestimated) due to its history and vitality. However, there is also a realization of the weaknesses of Russia: declining population and a non-diversified economy that is dependent on energy prices. Declining powers, however, can also be at least as disruptive as rising powers. The best way of dealing with declining powers is through firmness and awareness without illusions.

If Russia is considered a declining power, China is the opposite. China's status as a rising world power is by now clear, reflected in its economic power and growing military strength. Its position in Asia is well-established, and actions in the East China and South China Seas of late have rankled with the USA. Many of the oil producer countries in the Middle East are today highly dependent on oil export income from China. As interdependence in energy trade deepens over time, their corresponding importance to each other in business and strategic relations will also increase. The rising economic and military power will ultimately lead to political and security ambitions.

A regional angle

The Thirty Years' War in Europe (1618–1648) was a tragedy for the continent, a struggle over the political and religious order of Central Europe. It was a contest over political as well as religious power affecting and shaping the future of the Europe. The current political turmoil in the Middle East and North Africa indicates that the region seems to be on the verge of a conflict that can be described as a new Thirty Years' War. The region is threatening to slide into a conflict that is characterized by a disintegrating regional order, a contest between secular and religious concepts of domestic and regional politics, the potential for new and unlikely alliances, and all that within a disintegrating center. What is at stake is the future of the states in the region and the future political, religious system (Centre for Security Study, 2015).

What is unfolding now is characterized by a disintegrating regional order, a contest between secular and religious concepts of domestic and regional politics, and the potential for the breakup of the traditional alliances and creation of (unlikely) new alliances. In this process, regional actors (Iran, Turkey and Saudi Arabia) will be searching for political and economic support from global actors (China, Russia and later in the process even India) in order to create a dominant security and economic structure. The Middle East is again in the middle of a historical transformation. Almost 100 years ago, the fall of the Ottoman Empire and other external factors forced the region to undergo a significant structural change to come with the power struggle and external interventions. Today the Middle East and North Africa is still trying to find its identity, its political system, cultural and religious place in a world that is changing rapidly. As these changes take place, states that are pragmatic and adapt to the current needs of the people are those that can survive, strengthen their domestic legitimacy and enhance their regional capabilities, both economically and in terms of security. In this transformation, states that have realized the necessity of diversifying their economic foundation will strengthen their competitiveness and thus become a bigger player in the economic activities and security arrangements.

Saudi Arabia and Iran seem to be in direct confrontation in the geopolitics of the Middle East and North Africa. The House of Saud perceives its security under threat both from internal and external forces. The driver of the Iranian threat in Riyadh is primarily realpolitik. The kingdom fears that the balance of power in the Middle East will change in favor of Iran. Saudi Arabia is concerned that the US, its long-time ally, will continue to pursue a strategy of retrenchment from the Middle East and to refrain from providing support to traditional Arab allies in times of trouble. Saudi Arabia was upset by US policies during the early days of the Arab Spring. From the horizon of Riyadh, the presidency of Obama was very problematic and the new US administration is unpredictable, at least in the short term. This means that Riyadh must act to maintain its national interests in a fast-changing regional dynamic. Riyadh's involvement in Iraq, Syria and Yemen are clear indications of the new Saudi foreign policy in the broader Middle East and North Africa. Together with Iran and Turkey, Saudi Arabia will directly or indirectly play an important role in shaping the future of this turbulent region in the years to come.

Thus, it is important to note that the global and regional changes that are taking place raise the question about the future world order and a different value system compared with the one created by the Western countries after WWII. The whole Western architecture based on democratic values, openness and free trade is no longer something that can be taken for granted. In this new period of uncertainty and new world order even powerful regional states will take a much more active role in shaping the regional security and economic architecture.

Notes

1 In some other aspects like the job market the integration is more advanced. Many Egyptians and Yemenis are working in the richer Gulf countries, likewise people from Tunisia working in Libya. These workers send substantial remittances back to their home countries. Besides, richer Gulf countries are investing in poor Arab countries through development aid.
2 Other important countries in the Gulf region, like Israel, Egypt and even smaller countries, play an important role in the region. However, due to limited scope the chapter focuses on three regional actors, Iran, Turkey and Saudi Arabia.

References

ABC News (December 29, 2016). "Syrian Ceasefire a Sign of Russian Might and Waning US Influence". ABC News. www.abc.net.au/news/2016-12-30/syria-ceasefire-sign-russian-might-waning-us-influence/8153738

Al-Tamimi, N.M. (2014). *China Saudi Arabia Relations 1990–2012, Marriage of Convenience or Strategic Alliance?* Oxford: Routledge.

Bergenwall, S. (2016). *The Assertive Kingdom, Saudi Arabia's Threat Perception, Capabilities and Strategies.* Stockholm: FOI.

BP (2017). *World Energy Review 2017.*

Cammett, M., Diwan, I., Richards, A., and Waterbury, J. (2015). *A Political Economy of the Middle East.* 4th edn. Boulder: Westview Press.

Centre for Security Study (2015). *Strategic Trends 2015, Key Development in Global Affairs.* Zurich: Centre for Security Study.

Eurostat (2017). "The EU in the World – Economy and Finance". https://ec.europa.eu/eurostat/statistics-explained/index.php/The_EU_in_the_world_-_economy_and_finance

Feng, C. (April 2015). *Embracing Interdependence: The Dynamics of China and the Middle East.* Brookings Institution.

Fischer, S., Hausman, L.J., Karasik, A.D., Schelling, T. (1994). *Securing Peace in the Middle East, Project on Economic Transition.* London: The MIT Press.

Foreign Affairs (November 24, 2016). "Turkey's Post–Arab Spring Foreign Policy".

Foreign Policy (September 13, 2016). "Russia's Middle East Offensive".

Foreign Policy (March 16, 2017). "Saudi Arabia, China Sign Deals Worth Up to $65 Billion".

Gardner, D. (February 7, 2017). "Turkey's Strategic Direction is in Play in Syria". *Financial Times.*

Hindy, L. (April 2017). "A Rising China Eyes the Middle East". The Century Foundation. https://tcf.org/content/report/rising-china-eyes-middle-east/?agreed=1

Hsu, S. (2016). "China's Relations with Iran: A Threat to the West?" *The Diplomat.*

International Energy Agency (2017). *World Energy Outlook 2017.*

International Monetary Fund (2017). *World Economic Outlook Database.* Washington: IMF.

Karasik, T. (February 24, 2014). *The GCC's New Affair with China.* The Middle East Institute.

Katzman, K. (2017). *Iran's Foreign and Defense Policies.* Congressional Research Service.

Khouri, R.G. (2017). "The Modern Arab State's Elusive Quest to Anchor Sovereignty in the Hands of its Citizens". In: A. Alkebsi, N.J. Brown, and C. Sparre, eds, *Restructuring the Middle East Political and Economic Policy,* 1st edn. London and New York: Routledge.

Milton-Edwards, B. and Hinchcliffe, P. (2007). *Conflicts in the Middle East since 1945.* London and New York: Routledge.

National Intelligence Council (2012). *Global Trends 2030 Alternative Worlds.* Washington: NIC.

RAND Corporation (2016). *China in the Middle East: The Wary Dragon.*

Richards, A. and Waterbury, J. (1990). *A Political Economy of the Middle East – State, Class, and Economic Development.* Boulder: Westview Press.

Rouis, M. and Tabor, S. (2013). *Regional Economic Integration in the Middle East and North Africa.* Washington, DC: World Bank.

Stockholm International Peace Research Institute (2017). *SIPRI Year Book 2017.* Stockholm: SIPRI.

Strategic Analysis (2014). *Strategic Trends in a Global Perspective, 2025 a Completely Different World.* Stockholm: Government Office of Sweden.

The Atlantic (October 9, 2015). "Islamism, the Arab Spring, and the Failure of America's Do-Nothing Policy in the Middle East".

The Economist (25–31 March 2017). "In the Middle East Russia is Reasserting its Power".

The Guardian (12 March 2017). "The Observer View on Sending US Troops to Syria".

Trenin, D. (2016). *Russia in the Middle East: Moscow's Objectives, Priorities, and Policy Drivers.* Moscow: Carnegie Center.

UNDP (2002). *Arab Human Development Report 2002.* New York: UNDP.

UNDP (2016). *Arab Human Development Report 2016.* New York: UNDP.

UN Population Division (2017). *World Population Prospects, Population Trends.* New York: UN Department of Economics and Social Affairs.

US Energy Information Administration (2017). *Current Issues and Trends.* EIA.

Wang, J. (May 9, 2017). "'One Belt One Road': A Vision for the Future of China-Middle East Relations". *Al Jazeera*.

Weidokal, M. (2016). *The Power Vacuum in the Middle East and North Africa*. International Strategic Analysis.

World Bank (May 14, 2017). *Water Management is Key to Sustainable Development and Stability in the Middle East and North Africa*.

World Trade Organization (2017). *Statistics Database on World Trade*.

3

CONFLICTS IN THE MIDDLE EAST AND NORTH AFRICA

An attempt at reframing

Joost R. Hiltermann[1]

Introduction: Writing about conflict in MENA

To write about conflicts, or conflict, in the Middle East and North Africa (MENA) is to talk about the way in which millions of people live their daily lives. Even those not in a war zone still live in fear that conflict might descend on them as suddenly as it did on their neighbors: some form of armed conflict is never far away. That fear – informed also by the memory of conflicts past – may itself act as inoculation against an outbreak of fighting, but in the end it rarely is "the people" who choose to wage war. It is their political leaders who do – leaders who are seldom elected and even more rarely subject to peaceful rotation from office. Instead, they cling to power with a combination of habit, greed and self-preservation.

To write intelligibly about armed conflict in the MENA region is to offer, first off, a kaleidoscopic view of the political and historical landscape, and provide the beginnings of a typology for the past 50 years. (I have included an attempt in the appendix to this chapter.) The result is a bewildering (and far from exhaustive) list that obscures as much as it clarifies, and upon close examination is more likely to provoke controversy than consensus. It suggests that any attempt at a typology inescapably leads to three principal conclusions: that MENA conflicts are wildly varied, indeed unique, in origin, character and evolution; that despite the endurance of certain conflicts, they do not come to us "from time immemorial", the result of supposedly primordial differences (Jews vs Muslims; Sunni vs Shia); and that they betray no defined patterns or rules for why or how they begin, continue in a constant ebb and flow, and eventually – usually after a long many years and great violence – come to an end. There can be no "theory of MENA conflicts" but at most an attempt to understand their idiosyncrasies, how they are linked, and how patterns of governance, the obsolescence of social contracts and growing illegitimacy contribute to their outbreak.

Nor will we get very far if we study "deep causes", such as poverty, inequality, resource competition, poor governance, injustice, political repression, social fissures, ethnic divisions, religious schisms and so forth. These phenomena, which are not unique to the MENA region, prevail long before conflict breaks out, survive and are compounded by it, and usually persist long afterward. However, they may help explain conflict's endemic nature and recurring cycles in societies over decades. More interesting are causes external to the region that play a determinant role. The Cold War, for instance, structured conflicts within a global geopolitical struggle in which Middle Eastern actors were not key shapers but could position themselves. The 9/11 attacks are another example, with Washington reshaping the "resistance axis" that arose from the Arab–Israeli conflict and the "Three No's" of the 1967 Arab League summit in Khartoum into an "axis of evil", despite the fact that the actors concerned (Iraq, Iran, Hezbollah and to a lesser extent Syria) had nothing to do with the attacks.

Generally, it would be more useful to look at "proximate causes", aka catalysts or triggers. These are due to human actions that have immediate impact and feed on those deeper trends, exploit and politicize them, and turn them into weapons: poverty as weapon, water as weapon, oil as weapon, inequality as weapon, religious difference as weapon, etc. Examples of proximate causes are: a perceived opportunity (e.g., a sudden vulnerability in a rival), fear of attack by an adversary, revenge for a recent slight or old grievance, an acute financial crisis, pressing resource scarcity, or, simply, an accident: a miscommunication, a misread signal, a misinterpretation of an event. The possibilities are legion, and I suspect we can find examples of all of these in MENA conflicts over the past 50 years.

Of lineages and earthquakes

Even if we cannot fashion an overall theory of conflict in MENA, it may be useful to look at conflict genealogies; these may at least elucidate a certain internal logic and trajectory, if not outcomes, of clusters of associated conflicts. These lineages often start with a political earth-quake – itself the result of a long build-up of pressures – which generates rolling tremors as well as new fissures, and unleashes a proliferating series of secondary struggles. The biggest earth-quake (Cluster I) was the disintegration of the Ottoman Empire, which has its own genealogy, its own internal logic and dynamic, and its own consequences, yielding a "rolling" and pervasive disorder, visible until this day.

Starting with the dramatic changes wrought by World War I is admittedly somewhat arbi-trary; the region's "pre-history" cannot be ignored in any serious study of its 20th-century his-tory leading up to today. However, one of this essay's principal theses is that it is the impact of post-World War I Western dominance on what existed in the region that decisively shaped what form local political systems and governance took in subsequent decades, with variations attrib-utable precisely to that pre-history. Hence the focus on that interaction and its consequences.

The Empire's demise set off at least four other major earthquakes within the MENA region during the past century and has sustained the conflict clusters to which these gave birth. The 1948 creation of the state of Israel was one such earthquake (Cluster II). Then followed the 1979 Islamic Revolution in Iran (Cluster III) and the siege of the Grand Mosque in Mecca that same year (Cluster IV). The 2011 Arab uprisings, which spread hope through the region even as they, and the violent response to them, profoundly destabilized it, promised to drive a nail in the post-Ottoman order's coffin (Cluster V). (I will describe region-shaking external interference, such as the 2003 US invasion of Iraq and the 2015 Russian military intervention in Syria, sep-arately below.) The classification of these lineages is admittedly arbitrary; they serve to elucidate and initiate a debate, not to be the definitive way of grouping conflicts in the MENA region (Hiltermann, 2018).

The conflict clusters – described in more detail below – can be viewed independently of each other, yet this does not mean they are not linked; after all, they share the same brutal pater-nity, and therefore the same violent pathology. In its construction, the post-Ottoman order/ disorder and associated colonial enterprise allowed for the creation of Israel, starting with the 1917 Balfour Declaration, even as it denied a state to the Kurds in the 1923 Treaty of Lausanne. The same post-Ottoman order, as it aged, gave rise to ideological projects challenging it – Arab secular nationalism, Cold War socialism, Baathism, liberal capitalism, Islamism – culminating in the non-ideological Arab uprisings in 2011. The Iranian Revolution was one such challenge to secular, Western neo-colonialism. Indeed, the Arab uprisings, the Iranian Revolution, and post-Mecca-siege Sunni radicalization have a lot in common: all three are responses to aspects of the non-functioning post-Ottoman order. Even the Algerian civil war (1992–1999) may be seen in this context – as an early Islamist challenge to secularism, which was crushed and may yet rebound. Yet we should understand that it also emanated from a French colonial project that predated the end of Ottoman rule.

Cluster I: The post-Ottoman order/disorder[2]

The Ottoman Empire collapsed from the weight of its own contradictions, helped by a push from its enemies, including the two main Western colonial powers, Britain and France, which helped dismantle it and picked over its leftovers. These two states stepped into the military, political and administrative vacuum, dividing the spoils between them, and endeavoring to fashion a new order in the territories they acquired. This led to a chronic legitimacy crisis from which the region has not been able to recover and which, as the Arab uprisings intimated, may prove terminal. France and Britain imposed new borders and new political systems that reflected their own interests focused in particular on access to resources. Moreover, by grafting tissue carrying their cultural and legislative DNA onto new systems of governance, these came to reflect not just their own interests but themselves. Yet local realities gave the emerging power structures and administrations a hybrid quality, recognizable but different, functioning but not well-adapted (Sluglett, 2014).

Resistance to the new order soon began to build. Its first target was foreign control; its agent was the very secular elites trained by the colonial powers themselves, now turned against their mentors and enablers in a fury of nationalist pride (Dawn, 1991). These Arab nationalist elites governed for decades, using the ill-suited structures they had inherited, rotating through intra-elite military coups, and aligning themselves with outside powers – including their erstwhile colonial masters – to receive protection against growing opposition to their autocratic rule. Over time, new rulers were able to thoroughly overhaul governing systems and even book economic successes. In quite a few Arab countries, rulers made serious attempts to rework the institutional framework and establish a developmental state, expand education, provide universal health care and escape economic dependency (Owen, 2004).

The problem is that, in the end, all these attempts faltered. The reasons for this are many, but much can be attributed to rapid social and economic transformation that created stark dynamics of inclusion/exclusion along the lines of social class and center vs periphery, often intertwined. These failures ultimately led to the collapse of social contracts that had established a degree of legitimacy despite a lack of political participation and persistent inequality. It would be too easy, however, to dismiss the post-colonial secular regimes as total and utter failures; they achieved a fair amount. But they were brittle, their evolution greatly hampered and weakened by external interventions (the Israel project, the Cold War, the 2003 US invasion of Iraq), even as power struggles outside the region in some cases helped regimes to survive. It is fair to ask whether MENA conflicts occurred because the regimes faltered or whether the regimes faltered because they were in a state of permanent mobilization for conflict. The answer may be: a little bit of both.

Opposition to secular rulers eventually came from the religious corner. Clerics and other adherents mobilized the masses to confront a secular ideology associated with Western domination and the reigning order's failure to adequately address, much less resolve, the daunting economic and social challenges it faced – dependent as it was on the vagaries of a world economy steered by greater powers. The main carrier of popular discontent was the Muslim Brotherhood, founded in Egypt but branching out throughout the Sunni world. The new opposition sought to establish a new social contract (International Crisis Group, 2005).

Groups taking power soon found they had no choice but to permit themselves to be co-opted if they wished to survive and thrive, or risk becoming isolated and suffer (the fate of post-1979 Iran). This also meant new rulers had to choose sides, as during the Cold War; this in turn affected the character of the ruler-opposition dynamic. Challengers invariably constructed ideological frameworks to appeal to the public and mobilize opposition; these frameworks often had foreign roots as well. Take for instance socialism (inscribed in the opposition, then ruling ideology of countries as diverse as Algeria and South Yemen, along with its Baathist variant in Iraq and Syria). Yet ideological jackets fit only as long as the opponent-turned-ruler delivered the goods, but since MENA states' challenges remained as daunting as ever while aforementioned ill-suited structures began to atrophy, each successive ideology was shown ultimately to be bankrupt.

In sum, this evolving post-Ottoman order was congenitally unstable and riven by violent conflict. Algeria provides apt examples of both major transitions: its war of independence against France (1954–1962), and the civil war that erupted when the military, backed by post-independence secular elites, ejected the surging Islamists' 1991 electoral victory. Interestingly, such instability was more pronounced in former French colonies with their republican systems, sometimes with democratic trappings, than in their British-imbued counterparts, many of which were monarchies and which survive until this day, having withstood shocks of the 2011 Arab uprisings. While both types have generally been repressive and afflicted with rubber-stamp parliaments, the diverging trajectory may be attributable to the monarchies' additional layer of legitimacy, whose hereditary practices their populace accepted as legitimate and normal, whereas presidents' attempts to hand power to their sons more commonly provoked outrage.[3] Moreover, oil-producing countries of either type may have benefitted from social contracts they had a greater ability to uphold – until oil prices collapsed (Bellin, 2004).

Cluster II: The Arab–Israeli conflict

One fateful feature of the post-Ottoman colonial enterprise was the effort to create a home for the Jewish people, persecuted throughout Europe, in one of the former empire's backwaters, the area later known as Palestine. It set off an enduring struggle between Israel and the indigenous Palestinian population and its chosen representatives – the latter backed with varying degrees of sincerity by Arab states – which has shaped perceptions in the region for longer and arguably more intensely than any other. It has assumed various forms since the state's violent founding in 1948 (or earlier, if one wishes to look at its roots in Theodor Herzl's Zionist enterprise in the late 1800s and the 1917 Balfour Declaration), with Israel taking additional territory in 1967. It is not that this conflict has caused the region's many other wars since then, although it did cause some, but that the region's people perceive it as a grievous injustice, a festering wound, and a glaring example of their leaders' impotence in reversing it. That perception prevails even in non-Arab states such as Turkey and Iran. This is because it has an important Islamic dimension, but also because people there see the Israel/Arab conflict as representing an unremitting Western effort to divide, undermine and destroy the entire region, not just Palestine or the Arab order midwifed by European powers after they brought the Ottomans to their knees. They see it as a form of European settler colonialism, and resent the double standards Western powers have employed to protect Israel from its enemies (for background, see *Middle East Report*, 2014).

The persistence of the perception of Israel as a Western foothold and unfinished neo-colonial project has infected regional politics and pushed other factors (the "deep causes") to the background, at least before the 2011 Arab uprisings. People blamed their leaders for failing to stand up effectively to Israel, despite wars that demanded great sacrifice and enabled authoritarian rule. And they (and their leaders, for reasons of self-interest) blamed external actors for the latter's support of Israel as a vector of their assumed neo-colonial ambitions. Even the 2003 US invasion of Iraq was seen that way by many Iraqis. (Control of oil fields was another frequently mentioned explanation, linked to those same ambitions.)

Perceptions, at times more than "objective" reality itself, are the primary shapers of responses to events. The injury of Israel's creation, *and what it was seen to signify*, was one of the primary sources for the rise of pan-Arab populism, which fed on the broader experience of Western colonial control (through mandates, direct rule, or otherwise) of the post-Ottoman world. Post-1948, it spread with successive coups in Syria, Egypt and Iraq, taking the form of Nasserism and Baathism, and fueling popular support for the 1967 and 1973 wars. It also informed the assassination of Anwar Sadat, the peacemaker/traitor. And it gave rise to the PLO and, once the PLO came to be seen as trading away Palestinian rights, to Hamas, with more radical groups sprouting up (Islamic Jihad, Islamic State), still weak but primed to leap into the vacuum as their predecessors fail to deliver a viable independent Palestine.

The original conflict took on a logic of its own, setting off an uncontrolled chain reaction of events that continues to roil the wider region. The conclusion of one round of fighting merely laid the ground for the next. The 1967 Palestinian refugees, added to the initial 1948 wave, undermined the stability of Hashemite rule in Jordan. In a brief war in 1970–1971, Jordanian forces supported by Israel expelled PLO fighters to Lebanon; here they created a state within a state in the camps erected in 1948, using these as launching pads for cross-border operations in Israel. Israel responded in 1982, occupying southern Lebanon. This provoked resistance from the local population, supported by Iran and Syria, taking the form of the guerrilla movement known as Hezbollah (the Party of God). Today Hezbollah is fighting in Syria to keep alive its regional sponsor the Assad regime. If victorious, its very success and spreading strength could trigger a new round of war with Israel after the previous ones in 1993, 1996 and 2006, which left large swathes of Lebanon devastated, even if Hezbollah, basing itself on a strategy of mutual deterrence, has conspicuously avoided a new conflict with Israel since 2006 (International Crisis Group, 2018b).

The following sequence of events unfolded inside the territory controlled by Israel: a harsh military occupation from 1967 onward, popular resistance to it, an escalation of land grabs, violent acts of rebellion, more severe and collective punishments (detention without trial, mass imprisonment, systematic torture, house demolitions and deportation of local leaders), popular uprisings (1988, 2000), and yet harsher repression. In Gaza, the same, and then also three rounds of war (2008, 2012, 2014) following Israel's 2005 unilateral withdrawal that have left the population defeated, demoralized, and desperate (Halbfinger, 2018). Yet their very desperation will almost surely inform their readiness for the next round, as seemingly nothing else can bring a peace allowing them to live ordinary lives. The situation in the West Bank is no more sustainable: land expropriation and settlement construction proceed without significant external constraint. Meanwhile, Jerusalem and its holy sites representing the three monotheistic religions remains a focal point for contending forces from across the region, a tinder box waiting to be set alight – along with everything around it – by a single act of brazen foolishness (International Crisis Group, 2016c).

There is another dimension to the Arab–Israeli conflict that may be profoundly destabilizing for the region. Initially, the Zionist endeavor was a 19th century nationalist project; its religious dimension was mostly absent. As nationalism has aged, Jewish nationalism has aged along with it, and a submerged ethno-religious dimension of the Israel phenomenon has come to the surface (for example, in use of the term the "Jewish state").[4] This raises questions for states that are not based on a particular religious conviction, such as Israel's immediate neighbors.[5]

Cluster III: The 1979 Islamic Revolution: The rise of Shia Iran

The Iranian Revolution upended the precarious balance in the Gulf, where Western allies had long resisted Soviet attempts at making strategic inroads. To the extent that Baathist Iraq had moved into Moscow's orbit – it never fully did – it now determinedly moved away from it by restoring relations with Washington, with whom it shared a fear of spreading Shia Islamist fervor. When the Iranian revolution was still young, the domestic situation chaotic, the future and who would lead unclear, Saddam Hussein made a move aimed at precipitating a political change in Tehran favorable to Iraq's interests. He sent his forces across the border into Iran's oil-rich, majority-Arab province of Khuzestan, viewing it as Iran's Achilles' heel that would ensure a swift military victory and resultant political payoff. It was a miscalculation of his own military's strength as well as of his opponents' readiness to rally around the flag: it helped solidify, not undermine, the nascent Islamist order.

Eight years of war ensued, with human losses in the hundreds of thousands. It left deep psychological scars after the war ground to a UN-mediated halt following a political understanding between Washington and Moscow (Razoux, 2015). Iran's top leadership and military command today derive entirely from this war generation: hardened, embittered, distrustful of the West, determined never to leave the country again vulnerable to external aggression (Hiltermann, 2010).

Iraq, by contrast, despite its apparent qualitative edge at war's end, went into a tailspin, as Saddam Hussein, eager to recoup his financial losses, turned on his country's principal creditor, Kuwait, and threatened the other, Saudi Arabia. This triggered a successful US-led military effort to dislodge Iraqi forces from the small Gulf state and the imposition of crippling UN sanctions. The decade-long degeneration of Iraqi society weakened it to the point of collapse (Graham-Brown, 1999); the 2003 US invasion did the rest. Washington's ignorance of the local state of affairs informed the fatal errors it ended up making as it basked in the glow of its lightning military triumph: dismantling the army, selective de-Baathification, promoting former exiles to leadership positions, and a highly destructive manipulation of ethnic and sectarian identities that empowered Shias and Kurds while alienating Sunni Arabs (International Crisis Group, 2003). The resulting security vacuum gave rise to an escalating conflict between Sunni insurgents and government-allied Shia militias, with young men recruited into either camp to the detriment of the country's development, its enormous potential squandered despite its oil wealth but especially through misallocation of funds and pervasive corruption (International Crisis Group, 2016b).

The Islamic Revolution did not come out of nowhere, of course. The fault lines were there. It started as a popular revolt against the established order, which was dictatorial, highly repressive and heavily dependent on US support. In fact, the Shah owed his tenure to the US and UK, which engineered a coup against the democratically elected Prime Minister, Mohammad Mossadegh, in 1953, after he tried to extend national control over the oil industry (Kinzer, 2008). More broadly, therefore, the movement to oust the Shah was a revolt against a neo-imperial order established during the Cold War that controlled the region through client regimes. It took on a predominantly Islamist form because the repressive order it replaced had been secular – secularism being seen as an inauthentic, alien ideology, reflecting values imposed by the West to open Iran up to Western exploitation. This Islamist awakening, which was Shia in character because it happened to take place in majority-Shia Iran, electrified believers across the Muslim world, Sunni as well as Shia (see also Scott Peterson, 2010 and Christopher de Bellaigue, 2004). Indeed, it was this sudden threat to the ruling monarchies – not all secular, but many seen as Western puppets – that triggered a dual response, led by Saudi Arabia, the richest among them: to isolate Iran by financially supporting Iraq in its war effort; and to foment a world-wide Sunni resurgence to counter the Shia one by promoting Saudi Arabia's (virulently anti-Shia) Wahhabi creed through mosque-building, distribution of religious literature and salary payments to willing clerics (Shane, 2016).

In sum, these spiraling extremes – politicized Shiism vs politicized Sunnism – gathered strength, feeding off one another. To the extent the power competition between Saudi Arabia and Iran could be called an ethnic Arab-Persian one – both sides used ethnic slurs during the Iran–Iraq war – it now gained a sectarian overlay: the use of sectarian markers to whip up popular support inside and beyond their borders. While ethnic and religious differences have ancient origins, there is nothing primordial about the Saudi–Iranian rivalry: at heart it is a struggle between two regional powers that tried to find ways to accommodate each other but whose relationship came unstuck as a result of war (the Iran–Iraq war; Iraq's aggression against Kuwait) and external intervention (the war to drive Iraqi forces from Kuwait; the US invasion of Iraq). Such manipulation of emotive identities succeeds because these societal divides are real, even if not inherently inimical. Yet in doing so its proponents have given rise to a dynamic that may prove a great deal easier to generate than to suppress, as it permeates and contaminates politics throughout the region. The question is whether political leaders will exhibit a similar capacity and willingness to suppress the sectarian rage they have fomented before the entire region bursts into flames, sparing not even them. Yet political leaders calculate their interests in the short term; few have strategic vision or, even if they have one, the capability to implement it (Gause, 2014).[6]

Cluster IV: The 1979 siege of Mecca: Sunni radicalization

The perceived threat from an Iran-led revolutionary Shiism was not the only factor precipitating a turn toward Saudi-led Sunni radicalization. The two-week siege of the Grand Mosque in Mecca by religious puritans in 1979 represented a radical contestation of the Saudi ruling dynasty from within the Sunni Muslim community, and prompted the House of Saud to bolster its Wahhabi base by championing (Sunni) Islamist causes, such as the effort to drive Soviet troops from Afghanistan (Trofimov, 2007). In other words, the Saudis' "weaponization" of Wahhabism not only was a rallying cry against the Iranian/Shia surge but also a useful externalization of a domestic legitimacy crisis generated by a distorted transition based on exclusion/inclusion (Armstrong, 2014).

The region had a long post-Ottoman tradition of Sunni activism, starting with the Muslim Brotherhood. The movement, which had its genesis in the nationalist fervor of 1920s Egypt, was at times courted, at other times suppressed by the rulers of the day. Following their humiliating defeat in the 1967 war with Israel, Arab regimes empowered the Brotherhood and other Islamists to insulate themselves against Communist and other leftist critiques of their failure. Without this, the Islamists of today arguably would never have emerged as strongly as they did. The Saudis and other Gulf monarchies such as the United Arab Emirates, which had not taken part in the 1967 war, resisted this approach. The Brotherhood's republicanism, professed readiness to participate in parliamentary politics and explicitly politicized form of Islam that differed from their own posed an additional threat to their legitimacy.

Saudi proselytizing in and of itself did not radicalize the vast majority of Sunni Muslims but it fertilized the fields sufficiently that, when the proper conditions arose, a small vanguard of radical preachers was able to find and nurture a willing audience. What were these conditions? A convergence of economic crisis (especially joblessness and subsidy cuts) and deteriorating governance and politics (poor service delivery, increasingly conspicuous corruption at the highest levels of state, and presidents mimicking monarchical rule by introducing dynastic practices). Jointly and cumulatively: a growing perception of injustice, a breakdown of the social contract between rulers and ruled, and, ultimately, a severe crisis of legitimacy.

At first, republics and monarchies alike sought to deflect criticism by facilitating the departure of their restless young to Afghanistan to fight the godless Soviets. This strategy backfired. The victory by the religiously inspired mujahedin empowered these young fighters, once they returned home, to challenge local rulers using the militant Islamist discourse they had developed in combat. Initially welcomed as heroes, the "Arab Afghans" soon came to be seen as established regimes' mortal enemies. Embattled leaderships responded by doubling down, establishing intrusive police states that operated through extensive informant networks, compliance enforced by issuing or withholding a range of administrative permits (conditioned on the provision of information), and torture and imprisonment of hard-core elements, in particular non-compliant returnees. This had the effect of spawning jihadist groups, Al-Qaeda most prominent among them. The "Arab Afghans" were particularly successful in Algeria, where they fueled the Islamist insurgency in the 1990s, and in Egypt, where they inspired the group that called itself Islamic Jihad, led by Ayman al-Zawahiri (who later succeeded Osama bin Laden as Al-Qaeda leader) (Ould Mohamedou, 2011; International Crisis Group, 2016a).

Initially, these groups proved unable to spring the constraints of their own radical ideas and practices. Their inflexibility and violent excesses alienated most Sunni Muslims and permitted repressive rulers to pose as guarantors of security and stability. The next earthquake changed that, however.

Cluster V: The 2011 Arab uprisings

The Arab uprisings – in their Tunisian origin a popular response to the pervasive, vindictive rule by lowly police officers at neighborhood level – inspired hope that, in fact, change was possible, that defunct social contracts could be renegotiated, and that newly hereditary and thoroughly corrupt autocracies could be overthrown. As an expression of popular discontent, these uprisings were spectacularly successful. Yet as spontaneous eruptions aimed at replacing autocratic regimes the picture is decidedly mixed. Protesters' success in Egypt inspired the young throughout the Arab world (and even among Iraqi Kurds) to emulate tactics. (Popular protests following contested election results in Iran in 2009 may have served as a model for the Arab uprisings two years later.) Yet regimes also learned from each other's experiences, exploiting societal divisions to ensure quiescence by holding up the specter of chaos and sectarian war (Lynch, 2016).

Foreign military and diplomatic interventions played an increasingly important role and often promoted winner-takes-all rather than negotiated solutions: in Libya, to overthrow Muammar Qaddafi and his clique; in Yemen, to nudge out Ali Abdullah Saleh in favor of his deputy; and in Bahrain, to bolster the regime of King Hamad Al Khalifa. In Syria, both protesters and the Bashar Assad regime appealed for outside support, initiating a regional proxy war, which then metastasized to draw in global powers. Both regional and global rivalries played out in these various theatres: in Syria and Libya, between Egypt, UAE and Saudi Arabia vs Qatar and Turkey (concerning the Islamist question); in Syria, between Russia vs the West, in addition to regional actors.

The uprisings failed in most cases – Tunisia being the exception – because the young protesters had no plan for alternative rule, no unified leadership, nor a political strategy for realizing their hopeful visions, only a pent-up desire to exercise a "no" vote in the street. The sole organized societal force capable of filling the vacuum, the Muslim Brotherhood, proved clumsy and inept at making the transition from opposition to government, and its rule was promptly contested (Brown, 2012). In Egypt, the military tolerated yet undermined the Brotherhood, whose leaders stacked error upon error from lack of experience and a short-sighted resistance to the principle of political inclusivity (International Crisis Group, 2013). The Saudi and UAE-backed July 2013 coup polarized Egyptian society further, inducing many secular young to side with the military (an updated, more repressive version of the Hosni Mubarak regime) in its repression of the Brotherhood and anyone suspected of supporting it. Extrajudicial killings, imprisonment and torture became widespread, radicalizing many (Human Rights Watch, 2014). (By contrast, in Tunisia, the local Brotherhood – the ruling An-Nahda party – pre-emptively stepped down from government following the Egypt coup and agreed to share power.) (International Crisis Group, 2014)

The coup exposed a widening intra-Sunni Islamist fault line between the Brotherhood's defenders and opponents throughout the region. This encouraged radicalization: now, mobilized youth – the failed uprisings' flotsam – had an address to which they could turn to express their anger and frustration, groups that were worth joining because they achieved military victories and provided a sense of identity, purpose and belonging. Jihadist groups began to gain traction and thrive, especially in war zones – Syria, Iraq, Yemen and Libya – and "ungoverned spaces" – the Sinai, the Sahel, Hadramawt and elsewhere. Al-Qaeda grew, then split (in Syria), giving rise to the Islamic State, an insurgent group whose roots and drivers lay in the 2003 US invasion of Iraq. The two groups evolved diverging ideologies and pursued opposing objectives, using different methods; the outcome of their violent rivalry remains uncertain, but as long as they can operate in chaos and war, their potential for growth remains formidable despite internecine strife or momentary military defeats, such as in Libya, Iraq and Syria (International Crisis Group, 2016a).

External intervention as compounding factor

The picture, as seen through the analytical frame of these conflict clusters, is complicated by two factors: external intervention and conflicts' post-2011 intersecting nature. To start with the first: From the Middle Easterner's viewpoint, the region has been the target of an unending series of alien invasions that have preyed on divisions and filled vacuums, and have varied in form and impact but rarely helped calm the waters, much less brought peace. That same perspective argues that while MENA states may have lashed out at nearby enemies (witness Egypt/Yemen, Iraq/Iran, Iraq/Kuwait), they have never done so outside the region, which has chronically been on the defensive, trying to recover from the shock of post-Ottoman division and disempowerment.

The Cold War

During the Cold War, elites – whether in power or opposition – made their choices, altering the region's power configurations through shifting allegiances. Regimes rose and fell as a result of the superpower struggle, and if a regime's orientation was uncertain, as was the case of Gamal Abdel Nasser's Egypt, Moscow and Washington would compete in wooing it, expending great resources, or seek to replace it with one whose loyalty could be bought. Think of the 1953 Mossadegh coup, the 1958 Lebanon crisis, or the 1955–1979 Baghdad Pact.

They would also exploit internal rifts to undermine one another, precipitating armed conflict, as in the case of Iraq and the Kurds (1961–1975) (Gibson, 2015), or keeping existing conflicts or standoffs alive, giving them the appearance of intractability. The conflict between Israel and the Palestinians is one example, between Israel and Syria another.

The 1956 Suez crisis was a late-colonial attempt by Israel, the UK and France to wrest control over this vital waterway from Egypt's nationalist president Gamal Abdel Nasser. The combined pressure from the US and Soviet Union, this time acting in concert, forced the parties to withdraw. In Lebanon, efforts by the so-called Multinational Force (MNF) (US, UK, France and Italy) to bring fighting to an end in the aftermath of the Israeli invasion, compel foreign forces to withdraw, and restore the legitimacy of the Lebanese government and institutions (1982–1984) ran aground amidst an escalating civil war to which the MNF contributed by shelling militia positions and civilian areas.

The US decade

The end of the Cold War brought new regional equations (Syria joining the US-led war in Kuwait) and amalgamations (the unification of north and south Yemen), as well as new military interventions by the remaining superpower, the US. Washington tried to operate under the mantle of international legitimacy whenever it could, whence the 1990–1991 "coalition of the willing" it led. The effort to oust Iraqi forces from Kuwait may be the only notable exception to the notion that external interventions in MENA have made matters worse, not better. Yet even in this case, the salutary results (liberating Kuwait) were eclipsed by its unintended consequences: the rise of Al-Qaeda motivated by the stationing of Western troops on Saudi soil; and the Shia and Kurdish uprisings in Iraq. Moreover, the need to contain Iraq led to systematic infringements of Iraqi sovereignty: draconian UN "dumb" sanctions that caused the Iraqi infrastructure's progressive collapse and emasculated its middle class; two no-fly zones, as well as a safe haven for Iraqi Kurds; the UN-led effort to dismantle Iraq's weapons of mass destruction (WMD) programs; and US strikes at regime targets in 1993 and 1998. In other words, an invasion justified by the act of aggression that preceded it, blessed by international legitimation, and successful in achieving its primary and limited objective of freeing Kuwait (rather than ousting the Iraqi regime) ended up by setting in motion a new and deeply destabilizing dynamic, one that empowered new actors (Shia Islamists, Kurds) and brought the country to near-collapse – a growing vacuum waiting to be filled (Cockburn and Cockburn, 2000).

The 2003 US invasion of Iraq was arguably the most consequential foreign intervention in MENA since World War II. It compounded Iraq's post-1991 territorial vacuum and tilted the strategic advantage toward Tehran in the regional Cold War between Iran and Saudi Arabia. It also provided oxygen to an Al-Qaeda reeling from defeat in Afghanistan. The group thrived in Iraq's chaos, sprouting an even more brutal permutation, the Islamic State. Though greatly weakened by an alliance of US forces with local tribes, it survived the US occupation and gained a new lease of life when neighboring Syria descended into turmoil in 2011. Resurrected, it returned to Iraq in 2013–2014, feeding on the Sunni Arab population's deep grievance toward the Shia Islamist rulers in Baghdad, whom they deemed Iranian proxies (International Crisis Group,

2016a). This then necessitated renewed US military intervention, joined by other Western as well as Arab states. This campaign, focused on defeating IS in both Iraq and Syria, led to IS's territorial defeat in Iraq and Syria in 2017, but its ultimate success will hinge on the nature of post-conflict governance.

The Iraq invasion's dismal failure triggered a partial US retreat from the region. President Obama argued that states should sort out their own problems; the US would act only to protect what it saw as its vital interests (Lynch, 2015). This was first visible in Libya in 2011, when the UK and France took the lead in protecting Libyan civilians from the Qaddafi regime, with the US "leading from behind". The NATO intervention was empowered under the principle of the Responsibility to Protect (R2P), but acted beyond that mandate to help oust Qaddafi. This precluded international consensus on how to address the subsequent crisis in Syria, another country whose internal affairs the US did not deem a strategic interest (Goldberg, 2016). Instead, a popular uprising turned into an armed rebellion, then into a proxy war involving Iran, Turkey and the Gulf states. In the absence of a shared understanding between the US and Russia on how to resolve the conflict, UN-mediated talks faltered and were joined by a parallel track in Astana involving the main stakeholders on the ground: Russia, Iran and Turkey; regardless, the emergence of a shared understanding might not have sufficed to yield an end to the war, given the multiplicity of actors. Today we see the original conflict between a regime and its people, having morphed into a proxy war, giving rise to secondary conflicts that could be even more dangerous to regional stability: between Israel and Hezbollah/Iran, between the US People's Protection Units (YPG) and regime/Iran/Russia in eastern Syria, and between the regime and the People's Protection Units; in the latter, Turkey also pursues the YPG without, however, being able to strike a deal with the Assad regime, which brooks no Turkish interference (Lund, 2017; Heller, 2017).

Yet US strategic interests did come into play, and provoked responses: first in 2013, when the regime crossed the Obama administration's declared red line by chemically attacking civilian neighborhoods; in this case, the threat of military force prompted the regime to consent to an international effort to dismantle its chemical weapons program. Next, the rise of jihadist groups with transnational aims provoked a US-led military intervention in 2014. And then, Russia's September 2015 intervention tipped the military scales, precluding US-led no-fly zones or US-protected safe havens. This triggered no response apart from an offer of closer coordination; at that point, however, the US was approaching, then underwent, a political transition in Washington that removed it as a key player in Syria for the time being.

Russia's resurgence

Moscow's decision to launch an air campaign in support of the Assad regime and its regional backers Iran and Hezbollah was inspired by its assessment that its ally in Damascus was about to collapse. By late 2018, this effort seemed to have paid off: the regime, though weakened and fractured, appeared secure and in control of the country's main cities, with only a last rebel holdout in the province of Idlib. With the US inward looking and in political turmoil, Russia placed itself in the driver's seat, but a political process it launched in Kazakhstan (the "Astana process") has sputtered along, raising questions over President Putin's capacity to deliver, if not his intentions. The military intervention did little to stabilize Syria, or to defeat jihadist rebels occupying major tracts of territory, for example in Idlib. Instead, it aggravated long-term governance challenges whose continuance foretells endemic violence and strife (International Crisis Group, 2018a).

Turkey's defensive aggressiveness

Turkey's role also has been important. The country is both *of* the region and…not so much. It was the seat of the Ottoman Empire, but when that fell and Turkey's modern borders were set, its ambitions were clipped along with its territory. Today it holds no realistic aspiration to rule its former domain, but merely seeks to do business with the states that emerged. A non-Arab Muslim state and NATO partner, Turkey also has endeavored to serve as a bridge between its Western allies and a post-Cold-War Arab world. For some time before 2011, it appeared to pursue an arrangement that Arab elites derisively referred to as "neo-Ottomanism" – Turkish economic rather than administrative domination. Its spearhead was the AK Party, which received its economic power from unlocking the Turkish interior and mobilizing an aspiring new middle class. Its standard-bearer, Prime Minister Recep Tayyip Erdoğan, strengthened economic ties throughout the region, including with Assad's Syria. Yet the AK Party was inspired by the Muslim Brotherhood, and so when popular uprisings shook the Arab world in 2011, Turkey faced a dilemma: back the besieged regimes or shift its support to the only organized, viable alternative, its ideological ally, the Muslim Brotherhood? It settled on the latter – in Egypt, Tunisia, Libya and Syria, even in Yemen.

This proved the wrong bet, as the counter-revolution – led by Egypt's "deep state" and backed by Saudi Arabia and the UAE – was more determined, unleashing a military power that overturned the nascent regional economic order Turkey tried to build. Meanwhile, Turkey experienced internal convulsions (Erdoğan's bid to install a presidential system; a return to war with the Kurdistan Workers' Party, PKK; an attempted military coup) while becoming embroiled in foreign military adventures: against the Islamic State in Syria and Iraq, but also and especially against the PKK and its affiliates in these two countries. Its friendship with Israel suffered over Ankara's support of Palestinians in Gaza (and an activist-led attempt to provide aid to the besieged territory), then partly recovered. A dangerous confrontation with Russia in the skies above the Turkey-Syria border in 2015 triggered a year-long stand-off, diffused as suddenly as it had come about, with Turkey acknowledging Russia's dominant role in Syria. Relations with Iran deteriorated over the latter's support of the Assad regime and a growing presence – by proxy – in northern Syria and northern Iraq. As Ankara lashed out at both internal and external enemies, it was not the first, nor the last, to discover that often it is easier to get in than to get out, and to start a war than to end it (Bechev and Hiltermann, 2017).

The EU as paying bystander

Finally, a word about the European Union. It is somewhat of a cliché that the EU, unable to reach foreign policy consensus across its 28 member states, has been more of a payer than a player in MENA. This has been true with one notable exception: the High Representative's office was prominent in helping secure the 2015 nuclear deal between the EU3+3 and Iran. EU diplomatic efforts in finding a just settlement to the Israel–Palestine conflict have been tepid and yielded no results. At times, the EU has patted itself on the back merely for being involved, as if the act of trying, rather than getting things done, counted more. This was its attitude in post-coup Egypt, when it heralded its mediation attempts as a success – and proof that the union mattered – even through it was being used by the regime to buy time.

Elsewhere in the region, the EU has been better known for providing humanitarian and development aid, and promoting economic integration and democratic reform. Like any large conglomeration of states, the EU has been sluggish in responding to breaking crises, which has encouraged an overly securitized approach to what are fundamentally political problems.

Witness its participation in the anti-IS campaign and military support of local proxies, such as Iraqi Kurds, while neglecting to address Sunni grievances in Iraq and Syria; and its use of naval power to interdict people-smugglers and rescue migrants crossing the Mediterranean (EUNAVFOR MED) (Hiltermann, 2015).

Moreover, the EU has yet to become more than the sum of its parts; instead, member states have undermined unity at times, and thus its reputation. Some of them also have been openly interventionist, unlike the EU (which doesn't have common foreign or defense policies), whether through NATO (Libya) or individual membership in US-led alliances (e.g., in Iraq/Syria). The UK, France and Germany have taken differing approaches toward the migrant/refugee crisis and jihadist threat, and sometimes different sides in the conflicts in Syria, Yemen and Libya. In Yemen, in particular, the EU shone by its neutral approach to the war that started in 2015. It reached out to all sides and strongly backed UN mediation, even as the UK and France supported Saudi Arabia and its Gulf allies in the UN Security Council (the shamefully one-sided Resolution 2216 of April 2015) and in their warfighting capability (through weapons sales). Such contradictory actions serve merely to compound crises like the one in Yemen.

In sum, the common characteristic of perhaps all external interventions – military, political or economic – is that they are driven by motivations that have nothing to do with the region's welfare and stability. Instead, they deepen the crisis of legitimacy that all states face, thus making the next round of problems worse and increasing the chances of further conflict.

Intersecting trajectories

The challenge we face today is that subsets of the five conflict clusters, set off by their respective earthquakes, have started to bleed into one another. Seemingly strong authoritarian states have collapsed in the Arab uprisings' popular fervor, and geographically limited conflicts have begun to metastasize beyond post-Ottoman borders. Each conflict cluster has its own drivers and actors, its own logic and dynamic, but when they become intertwined, things are mixed up: conflict actors form unlikely new alliances because their interests have become tactically aligned, and they dilute their ideologies to attract manpower and rule territories they acquire.

Moreover, when lines are blurred, conflict discourse becomes confusing. When Saudi Arabia states, as it does, that Iran has no right to stick its nose in Arab affairs (in Lebanon, Syria, Iraq, Bahrain, or Yemen), it is seeing Iran in light of the 1979 Islamic Revolution, its leaders striving to export their model across Shia populations and beyond through conversion (Cluster III). However, for Iran, its support of Hezbollah and the Assad regime is not primarily related to its wish to protect Shia populations and simultaneously implant the Velayet-e Faqih doctrine. Tehran is far more concerned by the threat it sees emanating from Israel and its offensive nuclear capability (Cluster II); in response, it supports Hezbollah as an instrument of "forward-defense", and it backs the Syrian regime as essential to securing its arms channel to Hezbollah. The presence of a Shia population in southern Lebanon has been a facilitating factor, one that it has skillfully exploited. The same goes for its declared solidarity with the Palestinian people. For Iran, the original driver is key, but Saudi Arabia does not see it that way.

The argument concerning Iraq is different. Here Saudi Arabia is correct to view Iran's assertive presence (military advisers, weapons training and supplies, political manipulation) as an effort to supplant Sunni political dominance; given Iran's experience in the 1980–1988 war with Iraq (Cluster III), this cannot be a surprise. Yet that presence should be understood also in the context of the political-security vacuum created by the US in 2003. In other words, unlike its Syria role, Tehran's Iraq posture today is a legacy of the Islamic Revolution – and the Saudi–Iranian competition that escalated in its wake – *as mediated by external intervention*, and also informed by Tehran's need to protect its "near-abroad".

One could argue that Israel remains Iran's most dangerous enemy, requiring it to protect its Hezbollah alliance at all cost, whereas Iraq offers Iran strategic depth against a chaotic region with hostile neighbors and radical Sunni jihadist enemies. At the same time, Iran stands accused of trying to link its chance post-2003 Iraq role to post-2011 events in Syria, namely by endeavoring to forge a land corridor from Iran through central Iraq westward into Syria and, finally, Lebanon and the Mediterranean to supplement its air supply channel to Hezbollah. In other words, Iran could be marshalling its Cluster III advantage in Iraq to bolster its Cluster II "forward-defense" stance. For some, this apparent project is merely a cover for Iran's millennialist ideology, which seeks regional hegemony (Al Shihabi, 2016).

Iran's recent influence in Yemen and Bahrain (though much less so in the latter) also stems from the Saudi–Iranian rivalry (Cluster III). Yet in both cases, it was enabled by the breakdown of the prevailing order in the Arab uprisings (Cluster V). Sectarianism was not the driver of events in 2011, yet it is increasingly becoming so, as Iran and Saudi Arabia both appeal to people's insecurity as threatened *religious* groups. It is understandable that Saudi Arabia would view Iran's minimal interference in Bahrain and limited but growing support of the Houthis in Yemen as part of their post-1979 competition, but one must query the wisdom of the way in which Riyadh has chosen to counter its adversary.

Now let us look at Hezbollah. The group established itself, with Iranian help, in response to the 1982 Israeli invasion of Lebanon, which was directed against the PLO. It therefore is a creature of the Israeli–Palestinian conflict (Cluster II). While pro-Shia in origin – defending Lebanon's Shia community from external aggression and promoting it within the Lebanese political system – the group never profiled itself explicitly as sectarian until it was drawn into the Syrian war. Even then, it argued it was fighting a Sunni *jihadist* threat to the regime, not Sunnis as such (i.e., religion-based political formations, not a religious group). The primary reason for its involvement in Syria was the fear the regime might collapse, endangering the Iran-Hezbollah arms channel and thus Hezbollah's survival as a militia standing up to Israel. At heart, Hezbollah remains a Cluster II actor, but a Cluster V conflict (arising from the Arab Awakening in Syria) compelled it to take on a new role, one that converged with a Cluster III (sectarian) role as the Syrian conflict became regionalized. In other words, the original conflict driver remains critical to Hezbollah even as its immediate objectives and character are changing by its need to adapt to new circumstances.

If the joint Saudi-UAE 2015 military intervention in Yemen can be explained by these two countries' enmity toward Iran, their role in North Africa has an altogether different source. Here – in Egypt, Libya and Tunisia – the two Gulf states (mostly the UAE) bring their financial and, in the case of Libya, military weight to bear in opposition to the Muslim Brotherhood (Cluster IV). This reflects an intra-Sunni-Islamist struggle unleashed by the Arab uprisings (Cluster V). It places the two Gulf states in opposition to Turkey and Qatar, which champion the Brotherhood's cause for reasons of both ideological affinity and business interest (Cluster IV). This conflict further saps the energies of Gulf states, which face economic pressures as a result of low oil prices while being overly reliant on oil (a Cluster I feature of post-Ottoman order/disorder), and which may be heavily armed but are limited in their capacity to project themselves militarily.

And so, even if Iran has no hegemonic ambitions, it has projected military power in the region by filling sudden security vacuums and pocketing the mistakes of its adversaries – *if* it can avoid over-reach and a protracted entanglement in the Syria and Iraq theatres. The situation is even more complex in Yemen, where Saudi Arabia's objection to the local branch of the Muslim Brotherhood, the Islah party, is not as strong as the UAE's (Cluster IV). The UAE's opposition to Islah weakens, possibly fatally, the anti-Houthi front (Cluster III). This leaves little space for a swift political resolution of the conflict, while outright military victory for either side seems equally improbable (International Crisis Group, 2016d).

Initiatives are afoot to forge a novel regional anti-Iran alliance (Cluster III) combining Israel with Sunni Arab states (Lerman, 2016). At once, such a project runs into obstacles. The most important one is that Arab states cannot afford to ally themselves openly with Israel – not even against common enemy Iran – as long as Israel, in their eyes, fails to make the necessary concessions to reach an acceptable outcome of its conflict with the Palestinians (Cluster II). It is difficult to envision any progress on that front; more likely, a new round of war will break out in Gaza, and even in the West Bank – if the Trump administration rolls out and seeks to implement a peace plan largely favoring Israel (Zalzberg and Thrall, 2017).

Another obstacle is Egypt, which has the same concerns but is resentful of its financial backers in the Gulf and whose president, Abdel-Fattah Sisi, has not concealed his admiration for his fellow survivor (Cluster V), Bashar Assad, who is the Gulf states' enemy to the extent he remains in Iran's camp (Cluster III). Egypt, in other words, would not be an enthusiastic partner in any anti-Iran alliance with Israel (its original Cluster II enemy), even as its military relationship with Israel has reached unprecedented levels in the two states' common struggle against jihadists in the Sinai (Sabry, 2015).

What does it all mean?

Conflict is endemic in society; in this respect, the MENA region is no different from any other. Moreover, MENA conflicts, like conflicts elsewhere, are unique in their origin, evolution and defining characteristics. Yet it is possible to group these conflicts into five distinct conflict clusters whose members share a common genealogy and drivers even as they morph over time to draw in more actors motivated by new or different grievances. This analysis suggests three main, related conclusions.

First, there is utility in grouping conflicts this way. It helps explain the persistence of the original conflict drivers as conflicts belonging to different clusters start to bleed into one another, and brings them back from the relative obscurity to which the current mayhem has consigned them. And it forces the following questions: How can we even begin to tackle today's conflicts if we fail to recognize their original sources? Aren't we merely scratching the surface while the forces struggling below generate yet new generations of conflicts? Isn't it likely that we do more harm by providing the wrong treatment based on misdiagnosis? And what can we effectively do to address the systemic crises that have rotted the post-Ottoman order from within?[7]

Second, the growing, deeply alarming convergence of the five conflict clusters, aggravated by external intervention, has rendered individual states' social contracts unsustainable, precipitated the collapse of state structures, exposed ideologies promising salvation to be bankrupt or a sham, forestalled urgently needed efforts to tackle tough social, economic and environmental challenges and rapidly depleting resources, and left old injustices to fester and deepen. This disaster is exploited by new, assertive actors using violent, even brutal tactics, to replace the old with something new.

Yet what can that be? Dynamic actors such as the Kurds want their own state, claiming today what was denied them a century ago, even as the Arab nation-state model as a form of governance is disintegrating in front of their eyes. Moreover, they are concerned only with their own fate as Kurds; they have no vision for a new regional architecture (Hiltermann, 2008).

Jihadist groups such as Al-Qaeda and the Islamic State are more potent, having much broader, more revolutionary, ambitions. One way or another, they aspire to resurrect the Caliphate, abolished by the truncated and stridently secular Turkish state that arose from the Ottoman Empire's ashes. Yet while their methods are hyper-modern, their ideology is regressive and their predominant method no less repressive than that of the states they are seeking to supplant. Nor have they given any indication that they can offer solutions to the region's problems, or provide an alternative and workable social contract. Their project is therefore bound to fail, no less than their ideological predecessors' projects.

And, third, the global retreat of the United States as the unipolar power of its era is leaving the region prey to a multiplication of conflict nodes with not a single one capable of imposing overall dominance, not even within "camps" (e.g., pro-Iranian vs pro-Saudi) that could provide a measure of stability by cordoning off conflicts. The primary organizing principle is gone, and nothing has yet replaced it. As Antonio Gramsci put it with great eloquence: "The crisis consists precisely in the fact that the old is dying and the new cannot be born; in this interregnum a great variety of morbid symptoms appear" (Gramsci, 1971).

As internal contradictions mount and external intervention escalates, the post-Ottoman order/disorder appears ruined beyond repair; the outlines of what might replace it remain far from discernible. There is little that states outside a disintegrating MENA, fearing the fallout, can do until and unless MENA actors themselves gather the capacity and will to create a new order (or face the possibility that external powers will impose another ill-fitting structure on them). Yet conflicts can be managed, avoided or prevented, and even brought to an end, whether through victory/defeat or, preferably, negotiation. This is hard work, and the first impulse should always be: Do no (further) harm. This means: no unilateral military intervention, nor arms sales to conflict actors except for strictly defensive purposes; instead, redoubled efforts to support negotiated settlements, stepped-up humanitarian assistance, bolstering of technocratic institutions to prevent financial collapse, promises of reconstruction funds conditioned on conflict actors upholding international law and negotiating inclusive peace settlements, and cautious backing of the states still standing conditioned on their willingness to institute reforms.[8]

An afterthought

One could take the metaphor of five earthquakes and their aftershocks a step further into the realm of shifting and colliding tectonic plates. As the post-Ottoman MENA conflict clusters continue to spawn new wars and hollow out states, actors and conflicts external to the region will impose themselves. Over time, the post-Ottoman order/disorder is likely to give way to an altogether new formation, one with its own violent eruptions and its own internal logic, drivers and actors. May the region's people be the primary drivers and shapers of whatever emerges.

Appendix: An attempt at a typology of MENA conflicts of the past 50 years

- Interstate wars (Iran vs Iraq, 1980–1988; Israel vs Lebanon, 1978, 1982, 1993, 1996, 2006, also listed below) and internationalized interstate wars (Iraq vs Kuwait, 1990, turned into Iraq vs US-led international coalition, 1991, including Iraqi rocket attacks on Israel)

Conflicts in the Middle East

- Civil wars (Jordan, 1970–1971; Algeria, 1992–1999; Iraqi Kurdistan, 1994–1998; Iraq, 2005–2007; Libya, 2014–today), including wars of secession (Yemen, 1994), and metastasizing/regionalizing civil wars (Yemen, 1962; Lebanon, 1975–1990; Syria, 2012–today; Yemen, 2015–today, also listed below)
- Violent uprisings/revolutions (Iran, 1979) and those provoking external intervention (Libya, 2011; Bahrain, 2011; Syria, 2011)
- Violent insurgencies and counter-insurgencies (Iraq/Kurds, intermittently 1960s–1991; Turkey/PKK, intermittently 1980s–today; IS in Iraq, Syria, Libya and Sinai, 2013–today)
- Violent internal repression, perhaps following – failed or successful – coups d'état (Syria, 1982; South Yemen, 1986; Iran, 2009; Egypt, 2013; Turkey, 1960, 1980, 2016)
- Military occupations (Israel in Lebanon, 1982–2000; Syria in Lebanon, 1976–2005; Iraq in Kuwait, 1990–1991; US in Iraq, 2003–2011), with cyclical fighting (Israel in Palestine, 1967–today, including two uprisings, 1988, 2000, and three Gaza wars, 2008–2009, 2012, 2014)
- Cross-border wars between state and non-state actors (Israel vs Hezbollah in Lebanon, 1993, 1996, 2006; Kingdom of Saudi Arabia/UAE vs Houthis/Ali Abdullah Saleh in Yemen, 2015–today; Islamic State in Syria/Iraq, 2012–2017)
- Wars of national liberation (Palestine vs Israel; Algeria vs France; Western Sahara vs Morocco)
- Wars over resources? (Iran vs Iraq, 1980, maybe; Iraq vs Kuwait, 1990–1991, maybe; use of oil as a weapon in Kuwait, 1991, and in Qayyara/Iraq, 2016; Kirkuk/Iraq as pre-conflict over oil, 2003–today; use of water as a weapon by and against IS in Iraq and Syria, 2014–2017)
- Genocide/genocidal acts/ethnic "cleansing" (Israel vs Palestinians, 1948, 1967; Iraq's counter-insurgency vs Kurds, 1987–1988; Sunni vs Shia violence in Iraq, 2005–2007; Islamic State vs Iraqi Yazidis, 2014)

Notes

1 Program Director, Middle East & North Africa, International Crisis Group. This essay is based on field research conducted by my Crisis Group colleagues and myself, as well as historical insights I gleaned from teaching a course on the politics of the Middle East at the University of Kent's Brussels School of International Studies in 2016 and 2017. I wish to thank Issandr El Amrani (who had an early idea for the proposed new approach to conflicts in the Middle East), Jean-Marie Guéhenno, Robert Blecher and Heiko Wimmen for reviewing an earlier draft and providing helpful comments. Responsibility for any errors of fact or historical judgment is entirely mine.

2 I have gone back and forth on whether the post-Ottoman order/disorder should be regarded a conflict cluster or addressed separately for having informed all subsequent conflicts in the region. I ended up labelling it a cluster in its own right, because the types of conflicts it has spawned concern the foundations of state legitimacy, whereas this is not necessarily true of clusters two, three and four. Cluster five, however, constitutes the culmination of cluster one's internal contradictions, and has ushered in a new set of conflicts.

3 As Jean-Marie Guéhenno pointed out in comments (here paraphrased) on an earlier draft of this chapter, the logic of democracy in republican systems introduces the logic of numbers and majority rule in fragile polities. The question of legitimacy after the demise of the Ottoman Empire is a central one that was not addressed very well by either Britain or France.

4 I am grateful to Jean-Marie Guéhenno for his insights on this matter. See also, Ofer Zalzberg (2018).

5 On the inadequacies of the "peace process" (a term that seems to uniquely evoke the Israeli–Arab conflict, despite the great number of conflicts around the world (Middle East and North Africa Report (International Crisis Group))), see Crisis Group, 2012).

6 For a nuanced take on sectarianism, see Ussama Makdisi (2017).

7 For interesting takes on this, see James L. Gelvin (1999) and Eva Bellin (2012).

8 I have elaborated these ideas in my commentary "Tackling the MENA Region's Intersecting Conflicts" (Hiltermann, 2018).

References

Al Shihabi, Ali (2016). *The Saudi Kingdom: Between the Jihadi Hammer and the Iranian Anvil* (Princeton, NJ: Markus Wiener Publishers).

Armstrong, Karen (2014). "Wahhabism to ISIS", *New Statesman* (November 27), online at www.newstatesman.com/world-affairs/2014/11/wahhabism-isis-how-saudi-arabia-exported-main-source-global-terrorism, accessed 23/9/18.

Bechev, Dimitar, and Hiltermann, Joost R. (2017). "Turkey's Forays into the Middle East", *Turkish Policy Quarterly* (December 14), online at http://turkishpolicy.com/article/879/turkeys-forays-into-the-middle-east, accessed 23/9/18.

Bellaigue, Christopher de (2004). *In the Rose Garden of the Martyrs: A Memoir of Iran* (London: HarperCollins Publishers).

Bellin, Eva (2012). "Reconsidering the Robustness of Authoritarianism in the Middle East: Lessons from the Arab Spring", *Comparative Politics*, Vol. 44, No. 2 (January).

Bellin, Eva (2004). "The Robustness of Authoritarianism in the Middle East: Exceptionalism in Comparative Perspective", *Comparative Politics*, Vol. 36, No. 2 (January).

Brown, Nathan (2012). *When Victory Becomes an Option: Egypt's Muslim Brotherhood Confronts Success*, Carnegie, online at http://carnegieendowment.org/files/brotherhood_success.pdf, accessed 23/9/18.

Cockburn, Andrew, and Cockburn, Patrick (2000). *Out of the Ashes: The Resurrection of Saddam Hussein* (New York: HarperCollins).

Dawn, Ernest (1991). "The Origins of Arab Nationalism", in Khalidi, Rashid, Anderson, Lisa, Muslih, Muhammad and Simon, Reeva, eds. *The Origins of Arab Nationalism* (New York: Columbia University Press), pp. 3–30.

Gause, Gregory (2014). *Beyond Sectarianism: The New Middle East Cold War*, Brookings Doha Center Analysis Paper, No. 11, online at www.brookings.edu/~/media/research/files/papers/2014/07/22-beyond-sectarianism-cold-war-gause/english-pdf.pdf, accessed 23/9/18.

Gelvin, James L. (1999). "Modernity and its Discontents: On the Durability of Nationalism in the Arab Middle East", *Nations and Nationalism*, Vol. 5, No. 1, pp. 71–89.

Gibson, Bryan (2015). *Sold Out? US Foreign Policy, Iraq, the Kurds, and the Cold War* (Basingstoke, UK: Palgrave Macmillan).

Goldberg, Jeffrey (2016). "Obama's Former Middle East Adviser: We should Have Bombed Assad", *The Atlantic* (April 20), online at www.theatlantic.com/international/archive/2016/04/philip-gordon-barack-obama-doctrine/479031, accessed 23/9/18.

Graham-Brown, Sarah (1999). *Sanctioning Saddam: The Politics of Intervention in Iraq* (New York: I.B. Tauris).

Gramsci, Antonio (1971). *Selections from the Prison Notebooks*, "Wave of Materialism" and "Crisis of Authority" (New York: International Publishers).

Halbfinger, David M. (2018). "With Gaza in Financial Crisis, Fears that 'an Explosion is Coming'", *The New York Times* (February 11).

Heller, Sam (2017). "The Signal in Syria's Noise", *War on the Rocks* (June 30), online at warontherocks.com/2017/06/the-signal-in-syrias-noise, accessed 23/9/18.

Hiltermann, Joost R. (2008). "To Protect or to Project? Iraqi Kurds and their Future", *Middle East Report*, Vol. 38 (Summer), online at www.merip.org/mer/mer247/protect-or-project, accessed 23/9/18.

Hiltermann, Joost R. (2015). "Europe's Middle East Myopia", *Politico* (August 12), online at www.politico.eu/article/europes-myopia-civil-wars-middle-east-north-africa-humanitarian-crisis, accessed 23/9/18.

Hiltermann, Joost R. (2010). "Deep Traumas, Fresh Ambitions: Legacies of the Iran-Iraq War", *Middle East Report*, Vol. 40 (Winter), online at www.merip.org/mer/mer257/deep-traumas-fresh-ambitions, accessed 23/9/18.

Hiltermann, Joost R. (2018). "Tackling the MENA Region's Intersecting Conflicts", online at www.crisisgroup.org/middle-east-north-africa/eastern-mediterranean/syria/tackling-mena-regions-intersecting-conflicts, accessed 23/9/18.

Human Rights Watch (2014). *Egypt: Rab'a Killings Likely Crimes Against Humanity*, online at www.hrw.org/news/2014/08/12/egypt-raba-killings-likely-crimes-against-humanity, accessed 23/9/18.

International Crisis Group (2003). *Baghdad: A Race Against the Clock*, online at www.crisisgroup.org/middle-east-north-africa/gulf-and-arabian-peninsula/iraq/baghdad-race-against-clock, accessed 23/9/18.

International Crisis Group (2005). *Understanding Islamism*, online at www.crisisgroup.org/middle-east-north-africa/understanding-islamism, accessed 23/9/18.

International Crisis Group (2012). *The Emperor Has No Clothes: Palestinians and the End of the Peace Process*, online at www.crisisgroup.org/middle-east-north-africa/eastern-mediterranean/israelpalestine/emperor-has-no-clothes-palestinians-and-end-peace-process, accessed 23/9/18.

International Crisis Group (2013). *Marching in Circles: Egypt's Dangerous Second Transition*, online at www.crisisgroup.org/middle-east-north-africa/north-africa/egypt/marching-circles-egypt-s-dangerous-second-transition, accessed 23/9/18.

International Crisis Group (2014). *The Tunisian Exception: Success and Limits of Consensus*, online at www.crisisgroup.org/middle-east-north-africa/north-africa/tunisia/tunisian-exception-success-and-limits-consensus, accessed 23/9/18.

International Crisis Group (2016a). *Exploiting Disorder: al-Qaeda and the Islamic state*, online at www.crisisgroup.org/global/exploiting-disorder-al-qaeda-and-islamic-state, accessed 23/9/18.

International Crisis Group (2016b). *Fight or Flight: The Desperate Plight of Iraq's "Generation 2000"*, online at www.crisisgroup.org/middle-east-north-africa/gulf-and-arabian-peninsula/iraq/fight-or-flight-desperate-plight-iraq-s-generation-2000, accessed 23/9/18.

International Crisis Group (2016c). *How to Preserve the Fragile Calm at Jerusalem's Holy Esplanade*, online at www.crisisgroup.org/middle-east-north-africa/eastern-mediterranean/israelpalestine/how-preserve-fragile-calm-jerusalem-s-holy-esplanade, accessed 23/9/18.

International Crisis Group (2016d). *Yemen: Is Peace Possible?*, online at www.crisisgroup.org/middle-east-north-africa/gulf-and-arabian-peninsula/yemen/yemen-peace-possible, accessed 23/9/18.

International Crisis Group (2018a). *Averting Disaster in Syria's Idlib Province*, online at www.crisisgroup.org/middle-east-north-africa/eastern-mediterranean/syria/b56-averting-disaster-syrias-idlib-province, accessed 23/9/18.

International Crisis Group (2018b). *Israel, Hizbollah and Iran: Preventing Another War in Syria*, online at www.crisisgroup.org/middle-east-north-africa/eastern-mediterranean/syria/182-israel-hizbollah-and-iran-preventing-another-war-syria, accessed 23/9/18.

Kinzer, Stephen (2008). *All the Shah's Men: An American Coup and the Roots of Middle East Terror* (Hoboken, NJ: John Wiley & Sons).

Lerman, Eran (2016). *The Game of Camps: Ideological Fault Lines in the Wreckage of the Arab state System*, Begin-Sadat Center for Strategic Studies, online at https://besacenter.org/mideast-security-and-policy-studies/124-lerman-game-of-camps, accessed 23/9/18.

Lund, Aron (2017). "How Assad's Enemies Gave Up on the Opposition", The Century Foundation, online at https://tcf.org/content/report/assads-enemies-gave-syrian-opposition, accessed 23/9/18.

Lynch, Mark (2015). "Obama and the Middle East: Rightsizing the US Role", *Foreign Affairs* (September/October), online at www.foreignaffairs.com/articles/middle-east/obama-and-middle-east, accessed 23/9/18.

Lynch, Mark (2016). *The New Arab Wars: Uprisings and Anarchy in the Middle East* (New York: PublicAffairs).

Makdisi, Ussama (2017). *The Mythology of the Sectarian Middle East*, Center for the Middle East at Rice University's Baker Institute for Public Policy (February), online at www.bakerinstitute.org/media/files/files/5a20626a/CME-pub-Sectarianism-021317.pdf, accessed 23/9/18.

Middle East Report (2014). "Primer on Palestine, Israel and the Arab–Israeli Conflict", online at www.merip.org/primer-palestine-israel-arab–Israeli-conflict-new, accessed 23/9/18.

Ould Mohamedou, Mohammad-Mahmoud (2011). "The Militarization of Islamism: Al-Qā'ida and Its Transnational Challenge", *The Muslim World*, Vol. 10, No. 2 (April), pp. 307–23.

Owen, Roger (2004). *State, Power and Politics in the Making of the Modern Middle East* (New York: Routledge).

Peterson, Scott (2010). *Let the Swords Encircle Me: Iran – A Journey Behind the Headlines* (New York: Simon & Schuster).

Razoux, Pierre (2015). *The Iran-Iraq War* (Cambridge, MA: Harvard University Press).

Sabry, Mohannad (2015). *Sinai: Egypt's Lynchpin, Gaza's Lifeline, Israel's Nightmare* (New York: The American University in Cairo Press).

Shane, Scott (2016). "Saudis and Extremism: 'Both the Arsonists and the Firefighters,'" *The New York Times* (August 25), online at www.nytimes.com/2016/08/26/world/middleeast/saudi-arabia-islam.html, accessed 23/9/18.

Sharabi, Hisham (1992). *Neopatriarchy: A Theory of Distorted Change in Arab Society* (Oxford: Oxford University Press).

Sluglett, Peter (2014). "An Improvement on Colonialism? The 'A' Mandates and their Legacy in the Middle East", *International Affairs*, Vol. 90, No. 2, pp. 413–427.

Trofimov, Yaroslav (2007). *The Siege of Mecca: The Forgotten Uprising in Islam's Holiest Shrine and the Birth of Al Qaeda* (New York: Anchor Books).

Zalzberg, Ofer (2018). "In Ireland, Israel's Religious Right Engages with Ideas for Peace", online at www.crisisgroup.org/middle-east-north-africa/eastern-mediterranean/israelpalestine/ireland-israels-religious-right-engages-ideas-peace, accessed 23/9/18.

Zalzberg, Ofer, and Thrall, Nathan (2017). "Counting the Costs of US Recognition of Jerusalem as Israel's Capital", online at www.crisisgroup.org/middle-east-north-africa/eastern-mediterranean/israelpalestine/counting-costs-us-recognition-jerusalem-israels-capital, accessed 23/9/18.

4

US MIDDLE EAST POLICY

Stephen Zunes

The evolution of US policy

The State Department once described the Middle East as "a stupendous source of strategic power, and one of the greatest material prizes in world history,…probably the richest economic prize in the world in the field of foreign investment" (Kolko and Kolko, 1972). President Dwight Eisenhower referred to the region as the most "strategically important area in the world" (Spiegel, 1985). American oil interests, particularly in Saudi Arabia, led to an expanded US role in the region during World War II. This involvement increased still further with the close American relationship with the Shah of Iran after the CIA restored him to the throne in 1953, supplanting Great Britain as the primary outside power in that oil-rich country. Though the British and French played a significant role in enforcing Western interests in the Middle East and North Africa for the first quarter century of the Cold War, the United States increasingly asserted its primacy over these declining European colonial powers, particularly as left-leaning nationalist governments allied with the Soviet Union emerged in a number of Arab countries.

Security in the Persian Gulf was seen primarily as a British responsibility until Prime Minister Harold Wilson announced in 1969 that Great Britain would withdraw most of its security commitments from areas east of the Suez Canal, a reflection of Britain's declining global power as well as a result of American pressure to take on the lead role in Middle East security. Since the Vietnam War had led to a large-scale skepticism over direct US military involvement overseas, President Richard Nixon decided to engage in a surrogate strategy, announced in 1971, which became known as the Nixon Doctrine. According to Nixon, "we shall furnish military and economic assistance when requested … But we shall look to the nation directly threatened to assume the primary responsibility of providing the manpower for its defense" (Nixon, 1969).

The Persian Gulf became the first testing ground for using a regional *gendarme* to promote US interests, essentially an extension of the Vietnamization program of training and arming locals to enforce the US security agenda. The Shah of Iran owed his throne to the United States, had lots of money from the rise in oil prices with which to purchase weapons, and a desire to feed his megalomania – all of which made him a well-suited surrogate. Throughout the 1970s, the United States sold over USD 20 billion in advanced weaponry to the Shah (with an additional USD 20 billion on order.) In addition, there were as many as 30,000 American advisors and trainers – mostly working for private defense contractors – in Iran in order to transform the Iranian armed forces into a sophisticated fighting force capable of counter-insurgency operations. This policy was successfully implemented when Iranian troops – with American and British support – intervened in support of the Sultan of Oman against a leftist rebellion in the Dhofar province in the mid-1970s. In 1979, however, Iran's Islamic Revolution brought this policy crashing down, replacing the compliant Shah with a regime stridently opposed to Western interests.

In response to this shocking recognition of the limits of surrogate strategy, the Carter Doctrine was announced in 1980, in which the United States would no longer rely on potentially unstable allies and their armed forces, but would be able to intervene directly through the Rapid Deployment Force, later integrated into the Central Command. An agreement was reached with the Saudi Government whereby, in exchange for the sale of an integrated package of highly sophisticated weaponry, the Saudis would build and pay for an elaborate system of command, naval and air facilities large enough to sustain US forces in intensive regional combat. For example, the controversial 1981 sale of the sophisticated AWACS airborne radar system to Saudi Arabia was to be a linchpin of an elaborate communications system comparable to that of NATO. According to a *Washington Post* report at that time (then denied by the Pentagon), this was to be part of a grand defense strategy for the Middle Eastern oil fields that included an ambitious plan to build bases in Saudi Arabia, equipped and waiting for American forces to use (Armstrong, 1981). In the event of war, American forces would be deployed so quickly and with such overwhelming force that the casualty ratio would be highly favorable and the length of the fighting would be short. The result would be that disruptive anti-war protests from the American public would be minimal. This was of particular concern since Congress had recently passed the War Powers Act, whereby the legislative branch could effectively veto a president's decision to send American troops into combat after 60 days. Though the exact scenario in which US forces would be deployed could not have been predicted at the time, the Carter Doctrine helped make possible the American military and political successes in the 1991 Gulf War against Iraq.

During the Iran–Iraq War between 1980 and 1988, the United States armed one side and then the other as a means of insuring that neither of the two countries could become dominant in the region. When the Clinton administration came to office in 1993, the policy was shifted to that of "dual containment", seeking to isolate both countries, which the United States saw as potentially dangerous and destabilizing forces in this strategically important region, labeling them both as "rogue states". As defined by US national security managers, rogue states were countries that possess substantial military capability, seek the acquisition of weapons of mass destruction and violate what are seen as international "norms". President Clinton's first National Security Advisor Anthony Lake put the matter clearly: "Our policy must face the reality of recalcitrant and outlaw states that not only choose to remain outside the family [of nations] but also assault its basic values …[and] exhibit a chronic inability to engage constructively with the outside world …" Lake argued further that just as the United States took the lead in "containing" the Soviet Union, it must now also bear the "special responsibility" to "neutralize" and "contain" these "outlaw states" (Klare, 1994). In addition to Iraq and Iran, Libya and Sudan were also widely considered as rogue states, with Syria sometimes included on the list by certain foreign policy hawks. (The only countries outside the region given such a label were communist North Korea and Cuba.)

Despite legitimate concerns voiced by the US Government regarding Iran and Iraq's human rights records and violations of international norms, neither country was unique in the region in such transgressions. For example, due to its powerful armed forces, nuclear arsenal, conquests of neighboring countries and violations of international legal standards, a case could be made that Israel – America's chief partner in the region and the world's largest recipient of US economic and military support – would also fit this definition. Yet the label of "rogue state" had a clear function in US foreign policy independent of any objective criteria. Iran and Iraq were the only two countries in the Middle East that combine a large population, adequate water resources and oil wealth to be major independent players that had the ability to challenge American hegemony in the region. These two countries were labeled rogue states ultimately because of their failure to accept the post-Cold War order that requires accepting the American strategic and economic agenda. Prior to the arrival of the regimes seen as so antithetical to American interests, these countries engaged in large-scale military procurement with the support or acquiescence of the United States as well as engaging in major human rights abuses without American objections. Once their cooperation with the United States ended and their hostility toward American interests emerged (through revolution in the case of Iran and policy shifts in the case of Iraq), their long ignored human rights abuses and militarization became a focal point for their vilification.

Following the end of the Cold War, American officials were no longer concerned that the region might fall to Soviet influence, yet the United States also had a long-standing concern about the influence of indigenous movements that could potentially challenge American interests. There was a perception of an ongoing threat from radical forces – both Islamist and secular – as well as concern over the instability that could result from any major challenges to the rule of pro-Western regimes, even if led by potentially democratic movements. This resulted in a policy where the United States supported the maintenance of the status quo regardless of a given regime's level of commitment to democracy or human rights.

In the decades following World War II, US administrations – to varying degrees – saw American dominance as exercised though multiple independent centers of power, such as the United Nations and other inter-governmental organizations, with increasing emphasis during the 1990s on the role of international financial institutions, such as the World Bank and the International Monetary Fund. International law was seen as a vehicle that would help facilitate the use of America's preeminent military and economic power in the interest of world order. While certain elements of international law could occasionally be stretched or quietly undercut, the prevailing view in Washington had been that the United Nations system allowed for a relatively stable world order in which the United States and its allies could usually get its goals accomplished and was far less dangerous than a more anarchic system.

However, as a result of the United States emerging as the world's one remaining superpower following the collapse of the Soviet Union, with US military spending higher than almost all of the rest of the world's governments combined, and with American commercial and cultural influence far greater than any other country, a sense emerged among many leading policymakers that the United States could go it alone. The UN system, according to this view, was seen as a constraint and an anachronism, so the United States no longer had to play by the rules and had the right and the ability to impose a kind of Pax Americana on the Middle East and the rest of the world.

This resulted in a number of other policy shifts, such as the broad bipartisan consensus in Washington (despite some occasional reservations expressed regarding some specific policies) to provide unconditional support for a series of right-wing Israeli governments in their ongoing occupation and colonization of territories seized in the June 1967 War, as well as their military offensives resulting in large-scale civilian casualties; ending support for the referendum process allowing for self-determination in Moroccan-occupied Western Sahara in favor of a dubious Moroccan-instigated "autonomy" plan; and, a series of unilateral military actions in the greater Middle East without UN authorization. In his introduction to the 2002 National Security

Strategy, President George W. Bush asserted that the United States represented "a single sustainable model for national success" (Bush, 2002). In particular, according to the president,

> I believe the United States is *the* beacon for freedom in the world. And I believe we have a responsibility to promote freedom that is as solemn as the responsibility is to protect the American people, because the two go hand-in-hand.
>
> *(Woodward, 2004)*

Historian Margaret Macmillan writes, "Faith in their exceptionalism has sometimes led to a…tendency to preach at other nations rather than listen to them, a tendency [to believe] that American motives are pure where those of others are not" (Hiro, 2003). Journalist Eric Zuesse observed how Bush "made clear right at the start that the United States had to be accepted by other nations as being not merely the first among equals, but a role apart, which simply mustn't be judged like other countries" Furthermore, notes Zuesse, Bush "gives every indication that he hates Man-made international law, and really believes he's serving God through his campaign to destroy and replace it by his standing *above* it" (Zuesse, 2004).

The National Security Strategy (NSS) also marked a more radical view of US hegemonic priorities by arguing that the United States should strike preemptively at any country it believes is developing biological, chemical or nuclear weapons: "America will act against such emerging threats before they are fully formed" (Bush, 2002). This underscores the basis of the Bush administration's post-invasion rationale – initially backed by Senators John Kerry, Hillary Clinton, Joe Biden, Chuck Schumer, and a number of other leading Democrats as well – that, while Iraq may not have actually had any "weapons of mass destruction" (WMDs), offensive delivery systems, or WMD programs as claimed, even just having the potential to develop such weapons programs and weapons systems sometime in the future was enough to justify the invasion. The invasion of Iraq, therefore, was not a "preemptive" war but a "preventive war". The 2002 NSS argues that since it is hard to know when or how terrorists might strike, it is therefore justifiable to attack any country which might be developing a weapons potential that might someday be used against US interests.

Supporters of an American hegemonic order were initially able to take advantage of the very real security concerns in the aftermath of the September 2001 Al-Qaeda attacks on the United States to engage in a series of policy initiatives, initially with the support of a broad cross-section of US political and intellectual opinion, which posed a direct challenge to the post-World War II international legal order. The doctrine of preventive war, the use of extraordinary rendition and torture, the invasion and occupation of Iraq, threats against Iran, the aggressive counter-insurgency operations and air campaigns in Afghanistan, the backing for some of the more militaristic and expansionist elements in Israel, and related policies have served to alienate the United States from many of the governments and a large cross-section of the Middle Eastern and North African population – ironically, those whose cooperation has been most important in the struggle against terrorist groups and other extremist elements in the region.

Subsequent events

The disastrous outcome of the Iraq War tempered the more extreme hegemonic goals coming out of Washington. Barack Obama was elected president in 2008 in large part because he recognized that that there were limitations to American power, particularly in regard to military force. Among the American electorate, support for military intervention declined greatly after the invasion of Iraq. Democratic politicians who supported the Iraq War suffered politically and likely contributed to the narrow losses of the pro-Iraq War Democratic nominees for president in 2004 and 2016. John Kerry's support for the Iraq War led to a campaign reminiscent to the 1968 contest between Humbert Humphrey and Richard Nixon, where anti-war elements that would have otherwise voted Democrat declined to do so and Kerry's tentative reservations against the war opened him up to charges of "flip-flopping". Similarly, Donald Trump's disingenuous claim that he opposed the war played an important role in defeating his hawkish Republican rivals for the nomination and led enough libertarian and other anti-interventionists to support him over the pro-interventionist Hillary Clinton to have made the difference in the general election (Kriner and Shen, 2017). Despite this, the Trump administration has amplified the militarization of US policy in the region, with increasing attacks against suspected terrorists and the concomitant increase in civilian casualties. No longer even pretending to support democratization or an end to the Israeli occupation, Trump has eschewed any idealistic rationalizations for US policy, saying that the United States should have taken control of Iraqi and Libyan oil fields following US military intervention in those countries (Trump, 2016).

In addition to the enormous humanitarian, fiscal and environmental costs of the war, the invasion seriously strained relations with most of Washington's Arab allies, lowered public opinion towards the United States in the greater Middle East to record lows, and encouraged the rise of Islamist extremists. Indeed, virtually the entire political and military leadership of the so-called "Islamic State" (ISIS) are Iraqis radicalized during the US occupation and counter-insurgency war, many of whom having suffered abuse in American-run military prisons. Ironically, however, the United States has used the threat from ISIS as an excuse for further militarization, military intervention, and support for armed groups and autocratic governments – the very failed policies which have contributed so greatly to the region's suffering and the rise of extremist groups. This has underscored the paradox that the greater the assertion of military force by the United States, the greater the threat of radicalization and the more rapid the decline in US influence.

Washington was totally unprepared for the wave of popular uprisings that swept the Middle East in the early 2010s. It had long been assumed that the autocratic leadership of most Arab countries was firmly entrenched and there was little risk of destabilization. Though the foreign policy establishment was divided between those willing to quietly encourage limited democratic reforms and those rooted to a realpolitik view that had no qualms about continued dictatorial rule as long as it was pro-Western, few believed that the desire for greater freedom and justice – particularly among a younger generations of Arabs – would result in a series of popular uprisings challenging both allied and adversarial dictatorships. Despite the failure of the uprisings (outside of Tunisia) to create a more democratic and stable order, it served as a reminder that civil society, transnational movements, and other factors have reduced the ability of the United States and other foreign governments to impact the fate of nations in the greater Middle East. Clandestine operations by intelligence agencies, secret agreements and even full-scale military invasions and occupations can no longer insure that the United States can impose its agenda.

This has not, however, prevented the United States from trying to influence the outcome of such rebellions. Indeed, whether the motivation for direct or indirect US military intervention in the greater Middle East in recent years has been based on crass imperialism, sincere (if sometime misguided) liberal internationalism, or other reasons, the United States still maintains a major presence in the region. While the Obama administration recognized that the reckless interventionism of the Bush administration actually hurt US strategic objectives, President Obama still saw the United States as the "indispensable nation" and still supported a leading role for the United States, albeit more nuanced. Despite criticisms by Republicans and some hawkish Democrats that he was being too cautious and too reluctant to use military force,

President Obama ordered the bombing of no less than seven countries in the greater Middle East during his eight years in office. Similarly, through the use or the threat of US veto power in the UN Security Council, the influential role in international financial institutions, and other diplomatic efforts – as well as its role as the principal arms supplier to the region – the Obama administration vigorously pursued an agenda supportive of its allies and interests and detrimental to perceived adversaries regardless of America's stated support for human rights and international law. The Trump administration has indicated that it has even less regard for those principles in pursuing what it sees as US interests in the greater Middle East.

The US role in the 2011 NATO intervention in Libya was characteristic of Obama's desire to exert American power in the region without the unilateralism and overreach characteristic of the Bush administration. Declaring that the United States was "leading from behind", President Obama acted only after a large-scale indigenous uprising against the regime of long-standing dictator Muammar Qaddafi was underway, the Arab League requested and the UN Security Council approved the use of force, and British and French forces demonstrated their willingness and ability to take primary responsibility for the air campaign. The Obama administration, however, joined its NATO and Arab allies in going well beyond the Security Council mandate to provide a no-fly zone to protect civilians to instead effectively become the air force for the coalition of rebel armies. The subsequent collapse of the Libyan state, however, the ongoing violence between various armed factions, and the rise of radical Islamist groups in the country has raised questions about even this relatively modest intervention. Trump criticized the Libya intervention as misguided and Obama himself has acknowledged the failure of the United States to play a more assertive role in trying to promote post-Qaddafi stability in the country as perhaps the greatest regret of his presidency (Rhodan, 2016).

The Obama administration tried to walk a similar fine line in regard to Syria's civil war, but was challenged domestically from both the right and the left. Furthermore, even Syrian opponents of the Assad regime were suspicious of US motivations as a result of bipartisan policies of earlier years in which the United States employed punitive sanctions, demanded unilateral disarmament, supported the Israeli occupation of the Golan province, attacked Syrian forces in Lebanon, and made a series of exaggerated and unfounded charges – along with military threats – regarding the country's alleged culpability in terrorism and danger to regional security (Zunes, 2004). Charges that the Obama administration and other Western powers were behind or otherwise responsible for the initial popular revolt against Syria's corrupt and autocratic regime, however, are groundless.

In mid-2011, after the indigenous popular nonviolent uprising had been waging for a couple of months, the State Department established a small office in Istanbul which provided workshops, information and some logistical support for some nonviolent pro-democracy activists, but it is unclear if it had much impact. As hundreds of armed militia sprung up under the loose banner of the Free Syrian Army in early 2012, several US agencies provided a limited amount of arms and funding to some "moderate" rebel factions, but a combination of their failure to gain traction militarily and some of them being incorporated into coalitions with hardline Islamists resulted in Washington largely scuttling such efforts by 2014. Indeed, after the rise of ISIS that same year, the United States began providing arms almost exclusively to groups fighting that Islamist cult rather than the Syrian regime.

Perhaps the most significant factor the Syrian crisis has played in regard to US hegemony is that it has become the vehicle through which Moscow has reasserted its role in the Middle East. Since the breakup of the Soviet Union, its former allied regimes in the region – initially Afghanistan and South Yemen, and subsequently Iraq and Libya – have fallen, with US intervention having varying degrees of responsibility in three of those cases. Combined with the

US Middle East policy

eastward expansion of NATO and growing US ties with some of the Caucasus republics, it has led the Kremlin to reassert its perceived strategic interests by throwing its support behind the Syrian Government despite the large-scale atrocities by the Assad regime. This has limited the military options the United States may have had to force regime change by military means or even to simply protect the civilian population.

Even when there is neither warfare nor Russian influence, the limits of US power to control events became apparent during the 2011 Egyptian revolution which overthrew a long-standing autocratic American ally, the subsequent election of a conservative Islamist as president and the military coup and reinstallation of authoritarian military rule that followed. Despite various conspiracy theories regarding supposed US instigation of the uprising or the military coup, policy-makers in Washington were in fact scrambling to anticipate or even keep up with events, much less influence them. Despite billions of dollars' worth of economic and military aid and decades of close military cooperation, the ability of the United States to affect the outcome of events in that nation of nearly 100 million people was and remains minimal.

Meanwhile, in the Persian Gulf, with important military installations in Bahrain and an exaggerated concern over Iranian influence among that country's Shia majority, the US Government expressed little public concern over the brutal repression by the Bahraini regime and Saudi-led foreign forces against the popular nonviolent pro-democracy movement in that island nation. However, given the determination by those monarchies to prevent a democratic opening in the Gulf, there was little the United States could have done to have prevented it anyway. Similarly, the United States had little influence in the more positive outcome in Tunisia, particularly given that France, as the former colonial power, was the dominant foreign influence.

The United States did play a more active role in Yemen, however, as a stalemate developed in 2011 between President Ali Abdullah Saleh and the broad alliance of oppositionists which had staged a largely nonviolent civil resistance campaign to his authoritarian regime. Rejecting proposals by the opposition for a National Council consisting of 143 opposition representatives to form a provisional government and oversee democratic multiparty elections, the United States instead backed a Saudi-led plan by the autocratic monarchies of the Gulf Cooperation Council in which Saleh would be replaced by his vice-president, Major General Abd Rabbuh Mansur Hadi. The result was the Houthi uprising and civil war, the devastating Saudi military intervention, the growing influence of Al-Qaeda, and an increase in US drone strikes and commando raids. As a result, the one country on the Arabia Peninsula that was poor and dependent enough for the United States to have potentially impacted the outcome in a positive manner by supporting pro-democracy forces, the Obama administration instead sided with the autocratic Gulf monarchs in imposing what they apparently believed would result in a more stabilizing transition which would enhance US influence. Instead, US policy contributed to a dramatic destabilization and tragic humanitarian consequences. The United States has continued to support the ongoing Saudi bombing campaign in the country, which has killed thousands of civilians.

Though Trump initially sided with the Saudis and their allies in their dispute with Qatar, the State Department has subsequently taken a more neutral stance in trying to resolve the conflict between these US allies. The bipartisan support for increasing ties with the family dictatorships which rule the Arab Gulf states remains largely unquestioned.

Despite the desire by President Obama and others to focus US policy more on East Asia, the ongoing turmoil in the region has resulted in the greater Middle East remaining the most important region in terms of US security interests. As of 2018, the United States had an estimated 5200 troops in Iraq, 11,000 in Afghanistan, and 700 in Syria, many of whom are in combat zones. In addition, there are an estimated 15,000 US troops stationed in Kuwait, 10,000 in Qatar, 7000 in Bahrain, 5000 in the United Arab Emirates, 2500 in Turkey, and 1500 in Jordan, as well as 20,000 sailors and marines aboard the two aircraft carriers and 20 additional ships in the Fifth Fleet. Currently, the State Department's Bureau of Near Eastern Affairs lists the priorities of US policy in the region as:

- Helping Iraqis build a unified, stable and prosperous country
- Renewing progress toward the two-state solution to the Palestinian–Israeli conflict
- Working against terrorists and their state sponsors, as well as against the spread of weapons of mass destruction
- Supporting efforts at economic and political reform in the region

By most measures, however, the United States is failing at each of these, and there are serious questions as to whether the US even supports the second and fourth of these goals.

Nuclear non-proliferation

Concerns over the acquisition of nuclear weapons by Middle Eastern countries hostile to US interests has been a major concern for successive administrations. Despite claims to the contrary, it is hard to imagine that should any such country actually obtain nuclear weapons that they would launch a suicidal first strike against US bases or American allies. (None of these countries is anywhere close to developing the capability to attack the United States itself.) The actual concern may be related more to a determination to prevent any potential adversary from developing a nuclear deterrent that might limit Washington's ability to intervene militarily in the region or limit its allies – such as Israel and Saudi Arabia – from similarly engaging in unfettered military operations beyond their borders. Successive administrations have largely rejected universal, law-based and reciprocal arms control agreements and instead insisted that the United States and its allies should be allowed to develop and deploy nuclear weapons and delivery systems while subjecting perceived adversaries to sanctions, threats of war, and even invasion and occupation for allegedly developing even just the potential of such technologies (Zunes, 2009). For example, in 2002, the US House of Representatives passed a resolution by a 401–11 margin urging the president to oppose any policy toward Iran "that would rely on containment as an option in response to the Iranian nuclear threat" and threatening unilateral military action to prevent Iran from simply having "nuclear weapons *capability*" – not necessarily any actual weapons or an active nuclear weapons program (US House of Representatives, 2012).

UN Security Resolution 687 (1991), which demanded Iraqi disarmament, did so within the context of "establishing in the Middle East a zone free of weapons of mass destruction". It was alleged violations of this resolution that the Bush administration used to justify the invasion of Iraq in 2003, even though Iraq was actually in full compliance with the resolution for nearly a decade prior to the war and the United States discouraged implementation of the provision regarding a WMD-free zone. Nuclear-weapons free zones (NWFZs) have been successfully established in Latin America, Africa, Antarctica, the South Pacific, Southeast Asia, and Central Asia, but the United States has repeatedly blocked United Nations efforts for an international conference to establish such a regime in the Middle East. US opposition to NWFZs in the Middle East and elsewhere has stemmed largely due to the desire for the United States to move its tactical nuclear weapons around the world. This is why Israel – which possesses hundreds of nuclear weapons – is actually correct in insisting that they would not be the first country to introduce nuclear weapons in the region, since US aircraft carriers first brought atomic bombs into the eastern Mediterranean in 1958. Successive US administrations have either acquiesced or quietly supported the development of Israel's nuclear arsenal.

Israel continues to be in violation of UN Security Council resolution 487 (1981), which calls on Israel to place its nuclear facilities under the trusteeship of the International Atomic Energy Agency, while Pakistan and India have been in violation of UN Security Council resolution 1172 (1998) which calls on those nations to end their nuclear weapons programs and eliminate their long-range missiles. The United States had blocked enforcement of those resolutions, however, while demanding – under threat of war – that Iraq and Iran unilaterally eliminate their nuclear programs. Congress went on record defending Israel's 1981 bombing of an Iraqi nuclear reactor, demonstrating a strong bipartisan preference for selective counter-proliferation over a more universal non-proliferation. Indeed, the bipartisan consensus in opposition to the United Nations or diplomatic measures was reflected in a near-unanimous Congressional resolution in March 2003 declaring that – despite the successful efforts by the United Nations to eliminate Iraq's nuclear, chemical and biological programs in the 1990s – the United States had the right to invade Iraq on the grounds that such "diplomatic and other peaceful means alone" would not "adequately protect the national security of the United States against the continuing threat posed by Iraq" (US House of Representatives, 2003). Similarly, when a protracted British-led diplomatic effort to eliminate Libya's nascent nuclear program reached a successful conclusion in December 2003, a large bipartisan majority of the US House of Representatives supported a resolution which declared – in direct contradiction of American diplomats involved in the talks (Leverett, 2004) – that the elimination of Libya's nuclear program "would not have been possible if not for…the liberation of Iraq by United States and Coalition Forces" (US House of Representatives, 2004).

The decision to overthrow the Iraqi Government in a US-led invasion and the Libyan Government in a US-backed uprising after both nations had given up even the potential for a nuclear deterrent may have contributed to Iran's initial reluctance to limit its nuclear program. Despite Iran's program being civilian in nature, the potential that it could eventually branch off into military applications became a major obsession for policy-makers. Most Democrats and almost all Republicans in Congress went on record insisting that Iran must capitulate to US demands that it end its nuclear program and opposed negotiations.

One factor often overlooked is that Article VI of the Nonproliferation Treaty – the supposed basis of US objections to Iraq and Iran's nuclear programs – requires countries in possession of nuclear weapons at the time of the signing to "pursue negotiations in good faith on effective measures relating to cessation of the nuclear arms race at and early date and to nuclear disarmament, and on a treaty on general and complete disarmament under strict and effective international control" (United Nations Office on Disarmament Affairs, 1968). Despite this, neither the United States nor the four other original nuclear powers have fulfilled this obligation. This underscores how the issue was never one of nonproliferation. Even if Iran indeed did intend to use the option of developing nuclear weapons, it would have almost certainly been for deterrence, given threats of regime change by the United States, the recent overthrow of governments to their immediate east and west, the existing nuclear arsenals of three neighboring countries, and the overthrow of the Iraqi and Libyan governments *after* they had eliminated their nuclear programs.

Obama agreed with the urgency of preventing Iran from obtaining a nuclear deterrent and threatened the use of military force if necessary, but he also recognized that Iran – which has been a regional power at various times for nearly 2500 years – could not simply be bullied into submission. Furthermore, he recognized that military options would have little international support, would likely fail in their strategic objectives, and have catastrophic results. He therefore had the United States join Russia, China, Great Britain, France and Germany – with the support of the United Nations Security Council, which imposed sanctions on Iran to encourage that government to compromise – in years of painstaking negotiations eventually resulting in an agreement – known as the Joint Comprehensive Plan of Action – which allows Iran to maintain a limited civilian nuclear program but with sufficient safeguards to preclude the physical possibility of developing weapons, along with one of the most rigorous inspection regimes in history to ensure their compliance. Despite this, there was strong opposition by Republicans, some Democrats, as well as Trump and others in his national security team, who have repeatedly exaggerated Iran's military prowess and support for insurgent movements and claimed it was a "one-sided agreement". (The agreement actually was one-sided, but against Iran: neither the United States nor the other powers have to give up any aspect of their nuclear programs in return.) On 8 May 2018, the Trump administration withdrew the United States from the treaty and re-imposed sanctions, including those against foreign companies which had begun investing and trading with Iran. This has left Iran with little incentive to uphold the agreement and sends a lesson to other nations that the United States cannot be trusted to keep its commitments.

Israel

For nearly a quarter of a century, Washington has played the contradictory role as the mediator in Israeli–Palestinian peace talks and the principal military, economic and diplomatic backer of the occupying power. This has included blocking enforcement of scores of UN Security Council resolutions as well as vetoing and weakening scores of others and rejecting efforts by the United Nations or other intergovernmental organizations as well as any other country from taking leadership in the peace process. In addition, both Republican and Democratic administrations have attacked the International Court of Justice and other UN bodies for documenting and passing judgment regarding ongoing Israeli violations of international humanitarian law (Zunes, 2017). Similarly, US political leaders across the ideological spectrum have condemned civil society efforts (such as calls for boycotts, divestment and sanctions (BDS) targeting Israel) to end the occupation. The bipartisan consensus is that any peace agreement must come only from direct negotiations between the Israeli and Palestinian governments without exerting any pressure on the former, which – given the gross asymmetry in power between the occupier and those under occupation – essentially means no settlement is possible except what is acceptable to Israel's right-wing government. This effectively precludes the establishment of an independent viable Palestinian state alongside Israel. As a result – despite the Palestine Authority, the Palestine Liberation Organizations, and the ruling Fatah party accepting a Palestinian ministate in the West Bank and Gaza Strip and recognizing Israel with security guarantees on the remaining 78% of historic Palestine – there has been no peace agreement.

There are serious questions, therefore, as to whether the United States even wants an equitable and lasting peace settlement, particularly in light of the important role that Israel – by far the region's most powerful armed force – plays in advancing the United States' long-standing strategic interests in maintaining and securing a pro-Western regional order that advances and legitimates US influence in the region and prevents anti-Western or independent-minded challenges to that order. As such, in a region where radical nationalism and Islamist extremism could threaten US control of oil and other strategic interests, Israel has played a major role in preventing victories by radical movements, not just in Palestine but in Lebanon and Jordan as well. The Israeli air force is predominant throughout the region. Israel's frequent wars facilitate battlefield testing of US weapons and Israel's arms industry has provided weapons and munitions for governments and opposition movements supported by the United States. Moreover, during the 1980s, Israel served as a conduit for US arms to governments and movements too unpopular in the United States to receive overt military assistance, including South Africa under the apartheid regime, Iran's Islamic Republic, Guatemala's rightist military juntas, the Nicaraguan Contras, and subsequently Colombian paramilitaries. Israeli military advisers assisted the Contras, the Salvadoran junta, and other movements and governments backed by the United States – most recently a number of Kurdish forces.

The Israeli intelligence agency Mossad has cooperated with the CIA and other US agencies in gathering intelligence and spearheading covert operations. Israel possesses missiles capable of striking targets thousands of miles from its borders and has collaborated with the US military-industrial complex in research and development for new jet fighters and anti-missile defense systems, a relationship that is growing every year. Israelis have trained US forces bound for Iraq and Afghanistan in counter-terrorism and counter-insurgency tactics. As one Israeli analyst described it during the Iran-Contra scandal, where Israel played a crucial intermediary rule, "It's like Israel has become just another federal agency, one that's convenient to use when you want something done quietly" (Glenn, 1986). Former US Secretary of State Alexander Haig once described Israel as the largest and only unsinkable US aircraft carrier in the world.

Indeed, history has shown that the stronger, more aggressive and more compliant with US interests that Israel has become, the higher the level of aid and strategic cooperation it receives. For decades, the United States has insisted on insuring Israeli qualitative military *superiority*, not just an adequate deterrent from potential aggressors. A militant Israel is seen to advance American interests. Indeed, an Israel in a constant state of war – technologically sophisticated and militarily advanced, yet lacking an independent economy and dependent on the United States – is far more willing to perform tasks unacceptable to other allies than an Israel at peace with its neighbors. As former Secretary of State Henry Kissinger (1982) once put it, in reference to Israel's reluctance to make peace, "Israel's obstinacy … serves the purposes of both our countries best".

For example, over the objections of leading Israeli generals, the United States put pressure on Israel to launch a major – and ultimately disastrous – war on Lebanon in 2006 as an effort to destroy the missile capabilities of Hizbullah, a pro-Iranian militia, in anticipation of a then-planned attack on Iran (Hersh, 2006). The United States also successfully pressured Israel to reject Syrian peace overtures in 2007 out of concern that a return of the Golan region would boost Assad's standing (Sciff et al., 2007). The Trump administration's support for Israeli colonization of the West Bank, the decision to formally recognize Israel's exclusive control of the multi-religious and multi-ethnic Jerusalem as its capital and moving the US embassy to the city, and its refusal to support an independent Palestinian state alongside Israel has further underscored how the United States is not really interested in Israeli–Palestinian peace.

Israel has long rejected calls by previous administrations to end their colonization drive in occupied Palestinian territories, withdraw from most of the occupied West Bank, and allow for the establishment of a viable Palestinian state. By contrast, the Palestine Authority agreed to all the terms put forward by the Obama administration for a peace agreement, including accepting large blocks of illegal Israeli settlements in return for an equivalent amount of land in Israel's Negev Desert, demilitarizing their state, allowing for international monitors, giving up the right of return for Palestinian refugees. However, the Obama administration then added a new requirement that Palestine explicitly recognize Israel as a "Jewish state", a demand that was not required of Egypt or Jordan in their peace treaties with Israel. Indeed, it would be the world's first peace treaty in which one party is obliged to recognize another country's ethnic or religious identity over that of others and politically unacceptable for any Palestinian leader, particularly in light of the 20% of the Israeli population who are Palestinian Arabs, thereby giving Washington grounds for saying neither side was willing to compromise.

Neither major political party has called for an end of the Israeli occupation and settlements. The Democratic platform didn't mention either, while criticizing the United Nations and civil society groups for challenging it and praising Israel for its commitment to "democracy, equality, tolerance, and pluralism" (Democratic National Committee, 2016) while the Republican Party platform stated that "We reject the false notion that Israel is an occupier" (Republican Party Platform, 2016). In both the 2016 platform and in statements by Trump himself, the Republicans dropped the call by Presidents Bush and Obama for Israel to allow for at least a mini-state for the Palestinians in parts of the West Bank. US ambassador to Israel David Friedman insists that the Israeli settlements are "part of Israel" and that Israel has a right to expand them further. Israel currently directly controls 60% of the West Bank and limits the Palestine Authority to control over the rest through dozens of non-contiguous cantons separated by Israeli checkpoints. Friedman, however, supports Israeli annexation of the entire occupied territories and insists the United States should end the "two-state narrative" (Friedman, 2016). And, he has called moderate pro-Israel Zionist groups like J Street worse than Nazi collaborators (Levitz, 2016). Trump's senior director for international negotiations which oversees Israeli–Palestinian peace talks is conservative blogger Victoria Coates, who also supports Israel's annexation of occupied Palestinian territories.

Conclusion

Despite the end of the Cold War and the Arab Spring, US security policy in the Middle East – with a few minor exceptions – has changed little despite its poor record for advancing the interests of the United States or the well-being of the peoples of the region. Opposition to such policies has been both principled – in the sense that there are serious moral and legal implications – as well as practical, particularly in regard to the overemphasis on military means to address complex political, social and economic problems, which has emboldened extremists and weakened moderate voices, resulting in a more anarchic international order that makes legitimate counter-terrorism efforts all the more difficult. While the militarism of the Trump administration and its lack of concern for human rights and international law has sparked concern both in the United States and internationally, in many key respects such dangerous priorities have shaped US Middle East policy for years.

References

Armstrong, S. (1981). "Saudis' AWACS Just a Beginning of a New Strategy". *Washington Post*, November 1.
Bush, G. (2002). "Introduction". *The National Security Strategy of the United States of America,* Washington DC: White House, p. 4.
Democratic National Committee (2016). "Democratic Party Platform" [online]. Available at: https://democrats.org/about/party-platform/
Frankel, G. (1986). "Israeli Reportedly Set Up First US-Iran Arms Deal". *Washington Post*. November 19.
Friedman, D. (2016). "End the Two-state Narrative". *Israel National News* [online]. Available at: www.israelnationalnews.com/Articles/Article.aspx/18368
Hersh, S. (2006). "Watching Lebanon: Washington's Interests in Israel's War". New Yorker, August 21.
Hiro, D. (2003). *Secrets and Lies: Operation Iraqi Freedom and After: A Prelude to the Fall of US Power in the Middle East?* New York: Nation Books, p. 388.
Kissinger, H. (1982). *Years of Upheaval*, Boston: Little, Brown, p. 621.
Klare, M. (1994). "Making Enemies for the '90s: The New 'Rogue States' Doctrine" *The Nation*, p. 625.
Kolko, G. and Kolko, J. (1972). *The Limits of Power*, New York: Harper & Row, p. 45.

Kriner, D. and Shen, F. (2017). *Battlefield Casualties and Ballot Box Defeat: Did the Bush-Obama Wars Cost Clinton the White House?* (June 19, 2017) [online]. Available at http://dx.doi.org/10.2139/ssrn.2989040.

Leverett, F. (2004). "Why Libya Gave Up on the Bomb", *The New York Times*, January 23, p. A23.

Levitz, E. (2016). "Trump Picks Lawyer Who Says Liberal Jews are Worse than Nazi Collaborators as Israel Ambassador". *New York Magazine* [online]. Available at: http://nymag.com/daily/intelligencer/2016/12/trumps-israel-ambassador-likens-left-wing-jews-to-kapos.html.

Nixon, R. (1969). *Address to the Nation on the War in Vietnam.* 3 November, Washington, DC: White House.

Republican National Committee (2016). "Republican Party Platform", p. 47 [online]. Available at: www.gop.com/the-2016-republican-party-platform/

Rhodan, M. (2016) "President Obama Admits the 'Worst Mistake' of His Presidency", *Time*, April 11.

Schiff, Z., Amos, H., and Stern, Y. (2007). "US Takes Harder Line on Talks between Jerusalem, Damascus". *Haaretz,* February 24.

Spiegel, S. (1985). *The Other Arab–Israeli Conflict.* Chicago: University of Chicago Press, p. 51.

Trump, D. (2016). Transcript of "Commander-in-Chief Forum". *Time Magazine* [online]. Available at: http://time.com/4483355/commander-chief-forum-clinton-trump-intrepid/

United Nations Office on Disarmament Affairs (1968). *Treaty on the Non-Proliferation of Nuclear Weapons,* Article VI.

United Nations Security Council (1981). Resolution 487 [online]. Available at: http://unscr.com/en/resolutions/487

United Nations Security Council (1991). Resolution 687 [online]. Available at: http://unscr.com/en/resolutions/687

United Nations Security Council (1999). Resolution 1172 [online]. Available at: http://unscr.com/en/resolutions/1172

US House of Representatives (2003). House Concurrent Resolution 104. 108th Congress, 1st session. March 21.

US House of Representatives (2004). House Amendment 601. 108th Congress, 2nd session. November 22.

US House of Representatives (2012). House Resolution 568. 112th Congress, 2nd session. May 17.

Woodward, B. (2004). *Plan of Attack: The Definitive Account of the Decision to Invade Iraq,* New York: Simon & Schuster, p. 88.

Zuesse, E. (2004). *Iraq War: The Truth,* Boise: Delphic Press, pp. 118, 121.

Zunes, S. (2004). "US Policy toward Syria and the Triumph of Neoconservatism", *Middle East Policy*, vol. XI, no. 2.

Zunes, S. (2009). "The United States and the Undermining of the Nonproliferation Regime", in David Krieger, ed., *The Challenge of Abolishing Nuclear Weapons*, New Brunswick, NJ: Transaction Publishers.

Zunes, S. (2017). "The United States and Israeli Violations of International Humanitarian Law", in Anthony Chase, ed., *Handbook on Human Rights and the Middle East and North Africa*, Abingdon and New York: Routledge, pp. 142–154.

5

EXTERNAL INTERVENTION IN THE GULF

Matteo Legrenzi and Fred H. Lawson

Introduction

External powers have played a crucial role in cultivating, maintaining and jeopardizing Gulf security for many centuries. In the early 1800s, Great Britain took command of the most important port communities situated on both shores of the Gulf and set up an integrated structure that protected the primary strategic and commercial interests of the imperial administration in India (Kelly, 1968). Iran and the coastal principalities of Kuwait, Bahrain, Qatar, the Trucial States and Oman became protectorates of the British-Indian Empire, and their relations with states outside the region were tightly regulated by the British diplomats and military commanders that effectively governed the area (Onley, 2007). British-Indian officials engaged in a complex set of maneuvers, collectively known as The Great Game in Asia, which was designed to prevent any external actors from posing a severe threat to the imperial order (Ingram, 1979). By playing this game, they managed to preserve the empire's exclusive position in the Gulf from the first decades of the 19th century to the late 1930s.

Emergence of US dominance in the Gulf

External intervention in the security affairs of the Gulf shifted decisively during the course of World War II. The United Kingdom (UK), which enjoyed a preeminent position in Iran, Iraq, Kuwait, Bahrain, Qatar, the Trucial States and Oman, found itself challenged by initiatives undertaken by the United States as the war progressed. American military forces played a key role in transporting armaments and foodstuffs to the Soviet Union through the ports of southern Iran beginning in the winter of 1941–42. At the same time, the US Army Air Corps acquired landing rights at a string of British military airfields along the southern shore of the Gulf – most notably the large Royal Air Force base at al-Muharraq in Bahrain and the secondary staging facility at Sharjah in the Trucial States (Peterson, 1986). American commanders in the region began reporting directly to the Department of War in December 1943 under the auspices of the US Persian Gulf Command.

Washington's growing military involvement in the Gulf accompanied a steadily expanding economic presence. US-based Standard Oil of California (SOCAL) acquired the rights to explore for hydrocarbons in Bahrain and the Eastern Province of Saudi Arabia after British

External intervention in the Gulf

geologists concluded that these two territories lacked sufficient deposits to be worth pursuing. In May 1932, commercially viable amounts of petroleum were discovered in Bahrain, and a year later SOCAL convinced the ruler of Saudi Arabia, King 'Abd al-'Aziz bin 'Abd al-Rahman Al Sa'ud, to grant it a concession to tap the new-found oil resources of the Eastern Province, despite belated efforts by the British-owned Iraq Petroleum Company to catch up. In 1944, as SOCAL transformed into the Arabian American Oil Company (ARAMCO), the US Department of State opened a consulate at Dhahran in the Eastern Province after conceding to London that this diplomatic outpost would handle all matters involving American interests in Saudi Arabia and Bahrain.

As the war drew to a close, the US strengthened its position in Saudi Arabia. Partly to offset British prerogatives and Soviet ambitions in the region, and partly as a means of subsidizing the cash-strapped Saudi government, American commanders constructed a large air base at Dhahran (Lawson, 1989). Saudi officials insisted that US military personnel wear civilian clothing while working on the project, so as not to inflame local sentiment against the presence of non-Muslims on sacred soil. After Japan surrendered, the Dhahran air base was transformed from a transit hub to a forward staging facility for US strategic bombers. In 1946 Riyadh contracted with the US-based Trans World Airlines (TWA) to set up and manage the local air carrier, Saudi Airlines. These initiatives contributed to a short but intense regional crisis between the US and the Soviet Union in the spring of 1946 (Fawcett, 1992).

By the early 1950s, the broad contours of the US presence in the Gulf had become consolidated (O'Reilly, 2008). ARAMCO maintained exclusive rights to exploit the vast pool of hydrocarbons lying beneath eastern Saudi Arabia and Bahrain. US military personnel took charge of training and equipping the armed forces of both countries, but did so as unobtrusively as possible. The Dhahran air base was formally transferred to Saudi control in March 1949, although the US Air Force insisted on retaining exclusive rights to use the facility. That same year, the US Navy deployed a pair of destroyers to the Gulf on a permanent basis under the auspices of the US Middle East Force, whose headquarters was set up on a supply ship docked at the Bahraini port of Jufair (Palmer, 1992). The Eisenhower administration stepped up the delivery of advanced weaponry to the Saudi armed forces in response to Riyadh's hints that it might respond positively to overtures from Moscow. Persistent Arab nationalist criticism of the US military presence at Dhahran, combined with the gradual diminution of the facility's role in US strategy toward the Soviet Union, led the US to evacuate the air base in April 1962.

During the early 1970s relations between Washington and Riyadh chilled dramatically. Saudi Arabia orchestrated an embargo of oil shipments from the Arab oil-producing countries to the US, the UK and the Netherlands in the aftermath of the October 1973 Arab–Israeli war, prompting public figures close to the Nixon administration to debate the advantages of dispatching US troops to seize the oil fields of the Gulf (Buheiry, 1980). Such public speculation left a legacy of mistrust in Arab Gulf capitals concerning American intentions, which was exacerbated by the close cooperation that took shape between Washington and Tehran during the mid-1970s (Wright, 2007). According to the Nixon Doctrine, powerful client states were accorded responsibility to preserve order in strategically vital parts of the world, in line with underlying US interests. Iran shouldered Saudi Arabia aside in performing that task in the Gulf. The resulting friction between Washington and Riyadh made Saudi officials receptive to overtures from Moscow (Page, 1984).

This regional security arrangement was thrown into disarray by the Iranian revolution of 1978–79. All US forces were expelled from the new Islamic Republic of Iran, and Tehran declared that it would no longer act as the client of any external power, a stance called "Neither East nor West". Saudi Arabia and the smaller Arab Gulf states expressed concern that Iranian-sponsored organizations would take steps to undermine existing regimes throughout the Gulf, particularly since Saudi Arabia, Bahrain and Kuwait harbored sizable Shi'i communities that might rise up in support of the Islamic Republic. These fears were compounded when Soviet troops intervened in the civil war in Afghanistan in December 1979 (Khalilzad, 1980; Halliday, 1981). The convergence of Iranian militancy and Soviet assertiveness led US President James E. Carter to proclaim in January 1980 that Washington would resist any attempt by outside forces to challenge American predominance in the Gulf, if necessary by military means. This policy came to be known as the Carter Doctrine.

Zenith of US predominance

As a way to implement the Carter Doctrine, US policy-makers created a new expeditionary force charged with reacting to threats in the Gulf. It was christened the Rapid Deployment Joint Task Force (RDJTF), and consisted of bits and pieces of units stationed in West Europe and the continental United States with headquarters at McDill Air Force Base in Florida (Record, 1981). American commanders then went in search of local governments that would agree to cooperate with the new formation. Only Oman agreed to allow US warplanes to make use of airfields on its territory, and to permit its armed forces to take part in military exercises orchestrated by the RDJTF. The Carter administration's efforts to persuade other Arab Gulf states to collaborate with the RDJTF collapsed in September 1980, when the Iraqi army invaded Iran.

As soon as it took office in January 1981, the Reagan administration authorized the deployment of US Air Force Airborne Warning and Control Systems (AWACS) aircraft to Saudi Arabia (Lawson, 1984). US commanders invited the Saudi armed forces to create a comprehensive mutual security arrangement, but the Saudi authorities demurred. Washington nevertheless continued to allocate more units and resources to the reconfigured Rapid Deployment Force (RDF), and in January 1983 designated the formation as the US Central Command (CENTCOM). As one of six unified, multi-service commands of the American armed forces, CENTCOM was given responsibility for contingency planning, undertaking military exercises and administering US military assistance to local allies throughout the Gulf, Southwest Asia and Northeast Africa (Waltz, 1981). It initially consisted of the Middle East Force, three US Navy aircraft carrier groups, seven tactical fighter wings, one Marine amphibious division, the 82nd Airborne Division, the 101st Airborne Division and the 24th Mechanized Infantry Division, for a total of just under 300,000 troops.

Meanwhile, the US Army Corps of Engineers initiated several large-scale construction projects on behalf of Saudi Arabia and Bahrain (McNaugher, 1985). The most significant was a pair of modern air bases at King Khalid Military City outside Hafr al-Batin, on the border with Iraq and Kuwait. They were complemented by a new air base at the southern end of the main island of Bahrain. All three facilities were notably overbuilt, that is, designed to handle many more aircraft than the Saudi and Bahraini air forces possessed and capable of accommodating the huge C-5A transports used by the US Military Airlift Command.

Direct US military involvement in the Gulf increased sharply during the spring of 1987. US officials raised the American flag on 11 Kuwaiti oil tankers that March, and ordered US Navy warships to begin escorting the vessels through the Gulf. Two months later, Iraqi aircraft fired missiles at the destroyer USS *Stark*, thereby convincing the Reagan administration to extend the reflagging program (Stein, 1988–89). US commanders placed all US ships operating in and around the Gulf on Condition One alert in early August 1987 in the wake of rioting by Iranian pilgrims in Mecca, and then staged mock air attacks against the coast of Iran. A month later,

US warships seized an Iranian boat that was laying mines in international waters, and a month after that destroyed a pair of Iranian oil drilling platforms at the southern end of the Gulf in retaliation for an Iranian missile strike on a US-owned tanker off Kuwait. US forces in April 1988 launched coordinated attacks against six Iranian gunboats and two more oil platforms, following a mine explosion off Qatar that damaged a US frigate. That July, a US Aegis missile cruiser operating off the United Arab Emirates (UAE) shot down an unidentified aircraft that was approaching low and fast from the north; the plane turned out to be an Iranian airliner coming in for a landing at Dubai.

These combat operations accompanied persistent US requests for direct access to local air and naval installations throughout the Gulf. The Iran–Iraq war drew to a close, however, before Washington's attempts to gain a foothold on the Arabian Peninsula bore fruit. US officials subsequently made a concerted effort to forge security ties to Iraq, building upon the intelligence sharing and supplying of dual-use equipment that had taken place during the last months of the war with Iran. In October 1989, the Bush administration issued National Security Directive 26, which instructed US government agencies to use economic inducements to dampen Iraqi belligerence and improve relations with Baghdad. Washington then extended USD 1 billion in agricultural credits to Iraq, along with USD 200 million in loans from the Export-Import Bank.

Rapprochement between the US and Iraq irritated the state of Israel. In December 1989, Baghdad successfully tested an intermediate-range ballistic missile (IRBM) and claimed that a version with a much longer range was under development. These events sparked an exchange of belligerent accusations between Israeli and Iraqi officials, which culminated in an April 1990 address by Iraq's President Saddam Hussein, in which the Iraqi leader threatened that "We will make fire eat up half of Israel if it tries to do anything against Iraq" (Freedman and Karsh, 1993, 32). A month later, Saddam Hussein charged that the US intended to dominate the Gulf in the post-Cold War era and was backing Kuwait in its campaign to damage the Iraqi economy. In late July, US Ambassador to Baghdad April Glaspie was summoned to the Iraqi foreign ministry to meet with Saddam Hussein, who told her that the US was encouraging Kuwait and the UAE to strangle Iraq. Glaspie replied that Washington took no position regarding "inter-Arab disputes such as your border dispute with Kuwait" and urged the Iraqi leader to find a peaceful way to end the crisis (Freedman and Karsh, 1993, 53). Shortly after this incident, the UAE navy engaged in joint exercises with CENTCOM. US commanders offered to deploy warships to Kuwait as well, but that principality declined the offer on the grounds that such a deployment would aggravate tensions with Baghdad.

On 2 August 1990, the Iraqi armed forces rolled across the border into Kuwait. US President George H.W. Bush immediately asked the Saudi government for permission to dispatch a squadron of fighter-bombers to the kingdom, but King Fahd bin 'Abd al-'Aziz ignored the request. The Central Intelligence Agency then reported that the Iraqi offensive looked ready to push into the Eastern Province, and US Secretary of Defense Richard Cheney was sent to Riyadh to inform the Saudi authorities of the imminent danger (Gause, 2010: 105). Cheney convinced King Fahd to allow 250,000 US soldiers to take up positions on Saudi territory. By mid-August, US commanders had started to prepare a counteroffensive to expel Iraqi troops from Kuwait. Operation Desert Storm got underway on 17 January 1991, with massive US air strikes all across Iraq.

Russian officials in early February 1991 tried to mediate the conflict. Baghdad accepted the mediation initiative, but demanded that Israel withdraw from the Palestinian lands it had occupied in June 1967. A succession of proposals and counter-proposals followed, all of which the US government flatly rejected. President Bush then called on the Iraqi populace to rise up and overthrow Saddam Hussein. On 22 February, he announced that Iraq had 24 hours to pull its forces out of Kuwait. As soon as the deadline arrived, the ground assault against Kuwait started; it lasted for four days, during which Iraqi battle deaths were estimated at 35,000 and US losses totaled 148 killed and 458 wounded. Clusters of retreating Iraqi soldiers outside the southern port town of Zubair revolted against their commanders on 28 February; the uprising quickly spread to the southern cities of Basrah, Najaf and Karbala, as well as to the predominantly Kurdish areas of northern Iraq. US officials publicly praised the rebels, but provided them with no material support. Secretary of State James Baker later claimed that Washington had kept its distance from the revolt "primarily out of fear of hastening the fragmentation of Iraq and plunging the region into a new cycle of instability" (Pollack, 2004, 247). US commanders did, however, take steps to protect rebels in the north; a no-fly zone was declared in early April to prevent Iraqi aircraft from attacking Kurdish fighters.

Washington turned to the United Nations (UN) to codify the terms of post-war security in the Gulf. UN Security Council Resolution 687 maintained the economic sanctions that had been imposed on Iraq in the run-up to the war, and ordered that they remain in place until the authorities in Baghdad agreed to recognize the sovereignty of Kuwait, return all property seized during the occupation, release all Kuwaiti prisoners, make restitution to all countries damaged during the war and terminate all activities aimed at developing weapons of mass destruction (WMD). Resolution 687 authorized the UN to send inspectors to verify that WMD production had stopped, the UN Special Commission on Iraq (UNSCOM). Iraqi troops advanced into the northern provinces in late March 1991, after rival Kurdish militias clashed with one another. The US then pushed through UN Security Council Resolution 688, which created a so-called "safe haven" in the north enforced by 10,000 troops. In August 1992, US commanders set up a no-fly zone in the south. Iraqi forces challenged the southern zone that December, and US forces responded by carrying out a wave of air strikes against military targets.

Two elite Iraqi army divisions moved into positions along the border with Kuwait in October 1994. At the same time, Iraqi officials threatened to expel UNSCOM. US commanders quickly augmented air, ground and naval forces in the Gulf, and convinced the UN Security Council to adopt Resolution 949 that imposed strict constraints on the operations of the Iraqi armed forces near the Kuwaiti border. Fighting resumed between Kurdish militias in northern Iraq in August 1996, and Iraqi troops once again crossed into Kurdish areas. In response, the US launched four dozen cruise missiles against Iraqi military installations in the south, and enlarged the southern no-fly zone. Iraqi officials in October 1997 threatened to shoot down US surveillance aircraft and expel all members of UNSCOM who held US citizenship. UNSCOM pulled out of the country, and Washington ordered an aircraft carrier group to take up positions in the Gulf and deployed B-52 heavy bombers to Diego Garcia in the Indian Ocean. The Iraqi government then readmitted all UNSCOM inspectors.

Iraq interfered with UNSCOM operations once more in January 1998, and the US responded by sending an aircraft carrier group and Marine expeditionary force to the Gulf. That October Baghdad demanded an end to the UNSCOM mission, and the inspectors departed in early November. US commanders issued orders to attack Iraqi targets, but while the warplanes were in the air Baghdad announced that the inspectors could resume their activities. UNSCOM reported in December 1998 that the Iraqi Government was not complying with the terms of Resolution 687, and pulled out once again in protest. The US military reacted by carrying out 600 air strikes and launching 400 cruise missiles against the south. Throughout 1999–2000 US military aircraft continued to bombard Iraqi command centers and military facilities. Saudi

External intervention in the Gulf

Arabia and Turkey grew increasingly discomfited by the unrelenting and largely ineffective air strikes, and gradually narrowed the range of actions that they permitted from bases located on their territories.

While Washington sparred with Baghdad during the 1990s, US relations with Iran went from bad to worse. Tehran adopted a neutral stance toward the 1990–91 war, criticizing Iraq for occupying Kuwait while condemning the other Arab Gulf states for inviting US troops into the Gulf. The Bush administration in turn hinted that Washington might release the financial assets that had been frozen since 1979, if the Iranian government would explicitly renounce terrorism and exert pressure on the Lebanon-based Islamist movement The Party of God (Hizbullah) to scale back its military operations. Iranian President Akbar Hashemi Rafsanjani did disavow the use of terrorist tactics in his Friday sermon on 20 December 1991.

Nevertheless, the Clinton administration stopped making overtures to Tehran, and instead pursued a policy of combating Iranian influence while at the same time inflicting punishment on Iraq – a policy known as Dual Containment (Gause, 2010, 127). Confronted with a more belligerent posture on Washington's part, the Iranian government took steps to acquire a variety of new weapons. Surface-to-surface and ground-to-sea missiles were purchased from the People's Republic of China (PRC); SCUD-C IRBMs arrived from the Democratic People's Republic of Korea, along with technology found in the more advanced No Dong 1 missile. These acquisitions accompanied the resumption of the 1960s-era program to generate electricity using nuclear power. In 1992, Russia agreed to bring the nuclear station at Bushehr back on line. Three years later, Moscow agreed to supply Iran with a gas centrifuge uranium enrichment plant, but ended up cancelling the agreement under pressure from Washington. Russia subsequently provided the Islamic Republic with light water enrichment equipment, which was less capable of producing weapons-grade plutonium.

US Secretary of State Warren Christopher condemned Iran before the UN General Assembly in September 1995, on the grounds that Tehran was sponsoring terrorism throughout the Middle East and attempting to amass a nuclear arsenal. Washington accused Tehran of playing a role in the bombing of a US military installation outside Dhahran in June 1996; Iranian officials denied the charge, but reaffirmed their intention to resist American predominance in the region. US officials a month later blamed Iran for the crash of a TWA airliner off the coast of Long Island, as well as for a bombing at the Olympic Games in Atlanta. These events prompted the US Congress to approve the Iran-Libya Sanctions Act (ILSA), at whose signing President Clinton remarked that "Iran and Libya are two of the most dangerous supporters of terrorism in the world" (C-SPAN, "Iran and Libya Sanctions Signing", 5 August 1996). Relations between Washington and Tehran remained frigid during the late 1990s, even as the Islamic Republic made overtures to Saudi Arabia, Qatar and the UAE.

Iranian President Muhammad Khatami in January 1998 called for "a crack in this wall of distrust" during an interview with the US-based Cable News Network (Gause, 2010, 131–132). He expressed regret for the 1979 seizure of the US embassy in Tehran, and proposed a series of bilateral cultural and academic exchanges. That February, a US wrestling team travelled to Tehran, and in June 1998 the US played the Iranian national team in a football match in Lyon from which the Iranians emerged victorious. Despite this window of opportunity for improved relations, Iranian officials expressed sympathy for Baghdad during the successive confrontations with Washington that took place during the course of 1998. Iraq subsequently agreed to permit 3000 Iranian pilgrims to visit the Shi'i shrines at Najaf, Karbala, al-Kadimain and Samarra. The thaw in Iraqi-Iranian relations set the stage for Moscow to announce that it planned to sell additional nuclear reactors to the Islamic Republic.

Deterioration of US predominance

Shortly after taking office in January 2001, the US administration headed by President George W. Bush implemented additional measures to disarm Iraq. On one hand, it adopted so-called "smart sanctions", which were designed to incur less damage on the Iraqi populace; on the other, it stepped up air strikes (Gause, 2010, 188–189). US and British warplanes in February attacked targets outside the southern no-fly zone for the first time since 1991. A second round of bombings took place a month later, after Iraqi air defense units locked their radars on American aircraft. Further strikes were carried out in April, May and August. In the aftermath of the September 2001 attacks by al-Qaeda on New York City and northern Virginia, Iraqi air defense units stopped challenging US forces for two months. Yet in his January 2002 State of the Union address, President Bush included Iraq as part of the global "axis of evil", and told reporters six months later that "It is the stated policy of this government to have regime change [in Baghdad]. ...And we'll use all the tools at our disposal to do so" (Public Papers of the Presidents 2004, 1190).

Meanwhile, relations between Washington and Riyadh cooled off. When US officials refused to criticize large-scale Israeli military operations in the West Bank during the summer of 2001, Saudi Crown Prince 'Abdullah bin 'Abd al-'Aziz notified President Bush that "from now on, you have your interests and the kingdom has its interests, and you have your road and we have our road" (Gause, 2005, 142). The Saudi government denied that Saudi citizens were involved in the September 2001 attacks, and refused to allow US forces to operate from bases on Saudi territory when the air offensive against Afghanistan got underway that October (Gause, 2004). The frostiness that pervaded US-Saudi relations thawed a bit in April 2002, when 'Abdullah visited the Bush family ranch at Crawford, Texas. The two leaders worked out several areas of collaboration regarding intelligence gathering and processing, and the Saudi authorities started to crack down on the financial networks through which funding for militant Islamist organizations flowed.

President Bush told graduates of the US Military Academy at West Point in June 2002 that deterrence and containment were no longer sufficient to protect American interests from pressing security threats, although he did not mention Iraq by name. His words marked a shift toward preventive warfare, which by September 2002 had coalesced into the Bush Doctrine (Gresh, 2015). The new posture accompanied a marked escalation in the number and severity of air strikes against Iraqi military installations, which culminated in the return of UNSCOM that October. It also entailed a massive build-up of US ground forces in the Gulf (Lawson, 2004). In February 2003, US Secretary of State Colin Powell presented evidence to the UN Security Council that Iraq was continuing to pursue WMD development, and on 17 March President Bush threatened to attack Iraq if Saddam Hussein did not relinquish power within 48 hours. At the deadline Washington carried out a cruise missile strike on the house in which the Iraqi president was reported to be spending the night. Hours later, US and British troops advanced into Iraqi territory from Kuwait. Baghdad was occupied on 9 April, and the northern city of Musil seized by US and Kurdish forces two days after that.

Meanwhile, the National Council of Resistance of Iran in August 2002 released details of three previously undeclared nuclear research facilities in the Islamic Republic. Tehran did not deny the report, and intimated that such activities were legitimate since they were taking place in accordance with the terms of the Non-Proliferation Treaty. In February 2003, President Muhammad Khatami invited the International Atomic Energy Agency (IAEA) to visit the uranium enrichment plant at Natanz and promised to allow regular inspections. A month later, however, the IAEA criticized Iran for not fully disclosing all aspects of its nuclear program.

As US forces poured into the Gulf during the spring of 2003, Washington avoided provoking greater confrontation with Iran. The Bush administration even sent signals to Tehran concerning

External intervention in the Gulf

the possibility of cooperation with regard to Iraq. Such signals set the stage for the delivery to US representatives of a secret note that offered a grand bargain, in which Iran would terminate its nuclear research program and moderate its anti-Israel rhetoric in exchange for an end to US-sponsored economic sanctions. Officials in Washington refused to acknowledge the existence of the offer, and charged that the Islamic Republic was harboring members of al-Qaeda who had escaped from Afghanistan. Commanders of the Islamic Revolutionary Guards' Corps (IRGC) then accelerated the drive to achieve military self-reliance, predicated on strategic deterrence and a wide range of new armaments. The US responded by flying surveillance drones over Iran, and in the summer of 2004 US Special Forces personnel carried out reconnaissance missions inside Iranian territory. These operations made it impossible for the Iranian national assembly to ratify a provisional agreement that had been drawn up in October 2003 with the United Kingdom, France and Germany to suspend uranium enrichment; assembly members instead ordered enrichment to resume, and in February 2005 US Secretary of State Condoleezza Rice denounced the moribund agreement.

Iranian President Mahmud Ahmadinejad took office in June 2005, firmly convinced that negotiations with the West were futile and that the US only understood brute force. His administration celebrated an upturn in enriched uranium production in April 2006, and dismissed UN Security Council Resolution 1696 of July 2006 that demanded an end to further enrichment activities. President Bush observed in October 2007 that the emergence of a nuclear-armed Iran was likely to lead to "World War Three" (Stolberg, 2007).

US policy toward the Arabian Peninsula after 2003 was bound up with developments in Iraq. Saudi Arabia, Qatar and the UAE distanced themselves from Washington as chaos spread across Iraq during 2005–06. When the Bush administration entreated governments throughout the region to provide material and moral support for the new leadership in Baghdad, these countries instead cultivated economic and strategic ties with Turkey and the PRC. China's President Hu Jintao paid an official visit to Riyadh in April 2006. CENTCOM then scrambled to prop up America's deteriorating position in the Gulf, and in October 2006 orchestrated joint naval and air exercises with the armed forces of Bahrain, Qatar and the UAE. By the spring of 2007, CENTCOM had persuaded policy-makers in Washington to boost arms sales to the Arab Gulf states. The flow of US-made weaponry to the region jumped after President Barack Obama took office in January 2009. Saudi Arabia and the UAE contracted to purchase Patriot anti-missile batteries and Terminal High Altitude Area Defense (THAAD) systems. In 2010, the UAE augmented its arsenal with 80 F-16 fighter-bombers equipped with electronics more advanced than those fitted in the F-16s used by the US Air Force.

Iranian leaders greeted Obama's presidency with guarded optimism, but saw no fresh faces in the administration's foreign policy team – which consisted almost entirely of former Clinton advisers. Tehran consequently reiterated a list of long-standing demands: a guarantee that the US not interfere in the domestic politics of Iran, the release of frozen assets, the lifting of economic sanctions, the withdrawal of US troops from the Gulf and an end to the West's lopsided posture toward the Arab–Israeli conflict. Still, the Obama administration expressed a willingness to engage in talks with Tehran, and it was not until July 2009 that the president declared that if the Iranian authorities had not agreed to resume negotiations by September, the US would consider punitive measures. Secretary of Defense Robert Gates in December 2009 announced that Washington was imposing new economic sanctions on the Islamic Republic to compel it to act responsibly. A month later, US commanders deployed Patriot anti-missile batteries to Kuwait, Bahrain, Qatar and the UAE. A pair of US Navy Aegis missile cruisers moved into the Gulf as well, assigned to patrol the Iranian coast on a permanent basis.

By the spring of 2010, Washington had firmly recommitted to coercive policies in its dealings with Tehran. Reports surfaced in mid-March that US commanders had transported more than 190 Blu-117 "bunker buster" bombs to Diego Garcia in the Indian Ocean. Iranian leaders reacted by announcing that they would develop a new generation of gas centrifuges and set up ten more uranium enrichment plants. This announcement provoked the UN Security Council to adopt Resolution 1929, which demanded an immediate end to the construction of heavy water reactors and a stop to further IRBM development.

Washington voiced sympathy for the popular uprisings that erupted across the Middle East and North Africa during the winter of 2010–11. The governments of the Arab Gulf states, by contrast, tended to back the old regimes. Riyadh was particularly aggravated by the Obama administration's insistence that the authorities in Bahrain engage in negotiations with its domestic critics. Saudi officials considered the Bahraini opposition to be agents of Iran, and ordered Saudi troops to intervene to crush the uprising. The Saudi authorities were reportedly incensed that Washington abandoned Egypt's President Hosni Mubarak, and Secretary of State Hillary Clinton and Secretary of Defense Gates were informed that King 'Abdullah was too ill to see them when they arrived in Riyadh in March 2011. At the end of March, a senior member of the Al Sa'ud told a conference in the UAE that the six countries of the Gulf Cooperation Council (GCC) must look out for themselves: "Why not seek to turn the GCC into a grouping like the [European Union]? Why not have a unified Gulf army? Why not have a nuclear deterrent with which to face Iran …or Israeli nuclear capabilities?" (Berger, 2014).

US relations with the GCC states recovered marginally during the winter of 2011–12. At the inaugural meeting of the newly created GCC-US Strategic Cooperation Forum in April 2012, Secretary of State Clinton proposed that a region-wide anti-missile infrastructure be set up. Yet at the same time the Obama administration announced its intention to reorient US grand strategy away from the Middle East and in the direction of East Asia, undertaking a Pivot to Asia that would entail a larger military presence in the South China Sea and closer collaboration with India, Indonesia and Vietnam. Saudi Arabia found itself at odds with US policy toward the Islamic Republic as well: Riyadh was excluded from negotiations over the Iranian nuclear program during 2012–13, and complained that Tehran posed a severe threat to regional stability in Syria and Yemen. Saudi officials were reported to have been furious with Washington after the US refrained from taking military action against Syria in response to an August 2013 gas attack against civilians outside Damascus.

US policy-makers took steps to reconcile with the GCC states in early 2014. Washington appointed a special ambassador to the Gulf, and President Obama visited Saudi Arabia that March. The US Congress in May 2014 adopted a defense appropriations bill that urged US military commanders to restore "a robust forward presence and posture" in the region (Pecquet, 2014), and Secretary of Defense Charles T. Hagel promised during a tour of the GCC countries to maintain a large force even if some sort of agreement were to be concluded with Iran. After a new provisional nuclear deal was drawn up in March 2015, Secretary of State John Kerry visited the GCC states to reassure their leaders that the US would continue to resist Iranian initiatives in the Gulf. Kerry invited GCC foreign ministers to come to Washington to discuss plans for the future. The meeting took place in May 2015, and closed with a statement that "the US policy to use all elements of power to secure our core interests in the Gulf region, and to deter and confront external aggression against our allies and partners, as we did in the [1990–91] Gulf War, is unequivocal" (Hammond, 2015). US officials reiterated support for a regional anti-missile structure, but avoided discussing the sale to Saudi Arabia of F-35 fighter-bombers and Aegis missile defense systems. After the meeting ended, officials in Riyadh hinted that the kingdom might initiate a nuclear research program of its own, perhaps in collaboration with Pakistan.

Iranian officials sat down with representatives of the US, Russia, the UK, France, the PRC and Germany in Istanbul in April 2012 to discuss ways to defuse the ongoing crisis over the Islamic Republic's nuclear research program. As the meeting broke up, US officials remarked that Iran might be permitted to continue to produce enriched uranium, provided that Tehran give firm assurances that it would not build nuclear weapons and would allow full IAEA inspections. US diplomats then embarked on a series of talks with their Iranian counterparts, brokered by Oman. The talks collapsed after the US Navy moved additional warships into the Gulf and Washington imposed sanctions on banks based in Iraq and the PRC on the grounds that they were acting as surrogates of Iranian financial institutions. When Iran's Supreme Leader 'Ali Khamene'i proposed that October to dismantle the enrichment plants in exchange for a reduction in sanctions, US officials ridiculed the offer.

US representatives nevertheless resumed direct talks with Iranian representatives in Oman during March 2013. The negotiations led the two parties to prepare an interim agreement regarding Iran's nuclear program, rather than pursuing a comprehensive settlement at once. In June 2013, Hasan Ruhani was elected president of the Islamic Republic, and expressed a commitment to finding a mutually acceptable solution to the dispute (Parsi, 2017, 216). The Obama administration in early September relaxed restrictions on cultural and athletic exchanges between the US and Iran, including disaster relief and wildlife conservation projects. High-level talks resumed in New York in September and in Geneva in October. They culminated in the November 2013 Joint Plan of Action, whereby Iran agreed to stop uranium enrichment and refrain from replacing old centrifuges with new models; the US, Russia, the UK, the PRC, France and Germany agreed to ease sanctions in a "limited, temporary, targeted and reversible" way (Radio Free Europe/Radio Liberty, 2014). Subsequent negotiations resulted in the April 2015 Joint Comprehensive Plan of Action (JCPOA), which put permanent limits on Iran's enrichment activities, reduced the number of operational centrifuges for the next ten years, required the nuclear reactor at Arak to be redesigned so as to become incapable of producing plutonium, mandated complete monitoring by the IAEA and ordered Tehran to work with the IAEA to formulate a "road map" for comprehensive inspections (Arms Control Association, 2018).

GCC governments voiced no public criticism of the JCPOA, and expressed hope that the pact would reduce the potential for conflict in the Gulf. Saudi officials found little to like about the agreement, however, and worried that it only postponed – rather than eliminated – the prospect of a nuclear-armed Iran. Furthermore, Riyadh expected the JCPOA to release the Islamic Republic from the constraints that had prevented it from being a full player in regional affairs. Saudi misgivings appeared to be confirmed by subsequent developments in the civil war in Yemen, as well as by a notable increase in Iranian intermediate-range ballistic missile testing.

External rivals gain strength in the Gulf

During the years of the Cold War, the chances that the Soviet Union might successfully challenge US predominance in the Gulf remained miniscule (Golan, 1990). Moscow tended to back away from overt confrontation with US forces in the Middle East (Fukuyama, 1981), and physical geography put almost insurmountable obstacles in the path of any attempt by the Red Army to push southward from the Caucasus (Dunn, 1981; Epstein, 1981). In addition, the Soviet Union had formal diplomatic relations with only two states in this part of the world: Iraq and Kuwait.

Moscow restored diplomatic relations with Riyadh in 1991, but connections between the two governments languished until fighting between the Russian authorities and militant Islamists in the North Caucasus came to an end in 2003 (Smith, 2007). At that point King

'Abdullah traveled to Moscow to explore the possibility that Russian state oil companies might be willing to look for natural gas in the remote southeastern corner of the kingdom. A Russian-Saudi Business Council was set up in May 2005, and Russian President Vladimir Putin paid official visits to Saudi Arabia and Qatar in January 2007. Putin reportedly offered to supply the Saudi armed forces with T-90 main battle tanks and construct nuclear reactors in the kingdom. King 'Abdullah reciprocated by visiting Moscow again that November. Russia delivered some 150 tanks and 200 military helicopters to the Saudi armed forces during the course of 2007–09.

Any subsequent improvement in bilateral ties ran afoul of the 2010–11 uprisings, which tended to pit Russia and Saudi Arabia on opposite sides of each particular contest. It was not until June 2015 that the prospects for bilateral cooperation brightened: Saudi Minister of Defense Muhammad bin Salman traveled to St Petersburg to confer with President Putin, who proffered additional armored vehicles and helicopter gunships. More important, the two leaders agreed that Russia would build 16 nuclear power plants on Saudi soil and Saudi Arabia would invest some USD 10 billion in the Russian economy. A follow-up visit by Saudi Foreign Minister 'Adil al-Jubair proved less productive: the two governments disagreed over Russian policy toward Syria and the future of Iran's nuclear program.

Russian relations with Iran, by contrast, cooled dramatically during the first decade of the 21st century (Omelicheva, 2012). Moscow voted in favor of UN Security Council Resolution 1696 and acquiesced in later sanctions against the Islamic Republic implemented by the UN, the US and the European Union (EU). It supported as well Security Council Resolution 1929 of June 2010, which banned arms sales to Iran; President Ahmadinejad called Russian President Dmitry Medvedev "a messenger for Iran's enemies" in response to that vote (Dunaeva, 2013). Developments in the Syrian civil war laid the groundwork for a rapprochement between Moscow and Tehran, however, and in November 2015 Tehran reached a deal with Moscow to buy advanced S-300 anti-aircraft missile batteries. By the spring of 2016, the two countries were discussing a range of collaborative economic initiatives, including the construction of a deep-water canal from the Caspian Sea to the Gulf (Paulraj, 2016). That August Russian military commanders disclosed that they had used a military airfield outside the Iranian city of Hamadan to carry out an attack against the Islamic State in Syria; the revelation sparked intense criticism among members of Iran's national assembly, since the Islamic Republic's constitution explicitly prohibits foreign bases on Iranian territory.

Recent Russian initiatives in the Gulf have been matched by the People's Republic of China, whose industrial sector has grown increasingly reliant on uninterrupted shipments of hydrocarbons from Iran and the Arab Gulf states (Kemp, 2012). To offset the eastward flow of oil and natural gas from Saudi Arabia, Qatar and the UAE, officials in Beijing proposed in 2005 to set up a free trade area with the GCC. The effort collapsed four years later, when it became clear that the PRC intended to block Gulf-based petrochemical companies from gaining access to the Chinese domestic market. When PRC officials in October 2013 unveiled plans for the ambitious commercial and transportation network known as the One Belt, One Road initiative, the two primary routes conspicuously avoided traversing the Gulf and the Arabian Peninsula.

Iran, by contrast, stands at the heart of the PRC's strategic ambitions in this part of the world (Abidi, 1982). Chinese state oil companies took advantage of the imposition of UN, US and EU sanctions against the Islamic Republic to make extensive investments in the country's hydrocarbons sector (Hong, 2014). Between 2003 and 2011, the PRC's annual foreign direct investment in Iran soared from USD 7.8 million to USD 616 million. The China National Petroleum Company in February 2010 contracted to develop Phase 11 of the massive South Pars offshore natural gas field to the tune of USD 4.7 billion. Such investments compelled Beijing to balk at supporting UN Security Council Resolution 1929. PRC representatives voted for the measure only after they had orchestrated a six-month delay in the proceedings, during which time Tehran was able to implement significant countermeasures (Harold, 2015). Iranian officials rewarded Beijing by opening the doors to a wide range of infrastructure projects associated with the One Belt, One Road initiative.

Growing commercial and financial ties between the PRC and Iran accompanied a surge in Chinese military operations in and around the Gulf. Components of the People's Liberation Army Navy (PLAN) started to engage in anti-piracy patrols in the Gulf of Aden in December 2008; the patrols included sporadic stopovers at Omani and Saudi ports (Weitz, 2009; Lanteigne, 2013). Iranian warships began to take part in the patrols three years later. In May 2013, a flotilla of Iranian warships made the journey to the PRC's southernmost naval base on Hainan Island. Beijing reciprocated in September 2014 by sending a guided missile destroyer and a guided missile frigate, including the flagship of the PLAN's task force in the Gulf of Aden, to call at Bandar Abbas; the vessels then carried out joint exercises with Iranian warships. These maneuvers were followed by a visit to Tehran by the commander of the PLAN, which resulted in a memorandum of understanding between the two governments concerning combined counter-terrorism operations and training missions. Just before the commander's visit, Beijing welcomed the commander of the Saudi navy to the headquarters of the PLAN's South Sea Fleet at Zhanjiang.

PRC President Xi Jinping arrived in Tehran in January 2016 and signed a bilateral security cooperation treaty that was scheduled to last until 2041. In the wake of the visit, Chinese officials began to talk about creating a Persian Gulf Chain of Pearls that would complement the One Belt, One Road initiative. February 2017 saw a PLAN task force consisting of a guided missile destroyer, a guided missile frigate and a supply ship call at ports in the UAE, Qatar, Saudi Arabia and Kuwait.

Conclusion

American predominance in the Gulf has deteriorated in recent years, but the United States remains the indispensable external actor without which any discussion of Gulf security would be moot. The questions remain whether Russia will play as active a role in the Gulf as it has assumed in other parts of the Middle East and whether the PRC's economic interests will translate into a direct security presence. EU member-states in the meantime have not managed to adopt a unified stance toward the region, as past attempts to engage the GCC collectively have failed and the rift between Saudi Arabia and Qatar makes it even less likely such initiatives will succeed in the foreseeable future. Nevertheless, the EU might well stake out a unified posture vis-à-vis Iran, if it manages to withstand the secondary sanctions that could be imposed by Washington after its decertification of the JCPOA. In short, the deterioration of US strategic predominance is likely to pave the way for other external powers to become influential security actors in the Gulf, although American actions will remain pivotal.

References

Abidi, A.H.H. (1982) *China, Iran and the Persian Gulf.* Atlantic Highlands, NJ: Humanities Press.
Arms Control Association (2018) The Joint Comprehensive Plan of Action (JCPOA) at a Glance. www.armscontrol.org/factsheets/JCPOA-at-a-glance, May 2018.
Berger, Linda (2014) The Gulf Cooperation Council between Unity and Discord towards the Arab Uprisings. *Sicherheit und Frieden* 32: 260–264.
Buheiry, Marwan R. (1980) *US Threats of Intervention against Arab Oil: 1973–1979.* IPS Papers No. 4. Beirut: Institute for Palestine Studies.

Dunaeva, Elena (2013) Russo-Iranian Political Relations in the First Decade of the Twenty-First Century. *Iranian Studies* 46: 443–469.

Dunn, Keith A. (1981) Constraints on the USSR in Southwest Asia: A Military Analysis. *Orbis* 25: 607–629.

Epstein, Joshua M. (1981) Soviet Vulnerabilities in Iran and the RDF Deterrent. *International Security* 6: 126–158.

Fawcett, Louise (1992) *Iran and the Cold War*. Cambridge: Cambridge University Press.

Freedman, Lawrence and Efraim Karsh (1993) *The Gulf Conflict 1990–1991*. Princeton: Princeton University Press.

Fukuyama, Francis (1981) Nuclear Shadowboxing: Soviet Intervention Threats in the Middle East. *Orbis* 25: 579–605.

Gause, F. Gregory III (2004) *Relations between the Gulf Cooperation Council States and the United States*. Dubai: Gulf Research Center.

Gause, F. Gregory III (2005) Saudi Perceptions of the United States since 9/11. In *With Us or Against Us: Studies in Global Anti-Americanism*, eds. Denis Lacorne and Tony Judt. New York: Palgrave Macmillan.

Gause, F. Gregory III (2010) *The International Relations of the Persian Gulf*. Cambridge: Cambridge University Press.

Golan, Galia (1990) *Soviet Policies in the Middle East from World War II to Gorbachev*. Cambridge: Cambridge University Press.

Gresh, Gregory F. (2015) *Gulf Security and the US Military*. Stanford, CA: Stanford University Press.

Halliday, Fred (1981) *Soviet Policy in the Arc of Crisis*. Washington, DC: Institute for Policy Studies.

Hammond, Jeremy R. (2015) How the US Provides "Security" to the Persian Gulf Region. https://foreignpolicy.com, 18 May.

Harold, Scott W. (2015) Opportunistic Cooperation under Constraints: Non-Proliferation, Energy Trade and the Evolution of Chinese Policy towards Iran. *The Chinese Journal of International Politics* 8: 59–88.

Hong, Zhao (2014) China's Dilemma on Iran: Between Energy Security and a Responsible Rising Power. *Journal of Contemporary China* 23: 408–424.

Ingram, Edward (1979) *The Beginning of the Great Game in Asia 1828–1834*. Oxford: Clarendon Press.

Kelly, J.B. (1968) *Britain and the Persian Gulf 1795–1880*. Oxford: Clarendon Press.

Kemp, Geoffrey (2012) *The East Moves West*. Washington, DC: Brookings Institution Press.

Khalilzad, Zalmay (1980) The Return of the Great Game: Superpower Rivalry and Domestic Turmoil in Afghanistan, Iran, Pakistan and Turkey. Discussion Paper No. 88. The California Seminar on International Security and Foreign Policy. Los Angeles.

Lanteigne, Marc (2013) Fire Over Water: China's Strategic Engagement of Somalia and the Gulf of Aden Crisis. *Pacific Review* 26: 289–312.

Lawson, Fred H. (1984) The Reagan Administration in the Middle East. *MERIP Reports* 14: 27–34.

Lawson, Fred H. (1989) The Iranian Crisis of 1945–1946 and the Spiral Model of International Conflict. *International Journal of Middle East Studies* 21: 307–326.

Lawson, Fred H. (2004) Political Economy, Geopolitics and the Expanding US Military Presence in the Persian Gulf and Central Asia. *Critique: Critical Middle East Studies* 13: 7–31.

McNaugher, Thomas L. (1985) *Arms and Oil: US Military Strategy in the Persian Gulf*. Washington, DC: Brookings Institution.

Omelicheva, Mariya Y. (2012) Russia's Foreign Policy toward Iran: A Critical Geopolitics Perspective. *Journal of Balkan and Near Eastern Studies* 14: 331–344.

Onley, James (2007) *The Arabian Frontier of the British Raj*. Oxford: Oxford University Press.

O'Reilly, Marc J. (2008) *Unexceptional: America's Empire in the Persian Gulf, 1941–2007*. Lanham, MD: Lexington Books.

Page, Stephen (1984) Moscow and the Arabian Peninsula. *American-Arab Affairs* 8: 83–93.

Palmer, Michael A. (1992) *Guardians of the Gulf*. New York: The Free Press.

Parsi, Trita (2017) *Losing an Enemy: Obama, Iran and the Triumph of Diplomacy*. New Haven, CT: Yale University Press.

Paulraj, Nansi (2016) The JCPOA and Changing Dimensions of the Russia-Iran Relations. *Contemporary Review of the Middle East* 3: 95–110.

Pecquet, Julian (2014) Defense Bill Calls for Military Pacts with Gulf States. www.al-monitor.com/pulse/originals/2014/05/military-pact-gulf-states-house-bill-us.html, 6 May.

Peterson, J.E. (1986) *Defending Arabia*. New York: St Martin's Press.

Pollack, Kenneth M. (2004) *The Persian Puzzle*. New York: Random House.

Public Papers of the Presidents (2004) *Public Papers of the Presidents of the United States: George W. Bush, Book 1: January 1 to June 30, 2002.* Washington, DC: United States Government Printing Office.

Radio Free Europe/Radio Liberty (2014) Key Points of Iran Nuclear Deal, 20 January.

Record, Jeffrey (1981) *The Rapid Deployment Force and US Military Intervention in the Persian Gulf.* Cambridge, MA: Institute for Foreign Policy Analysis.

Smith, Mark A. (2007) *Russia and the Persian Gulf: The Deepening of Moscow's Middle East Policy.* Occasional Paper No. 07/25. London: Conflict Studies Research Centre.

Stein, Janice Gross (1988–89) The Wrong Strategy in the Right Place: The United States in the Gulf. *International Security* 13: 142–167.

Stolberg, Sheryl Gay (2007) Nuclear-Armed Iran Risks World War, Bush Says. *New York Times*, 18 October.

Waltz, Kenneth N. (1981) A Strategy for the Rapid Deployment Force. *International Security* 5: 49–73.

Weitz, Richard (2009) Operation Somalia: China's First Expeditionary Force? *China Security* 5: 27–42.

Wright, Steven (2007) *The United States and Persian Gulf Security.* Reading, MA: Ithaca Press.

6

THE SECURITY IMPLICATIONS OF THE ISRAELI–PALESTINIAN CONFLICT

Michael Schulz[1]

The Israeli–Palestinian conflict

The Israeli–Palestinian conflict (Hebrew: יניטסלפ-ילארשיה ךוסכסה, transliterated *Ha'Sikhsukh Ha'YIsraeli-Falestini*; Arabic: يليئارسإلا-ينيطسلفلا-عازنلا, transliterated *al-Niza'a al-Filastini-al-Israili*), the longest-running armed conflict in the world, has many security ramifications, from the direct personal physical security of Israelis and Palestinians to the global scale of peace and security. This chapter deals with the security implications linked to the Israeli–Palestinian conflict, and what these imply for the core parties to the conflict, the Middle East region, as well as for the rest of the world. The Israeli–Palestinian conflict has security ramifications for others than the conflict parties themselves. Others have written about different security aspects of conflicts in the wider Middle Eastern region (Fawcett, 2016; Bilgin, 2005; Maoz, 1997), as well as Middle Eastern conflicts' internal security dynamics (Harders and Legrenzi, 2008; Lindholm Schulz and Schulz, 2005), and its global implications (Fawcett, 2016; Tibi, 1991). Despite the large number of published articles and books, we cannot find a contribution that systematically enquires into the various security implications that follow from the Israeli–Palestinian conflict. This chapter intends to fill this gap of security studies related to the case of the Israeli–Palestinian conflict.

With the changing political map, following the two world wars, the "new" states have striven to build and consolidate their nation-state status. Security politics have been their most important concern, and resources have been allocated accordingly. States such as Israel, Lebanon, Syria, Jordan and Egypt have invested huge resources in safeguarding their territorial borders against each other. Israel, furthermore, allocates huge resources to protect its territory from Arab and Palestinian attempts to recapture historical Palestine. A bitter and implacable conflict, which has spread to all the states in the region, and beyond the region itself, has resulted in intense armament build-up. Thus, the conflict clearly has wide ramifications for other conflicts and crises in the Middle East region and connects to actors on the global arena. An analysis of the Israeli–Palestinian case from the perspective of regional security theories will hopefully contribute to an understanding of the conflict pattern, its forces of change, and how it has implications also for regional and global security.

Israeli–Palestinian conflict

Brief historical overview of changing conflict dynamics

To analyze the security impacts from the Israeli–Palestinian conflict, one can identify key events and the transformations of the conflict dynamics that followed, and see the wider security ramification for the Middle East region and global security. Within each conflict period, with its specific dynamics, the conflict impacted on security in various different contexts and spaces. Four time periods can be identified:

- Before 1948, the character of the conflict was more of a civil war-like situation between primarily Jewish nationalists (Zionists) and Palestinian Arab nationalists in Palestine as part of the Ottoman Empire, and after World War I within the British Palestine mandate (1920–1948)
- Between 1948 and 1973, the security impacts and conflict dynamics were mainly centered on the interstate relations, and four rounds of interstate wars between Israel and the Arab states (Egypt, Jordan, Lebanon and Syria) that took place in 1948–49, 1956, 1967 and 1973
- Between 1964 and 1993, a Palestinization of the conflict followed (i.e. Palestinians were seen as the other core actor next to Israel), and the Palestine Liberation Organization (PLO) became a key player in the conflict, but also the Arab states became split due to Egypt's peace accord with Israel in 1977. It was a period in which military confrontation between the PLO and Israel increased, partly also on Lebanese soil (1978 and 1982) and eventually led to a Palestinian popular (mainly) unarmed uprising (1987) against the Israeli occupation
- From 1993 to 2000, we had the Oslo process, which included several completed agreements (Oslo I 1993, Paris protocols 1994, Oslo II 1995, Hebron 1997, Wye River 1998, Taba 1999), and mutual recognition by Israel and the PLO, but not a final political settlement of the conflict's overarching key issues: Palestinian future status of self-rule, Israeli settlements, Jerusalem's future status, and the future of Palestinian refugees. In addition, this period includes a completed peace agreement between Israel and Jordan (1994 and 1995).
- From 2000 until the present time, we have also witnessed several unfinalized negotiations that followed the outbreak of the violent Al-Aqsa uprising period (2000–2005) and beyond. Further, several rounds of direct violent confrontations between Israelis and Palestinians took place, but also between the two major Palestinian political movements, Fatah and Hamas, which led to a political separation of the West Bank (Fatah controlled) and the Gaza Strip (Hamas controlled) until 2017.

The conflict between Israel and its neighbors, the Arab states and the Palestinians, has lasted for over a century and has gone through several conflict dynamical changes that affected the position around the key issues. In short, the conflict began as a result of colliding and conflict-escalating processes between immigrating Jewish nationalist (Zionists) and the Arab–Palestinian inhabitants of Palestine. Nationalist aspirations on both sides were to take control over the same territory, the land of Palestine, first primarily from the Ottomans, later from the British and eventually from each other. Both aimed at statehood, but with different contents of the state- and nation-building projects. Both nationalist movements' contradictory positions led to an armed civil war, and towards the end of the British mandate period (1920–1948), the British asked the newly established United Nations (UN) in 1946 for help to solve the Palestine situation.

The UN General Assembly accepted a partition plan (UN GA res 181) of Palestine in November 1947, which implied a partition of Palestine into one Arab and one Jewish state, with a joint economic union, and Jerusalem as an open international city. Because the parties did not agree over the resolution, and the Zionists declared Israel as a new state, with its independence on 14 May 1948, the Arab neighbors (Egypt, Jordan, Syria and Lebanon) declared war and attacked Israel. This first Arab–Israeli interstate war, in a series of four wars (1948, 1956, 1967 and 1973), ended with Israeli military victories, although political gains did not always follow. The wars often were seen, and also often analyzed, within the Cold War dynamics, and the Palestinians had a background role in the conflict (Tibi, 1991). This all changed with the establishment of the PLO, and the humiliating loss of the Arab states in the 1967 War, in which Israel expanded its territorial control further, and occupied parts of Syria (Golan Heights), parts of Jordan (the West Bank) and parts of Egypt (Gaza and the Sinai Peninsula). Approximately 1,500,000 Palestinians living in the West Bank and in the Gaza Strip now came under direct everyday contact with the Israeli occupation forces, simultaneously a Palestinization of the conflict began.

The Palestinization of the conflict led to increased direct-armed confrontations between Israel and the PLO, in which Israel considered the PLO as a terrorist organization, and the PLO saw Israel as a brutal occupant and refused to recognize Israel, or its right to exist. This direct military confrontation led to Israel's incursions into Lebanon in 1978 and was followed by occupation between 1982 and 1985, an invasion that aimed at defeating the PLO, which partly succeeded. However, the invasion backlashed also for Israel. Despite the PLO having to leave Lebanon for new headquarters in Tunis, the complex internal Lebanese situation turned against the Israeli occupation. Not least, when the newly established Shia militia Hezbollah began to attack Israeli positions and eventually forced Israel to withdraw from Lebanon (completed fully in 2000).

Meanwhile, the Palestinians in the West Bank and the Gaza Strip began in 1987 the first public unarmed resistance campaign against the Israeli occupation. Partly, this contributed to encouraging the top leaders to enter negotiations, and the so-called back-channel talks in Oslo resulted in the Oslo Accords (1993). In this agreement, Israel and the PLO mutually recognized each other and decided that a final peace agreement should be signed after five years of gradual transfer of political authority from Israeli occupation to Palestinian self-rule in the areas of civilian affairs. The Oslo process saw some steps forward in terms of the establishment of a Palestinian Authority, and the expansion of this Palestinian self-rule in the West Bank and the Gaza Strip (1994, 1995, 1997, 1998, 1999). However, the process faltered, and shortly after the failed negotiations at the summit at Camp David in 2000, the al-Aqsa *intifada* (2000–2003), the second Palestinian (mainly) armed uprising began against Israeli occupation. The public on both sides, who initially showed support for the Oslo agreements, increasingly distanced themselves from the Oslo Accords. Since 2000, although low intensive confrontations take place on a daily basis in the occupied territories, several more serious armed confrontations between Israeli and Palestinian forces have also taken place (2000–2003, 2006, 2007, 2008/09, 2012, 2014). In addition, some attempts at negotiations followed, in which the USA tried to mediate (most importantly in 2008 and 2014), but the parties have until the present time, not reached a final political agreement that all parties can live with.

The Israeli–Palestinian security complex

To analyze the security implications of the Israeli–Palestinian conflict, I will apply a theoretical framework that is inspired by Buzan's, as well as Buzan and Waever's broader definition of security, implying that security is not merely linked to the state and society, but also links to various aspects of human security (Buzan, 1983, 1991; Buzan and Waever, 1998). In this chapter, Buzan's framework will be applied as an analytical tool for the Israeli–Palestinian conflict. However, theoretically, the conflict must also interrelate security with the concept of peace. Precisely because most key actors in the conflict have concern for national security, it requires a deeper analysis of what the security needs imply in terms of peace. When applying Galtung's (Galtung, 1996) understanding of peace, as either negative (absence of direct violence) or positive (absence of direct and structural violence), we could argue that security also can be linked to the concept of peace. Hence, a situation of absence of direct violence is a security situation that is rather unstable, while the absence of both direct and structural violence is a security situation that could be labeled as a security community. According to Barry Buzan's definition of the regional security complex, '... as a group of states whose primary security concerns link together sufficiently closely that their national securities cannot realistically be considered apart from one another' (Buzan, 1983: 106). In this chapter, it does not solely refer to states, but also individuals, organizations and societies. It is also argued that key security *issues* among the actors of the Israeli–Palestinian security complex (IPSC) *link their security concerns* together in a web of amity/enmity. The Israeli and Palestinian national movements' clash over the same territory is the key issue.

The Middle East could also be seen as a regional security complex full of other *sets* of security complexes, or sub-complexes, which all have their own security issues that connect the states together in inextricably entangled relations. The Palestinian issue is a security concern for many states and other actors in the region and forms thereby, in an analytical way, the Israeli–Palestinian–Israeli security complex (Schulz, 1989). Further, each sub-complex can be more or less secure, and if it has changed towards a security community, it has reached a situation of positive peace.

> Security communities might be seen in one sense as resolved or matured security complexes in which basic conflicts and fears have been worked out, resulting in an oasis of relatively mature anarchy within the more fractious field of the international anarchy as a whole.
>
> *(Buzan, 1983, p. 115)*

This chapter also applies the *security complex theory* of Buzan (Buzan, 1983, 1991; Buzan, Waever and De Wilde, 1998; Buzan and Waever, 2003), which I have defined elsewhere as the IPSC (Schulz, 1989). The IPSC involves those actors whereby the nation-state project Israel and the rival project to realize the nation-state of Palestine is the main common security issue. The actors constituting parts of the IPSC are the state of Israel, the Palestinians, Palestinian organizations, the Palestinian Authority (PA)/PLO and the Arab states that have been, or still partly are, under Israeli occupation, namely Egypt, Jordan, Lebanon and Syria. The changing conflict patterns of the IPSC so far have been a story of going from one insecure security situation to another and has not reached what Buzan labeled a "mature security complex" (Buzan, 1983:115). However, some smaller steps have been taken towards a future potential change. A mature security complex situation would imply that basic conflicts and fears have been resolved between antagonistic parties, and some sense of trustworthy and close relations has developed between the actors of the security complex.

The IPSC has security ramifications outside the historical territory of Palestine. For instance, when the PLO lost its political power and military strongholds inside Jordan, after the military defeat against King Hussein in September 1970 (the "Black September"), it started to reorganize and establish itself inside Lebanon. This changed the power structure inside Lebanon and challenged the ruling Christian Maronite and Sunni elites. Therefore, the transnational Israeli–Palestinian conflict has automatically shaped the regional security complex in such a way that intra- and interstate conflicts between ethno-religious groups and their "states" have become inevitable. This, in turn, creates several new sub-complexes with their own security structures, which affect the IPSC as a whole.

Each of the actors of the IPSC are linked to other security complexes, with other security issues, inside the Middle East region. States such as Iraq, Saudi Arabia and Libya can also be viewed as parties involved in the conflict, though they are often connected to other complexes with security issues with a higher priority than the Israeli–Palestinian conflict. These states will be further investigated and the Palestinian–Israeli complex will be related to other security complexes inside as well as outside the Middle East region. During the Cold War, the superpowers must also be related to this regional security complex as external forces that intensify the conflict. Even if the superpowers have been involved mainly as arms providers, but also as political actors, in the wars between Israel and its Arab neighbors, they have avoided sending troops of their own to the war zone. It also became evident that the superpowers, despite their work to thwart it, could not prevent the outbreak of wars between Israel and the Arab states. On the contrary, it became evident that an escalation between them was at risk when war had broken out, and common interest developed to end the wars (Ben-Zvi, 1986; Jönsson, 1984).

Hence, the superpowers (USA and USSR) during the Cold War, and even more so after the Cold War (USA and Russia, jointly with the UN and the EU in the so-called quartet that tried to implement the roadmap of 2002), gradually developed a mutual interest in trying to solve the Palestinian–Israeli conflict. This consensus is an overall strategy from both sides since the end of the Cold War, also resulting in the adoption of the UN SC resolution 1397. This resolution implies that the conflict shall end with a Palestinian State placed next to Israel and that Israelis and Palestinians should agree on the details (i.e. the core issues). The great powers' actions and influence have also contributed to the creation of several sub-conflicts, which have their ramifications for the primary security issue. Since the end of the Cold War, it has mainly been USA that has been involved in the IPSC, but also actors such as the EU, UN and Russia, as well as smaller states such as Norway and Sweden.

Personal and State security implications of the IPSC

The IPSC, with its root cause, or primary conflict issue, linked to the historical struggle over Palestine, which constitutes the main security issue for those states involved in the IPSC. The foundation of Israel and its very existence became a security issue for the Arab world, in particular, the Palestinians, but also for the states that border Israel, as well as Israel itself. However, from a closer perspective, the conflict's main actors, the Israeli citizens since 1948, and the Palestinians living inside Israel and holders of Israeli citizenship, or stateless Palestinians since the 1967 occupation of the West Bank and the Gaza Strip, or Palestinian refugees in the Diaspora in mainly neighboring countries of Lebanon, Jordan and Syria, have all perceived the conflict from an individual and personal security perspective.

The victims of the armed conflict confrontations in several rounds of full-scale wars, and low-intensity armed confrontations and terrorist acts, have since the second uprising – the Al-Aqsa *intifada*, begun in September 2000 – amounted to 1242 Israeli and 9510 Palestinian battle-related deaths (B'Tselem, 2017). The number of Israeli and Palestinian battle-related deaths from 1948 to 1996 is estimated as 13,000, of which the vast majority are Palestinians. Many more

Israelis and Palestinians have been wounded. Add at least 55,000 battle-related deaths from the four major Arab–Israeli interstate wars of 1948–49, 1956, 1967, 1973, and Israel's Lebanon war in 1982 (against the PLO) and 2006 (against Hezbollah).[2] This gives an average of more than 1000 battle-related deaths annually since the establishment of the state of Israel, which usually is the threshold of a major armed conflict (i.e. full-scale war). The long-standing conflict thereby creates negative psychological impacts on Israelis and Palestinians, in which they sense that they are living in a highly insecure and fearful environment.

Israelis and Palestinians consider the conflict to be an existential zero-sum conflict, and that the victory of one side will be at the expense of the other side. However, since Israel has achieved statehood, Israelis, in general, do fear mostly Palestinian terror attacks against civilians, while Palestinians relate their sufferings to the non-statehood situation in which Israel continues to occupy large parts of the West Bank. Hence, Palestinians relate their security concerns to justice issues, such as the absence of real Palestinian statehood, abolishment of the illegal Israeli settlements in the West Bank, the sovereignty question over Jerusalem and the Palestinian refugee issue (Meital, 2006; Shikaki, 2006; Klein, 2003).

Both Israelis and Palestinians also link their personal security to the state. Israelis, generally, do consider the mere existence of Israel as a security guarantee for Israeli Jews. Some would even say that the state of Israel is a global security guarantee for all Jews. The so-called law of return, which gives the right for every Jew in the world to migrate to Israel, and instantly become an Israeli citizen is seen as such a security guarantee (Schulz, 1996).

The Israelis do not see peace with the Palestinians as the most prioritized issue for the future of Israel. In the so-called peace index questionnaire, from which the Israeli Peace Index (Peace Index, 2017) produces monthly opinion polls with the Israeli public, we see that in October 2017 only 11.6% of Israelis place "peace with the Palestinians" as the most prioritized issue for Israel's future (only after "reducing tensions between different sectors of Israeli society" (26.5%), "improving the education system" (22.6%), "strengthening of the IDF" (16.1%) and "the development of the Israeli economy" (14.8%)).

However, Palestinians perceive the future establishment of a Palestinian state as the solution that can bring increased Palestinian personal security. Although variations exist among the Palestinians of which parts of historical Palestine should constitute the Palestinian state (see Table 6.1), most Palestinians perceive the establishment in itself as an end-goal, when Palestinian suffering will see an end.

The Palestinians do not consider the PA as a state, despite the fact that 136 UN member states already have recognized Palestine. In general, Palestinians do not consider the PA as being sovereign and independent due to Israel's *de facto* control of the West Bank and the PA's weak position vis-à-vis Israel. In a poll conducted by the Palestinian Centre for Policy and Survey Research in October (PCPSR, 2017), as many as 40% of the Palestinian public believe that the first and most vital goal for them is to end the Israeli occupation of the areas occupied by Israel in June 1967, and build a Palestinian state in the West Bank and the Gaza Strip with Jerusalem as its capital (with 33% who believe that the "right of return of refugees to their 1948 towns and villages", 15% "to build a pious or moral individual and a religious society, one that applies all Islamic teaching" and 12% to "establish a democratic political system that respects freedoms and rights of Palestinians").

The link between personal security and state security can be seen as the remains of a Westphalia logic (Hettne et al., 2000), stemming from the idea that the state is the prime provider of security for its nation or citizens. In contrast to many other parts of the world, Middle East states have much higher expectations that the state will provide personal security, despite the fact that most states in the region have a long history of authoritarianism, with

Michael Schulz

Table 6.1 The preferred solution to the Israeli–Palestinian conflict according to the Palestinians in the West Bank and Gaza Strip[3]

What, according to you, is the preferred final solution to the Palestinian–Israeli conflict?	1997	2001	2006	2009	2016
Islamic state in the whole of Palestine	34.9	43.6	52.5	35.9	22.4
Arab state in the whole of Palestine	13.9	12.2	12.9	27.8	16.0
Secular and democratic state in the whole of Palestine	6.4	1.8	3.6	3.5	2.5
Bi-national state in the whole of Palestine	2.1	3.8	3.0	5.8	8.8
Palestinian independent state according to UN 1947 partition plan	7.9	6.2	11.6	9.1	11.3
Independent state in the West Bank and Gaza	28.4	22.9	14.6	15.6	26.2
Palestinian entity in the West Bank and Gaza in confederation with Jordan	1.5	0.5	1.0	1.1	1.8
Other	4.9	8.9	0.8	1.3	5.2
Do not know					3.3
No answer					2.0
Total	100.0	100.0	100.0	100.0	100.0
	(1278)	(1487)	(1481)	(1504)	(1200)

little regional cooperation or integration (Schulz et al., 2001). This is also why Israelis and Palestinians do identify strongly with the state building projects and expect that the state will also guarantee personal security. Hence, Israelis believe in a strong (i.e. military capacity) state, while Palestinians believe that once they establish their independent state and end the Israeli occupation, personal security will follow. The Oslo process that began with secret back-channel talks in Norway and Sweden in 1993 (Eriksson, 2015), and was formalized with the signing of the Oslo Accords on 13 September 1993 aimed at mutual recognition, and initiating a transitional process towards a final political settlement of the conflict. However, with the violent spoiling activities, mainly from the side of religious Israeli nationalist settlers and Palestinian Hamas members, the support for the Oslo process eroded (Schulz, 2011; Shikaki, 2006, 1996a, 1996b).

The security implications for sub-complexes of the IPSC

The IPSC has had security ramifications for the wider Middle East region in several ways. First, there are regional security spill-overs to the Arab states of the IPSC, in particular to neighbors bordering Israel, namely Egypt, Jordan, Lebanon and Syria, who all have been at war with Israel, and have had parts of their territories occupied, or still have parts occupied. Second, both Israel and the PLO, and later PA and Hamas, have been involved in other regional conflicts of the Middle East. Third, many of the regional conflicts also had spill-over effects on the IPSC, and the most recent example is the so-called Arab Spring that had repercussions also for the IPSC dynamics. Within the IPSC, we can identify several sub-complexes, which are all related to the main security issue.

The Palestinian diaspora

The Palestinians' refugee status and the position of the PLO in the various states have contributed to establish these sub-complexes. The PLO must be seen as a rather specific actor because the organization does not represent a government or state. The Palestinian diaspora is connected to many states both within and outside the Middle East region because Palestinians are "guests" and refugees in most of the Middle Eastern states. Some are living in refugee camps under the supervision of the UN, such as in Lebanon, Jordan and the occupied West Bank and Gaza Strip, while others are guest-workers in the Gulf states, and still others are political advisors in the Gulf states, as in Kuwait (MRG, 1987). In Jordan, most Palestinians have Jordanian citizenship, although a Palestinian who fled in 1948 and originates from the Gaza Strip still is registered a refugee. An estimate of the Palestinian population varies from one source to another, mainly due to the unreliable statistics from most Gulf states, as well as other Middle Eastern states that host Palestinian refugees. Conservative estimations speak about approximately 5 million Palestinians living in the diaspora, both inside and outside the Middle East (including both refugees and non-refugees that are partly or fully integrated into the host society), but some estimations reach 10 million or above (see UNRWA 2015). The Palestinians living in the Arab states have contributed often to alter the internal power balance, and influenced the development of events. In ethno-religious conflicts, such as the one currently in Syria, and in the past in Lebanon (1975–1990), the Palestinians and the PLO have a direct impact on the security situation. While the PLO's official policy has always been to stay out of each Arab state's internal affairs, the organization itself has caused tremendous policy changes by the various Arab governments.

Jordan–Israel–the Palestinians

The Hashemite Kingdom of Jordan, with its ruling Hashemitic Bedouin minority, rules the country's majority, the Palestinians. The king gets his primary political support from the Hashemite Bedouins. The Palestinian population constitutes between 50 and 60% of the total population; in the capital Amman, the Palestinian population is estimated to constitute 75% of the inhabitants. Around 20% of the Palestinian population belongs to the middle and upper classes in Jordan. These Palestinians feel like Jordanians and identify themselves with the monarchy (Persson, 1989: 40 ff., 2012).

The Kingdom of Jordan was directly involved in large-scale wars with Israel in 1948 and in 1967. In 1949–50 Transjordan annexed the West Bank, which Jordan subsequently lost in the 1967 War when Israel occupied the area, although the area was under Jordanian jurisdiction until 1988. Jordan's relationship with Israel since the 1967 War had been a state of "no peace and no war". However, as an outcome of the Oslo agreement of 1993 between Israel and the PLO, Jordan decided that the time was ripe to sign a peace agreement with Israel in 1995. The Royal House of Jordan has constantly lived with the risk of being seen as "betrayers" of the Palestinian cause, due to the historical events in 1970 when the PLO was a military threat to Jordan, leading to the bloody civilian conflict in the "Black September" war of that year. Jordan is still conscious of the Palestinian factor, and tries to mitigate without risking an uprising in the country. The king has so far managed to maintain a political balance between Israeli and Palestinian demands. Currently, political challenges come from other groups in the country, not least the Islamists, but also from a disappointed broader public that reacts against decreased socio-economic conditions. Public mass demonstrations against the policies of the government followed on several occasions, and also with the so-called Arab Spring period that spread all over the Arab world in 2011. In many ways, the Jordanians have tried to find a balance between the

Israeli and Palestinian political positions, but also those of the other Arab states, not least Syria, which, before the Arab Spring, often pressured Jordan.

Israel–Syria–the Palestinians

Before the Madrid negotiations in 1991, Syria was the leading state of the so-called "resister states", which refused to negotiate with Israel and which connected their own territorial security issues to the Palestinian issue. Before the civil war broke out in 2011, Syria had approximately 21 million inhabitants,[4] including 540,000 Palestinian refugees (UNWRA, 2017). Since 1993, the authoritarian system, led by the Baath party, and one President, which from 1970 to 2000 was President Hafez al-Assad, and currently his son, President Bashar al-Assad. The ruling minority in Syria mainly comes from the Shia Alawi minority, which constitutes approximately 12% of the population. Syria has always linked its security concerns to the Palestinian security issue and has openly supported the Palestinians ever since the first war with Israel in 1948–49. Militarily, Syria was never strong enough to fight a war alone against Israel, and in the three large-scale wars against Israel, the country cooperated with Egypt (Israel's War of Independence in 1948, The Six-Day War in 1967 and the October War in 1973) and Jordan (1948 and 1967).

After the Six-Day War in 1967, Syria lost the Golan Heights, which for both Israel and Syria is a high-security concern. However, Syria has linked a solution of the Palestinian issue, including the Palestinian refugee problem, to the return of the Golan Heights. Further, Israel's dependence upon the Sea of Galilee and the headwaters of the Jordan River has been a chronic cause of tension and conflict between it and Syria. However, with the Oslo Accords of 1993 and 1995, an Israeli–Syrian back-channel was established, and went on until Israeli Prime Minister Rabin was assassinated in November 1995.

Up to the present time, and even more so due to the enduring globalized civil war in Syria that broke out in 2011, the Israel–Syrian enmity has been preserved. In addition, historically, Syria sheltered several of the worst enemies of Israel, in particular, several of the leaders and their organizations' headquarters, such as hardliner Palestinian organizations Popular Front for Liberation of Palestine (PFLP), PFLP-General Command, and until 2011, Palestinian Hamas. This state of hostility between Israel and Syria has not changed despite several official talks (that began in Madrid 1991), as well as secret negotiations that began during the 1990s (Rabinovich, 2004, 2012; Ma'oz, 1999), in attempts to reach a political settlement. Syria became ready to talk with Israel due to the opening between Israel and the PLO, and the Oslo process that followed in 1993. In 2000, both Syrian President Hafez al-Assad and Israeli Prime Minister Ehud Barak met with US President Clinton in Geneva; however, due to newly raised last-minute conditions, the expected signing ceremony of a final peace deal faltered (Quandt, 2005). Continuous mutual fears, and politically inconciliatory positions, make the Syrian–Israeli enmity relationship within the IPSC a risk factor.

Lebanon–Israel–the Palestinians

The smallest state in the complex is Lebanon, where the state apparatus was almost completely eradicated during the civil war that raged between 1975 and 1990. After the PLO established bases in Lebanon in 1970, and as a result of its loss against the Hashemite Kingdom of Jordan during the "Black September" war, Israel's security interests increasingly oriented its focus on Lebanon's internal affairs. Lebanon became a sub-complex in itself during the civil war period with many states involved, both horizontally and vertically. Syria and Israel have for a long time had a strategic interest in Lebanon. Almost every state in the Middle East has an interest in Lebanon, which risks escalating, and again bringing the various groups into armed confrontations. Historically, Israel has carried out military operations on Lebanese territory in retaliation against the PLO. In 1978, Israel carried out "Operation Litani", followed by Israeli occupation of parts of southern Lebanon up to the Litani River. Israel used a proxy force with the help of a Christian leader, Major Haddad, that was established to monitor the borders between Lebanon and Israel. However, these buffer zones could not prevent the PLO from continuing its raids against Israel. In 1981, Israel carried out intensive bombing against Palestinian targets in Lebanon. The war ended with a cease-fire agreement on 24 July 1981 between Israel's government and Lebanon's president (Persson, 1983).

In 1982, Israel entered Lebanese territory in an attempt to crush the PLO militarily. On 14 June, Beirut, where the PLO's headquarters was located, was surrounded by Israel's army and navy. Israel's forces had thereby allied themselves with the Christian Falangist militia in East Beirut, and taken control of the road between Beirut and Damascus. The PLO had to leave Beirut and seemed to have lost its influence and power in Lebanon. Under Israeli occupation, hundreds of Palestinians were massacred in the refugee camps Sabra and Shatila, presumably by Christian militiamen (Nuwayhed al-Hout, 2004). The USA reacted strongly to the massacres in Sabra and Shatila, and President Reagan claimed that he was determined to see Israel leave Lebanon. The reaction against Israel was strong all over the world, especially in France, Italy and Great Britain.

However, after strong pressure, particularly domestically, Israel announced on 28 January 1985 that its troops would withdraw from Lebanon. In June 1985 the South Lebanese army guaranteed Israel's security along the northern border. Israel had managed to defeat the PLO, but Syria remained, as well as the Shia movement Hezbollah, which began to carry out raids, including suicide attacks, against Israeli targets. The confrontations between Hezbollah and Israel continued, despite a Lebanese peace agreement that followed in 1990; Hezbollah was the sole group that was not disarmed and merged into the Lebanese defense forces and argued that it needed, for the sake of Lebanon, to continue to struggle for liberation of Lebanese soil from Israeli occupation. Hezbollah also has argued that they are defending the Palestinians, and have developed good relations with Palestinian Hamas. Hezbollah and Israel have developed enmity relations, and have attacked each other since 1982, and ended up in direct escalated wars on several occasions, not least when Israel entered Lebanon in 2006, in an attempt to crush militarily the Hezbollah military capacity. By 2000, though, Israel decided unilaterally to withdraw from Lebanon and thereby fulfilled the requests of UN SC resolution 425. However, Hezbollah declared that Israel had not left Shebaa's farms, a small territorial slot on the Syrian–Lebanese border towards Israel. This land is a disputed area, and claims are made from different positions that it is either Lebanese or Syrian territory, occupied by Israel. The UN has not managed to facilitate a deal that all parties can accept, hence, the confrontation between Hezbollah and Israel continues. Israel also on several occasions has attacked Hezbollah forces inside Syria, or vehicles with suspected military material underway from Syria to Lebanon, with the argument that it is preventing Hezbollah from preparing for a new war against Israel. Hezbollah's position has also divided Lebanon internally; in particular the current Sunni Prime Minister Hariri has been a long-standing critical voice against Hezbollah's armed forces, arguing that they need to merge with the Lebanese armed forces. The Palestinian refugees in Lebanon have had a difficult position in relation to the Lebanese state and society, and in particular, after the PLO moved its headquarters out of Lebanon in 1982 to Tunisia. Lebanese–Palestinian relations have always been complicated. Palestinians are often blamed for the country's political and socio-economic problems and are placed in limbo by not being able to return to Palestine, or integrate into Lebanese society, due to discriminatory policies. A long-term solution for the Palestinians is urgently needed, but is far from emerging given the stalemate between the Israelis and PA/PLO, and even more so with Hamas. The Syrian civil war has further complicated their situation.

Egypt–Israel–the Palestinians

Egypt is the largest state in the complex in terms of territory and population, and was involved in full-scale wars with Israel in 1948, 1956, 1967 and 1973. Egypt has always been one of the most influential states in the Arab world. As early as the 1950s, President Nasser of Egypt had the lead role in trying to unite the Arab world against Israel and supported the liberation of Palestine. In 1970, Egypt also played a mediating role in the civil war between the PLO and Jordan. When Egypt finally signed the Camp David accord in 1979, this was seen by the Arab states as a step away from the agreed Arab collective action plan, and therefore seen as treason. Israel returned the Sinai Peninsula, which was occupied in the 1967 war, and thereby had succeeded in neutralizing the largest Arab state. Egypt was expelled from the League of Arab States and only returned as a full member at the summit in Casablanca in 1989. Because of Israel's Lebanon wars, Egypt kept a very low profile towards Israel, and until current times, the peace between Israel and Egypt has always been considered to be a cold peace. During the Oslo process, President Mubarak, jointly with King Hussein of Jordan, were seen as the facilitating actors, and part of the so-called peace camp in the Arab world. Despite its own peace agreement with Israel, Egypt has continuously pushed for fair and lasting solutions for the Palestinians. At the Camp David talks in 1978–79, Egypt agreed to include a point in which it would negotiate with Israel about Palestinian autonomy on the West Bank and in Gaza. Even after the downfall of President Mubarak following the Egyptian revolution in 2011, and Muslim Brotherhood candidate Morsi was elected President of Egypt, the peace agreement with Israel was not cancelled. However, the relations with Palestinian Hamas, which controls the Gaza Strip, improved radically. Borders between Egypt and Gaza became more open after years of more or less isolation of Palestinian entries to Egypt. With the downfall of Morsi and the Muslim Brotherhood, and President Sisi seizing power, Hamas and Egypt again have had a period of soured relations. However, when Fatah and Hamas reconciliation talks took place in Egypt, leading to a new political deal where Fatah will gradually take over the PA also in Gaza, the Egyptian–Hamas relations have somewhat improved. In general, Hamas's readiness to step down partly from the PA control in Gaza is much linked to the changed political landscape in the Middle East, and the loss of previous close allies (Iran, Syria and Turkey). Egypt's facilitation role will play an important part in the future Israeli–Palestinian relations (Persson, 2012; Meital, 2006).

The IPSC's security implications for the Middle East

The Middle East region is characterized by a variety of state-building processes, each state containing several different ethnic or ethno-religious groups. Because of direct or indirect great-power assistance in creating "new" states within the region after World War I, these groups extend over one, or in most cases several, territorial borders. The Middle East, which is formed by a web of interactions along various security issues, and creates various enmity/ amity relations, includes all the North African states, the states of Israel, Syria, Jordan, Lebanon, Iraq, the Arab peninsula states, as well as Turkey and Iran. One can identify a whole set of sub-complexes within the broader Middle East.

Depending on the security issue at the focus, we attain different analytical regions rather than more or less permanent historical formations. For example, we can delimit the states of Iran–Iraq, or Syria–Iraq, as two security complexes concerning political, cultural and

Israeli–Palestinian conflict

geopolitical, as well as security, issues. In this way, we can also delimit and define the IPSC, in which the security dimension is the main focus, and view it as an analytical region, which affects the Middle East as a whole. As mentioned earlier, the states included in the IPSC are also related to other complexes within the Middle East region. Syria had a very tense relationship with Iraq, a relation that was hostile during the Iran–Iraq war (1980–1990) in which Syria supported Iran. Syria is also involved with the Kurdish question. The Kurdish minority lives in the states of Turkey, Syria, Iraq, Iran and the Soviet Union. The Kurds' demand for autonomy, or even for an independent "Kurdistan", creates a security issue for the states involved (MRG, 1985b).

The establishment of the Gulf Cooperative Council (GCC) in 1981 was very much a response to a crisis. The Iranian Revolution of 1978–79 served as a catalyst for Bahrain, Kuwait, Oman, Qatar, Saudi Arabia and the United Arab Emirates to form the GCC, which has, so far, basically served as a security regime. The Iran–Iraq War of 1980–1988 and the Gulf War of 1990–91, as well as the US-led invasion of Iraq in 2003, have forced the GCC members to continual crisis response. However, there has been recent conflict within the GCC states, where mainly Saudi Arabia is upset with Qatar, which is seen to not follow the anti-Iranian line. Simultaneously, Qatar has had close relations with the Brotherhoods movements primarily in Egypt and Syria, as well as with Palestinian Hamas.

Another sub-complex is the Arab Maghreb Union (AMU), which was established in 1989 with the aim to create a customs union along the same lines as the (then) European Community. The AMU was meant to be an area with open borders for free movement of goods, services, capital and persons, as well as cultural cooperation. The relations to actors in the IPSC have been relatively few, besides the standard support for the Palestinians, although Morocco had warmer relations with Israel since 1986, when King Hassan II invited Prime Minister Shimon Peres to Morocco. When the Oslo Accords were signed, economic cooperation also developed between the two countries.

Historically, almost all of the Middle Eastern states have had a hostile attitude towards the state of Israel. Only Egypt and Jordan have, so far, recognized the state of Israel, and have full peace agreements. Although the various Arab states have been verbally united in their support for the Palestinians, there have been very few occasions of direct united action. The three no statements (no to negotiations, recognition and peace with Israel) by the League of Arab States following the end of the 1967 war is one such example. The oil embargo of 1973–74 could be seen as another occasion when primarily the oil states tried to pressure the USA and the West for supporting Israel in the October War of 1973 (Karlsson and Tompuri, 1981). The first opening of hostility in the Middle East came when Egypt's president Al-Sadat visited Israel in 1977 and paved the way for the Camp David peace accord between Egypt and Israel. In the 1980s, it was only King Hassan of Morocco, apart from Egypt, who met representatives from the Israeli Government. Israel has on its part, never hesitated to attack Arab regimes when it felt threatened. Israel attacked Iraq in 1981 when France helped Iraq build a nuclear power station. Israel's air force bombed and destroyed the nuclear plant. Israeli fears that an Arab state should develop a nuclear bomb made Israel ready to take preventive actions, and during the last decade, Iran has been seen as a potential threat to Israel. However, all sub-complexes have had actors that over time have gradually reconciled with Israel without abandoning support for the Palestinians. In 2002, at the League of Arab States meeting in Beirut, Crown Prince Abdullah of Saudi Arabia managed to gain unanimous support from all Arab states for a peace plan that was offered to Israel. The main offer to Israel was a full-fledged peace agreement with the entire Arab world if it would accept the establishment of a Palestinian state in the West Bank and the Gaza Strip, with East Jerusalem as its capital.

The global IPSC security implications

When US President Trump announced on 6 December 2017 that the US recognizes Jerusalem as Israel's capital, it was instantly followed by demonstrations and riots that protested the decision in the Israeli occupied territories, as well as in the wider Middle East, and many other places worldwide. For instance, in Gothenburg in Sweden, an attack in the form of people throwing burning objects against the synagogue buildings followed. Representatives from the synagogue made a statement that they believed the attack was due to Trump's statement on Jerusalem (Sydsvenskan, 2017). This example shows the broader IPSC implications for global security. However, there are several more ways in which global security is affected by the IPSC. These can be listed as follows:

1) Direct reactions, in the form of protests, demonstrations, riots and terror acts, due to external actors' statements or decisions (such as President Trump's decision to declare Jerusalem as Israel's capital, which was followed by riots and confrontations in the West Bank between Palestinian protestors and Israeli security forces)
2) Actors, such as the superpowers during the Cold War, are dragged into the confrontations, and risk escalating into direct armed conflict with each other. The 1973 war is a relevant example, in which the superpowers (USA and USSR) nearly ended up in a nuclear confrontation due to the events on the ground in the war between Israel and the united front from Syria and Egypt (Tibi 1991)
3) A third party is criticized or even attacked, for instance as Jewish minorities are attacked, due to the attacker's view that Jewish minorities outside Israel are responsible for actions taken by Israel or its allies. Likewise, the Arab minorities in various host societies are seen as equally responsible for actions taken by Palestinians, mainly the PLO, PA or Hamas. Another example is when the multinational peacekeeping forces were sent to Beirut in August 1982 to oversee the evacuation of the PLO (US, Italian and French forces), which came as a result of the Israeli occupation of the city. Soon they came to be seen as partial actors, and in October 1983 the US and French headquarters were attacked by suicide drivers from the Shia Lebanese movement Hezbollah.
4) Various countries, but mainly the great powers, are involved and influence the IPSC by trading arms with the actors that are directly part of the IPSC, as well as with actors within the broader Middle East context. Since the so-called Arab Spring began in 2011, five of the world's top-ten receivers and buyers of arms have been located in the Middle East (highest country first: Saudi Arabia, United Arab Emirates, Algeria, Turkey and Iraq). Unsurprisingly, the top suppliers of arms are primarily the great powers of the world (highest country first: USA, Russia, Germany, China, France and the UK) (SIPRI, 2017a).

Further, the UN has been involved in the IPSC and has held numerous sessions in the General Assembly, as well as in the Security Council, concerning the Israeli–Palestinian conflict. The IPSC has a global reach and continuously engaged many actors directly and indirectly. Besides the UN's own mediation attempts, which have sent three of its UN peacekeeping/observing units to the IPSC (UNDOF 1974, UNIFIL 1978 and UNTSO 1948), several countries have made many attempts to mediate/facilitate in the IPSC. The most well-known examples are the mediators coming from the US, EU, Russia, Norway and Sweden, who have had different roles since 1948 (Schulze, 2017; Eriksson, 2015). However, during the Cold War, UN mediation became difficult due to the political deadlock between the US and the USSR. After the Cold

War, the UN, US, EU and Russia could agree on what was to be called the roadmap for peace that was adopted by the UN in 2002 (linked to UN SC resolution 1397).

Conclusion

The security implications of the IPSC are wide and reach far beyond the personal and direct security of Israelis and Palestinians in the core areas of the conflict. With an applied analytical tool, i.e. the security complex theory, the analysis showed what security implications the IPSC has. This chapter showed that the Israeli–Palestinian conflict has serious consequences for a whole range of security fields. This result implies that the Israeli–Palestinian conflict is an issue that has security implications for the entire world, and should therefore also be treated as a global peace and security concern. This is not to say that the core actors to the conflict, primarily the key actors of the IPSC, do not own their conflict. However, the development of the IPSC has security concerns for the entire Middle East, as well as for the globe, and should involve the UN. A solution, which all parties can live with, of the complex key issues in the IPSC, should also have a positive effect for other sub-complexes in the Middle East and beyond.

Notes

1 Contact details: Michael Schulz, Associate Professor, School of Global Studies, University of Gothenburg, e-mail: michael.schulz@globalstudies.gu.se.
2 The figures do not include Israelis killed during armed conflicts with the Arab neighbour states in the 1948–49, 1956, 1967 and 1973 wars. Source: SIPRI (2017b).
3 Five surveys were conducted by Michael Schulz and Mahmoud Mi'ari: November 1997, July 2001, April/May 2006, September 2009 and the most recent in August 2016. A random sample of 1308 Palestinians was selected for the 1997 survey, 1492 for the 2001 survey, 1500 for the 2006 survey, 1504 for the 2009 survey, and finally 1500 for the 2016 survey. The surveys contained approximately 150 to 200 questions. The target population was all individuals 18 years old or above who were residents of the West Bank and the Gaza Strip, or of the city of Jerusalem (under Israeli control). The data collection for the first four surveys was done in cooperation with the Palestinian Central Bureau of Statistics (PCBS), while the last was done in cooperation with the Jerusalem Media Communication Centre. Although between the five surveys some questions were changed, removed or added, several key aspects under study have been measured on all five occasions.
4 www.worldometers.info/world-population/syria-population/ (accessed 16 December 2017).

References

Ben-Zvi, A., 1986, *The American Approach to Superpower Collaboration in the Middle East 1973–1986,* Jerusalem: The Jerusalem Post Press.
B'Tselem, 2017, "Israelis and Palestinians Killed in Current Violence". http://israelpalestinetimeline.org/wp-content/uploads/2017/09/deaths.png (accessed 16 October 2017).
Bilgin, P., 2005, *Regional Security in the Middle East: A Critical Perspective,* New York: RoutledgeCurzon.
Buzan, B., 1983, *People, States and Fear: The National Security Problem in International Relations,* first edition. Brighton: Wheatsheaf Books.
Buzan, B., 1991, *People, States and Fear: The National Security Problem in International Relations,* second edition. Brighton: Wheatsheaf Books.
Buzan, B. and O. Waever, 2003, *Regions and Powers: The Structure of International Security,* Cambridge: Cambridge University Press.
Buzan, B., O. Waever, and J. de Wilde, 1998, *Security. A New Framework for Analysis.* Boulder/London: Lynne Rienner Publishers.
Eriksson, J., 2015, *Small-State Mediation in International Conflicts. Diplomacy and Negotiations in Israel-Palestine,* London & New York: I.B. Tauris.

Fawcett, L. (ed.), 2016, *International Relations of the Middle East*, Fourth edition, Oxford: Oxford University Press.

Galtung, J., 1996, *Peace by Peaceful Means: Peace and Conflict, Development and Civilization*. London: SAGE Publications. https://doi.org/10.2307/2623565

Harders, C. and M. Legrenzi, 2008, *Beyond Regionalism? Regional Cooperation, Regionalism and Regionalization in the Middle East*, Aldershot: Ashgate.

Hettne, B., A. Inotai, and O. Sunkel (eds.), 2000, *National Perspectives on the New Regionalism in the South*, Vol. III: *The New Regionalism Series*, London: Macmillan Press Ltd./United Nations University/WIDER.

Jönsson, C., 1984, *Superpower*, London: Frances Pinter.

Karlsson, S. and G. Tompuri, 1981, *Makten över oljan*, Lund: Studentlitteratur.

Klein, M., 2003, *The Jerusalem Problem. The Struggle for Permanent Status*, in association with the Jerusalem Institute for Israel Studies, Jerusalem, Israel, Gainesville: University Press of Florida.

Lindholm Schulz, H., and M. Schulz, 2005, "The Middle East: Regional Instability and Fragmentation," in Farell, Mary, Hettne, Björn, and Van Langenhove, Luk (eds), *Global Politics of Regionalism. Theory and Practice*, London/Ann Arbor: Pluto Press.

Ma'oz, M., 1999, *Middle East Journal*, Vol. 53, No. 3, Special Issue on Israel, pp. 393–416.

Maoz, Z. (ed.), 1997, *Regional Security in the Middle East. Past, Present and the Future*, London/Portland: Frank Cass.

Meital, Y., 2006, *Peace in Tatters. Israel, Palestine, and the Middle East*, Boulder/London: Lynne Rienner Publishers.

Minority Rights Group (MRG), 1985a, *Migrant Workers in the Gulf*, Report No. 68, London: Expedite Graphic Limited.

Minority Rights Group (MRG), 1985b, *The Kurds*, Report No. 23 (revised), London: Expedite Graphic Limited.

Minority Rights Group (MRG), 1986, *Lebanon: A Conflict of Minorities*, Report No. 61 (revised), London: Expedite Graphic Limited.

Minority Rights Group (MRG), 1987, *The Palestinians*, Report No. 24 (revised), London: Expedite Graphic Limited.

Nuwayhed al-Hout, B., 2004, *Sabra and Shatila September 1982*, London/Ann Arbor: Pluto Press.

Palestinian Centre for Policy and Survey Research (PCPSR), 2017, www.pcpsr.org/en/node/711 (accessed 12 November 2017).

Peace Index, 2017, www.peaceindex.org/indexMonthEng.aspx?num=326&monthname=October (accessed 12 November 2017).

Persson, S., 1983, *Lebanon and its Security*, FOA-rapport C 10236-M3, Stockholm: FOA.

Persson, S., 1989, "Kongedømmet Jordan: De palestinske elitenes rolle", *Internasjonal Politikk*, No. 1–2, pp. 37–59.

Persson, S., 2012, *Palestinakonflikten*, Lund: Studentlitteratur.

Quandt, W. B., 2005, *Peace Process. American Diplomacy and the Arab–Israeli Conflict since 1967*, Washington DC: Brookings Institution.

Rabinovich, I., 2004, *Waging Peace. Israel and the Arabs 1948–2003*. Princeton: Princeton University Press.

Rabinovich, I., 2012, *The Lingering Conflict. Israel, the Arabs, and the Middle East 1948–2012*, Washington: The Brookings Institution.

Schulz, M., 1989, "The Palestinian-Israeli Security Complex: Inconciliatory Positions or Regional Cooperation?" in Ohlsson, L. (ed.), *Case Studies of Regional Conflicts and Conflict Resolution*, Gothenburg: Padrigu Papers.

Schulz, M., 1996, *Israel between Conflict and Accommodation. A Study of a Multi-Melting Pot Process*, Gothenburg: Padrigu Thesis Series.

Schulz, M., 2011, "Palestinian Public Willingness to Compromise: Torn between Hope and Violence," *Security Dialogues*, No. 2, Year 1, pp. 117–140.

Schulz, M., F. Söderbaum and J. Öjendal (eds.), 2001, *Regionalization in the Post-Cold Era: A Comparative Perspective on Forms, Actors, and Processes,* London: Zed Books Ltd.

Schulze, K. E., 2017, *The Arab–Israeli Conflict*, third edition, London & New York: Routledge.

Shikaki, K., 1996a, "The Peace Process, National Reconstruction, and the Transition to Democracy in Palestine", *Journal of Palestine Studies*, Vol. XXV, No. 2 (Winter 1996), pp. 5–20.

Shikaki, K., 1996b, *Transition to Democracy in Palestine: The Peace Process, National Reconstruction and Elections*, Nablus: Center for Palestine Research and Studies.

Shikaki, K., 2006, *Willing to Compromise. Palestinian Public Opinion and the Peace Process*, Special Report, United States Institute of Peace, January 2006.

Stockholm International Peace Research Institute (SIPRI), 2017a, http://armstrade.sipri.org/armstrade/html/export_toplist.php (accessed 12 December 2017).

Stockholm International Peace Research Institute (SIPRI), 2017b, "Mid-Range Wars and Atrocities of the Twentieth Century" http://users.erols.com/mwhite28/warstat4.htm (accessed 9 November 2017).

Sydsvenskan, 2017, "Säpo utreder hotbilden mot synagogor" www.sydsvenskan.se/2017-12-10/sapo-utreder-hotbilden-mot-synagogor (accessed 12 December 2017).

Tibi, B., 1991, *Conflict and War in the Middle East, 1967–91, Regional Dynamic and the Superpowers*, London: The Macmillan Press Ltd.

United Nations Relief and Work Association (UNRWA), 2015, "In Figures" www.unrwa.org/sites/default/files/unrwa_in_figures_2015.pdf (accessed 14 November 2017).

United Nations Relief and Work Association (UNRWA), 2017, "What We Do; Protection" www.unrwa.org/what-we-do/protection (accessed 16 December 2017).

7

THE FUTURE OF IRAQ'S SECURITY

Ibrahim Al-Marashi

Introduction

By the end of 2017, Iraq's military forces had expelled Islamic State of Iraq and Syria (ISIS) from all Iraqi urban centers that it had seized since 2014. Nonetheless, an examination of Iraq's future security is ever more salient as ISIS morphs from a terrorist group which held Iraqi territory into a state-sponsor of regional and international terrorism. The Iraqi State faces daunting challenges in terms of maintaining security in this post-conflict scenario. This matter is contingent on how the Iraqi Government and sub-state actors, as well as international and regional partners, interact to deal with a wide array of security issues, such as ISIS terrorism and the proliferation of numerous militias and para-military actors. While state-centric strategies have prioritized dealing with these hard security issues, no coherent, sustainable strategy has been articulated by the Iraqi political elite to deal with pressing human security issues, ranging from internally displaced peoples (IDPs) to looming environmental dangers. Failure to deal with the human security issues will ultimately only exacerbate the hard security dilemmas in Iraq's future. Indeed, it can be argued that the failure of the Iraqi State to provide human security is what enabled the ISIS invasion in 2014 in the first place.

Iraq's hard security and soft security dilemmas represent continuities from the Baathist past. Hard security issues such as Arab-Kurdish tensions over territory and former Saddam-era Iraqi military officers in ISIS are examples of legacies influencing the present. In terms of human security, for example, the collapsing Mosul Dam is a problem inherited from Saddam Hussein's decision to construct this structure in a haphazard fashion in the 1980s. While the emergence of democracy, albeit flawed, is a positive development in Iraq from a normative perspective since 2003, politics still retains patterns from its Baathist past, such as kin, clan and tribal solidarity and pervasive patronage networks. Essentially Iraq has developed a democratic façade, where politicians run in competitive elections and field candidates to the Council of Representatives, thus making their power contingent on public opinion, votes and the election cycle. Thus, the failure to address the long-term sustainable solutions to the hard and human security issues in the present can also be attributed to the evolution of the Iraqi State since 2003. In Iraq's electoral cycle, delivering security on the street or providing jobs via the ministries and militias results in votes. The political class has little incentive to deal with the long-term soft security issues as they deliver fewer tangible monetary or political results. It is only when soft security issues reach a crisis point, such as the lack of water in the summer of 2015 or the protests in the southern city of Basra during the summer of 2018, or the possibility of the collapse of the Mosul Dam, that politicians react to these crises, often in an ad hoc manner with stop-gap measures.

Conceptualizing Iraq's security

Since the rise of ISIS in 2014, most analyses on Iraq have focused on traditional aspects of security, primarily focusing on the combat strategies and tactics of ISIS itself, the Iraqi armed forces and militias, and the role of regional and international actors in this military campaign. Yet Iraq also faces a myriad of non-traditional, human security challenges, the lack of social capital, poor governance, food security, and water scarcity, all of which will impact Iraq's traditional security concerns. Yet, compared with the study of hard security in the literature, the human security issues have been neglected in the study of Iraq.

In the most recent edition of *The Modern History of Iraq* (2017), historian of Iraq Phebe Marr and I have written a history of the nation that incorporates both traditional and soft security issues since the formation of the Iraqi State in 1920 to the rise of ISIS. We argue that Iraq's political past and future are predicated on the interaction of four interrelated challenges: 1) fostering Iraqi national cohesion, 2) strengthening national governance, 3) developing Iraq's economic and human resources, and 4) balancing foreign interests. In terms of Iraq's future, the question of whether Iraq will survive as an intact state has arisen, which I address in an essay "What Future for Iraq? Unity and Partition after Mosul", for the Milan-based policy institute (Al-Marashi, 2017b).

While many prognoses have raised the specter of continued sectarian violence destabilizing Iraq, "sectarianism" as analytical concept proves problematic, as argued by Fanar Haddad, in *Sectarianism in Iraq: Antagonistic Visions of Unity* (2011). I also refrain from delving into sectarian differences as a causative factor in Iraq insecurity. Ethno-sectarian differences are often seen as primordial and embedded in Iraqi society, yet I would conceptualize these tensions as Shia, Sunni and Kurdish narratives of victimization and trauma. These narratives seek to mask rivalries within each community, which I deem more of a looming danger. Rather than attributing violence in Iraq to mere extant sectarian or ethnic differences, contestation of votes and territory are more likely to lead to intra-sectarian and intra-ethnic conflict, as has already happened in Iraq since 2003. Sectarianism seen as a causal variable to Iraq's violence is superficial and reduces the complexity of this intra-communal conflict dynamic.

Two scholars are worth noting that delve into specific aspects of Iraq's security. For example, in terms of hard security, Andrew Rathmell (2005, 2007) was the first to publish on the oft-neglected topic of Security Sector Reform (SSR) in Iraq, and new developments have transpired since then. An example of crucial research in the realm of human security is the work of Eckart Woertz (2017) on food security in Iraq.

This chapter does not offer a forecast in terms of a discrete time period as to when the hard security or human security challenges will be or even can be resolved, but rather serves as a diagnosis of Iraq's current and future security dilemmas. The hard security issues in Iraq outlined in this chapter, focusing on military and state security, are analyzed separately from the soft security issues, such as underlying geographic and resource-based vulnerabilities in Iraq, but they are not mutually exclusive and are intricately linked.

Iraq's hard security dilemmas

Iraq's future security is contingent on three predominant hard security issues: 1) Iraq's duopolies of violence, 2) ISIS remnants in Iraq, and 3) Iraqi factional contestation over urban centers, some adjacent to oil fields. The multitude of parties involved in this issue, both domestic and international, portend that rivalry will be the norm in the future, rather than cooperation.

Iraq's future duopolies of violence

Iraq's armed forces are divided into those controlled by the Iraqi State and sub-state actors. The military of the Iraqi State is known as the Iraqi Security Forces (ISF), and the ISIS offensive into Mosul in June 2014 caused its collapse, the result of persistent problems, such as corruption, plaguing this institution beforehand (Al-Marashi, 2013).

The ISF are not deployed within the Kurdistan Regional Government (KRG) of Iraq, a federal entity that it has its own capital, Irbil, and its own security forces, drawn from the militias of the two dominant Kurdish parties, the Kurdistan Democratic Party (KDP) and the Patriotic Union of Kurdistan (PUK), collectively referred to in Kurdish as the *peshmerga*, or "those who face death". However, as result of the ISIS invasion, another Kurdish actor has entered this conflict, the Syrian-Kurdish People's Protection Units (referred to by its Kurdish acronym YPG), an affiliate of the Turkish Kurdistan Worker's Party, the PKK. Given the time the US needed to reconstitute the ISF, the defense of the governments in Baghdad and Irbil became dependent on the Iraqi Shi'a militias and Kurdish Peshmerga, respectively.

After 2014, Arab Sunnis have demanded an independent force to maintain security, answerable to provincial governments opposed to the central government, akin to the Peshmerga forces of the KRG. They will likely continue to articulate this demand even after ISIS is expelled from Mosul.

Reform of the regular military forces

The ISF have been reconstituted and reformed since the ISIS invasion, but for Iraq's long-term security the military will have to adopt the best practices of SSR to develop an ethos of professionalization, in order to become an inclusive national institution. Reform of the ISF will be crucial for dealing with the immediate problem of internally displaced peoples (IDPs), creating security for the long-term reconstruction and their integration of areas formerly held by ISIS.

From a human security perspective, it was the behavior of the ISF that alienated it from elements of society. The use of Iraqi security forces to attack protesters in the Arab Sunni town of Hawija in April 2013 is one of the factors that created resentment on the ground that led to the reemergence of ISIS. In terms of Iraq's future, the question remains as to how Iraqi Arab Sunnis, traumatized by both ISIS rule, in addition to the behavior of ISF in the past, will reconcile themselves with this latter institution representing the Iraqi State and nation.

Precedent demonstrates that units of the ISF can be reformed. Prior to 2014 the Counter-Terrorism Force, otherwise known as the "Golden Division", was beset with problems, derogatorily referred to as former prime minister Nouri al-Maliki's "private army" (Witty, 2015). Since the ISIS invasion, the force has reformed itself with the help of a US training mission, and has borne the brunt of most of the urban combat in cities like Falluja, Ramadi and Mosul, emerging as one of the few professional, inclusive Iraqi military institutions. However, even if the success of the Golden Division can be replicated to the much larger, regular Iraqi army, another problem has emerged in the wake of the ISIS invasion, the presence of numerous militias.

The issue of militias

As ISIS reached the outskirts of Baghdad in July 2014, the central government – first under premier Maliki and then Haydar al-'Abbadi – faced a military emergency and a security vacuum.

The defense of the capital and the south became dependent on militias, mobilized after a call by Iraq's most influential Shi'a cleric, Ali Sistani, to defend the nation. In terms of the Shi'a militias' numbers in this aftermath, they reached anywhere from 60,000 to 120,000 fighters, while the numbers of the Iraqi military after the fall of Mosul had dwindled to only 50,000 reliable forces (Katzman and Humud, 2016: 12). The militias supplemented, if not supplanted the regular military. These militias were subsumed under the government rubric, *al-Hashd al-Sha'bi* or the Popular Mobilization Units (PMU), an umbrella institution that sought to coordinate the wide array of para-military groups. In fact the constituent militias of the PMUs would eventually vie for power among themselves.

The Iraqi Shia militias had mobilized in response to the fall of Mosul in 2014, and Iraq's future security is contingent on the whether these militias will be demobilized once ISIS is expelled from this city. This issue is significant for the future as some of the militia leaders argue that they need to remain mobilized to continue fighting ISIS in Syria until they destroy it in its capital in Raqqa (Steele, 2017). As there are so many Shia militias, around 30 in number, some may go to Syria, while other militia leaders have stayed in Iraq and increased their power through the political process, by running in the May 2018 elections, coming in second place. The more precarious scenario is that some of the Shia militias may turn on each other, either violently or within the government, without a common enemy to unite them, as they rival each other for territory and authority.

The militia issue illustrates the challenge for Iraq's security in dealing with foreign influence and control. As the Iraqi State lacks a monopoly on violence, the US and Iraq's neighbors have intervened in Iraq via support of the national military or proxies in the form of militias. The American withdrawal after 2011 was matched by increased influence from regional competitors, especially Iran, but also Turkey and Arab neighbors, such as Saudi Arabia. The militias as proxies will allow regional forces to have considerable impact on Iraq's domestic political landscape in the future.

An American military presence equipped and trained the ISF to deal with the ISIS challenge after 2014, and as a result, both Iran and the US vied with each other for influence in the domestic Iraqi arena afterwards and have remained as influencers to prevent the reemergence of ISIS. Iran's influence increased through training and equipping domestic Shia militias often outside of government control. New militias emerged with Iranian support, usually with the Arabic word for "brigade" (*kata'ib*) preceding it, such as Kata'ib Imam Ali and Kata'ib Hizbullah (Al-Ghazi, 2016). Qasim Sulaimani, commander of the Quds Force of the Iranian Revolutionary Guards, was often seen on the Iraqi frontlines, alongside Iraqi Shi'a militias.

The Shi'a militias, Iran and the US maintained an uneasy, de facto alliance against ISIS, and in the future this modus vivendi will become precarious once the Islamic State collapses. Al-'Abbadi would like the American training mission to remain in Iraq, even though its current level of 5,000 advisors might be reduced (Steele, 2017). After the defeat of ISIS, the Iranian Revolutionary Guards and its advisors in Iraq have created a flashpoint with the Trump administration, which appears to be looking for reasons to ratchet up tensions with Iran, particularly after Washington withdrew from the Iranian nuclear deal in 2018.

Turkey and the Gulf states will try to influence domestic politics to the benefit of their foreign policy goals. The Gulf states, particularly Saudi Arabia, will try to limit Iranian influence by allying with local Arab Sunni parties. Turkey's policy has been to ally with one Iraqi Kurdish faction, the Iraqi KDP, in order to curtail the resurgence of Turkey's own Kurds in the PKK. Turkey has also trained its own militia of Arab Sunnis, *al-Hashd al-Watani* (the National Mobilization Unit), from a base it established in the Iraqi town of Bashiqa, resulting in condemnation from the central government as a violation of its national sovereignty. The leader of the militia is Athil al-Nujaifi, the ousted governor of Mosul, who envisioned his force securing the city of Mosul after ISIS is expelled. The central government did not agree to his plan, setting up another looming conflict. One of the central issues behind this conflict is whether the Iraqi State will devolve more administrative powers to the Arab Sunni regions, including the demands of Arab Sunni politicians for a local national guard to maintain security in its areas.

In terms of SSR, the US military training presence in Iraq has become more robust after the ISIS invasion, and Washington will most likely use this leverage to pressure Iraq's leader to distance themselves from Iranian influence by reining in the power of the militias. However, for a sustainable SSR process, regional players such as Iran and Turkey, each of which have contributed to the proliferation of para-military groups, will need to be part of the solution. A legal framework was developed by the Iraqi State that formally integrates the militias in the armed forces with civilian, government oversight, but which ostensibly did little to control the de facto autonomy enjoyed by these forces. As of May 2018, these militias will essentially become part of the fabric of the state, blurring the distinction between para-military actors and the executive and legislative branches of the Iraqi Government.

Dealing with ISIS remnants

The most pressing issue for Iraq's future security is the survival of ISIS remnants (Mironova and Hussein, 2017). As ISIS initially started to lose territory in Iraq and withdraw from the Iraqi cities in the summer of 2015, it resorted to launching car bombs in urban centers. One of the most devastating attacks occurred on 3 July 2016 in the Karrada district of Baghdad, killing 300 (Mamouri, 2016). Such indiscriminate tactics were ostensibly aimed to sap the morale of the civilian base of its enemies in Iraq, but also to revert back to ISIS's progenitor, Abu Mus'ab al-Zarqawi's plan of targeting Shia civilians to provoke retaliation against Arab Sunnis. Even with ISIS's final loss of control over cities in Iraq at the end of 2017, it demonstrated its ability to use suicide bombers, exemplified by the January 2018 attack that killed 35 street vendors in a Baghdad square (Hassan and Coker, 2018). The possibility always exists of ISIS remnants attacking a Shia structure or procession, such as pilgrimages to Najaf and Karbala. Such an action might provoke another series of retaliatory killings, as occurred with the bombing of the sacred Shia al-'Askari shrine in Samarra in 2006.

Furthermore, ISIS remnants, otherwise referred to as "sleeper cells", can still intimidate civilians in urban centers which are nominally under Iraqi Government or KRG control. ISIS's ability to continue to project fear even in liberated spaces is problematic. From a policing perspective this will deprive security forces of the human intelligence needed to combat ISIS remnants.

The battle over urban centers

As ISIS was expelled from Iraqi towns such as Tikrit, Falluja, Ramadi and Sinjar in 2015, the problem of how the central government will manage resettlement of these urban centers emerged. Arab Sunnis fear that after a victory over ISIS, a Shia-dominated government will rule as a conqueror of this territory, largely supported by the Shia militias. For the Kurdish side, they will remember how vulnerable Irbil was in August 2014 to an ISIS assault, and they will seek to secure enough territory, such as Sinjar and Kirkuk, to protect the KRG flank, which the central government will most certainly demand reverts to its control.

Mosul and Kirkuk

When the battle for Mosul commenced in October 2016, there was no political consensus as to who will control the city after ISIS is expelled. The central government assumed control after the ISIS defeat by July 2017; however it was Baghdad's governance of this city that led to the conditions to allowed ISIS to find fertile ground in Mosul in the first place. The question for Iraq's future remains as to how will Arab Sunnis in this city, and in Anbar and Salah al-Din provinces, compromise with the central government on reconstructing and maintaining security in the city.

The notions of the territorial sovereignty of the central government came to the fore not only over Mosul, but Kirkuk as well, which did bode well for the historic tense relations between Baghdad and Irbil. In order to preempt ISIS's advance as of June 2014, Kurdish forces had seized the city of Kirkuk, which lay outside of the KRG's jurisdiction, but had long been coveted as an integral part of Iraqi Kurdistan. The KRG held a referendum on declaring independence from Iraq on 25 September 2017. The central government of Iraq ignored the vote and deployed Iraqi military forces to retake Kirkuk in October (Al-Marashi, 2017). The KDP and its leader Masoud Barzani, took a gamble with his failed push for an independence for Iraq's Kurds, and its rival, the PUK, failing to wholeheartedly endorse this effort, tacitly ordered its forces in Kirkuk to stand down, allowing the oil-rich city to revert to Iraqi Government control.

A future conflict still looms between these two sides over Kirkuk. This city, adjacent to one of Iraq's largest oil fields, ultimately involves the complex issues of resource nationalism. Resolving the tensions over allocation of oil between Irbil and Baghdad will determine whether Iraq survives in the most optimistic scenario as a loose Shia-Kurdish alliance.

The battle for smaller towns

The situation in smaller towns held by ISIS, such as Sinjar, Tal Afar, and Tuz Khurmato serves as a microcosm of Iraq's intra-ethnic and intra-sectarian tensions, in both the present and the future.

In Tal Afar in the Ninawa province, the Shia residents fled or were massacred when ISIS forces took the town in the summer of 2014. ISIS forces were expelled in September 2017 by a combination of Iraqi military forces and Shia militias. It could witness a conflict between Shia and Sunni Turkmen in the town, with the former, who were expelled by ISIS, seeking out reprisals against the latter for having collaborated with the Islamic State.

The town of Sinjar's inhabitants were primarily Yezidis, a Kurdish people practicing a syncretic faith. Yezidis became alienated from the KRG parties and security forces for abandoning them as ISIS forces entered their towns in 2014 (Goudsouzian and Lara Fatah, 2015). The Syrian Kurdish YPG forces came to their rescue, helping a good number flee to Syria, and then liberated their town after expelling ISIS in November 2015. Thereafter the YPG threatened the KDP's hold over Sinjar, technically not within the boundaries of the KRG, but an area the KRG had hoped to incorporate, along the lines of Kirkuk. The KDP forces have since sought to push the YPG out of Sinjar. By that point each faction had set up their own Yezidi militias, the YPG-affiliated Sinjar Resistance Units and the KDP-affiliated Rojava Peshmerga, which fought street battles with each other in March 2016 (Al, 2017).

The town of Tuz Khurmato is divided in half, one side controlled by the Kurdish forces, the other by Shia militias, ostensibly protecting the town's Shia Turkmen. Like in Sinjar, the problem of intra-sectarian tensions was illustrated in June 2016, when members of two Shia militias, the Badr Organization and Asa'ib Ahl al-Haq, fought street battles there, after the latter group kidnapped a member of the former. Thus, the town represents not only ethnic tensions, between Arab Shias, Kurds and Turkmen, but intra-sectarian tensions as well. Furthermore, Asa'ib Ahl al-Haq is itself a splinter of the Shia cleric Muqtada al-Sadr's Mahdi Army, and the Badr Organization splintered from the Islamic Supreme Council of Iraq (ISCI), demonstrating that Shia political plurality and rivalry has been the norm in Iraq, and will most likely continue in the future once there is no common foe in the form of ISIS, just as the electoral results of May 2018 have demonstrated.

Human security dilemmas

Human security in Iraq after ISIS will be precarious. Citizens lack sufficient protection, either from government or social institutions, to allow for engagement in politics, the private sector, or education. Iraq has witnessed societal erosion by three wars since 1980, sanctions after 1991, and then occupation, a civil war and the conflict with ISIS, resulting in massive costs, internal population displacement and flight from Iraq.

Even prior to the ISIS invasion, Iraq was left with its education and health sectors devastated, with rising unemployment and a middle-class flight that continued to deprive the country of its most precious resource. As a result, Iraq has an impoverished population that has suffered from a lack of basic services and few employment opportunities. Unemployment is high as of 2017, officially reported at 16%, but unofficially considered to be at least 30% (CIA World Fact Book, 2018). Most jobs are in the military, security-related services and government. An estimate of the labor-force distribution showed about 21.6% in agriculture, 18.7% in industry, and almost 59.8% in services (ibid.). As of 2017, over one-third of the labor force was working for a bloated public sector (Economist Intelligence Unit, 2015: 7). The development of a private sector to employ Iraqis remained hampered by insecurity and bureaucratic hurdles that discourage entrepreneurship.

The soft security issues in Iraq are clustered in six broad categories, not listed in priority, but are intricately linked. They are: 1) population displacement and refugees, 2) youth security and education, 3) security for minorities and their heritage, 4) gender security, 5) public health, and 6) environmental, energy and food security. The security concerns laid out below are not merely an indictment of the failures of the Iraqi State to manage them, but long-term issues that will affect Iraq's future, and will require massive investment and political capital to mitigate, never mind transform.

Population displacement and refugees

Population displacement began with the brain drain of the 1990s and the sanctions era and continued after 2003. The number of refugees and IDPs increased dramatically after the Iraqi civil war from 2006 to 2008, and again after the ISIS invasion.

The effects of brain drain

Iraq had been undergoing a flight of its educated professional middle class for years, especially doctors, professors, lawyers, engineers, scientists, artists and bureaucrats, fleeing to Europe or the US (Wasim, 2015). Writers, artists, journalists, scholars and others responsible for shaping the nation's intellectual and cultural life have also fled (Sassoon, 2008: 140–151).

The impact of the brain drain will manifest itself in the health and education sectors, and with economic development and the bureaucracy. Government institutions, bereft of an experienced civil service, have been crippled in their ability to deliver much-needed services. Economic development, including in the oil industry, advanced slowly in the absence of technical experience.

Internal displacement

After the 2003 war, occupation and violence from insurgencies had inflicted considerable population losses on Iraq, and according to the United Nations High Commissioner for Refugees (UNHCR), the number of Iraqi refugees ranges from 1.7 to 2.3 million (UNHCR, no date). Those are conservative estimates and are not up-to-date.

An unprecedented population shift resulted from the displacements of the civil war from 2006 to 2008 and the reemergence of ISIS, with both an exodus of refugees from the country and IDPs (Swain and Jägerskog, 2016: 140–142). The population shifts have affected the ethnic and sectarian balance in the country and created segregation in living patterns, affecting political and intellectual life, particularly in the capital Baghdad. All of these developments contributed to ethnic and sectarian segmentation and sharpened communal identity. Furthermore, the displacement of Iraq's non-Muslim minorities contributed to an increased Islamization of society and reduced diversity. Rapid and disruptive social change threw Iraqi society back on traditional social mechanisms and institutions for survival – family and religion.

Dealing with population displacement in the future

The military campaign against ISIS led to the destruction of numerous towns and cities, leading to a flood of IDPs within Iraq to refugee camps in the south and KRG. Approximately 2.5 million were initially displaced by ISIS's invasion of 2014, 46% fleeing to the KRG, suddenly increasing its population by 28% (Marr and Al-Marashi, 2017: 325). According to UN figures as of March 2017, there were 3,073,614 IDPs in Iraq, but by September the number fell to 1,904,520 (Iraq Mission, 2018).

The paramount humanitarian issue the Iraqi State faces in its near-term future is this displacement and how to reincorporate previously held ISIS territories and those who lived under ISIS rule. This process has been complicated by political battles over who is going to secure and govern these areas, who will get to live there in the resettlement process, and how to reintegrate the IDPs. Despite the military victories against ISIS, IDPs have not been able to return to their homes, as most have been destroyed, but also due to political considerations. Many of the refugees, mostly Arab Sunnis, are wary of returning to a post-conflict zone where the Shia militias are in control.

This problem will also hinge on the pace of reconstruction of the ISIS-held areas. For this to occur, the Iraqi Government on the national, provincial and municipal level will have to cooperate to restore essential services, and then begin reconstruction of damaged homes and buildings. One of the greatest obstacles to reconstruction is not just financing the process, but the long, delicate process of removing improvised explosive devices (IEDs) from former ISIS-held territories such as Ramadi, Falluja and Sinjar, and which most likely will be ubiquitous in Mosul.

In terms of reconstruction, small non-governmental and civil society organizations will be best positioned for this task, employing members from the affected communities. If the central government and international governments and organizations adopt this strategy, it would promote a sense of local ownership in this post-conflict scenario, in addition to the more immediate need of offering income to those in the affected regions (Schweitzer, 2017).

Youth security and education

The vicissitudes Iraq has endured since 1990, including the Gulf War and sanctions, the post-2003 conflicts, and the rise of ISIS, have had a dramatic impact on the younger generation. Many Iraqis came to maturity under these disruptions, which undercut their education and job opportunities.

Education at every level, from kindergarten to the university, has suffered since 2003, particularly from the scarcity of qualified teachers (Sassoon, 2008: 148–149). The brain drain was also exacerbated by the flight of Iraq's academics, who fled targeted assassinations and intimidation. Often the motivations for the murder of academics were unknown, as was the exact toll of assassinated academics. Academics have been killed for a variety of reasons, either nominally belonging to the former Ba'ath Party, for failing to adhere to a sectarian curriculum in the classroom, or simply giving a student a poor grade.

Finally, there is also considerable frustration among the youth. A 2016 study by the International Crisis Group (2016) points to the problems and frustrations of "Generation 2000", Iraqis between the ages of 15 and 24, which grew up during the occupation, insurgencies and the ISIS incursion. In 2016, this generation constituted almost 20% of the population (International Crisis Group, 2016: 1). They faced declining employment, a sense of disempowerment and, according to interviews, a lack of direction. As one NGO worker declared, "They have come into a world that offers them no points of reference" (ibid.).

This generation essentially has three choices for their future. First, for those with an education, a job in the public sector is the sole source of work, but these jobs could only be secured through patronage, via one of the political parties that controls the bureaucracy. The patronage system even affects getting an education, since many secondary school teachers, on meager salaries, provide private tutoring for a fee, thus assuring that a privileged minority obtained access to limited places in the higher education system and, therefore, the bureaucracy (ibid., p. 7).

A second choice, especially after 2014, has been joining a militia, an option that attracted many youth, particularly those with less education. Sunni youth were often recruited by ISIS or its affiliates as they swept into Iraq from Syria; young Kurds and Shia often volunteered for one of the numerous militias fighting ISIS. As a result, a substantial portion of this generation was not only "militarized" but also "sectarianized". The new militias offered salaries but also more intangible benefits such as a sense of empowerment and belonging, a substitute for frayed family and other social ties. This development has not only heightened sectarian identity but will set up the problem of future demobilization of the Shia and Kurdish militias once the struggle with ISIS had subsided.

A third, more difficult, choice is emigration, which became increasingly attractive after 2014, when oil prices fell and government jobs declined. In June 2014, for example, for the first time in a decade, ministries did not post any new jobs. One report claimed that 16,000 new civilian jobs were unassigned due to a shortage of funds; at the same time 30,000 new positions were assigned to pay for militias (ibid., p. 23).

The deterioration of Iraq's education infrastructure does not bode well for the country's future. As of 2018, the literacy rate for those over 15 years old was 79.7%, relatively low compared with Iraq's neighbors. In the same period Jordan's literacy rate was almost 95.4% (CIA World Fact Book, 2018). The interruption of education for many of Iraq's youth, the continued flight of academics, and the failure of the state to keep up with the number of students all indicate that education in Iraq will not improve in the near future. Iraq will require a major investment in its youth, yet the situation in the present does not augur well for this issue being addressed in the future.

Security for minorities

The rise of ISIS reshaped the cultural fabric of Iraq, obliterating the multidenominational history of the region and targeting women and children from religious minorities. ISIS sought to create a homogeneous, transnational nation of believing Sunni Muslims by destroying the heterogeneity of the north of Iraq, which resulted in the mass expulsions and executions of Iraqi Christians, and other syncretic minority faiths in Mosul and northern Iraq, such as the Yezidis, Shabak and Kakais.

Prior to the resurgence of ISIS, Christians generally fled from mixed areas in the center of Iraq to religious enclaves in the north in Mosul and the Ninawa plain. In the wake of several spectacular attacks on churches and clergy up to 2010, many feared the ultimate disappearance of the Christian community, much like that of the Iraqi Jews earlier. Christians, who had once totaled 800,000–1.2 million (about 3% of the population), may have been reduced to less than 500,000 after the ISIS invasion (Iddon, 2016).

Before ISIS invaded in 2014, the Iraqi Yezidi population was estimated at around 600,000 to 620,000, with the vast majority concentrated in northern Iraq (Acikyildiz, 2014: 34). ISIS, having accused the Yezidis of being "devil worshippers", pursued a strategy of eliminating their presence entirely, destroying any physical vestiges of their culture and the structures they venerated, and killing Yezidi men and enslaving women. The ISIS offensive in the summer of 2014 led to the displacement of 130,000 Yazidis, including 40,000 stranded on Mount Sinjar (Chulov, 2014). Many sought refuge in the Yezidi spiritual city Lalish, or Irbil, the capital of the KRG, or escaped into Syria. The recent violence by ISIS has caused more Iraqi Yezidis to seek asylum in Europe, with 70,000 people, or about 15% of the Yezidis in Iraq, fleeing to join the preexisting Yezidi diaspora communities in Germany, the US and Canada (Jalabi, 2014).

Yezidis have begun to return to Sinjar and Christians to towns such as Bartella and Tel Kayf, all of which have incurred significant damage, with little public services having been restored. However, the damage to their spiritual heritage, such as the destruction of Yezidi temples and Christian churches by ISIS, in addition to forced expulsion and sexual slavery, will require both physical reconstruction as well as investing in a mental health infrastructure, which is practically non-existent in Iraq or the KRG. The ordeal suffered by the Yezidis under ISIS is closely implicated to the status of gender security in Iraq.

Gender security

One of the most insidious legacies of ISIS's presence in Iraq was the enslavement of Yezidi women, some of whom were held captive and raped by multiple "owners" in a form of chattel and sexual slavery. As of 2016, some 1,500 Yezidi women had escaped, or had been freed by the captors before they went on to conduct suicide missions. Nearly 2,000 Yezidi women remained in captivity.

The fate of Yezidi women has to be contextualized in terms of gender security, or the lack of it, in Iraq. Legal frameworks in post-2003 Iraq were inadequate to prevent domestic abuse and honor killings, and the infrastructure remained woefully inadequate with regard to women's education and health. The greatest and perhaps most significant challenge has been the resurgence of patriarchal values that were firmly embedded in Iraqi Arab and Kurdish society and that have reemerged with the departure of Iraq's more educated, cosmopolitan elite. There has been a return to forced marriages and tribal customs, embedded in "honor killings", for immoral behavior, as older social norms surfaced. The incidence of honor crimes has risen throughout Iraq, even in urban areas, with the legal systems in both Baghdad and Irbil failing to deter or sufficiently punish the perpetrators (Wasim, 2013). These trends will unfortunately continue in the future.

For those Yezidi women who survived their ordeal of sexual slavery and returned to Iraq, primarily to the KRG, they often experienced stigma of rape in their own community (Wheeler, 2016). This issue ultimately leads to an examination of Iraq's public health infrastructure.

Health security

One of the most pressing emergency mental health crises in Iraq and the KRG is that of the Yezidi women who were held captive by ISIS, or witnesses to its violence in towns such as Sinjar. As a result of the degradation that occurred in Iraq's public health sector, it lacks proper facilities and qualified physicians, and there is insufficient mental health infrastructure to deal with the nation's traumatized population.

As a rentier-state, the Baath government (1968–2003) leveraged the increase in oil revenues around 1973 to subsidize public loyalty. One of those strategies included the state's provision of health care. A dire medical crisis in Iraq began during the sanctions that began after 1991, and the effects of depleted uranium from the wars in 1991 and 2003. The collapse of the state in 2003 exacerbated the decline of the health sector, already eviscerated by the UN-imposed sanctions.

The brain drain had dire ramifications for Iraq's health sector. The Iraqi Red Crescent believed that about 50% of Iraq's doctors and 70% of medical specialists left in the exodus (Al-Khalisi, 2013). Hospitals and clinics had been degraded by war, insurgency and violence. Health improvements have taken place: life expectancy had been 64 in 1990; in 2018 it had improved, but still was only 74.9. Infant mortality was still high at 37.5 per 1,000 (CIA World Fact Book, 2018).

A health issue has been the impact of trauma. An Iraqi health survey estimated that almost one in five Iraqis had some mental illness (Ditmars, 2016). A survey of school children in Mosul found that almost four of every ten children under 16 had a mental disorder (Marr and Al-Marashi, 2017: 326).

Post-conflict humanitarian medicine in Iraq will be complicated by political rivalries, including the federal-level Ministry of Health of Iraq, and its rival, subnational Ministry of Health in the KRG. This rivalry has only complicated the Iraqi State's capacity to interact with donor nations such as the Netherlands and Germany, the World Health Organization, and transnational medical organizations such as Doctors Without Borders (MSF), who are designing humanitarian strategies for dealing with the conflict.

These crises are also compounded by the socio-historical legacy of stigmas surrounding both rape and seeking mental health care as a sign of weakness in Iraq. Nevertheless, these problems for Iraq's future should not be reduced to an essentialist understanding of these stigmas surrounding mental health as a result of a cultural Middle Eastern or Islamic setting. The Iranian system has developed a network of mental health and addiction services centers that could provide a local model for Iraq and international organizations operating there.

Environmental security, energy security and food security

The environment, oil, energy and food are all interconnected in Iraq. Oil is the source of most of Iraq's revenue, but also the base of the nation's domestic energy needs. Energy also comes from hydroelectric infrastructure, its dams, which also regulate the flow of water for irrigation, which ultimately then relates to Iraq's food security. All of the aforementioned areas face a precarious future.

Oil

Foreign investment and oil contracts, as well as trade and local business, began to revive prior to the ISIS invasion in 2014, but development of Iraq's economic resources will be hampered by government divisions, corruption and inefficiency. Furthermore, Iraq's security in the near and long term will depend on the fluctuating price of oil. The reconstruction of Iraq has already been handicapped by years of low prices, compounded with the expenses incurred by combating ISIS. Complicating these matters are the tensions between the central government and the KRG, which have had a tumultuous past in agreeing on a revenue sharing deal, and as a result full-scale oil development will be hampered, particularly over the future status of Kirkuk.

Cooperation with foreign oil firms will be necessary to remedy the infrastructural problems in Iraq's lagging oil industry, as it needs water or gas injection for wells, greater supplies of electrical power, and major upgrades to refining and export facilities, such as pipelines. The same foreign cooperation will also be necessary for its hydroelectric infrastructure.

Hydroelectric infrastructure

Iraq's infrastructure, especially the hydroelectric system, is in a poor state owing to the long era of sanctions, wars and destruction or manipulation by insurgents. For example, ISIS's control of territory in Iraq enabled it to manipulate the flow of the Tigris and Euphrates rivers, either flooding or withholding water from downstream areas, while delivering water and electricity to its citizens to gain legitimacy. In early June 2015, after capturing Ramadi, ISIS closed the gates of a dam near the city, depriving downstream areas under Iraqi Government control of water.

When the United States agreed to fight ISIS, one of its first objectives was to eliminate targets around the Mosul dam. It was feared that ISIS could destroy the dam, creating a scenario where a 15-foot wall of water would crash into Baghdad, killing an estimated 500,000 people (Al-Marashi, 2015). US airstrikes enabled Iraqi forces to recapture the site in August 2014. Nonetheless, as of 2017, the Mosul dam still threatens to break due to a much older problem, erosion of its foundation and structural fatigue, and the risk would increase if there were rains that raised the water level. The Iraqi Government and an Italian company signed a USD 300 million deal to relieve fatigue on the dam, but an Iraqi environmentalist, Azzam Alwash (2016), argued this would only serve as a stop-gap measure. The cooperation of an upstream riparian, Turkey, was necessary to alleviate the stress on the dam by reducing the flow of the Tigris River.

Water and food security

Iraq's future in terms of hydroelectric energy and water for irrigation ultimately hinges on its upstream riparians, Turkey, which controls the headwaters of the Tigris and Euphrates river, in addition to Syria, which has dams on the Euphrates. Relations with Iran and its rivers will also affect Iraq.

Iraq will need to cooperate with all its upstream riparian neighbors to manage the problems of desertification and salination. For example, the Shatt al-Arab waterway has suffered from the diversion of rivers in Iran, mostly the Karun which had completely dried up where it flowed into the Shatt. The result was a backflow of seawater into the Shatt, which caused a shortage of drinking water in Basra as well as salinization of the soil. Seawater in the Faw district caused farmers to stop irrigating crops or breeding cattle (Marr and Al-Marashi, 2017: 321).

More modern methods were necessary to save and manage water resources. Increased aridity in southern Iraq also created creeping desertification of once arable land and an increase in sandstorms. Drought and lack of irrigation had turned fields around Amara in the south into dry beds. Iraq has also restored the southern marshlands and the wetlands habitat (which Saddam Hussein intentionally had dried up to curtail dissent in the area) and with them the fishing industry. The water ministry noted that it would take years to clean and restore Iraq's nearly 75,000 miles of canals (ibid.).

Conclusion

The survival of ISIS remnants and a civil war in neighboring Syria will continue to undermine Iraq's future security. A greater Iranian-Saudi competition for hegemony in the region will not abate anytime soon, and Iraq will become an arena for this conflict. Thus, the status of the Iraqi State itself remains more precarious than at any time in its history; the same could be said for its citizens who lack sufficient protection, either from government or social institutions, to allow for engagement in politics, the private sector, or education.

Iraq's greatest need for its future is the development of its human resources. Replenishing Iraq's skills, however, would take decades, and initiatives so far have yielded slow progress. From 2003 onwards, Iraq was left with its education and health sectors devastated, with rising unemployment and a middle-class flight that has deprived the country of its most precious resource. Iraq's political class need to make major investments, particularly in its youth, the generation from primary school to university whose education had been interrupted by the emergence of ISIS. The failure of the state to ameliorate the human security dilemmas outlined in this chapter creates the underlying conditions for alienated Iraqis to join groups like ISIS or the Shia militias, a lesson that the Iraqi political elites may have learned since 2014, but unfortunately lack the political unison and state capacity to address in the future.

References

Acikyildiz, B. (2014) *The Yezidis: The History of a Community, Culture and Religion*. London: I.B. Tauris.

Al-Ghazi, M. (2016) "La nihaya lil-milishiyyat fil-'iraq," ["No end to the militias in Iraq"], *Al-Monitor*, 7 August. Available at: www.al-monitor.com/pulse/ar/originals/2016/08/jaish-al-moumal-muqtada-sadr-iraq-iran-shiite-militias.html (Accessed: 19 September 2018).

Al-Khalisi, N. (2013) "The Iraqi Medical Brain Drain: A Cross-sectional Study", *International Journal of Health Services*, 43(2), pp. 63–78.

Al-Marashi, I. (2013) "Iraq's Security Outlook for 2013", Istituto per gli Studi di Politica Internazionale [Institute for the Study of International Politics], ISPI, Milan, 3 October. Available at: www.ispionline.it/it/pubblicazione/new-iraq-ten-years-later-9135 (Accessed: 19 September 2018).

Al-Marashi, I. (2015) "The Dawning of Hydro-Terrorism", *Al-Jazeera*, 19 June. Available at: www.aljazeera.com/indepth/opinion/2015/06/dawning-hydro-terrorism-150617102429224.html (Accessed: 19 September 2018).

Al-Marashi, I. (2017a) "How to Resolve the Kirkuk Crisis", *Middle East Eye*, 17 October. Available at: www.middleeasteye.net/columns/how-resolve-kirkuk-crisis-1758586344 (Accessed: 19 September 2018).

Al-Marashi, I. (2017b) "What Future for Iraq: Unity and Partition after Mosul", ISPI, Milan. Available at: www.ispionline.it/it/pubblicazione/after-mosul-re-inventing-iraq-17080 (Accessed: 19 September 2018).

Alwash, A. (2016) "The Mosul Dam: Turning a Potential Disaster into a Win-Win Solution", *Wilson Center*, 6 April. Available at: www.wilsoncenter.org/publication/the-mosul-dam-turning-potential-disaster-win-win-solution (Accessed: 9 November 2018).

Chulov, M. (2014) "40,000 Iraqis Stranded on Mountain as ISIS Jihadists Threaten Death", *The Guardian*, 7 August. Available at: www.theguardian.com/world/2014/aug/07/40000-iraqis-stranded-mountain-isis-death-threat (Accessed: 19 September 2018).

CIA World Fact Book (2018) "Iraq". Available at: www.cia.gov/library/publications/the-world-factbook/geos/iz.html (Accessed: 19 September 2018).

Ditmars, H. (2016) *Iraqi Narrative of US Invasion Struggles to Be Heard*, Middle East Institute, Washington DC, 26 May. Available at: www.mei.edu/content/article/iraqi-narrative-us-invasion-struggles-be-heard (Accessed: 19 September 2018).

Economist Intelligence Unit (2015) "Iraq". Available at: http://country.eiu.com/iraq (Accessed: 19 September 2018).

Goudsouzian, T. and Fatah. L. (2015) "Is Sinjar the New Kobane?" *Al-Jazeera*, 13 November. Available at: www.aljazeera.com/indepth/features/2015/11/analysis-sinjar-kobane-151113081340990.html (Accessed: 19 September 2018).

Haddad, F. (2011) *Sectarianism in Iraq: Antagonistic Visions of Unity*. New York & London: Hurst & Co.

Hassan, F. and Coker, M. (2018) "Suicide Bombings in Baghdad Puncture Newfound Hope", *New York Times*, 15 January. Available at: www.nytimes.com/2018/01/15/world/middleeast/baghdad-bombings.html (Accessed: 19 September 2018).

Iddon, P. (2016) "The Death Knell of Iraq's Christian Community", *Rudaw*, 1 June. Available at: http://rudaw.net/english/middleeast/iraq/06012016 (Accessed: 19 September 2018).

International Crisis Group (ICG) (2016) "Fight or Flight: The Desperate Plight of Iraq's 'Generation 2000'," *Middle East Report* No. 169, Brussels, 8 August. Available at: www.crisisgroup.org/middle-east-north-africa/gulf-and-arabian-peninsula/iraq/fight-or-flight-desperate-plight-iraq-s-generation-2000 (Accessed: 19 September 2018).

Iraq Mission (no date) Displacement Tracking Matrix, The International Organization for Migration. http://iraqdtm.iom.int/ (Accessed: 19 September 2018).

Katzman, K. and Humud, C. (2016) *Iraq: Politics and Governance*, Congressional Research Service, Washington DC, 16 September, pp. 1–40.

Mamouri, A. (2016) "Ba'ad tafjirat al-Karada tawajah al-hakuma dhagutan ijtima'iyya l-tahsin al-amin" ["After the Explosions in Karada, Social Pressure on the Government to Improve Security"], *Al-Monitor*, 13 July. Available at: www.al-monitor.com/pulse/ar/originals/2016/07/iraq-karrada-security-baghdad.html (Accessed: 19 September 2018).

Marr, P. and Al-Marashi, I. (2017) *The Modern History of Iraq*. 4th ed. London and New York: Routledge.

Mironova, V. and Hussein, M. (2017) "The New ISIS Insurgency: What Jihadists Do after Losing Territory", *Foreign Affairs*, 9 January. Available at: www.foreignaffairs.com/articles/iraq/2017-01-09/new-isis-insurgency (Accessed: 19 September 2018).

Rathmell, A. (2005) *Developing Iraq's Security Sector: The Coalitional Provisional Authority's Experience*, RAND Corporation, Santa Monica, CA. Available at: www.rand.org/pubs/monographs/MG365.html (Accessed: 19 September 2018).

Rathmell, A. (2007) *Fixing Iraq's Internal Security Forces: Why Is Reform of the Ministry of Interior So Hard?* Center for International and Strategic Studies, Washington DC, pp. 1–21.

Raya J. (2014) "Who are the Yazidis and Why is ISIS Hunting Them?" *The Guardian*, 11 August. Available at: www.theguardian.com/world/2014/aug/07/who-yazidi-isis-iraq-religion-ethnicity-mountains (Accessed: 19 September 2018).

Sassoon, J. (2008) *The Iraqi Refugees: The New Crisis in the Middle East*. London: I. B. Tauris.

Schweitzer, M. (2017) "Beyond a Military Victory: Reconstructing Iraq after ISIS", *The Global Observatory*, 17 January. Available at: https://theglobalobservatory.org/2017/01/isis-iraq-united-nations-reconstruction/ (Accessed: 19 September 2018).

Steele, J. (2017) "Sectarian Militias Have No Place in Iraq, Says Muqtada al-Sadr", *Middle East Eye*, 20 March. Available at: www.middleeasteye.net/news/muqtada-al-sadr-iraq-1637609574 (Accessed: 19 September 2018).

Swain, A. and Jägerskog, A. (2016) *Emerging Security Threats in the Middle East: The Impact of Climate Change and Globalization*. Lanham, MD: Rowman and Littlefield.

UNHCR (no date) "Iraq". Available at: www.unhcr.org/iraq.html (Accessed: 19 September 2018).

Wasim, B. (2013) "Ghasal al-'ar:'alaqah jadaliyya bayn al-dam wa al-sharaf", ["Honor Killing: The Current Relationship between Blood and Honor"], *Al-Monitor*, 11 October. Available at: www.al-monitor.com/pulse/ar/contents/articles/originals/2013/10/iraq-honor-crimes-increase.html (Accessed: 9 November 2018).

Wasim, B. (2015) "Hal mazalit mawasim al-hijra min al-'iraq maftuha?" ["Does the Open Seasons of Migration from Iraq Continue?"] *Al-Monitor*, 19 April. Available at: www.al-monitor.com/pulse/ar/contents/articles/originals/2015/04/iraq-youth-emigration-lack-security-west.html (Accessed: 9 November 2018).

Wheeler, S. (2016) "Yazidi Women after Slavery: Trauma", *Open Democracy*, 18 April. Available at: www.opendemocracy.net/5050/skye-wheeler/yazidi-women-after-slavery-comes-lasting-trauma (Accessed: 19 September 2018).

Witty, D. (2015) *The Iraqi Counter Terrorism Service*, Brookings Institution, Washington DC, March, pp. 1–45.

Woertz, E. (2017) "Food Security in Iraq: Results from Quantitative and Qualitative Surveys", *Food Security*, 9(3), pp. 511–512.

8

SECURITY AND SYRIA

From "the security state" to the source of multiple insecurities

Philippe Droz-Vincent

Introduction

Syria is without comparison a subject for the study of security in the Middle East. Since independence, Syria has harbored a deep paranoia over its security as a result of the strategic positioning of the country, in particular as a major party to the Arab–Israeli conflict. The unquestioned postulate, cultivated especially during Hafez al-Assad's years, was that Syria was in search of security based on military means and was a key to broader security perspectives in the Middle East, hence displaying the picture of a state whose security perspective was cast in conventional (realist) alloy.

Such a view could be questioned in line with new visions of security fashionable since the 1990s: with the central role of levels (from individuals to states to regions and to system) and different sectors (not just through the lens of the military-strategic activity). Security in Syria could then be understood as a complex construction emerging not just from a balance of power or a balance of threats. Power with the accumulation of military capabilities concealed the building of an enduring authoritarian regime and offset many state weaknesses behind the maintenance of a pervasive internal security apparatus. As a consequence, individuals and sub-state units as crucial security referents would harbor very different visions of (in)security. And conversely for the Assad regime, domestic threats were not separated from the influence of outside powers in a model of security (*mukhabarat*) state.

The surprising events of March 2011, namely an uprising in a particularly "securitized" setting where few would have forecast it before, allowed, at least among some sectors of society, the emergence of new hopes of transforming state–security relations from bottom up and hence how security was conceived in Syria. That was lost after 2012–13 with the descent of the uprising into the chaos of a civil war, a card also played by the Syrian regime to survive in power. And external calculations about a renewed regional security architecture in the Middle East based on the potential transformation of Syria proved elusive. Rather than helping rebuild the region, Syria has been transformed into a wellspring of insecurities connected to other regional and even international sources of threats.

Philippe Droz-Vincent

Syria as the archetypical insecure state in the Middle East

All states do not face the same degree of dangers and Syria is a particularly threatened state. Syria as a nation-state was a relatively new state carved out of the ashes of the Ottoman Empire by the French mandate under the League of Nations (1920). Security was very early elevated to a prominent role in independent Syria (1946). Syria was in a precarious position and under constant threat of submergence by great powers or the intrigues of regional powers: the impact of the Cold War (in the 1950s the US wanted a trans-Syrian pipeline to carry Saudi oil to the Mediterranean when the USSR supported Syrian independence); competing Cold War alliances around the Baghdad Pact and the Eisenhower doctrine; the appetites of the Hashemites from Transjordan considering Syria as the mother country of the Arabs and intriguing with Syrian politicians; the Iraqi influence; the creation of Israel which bordered Syria; and the first Arab–Israeli war. In the 1950s–1960s, international, regional and domestic politics came together in an unprecedented degree of turmoil for Syria, displaying the (regional) "Struggle for Syria" to borrow the title of the classic book by Patrick Seale (1965). No wonder that Syria has harbored an active concern about lack of security.

As stated by Arnold Wolfers (1962) (recalling Walter Lippman), security points to the protection of values or the absence of threats to acquired values. And then the demand for national security is primarily normative in character. The creation of Syria was accompanied by various nationalist traumas and a sense of territorial amputation with enduring effects that impacted on national security threat assessments: with boundaries inherited from colonial mandates in the context of the Sykes-Picot drawing of zones of influence; the Hussein (the Hashemite family)– MacMahon secret correspondence and the Balfour declaration; the detachment of Lebanon from geographical Syria (*al-Sham*) in 1920 and of the Alexandretta (Hatay) *sandjak* ceded to Kemalist Turkey in 1939 (Lundgren, 2014). States of the Middle East like Syria do not constitute the textbook entities much loved by political science (Korany et al., 1993; Azar and Chung in Moon, 1988). In Syria, the specific feature adding a dimension of complexity was that the range of "national interests" or core values due to be "secured" varied and ranged from the narrow cause of the national self (the Syrian nation-state as inherited from the French mandate, or *watan* in Arabic) to larger interests with regional dimensions, in particular related to the prospect of a single Arab nation (*qawm*) and Syria as the guardian of some Arab nationalist ideals. References to a geographic Syrian entity (*bilad al-Sham,* Greater Syria) understood as a political project due to be undertaken under the leadership of Damascus and which included Lebanon, Jordan and the former Palestine mandate, shaped some influential visions of (Greater) Syrian interests equated with those of the Arabs elsewhere, in a kind of mission on behalf of them. Security in Syria was then associated with demands which were ascribed to various supra-national levels and earned it a poor reputation as a neighbor (Kerr, 1971; Colombe, 1973).

Whatever the precise meaning of security, no other state has been so resolute in protecting its position and so adept at muscling its way to center stage to ensure that its security interests must be accommodated. If the "referent" of security (the Syrian nation-state, Greater Syria, an Arab entity) was changing, it was underpinned by military power in the eyes of Damascus rulers, so that Syria has been cast from conventional (realist) alloy in terms of security. Syria ranks among those nations which have experienced wars and high degrees of tension, a setting that exerted fascination for Kissinger to whom the aphorism "you can't make war in the Middle East without Egypt and you can't make peace without Syria" was attributed. The search for security by Syrian leaders took the form of an unrestrained race for armaments. It was at the core of Syria's alliance with the USSR: Syria first purchased Soviet arms in 1955 reinforced by a major economic and technical agreement in 1957; relations blossomed after the Ba'athi coups in 1963 then 1966 and Soviet involvement increased after each war with Israel.

Furthermore, new political actors were embodying Syria's endeavor to maximize its security. Hectic internal debates over security coincided with the rise of new political currents expressing high expectations for the country, especially middle-class officers coming out of the Homs military academy – whose entry was eased as the newly independent Syrian State was building its army, a key attribute of new-found sovereignty – and new politicians related to the Ba'ath party and various revolutionary nationalist trends. *Coups d'état* by nationalist officers (three in 1949 alone) in various relations with new civilian politicians signaled the strong endeavor of these new elites to foster changes. This new leadership was particularly sensitive to security threats, either in the objective sense (the absence of threat) or in the subjective sense (the absence of fear about core values), and to the search for stability in Syria. In the name of security and stability, they even surrendered for some time Syria's sovereignty into a total union with Egypt during the short-lived United Arab Republic (1958–1961).

After his arrival by a coup in November 1970, General Hafez al-Assad embodied this perspective. He astutely exploited Syria's location to transform his country from a weak and insecure state ("The Struggle for Syria") where numerous rivalries were played to a militarily powerful and assertive one ("the Struggle for the Middle East" to borrow the tile of another classic by Patrick Seale 1989). Syria borders Israel, Lebanon, Jordan, Turkey and Iraq and is a key crossroads between the Mediterranean and the Gulf, with its doors open to many geopolitical realms and security topics (the Palestinian–Israeli conflict, the Kurdish problem, the regional sharing of water, the expansion of Iran in the Levant after the 1979 revolution, etc.), hence constituting Syria as a key player, also in search of its own security. Through tenacious diplomacy over three decades, Hafez al-Assad made Syria a player in its own right. His foreign policy became more "state-like", though pan-Arab slogans were still used to legitimize enduring regional endeavors. Hafez al-Assad struggled to mobilize all available resources to foster Syria's security and further relied on Soviet military, economic and diplomatic assistance, making Syria one of the closest Soviet allies (along with Iraq) and one of its major clients, with a Treaty of Security and Cooperation signed in October 1980. He built Syria as a major party to the Arab–Israeli conflict and after 1974–1978 the only frontline Arab state that posed a military threat to the Syrian–Israeli border, complemented by a Syrian–Israeli interface or deterrence relation in Lebanon (Evron, 1987; Ma'oz, 1995; Dawisha, 1980). He built Syria as a state uniquely positioned either to facilitate an Arab–Israeli peace settlement or at least to endow it with credibility, or conversely to impede peace by mobilizing rejectionists (and even terrorist means), intimidating those willing to sign for peace and rejecting the legitimacy of an agreement. In the 1970s–1980s, in the name of security, Syria under Assad variously intervened in Lebanon (1976–2005), supported Turkey's Kurds until on the verge of war with Turkey in 1998 (Lawson, 1996), threatened to invade Jordan, blocked Iraqi oil shipments to the Mediterranean to support Iran during the Iran–Iraq war (1980–88), interfered with the Palestinian movements (Sayigh, 1997), maintained the instability of Israel's northern border, and even intimidated Gulf countries despite not having the capabilities to project power there. The security trigger was expansive and set high by the Assad regime: Syria became a power casting its shadow and influence beyond its borders.

The un-mature "regional security complex": An insecure community in the Middle East

During the Hafez al-Assad years, Syria concentrated its energy on the struggle for the Middle East, viewing it mainly as a fierce contest with Israel. Threats from other neighbors were prevalent, not just because of proximity, others' capabilities, the ensuing security dilemmas – for instance with Turkey over borders, water or the latter's cooperation with Israel in the 1990s – and possible shifts in their intentions (from defense to offense). This "regional security complex" (Buzan and Waever, 2009) was also complexified by a pervasive game of regional identity politics based on the discourse and symbols of Arab nationalism with internal security consequences, hence the historic rivalry with brotherly Ba'athi Iraq (Barnett, 1998; Mufi, 1996).

Beyond the stated principal strategic goal of the return of the Golan heights to its control, Syria's search for security was mainly driven by a pervasive balance of threats against Israel (on the difference between balance of threats and balance of power, see Walt, 1990). Neighboring Israel was a state that combined power proximity to Syria's soft underbelly – Damascus is not far from Israeli borders; the Beqaa valley and the Damascus–Beirut road are an open corridor into Syria – a nuclear deterrent capacity, an offensive edge, a powerful external ally (the US) and a tendency to pre-empt threats and act offensively. By contrast, Syria had few offensive capabilities –mostly air defenses, most of its forces were built and deployed operationally to secure the regime in Damascus – neither a nuclear deterrent nor a potent ally (the USSR did not play for Syria the role of the US for Israel). Tellingly, the Golan front remained quiet despite repeated military confrontations with Israel in Lebanon, directly or through Hezbollah. Syria rather grappled with acquiring the means to build a "power of resistance" (Wolfers, 1962), a topic also boasted by the Assad regime with the thematic of the "resistance" (*al-muqawama*), namely the means to resist an attack or deter a would-be attacker rather than to win in wars against Israel: with chemical weapons and ballistic missile capabilities; with the Iranian alliance since 1979; and with Syria's ability to entangle Israel by keeping a domineering influence on Lebanon.

Furthermore, Syria moved in a particularly challenging environment. And Hafez al-Assad showed an ability to reposition Syria favorably within the regionally changing concert/balance. Many Syrian security assumptions were based on a relatively stable bipolar world. The Gulf war of 1991, then the end of the Soviet Union, proved the inaccuracy of such assumptions in the Gorbachev era. Yet Syria repositioned itself with its decision to attend the international conference to resolve the Arab–Israeli conflict sponsored by a dominant US (and a declining USSR) in July 1991. Syria's security search was also made paranoid (for good or bad reasons) by the fact that many US administrations excluded Syria, in particular from the peace process, or at least did not fully involve it, favoring separate tracks between Israel and, respectively, Egypt (1978), the PLO (1993) and Jordan (1994). Syria reacted to policies followed by the US, from the Reagan administration that viewed Syria as a Soviet surrogate and a terrorist state to be punished or contained to the George W. Bush administration after the invasion of Iraq in 2003 (Drysdale and Hinnebusch, 1993; Rabinovich, 2008). The hectic and changing regional context was again replicated in the 2000s. It did not seem threatening as Syria concentrated on presidential succession in the summer of 2000; yet two months later the second *intifada* began and Ariel Sharon was elected as Prime Minister in Israel; September 11 then radically revamped the regional balance and, as a consequence of the US invasion of Iraq in 2003, the US became virtually Syria's neighbor, with neo-conservatives in power in Washington airing direct threats against Syria as "the next one" (after Iraq), on par with Iran (Droz-Vincent 2007).

It is difficult to tell how far Syria deviated from a rational reaction to objective threats. Yet the un-mature Middle Eastern security community left Syria in a frantic struggle for more security or at least highly sensitive to balances of threats or fear. Syrian decision-makers have tended to view relations with third countries in terms of how they impacted upon their regional balance with Israel with the necessity to maintain what they called the strategic parity, *al-tawazon al-istrateji*. And they harbored a deep suspicion of the US because of its support for Israel; however, in the 1990s–2000s they acknowledged that a settlement with Israel would come out under

US facilitating support. As a consequence of their active concern for security, Syrian leaders felt entitled to additional guarantees of security. In the 1980s, they amassed power sufficient to achieve an appreciable defense capability against Israel. What Syrians in the 1990s understood as "an honorable settlement" with Israel entailed not only the return of occupied Golan (the return to the lines of 6 June 1967) but also an acceptable outcome on the Palestinian–Israeli negotiations and some specific relations between Syria and Lebanon whereby the status of Lebanon would be under Syrian hegemony and not fall under Israeli influence (Cobban, 2000; Rabinovich, 2009). The alliance with Iran was an unnatural one between an Islamist revolution and the Hafez al-Assad regime (that crushed the Muslim Brothers' insurgents in 1982), not based on ideological solidarity but rather on a common search for security. It was seen as teetering in the 1990s but it endured as a key pillar under Hafez al-Assad and was reinforced under Bashar al-Assad. The pursuit of militarized security was also likely to ring a sympathetic chord inside Syria. Even opposition figures in the 1990s lauded Assad's foreign policy record. Conversely, external powers, in the first place the US, tended to view Syria as a hard-line maximalist actor with a record of obstructing peace processes. And high security aspirations in Syria tended to make it suspect of hiding aggressive aims, displaying an irredentist pan-Arab ideology and even using terrorism. And the dangers of the defense dilemma (the fear of war, the fear of dynamics that weapons might usher in; Buzan, 1991) did not distract Syria from the search for security by military means.

There were few moments during which security in Syria was not understood practically with the formula of militarized realist security and according to a zero-sum logic – what Syria or Arabs will lose, Israel will gain. Syria has not been a country that placed confidence in international negotiations, cooperation or model behavior (the role of norms) to fulfill its security interests. In the first half of the 1990s prospects for peace for a short moment raised in Damascus the possibility of some cooperative behavior – though fears of an Israeli economic dominance even in peace time mitigated such views in Damascus (Perthes, 1994). In the beginning of the 2000s, when Bashar prioritized what he called internal "modernization", some members of his team were prepared to offer a more accommodating regional and international foreign policy (Perthes, 2006). But these rare moments did not allow a reformulation of security in new terms. Security is in general a burden (as materialized in the first instance with the heavy burden of extravagant defense expenses), hence the tendency of nations to minimize such efforts. The limits to efforts for security in the Syrian State were placed very high and security was paid by sacrifices of other values or objectives as everything was expedient for the purpose of enhancing security. The overriding and permanent concern for security was a domineering constraint that justified everything at least until a severe economic crisis in the mid-1980s and until economic reforms (and social expenditures) were allowed by Hafez al-Assad to become competitors with the defense budget in the 1990s.

The security state, **mukhabarat** *everywhere, the absence of human security and the prevalence of fear*

Theoretical reflections in general on what security is and that have gained some prominence after the end of the Cold War help focus on new ways to unpack security. Whatever the importance of militarized security as embodied by the state in Syria, other and (at the time) unseen dimensions of (in)security away from a military strategic perspective rooted in the status quo proved critical and with a potential for change in 2011, at least for a brief moment.

On the one hand, the "horizontal" broadening of the meaning of security points to a necessary shift in the analytical focus from a military-only perspective to other (political, economic, social, environmental) sectors that are crucial to assess security and weight security differently from classic realist analysis (Buzan, 1991). For instance, concerning the economic sector, emerging new trends unrelated to security at first sight proved critical. In the 2000s under Bashar al-Assad, the reform process (called "modernization") of the Syrian economy deeply polarized Syrian society between the countryside/rural areas and the urban centers of Damascus or Aleppo where most of the investments took place in the hands of a select group of private entrepreneurs close to the Assad family and its associates. That created a huge gap, unprecedented in Syria's history since at least the 1950s, and shattered the equilibriums based on redistribution established by Hafez al-Assad after 1970 (Heydemann, 1999). Syria's rural regions around Deraa, Jisr al-Shughur, Idlib, Douma, Homs and Hama suffered from disinvestments, reduction in the availability of Ba'ath-supplied services (fertilizers), and decrease in public employment (UNDP, 2005; Khaled et al., 2011;[1] De Châtel, 2014) – the regime grew out of some of the same rural provinces (the Hawran, the Mediterranean coast, Deir ez-Zor) in the 1960s. Furthermore, Bashar al-Assad's institutional reforms (Hinnebusch, 2011), by removing old guard figures, broking personal fiefdoms and promoting a new generation, in fact kept institutions (parliament, municipal councils, branches of the Ba'ath) dysfunctional and overinvested in the security state. Security services, a predominantly 'Alawi, thuggish and arrogant force, took on their tasks of day-to-day governance – and local administrative bodies became the embodiment of a predatory culture in which resources were skimmed off for the benefit of the *mukhabarat*. The domineering state apparatus with its predatory rent-seeking elites and bureaucracies sapped the wealth of the country and created the seeds of a politics of social despair that exploded in 2011.

Also with huge medium-term consequences, the environmental sector let its importance be known. A prolonged period of lingering drought starting in 2003 plagued the country, in particular rural areas, in a general context of Syrian reckless policies which had been carried out under the name of "food security" and that resulted in a gradual deterioration of the country's water resources (Mohtadi, 2012). Rural Syria (and its peasantry) was furthermore hit by an especially severe drought from 2007 to 2010. To some extent this environmental factor was beyond the regime's control, but inept and corrupt government exacerbated matters through mismanagement of agricultural resources and corruption. Security services took bribes linked to endemic illegal drilling. And the plundering of underground water prompted displacement of hundreds of thousands (possible even 1.2 to 1.3 million), creating a wave of migrations from the countryside to over-crowded cities, at a time when Bashar's reforms shrank the labor market's demand in poorly skilled jobs. Most of the migrations flooded toward small or medium cities like Hama, Homs or cities on the coast that lacked infrastructures or capabilities to absorb such flows, with the parallel reduction of subsidies and disinvestment – and after 2003, Syrian cities had already to absorb huge Iraqi migrations. That transformed these cities into a boiling social pot in 2011.

On the other hand, the "vertical" expansion of security does not consider relevant threats only at the state level but also in terms of "human security" as defined by the Human Development Reports of the UNDP since the 1990s (in particular UNDP, 2009). It raises a wider net of relevant issues at various levels of insecurity from the individual (human rights), the intermediate (ethnic or confessional groups) and the global levels, along with the nation-state, all interacting to produce resulting security predicaments.

Most importantly, the focus on state security can also serve as a cloak for other objectives: national security is not just an ambiguous symbol but also a code word for regime security. Hafez al-Assad was said to have engineered the most systematic development of institutions in Syria since independence (Seale, 1991). But these institutions were an instrument of power building and the way in which power networks related to him were infused into the state from top to local levels (governors, Ba'athi branch leaders, technocrats in state enterprises, security heads, parliamentarians, mayors, etc.). Hafez al-Assad used the state and the Ba'ath party to build a network (neo-*asabiyya*) of power with a permanent concern for the security of the state and the regime – and both were equated in the regime's propaganda (Droz-Vincent 1999). From 1963 onwards, the Syrian regime continuously operated under emergency rule which suspended all rights and liberties for citizens. The security paradigm in Syria functioned as a way to protect and safeguard the Assad regime against both internal and external threats.

Concretely, a lot of questions or even areas were "securitized" or considered of strategic importance. The southern border with Jordan was deemed of military strategic value. In Deraa from where protests scaled up into a national movement in 2011, security services took advantage of a 2008 presidential decree that subjected land sales and construction in cities close to border areas to their prior approval, hence extortion. And, in a concrete way, on many topics, the man responsible for security – known by the generic name of *mukhabarat* by Syrians to encompass various rival services working in parallel under the interior or the military – had the final say on numerous matters. Tellingly, the first demands of the 2011 uprising were not "the fall of the regime" (*isqat al-nizam*) but the end of the tentacular grip of the security services on daily life that did not allow Syrians to proceed with any administrative or commercial matter without their approval.

Security in Syria was not just a function of the will of others and neighbors (in the first place Israel) but also expanded in a kind of compulsion for national security constantly reinstated by the Assad regime. The Syrian regime felt beleaguered by various threats, from Israel to a number of Arab opponents and, at home, it felt unsecure, a feeling said to have caused Assad to run a repressive system internally and to rely on tight 'Alawi networks. The sense of being plagued by internal political and economic vulnerabilities and by the uncertainty of external support to a Syrian power allegedly said to be in constant decline was a constant fear among elites in power in Damascus. Therefore, the security of the Syrian State/regime was not synonymous with the security of all its peoples: security for 'Alawi-dominated Syria was tied to a mythology of Syria as an embattled country and the core of Arab struggles; and conversely, the insecurity of the 'Alawi-dominated power could be conceived as a source of insecurity for its Sunni "plurality", if it existed, with huge differences between a Damascene and a Sunni of Aleppo or between urban and rural Sunnis (from Deraa, *rif* Dimachq or Idlib) or between Kurds and Arabs. The pervasive role of security was related to the specific nature of the state and its governing elites in this respect.

In Syria, security (*al-amn*) had a dreadful meaning well understood by Syrians (Pearlman, 2016), a very pervasive definition whereby its external and internal dimensions were conflated. A casualty of the need for security was the ordinary citizen who felt defenseless vis-à-vis the state, however rich or eminent he or she might be – and all 'Alawis did not feel secure (from the threat/scrutiny of the *mukhabarat*) when they were not part of the regime's core networks. Security at the top created a whole perception of insecurity among individuals, families, communities, villages. The conclusions of the Arab Human Development Report of 2009, when it stated that state security might at times be achieved at the expense of the individual security of its citizens, well applied to Syria. Human security with its focus upon emancipation from oppression as well as want was clearly lacking in Syria. For 40 years, the Assad regime (whether father or son) functioned on the basis of violence, with massacres (most prominently in Hama in February 1982) and prisons (hundreds or even thousands of people were detained as political prisoners), or at least the prospect of them ("the wall of fear", *hajez al-khawf*) – see the so-called "prison literature" (*adab al-sujun*) by novelists Mustafa Khalifa, Ghassan al-Jabai, Ibrahim Samuil, Hasiba Abd al-Rahman and Barra al-Sarraj. The only and brief change occurred when

Bashar al-Assad came to power and promised reforms in his inaugural speech, a period called the 2000 Damascus Spring (*rabi'a Dimachq*). The authoritarian security paradigm enforced in Syria has utterly failed in providing security in its enlarged meaning and with society as its "referent".

The 2011 uprising and the crushing of the demand for human security

Security resurfaced at the core of the 2011 uprising, in a surprising new way for a country where security seemed monopolized by the Assad regime for years. The 2011 uprising was a kind of emancipation move whose basic referent was society and individuals (Booth, 1991): it was an endeavor to rebuild new state–security relationships based on human security and to dislodge the "security state" (*mukhabarat* state) as the primary referent of security. The root causes of the uprising lay here: the spark came from the model of Tunisia and Egypt, but the root causes were a sense of social insecurity that was reflected in the enlarged nature of the protest movement. Syrian citizens understood their own state as the primary source of insecurity, with threats to the well-being of individuals and their interests deriving not from their neighbors' armed forces (in the first place the occupation of the Golan), but from political oppression, economic collapse, overpopulation, confessional manipulations, scarcity, etc. Demonstrations expressed the depth and breadth of years of frustration and sufferings. The uprising gave rise to an unprecedented sense of awareness and responsibility among huge strata of the Syrian population. And in particular, the young organizers of the various Facebook pages "Syrian Revolution 2011" didn't have the ten years of infrastructure that social movements had in Egypt, but they understood that this was a defining moment and they thought it was their chance to promote change – also because many knew what the Assad regime was capable of.

Sowing insecurity from above: Counter-insurgency without "winning hearts and minds"

The beginning of the uprising was a rebuke to those pessimists who ruled out the possibility of change, in a bottom-up perspective on security. March 2011 was a defining moment that might have changed the ideas that had helped Syria in developing its security perspective, with more emphasis on cooperation rather than on the raising of arsenals. This was lost quickly, furthermore when the regime stuck to power and played another strategy, namely the systematic sowing of insecurity inside society.

The regime was obsessed with a desire to contain and crush demonstrations: in a much anticipated speech before parliament in March 2011, Bashar al-Assad never apologized nor offered real reforms; from late July 2011, the regime chose what was called the "security solution" (*al-hall al-amni*) based on the conviction that excessive leniency was the problem – a special committee whose conclusions were leaked to the opposition concluded that the reason for the fall of Tunisian President Ben Ali and Egyptian President Mubarak had been their failure to crush protests at the moment of their inception (Abbas, 2012). The killing of 100 soldiers around Jisr al-Shughur in June 2011 – a town where Hafez al-Assad in 1980 ordered a helicopter raid that killed hundreds – changed the nature of the uprising. The official media sought to disparage the opposition's protests equating them with support for Israel's bad tricks, US hegemony, Saudi or Qatari involvement, sectarianism, Syria's partition and terrorism. Then, at the end of 2011, the military effort (*al-mahjub al-harbi*) became the official narrative with the rationale that a handful of decisive military operations against residual pockets stood between the crisis and its resolution. By seeking to force consent by repression, the Assad regime pushed the uprising toward armed resistance. It was also a way to dismiss the protest movement, disparage its nature (and its pacific, *selmiyye*, character) and tip the balance to a vicious cycle of nascent civil war. In early 2012, armed opposition began to adopt new methods and increasingly relied on guerrilla warfare with the rising efficiency of the nucleus of the rebel Free Syrian Army (FSA). The regime lost ground in terms of its loss of control of large swaths of the Syrian territory and was no longer able to govern the entire territory (Droz-Vincent, 2014).

The regime also sowed the seeds of insecurity in the country. In this sense, the rise of sectarianism/confessionalism was not just a religious matter but also a social–political factor of prime importance. Divisions based on confessionalism existed in Syria – the regime was 'Alawi in its heights, but not necessarily in its policies – but, after 2011, they were used to create mechanisms of direct loyalty. Many 'Alawi or minority intellectuals and activists, either a number of old activists for decades or younger generations, were engaged in local coordination (*tansiqiyyat mahaliyya*) with the opposition in 2011. Yet, with violence and sectarian attacks on the rise, minorities in general became fearful for what could happen, with the Assad regime promoting itself as a shield of stability for the Syrian ethno-confessional mosaic and the guardian of minorities against the alleged Sunni majority and alleged extremists. The regime took 'Alawis and other minorities hostage. Numerous 'Alawis who had settled in areas around big cities to work for the state and who owed their presence in the city since the 1970s to the Hafez al-Assad regime were told that they were defending their lands and homes, hence bringing to the surface deeply ingrained feelings of insecurity among 'Alawis – the security services were not privileged elite army units but were composed of underpaid and overworked 'Alawis. The regime's rag-tag militias (called *Shabbiha* by Syrians) deliberately stirred up ethno-confessional violence to scare minorities and 'Alawis into backing the regime by deliberately and cynically staging sectarian incidents in confessionally mixed areas: the *Shabbiha* thugs were not uniformly 'Alawi, especially in Aleppo where they were Sunnis, but in other regions such as central Syria, they hailed from pro-regime communities and came to represent, in the eyes of many Sunnis, the 'Alawi sect. Communal strife with predominantly Sunni armed groups facing off with predominantly 'Alawi security forces, *Shabbiha* or neighborhood vigilantes involved in tit-for-tat killings, was the main source of insecurity. And in Syria, as in general, the rationale for conflict is always intimate (with neighbors) rather than based on big narratives.

And the regime polarized society and pushed it to the brink with measures designed to increase the suffering of beleaguered communities in the hope of making them bow in obedience. With one month of relentless bombing on a tightly knit conservative neighborhood of Homs – in 2011, the city was called "the cradle of the revolution", when the events of the 1980s were associated with the name of Hama – and summary killings, disappearances, arbitrary arrests, various forms of abuse, military operations that were tantamount to collective punishments, and starvation of rebel areas. Many Syrians shifted from blaming elements of the regime (*mukhabarat* figures) and economic profiteers (e.g. Rami Makhluf), to blaming the regime and finally the 'Alawi community as a whole. And armed opposition groups took on a more pronounced religious ideological underpinning. Taboos were broken in gruesome massacres and the dissemination of intolerant slogans and chants ("we did not use to hate the 'Alawi, now we do", "Sunni blood is one", "we will exterminate the 'Alawis" vs "God, Bashar and that's all"). This fueled confessional security dilemmas among citizens who for a long time, in their overwhelming majority, had not been motivated by sectarianism/confessionalism (Posen, 1993 on Yugoslavia; Stedman et al., 2002).

Emancipation from below foiled: Fragmented militias, recombinant regime, radical (takfiri) jihadists and refugees

At its inception in 2011, the protest movement was especially broad-based and cross-cutting in terms of confessions, generations or socio-economic boundaries – and in particular, many an 'Alawi whether intellectual or villager felt the neglect of the Bashar al-Assad regime and resented the way she or he was treated and how her or his community was taken hostage by the regime's wrongdoings. Elements of civil society emerged among young activists, businessmen, doctors, religious leaders, etc., in sophisticated forms of self-rule embodied by local coordination councils (*tansiqiyyat mahaliyya*) – at a time when the regime was hell-bent on proving that radical Islamists were in control, a false assumption as early as 2011.

Syrian society was able to develop collective action on a remarkable scale as the regime was no longer able to govern the whole territory after 2012. Local coordination emerged as a kind of new public space: they acted as spontaneous media (as citizen journalists); they organized the demonstrations and decided on the Friday slogans through the Syrian Revolution 2011 Facebook page with evidence of good coordination between local committees; they shielded people from the regime, arranging safe havens and helping citizens flee from the grip of security services; mid-2012, they acted as bottom-up institutions that filled the void left by the retreating regime. Further networking developed when they joined the National Coordination for Syrian Revolution and Opposition Forces (called *Al-I'tilaf...*) in November 2012 and provincial council movements in February 2013. They had tense and even conflictual relations over priorities with local armed groups co-opted under the large umbrella of the FSA. Some battalion (*kata'ib*) leaders started to act as warlords, were more interested in the lucrative war economy (siege-busting, tunnels, checkpoints, smuggling routes) or committed human rights violations. And *tansiqiyyat* were deliberately targeted by the regime, then by the Russian intervention (after 2015), and also by the Islamic State (Da'esh) and even the Kurdish PYD (see below). Local coordinations were surviving, sometimes repressed by local rebel commanders or at least with interferences from them, but they never managed to catch up (for the example of one region that was a strong place of civic activism, Douma in the Damascus Ghouta, see Lund, 2016).

The opposition found it difficult to join ranks. It prioritized fighting the regime at any cost rather than building an independent and broad-based movement and rooting itself deeply in local dynamics, because of the pressure of time (the fall of the regime was said to be imminent) and under the meddling of foreign patrons (Qatar, Saudi Arabia, Turkey, France, Great Britain, the US, etc.) with various and often contradictory directions. The FSA displayed an inability to unify really, raise an acceptable leadership and offer a credible alternative to the regime. The changing breakdown of groups and alliances with various names was indicative of the continuous difficulty to unify. Only two armed groups have had the ability to develop some form of governance (between 2014 and 2018) approximating the appearances of a state and what the Assad regime was: Da'esh/the Islamic State and the Kurdish YPG – along with al-Qaeda's offshoot *Jabhat al-Nosra* on some dimensions. Yet, both did not meet the aspirations of most Syrians. Da'esh presented itself as a realistic political alternative, however abhorrent, to the Assad regime beyond its publicized distributions of goods and services. Questions remain open whether it aimed at exerting true governance or was just carrying out systematic and organized control to loot and extract resources in the Ba'athi tradition of "security states". The end result was territorial fragmentation, especially between 2014 and 2018.

Conversely, the regime lost much ground to rebels, but stuck to power, maintained some of its infrastructural power (to govern), while destroying local initiatives in rebel-controlled areas with artillery, missiles, chemical weapons or barrel bombs. The Assad regime developed a new network of control based on numerous local militias manning checkpoints and controlling alleged loyal areas – loyalist militias numbered as much manpower as the regular forces (after the wave of defections in 2012–13) so that no single front has been entirely held by the Syrian army. They have been recruited along sectarian, ethnic ('Alawi, Shia, Druze) lines, among nationalist groups or political parties (the Ba'ath or Syrian National Socialist Party), among tribal groups, Palestinians, along with female militias, those linked to Lebanese Hezbollah, and those created by Syrian rich businessmen. The recombinant Assad state (in areas not lost) has maintained its appearances and its basic services (administration, public services, passports, school certificates, basic documents of daily life). Its ability to govern has been dwindling, with the lack of economic resources, the shortages of fighting manpower and the slow demoralization in its ranks. But the picture has been worse in most rebel-held areas and the regime has made sure that this continued to be the case through indiscriminate bombing, not to speak about development rollback, with GDP decline of more than 50% and a reduction in life expectancy (at birth) of 15 years. This race between two weaknesses benefited the Assad regime. Yet the latter could not fully turn up its enfeeblement. In 2016–2018, it went on the offensive to retake rebel-held areas one after another (Homs, Hama, Aleppo, the Ghouta, Deir ez-Zor, Deraa, etc.) with Russian and Iranian military support. But the Syrian regime could not fully reign in the fragmented maze of local loyalist militias (and "reconciled" rebels) under the framework of the (air force) intelligence apparatus and reinstate "normal" authoritarian rule as before 2011.

The Syrian uprising turned into a war of attrition. The descent into the chaos of civil war was long because the protest movement professed an overriding desire not to forfeit their recovered dignity by using violence and not to tarnish the way by which Syrians had retaken their destiny into their own hands. However, although the conflict has remained fundamentally asymmetric on behalf of the regime – with the government's capabilities and external alliances much more powerful than that of the oppositions when aggregated – both camps lost their moral standard in a new kind of existential struggle justifying abominable means and a zero-sum game (killing or being killed) (Harling and Birke, 2013) that illustrated the destructive potential of war processes (Wood, 2008).

The Syrian security nightmare and consequences of a divided opposition unable to offer an alternative and a cohesive regime sticking to power, with Iranian, Hezbollah and Russian help, can be assessed with two mounting trends that came to dominate after 2013, the rise of Islamist (and Salafi) jihadist extremist militants and the generalized "brutalization" (Mosse, 1991) of the Syrian population.

On the one hand, Syria has become the training ground of choice and a magnet for today's violent jihadists: their numbers in 2013–15 topped those in Afghanistan in the 1980s. In the beginning of 2012, with frustration before international inaction and the rise of the civilian death toll, opposition ranks were debating the topic of *jihad*, a view propounded for a long time (at least April 2011) on more militant forums but considered taboo among the mainstream civic activists. Two prominent armed groups *Jabhat al-Nosra lil Ahl al-Sham* (that revealed itself as a branch from al-Qaeda in Iraq) and *Kata'ib Ahrar al-Sham* (the most prominent Salafi group) rose to the fore, along with the Salafi *Liwa' Suqur al-Sham* (in the Idlib province) – a message from al-Qaeda's leader Ayman al-Zawahiri in February 2012 called on Muslims to support *jihad* in Syria. And Da'esh/the Islamic State emerged from the first group. Jihadists were well organized and well funded, took responsibility for huge suicide and IED attacks against security forces, were able to organize successful offensives against regime military bases and recruited large contingents.

Though the non-sectarian, activist, civil society dimension of the uprising has remained prevalent (however weakened or overshadowed), jihadist groups have transformed the uprising into a militant one, in particular moved its nationalist and civic core into an ostensibly Islamist or Salafi and increasingly sectarian movement: they have embraced and disseminated specific projects with a sophisticated online propaganda and an openly sectarian rhetoric against "the 'Alawi enemy" and "its Shiites patrons", all lumped together as *rawafidh* ("rejectionists of Islam"). The regime might tacitly have favored them by freeing Islamist militants (from the dreadful Sednaya prison in April 2011) and not bombing their areas to the same degree; hence it has presented itself as a bulwark against Sunni religious armed extremism. Jihadists have shaped Syrian political future with a more Islamist/Salafi sectarian profile. They were also a symptom of the enfeeblement of (civil) society: their militants were not just young and idle people – during the 2000s Gulf funds supported cultural and charity-based Islamic networking in Syria – or combatants going with them for money – they paid their fighters well and endowed them with large stocks of ammunition. But they also recruited doctors or engineers gained through proselytism (*da'wa*) by their discourses – despair was a key factor of recruitment, especially after the August 2013 chemical attacks and the international non-intervention.

On the other hand, Syrian society has been brutalized to a point never seen before, under the inexorable creep of war and also as a result of strategies deliberately adopted by actors (Syrian Center for Policy Research and UNRWA, 2013; Syrian Center for Policy Research, UNRWA, and UNDP, 2013; and for the example of Aleppo, Caerus-American Security Project, 2014). New wars are allegedly targeting mostly civilians (Kaldor, 1999). The Assad regime has systematically "insecuritized" civilian populations and deployed tactics as a way to make displaced residents feel that they could not return: with targeted attacks on civilians, the destruction of physical infrastructures (hospitals, bakeries, schools, etc.), high-profile massacres, looting by militias (fueling so-called "Sunni markets" of looted items in 'Alawi neighborhoods). Rape was used as a war weapon and the fear of rape helped to poison local social relations (on women as agents of security, see Enloe, 1989). Whole neighborhoods and cities were besieged, with starvation tactics and transfers of population. Weapons of mass destruction were repeatedly used to sow fear, with two landmark attacks in August 2013 in the Ghouta and in April 2017 in Khan Sheikhun near Idlib – and many other underreported chemical attacks. Hundreds of thousands (more than half) of Syrians have been driven from their homes in what also amounted to state-directed population displacements used as a punitive strategy to expel rebels and the population that supported them – the number of internally displaced persons was 6.3 to 7.6 million by mid-2015 (Doocy et al., 2015).[2] Depopulated rebel-held areas increased the number of Syrians living under the regime's ambit in the coastal area (Latakia, Banias, Jableh, Tartous) or in the Druze Suweida province. Sieges and subsequent transfers of population have allowed the regime to manipulate the population balance along sectarian lines in very symbolic places for the uprising, in Homs in 2014 (Human Rights Watch, 2012, UN, 2014), in Daraya (another symbol of the 2011 uprising) and other cities from the Ghouta in 2016 to Aleppo in 2016. And, the government intended to undertake rebuilding efforts to its own benefit with the support of foreign donors by capitalizing on areas destroyed to install a revamped urban constituency. Cities have been hollowed of their civilian population after local truces brokered by Iran and Russia (with or without the UN help) in besieged neighborhoods in 2014–16 – in Homs, the land registry office was destroyed by fire in July 2013. A new legislative decree regarding the digitalization of property records and erasing all records of the past was enacted by President Assad in May 2016 (UN-Habitat, 2014; Global Protection Cluster, 2014). The north (Aleppo until the end of 2016 and then the Idlib area) received an enormous influx of people living in opposition-held areas, loaded on green governmental buses, trapped in other areas and unable to return back home. Thirty percent of the total population has become external refugees, most of them Sunnis and, for the regime, prospective Sunni supporters of the rebellion. And the regime has been trying to hijack reconstruction to reassert its exclusive authority and revamp its economic networks with decree 68 of 2012, decree 19 of 2016, law n°5 of 2016 and law n°10 of 2016 (Heydemann, 2018).

Syria as a new regional and international security problem: A return to the classical security ritual?

Syria since 2011 has been at the center of waves of insecurity and has positioned itself as an essential threat "generator", with complex effects from the local to the regional then the international level. Bloody and open conflict in Syria led to destabilization in the region accompanied by huge waves of refugees in Turkey, Lebanon and Jordan (5 million registered, 306,000 children born refugees; UNICEF, 2016; UNHCR, 2017) and even in continental Europe (with a peak in the summer of 2015). Local insecurities have inflated to the point of contaminating or connecting with the whole web of regional insecurity. And, incidentally, the Assad regime has also played on the new leeway gained through this factor to survive in power, in the tradition of the "struggle for the Middle East" adopted by Hafez al-Assad in the 1980s –though Hafez was much more in control though severely contested, while Bashar in 2011–12 lost control. The decay of the Syrian State into civil war with the spill-over of waves of refugees across borders, open warfare, armed groups, Islamist activism and in particular the rise of Da'esh/ the Islamic State are all immediate indicators of security issues and securitization moves, with direct security consequences for immediate neighbors. A regional groundswell of insecurity has installed itself around Syria. And regional shock waves went farther and deeper in terms of generating vulnerabilities and threats.

As the civil war in Syria gained in intensity and in size, Iran saw the prospect of a strategically hostile regime in Damascus as alarming and extended support to the Assad regime, shifting from organizational help for repression, circumventing sanctions and monitoring the Internet to huge economic help, weapons delivery and boots on the ground by mobilizing allies (Hezbollah, Iraqi Shia militias, Shia mercenaries) and even its own special forces. Syria has been a vital strategic enabler of Iran's ambitions in the Near East (and also with the core Arab–Israeli issue) and its only Arab ally without which Hezbollah would lose strategic depth.

Conversely, dangers as seen from Iran were understood as opportunities by Qatar, a former close ally of the Syrian regime in the 2000s. Qatar flush from its apparent success, at least in 2011–12, to help overthrow Qaddafi in Libya, shifted from mediation to proactive diplomacy – Qatar held the rotating presidency of the Arab League in 2011–12 – then to intervention. Qatar began to feel that an opportunity existed to remake the regional balance of power in a way that would enhance its status: Qatar bet on the quick overthrow of the Assad regime – supporting the Syrian Muslim Brothers, which caused tensions with Saudi Arabia – then tended to support the most "successful" groups picked among the myriad of rebel groups operating in Syria whatever their nature or extremist ideology. Then Qatar's star faded in the Arab League and the limitation of Qatar's capabilities was exposed in 2013, as Saudi Arabia came to dominate support for Syria's armed opposition. Saudi Arabia, whatever its extensive links with Syrian tribes, business, its religious organizations and its significant money, has had no real ability to project power in Syria and no understanding of the Syrian complex setting and its divisive oppositions, and instead has been playing on Sunni militant discourses, another way for insecurities to diffuse across the region.

Insecurities further extended as politics (balance of power or of threats) has been mixed with sectarian discourses. Traditionally, in the Arab World, threats had come not just from neighbors' foreign armies but also from challenges to domestic legitimacy in the name of norms or transnational identities such as Arabism or pan-Islamism. After 2011–12, threats were based on the polarization of confessionalism and sectarian divisions such as Shias versus Sunnis. Since the mid-2000s and also as a result of the repositioning of the US policy (from George W. Bush to Obama then Trump, with very different overtones), Saudi Arabia has harbored a strong sense of regional insecurity, in particular of being encircled by Shia powers with Iran, a revamped Iraq after 2003, Hezbollah in Lebanon, 'Alawis in Syria (designated after 2011 in the Saudi discourse as Shias) and Zaydis insurgents in Yemen (viewed after 2014–15 in Riyadh as blindly aligned with Iran). Saudi Arabia began to perceive that an opportunity existed to tip the balance in its direction by pulling Syria out of an alleged Shia axis and aligning it with more conservative Sunni Gulf powers by empowering Sunni armed actors in Syria.

Gulf states, though not always aligned, also pressed Turkey to intervene as a lot of Syrian officers and soldiers defected to Turkey. With the impossibility of establishing no-fly zones in Syria under a UN umbrella and with the US help, Turkey bet on a blind support for any group fighting the regime (including jihadists from *Jabhat al-Nosra* and even from Da'esh) because the time frame for the fall of Assad was said to be short – until in 2015, after numerous bomb attacks on its territory, Turkey reassessed its policy to act more explicitly within the US-led coalition against Da'esh. The additional security conundrum seen from Ankara was that the Syrian regime's weakening empowered Syrian Kurdish groups affiliated with the PKK (the Democratic Union Party, DUP, whose militia is the PYD) – other parties supported by the Barzani family of Iraq were less influential – to take control of the Kurdish areas adjacent to Turkey (the "three" northern cantons of Afrin, Kobane and Hassake). That re-opening of the Kurdish question and the possibility that Syrian Kurds might pursue an autonomy agenda or even build a quasi-state along its borders was considered a serious threat by the Turkish Government, whose policy (until 2015) was to prevent the PYD from playing a bigger role, at the price of supporting or turning a blind eye on the worst players (jihadists, even Da'esh) because they were the most effective militarily and fought the Kurds. That undermining of one of Turkey's strategic options signaled that Syria has acted as a graveyard for the ambitious Turkish foreign policy of the 2000s.

And in September 2015, the Russian intervention signaled a new step with a revamped international level of (in)security. Russia threw its weight into the Syrian conflict and since then has guaranteed that the sudden implosion of the regime under its intrinsic weaknesses (its dwindling human and morale resources in 2013–15) and despite the support from Iran, Hezbollah, and Shia militias (from Iraq or recruited in Afghanistan) would not be an option. And Russia brokered local cease-fires, with a shrewd calculation of ties with pivotal actors such as Turkey, especially after the failed coup attempt against Erdogan in June 2016. The Assad regime has remained weak but the picture has been worse for its opponents with Russian decisive intervention. The Russian security rationale in supporting the Syrian regime has not been much related to the fate of the Assad family in power, but to bigger objectives, with Syria as a focal point, hence fueling a view of Syria as a regional and even worldwide security problem. The underlying drivers of Russian intervention have not only been linked to Russian direct interests (Tartous, the spread of Islamism, state collapse in Syria), in one of the few remnants of the post-Soviet presence in the Middle East, but also to perspectives related to the general securitization of the Syrian crisis by Russia as an existential fight between Assad and terrorists (variously defined), with the risk of an Islamist spill-over as a result of the collapse of the Syrian State. Furthermore, Syria as a security problem and the growing Russian clout in the Syrian crisis have been actively used by Russia to force the US to re-engage Russia in diplomacy on an equal standing in the context of the importance Russia attaches to the reaffirmation of its international status. Escalating its role in the Syrian crisis has been a way for Moscow to be accepted on equal terms (as an indispensable mediator or powerbroker) by Washington, in a kind of search for a Yalta II model. Syria as a security problem pivoted from a local conflict with huge regional consequences to one with worldwide security implications.

The complexity of the levels of insecurities involved in and around Syria has not diminished with the territorial collapse of Da'esh in Iraq (Mosul) then in Syria (Raqqa) at the end of 2017 and the apparent recovery by the Syrian regime, however heavily weakened, of most parts of its territory. On the contrary, the proxy wars waged by local, regional and international actors, mainly in the north-west (Idlib), in Afrin, in the north-eastern "Arab-Kurdish federation" (Kobane, Hassakeh), in the south-east (Deir-ez-Zor), in the south-west (Deraa), in the Golan, etc. have offered many newly revamped security dilemmas and balances of threats. In 2018, no real negotiation is in sight as the regime does plan to regain control over the remaining lost parts of its territory by military means, does not offer any power-sharing to its opponents and does not offer any credible commitment to a political solution. And the Russian method to defuse tensions with various so-called "de-escalation agreements" is a way to try to stabilize a negative peace littered with security dilemmas, rather than a real compromise addressing security stakes.

Notes

1 This paper (p. 15) signals that poverty levels decreased between 1997 and 2004 then increased in 2004–2007 with different regional patterns (Deraa was the least poor region in 2004 and was the second poorest in 2007).
2 See also UNOCHA, May 2017 (www.unocha.org/syria).

References

Abbas, Hassan, 2012, *The Dynamics of the Syrian Uprising,* Paris: Arab Reform Initiative.
Khaled, Abu-Ismail, Abdel-Gadir, Ali, and El-Laithy, Heba, 2011, *Poverty and Inequality in Syria,* background paper, New York: United Nations-UNDP.
Azar, Edward, and Chung in Moon (eds), 1988, *National Security in the Third World,* London: Edward Elgar.
Barnett, Michael, 1998, *Dialogues in Arab Politics,* Columbia: Columbia University Press.
Booth, Ken, 1991, "Security and Emancipation", *Review of International Studies,* 17(4), pp. 313–326.
Buzan, Barry, 1991, *People, States and Fear,* London: Harvester Wheatsheaf.
Buzan, Barry, and Waever, Ole, 2009, *Regions and Power,* Cambridge: Cambridge University Press.
Caerus-American Security Project, 2014, *Mapping the Conflict in Aleppo,* Syria, February.
Cobban, Helena, 2000, *The Israeli-Syrian Peace Talks,* Washington: USIP Press.
Colombe, Marcel, 1973, *Orient arabe et non-engagement,* Paris: Presses Orientalistes de France.
Dawisha, Adeeb, 1980, *Syria and the Lebanese Crisis,* London: Macmillan.
De Châtel, Francesca, 2014, "The Role of Drought and Climate Change in the Syrian Uprising", *Middle Eastern Studies,* 50(4), pp. 521–535.
Doocy, Shannon, Lyles, Emily, Delbiso, Tefera, and Rolins, Courtland, 2015, "Internal Displacement and the Syrian Crisis", *Conflict and Health,* 9, p. 33.
Droz-Vincent, Philippe, 1999, *Moyen-Orient: Pouvoirs autoritaires, sociétés bloquées,* Paris: Presses Universitaires de France.
Droz-Vincent, Philippe, 2007, *Vertiges de la puissance,* Paris: La Découverte.
Droz-Vincent, Philippe, 2014, "State of Barbary (Take Two): From the Arab Spring to the Return of Violence in Syria", *Middle East Journal,* 68(1), Winter, pp. 33–58.
Drysdale, Alasdair and Hinnebusch Raymond, 1993, *Syria and the Middle East Peace Process,* New York: Council of Foreign Relations Press.
Enloe, Cynthia, 1989, *Bananas, Beaches and Bases,* London: Pandora.
Evron, Yael, 1987, *War and Intervention in Lebanon,* London: Croom Helm.
Global Protection Cluster, 2014, *Humanitarian Evacuations in Armed Conflict,* Thematic Roundtable, November. www.globalprotectioncluster.org/_assets/files/news_and_publications/GPC-Seminar-Summary_Conclusions-04_2015-screen.pdf
Harling, Peter and Birke, Sarah, 2013, "The Syrian Heartbreak", *MERIP Online,* 16 April.

Heydemann, Steven, 1999, *Authoritarianism in Syria,* Ithaca: Cornell University Press.

Heydemann, Steven, 2018, *Beyond Fragility,* Washington: Brookings Institution.

Hinnebusch, Raymond, 2011, "The Ba'th Party in post-Ba'thist Syria", *Middle East Critique*, 20(2), pp. 109–125.

Human Rights Watch, 2012, *Syria, New Satellite Images Show Homs Shelling,* New York, 2 March.

Kaldor, Mary, 1999, *New and Old Wars,* Stanford: Stanford University Press.

Kerr, Malcom, 1971, *The Arab Cold War,* Oxford: Oxford University Press.

Korany, Bahgat, Brynen, Rex and Noble, Paul (eds), 1993, *The Many Faces of National Security in the Arab World,* London: Palgrave Macmillan.

Lawson, Fred, 1996, *Why Syria Goes to War,* Ithaca: Cornell University Press.

Lund, Aron, 2016, *Into the Tunnels,* New York: The Century Foundation.

Lundgren, Emma, 2014, *Beyond Syria's Borders,* London: Tauris.

Ma'oz, Moshe, 1995, *Syria and Israel,* Oxford: Oxford University Press.

Mohtadi, Shahrzad, 2012, "Climate Change and the Syrian Uprising", *Bulletin of the Atomic Scientists*, 16 August.

Mosse, George, 1991, *Fallen Soldiers,* Oxford: Oxford University Press.

Mufi, Malik, 1996, *Sovereign Creations,* Ithaca: Cornell University Press.

Pearlman, Wendy, 2016, "Narratives of Fear in Syria", *PS*, 14(1), March, pp. 21–37.

Perthes, Volker, 1994, "From Front-Line State to Backyard?", *Beirut Review*, 8, Fall, pp. 81–95.

Perthes, Volker, 2006, *Syria under Bashar al-Asad,* London: International Institute for Strategic Studies.

Posen, Barry, 1993, "The Security Dilemma and Ethnic Conflict", *Survival*, 35(1), Spring, pp. 27–47.

Rabinovich, Itamar, 2008, *The View from Damascus,* London: Vallentine Mitchell.

Rabinovich, Itamar, 2009, *The Brink of Peace,* Princeton: Princeton University Press.

Sayigh, Yezid, 1997, *Armed Struggle and the Search for the State,* Oxford: Clarendon Press.

Seale, Patrick, 1965, *The Struggle for Syria,* Oxford: Oxford University Press.

Seale, Patrick, 1989, *Asad, The Struggle for the Middle East,* Berkeley: University of California Press.

Seale, Patrick, 1991, "Asad: Between Institutions and Autocracy", in Antoun, R. and Quataert, D. (eds), *Syria: Society, Culture and Politics,* Albany: State University of New York.

Stedman, John, Rothchild, David, and Cousens, Elisabeth (eds), 2002, *Ending Civil Wars,* Boulder: Lynne Rienner.

Syrian Center for Policy Research, UNRWA, 2013, *The Syrian Catastrophe,* New York: United Nations.

Syrian Center for Policy Research, UNRWA, UNDP, 2013, *Syria, War on Development,* New York: United Nations.

UN, 2014, *Report of the International Commission of Inquiry on the Syrian Arab Republic,* New York, United Nations.

UN-Habitat, 2014, *Neighborhood Profile: Old City of Homs,* New York: United Nations.

UNDP, 2005, *Poverty in Syria,* New York: United Nations.

UNDP, 2009, *Arab Human Development Report,* New York: United Nations.

UNHCR, 2017, Situation Syria Regional Refugee Response, New York: United Nations. http://data.unhcr.org/syrianrefugees/regional.php

UNICEF, 2016, *The Impact of Five Years of War on Syria's Children and their Childhood,* New York: United Nations. www.unicef.org.hk/upload/NewsMedia/publication/Syria_5yr_Report.pdf

Walt, Stephen, 1990, *The Origins of Alliances,* Ithaca: Cornell University Press.

Wolfers, Arnold, 1962, *Discord and Collaboration,* Baltimore: The Johns Hopkins University Press.

Wood, Elisabeth, 2008, "The Social Processes of Civil War: The Wartime Transformation of Social Networks", *Annual Review of Political Science,* 11, pp. 539–561.

9

HUMANITARIAN AID TO A MIDDLE EAST IN CRISIS

Roger Hearn

Introduction

The civil war in Syria, and the ensuing regional humanitarian crisis, has seen a refocusing of attention toward the provision of humanitarian aid within the Middle East. This chapter explores how humanitarian responses interact with the broader security context of the Middle East and more directly, how some of the notable challenges faced by the aid industry play out within this increasingly turbulent region. From this analysis reflections can be made regarding the suitability of the current aid architecture to respond to a region potentially facing decades of instability.

Clearly the scope for review is broad, given, for example, the insights that could be gleaned from the long-standing Palestine refugee crisis, or the aid response in Iraq following the 2003 invasion. This chapter will however primarily focus on the humanitarian response to the crisis in Syria.[1] In 2013 the humanitarian appeal for Syria became the largest ever requested and, since then, billions of dollars have been expended (Tran, 2013). The lessons that can be drawn, particularly from a response of this size, are of significant interest given their relevance for future humanitarian engagements in the region. The context in Syria is illustrative given the manner with which the Syrian regime, as a party to the conflict, has been able to negatively impact the humanitarian response. The regime, responsible for much of the humanitarian catastrophe in the country, has been able to assume the role of gatekeeper to the official aid response. This, among other things, has seen a disproportionate flow of official international aid into government-controlled areas at the same time as a restriction of assistance to opposition areas, including those besieged by the regime via military means. The accusation has been made that the manipulation of international aid by the regime amounts to it being used as an instrument of war.

Ultimately the flaws experienced in the Syrian response pose serious questions regarding the future relevance and legitimacy of emergency aid within a region with a growing propensity for internal conflict. Given the extent to which the crisis in Syria has been permitted by the United Nations Security Council to metastasize, one can assume that the global conflict resolution architecture will be unable to prevent other conflicts breaking out in the region and described in other chapters. Given the humanitarian consequences of conflict and the increased likelihood of intrastate conflict being a feature in numerous countries within the region into the future, it is therefore likely that the conditions seen in Syria – with the dominant role of one of the antagonists in the conflict – will be repeated in future humanitarian responses.

Traditional humanitarian responses will not be able to meet the growing demands within the region either financially or because of a failure to negotiate appropriate levels of access. More troubling is the potentially negative role aid may provide in propping up repressive governments in the region. A new paradigm will need to be developed if the humanitarian needs of individuals caught up in various future crises are to be addressed.

Aid and conflict

There is a perception, held fervently by many in the aid community, that the humanitarian space – the opportunity for aid providers to access affected populations in disaster zones – is shrinking (see for example, Hubert and Brassard-Boudreau, 2010). While this view appears to be confirmed with the increase in attacks on aid providers – a common barometer for gauging humanitarian access – on closer analysis a different trend emerges (Hubert and Brassard-Boudreau, 2010). The past few decades have witnessed a mushrooming of humanitarian institutions providing assistance in a range of contexts fueled by billions of additional aid dollars. Indeed, the brands and reputations of the largest aid organizations; the United Nations agencies, international non-government organizations (INGOs) and the Red Cross have been built on the basis of being able to reach the most vulnerable wherever they may be found. Fast moving media images of natural disasters and civilians devastated by conflict interact with a highly competitive humanitarian industry where being first on the scene has become matter of organizational survival. As aid agencies respond to a growing list of global humanitarian crises, they have found themselves engaged – to a varying and at times questionable extent – in a range of wars and security challenges. From these encounters emerge a range of policy and practice debates regarding the relationship between aid and conflict and concerning how aid agencies should best navigate often treacherous contexts.

As their focus and breadth have expanded into a growing list of complex humanitarian emergencies, aid organizations have been increasingly accused of losing their way (Barnett and Weiss, 2008). Humanitarian action is either condemned for its narrow focus on saving lives while doing nothing to address root causes of conflict (Ferreiro, 2012), or attacked for departing from its central mission by doing just that (Rieff, 2003). Alongside and related to this long-standing debate within the sector are a range of issues including broader questions of neutrality and the independence of aid programs. In its most direct form, the relationship between humanitarian work and military campaigns in contexts such as Afghanistan and Iraq has seen accusations directed toward aid organizations regarding their loss of independence from the aspirations of their key donors (James, 2003).

The impact of aid on the longevity of war and the idea that aid might in some way prolong or feed into wars has also been subject to increasing analysis (for example, Uvin, 1998; Narang, 2015; Terry, 2013; Wood and Molfino, 2016). While the principle of *Do No Harm* (Anderson, 1999) is now widely known in theory across the humanitarian sector, the extent to which aid organizations have been able to abide by this principle remains a contentious question. Research from different contexts suggests a relationship between certain types of aid interventions and an increase in conflict in certain settings (Wood and Molfino, 2016). The inability of aid agencies to understand the contexts with which they engage appears to play a part. However, there appear to be some significant examples of organizations willingly entering into relationships with host governments which have led to accusations of bias. While holding on to notions of neutrality in how these agencies frame the narrative of their work, the real impact has often turned out to be less principled. The experiences in contexts such as Sri Lanka have pointed to a disturbing interaction between aid organizations and the more hostile actions of a host government. While using as a justification the importance of maintaining good relationships with government authorities to ensure ongoing humanitarian access, an internal review of the UN in Sri Lanka has highlighted the role played by government authorities in restricting UN aid flows, for example by artificially reducing the number of beneficiaries in opposition areas. The report highlighted the inability of UN officials to challenge a series of abuses (Secretary-General's Internal Review Panel on United Nations Action in Sri Lanka, 2012). As described later in this chapter, a number of failings outlined in the Internal Review, in terms of appeasement of government authorities and confusion in lines of command within the UN system, appear to have featured prominently in the humanitarian response to Syria.

A brief history of humanitarian assistance in the Middle East

The modern aid industry, complete with its policy and practice debates, suggests that humanitarian assistance is a recent and largely Western endeavor. Deeper analysis reveals that is not the case and there is a long and complex history within the Middle East region to responding to those suffering from displacement and deprivation (see, for example, Davey and Svoboda, 2014). While not the focus of this chapter, as explored later, it will be important to broaden the range of players and forms of assistance in the future to meet what will most likely be an expanding range of contexts where citizens require assistance. For the current study, however, the role of humanitarian agencies, including the United Nations and the key INGOs, will be the focus.

A band of authoritarian regimes spanning the Middle East have – until recently – provided a layer of stability that appeared immune to serious internal unrest. Unlike a number of other regions, the middle-income level status of the Middle East (with the exception of Yemen) could provide the basic necessities for its citizenry. While not offering sustainable models for longer-term development, the features of these states had meant limited humanitarian responses to the region. Indeed, if this chapter had been written 25 years earlier, the primary – and almost sole – focus would have been humanitarian assistance related to the unresolved Palestine refugee crisis.

Per capita support to Palestine refugees still makes up a significant component of humanitarian assistance to the region.[2] The United Nations Relief and Works Agency for Palestine Refugees in the Near East (UNRWA) has, since becoming operational in 1950, provided education, basic health services and more traditional relief in the form of food aid and cash assistance. While much of the funding for UNRWA came from the humanitarian windows of key donors, over the years, the assistance, for example providing primary and secondary education to millions of Palestinian children, came to resemble many of the functions of the social services arm of a government. There are multiple opinions regarding the role and mandate of UNRWA (for example see Hanafi, Hilal and Takkenberg, 2014). Even more has been written in the opinion pages of the media regarding the role of UNRWA in keeping alive the aspirations of refugees for the right to return. Depending on the editorial steer, the Agency has either softened the force of Israel's ongoing displacement of Palestine refugees (Baker, 2013) or it has played a hostile role toward Israel by keeping the plight of Palestinians in the public consciousness (Spyer, 2008). In reality, the longevity of the agency demonstrates that humanitarian funding is no substitute for effective political action. Sadly, however, it also demonstrates that the international community will fall back on humanitarian instruments in lieu of effective political settlement; for decades if necessary.

While UNRWA has a clear mandate in terms of the refugee population, the role played by a number of INGOs engaged in the Israeli/Palestinian conflict, particularly those with substantial USA support has been at times questionable. Present because of the dire conditions caused by the ongoing Israeli occupation of the West Bank and Gaza, some of these agencies have had trouble voicing this reality for fear of disrupting their donor base in the USA. Instead they contribute to an illusion that the longer-term development needs of Palestinians will be resolved by something other than a meaningful and comprehensive political resolution (see, for example, Qarmout and Béland, 2012).

It was not until the crisis stemming from the 2003 invasion of Iraq that the region saw another significant humanitarian response that for a number of years captured the attention of key donors.[3] While a component of the aid response focused on the large-scale exodus of Iraqi refugees into Jordan and Syria, the lion's share was geared toward supporting the state building project of the USA and its allies inside Iraq. The propensity of UN agencies and INGOs to actively engage alongside military actions inside Iraq was called into question by multiple analysts (for a review of the debates see for example Abiew, 2012 or de Montclos, 2014).

By late 2010, the Middle East operations of many international aid organizations were phasing out. With the exception of some larger humanitarian funded programs in Palestine and some longer-term USAID or EU projects in Egypt, the region was a small player in the larger global aid industry with more significant interests in sub-Saharan Africa and parts of Asia.

The Syria crisis

This waning humanitarian action in the region changed dramatically with the Syrian crisis, which for a number of years has resulted in a massive influx of humanitarian assistance within and around Syria.

The Syrian uprising initially played out as a human rights crisis beginning in Dara'a in March 2011. A large number of the state's citizenry, inspired by events taking place across the region and with the aid of social media became involved in a series of demonstrations that were quickly inflamed by a ham-fisted response from the regime. During the course of 2011 an uprising was in place across much of the country. While the international voices calling for the Assad regime to stand down intensified, a stalemate at the United Nations Security Council soon took hold. The Russians and to a lesser extent China were left feeling manipulated by UNSC resolution 1975 where the principle of *Responsibility to Protect* was used as a justification for a military intervention in Libya that quickly moved from protecting civilians into a full-blown regime change exercise. Beyond the perception of trickery, it was clear that the Russians had a longer-term strategic interest in Syria that would always make robust UNSC action unlikely if not impossible. The United Nations was unable to pursue meaningful actions inside Syria that would investigate the growing list of abuses from the regime or ultimately take steps to resolve the crisis. A United Nations Supervision Mission in Syria was established in April 2012 as part of a six-point plan aimed, among other things, at reducing the scale of fighting, ensuring timely humanitarian assistance to all areas and addressing some of the human rights issues in the country (UN Peacekeeping 2017). The mandate of the mission – compromised by the divisions within the UNSC – was never robust enough to be fulfilled and came to an early end in August of that year (Koops et al., 2015).

The escalation of the crisis during 2011 and its increasing militarization into 2012 began to sow the seeds for the massive humanitarian crisis both inside Syria and in surrounding countries. Refugee numbers went from a trickle (70,000 in mid-2012) to a flood (half a million by the end of 2012). In Jordan, Turkey and Lebanon a steady flow of refugees exceeded 2 million by the end of 2013. As of 2017 there were in excess of 5.2 million refugees, 6.3 million internally displaced and millions more requiring humanitarian assistance (UNOCHA Syria, 2017). The massive humanitarian crisis, well publicized in the international media, soon generated significant funds from bilateral donors and from the public fundraising efforts of key international agencies. Two UN appeal mechanisms were instigated: one for a regional response for Syrian refugees in surrounding countries and the other as a response program for Syrians still inside the country. Already in 2013, these appeals were the largest on record totaling USD 4.4 billion.

Given the scale of the humanitarian response inside Syria and the dire situation facing millions of Syrians, the provision of aid has been an important and life-saving endeavor. Food aid, medical assistance, shelter support and cash assistance have all played a critical part in supporting desperate populations. However, as the humanitarian program inside Syria began to take shape early in the crisis, a number of key inadequacies emerged. Despite the humanitarian budgets that ultimately totaled in the billions, huge pockets of the country – particularly in the earlier years of the response – remained under-supported by international assistance.

The Syrian Government was quick to put its stamp on the global humanitarian program, demanding that aid be distributed through its nominated providers and by playing a vetting role over the appeal processes of the United Nations. The Syrian Arab Red Crescent (SARC), along with a group of national NGOs approved by the government, was the key account holder and became the conduit for the expanding aid programs of the international aid community. While the UN agencies, a number of INGOs and the ICRC may have had their own donor funded programs, by and large these organizations were not responsible for the day-to-day delivery of these programs, a responsibility ceded to SARC, an institution described as "an auxiliary to the government" (Howe, 2016). While there have been multiple accounts of the neutrality shown by some SARC staff in the field, at a national level the leadership of the organization has struggled to demonstrate independence from the Syrian Government.

Aid organizations operating from Damascus found (and still find) that they were unable to verify the ultimate destination of aid despite the assurances from SARC. For example, the World Food Programme states in an internal evaluation that, "WFP staff monitor the situation when feasible, but most monitoring is conducted by partners and a third-party monitoring firm, which also has limited direct access to beneficiaries" (World Food Programme, 2015a). According to some reports, the amounts of resources flowing via agencies controlled or heavily influenced by the Syrian regime accounted for approximately USD 900 million out of the total allocated from the USD 1.1 billion response budget of 2015. As an example of this discrepancy at its worst, only between 1 and 2% of United Nations' food assistance was channeled to areas outside of the regime's control for the months of July, August and September during 2015 (World Food Programme, 2015b: 6).

The centralized control held by the Syrian Government to direct the location and types of aid flows meant that humanitarian assistance has not only benefited the regime (Martínez and Eng, 2016) but ultimately some claim it has been used as an instrument of war (Physicians for Human Rights, 2017). The Syrian regime was ultimately provided with a sign-off role in the narrative of the multi-billion-dollar appeal documents. This resulted in the lack of recognition of cross border aid which they considered "illegal". Similar to the situation in Sri Lanka, the regime would, among other tactics, dispute the population figures in opposition areas and reduce levels of aid (funded by Western donors and distributed through the UN) accordingly. Other forms of regime manipulation included the avoidance of phrases or concepts such as *sieges* or the notion that violence was a primary cause of displacement (Hopkins and Beals, 2016). Therefore, the Syrian Government, a pariah for most in the international community was (and to a large extent remains) in the dubious position of tacitly controlling billions of dollars of aid resources.

While acknowledging the immense difficulties associated with working within the Syrian context, the overall leadership of the humanitarian community within Damascus was subject to significant manipulation by the Syrian Government. The criticism of weak leadership and a propensity to work within the system "permitted" by the Syrian regime rather than working toward what was best for the entirety of potential aid beneficiaries (and according to humanitarian principles), has also been made by researchers, activists and aid practitioners (Howe, 2016; the Syria Campaign, 2016; Hearn, 2016). The weakness of certain UN agencies to assert themselves could be traced to the inability of those agencies to come to a unified position early in the crisis with the Syrian Government on what was not permissible (Hearn, 2016; the Syria Campaign, 2016b). As part of the overall control and manipulation of the international aid response in Syria, the Regime's Ministry of Foreign Affairs has played an explicit role. On a daily basis, ministry officials would be involved in the withholding of staff work permits, or the control of staff movement within the country.[4] The entire program of a UN agency or INGO could be stalled for months or permanently through the act of not granting work permits for key staff. For the leadership of various UN agencies working without a common and unified mandate, these measures had a cowering effect.[5]

The weak leadership of many United Nations agencies within Damascus was later compounded by turf battles between different agencies both within Syria and in relation to the regional leadership of the response (Sida et al., 2016). The multiple lines of reporting of the different UN agencies responding to the crisis and the limitations in the mandate of UNOCHA created a disharmony that was used by the regime to dictate the terms of the humanitarian response.

From the very beginning of the response, requests for aid convoys – cross line – into opposition-held areas were routinely denied or delayed by the Syrian Government, confirming the view of multiple aid personnel that approvals for access were not based on need but to serve the regime's agenda. Various reports to the Security Council outline the situation. For example:

> Despite our persistent and unrelenting efforts, our ability to access hard-to-reach and besieged locations remains severely hampered by the pitiful approval rate for inter-agency convoys by the Syrian authorities. In 2015, just over 10 percent of the 113 requests for inter-agency convoys resulted in the delivery of much needed humanitarian and life-saving assistance. A further 10 percent were approved in principle, but could not proceed due to a lack of final approval, insecurity, or lack of agreement on safe passage. The United Nations placed some three percent of requests on hold due to insecurity. And, almost 75 percent of requests went unanswered by the Government of Syria. Such inaction is simply unacceptable for a Member state of the United Nations and signatory of the United Nations Charter.
>
> *(UN Under Secretary-General for Humanitarian Affairs, January 2016)*

An unauthorized cross border aid response commenced during 2012 by a collection of INGOs and national or diaspora organizations – initially from Turkey but later from northern Iraq, Jordan and Lebanon (via local organizations). While necessary to ensure the flow of aid to opposition-held areas, it resulted in an uncoordinated national response. While funds began to flow unofficially across borders from surrounding countries and officially via cross line operations from Damascus, the formal UN appeal processes remained geared entirely toward Damascus. Aid toward opposition areas was either not provided through the formal appeal programs or as an add-on via the more problematic "cross line" operations operated from UN agencies working out of Damascus.

Growing criticism of the Damascus-centric nature of the response led to a series of United Nations Security Council Resolutions enabling cross border relief operations into Syria

(UNSC Resolutions 2165, 2191 and 2258). The overwhelming gap in terms of those not able to receive assistance because of the failure of agencies to use the cross border option was stated bluntly by the United States Ambassador to the United Nations reporting on a closed door meeting: "[Valerie] Amos [Under Secretary-General Humanitarian Affairs] was very clear and is always very clear – that 3.5 million people can be reached just … by giving consent, literally with a stroke of a pen, allowing the UN to use border checkpoints, all of them…" (Charbonneau, 2014).

Despite the mandate afforded to UN agencies there was a reluctance to robustly undertake cross border operations. Fearful of compromising relationships with the Syrian regime, most agencies continued cross line operations from Damascus (Lynch, 2014). These operations often appeared to many observers to be more tokenistic given the numerous difficulties associated with accessing, for example, border areas with Turkey from Damascus and described above (Sparrow, 2017). This included navigating multiple checkpoints and crossing lines of fighting rather than accessing these territories more simply from Turkey. The common defense from agencies working inside Damascus was that maintaining solid relationships with the regime enabled ongoing operations to continue in the limited humanitarian space available. This position has been contested by personnel across the humanitarian sector (Lund, 2016) who challenge the key argument that the agencies in Syria could not afford to jeopardize the larger components of the international aid effort, in particular the food aid program. As David Miliband states, "My argument is the Assad regime can't afford to kick the U.N. out of Damascus. The U.N. is feeding so many of [Assad's] own people" (Lynch, 2014).

While the discrepancies between the levels of aid delivered cross border and cross line have been significant, the (largely) regime use of laying siege to different parts of the country results in the most egregious outcomes for the official aid program. Sieges in the Syrian context have involved the sealing of specific suburbs, towns or regions via military containment. During 2016 these potentially affected over 1.3 million people (Physicians for Human Rights, 2017). These actions have usually been accompanied by air and land attacks on the trapped populations. The horror of these methods has been graphically displayed in the suburbs of Douma and what was the Palestinian dominated suburb of Yarmouk in Damascus. The use of a siege by the Syrian Government has meant that although only a few kilometers from downtown Damascus, areas consisting of hundreds of thousands of residents could be surrounded, contained and cut off from all assistance (including food, medical aid, sanitation services and other basic supplies) by the Syrian Government. At the same time, the bulk of the international humanitarian assistance would continue to be directed to the areas approved by the regime. It is difficult not to see this arrangement as an example of international aid being used as an instrument of war.

Martínez and Eng (2016) outline the impact of official and supposedly "neutral" food aid and the manner with which it has supported the Syrian regime; first, by assisting it to maintain welfare responsibilities and thus diffuse dissent in areas of its control. While an air of stability could be provided to regime-held areas, for those living under siege by the regime in opposition areas the situation was dramatically different. Martínez and Eng describe how residents in suburbs of Damascus and elsewhere, once cut off from food, medical and fuel supplies, began to question the authority of opposition leadership. They describe a situation where aid flows would commence once, for example, a truce was reached with the regime.

For aid providers conducting operations cross border via Turkey or Iraq or via local Syrian organizations, there were multiple challenges. The constantly changing security context was key, with an ever-changing array of armed actors, including those hostile to Western agencies. Local organizations began forming and operating outside of the legal parameters of the Syrian State from 2012 onwards. This included local coordinating committees, activists, community-based organizations and diaspora groups (Haddad and Svoboda, 2017). In a number of cases these organizations provided a credible alternative to international aid providers (for example see Howe, 2016). With limited international support, this group of responders attempted to provide assistance while avoiding attacks from both the Syrian regime and in later years ISIS. The humanitarian responses provided by these local groups were, however, not included as part of the overall humanitarian response plan channeled via Damascus. As the number of security incidents increased, including some notable kidnappings of international personnel, the interest of those INGOs operating cross border, to work via some of these local partner organizations, increased. As stated by Howe, the relationship between INGOs and their local partners was often more of a convenience with local organizations playing the role of service provider on behalf of their international counterparts.[6] Interestingly, while more than 75% of the actual delivery was performed by these local organizations during 2014, they only received 0.3% of funding directly from donors, with INGOs acting as the conduit for this funding (Els et al., 2016).

A further complicating feature of the cross-border operations within opposition-held Syria was the uneasy interface between humanitarian relief and the various anti-terrorism frameworks of donor nations (Burniske et al., 2015). While impossible to verify its full impact, it seems likely that these conditions served as dampener on humanitarian assistance in non-regime areas as aid agencies grew increasingly fearful of getting on the wrong side of law enforcement agencies in their own countries.[7]

A "Whole of Syria (WoS) approach" was instigated by the UN in early 2015 as an attempt to draw together the key components of the Syria response from the multiple hubs based in and around the country. While the intention was laudable – to increase the level of shared analysis and to ultimately reduce the number of gaps in the response – the results were harder to discern. The sense that the aid community based in Damascus was serving the purposes of the Syrian Government was still, in 2016, a common narrative from the large number of Syrian activists and aid providers not aligned with the regime, who concluded that:

> As if refusing to break the sieges were not enough, it now seems the UN is even afraid of uttering the words. For many of us in Syria, the UN has turned from a symbol of hope into a symbol of complicity. Two decades ago, in Srebrenica, we saw what happens when UN peacekeepers get dictated to by war criminals. Today in Syria, it seems to be the turn of UN humanitarians.
>
> *(Open letter to Stephen O'Brien, 15 January in The Syria Campaign, 2016a)*

The robust involvement of Russia coupled with the lack of engagement by the United States has seen the military situation in Syria change significantly. With the end of a viable opposition and the re-emergence of regime dominance (strengthened by a number of proxies), the aid response to Syria is likely to shift. For those agencies focused on large-scale, cross-border activities from Turkey the options for engaging with opposition areas at scale are reducing as the months draw on (despite what will be likely large pockets of unmet need in non-regime held areas). In response, more INGOs will seek to register in Damascus and work through the Syrian regime nominated aid providers with all of the compromises this entails.

It seems that the trajectory of the humanitarian response was set very early in the crisis. Patterns were established, for example, in relations with Syrian Government officials, that became difficult if not impossible to break. Failure to set a clear line in terms of permissible behavior (including not allowing a party to a conflict to have a sign-off role on humanitarian appeals or play such a dominant role in coordinating the aid response) meant a loss of control that was impossible to reassert. As aid agencies moving away from their cross-border operations seek to engage with Damascus in the future it will be hard if not impossible to negotiate appropriate humanitarian access because of the principles and standards previously set.

This analysis of the Syrian humanitarian response does not suggest that aid in regime-held areas should have been withheld and only be provided to opposition-held areas. Instead, the conclusion is that the basis of aid programs should be a thorough assessment of the total requirements in a country and the development of responses that provide assistance to those most in need wherever they may be located. This, sadly, did not occur in the Syrian humanitarian response (although there were attempts with the WoS approach a few years into the crisis). Ultimately it is impossible to conclude what impact the aid response had on the overall trajectory of the war in Syria. Clearly, the involvement of Russian airpower, Hezbollah and Iranian fighters, along with the anti-ISIS coalition, would have had a more profound impact on the end result in Syria compared with the impact of aid flows. However, it is clear that the use of humanitarian assistance has benefited the regime to a greater extent than opposition forces, leading to a conclusion that aid flows have played a role in the conflict inside Syria. It is also important to reflect on the precedent of the Syrian humanitarian response for future operations. Clearly, a rather disturbing message has been sent to future belligerents about the role they can play in manipulating aid programming.

Facing the future: Aid and conflict in the Middle East

If the inability of aid to adequately respond to the humanitarian crises currently sweeping Syria and elsewhere in the region is troubling, it is likely that much worse is to come. The Middle East is a region facing a significant period of instability and conflict, as unresolved governance issues continue to fester and interact with poor development prospects, unsustainable population increases and the growing reality of global warming.

Egypt fits many of these criteria and will likely pose profound challenges for the international community in years to come. With a population increasing by more than 1.8 million annually, services and infrastructure are at breaking point (Worldometers 2017). The impact of global warming will also directly impact the delta region of the country in the coming years, potentially leading to massive displacement and a significant diminishment of Egypt's ability to access adequate food and water supplies. The growing repression by the country's regime suggests that the compounding problems faced by the country will, when merged with unresolved governance issues, have the potential to explode over the next decade.

The population of the Gaza Strip, now at more than 2 million, has been subject to Israeli blockade for more than a decade. The underpinnings of the territory are fundamentally untenable: with an economy that has been unraveling since before the Hamas take-over of Gaza, and power supplies, water and sewerage all crumbling (United Nations Country Team in the occupied Palestinian territory, 2017). The UN concludes that the Gaza Strip will be uninhabitable by 2020 as it goes through a process of "de-development" (UNCTAD, 2015). For a population made up of predominantly young people, the territory, subject to three Israeli wars over ten years, has no sense of a future. The failure of political processes to resolve the longstanding political situation for Palestinians in the entire occupied Palestine territory results in an overreliance on humanitarian solutions.

These two examples of potential flash points – along with the ongoing crises in Syria, Iraq, Yemen and Libya and the likelihood of the further breakdown of Iraq, with its fractured governance model – not to mention the potential for conflict stemming from a regional water crisis and global warming, all point to significant humanitarian actions in the future. If agencies are unable to more appropriately engage in effective aid responses, they will continue to be accused of bias, incompetence or irrelevance. Just as critically, they will be unable to effectively meet the humanitarian needs of the millions likely to be affected by ongoing crises. While this will be devastating for individuals, it will also potentially play out via mass migration to less conflict prone regions. The Syrian regime effectively played the sovereignty card in relation to how aid could be delivered in the country and the bulk of UN agencies were quick to comply. It is likely that sovereignty will be used as a justification for controlling the actions of aid providers in future conflicts given the profusion of repressive states in the Middle East. UN agencies and other large-scale players in the humanitarian community will need to exhibit a more robust engagement with these states if they are to better fulfil their humanitarian mandates.[8] Going forward, aid agencies need to more competently grapple with profound questions concerning how far they will relinquish humanitarian principles to deliver aid and indeed at what point they need to hold back on delivery rather than acquiesce to governments willing to use aid as a weapon of war.

While underfunding per se was not the underlying reason for the lack of a comprehensive aid response throughout Syria, it has played a significant role. In future, when looking at the Middle East with its propensity for crisis and deprivation, mobilizing adequate humanitarian response funding will be a challenge. Humanitarian agencies are now overwhelmed with an escalation in humanitarian need (more than 120 million people in need of assistance globally) and massively underfunded humanitarian appeals (UNOCHA, 2017b). Despite fairly significant global coverage of the Syrian crisis and to a lesser extent the Iraq crisis, the funding for assistance does not cover needs. For countries under the global radar such as Yemen, with over 18.8 million people requiring humanitarian aid, or Libya, with significant portions of the country in desperate need, the situation is even more dire (UNOCHA, 2017a). The gap between needs and resources will likely widen in the years to come. The role of the Gulf and its expanding base of government-associated foundations will need to be factored into future humanitarian programs. While potentially providing a critical form of funding, these newer forms of funding will also at times challenge notions concerning the independence of aid.[9]

In addition to providing funding, donors will also need to closely scrutinize the impact of their own national anti-terrorism frameworks and legislation. If aid is to be provided to those most vulnerable in the Middle East context new modalities will need to be developed that do not limit the flow of aid as has been the case in Syria and the Gaza Strip (Burniske et al., 2015).

To ensure relevant and appropriate support to humanitarian responses, while most likely maintaining existing resource levels, local actors will need to be engaged to a more significant level. As found in the Syria response into opposition-held areas, local organizations can often better navigate the immense security challenges faced within a region prone to conflict while ensuring greater contextual relevance. A more significant engagement of local actors, including NGOs, the private sector and, where appropriate, local government will also reduce costs and potentially enable a broader system of resource flows, including remittances and private sector funding.[10] The Grand Bargain – the commitments emerging from the World Humanitarian Summit – has on a rhetorical level raised the stakes for humanitarian actors by pushing for a commitment of 25% of aid resources being provided directly to local actors. A review outlined in the 2015 World Disasters Report revealed that less than 2% of funding had, in recent times, gone directly local organizations, demonstrating distance that this shift needs to go (International Federation of the Red Cross and Red Crescent, 2015). As stated previously, in relation to Syria, the level of aid going directly to local providers was even lower than this low global average.

Despite the importance of enhancing the role and responsibility of national organizations, international humanitarian agencies will still have a role to play, particularly at the outset of a crisis. The disunity and disconnect between UN agencies and the limited mandate of UNOCHA to lead humanitarian responses need to be addressed. The multitude of humanitarian actors present during a crisis creates confusion and inefficiencies. As the case of Syria has demonstrated, the lack of unity among aid agencies can also result in the manipulation of humanitarian programs. While there are structural changes that can be made to ensure greater efficiency in aid delivery, there is also the question of leadership. A failure of leadership by key personnel within UN agencies and INGOs can imperil operations from the very beginning. The leadership gap has been recognized as a weakness in the UN system and plays a part with other humanitarian organizations. As demonstrated in Syria, even when the UN Security Council authorized cross border options, UN agencies were loath to engage and compromise working relations with the government. Alongside improved leadership, international organizations will also need to enhance their capacity to analyze and more deeply understand the contexts within which they work if they are to engage more thoughtfully in complex environments. As stated earlier, humanitarian actors are in a constant struggle to demonstrate that they are responding in those crises that are deemed news worthy. Failure to be "seen" by their key donors during these times becomes a matter of organizational survival for many aid groups. Aid providers however need to gauge the potential damage they may bring to a crisis from "being present" in a way that significantly jeopardizes their neutrality and independence.

With the massive escalation of crises across the Middle East, the region is now one of the larger recipients of humanitarian aid globally. Ultimately the lack of political solutions to pressing security challenges coupled with a range of structural issues, including the impact of global warming, will continue to see humanitarian actors placed in the middle of a range of complex challenges. While providing humanitarian relief in a war zone is always a game of compromise and imperfect arrangements, action must be taken to reduce the potential harm of aid. The clearest gauge for success should be that humanitarian assistance ultimately serves those most in need and not the interests of a repressive government.

Notes

1 This chapter only investigates humanitarian assistance (a term used interchangeably with emergency aid) and not other longer-term forms of aid including bilateral or multilateral development programs. This assistance includes emergency funding sources from governments and funds raised publicly by aid agencies to be used in humanitarian responses – i.e. to save lives and alleviate suffering. It includes, but is not limited to, contributions to UNOCHA funding appeals.

2 This assistance should also be seen alongside the longer-term development assistance geared toward the region. Significant aid has been related to the larger USA imperative of supporting Israel either directly or via massive financial support to the neighboring states of Egypt and Jordan willing to recognize Israel.

3 The much maligned Oil for Food Program which operated from 1995 until 2003 is not included in this brief overview.

4 Various Secretary-General reports outline the backlog of visa approvals and INGO requests for permission to operate inside Syria, for example, Report by the Secretary-General, Implementation of Security Council resolutions 2139 (2014), 2165 (2014), 2191 (2014), 2258 (2015) and 2332 (2016) 24 August 2017 (United Nations Secretary-General, 2017).

5 Clearly the ability of UN agencies to more firmly adhere to humanitarian principles, including those of neutrality, impartiality and independence goes beyond the capacity or willingness of UN leaders at a country level. The lack of coherence between the actions of the multiple UN agencies and the absence of global leadership over operations also plays a critical part.
6 As will be discussed later, the longevity of many of these "partnerships" will be tested as INGOs, fearing diminishing opportunities in opposition areas, attempt to register with the Syrian Government to operate out of Damascus.
7 It is also quite possible that the complete closure of INGO cross border programs to opposition areas – particularly in the governorate of Idlib – might ultimately be based on donor reactions to aid diversion by a listed terrorist group.
8 The division within the United Nations Security Council will not, however, make this a particularly easy task for UN agencies.
9 A recent example concerns the role of Saudi Arabia in Yemen which, while being a major protagonist in the conflict, has also offered significant amounts of humanitarian aid to the United Nations Appeal. This situation is not dissimilar to the role of United States Government aid programming to Iraq and its links with its own military campaign in that country.
10 Of course, a thorough assessment of "local actors" needs to take place to ensure that they are able to remain as independent and neutral as possible, something that has not been the case with, for example, the use of SARC in Syria.

References

Abiew, F.K., 2012. Humanitarian Action under Fire: Reflections on the Role of NGOs in Conflict and Post-conflict Situations. *International Peacekeeping, 19*(2), pp. 203–216.

Anderson, M.B., 1999. *Do No Harm: How Aid Can Support Peace – or War.* Boulder, CO: Lynne Rienner Publishers.

Baker, R., 2013. UNRWA Aid Sustains Palestinian Misery, *Al-Monitor*, 10 April. Available at: www.al-monitor.com/pulse/originals/2013/04/unrwa-sustains-israeli-occupation.html

Barnett, M. and Weiss, T.G. eds., 2008. *Humanitarianism in Question: Politics, Power, Ethics.* Ithaca, NY: Cornell University Press.

Burniske, J., Lewis, D.A. and Modirzadeh, N.K., 2015. *Suppressing Foreign Terrorist Fighters and Supporting Principled Humanitarian Action: A Provisional Framework for Analyzing State Practice.* Available at: http://dx.doi.org/10.2139/ssrn.2673502

Charbonneau, L., 2014. UN Urges End to Syria's "Convoluted" Aid Restrictions, *Reuters*, 26 March. Available at: http://uk.reuters.com/article/uk-syria-crisis-un/u-n-urges-end-to-syrias-convoluted-aid-restrictions-idUKBREA2R23620140328

Davey, E. and Svoboda, E., eds., 2014. *Histories of Humanitarian Action in the Middle East and North Africa.* HGP Working Paper. Available at: www.odi.org/sites/odi.org.uk/files/odi-assets/publications-opinion-files/9141.pdf

Els, C., Mansour, K. and Carstensen, N., 2016. *Between Sub-contracting and Partnerships.* Available at: www.local2global.info/wp-content/uploads/L2GP_funding_Syria_May_2016.pdf

Ferreiro, M., 2012. Blurring of Lines in Complex Emergencies: Consequences for the Humanitarian Community. *The Journal of Humanitarian Assistance.* Available at: http://sites.tufts.edu/jha/archives/1625#_edn1

Haddad, S. and Svoboda, E., 2017. *What's the Magic Word? Humanitarian Access and Local Organizations in Syria*, HPG Working Paper, ODI, March.

Hanafi, S., Hilal, L. and Takkenberg, L., eds., 2014. *UNRWA and Palestinian Refugees: From Relief and Works to Human Development.* London and New York: Routledge.

Hearn, R., 2016. How the Disunity among UN Agencies is Failing Syria, *Al Jazeera*, 5 July. Available at: www.aljazeera.com/indepth/opinion/2016/07/disunity-agencies-failing-syria-160705073104363.html

Hopkins, N and Beals, E., 2016. How Assad Regime Controls UN Aid Intended for Syria's Children, *The Guardian*, 29 August.

Howe, K., 2016. No End in Sight: A Case Study of Humanitarian Action and the Syria Conflict. *Planning from the Future. Component 2.* Available at: http://fic.tufts.edu/assets/syria_case_study.pdf

Hubert, D. and Brassard-Boudreau, C., 2010. Shrinking Humanitarian Space? Trends and Prospects on Security and Access. *The Journal of Humanitarian Assistance, 24.*

International Federation of the Red Cross and Red Crescent, 2015. *World Disasters Report, 2015, Focus on Local Actors the Key to Humanitarian Effectiveness*. Available at: http://ifrc-media.org/interactive/world-disasters-report-2015

James, E., 2003. Two Steps Back: Relearning the Humanitarian-Military Lessons Learned in Afghanistan and Iraq. *Journal of Humanitarian Assistance*. Available at: www.jha.ac/articles/a125.htm

Koops, J., Koops, J.A., MacQueen, N., Tardy, T. and Williams, P.D. eds., 2015. *The Oxford Handbook of United Nations Peacekeeping Operations*. Oxford, UK: Oxford Handbooks.

Lund, A., 2016. *The UN Enters Syria's Moral Labyrinth*, Carnegie Middle East Center, 9 September 2016.

Lynch, C., 2014. UN's Fear of Angering Assad Leaves Gap in Syria Aid Effort. Foreign Policy. Available at: https://foreignpolicy.com/2014/12/30/u-n-s-fear-of-angering-assad-leaves-gap-in-syria-aid-effort/

Martínez, J.C. and Eng, B., 2016. The Unintended Consequences of Emergency Food Aid: Neutrality, Sovereignty and Politics in the Syrian Civil War, 2012–15. *International Affairs*, 92(1), pp. 153–173.

de Montclos, M.A.P., 2014. The (de) Militarization of Humanitarian Aid: A Historical Perspective. *Humanities*, 3(2), pp. 232–243.

Narang, N., 2015. Assisting Uncertainty: How Humanitarian Aid Can Inadvertently Prolong Civil War. *International Studies Quarterly*, 59(1), pp. 184–195.

Physicians for Human Rights, 2017. *Access Denied: UN Aid Deliveries to Syria's Besieged and Hard-to-Reach Areas, March 2017*. Available at: https://phr.org/resources/access-denied-un-aid-deliveries-to-syrias-besieged-and-hard-to-reach-areas/

Qarmout, T. and Béland, D., 2012. The Politics of International Aid to the Gaza Strip. *Journal of Palestine Studies*, 41(4), pp. 32–47.

Rieff, D., 2003. *A Bed for the Night: Humanitarianism in Crisis*. New York: Simon & Schuster.

Secretary-General's Internal Review Panel on United Nations Action in Sri Lanka, 2012. *Report of the Secretary-General's Internal Review Panel on United Nations Action in Sri Lanka*, November, 2012. Available at: www.un.org/News/dh/infocus/Sri_Lanka/The_Internal_Review_Panel_report_on_Sri_Lanka.pdf

Sida, L., Trombetta, L. and Panero, V., 2016. *Evaluation of OCHA Response to the Syria Crisis*. Available at: https://docs.unocha.org/sites/dms/Documents/OCHA%20Syria%20Evaluation%20Report_FINAL.pdf

Sparrow, A., 2017. Enabling Assad. Foreign Affairs. Available at: www.foreignaffairs.com/articles/syria/2017-01-11/enabling-assad

Spyer, J., 2008. How UNRWA Became a Barrier to Peace, *Jerusalem Post*, May 27.

The Syria Campaign, 2016a. *Open Letter from Besieged Syrians to UN's Stephen O'Brien*, 15 January 2016. Available at: www.huffingtonpost.com/the-syria-campaign/open-letter-from-besieged_b_8979800.html

The Syria Campaign, 2016b. *Taking Sides: The United Nations' Loss of Impartiality, Independence and Neutrality in Syria*. Available at: http://takingsides.thesyriacampaign.org/wp-content/uploads/2016/06/taking-sides.pdf

Terry, F., 2013. *Condemned to Repeat: The Paradox of Humanitarian Action*. Cornell University Press.

Tran, M., 2013. Syria Appeal is Biggest in UN History, *The Guardian*, 7 June.

UNCTAD, 2015, September. *Report on UNCTAD Assistance to the Palestinian People: Developments in the Economy of the Occupied Palestinian Territory*. United Nations Conference on Trade and Development, Geneva. Available at: http://unctad.org/en/PublicationsLibrary/tdb62d3_en.pdf

Under-Secretary-General for Humanitarian Affairs and Emergency Relief Coordinator, 2016. Stephen O'Brien Statement to the Security Council on Syria, New York, 27 January 2016.

United Nations Country Team in the occupied Palestinian territory, 2017. *Gaza Ten Years Later*, July. Available at: https://unsco.unmissions.org/sites/default/files/gaza_10_years_later_-_11_july_2017.pdf

United Nations Secretary-General, 2017. *Implementation of Security Council Resolutions 2139 (2014), 2165 (2014), 2191 (2014), 2258 (2015) and 2332 (2016)*, 24 August 2017.

UNHCR, 2017. *Syria Regional Response Inter-Agency Information Sharing Portal*. Updated September. Available at: http://data.unhcr.org/syrianrefugees/regional.php

UNOCHA, 2017a. *Global 2017 Humanitarian Overview, June Status Report*. Available at: www.unocha.org/sites/unocha/files/GHO-JuneStatusReport2017.pdf

UNOCHA, 2017b. *Syrian Arab Republic*. September 2017. Available at: www.unocha.org/syria

Uvin, P., 1998. *Aiding Violence: The Development Enterprise in Rwanda*. Kumarian Press.

Wood, R.M. and Molfino, E., 2016. Aiding Victims, Abetting Violence: The Influence of Humanitarian Aid on Violence Patterns during Civil Conflict. *Journal of Global Security Studies*, 1(3), pp. 186–203.

World Food Programme, 2015a. *Emergency Food Assistance to the People Affected by Unrest in Syria, July, August, September 2015*. Available at: www1.wfp.org/operations/200339-emergency-food-assistance-people-affected-unrest-syria

World Food Programme, 2015b. *Evaluation Reports, Agenda item 7,* Summary Evaluation Report on WFP's Response to the Syrian Crisis (2011–2014), 25–28 May 2015. Available at: http://documents.wfp.org/stellent/groups/public/documents/eb/wfpdoc063892.pdf?_ga=2.165805630.1657222013.1505380001-1784047614.1505380001

Worldometers, 2017. *Egypt Population*. Available at: www.worldometers.info/world-population/egypt-population/

10
PEACEBUILDING IN THE MIDDLE EAST

Karin Aggestam and Lisa Strömbom

Introduction

The ongoing turmoil and unravelling conflicts in the Middle East present an infinite number of challenges to sustainable peace. The hopes for political liberalization generated by the Arab Spring have been pulled back by the restoration of military regimes as seen in Egypt and by the ongoing devastating warfare in Syria. The Israeli–Palestinian conflict seems more intractable than ever and the humanitarian situation in Yemen is dramatically deteriorating. In addition, international policies toward the region are strikingly incoherent despite various interventions that have been launched in recent years to counteract the spread of violence and terrorism by the Islamic State (IS). As a result, geopolitical influence has shifted toward regional power politics, exposing the deep rivalries between major states, such as Iran, Turkey and Saudi Arabia.

However, while the management of terrorism, power rivalries and civil wars are high on the international policy agenda, less attention is spent on the underlying conflict drivers, such as poverty, inequality and social exclusion, which are entrenched throughout the Middle East. The practice of peacebuilding is geared precisely toward such comprehensive societal analyses as it addresses the root causes of conflict. Yet, pessimistic and "doomsday" scenarios seem to dominate contemporary international discourses with emphasis on a negative notion of peace; that is, the absence of physical violence (Galtung, 1969). This generates short-term solutions, which primarily focus on the maintenance of status quo, stability and order (Ramsbotham et al., 2011). Yet, we argue that this is precisely the point in time when we simultaneously need to think beyond the physical manifestations of violence. Hence, our analysis of peacebuilding moves beyond negative peace by focusing on peacebuilding initiatives and efforts in various local contexts throughout the region. Consequently, the overarching aim of this chapter is to analyze some distinct peacebuilding strategies and the ways they are situated and implemented in the Middle East. With such an analysis, current enabling as well as restraining conditions for peacebuilding practices in the region are illuminated.

The concept of peacebuilding is an umbrella notion, which includes a broad set of activities that are related both to long- as well as short-term strategies in prevention, peace-making and post-conflict reconstruction. As such, it focuses on identifying root causes of conflict, which harbor the ability to generate deeper societal transformation and positive peace (Lederach, 1994). To delimit the scope of this chapter, we have chosen four peacebuilding domains, which we find particularly relevant for the construction of a long-term sustainable peace in the Middle East. These are linked to the contemporary research agenda on peacebuilding namely (1) institutionalization and security sector reform; (2) inclusion of youth in societal change; (3) gender equality and democratization; and (4) environment and sustainable peace. As countries and conflicts in the Middle East are diverse and face different challenges, we have chosen four empirical cases to illustrate these distinct peacebuilding efforts. Each case represents practices in one of the four domains of peacebuilding above and provides insight into the opportunities and restraints of conducting peacebuilding practices. The cases chosen are Tunisia, Lebanon, Iraq and Israel–Palestine, which provide multi-faceted illustrations and a broad set of problems pertaining to peacebuilding in the Middle East. Tunisia, the country where the Arab Spring set off in 2010 is currently going through major institutional changes, which include the security sector. Lebanon is formally in a post-conflict phase, but still plagued by intra-societal tensions caused by a long history of civil wars. Confronted with a massive influx of Syrian refugees the quest for preventive peacebuilding efforts among Lebanese youth is more urgent than ever. The third case focuses on the Middle East peace process where water has been a prioritized area for international peacebuilding actors since the 1990s. Finally, the last case concerns the people and state of Iraq, which are exposed to endemic violence since the US military intervention in 2002. Iraqi women in particular are vulnerable to sexual and gender-based violence. At the same time, as our analysis shows, women also serve as active agents for transformative change.

The chapter proceeds as follows. The first part provides a conceptual orientation on how peacebuilding can be defined in theory and in practice. It provides a brief overview of recent decades of international peacebuilding practices. The second part consists of four illustrative cases of peacebuilding. The first focuses on Security Sector Reforms (SSR) and how they have been practiced and implemented in the case of Tunisia since the ousting of the president Ben Ali in January 2011. The second case examines environmental peacebuilding efforts between Israelis and Palestinians as part of the Middle East peace process. It illustrates how local peacebuilding initiatives pertaining to environmental issues have sustained beyond the peace process. The third case analyzes how women have participated in the institutionalization of peace in Iraq and their struggle for gender equality. Finally, the last case illustrates how youth act as critical agents for peace and how their peacebuilding practices in Lebanon are performed. The chapter concludes on a note on the future of peacebuilding in the Middle East.

Peacebuilding in theory and practice

Peacebuilding is central to social progress as it seeks to address justice and the structural root causes of conflict (Mani, 2002; Aggestam and Björkdahl, 2013; Philpott, 2012). It is therefore closely related to social, economic and political progress by its ambition to build peace beyond the cessation of direct and organized violence. Peacebuilding activities are diverse and plural ways of transforming destructive, violent conflicts into constructive ones (Kriesberg, 2003). As such, it is related to positive peace (Galtung, 1969), which implies overcoming direct as well as structural and cultural violence. This section provides an overview of recent trends in the field of practice as well as in theory.

The peacebuilding field is relatively new and evolved as a response to the growing number of intrastate conflicts in the early 1990s. It was triggered after the end of the Cold War by the initial optimism about the prospects for collective actions within the United Nations (UN). At the same time, it was a response to the increasing number of intrastate conflicts with their devastating consequences, such as ethnic cleansings and genocides taking place in conflict zones such as the Western Balkans and Rwanda. A noticeable mobilization against these conflicts was observed on the international arena, which included humanitarian military interventions and long-term international engagement to build peace (Hoffman and Weiss, 2006; Philpott and Powers, 2010). Taking the lead, former UN Secretary-General Boutrous Boutrous-Ghali launched a new peacebuilding agenda in the document *Agenda for Peace* (1995) where peacebuilding is "defined as action to identify and support structures which will tend to strengthen and solidify in order to avoid a relapse into conflict". The document contained an ambitious agenda that underlined the responsibility of the international community to not only manage but also prevent conflict. Hence, peacebuilding was launched as an attempt to resolve problems associated with fragile, failing and dysfunctional states in order to transform them into robust, liberal democracies. The prospect of building peace and security was also to be bolstered and embedded by economic development, interdependence and regional cooperation. Consequently, comprehensive peace-support operations began to expand dramatically from the early 1990s onwards which was reflected not only in numbers but in their multifunctional tasks and mandates (Heldt and Wallensteen, 2006).

Peacebuilding is often described as the institutionalization of peace, which aims to balance the twin objectives of consolidating peace and averting a relapse into conflict (Mani, 2002). There are numerous definitions and concepts associated with peacebuilding, which reflect the broad range of activities associated with the term (Jeong, 2005; Call and Wyeth, 2008; Cousens and Kumar, 2001). Furthermore, the concept of peacebuilding serves as an umbrella notion, which overlaps with many other spheres of peacemaking, peacekeeping, development, reconciliation, institution building and democracy promotion.

Ramsbotham et al. (2011) suggest a useful analytical overview of peacebuilding, which is summarized in four dimensions. The first one regards *military/security*, focusing on establishing order and security in the post-conflict phase. For instance, peacekeeping troops can rapidly be deployed as a way to bolster a cease-fire, a peace agreement and to restore state control over the security sector after the violence has ceased. Thus, the quest to integrate various military branches into one and to transform rebel groups to political parties is of critical importance for security and order (Edmunds, 2008; Lyons, 2005; Sriram and Herman, 2009). This ambition is reflected in the number of programs that the international community has launched in recent years on Security Sector Reforms (SSR), in which strategies for Demilitarization, Demobilization and Reintegration (DDR) are often integrated. The second dimension of peacebuilding is *political/constitutional*, focusing on supporting the political and democratic transition from war to peace by assisting the establishment of the rule of law, for instance by drafting and making constitutional reforms and amendments, holding elections and strengthening civil society. In addition, one central aim is to introduce and build good governance and to establish a strong justice sector, which can monitor the adherence to human rights and democratic norms (Call, 2007; Jarstad and Sisk, 2008). The third dimension relates to *economic/social* peacebuilding practices, such as assisting with development and long-term sustainable macro-economic planning aimed to stabilize the economy of the state. Such efforts may include issues related to distributive justice and inequalities between groups, but may also comprise land ownership, property rights, employment and welfare programs (Berdal, 2009; Donais, 2005; Carey, 2012). The last dimension concerns the *psycho/social* dimensions of building peace in conflict-ridden and traumatized post-war societies. Thus, peacebuilding is here strongly associated with creating justice, reconciliation and the building of renewed societal relations after violence (Biggar, 2003; Murithi, 2009; Lederach, 1994).

The last two decades has seen a rapid professionalization of the peacebuilding field due to the increasing needs and demands of peace expertise, particularly from Western policy-makers. Yet, despite successful outcomes in some peace processes, the peacebuilding field is still struggling with a whole range of problems and challenges. These stem from various challenges to peace, such as collapsed peace processes (MacGinty, 2006), the non-implementation of negotiated peace agreements (Stedman et al., 2002), the resurgence of violence in post-conflict societies by so-called peace spoilers (Darby, 2001; Newman and Richmond, 2006), social exclusion of women and other marginalized groups (Paffenholz et al., 2016), and widespread peace fatigue in long-drawn peace processes (Perry, 2009; Aggestam and Strömbom, 2013). Hence, a number of assessment studies and evaluation programs have been conducted on peacebuilding practices that aim to distill lessons learned and identify best practices (see, for example, Reychler and Schirch, 2013).

The scholarly field of peacebuilding has also sought to generate policy relevant contributions, which for example is reflected in the large number of handbooks on peacebuilding produced, including tool-boxes and recommendations of suitable strategies and best practice (see, for example, UN, 2010). Several academic studies have also examined the correlation between peacebuilding and sustainable peace from a diversity of theoretical perspectives (Newman et al., 2009) and methodological approaches ranging from large N-studies (Wallensteen, 2015) to ethnographic studies (Paffenholz, 2001). Yet, despite their generic drive, these studies show that there is no universal blueprint for peacebuilding. Hence, greater attention is now paid to local ownership, institutions and capacity peacebuilding (MacGinty, 2006).

At the same time, these evaluations and assessments have triggered major debates among scholars who hold distinct ideas of what should be viewed as efficient as well as sustainable peacebuilding. Newman and others (2009) have identified three ideal types of peacebuilding: transformative, realist and liberal. Transformative peacebuilding focuses on resolving the underlying causes of conflict and strives to promote a durable peace, which rests on a positive interpretation of peace and social justice, as well as a desire to engage with local actors, bottom-up approaches and the promotion of human security. Accordingly, this is not a universalizing vision of peace but one that recognizes the importance of diverse contexts. In contrast, realist peacebuilding puts less emphasis on resolving conflict and more on managing and containing conflict escalation. An overriding strategic concern is the establishment of international stability and order by establishing strong states. Societal change on the other hand is delinked from international peacebuilding in this realist understanding (Barnett et al., 2014). Finally, liberal peacebuilding may be the one that most clearly articulates its vision of peace by its democracy promotion, market economy and state-building efforts. Thus, it has guided most peacebuilding interventions in recent years. This is also why the debates mostly have centered on liberal peacebuilding where critics highlight its limitations in practice (Campbell et al., 2011).

Contemporary peacebuilding practices have been criticized for their oftentimes top-down and hegemonic interventions, which tend to create more of virtual than real state institutions and hybrid forms of peace as a result of the international–local interplay (MacGinty, 2010). The ambition to rapidly promote democracy and market-based economic reforms in post-conflict societies risks causing counter-productive results, such as instability and even exacerbated conflict. In addition, ill-timed and poorly organized political elections may backfire and trigger ethnic tensions, which we have seen in Iraq. Scholarly work has highlighted the risk and vulnerabilities of conflict escalation particularly in partial democracies and transitional states. This is why Roland Paris (2004), for example, argues that institutionalization should precede liberalization.

As these debates reflect, peacebuilding in practice has in many instances failed to live up to its high expectations and ambitious normative agenda as articulated in the 1990s. Consequently, we are today witnessing an increasing pragmatism in peacebuilding (Barnett et al., 2014; Paris

2014), which is coupled with new major security and political challenges in global politics, such as the resurgence of authoritarianism and the Islamic State's (IS) spheres of influence in the Middle East and elsewhere. These are taking place in parallel with the increasing failures of regional and international institutions to cope with and manage security threats with cohesive, comprehensive and multilateral strategies, which the ongoing war in Syria tragically illustrates. Consequently, the concept of resilience in peacebuilding has taken hold and centers on capacity building and the strengthening of the ability of local communities themselves to prevent and manage conflict (Chandler, 2015). Resilient peacebuilding acknowledges the complexity and multi-layered nature of building peace in conflict societies, which are seen as being in constant state of flux. Hence, social and political progress should be understood in terms of adaptive cycles. States and societies need to embrace both complexity as well as various adaptive strategies in preventing and managing violence. Consequently, it signifies a major shift in the way the international community actors intervene to assist in peacebuilding. The overarching ambition is no longer to impose a specific model or agenda for peace, but rather to facilitate, strengthen and create space for existing national and local capabilities to cope with violent change and sustain peace.

Security sector reform in Tunisia

An integral part of many peacebuilding programs is the challenge of security sector reform (SSR), which refers to the structural transformation of former armies, militias and armed combatants into a reformed security sector that can anchor the peace in principles of democracy and rule of law (Lyons, 2005, Sriram and Herman, 2009). However, actors in the security sector are used to working in an environment of internal conflict and are thus seldom held accountable for their actions. It is therefore a daunting task to create a new security culture where former militias take part in a reshaped national army, which requires new practical routines as well as transformed mind-sets. Furthermore, the aim of SSR is to disarm, demobilize, and repatriate (DDR) former warring groups. This includes the construction of incentives for former combatants to give up their arms, which is difficult as they then can be seen as giving up their trump card to use violence to express their grievances. Furthermore, it points to the need to control small arms and light weapons and the reintegration of child soldiers. Hence, the overarching goal of SSR is to reconstitute national forces so they can remain under government control and have enough strength to outweigh possible challengers from below. It is therefore often argued that interveners and peacebuilders cannot withdraw from the mission until the security sector is fully reformed.

The Tunisian revolution broke out in December 2010, starting with a single fruit-vendor's individual protest against corruption, which triggered large-scale popular protest. The people of Tunisia thereafter mobilized against the authoritarian regime led by Ben Ali since 1987, which ended in the overthrow of the regime a month later. The revolt in Tunisia, the Jasmine Revolution, sparked uprisings against authoritarian rule all over the Middle East, which took place in Syria, Libya, Yemen and Egypt under the umbrella name "the Arab Spring". The historical record for many of these uprisings has subsequently become tainted as a majority of the political protests backlashed and the much-hoped for democracy came to a halt. Tunisia, however, is seen as one of the more successful cases where democratic rule has been established in a process toward rule of law, freedom of speech and the success of forming a new constitution.

Yet, one of the most challenging tasks in Tunisia's transition process toward peace and democracy to this date has been to reform the Tunisian security sector. Tunisia's political life is characterized by polarization between secular and religious groups and a growing split has become visible during the peacebuilding process (ICG, 2015:12). When the new constitution was finally in place in 2014, after concerted efforts from the dialogue quartet consisting of four national organizations,[1] intense attempts were made to embark on an ambitious SSR process. Tunisia's major security institutions were targeted for reforms, such as the Ministry of Defense, the Ministry of Interior, and the Ministry of Justice, which controls all personnel within the judicial sector (Hanlon, 2012).

The Tunisian SSR-process has mainly focused on regulating the Ministry of the Interior, which in practice controls the Ministry of Justice (Sayigh, 2015:6). This reflects political and popular demands as corruption and violence emanates from the security sector (ICG, 2015). Intense efforts have also been made at reforming the Ministry of Interior with the dismissal of a large number of executive personnel and the remaking of the structure of the police forces with recruitment of new heads of police nationally as well as locally. These forceful struggles to reform Tunisia's security sector were in turn supported by many external actors, including multi-national organizations, such as Democratic Control of Armed Forces (DCAF) and UNESCO (IFIT, 2013), as well as individual states, such as Qatar, Germany and the US (Kartas, 2014). The EU, for instance, contributed 23 million euros to SSR-programs, targeting Islamic terrorism and radicalization (EUAA, 2016:2). Doubtlessly, large resources have been spent nationally as well as internationally in order to reform Tunisia's security sector. Even though Tunisia is a successful example of democratization from a broader perspective of the Arab Spring, the SSR-process has been stained by major problems and the future process seems uncertain. Critics have argued that one contributing problem is that international actors have mostly invested in reforms aimed at their own security (Abrahamsen, 2016), such as anti-terrorism activities sponsored by the EU. Furthermore, single actors within the Ministry of Interior have used sporadic political turbulence to evade new reforms, claiming that they have to focus on the growing external threats from Islamic terror-groups instead of reforming the security sector from within (Sayigh, 2015). These actors have also successfully used social media to promote an image of acting in the interest of the people; thus, being able to escape heightened measures of external control of their actions. Despite intense efforts by new NGOs aimed at monitoring the reform of the security sector, such as the Tunisian Institutional Reform (TIR), many problems remain. For example, non-violent civil society organizations have been depicted as a threat to the state by the Ministry of Interior: organizations and mosques have been shut down; and there have been severe limitations to the right to demonstrate. Moreover, continuous accusations of corruption and violence from the state apparatus emanate from organizations as well as the public, which underline the complex and difficult path to transition from conflict to peace and democracy as well the challenging task of reforming a security sector, which has long been characterized by a paranoia that comes with authoritarian rule.

Environmental peacebuilding in Israel–Palestine

Projections of climatic change in the Middle East foretell rising temperatures and decreased precipitation, which will increase evaporation of surface water, slow down rejuvenation of groundwater and add to aridity in the whole region. Besides these direct threats to water resources, climate change will most likely have negative effects on economic growth, social stability and food security due to diminished production from local agriculture and higher global food prices. Future climate patterns are furthermore assumed to become more unpredictable, which may add uncertainty and contribute to the securitization of natural resources. Water resources are especially highly present in the framing of conflict scenarios. For instance, some analysts argue that one significant cause of the outbreak of civil war in Syria was water scarcity (Selby, 2017). However, in more recent years, water scarcity has also increasingly been associated with the potential for cooperation and peace. For instance, with the start of the Middle East peace process, water constituted one important area of the standing working groups within the multilateral framework, aiming to foster regional cooperation and sustainable peace (Peters, 1996).

With the Declaration of Principles in 1993, water was mentioned as a potential area of cooperation and economic growth in general terms. As a consequence, many hydro-peacebuilding projects between Israelis and Palestinians were launched and received generous funding under the assumption that cooperation over water, economic development and peace are strongly interrelated. Yet, as the first agreement in 1993 concerned general principles, it lacked specified criteria which could be agreed upon by all. Moreover, water rights and resource allocation were only vaguely mentioned. Many technical water projects in the West Bank and the Gaza Strip were initiated and funded in an effort to develop additional water supplies (Aggestam, 2015). Most of these efforts centered on cooperation in the eastern basin as well as in the Gaza Strip, which suffer severe salinization problems and brackish groundwater.

The second major interim agreement between Israel and the PLO from 1995 was more specific and stressed that cooperation on water resources was an imperative. Both parties were thus committed to develop water from the West Bank underground aquifers in order to meet the immediate needs of the Palestinians. This provided, according to Selby (2003: 125), a first step in the direction of an equitable water-sharing arrangement. Also, a Joint Water Committee was established with the aim of coordinating, protecting and managing water resources and sewage systems. In addition, a formal system of teams for supervision and monitoring was put into place. Yet, it is important to note that the Water Committee had no power to regulate or administer existing quantities of water as currently extracted by the Israeli Civil administration and the Jewish settlements (Schlütter, 2005: 628). This is why some scholars argue that the "Oslo II negotiations did little more than to formalise and legitimate management structures and relations, which were already very much in existence" (Selby, 2003: 127; see also Jägerskog, 2003).

Even though the Middle East peace process collapsed in early 2000, other local alternative peacebuilding efforts sustained despite the overall hostile environment between Israelis and Palestinians. One such organization is EcoPeace (former FOEME), which began its work at the start of the peace process by bringing together Jordanian, Palestinian and Israeli environmentalists.[2] The ambition of the organization has all along centered on building peace through cooperation in the field of environment and by transnational advocacy to protect shared environmental heritage. With the outbreak of the second *intifada* in 2000, its peacebuilding strategies focused increasingly on bottom-up, community-led activism. One such outcome is the "Good Water Neighbors project", which contains cross-border support of water supply and sanitation (Harari and Roseman, 2008). Initially, the project involved 11 communities, but has expanded to 26 (nine Palestinian, eight Israeli and nine Jordanian). Other significant projects focus on the rehabilitation of the Jordan Valley. The diversion of 96% of the fresh water from the Jordan River in combination with the discharge of large quantities of untreated sewage is causing irreversible damage to the Jordan Valley. Related to this are also efforts to stabilize the Dead Sea where the water level is dropping a meter per year. In addition to these peacebuilding efforts, EcoPeace has developed three Ecoparks in Jordan, Israel and Palestine in an effort to promote shared space and to preserve biodiversity. These parks are also used to promote environmental education and to foster concrete experiences of shared environments. What the work of EcoPeace illustrates is that peacebuilding needs to be locally anchored, long-term and sustainable despite the ongoing and intractable nature of the Israeli–Palestinian conflict.

Women and institution building in Iraq

The adoption of the Security Council resolution 1325 (SCR 1325) in 2000 constitutes a land-mark. For the first time, gender was placed at the core of peacebuilding processes. The resolution on Women, Peace and Security (WPS) underlines representation and participation of women in peacebuilding processes as well as at the negotiation table. Moreover, the SCR 1325 stipulates that women should be an integral part of conflict prevention, resolution and peacebuilding efforts at local, national as well as international levels (Pratt and Richter-Devroe, 2011). Iraq has a history tainted with conflicts, such as the long war with neighboring Iran, the conflict with Kuwait in 1991 and most recently its own civil war, triggered by the US-led invasion which sought to remove suspected chemical weapons and to overthrow Saddam Hussein's authoritarian regime.

Today the country is largely in turmoil, plagued with internal strife, terrorism, suicide bombings and a myriad of radical armed groups, which are competing for power in different parts of the country. Despite this tumultuous development, Iraq has simultaneously been undergoing an institution-building process with the aim of building a democratic peaceful state. Integral to this process has been a conscious effort to include women in the political process of building peace and institutions (WWICS, 2003).

With a highly ambitious agenda set out from the start, the goal has been to include women in all institutions and from all parts of society. Already in 2005, a 25% female quota in parliament was put in place with the aim of increasing women's participation and political influence in the Iraqi post-conflict phase. Yet, the quota failed to address women's specific needs and women are still vastly under-represented in most political forums. For instance, when a national reconciliation commission was created in order to promote values of tolerance, nonviolence and the rule of law, women were not included. Instead women were relegated to their "own" forum, the "Office for Women in the National Commission", which has little resources and no real influence over the wider political process (Khoudary, 2016).

Furthermore, the deteriorating security situation has hindered women from participating in political life since traditional culture in Iraq has been inclined to view women as security providers of the household, which consequently has meant that they have to stay at home to care for the family. Thus, women's participation in formal political institutions has been impaired and constrained by the patriarchal nature of Iraqi society. However, within the informal spheres where civil society (CSO) and community-based organizations (CBO) are vital, women play an important part. On the local level, women in CSOs play a crucial role in easing the suffering of women and children in conflict by working with legal channels as well as humanitarian aid (Khoudary, 2016). In 2014, following intense women's activism, the National Action Plan was put in place with the aim of implementing 1325 in Iraqi peacebuilding efforts. This proves that Iraqi women still struggle to have a voice in the peacebuilding process. They have further tried to influence the situation of women in the conflict in Syria and those affected by ISIS's land winnings in the Middle East. The National Action Plan has succeeded in changing facts on the ground, such as building shelters for women affected by violence and suggesting reformed legislation that supports women's rights. However, resources are scarce and the laws are seldom implemented due to a lack of resources and resistance from the patriarchal culture that prevails among men and women (WPP, 2015). The future of the WPS agenda in Iraq is therefore uncertain. Yet, the recent defeat of ISIS in important former strongholds such as Mosul has created a hope for a strengthened reconciliation process. Consultations with local and national women's groups have been held in order to strengthen women's rights and voice in the reconciliation process (UN Women et al., 2017). Thus, there is some hope for an enhanced representation of women in Iraqi peacebuilding if the country continues to tread a more peaceful path. Yet, given the historical turmoil and suppression of women during the conflict-ridden years since 2003, there are still dire challenges ahead.

Youth and peacebuilding in Lebanon

One of the most severe long-term challenges in the Middle East is how to cope with the rapid population growth. ". Youth under the age of 24 now makes up 50–65% of the population in most states in the Middle East (Youth Policy Organisation, 2017). This places an immense strain on the entire infrastructures, not least on the educational system that is already poor or in decline in many states. It also exacerbates social, political and economic problems that the region is facing (Monshipouri, 2014). In addition, youth participation in the workforce is the lowest among the developing regions and the discrepancy in participation between men and women is the highest in the world. As a consequence, unemployment is widespread and male youth in particular is increasingly associated with problems pertaining to crime and political violence (Youth Policy Organisation, 2017).

To counter these pessimistic scenarios, recent academic literature and policy reports have begun to highlight the ways in which youth can constructively contribute to peacebuilding (see, for example Pruitt, 2014; Williams, 2016). It is important to identify youth as a vulnerable group and how young people are affected by armed conflicts in multiple ways. At the same time, their wider socio-economic needs should be taken into account as their positions in society have a long-term bearing on their potential peacebuilding capacity and power. Yet, here lies an obvious tension between the young and old generations, which concerns among many other things the control of power and resources.

Recognizing the fact that the number of youth is the largest ever worldwide, the United Nations Security Council adopted a new resolution in 2015, number 2250 on Youth, Peace and Security, which follows resolution 1325 on Women, Peace and Security. Resolution 2250 focuses on youth aged between 18 and 29 and their participation in the prevention, protection and reintegration to society in the post-conflict phase. Furthermore, the resolution underlines how conflicts disrupt youth's social and economic development. It recognizes how this may lead to a rise of radicalization of violence and violent extremism. At the same time, it stresses how youth can be viewed as critical agents for change in the ways they can potentially play constructive roles in their communities as part of conflict prevention (United Nations, 2014). The UN resolution therefore corresponds with Agenda 2030, which focus on young people's empowerment, participation and well-being in one-third of the Sustainable Development Goals (The Global Survey on Youth, Peace, Security, 2016). At the same time, it is important to acknowledge the cultural, economic and political barriers that prevent broadened participation of youth in a region such as the Middle East.

In the case of Lebanon, the country continues to struggle with its legacy of a violent past, fragmented societal fabric, prolonged governmental crises and more recently by the huge influx of Syrian refugees, which has increased the resident population by nearly 25% in Lebanon (Bocco and Belhadj, 2014). The Lebanon Agreement, which was signed in 2007, puts a strong emphasis on political, economic and social reforms. Yet, sustainable peacebuilding efforts are constantly punctuated by broader regional dynamics and tensions, such as the ongoing Syrian conflict and the Sunni–Shia divide, which are affecting rivalries and alliance building in the region. Deep-seated sectarian animosities also persist in the country, which increase the likelihood for future political instability and violence in Lebanon. At the same time, the international engagement has prioritized post-conflict recovery activities, such as humanitarian aid, local development, security sector reform, reconstruction of infrastructure, public administration reform, and political stabilization in accordance with human rights (Bandini, 2012).

To prevent and mitigate conflict mobilization among youth along sectarian lines, a number of "multi-stakeholder strategies" have been launched by CSOs, such as Generations For Peace; Development for People and Nature Association; the Beirut Centre for Development and Human Rights (Wuerth, 2015). One such example is the "Youth Network for Civic Activism". To counter the common practice by political parties and other factions of using burning tires to block roads between communities as a form of protest, this network reframed the rites in the southern town of Nabatieh by painting the tires in bright colours and converting them into furniture and flower pots. Another example is the Eco Warriors who try to foster inclusive group identity around environmental issues as a way to counter and prevent extremisms among youth. Other forums, festivals and training for youth across the communities aim to enhance belonging and trust building. For instance, in the northern city of Tripoli vocational training is provided to diverse groups of youth. They all have different religious affiliations, but share a similar background of coming from economically marginalized areas. Through the training in communication skills, these young people have become more used to working together and friendships have thereby been formed (Wuerth, 2015).

In particular, sport- and art-based peacebuilding activities among youth have been recognized as a constructive entry point and platform for interaction and community building. With the Syrian refugee influx, many young people have felt isolated and rejected. ANERA is one such civil society organization, which uses a broad range of sport and other recreational activities to bring together youth to promote dialogue, empowerment and social integration among Palestinian, Syrian and Lebanese youth.[3]

In most youth peacebuilding initiatives, education is central. Yet, it is a major challenge to integrate peacebuilding into formal and non-formal education channels and school environments in Lebanon. The UNDP supports a wide range of local peacebuilding organizations, which aim to create "safe spaces" for groups to meet and discuss openly in partnerships with local governmental actors. One such example is the "Violence Free Schools Initiative", which focuses on "Codes of Conduct for Non-Violence" and other non-violent tools of dealing with conflicts. Another focus area is the training of youth leadership based on principles of conflict resolution. Here a number of initiatives have been taken in coordination with Lebanese American University and the Lebanese Conflict Resolution Network (Safa, 2007).

Conclusion

This chapter has discussed diverse contexts, challenges and a broad range of peacebuilding practices that exist in the Middle East. Yet, one overarching conclusion that can be drawn from the analysis is that heightened conflict and tension create less room for peaceful political and institutional change. Tunisia, with its relatively successful democratization process, is a deviant case in the way that it has been able to conduct deep structural change of its security sector, despite an uneven and troublesome transition phase. In the same vein, Lebanon is officially in a post-conflict phase, but continues to experience grave tensions and competition for power that the Hariri government confronted most recently in the last few months of 2017. Despite the vulnerability that Lebanon is facing in regards to spill-over effects from regional rivalries, the peacebuilding activities among Lebanese youth still hold the greatest prospect for a peaceful reconstitution of future societal relations between sectarian groups. In the cases of Iraq and Israel–Palestine, the peacebuilding efforts are highly restrained as both cases are stuck in destructive limbos between war and peace. Despite highly ambitious and costly peacebuilding initiatives, the structural power asymmetries between various ethnic groups inhibit any opportunities to achieve conflict transformation. At the same time, "islands of peace" at local levels and in specific issue areas can nevertheless be identified (Aggestam and Strömbom, 2013). Even though these peacebuilding initiatives seem to be disconnected from the overarching development in the countries, they still constitute ground-breaking work, which in the long run can lay the foundations for a sustainable peace in the Middle East.

Notes

1 These are the Tunisian General Labor Union, the Tunisian Confederation of Industry, Trade and Handicrafts, the Tunisian Human Rights League and the Tunisian Order of Lawyers.
2 See www.ecopeaceme.org
3 See www.anera.org

References

Abrahamsen, Rita, 2016. "Exporting Security Governance: The Tensions of Security Sector Reform", *Global Crime*, 17(3–4): 1–15.
Aggestam, Karin, 2015. "Desecuritisation of Water and the Technocratic Turn in Peacebuilding", *Journal of International Environmental Agreement. Politics, Law and Economics*, 15(3): 327–340.
Aggestam, Karin and Björkdahl, Annika, eds, 2013. *Rethinking Peacebuilding: The Quest for Just Peace in the Middle East and the Western Balkans*. London and New York: Routledge.
Aggestam, Karin and Strömbom, Lisa, 2013. "Disempowerment and Marginalisation of Peace NGOs: Exposing Peace Gaps in Israel and Palestine", *Peacebuilding* 1(1): 109–124.
Bandini, Duccio, 2012. "International Peacebuilding in Lebanon", *Conciliation Resources*. Available at www.c-r.org/accord-article/international-peacebuilding-lebanon-what-role-eu
Barnett, Michael, Fang, Songying and Zürcher, Christoph, 2014. "Compromised Peacebuilding", *International Studies Quarterly*, 58(3): 608–620.
Berdal, Mats, 2009. *Building Peace after War*. London: Routledge.
Biggar, Nigel, ed., 2003. *Burying the Past. Making Peace and Doing Justice after Civil Conflict*. Washington, DC: Georgetown University.
Bocco, Riccardo and Belhadj, Souhail, 2014. *Middle East: Regional Perspectives for the White Paper on Peacebuilding*, Geneva Peacebuilding Platform. Available at www.gpplatform.ch/sites/default/files/White%20Paper%20Series%20-%20Compilation.pdf
Campbell, Susanna, Chandler, David and Sabaratnam, Meera, 2011. *A Liberal Peace? The Problems and Practices of Peacebuilding*. London: Zed Books.
Call, Charles T., ed., 2007. *Constructing Justice and Security after War*. Washington, DC: United States Institute for Peace.
Call, Charles T. and Wyeth, Vanessa, eds, 2008 *Building States to Build Peace*. Boulder and London: Lynne Rienner Publishers.
Carey, Henry F., 2012. *Privatizing the Democratic Peace: Policy Dilemmas of NGO Peacebuilding*. Basingstoke: Palgrave Macmillan.
Chandler, David, 2015. "Resilience and the 'Everyday': Beyond the Paradox of 'Liberal Peace'", *Review of International Studies*, 41(1): 27–48.
Cousens, Elizabeth and Kumar, Chetan, 2001. *Peacebuilding as Politics*. Boulder: Lynne Rienner Publisher.
Darby, John, 2001. *The Effects of Violence on Peace Processes*. Washington, DC: United States Institute of Peace Press.
Donais, Timothy, 2005. *The Political Economy of Peacebuilding in Post-Dayton Bosnia*. London: Routledge.
EUAA, 2016. "Relations between the EU and Tunisia", *European Union External Action Factsheet*, 29 November 2016. https://eeas.europa.eu/headquarters/headquarters-homepage_en/16047/Relations%20between%20the%20EU%20and%20Tunisia.
Edmunds, Timothy, 2008. *Security Sector Reform in Transforming Societies*. Manchester: Manchester University Press.
Galtung, Johan, 1969. "Violence, Peace and Peace Research", *Journal of Peace Research*, 6(3): 167–191.

Hanlon, Querine, 2012. *The Prospects for Security Sector Reform in Tunisia: A Year after the Revolution*, The International Security Sector Advisory Team, The Geneva Center for the Democratic Control of Armed Forces. http://issat.dcaf.ch/Learn/Resource-Library/Policy-and-Research-Papers/The-Prospects-for-Security-Sector-Reform-in-Tunisia-A-Year-After-the-Revolution.

Harari, N. and Roseman, J., 2008. *Environmental Peacebuilding in Theory and Practice*. EcoPeace Friends of the Earth Middle East. www.foeme.org

Heldt, Birger and Wallensteen, Peter, 2006. *Peacekeeping Operations: Global Patterns of Intervention and Success, 1948–2004*. Stockholm: Folke Bernadotte Academy.

Hoffman, Peter and Weiss, Thomas, 2006. *Sword and Salve: Confronting New Wars and Humanitarian Crisis*. Oxford: Rowman and Little Publishers.

ICG, 2015. "Reform and Security Strategy in Tunisia", International Crisis Group, *Middle East and North Africa Report*, No 161, 23 July 2015. www.crisisgroup.org/middle-east-north-africa/north-africa/tunisia/reform-and-security-strategy-tunisia

IFIT, 2013. *Inside the Transition Bubble: International Expert Assistance in Tunisia*. Institute of Integrated Transitions. www.ifit-transitions.org/resources/publications/major-publications-briefings/inside-the-transition-bubble-international-expert-assistance-in-tunisia/inside-the-transition-bubble-en-full

Jägerskog, A., 2003. *Why States Cooperate over Shared Water: The Water Negotiations in the Jordan River Basin*. Linköping: Linköping Arts and Science.

Jarstad, Anna and Sisk, Timothy, 2008. *From War to Democracy: Dilemmas of Peacebuilding*. Cambridge: Cambridge University Press.

Jeong, H.-W., 2005. "Peacebuilding in Postconflict Societies", in Michael Keating, Anne Le More and Robert Lowe (eds.), *Aid, Diplomacy and Facts on the Ground*. Bristol: Chatham House.

Kartas, Moncef, 2014. "Foreign Aid and Security Sector Reform in Tunisia: Resistance and Autonomy of the Security Forces", *Mediterranean Politics*, 19(3): 373–391.

Khoudary, Yasmin, 2016. "Women and Peace-Building in Iraq", *Peace Review: A Journal of Social Justice*, 28: 499–507.

Kriesberg, L., 2003. *Constructive Conflicts*. Oxford: Rowman & Littlefield Publishers.

Lederach, John Paul, 1994. *Building Peace: Sustainable Reconciliation in Divided Societies*. Washington, DC: United States Institute of Peace Press.

Lyons, Terrence, 2005. *Demilitarizing Politics*. Boulder: Lynne Rienner Publishers.

Mani, Rama, 2002. *Beyond Retribution: Seeking Justice in the Shadows of War*. Cambridge: Polity Press.

MacGinty, Roger, 2010. "Hybrid Peace: The Interaction between Top-down and Bottom-up Peace", *Security Dialogue*, 41(4): 391–412.

MacGinty, Roger, 2006. *No War, No Peace. The Rejuvenation of Stalled Peace Processes and Peace Accords*. Basingstoke and New York: Palgrave.

Monshipouri, Mahmood, 2014. *Democratic Uprisings in the New Middle East. Youth, Technology, Human Rights and Foreign Policy*. Boulder: Paradigm Publishers.

Murithi, Tim, 2009. *The Ethics of Peacebuilding*. Edinburgh: Edinburgh University Press.

Newman, Edward and Richmond, Oliver, eds., 2006. *Challenges to Peacebuilding: Managing Spoilers During Conflict Resolution*. Tokyo: United Nations University Press.

Newman, Edward, Paris, Roland and Richmond, Oliver, eds., 2009. *New Perspectives on Liberal Peacebuilding*. Tokyo: United Nations University Press.

Office of the Secretary-General's Envoy on Youth, 2016. "Global Survey on Youth, Peace and Security". www.un.org/youthenvoy/2016/11/global-survey-youth-peace-security/

Paffenholz, Thania, 2001. *Peacebuilding: A Field Guide*. Boulder: Lynne Rienner.

Paffenholz, Thania, Ross, Nick, Dixon, Steven, Schluchter, Anna-Lena, and True, Jacqui, 2016. "Making Women Count – Not just Counting Women: Assessing Women's Inclusion and Influence on Peace Negotiations", *Report ITI, UN Women*, www.inclusivepeace.org

Paris, Roland, 2004. *At War's End: Building Peace after Civil Conflict*. New York: Cambridge University Press.

Paris, Roland, 2014. "The Geopolitics of Peace Operations: A Research Agenda", *International Peacekeeping*, 21(4): 501–508.

Perry, Valery, 2009. "At Cross Purposes? Democratization and Peace Implementation Strategies in Bosnia and Herzegovina's Frozen Conflict", *Human Rights Review*, 10: 35–54.

Peters, Joel, 1996. *Pathways to Peace? The Multilateral Arab-Israel Peace Talks*. London: Royal Institute of International Affairs.

Philpott, Daniel, 2012. *Just and Unjust Peace: An Ethic of Political Reconciliation*. Oxford: Oxford University Press.

Philpott, Daniel and Powers, Gerard, eds, 2010. *Strategies of Peace: Transforming Conflict in a Violent World.* Oxford: Oxford University Press.

Pratt, Nicola and Richter-Devroe, Sophie, 2011. "Critically Examining UNSCR 1325 on Women, Peace and Security", *International Feminist Journal of Politics*, 13: 489–503.

Pruitt, Lesley, 2014. *Youth Peacebuilding.* Albany, NY: SUNY Press.

Ramsbotham, Oliver, Woodhouse, Tom and Miall, Hugh, 2011. *Contemporary Conflict Resolution.* Oxford: Blackwell Publishers.

Reychler, Luc and Schirch, Lisa, 2013. *Conflict Assessment and Peacebuilding Planning: Toward a Participatory Approach to Human Security.* Boulder: Lynne Rienner Publishers.

Safa, Oussama, 2007. *Conflict Resolution and Reconciliation in the Arab World: The Work of Civil Society Organizations in Lebanon and Morocco.* Berghof Research Center for Constructive Conflict Management. Available at www.berghof-foundation.org/fileadmin/redaktion/Publications/Handbook/Articles/safa_handbook.pdf.

Sayigh, Yezid, 2015. "Missed Opportunity: The Politics of Police Reform in Egypt and Tunisia", *Carnegie Middle East Center*, March 2015. http://carnegie-mec.org/2015/03/17/missed-opportunity-politics-of-police-reform-in-egypt-and-tunisia-pub-59391.

Schlütter, B., 2005. "Water Rights in the West Bank and in Gaza", *Leiden Journal of International Law*, 18: 621–644.

Selby, Jan, 2003. "Dressing up Domination as 'Cooperation': The Case of Israeli–Palestinian Water Relations", *Review of International Studies*, 29(1): 121–138.

Selby, J., Dahi, O., Frölich, C. and Hulme, M., 2017. "Climate Change and the Syrian Civil War Revisited", *Political Geography*, 60: 232–244.

Sriram, Chandra Lekha and Herman, Johanna, 2009. "DDR and Transitional Justice", *Conflict, Security & Development*, 9(4): 10–11.

Stedman, Stephen, Rothchild, Donald S. and Cousens, Elizabeth M. (eds.), 2002. *Ending Civil Wars: The Implementation of Peace Agreements.* Boulder: Lynne Rienner Publishers.

UN Women, UN Assistance Mission for Iraq, Government of Iraq, 2017. "Women's Participation in Iraq's National Reconciliation Process Paramount", 21 July 2017. https://reliefweb.int/report/iraq/women-s-participation-iraq-s-national-reconciliation-process-paramount-enar.

United Nations, 2010. *Monitoring Peace Consolidation: United Nations Practitioners' Guide to Benchmarking.* New York: United Nations.

United Nations, 2014. "Security Council, Unanimously Adopting Resolution 2250 (2015), Urges Member States to Increase Representation of Youth in Decision-Making at All Levels", *Meetings Coverage.* website. www.un.org/press/en/2015/sc12149.doc.htm.

Wallensteen, Peter, 2015. *Quality Peace: Peacebuilding, Victory and World Order.* Oxford: Oxford University Press.

Williams, Margaret, 2016. "Youth, Peace, and Security: A New Agenda for the Middle East and North Africa", *Journal of International Affairs*, 69(2): 103–112.

WPP, 2015. "Interview with Susan Aref, director of Women's Empowerment Organization in Iraq, conducted by Margaret Williams", *The Women Peacemaker Program.* www.womenpeacemakersprogram.org/news/challenges-facing-womens-participation-in-peacebuilding-processes-in-iraq/

Wuerth, Oriana, 2015. "4 lessons on youth and peacebuilding in Lebanon." Available at www.devex.com/news/4-lessons-on-youth-and-peace-building-in-lebanon-85649

WWICS, 2003. "Building a New Iraq: Women's Role in Reconstruction: Women's Role in Strengthening Civil Society. Findings and Conclusions". *The Woodrow Wilson International Center for Scholars, Conflict Prevention Project, Middle East Project.* www.inclusivesecurity.org/wp-content/uploads/2012/09/20_building_a_new_iraq_women_s_role_in_reconstruction.pdf

Youth Policy Organisation, 2017. *Middle East and North Africa: Youth Facts.* Available at www.youthpolicy.org/mappings/regionalyouthscenes/mena/facts/

PART II

Energy, resource issues and climate change as security issues in the Middle East

11

THE WATER-ENERGY-FOOD NEXUS IN THE MENA REGION

Securities of the future

Martin Keulertz and Tony Allan

Introduction

Water in the Middle East and North Africa (MENA) region is a topic that has been high on the agenda of the region's decision-makers. The limits of natural resources are increasingly felt by populations across the region. Water has become one of the topics that could make or break economies and societies in the region. In particular, the water-food-energy nexus is a concept which has special relevance for the MENA region. The WEF Nexus, as it is frequently described, suggests that if water, energy and food systems are jointly managed, there could be trade-offs. Initially a concept developed by McKinsey consultants, the nexus has been promoted by European agencies in the MENA region to identify new holistic management approaches (Keulertz et al., 2016). Yet, the nexus has not been very successful thus far. Despite the millions of euros invested particularly by the German and Swedish governments in nexus approaches in the MENA region, the concept has not taken off. It has remained an apolitical approach to water management, which has only caught the imagination of academics and development experts: not governments and the private sector (Allan et al., 2015).

This chapter will provide an analysis on the nexus in the MENA region using a different approach. It will present the water predicament of the region using per capita statistics for current periods. It will be shown that all the countries are subject to water scarcity with respect to water for food production. This food-water scarcity has profound impacts on water security in the region, while water for drinking and sanitation services will be adequate, albeit at the cost of substantial investment in technology. The same is true for water for energy. However, water for food will be increasingly scarce, leaving the majority of economies in the region with no other alternative than downsizing their agricultural sectors and further embracing the "virtual water" option. The chapter will conclude with recommendations on how to manage the nexus with a new conceptualization of water for different uses.

The water security challenge in the MENA region

The MENA region hosts the most water-scarce countries in the world (see Figure 11.1). The GCC economies, Yemen and Jordan are among the most water-scarce countries in the MENA region. With exception of Turkey, Iraq and Iran, all countries of the region are living under

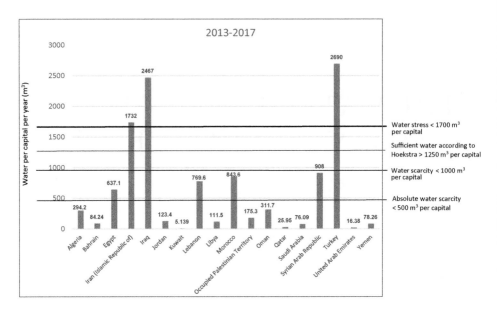

Figure 11.1 Water per capita in the Middle East and North Africa region
Source: Keulertz et al. (2016)

water scarcity conditions. Algeria, Bahrain, Jordan, Kuwait, Libya, the Palestinian Territories, Oman, Qatar, Saudi Arabia, the United Arab Emirates and Yemen are all subject to absolute water scarcity with less than 500 m³ per capita of water available to their citizens annually.

Translated into water use per capita in liters, the average citizen of the MENA region requires approximately 1 m³ of water per year for drinking; 100 m³ per year per person is sufficient for domestic and industrial use, e.g. for cooking, washing and industry use. This is termed "small water" (Allan, 2013). The "big water" on the other hand is embedded in food production and consumption. The average citizen of the MENA region consumes 900 m³ of water per day if on a vegetarian diet. A non-vegetarian consumes about 1800 m³ per day (Allan, 2011, 2013). This "big water" cannot be mobilized in any MENA economy.

The "big water" challenge

"Big water" has been a problem in the MENA region for decades. Most countries ran out of the "big water" devoted to food production in the 1970s to fully feed themselves (Allan, 2002). Land has also become a bottleneck. Due to population growth, cities have expanded into fertile land. At the same time, Egypt in particular has conducted horizontal agricultural expansion in desert areas using both water diverted from the Nile since the 1970s and more recently mainly with groundwater for food production (Ahmed and Fogg, 2014; McKee, 2017).

Egypt has a prominent position in the MENA region. It is currently the leading food producer in the Arab world (UNESCWA, 2017). Another demand for "big water" for agriculture is that driven by population growth. The MENA region is set to grow in absolute population numbers, hosting more people than China in 2100. Although fertility rates are declining, the region is going to double in the next 80 years from presently 500 million people to more than 1 billion people by 2100 (McKee et al., 2017). Approximately 80% of MENA citizens will live in cities, which are therefore set to become the key arena for decision-making with respect to water security in the region. More cities will generate an increasing demand for food, hence the shortage of "big water". The cities have to be largely fed from outside the MENA region.

"Big water" fortunately is available outside the MENA region. It is already evident that water is not available in MENA for the production of staple foods such as cereals for human consumption and animal feed. Perishables such as fruits and vegetables will continue to be grown in the MENA region, yet on a much smaller scale. These conditions have a profound impact on the water-energy-food nexus. This analysis will use the supply chain approach developed by Allan et al. This approach posits that there are two supply chains forming the nexus. These two supply chains need to be carefully examined to see what is possible in terms of water management (Allan et al., 2015).

The "small water" supply chain

The "small water" supply chain provides blue water – surface and groundwater – to urban consumers for domestic use and to serve the industrial/energy sector. This supply chain has a very important advantage as a water source: the blue water in this supply chain can be recycled and reused with treatment. For example, although households and industry withdraw approximately 30% of global blue water resources from the point source, they consume very little because the water goes back into the environment, where it can be treated to some extent in natural systems, or in a water treatment plant for potential reuse. Households and industry effectively consume only 3% and 5% of blue water resources, respectively, after treatment rather than the higher volumes to which they had access (Keulertz and Woertz, 2014).

Small water can be also be produced by desalinating sea water. The salt in sea water can be extracted through various methods of which the most common one today is reverse osmosis. It uses a high pressure pump to exert pressure on salt water and thereby force the water across a semi-permeable reverse osmosis membrane, leaving almost all (around 95–99%) dissolved salts behind in the rejected stream (Pure Tec, 2017). Desalinating water is however relatively costly at around USD 0.50 per cubic meter of water. This figure compares very favorably with the cost of delivering natural water to domestic and industrial users. For example, Europe's largest desalination plant in Barcelona produces 200 million m^3 per day for around 260,000 residents of the Catalan city. The costs to build this plant accumulated to EUR 159 million (USD 190 million) (Water Technology, 2017). This technique has especially been applied in the GCC economies where financial endowments are readily available for investments in desalination plants (Ghaffour et al., 2013).

An example of a city-state that has managed to fully address its water security challenges, Singapore has become one of the most water-secure cities in the world despite very limited access to fresh water. After decades of reliance on water from Malaysia for about 5% of its water needs and with increasing tensions over water transfers, Singapore has invested in its domestic water infrastructure – including both reuse and desalination technologies to become one of the most advanced urban water providers in the world (Tortajada, 2011). Under the supervision of the Public Utilities Board (PUB), Singapore recycles wastewater at levels exceeding US standards. At the same time, desalination plants provide water that is mixed with treated water. As the Singaporean case shows, this "small water" supply chain is mostly dependent on investment in water infrastructure such as water production, recycling and distribution. If its costs are fully recovered through consumer payment for water bills, the "small water" supply chain can be effectively addressed in the same way in the MENA region.

The "big water" supply chain

The other water supply chain is the "big water" or "food-water" supply chain. It is the water that is consumed by human beings in food supply chains. Although 70% of global blue water resources are withdrawn by the agricultural sector, very little of the water is recoverable through technology. Egypt is a very unusual case where the Nile River system is such that the water can be reused in irrigated farming 2.6 times. Egypt has very low rainfall. It depends on blue water for almost all its crop production (Elbana et al., 2017).

Across the region food supply chains consume about 93% of the region's blue water. If green water is also taken into account, the number increases to 99% of water resources (Bromwich et al., forthcoming). The food supply chain is globally the biggest water consumer (Keulertz and Allan, 2017). "Big water" is used, consumed and shipped all along the food supply chain. Unfortunately at the same time, "big water" is wasted, mismanaged and not valued in the food supply chain (Allan, 2013). It silently "flows" virtually through food supply chains and these economy securing processes are very poorly understood by society.

Farmers and "big water"/"food-water"

"Big water"/"food-water" is almost entirely managed by farmers, who operate almost everywhere and certainly in the MENA region in the private sector. Farmers depend on rainfall or access to ground- and surface water. This is particularly challenging in the MENA region where there is a drought every summer and periodic multi-year droughts. Water is a key bottleneck for economic development. Water scarcity is increasingly felt by farmers and decision-makers around the region.

Farmers are subject to numerous financial and institutional pressures. In the MENA region, being a farmer is a very challenging, high risk livelihood, further challenged as a consequence of water scarcity (see Table 11.1).

Farmers are at high risk of poverty unless they can irrigate crops or pursue mixed rainfed farming practices. Irrigation pays off because farmers grow high value vegetables and fruits. Mixed rainfed systems often produce legumes and tree crops such as olives. Farmers in highland and dryland mixed systems and pastoralists are subject to extensive poverty levels (Dixon et al., 2001). The absence of readily available food-water makes the livelihoods of farmers very challenging if not impossible. Thus, the "big water" supply chain's main feature is that it is associated with rural poverty. Only those who irrigate or grow high value crops such as olives or those with off-farm income can survive the climatic conditions of the MENA region.

However, the region is also diverse in terms of "big water" availability to support irrigation systems. The region has three major food bowls: the Jordan River Basin, the Euphrates and Tigris River Basin, and the Nile River Basin.

Population growth in the food bowls: Another key risk factor to "big water"

Inadequate local food-water in the food supply chains of the MENA economies is one of the major risk factors in the MENA region with respect to agricultural development. The food bowls of the region are subject to increased water risk resulting from overuse of water resources for irrigating crops and increasing demand for water resources due to population growth. The three major food bowls in the MENA region, the Arab part of the Nile Basin, the Jordan Basin, and the Euphrates and Tigris Basin, will all see extraordinary levels of population growth in the coming decades. Egypt and Sudan, which form the Arab part of the Nile Basin, will grow from

Table 11.1 Principal farming systems of the Arab countries

Farming system	Land area	% of the region's agricultural population	Main livelihoods	Prevalence of poverty
Irrigated	2	17	Fruit, vegetables, cash crops	Moderate
Highland mixed	7	30	Cereals, legumes, sheep, off-farm income	Extensive
Rainfed mixed	2	18	Tree crops, cereals, legumes, off-farm income	Moderate
Dryland mixed	4	14	Cereals, sheep, off-farm income	Extensive
Pastoral	23	9	Camels, sheep, off-farm income	Extensive
Arid zones	62	5	Camels, sheep, off-farm income	Limited

Source: UNESCWA (2017)

130 million people today to 330 million by 2100 (see Figure 11.3). With negligible rainfall of 50–200 mm in both countries (with a maximum of 700 mm in the most southern part of Sudan), the two economies are almost entirely dependent on irrigation (FAO, 2005, 2017). Similar rainfall patterns are true for eastern Syria and southern Iraq. The two Arab riparians of the Euphrates and Tigris are also fully dependent on irrigation. Their total population will reach about 200 million in 2100 (see Figure 11.2). Jordan, Israel and the Palestinian Territories are almost facing a population growth contest reaching about 55 million people by the end of the century.

A sober look at the agricultural potential of the MENA region

This brings the chapter to the question of what is possible in the MENA region in relation to mobilizing "big water" in domestic food supply chains. A recent study by Mulligan et al. (2017) on environmental factors in the MENA region concluded that 81% of the MENA region has close to zero agricultural potential. Only in very few areas such as in the food bowls, can agriculture be moderately expanded. These areas are especially in Turkey and Syria. There are some opportunities for the MENA region economies despite increasing climate fluctuations (Mulligan et al., 2017). But, this agricultural expansion potential cannot meet the food demands resulting from population growth. It can only optimize water use in areas with sufficient rainfall.

Only rainfed agriculture and a cautious planning of reduced irrigation in most areas and a modest expansion in irrigation some regions with an emphasis on high value crops is possible in the MENA region. The economic importance of agriculture in the MENA region will have to decline in the coming years to prioritize "small water" to serve the high value domestic and industrial consumption. Reducing agricultural activity to save water resources has however quite serious security implications on the street where the state of the region's water resources are poorly understood. Communicating these risks to ordinary citizens will be mandatory to achieve "big water" security.

"Big water"/"food water" security threats

It has been shown that farmers in the MENA region are exposed to the risks associated with poverty. Water scarcity and the need to prioritize "small water" will inevitably have impacts on

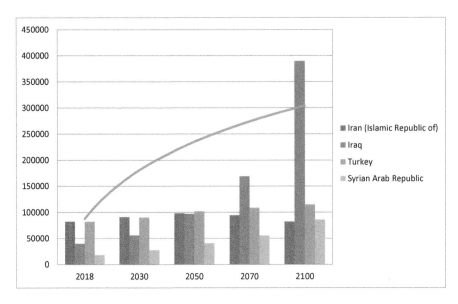

Figure 11.2 Population growth – in thousands – in the Euphrates and Tigris Basin countries
Source: UNDESA (2017)

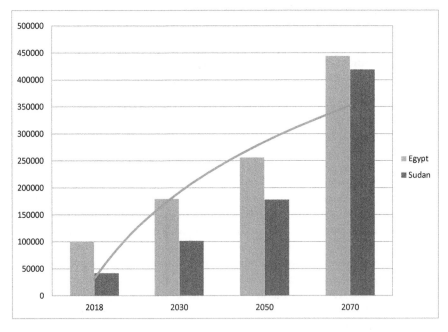

Figure 11.3 Population growth – in thousands – in the Arab Nile riparian countries
Source: UNDESA (2017)

Water-energy-food nexus in the MENA region

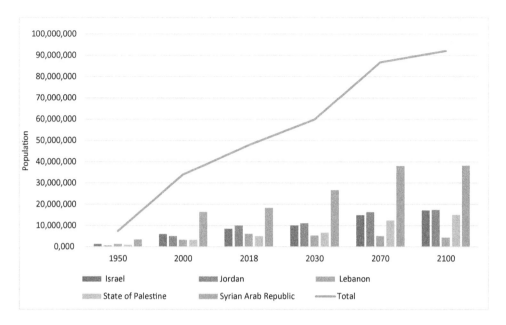

Figure 11.4 Population growth - in thousands - in the Jordan River Basin countries
Source: UNDESA (2017)

family and national security. If rural development is not addressed with an emphasis on water scarcity conditions, the MENA region could see dramatically increased levels of poverty in the countryside. The most likely outcome of poverty in rural areas is a further exodus to cities (McKee et al., 2017). These processes will in turn require even more attention to the "small water"/"non-food" supply chains.

The scarcity of food-water in the MENA region means that the region will experience a transition with more people leaving the once prosperous countryside to migrate to cities. This transition period is associated with risk. Although poverty and violent activities are linked, recent empirical studies have shown that it is not the poorest of the poorest that become members of terrorist organizations but unemployed, skilled, middle class citizens (Krueger, 2007; Benmelech et al., 2010).

The cities will have to absorb millions of former farmers and their families in the future, who need to be employed. Urbanization trends have already been observed in many MENA economies as young people seek new livelihoods in cities as opposed to the countryside (McKee et al., 2017). The lack of sufficient "food-water" will only intensify these trends. The exodus of farming families from the countryside to cities means that food security cannot be achieved domestically or even regionally.

"Food-water" scarcity has the potential to impact the MENA region very seriously both socially and economically. This means that new livelihoods have to be conceived in urban areas to avoid further social and political unrest, which has been shown to be disastrous for the MENA region as a whole for the past seven years. "Food-water" scarcity could lead to local conflict between farmers over water with a potential destabilizing impact at the national level (Keulertz, forthcoming). Moreover, rural out-migration to cities may not be limited to cities but could potentially reach other world regions such as Europe. These risks are so clear that there is no alternative to "importing" "food-water" in economically and politically sustainable ways via trade.

Alternatives to managing the "big water" supply chain

The MENA region has for decades pursued a silent strategy to meet its food-water needs resources with "virtual food-water imports". Virtual water is the "volume of water used to produce a commodity or manufactured item, measured at the place where the product was actually produced" (Chapagain and Hoekstra, 2008). Translated into practice, there are a few world regions such as North and South America, the former Soviet Union states and to a lesser extent Australia and India that provide "virtual water exports" to water-scarce regions such as the MENA region (Keulertz, 2013). These silent "virtual water flows" are carried out by large agribusiness conglomerates such as Archers Daniels Midlands, Bunge, Cargill and Louis Dreyfus (the ABCD companies), which control the vast majority of agricultural trade (Sojamo et al., 2012). In recent years, these Western companies have been joined by East Asian competitors such as Noble, Olam and Wilmar (the NOW companies) (Keulertz and Woertz, 2015). These companies are strategic global traders. This characteristic is particularly true for the recently established Asian companies, which are owned by the Chinese and Singaporean government. They are challenging the Western hegemony over global food trade (Keulertz and Woertz, 2015).

The MENA region has no such trading company. Despite several attempts to establish a strategic trading company, the grand ministerial announcements by some of the Gulf states have not materialized (Woertz, 2013). The Arab Authority for Agricultural Investment and Development (AAAID), based in Khartoum and Dubai, is another example of a failed attempt to strategically grow a food system that procures food through foreign direct investment in north-east Africa (Keulertz, 2013). Although Abu Dhabi announced in 2012 the establishment of a trader similar to the NOW companies in Asia, no progress has been made in the last few years. In practice MENA food importers rely on Western companies. At the same time, strategic cereal commodity imports have been used by the Russian President Vladimir Putin to offer cheap wheat exports to countries such as Egypt as a geopolitical tool in the MENA region to exert influence over governments and societies (Borshchevskaya, 2015). However, trade between Egypt and Russia was partially suspended due to quality concerns by Egypt over Russian wheat (Ahram Online, 2016). Yet, as these examples show, the formation of "big water" supply chains is barely managed. In order to address the future challenges in the MENA region, the WEF nexus can play an important role.

Lessons from the WEF nexus: Pursuing what is possible

It has been shown that, "food-water" scarcity in the MENA region determines that there can be little scope for limited agricultural expansion at the national and regional levels. However, if the two supply chains are properly understood, important lessons can be drawn by decision-makers in the MENA region.

First, the "non-food water" supply chain requires investment in well-tested infrastructure where the risks are widely understood within the region. Investing in water infrastructure to produce, deliver and distribute water equitably and cost-effectively to urban residents and industry will be a key issue in the future but one that is eminently addressable. Trade-offs can be achieved by reusing wastewater to irrigate urban landscapes. Studies have shown that cities such as Munich can provide 66% of their fruits and 246% of their vegetable requirements through urban agriculture (Gondhalekar and Ramsauer, 2017). Peri-urban agricultural parks, which pursue integrated management strategies such as using solar power for sea water desalination to irrigate fruit and vegetable production, can support food security strategies. In Australia, the nexus-inspired Sundrop Farms produce 15% of the country's tomato production for Coles Supermarkets (Klein, 2016). Similar strategies could be pursued in the MENA region. Among the core challenges will be to establish an inclusive private sector and therefore new policy institutions. However, this will have to involve a paradigm shift. As the former Jordanian Minister of Finance, Bassem Awadallah, and Adeel Malik from the University of Oxford have noted "a singular failure of the Arab world is the absence of a private sector that is independent, competitive, and integrated with global markets" (Malik and Awadallah, 2013). Establishing a private sector similar to other world regions will not be an easy task. It will require significant risk-taking by governments to introduce policy reforms aimed at reducing corruption and increasing competition.

Policy shifts akin those envisaged by Malik and Awadallah are politically costly. However, they are mandatory for making investments work for farms such as the Sundrop example from Australia. At present, they are too expensive for the large number of mid-income countries in the MENA region. Moreover, these farms can only provide a limited range of food items such as fruits and vegetables, which are unlikely to be a problem in the MENA region despite its water scarcity. Such farms may also compete with existing smallholder farmers, who produce perishables in small plots to support livelihoods (Zurayk, 2011).

The real "food-water" supply chain is located in cereal production for both human and animal consumption. Cereals and animal feed can only be produced on a large-scale in the MENA under rainfed conditions. However, climate change and the subsequent erratic rainfall patterns will induce major challenges for rainfed agriculture (Mulligan et al., 2017). It will remain a risky strategy to grow staple food commodities domestically.

The already proven solution of the "food-water" deficits involves the import of food commodities via the existing international trading system or to establish a trading house that can procure food on the global market specifically to meet the food-water needs of the region's growing population. The MENA region is a major player in global food trade. It is already a very significant driver of global food prices (Nigatu and Motamed, 2015). The combined efforts by the private sector and governments could leverage the region out of its food insecurity predicaments. Yet, this has to go hand in hand with foreign policy strategies aimed at keeping global agricultural trade open and increased joint efforts by countries in the region. The recent political developments between Saudi Arabia and Qatar, Saudi Arabia and Lebanon and the numerous actors in the Syrian conflict pose the questions of whether combined efforts are politically wanted.

Finally, all solutions to the "food-water" problem in the MENA region must come from the upstream "food-water" supply chain such as increased attention to food processing and storage. Most importantly, MENA governments and the private sector must begin to provide employment for urban dwellers to allow a diversification of the economies. However, all of these processes are highly political, which will be extremely challenging in one of the most politicized regions of the world.

Conclusions

This chapter has introduced a different conceptualization of the WEF nexus. It has shown that the nexus is best understood through a supply chain approach. The first supply chain is the "non-food water" supply chain. It can be managed through investments in infrastructure. The second supply chain is the "big water" supply chain, which is far more difficult to manage. It requires attention to ecologically sound practices such as rainfed agriculture and some technology investments. However, the most viable way to address the "big water" supply chain is to combine efforts on the global food market to procure food from the world's food bowls in

North and South America, the former Soviet Union and other countries. This approach, placing a higher emphasis on "importing virtual water", is highly political, which will in turn need novel policy approaches between governments in a politically very volatile region.

"Big water" in the MENA region is one of those topics that will present the region with risks and opportunities. If it remains unmanaged, the MENA region could further destabilize. If, however, it is managed, "big water" could help the region to transform internally to finally utilize the opportunities it has on a global scale. After all, high population growth means that a very sizable number of consumers will be based in the MENA region. Reaching their potential could boost global trade and regional economic prosperity.

References

Ahmed, A.A. and Fogg, G.E., 2014. The Impact of Groundwater and Agricultural Expansion on the Archaeological Sites at Luxor, Egypt. *Journal of African Earth Sciences*, 95(Supplement C), pp. 93–104. Available at: www.sciencedirect.com/science/article/pii/S1464343X14000338

Ahram Online, 2016. Egypt Resumes Fruit, Vegetable Exports to Russia: MENA. Ahram Online. Available at: http://english.ahram.org.eg/NewsContent/3/12/245127/Business/Economy/Egypt-resumes-fruit,-vegetable-exports-to-Russia-M.aspx

Allan, J.A., 2002. *The Middle East Water Question: Hydropolitics and the Global Economy*, London and New York: I.B. Tauris.

Allan, J.A., 2013. The Food-Water Value Chain. In M. Antonelli and F. Greco, eds. *L'acqua che mangiamo: Cos'è l'acqua virtuale e come la consumiamo*, Milano: Edizione Ambiente.

Allan, T., 2011. *Virtual Water: Tackling the Threat to our Planet's Most Precious Resource*, London: I. B. Tauris.

Allan, T., Keulertz, M. and Woertz, E., 2015. The Water–Food–Energy Nexus: An Introduction to Nexus Concepts and some Conceptual and Operational Problems. *International Journal of Water Resources Development*, 31(3), pp. 301–311. Available at: http://dx.doi.org/10.1080/07900627.2015.1029118

Benmelech, E., Berrebi, C. and Klor, E.F., 2010. *Economic Conditions and the Quality of Suicide Terrorism*. Working Paper Series, No. 16320. National Bureau of Economic Research. Available at: www.nber.org/papers/w16320

Borshchevskaya, A., 2015. How to Judge Putin's Trip to Egypt. The Washington Institute (February 2015). Available at: www.washingtoninstitute.org/policy-analysis/view/how-to-judge-putins-trip-to-egypt

Bromwich, B., Allan, J.A., Colman, A.J. and Keulertz, M., forthcoming. Introduction. In J. A. Allan, M. Keulertz, A.J. Colman and B. Bromwich, eds. *Handbook of Water, Food and Society*, New York: Oxford University Press.

Chapagain, A. and Hoekstra, A., 2008. *Globalization of Water*, London: Wiley & Sons.

Dixon, J., Gulliver, A. and Gibbon, D., 2001. *Farming Systems and Poverty*, Rome: FAO.

Elbana, T.A., Bakr, N. and Elbana, M., 2017. *Reuse of Treated Wastewater in Egypt: Challenges and Opportunities*, Berlin, Heidelberg: Springer, pp. 1–25. Available at: https://doi.org/10.1007/698_2017_46

FAO, 2005. *Country Profile Sudan*. Available at: www.fao.org/docrep/017/aq044e/aq044e.pdf

FAO, 2017. Country Profile Egypt. *Aquastat, Version 2010*. Available at: www.fao.org/nr/water/aquastat/countries_regions/EGY/

Ghaffour, N., Missimer, T.M. and Amy, G.L., 2013. Technical Review and Evaluation of the Economics of Water Desalination: Current and Future Challenges for Better Water Supply Sustainability. *Desalination*, 309(Supplement C), pp. 197–207. Available at: www.sciencedirect.com/science/article/pii/S0011916412005723

Gondhalekar, D. and Ramsauer, T., 2017. Nexus City: Operationalizing the Urban Water-Energy-Food Nexus for Climate Change Adaptation in Munich, Germany. *Urban Climate*, 19(Supplement C), pp. 28–40. Available at: www.sciencedirect.com/science/article/pii/S2212095516300542

Keulertz, M., 2013. *Drivers and Impacts of Farmland Investment in Sudan: Water and the Range of Choice in Jordan and Qatar*, London: King's College London.

Keulertz, M. (forthcoming). The Hydro-Agrarian Question of the 21st Century. In R. Bahn, R. Zurayk, and E. Woertz, eds. *Agriculture, Conflict and the Agrarian Question in the 21st Century*, London: Zed Books.

Keulertz, M. and Allan, J.A., 2017. What is Food-Water and Why Do We Not Account for it? In *The Oxford Handbook of Water Politics and Policy*, New York: OUP.

Keulertz, M. and Woertz, E., 2014. Financial Challenges of the Nexus: Pathways for Investment in Water, Energy and Agriculture in the Arab World. S.W.I. Paper, ed. *Igarss 2014*, 68(1), pp. 1–5. Available at: http://dx.doi.org/10.1080/07900627.2015.1019043

Keulertz, M. and Woertz, E., 2015. State Actors in International Agro-Investments: The role of China, Russia and Gulf. *Development Policy*, 6(1), pp. 20–32.

Keulertz, M., Mulligan, M., Woertz, E., Menichetti, E. and Biskup, S. 2016. *Material Factors for the MENA Region: Data Sources, Trends and Drivers*, Methodology and Concept Papers (3). MENARA Project. www.iai.it/sites/default/files/menara_cp_3.pdf

Keulertz, M., Sowers, J., Woertz, E. and Mohtar, R., 2016. *The Water-Energy-Food Nexus in Arid Regions*, Available at: http://oxfordhandbooks.com/view/10.1093/oxfordhb/9780199335084.001.0001/oxfordhb-9780199335084-e-28

Klein, A., 2016. First Farm to Grow Veg in a Desert Using Only Sun and Seawater. *New Scientist*.

Krueger, A.B., 2007. *What Makes a Terrorist*, Princeton University Press. Available at: www.jstor.org/stable/j.ctt7t153

Malik, A. and Awadallah, B., 2013. The Economics of the Arab Spring. *World Development*, 45, pp. 296–313. Available at: http://dx.doi.org/10.1016/j.worlddev.2012.12.015

McKee, M., 2017. *Just Add Water: The Alchemy of Authoritarian Rule in Desert Land Development in Egypt during the Mubarak Era*, London: SOAS.

McKee, M., Keulertz, M., Woertz, E. and Habibi, N., 2017. *Working Paper on Demographic and Economic Material Factors in the MENA Region*, MENARA Project. Rome: IAI.

Mulligan, M., Keulertz, M. and McKee, M., 2017. *Working Paper on Environmental Factors in the MENA Region: A SWOT Analysis*, MENARA Project. Rome: IAI.

Nigatu, G. and Motamed, M., 2015. *Middle East and North Africa Region: An Important Driver of World Agricultural Trade*, Washington, DC. Available at: www.ers.usda.gov/webdocs/publications/35796/53335_aes88.pdf?v=0

Pure Tec, 2017. What is Reverse Osmosis? Available at: https://puretecwater.com/reverse-osmosis/what-is-reverse-osmosis

Sojamo, S., Keulertz, M., Allan, J.A. and Warner, J., 2012. Virtual Water Hegemony: The Role of Agribusiness in Global Water Governance. *Water International*, 37(2), pp. 169–182.

Tortajada, C., 2011. Water Management in Singapore. *International Journal of Water Resources Development*, 22(2), pp. 227–240.

UNDESA, 2017. *United Nations World Population Prospects: The 2017 Revision*, UNDESA.

UNESCWA, 2017. *Arab Horizon 2030: Prospects for Enhancing in the Arab Region*, Beirut, Lebanon.

Water Technology, 2017. Barcelona Sea Water Desalination Plant, Spain. Water Technology. www.water-technology.net/projects/barcelonadesalinatio/

Woertz, E., 2013. *Oil for Food. The Global Food Crisis and the Middle East*, Oxford and New York: Oxford University Press.

Zurayk, R., 2011. *Food, Farming and Freedom: Sowing the Arab Spring*, Charlottesville, Virginia: Just World Books.

12

THE MULTIDIMENSIONAL ASPECT OF WATER SECURITY IN THE MIDDLE EAST AND NORTH AFRICA[1]

Neda A. Zawahri

Introduction

The Middle East and North Africa[2] (MENA) is the most water-stressed region in the world. Water is not only scarce but a large share of the region's water supply is located in transboundary rivers and aquifers that cross the border of states with a history of animosity and conflict. Due to a combination of factors, the region's supply of water is under threat. As this chapter will demonstrate, population growth, socio-economic development, climate change and ineffective management of existing supplies mean that the region's water crisis is expected to get worse in the near future, which can have devastating impacts on regional and domestic stability along with individual security. As the 2011 Arab uprising that swept across the region demonstrated, the failure to provide society with adequate access to water, food, energy and jobs can contribute to popular protests against ineffective regimes. Access to water is related not only to political stability but also to national security, individual security and food security, and in times of war hydrological infrastructure and water resources become weapons used by warring factions to inflict losses on enemies. The objective of this chapter is to reveal and demonstrate the multi-faceted nature of water security in the MENA and discuss means by which adaptive capacity can be built to address this impending crisis.

Before demonstrating this argument, an overview of the region's water supply and demand is considered along with the factors that are combining to challenge states' ability to meet domestic demands. The chapter then discusses MENA's transboundary water and the challenges riparian states confront as they look toward their shared resources to meet increasing demand. Then the discussion moves to the multidimensional aspect of water security in the region. The conclusion considers factors that can mitigate the region's water crisis.

Water scarcity

The MENA region has an arid and semi-arid environment where 85% of the land is desert. Due to this relative aridity, it is the most water-stressed region in the world (World Bank, 2007). While there is some variance across the MENA – with the Mashreq having more water than the Gulf Cooperation Council (GCC) states – the majority of the states are water poor. Containing

6% of the world's population, the MENA has less than 2% of the planet's renewable fresh water supply (World Bank, 2007). In fact, the 12 most water scarce states in the world are located in this region (Al-Otaibi, 2015).[3] For example, the per capita water availability in Jordan, Yemen, Saudi Arabia and the GCC states is below 200 cubic meters per year (m^3/yr), which is much less than the 500 m^3/yr international water poverty line (Droogers et al., 2012). Approximately half of the Arab world's population lives below the water poverty line (United Nations World Water Development Report, 2015).

Several factors are combining to aggravate the region's water crisis and increase the likelihood that more states in the region will cross into the water poverty line. These factors include population growth, socio-economic development, climate change and ineffective management of existing supplies. MENA states confront some of the highest population growth rates in the world. In 2015, Yemen's average annual population growth rate was 2.57%, in Oman it was 7.9%, in Jordan it was 3.01, and in Saudi Arabia it was 2.32% (United Nations Department of Economic and Social Affairs Population Division, 2016). MENA's population is expected to increase from 480.7 million in 2010 to 771.2 million by 2050, a 57% increase (ibid.). An increasing population means added pressure on existing supplies of water, food and energy. As MENA states developed, industrialized and confronted increased urbanization, residents experienced improvements in their living standards, which further increased demand for water along with energy and food.

Complicating these increasing demands is the influence of climate change, which has already been impacting the region. According to the Intergovernmental Panel on Climate Change (IPCC), by 2030 the MENA can expect a rise in temperature (between 1 to 2 degrees Celsius and increasing to 3 degrees Celsius by 2065), a decrease in precipitation (between 10 to 20%), and an increase in the evaporation rate along with more frequent and prolonged droughts (IPCC, 2007; Immerzeel et al., 2011; Droogers et al., 2012). The region is also expected to experience periodic flash floods and a rise in sea levels. While many climate change projections cover the next 20 or so years, the MENA has already been experiencing the impact of climatic variability. The region's temperature since the mid-20th century has been warming (Donat et al., 2014). Droughts have been more frequent and prolonged, and there have been intensive flash floods that have destroyed infrastructure in the Gaza Strip, Oman, Saudi Arabia and Tunisia (United Nations World Water Development Report, 2015). As for the impact of climatic variability on existing water supplies, models tend to be in agreement that the available supply of water in the MENA is expected to decrease but they disagree on the exact magnitude of the decline (IPCC, 2007).

While there is no doubt that climate change will aggravate the region's water crisis, the general expectation is that its contribution is an estimated 20% of the shortage, while population growth and economic development drive about 80% of the shortage (Food and Agricultural Organization of the United Nations, 2015; Droogers et al., 2012). Accounting for not only climate change but also population increases and economic development, Droogers et al. (2012) find that the MENA can expect an overall decrease in water supplies and an increase in demand in the near future. Together, demand is expected to increase by 50% and unmet demand is expected to increase by 370% by 2050 (Droogers et al., 2012; Immerzeel et al., 2011). Increase in annual water demand across the MENA from 2005 to 2030 is expected to be 47% (2030 Water Resources Group, 2009).

In addition to high population growth rates, socio-economic development and climate change is the impact of ineffective management of existing supplies. As with many regions throughout the world, the agricultural sector in the MENA is the greatest consumer of water, consuming on average 83% of the domestic budget (Food and Agricultural Organization of the

United Nations, 2015). There is, however, some variance in the agricultural consumption rate within the region, with states such as Jordan, Israel and Palestine consuming less than 65% and Saudi Arabia, Oman and Yemen consuming more than 85% (ibid.). Historically farmers have been powerful political forces across the MENA and their use of water has been inefficient, which has contributed to wasting a scarce resource. Throughout the region, farmers have used highly subsidized scarce fresh water to grow water intensive and low value crops. Municipal water supply is also heavily subsidized throughout the MENA countries. Due to its low price, high income households and residents in oil rich states have high per capita water consumption rates and they tend to resist government efforts to decrease subsidies on household water (Michel et al., 2012; Zawahri, 2012).

To meet every increasing demand for water, regimes across the MENA have pursued the construction of hydrological infrastructure such as inter-basin transfer of water, dams and desalination plants, and mining groundwater aquifers. The general preference of the region's leadership has been for these short-term projects that can augment immediate supplies to meet today's needs, while avoiding consideration of the long-term consequences of unsustainable policies. In fact, over 75% of the world's desalinized water is located in the MENA, more specifically in Israel, the oil rich GCC states and Saudi Arabia (Al-Otaibi, 2015). Energy poor states are also interested in building desalination plants to augment domestic supplies of water. Energy poor Jordan, for example, looks to construct the Red-Dead water canal that contains plans for several desalination plants (Zawahri and Weinthal, 2014).

As a result of decades of policies that neglected to consider long-term water sustainability, the region's hydrological systems, transboundary rivers and aquifers have been exploited at an unsustainable rate (Michel et al., 2012). Moreover, municipal and industrial dumping into rivers and lakes, solid waste deposits, seepage from landfills and contamination by agricultural runoff are all threatening the water quality throughout the region (Food and Agricultural Organization of the United Nations, 2015). Across the MENA groundwater has been overexploited and polluted by seawater intrusion and seepage of pollution, and the future of this important source of water is endangered (Shetty, 2006). For example, the groundwater extraction levels in Gaza, Yemen, Jordan, Egypt, Syria, Saudi Arabia and the GCC states are beyond annual recharge rates resulting in their contamination. In the case of Saudi Arabia, for example, over-extraction of one of the world's oldest aquifer system by 954% resulted in its exhaustion and increasing dependence on desalination to meet domestic needs (United Nations World Water Development Report 4, 2012). By 2060, Jordan will exhaust its groundwater resources (Mercy Corps, 2014). This ineffective and inefficient management of domestic and transboundary water supplies across the region will compromise states' ability to adapt to the increasing demand along with climatic variability.

Transboundary water

Over 60% of MENA's water supply is located in transboundary rivers, such as the Euphrates, Tigris, Asi, Jordan and Nile, which cross through states with a history of animosity and conflict (United Nations World Water Development Report, 2015). Moreover, states across the region are heavily dependent on their transboundary water resources to meet domestic demand for water and energy. For instance, over 80% of Syria's water comes from the Euphrates River, while over 90% of Iraq's water comes from the Euphrates and Tigris Rivers. The Jordan River is the only perennial river for Israel, Jordan and Palestine, and the Nile is Egypt's lifeline. A history of political instability, both domestically and regionally, has compromised the ability to build institutions, such as treaties and river basin commissions, to cooperate in an attempt to achieve an effective management regime to govern MENA's transboundary water resources. The region has few ratified treaties governing shared water resources, and many that do exist tend to govern the basin in a fragmented manner with bilateral or sub-basin accords governing multilateral basins. For instance, while the Jordan River is shared by Lebanon, Syria, Israel, Palestine and Jordan, it is governed by a series of bilateral accords between a few of the riparians. Similarly, flowing through Turkey, Syria and Iraq, the Euphrates River is governed by a couple of bilateral protocols. Fragmented governance is ineffective because it prohibits the internalization of externalities, increases transaction costs of negotiating and sustaining cooperation, and complicates implementation of agreements (Zawahri and Mitchell, 2011). Another weakness of the region's treaties is that they tend to focus on quantitative allocations and discount groundwater resources along with considerations of the ecosystem and water quality. The region's international basins are also heavily developed and polluted. Due to upstream diversion and consumption of the Jordan River system, it is no longer capable of replenishing the Dead Sea, which has been shrinking by one meter per year (Farber et al., 2004). In fact, the lower Jordan River is made up of runoff water from the agricultural sector and fisheries along with untreated wastewater. Similarly, the Euphrates, Tigris and Nile basins are also considered "closed" or nearly so because the basins' waters are in use and little remains to meet any additional needs. Therefore it can be argued that there is a general disregard for the integrated management of the region's transboundary basins between riparian states (Zawahri, 2008a).

Multidimensional water security

Across the MENA water supply is integral to national security, political stability, regional stability, food security and human security. This perception means that water has a multidimensional security perspective in this region that is already plagued by conflict. Through an understanding of these various dimensions of water security we can begin to appreciate the challenges that the region's regimes, policy-makers, and residents confront. We can also begin to appreciate why increasing water scarcity can contribute to regional instability or tension, challenge economic development and threaten social order along with contributing to state failure. It can also compromise states' ability to comply with existing treaties or protocols governing the region's transboundary water resources (Zawahri, 2017). As an assessment by the US intelligence agencies concluded "water problems – when combined with poverty, social tensions, environmental degradation, ineffectual leadership, and weak political institutions – contribute to social disruptions that can result in state failure" (Intelligence Community Assessment, 2012: iii). An understanding of this multidimensional aspect of water security in the MENA can also help in formulating policy prescriptions that can build adaptive capacity to climate change and minimize the impact of increasing water shortages.

Human security

Access to clean water and safe sanitation systems is integral to human welfare, human security and livelihoods along with poverty reduction. Household access to safe quality and sufficient quantity of water is critical for human health and social dignity. Among the Arab population in the MENA, about 75% live under water scarcity levels, and half live under extreme water scarcity (United Nations World Water Development Report, 2015). Anything below 500 m³/yr is considered a *water barrier* to growth, because people's lives become focused on water scarcity and economic development will be limited. Contaminated or insufficient water along with poor sanitation endanger the health and well-being of families and inflict a financial cost on those living near or below the poverty line. As poor families struggle to secure and pay for safe water, they can divert resources away from health care and education, and thus harm their future earnings while perpetuating a cycle of poverty.

Leaders throughout the MENA have done well in terms of providing citizens access to water and sanitation. On average, across the region over 90% of urban area residents have access to piped water in their homes (Joint Monitoring Program Data for Water Supply and Sanitation, 2017). However, securing a connection to household water lines does not guarantee regular delivery of water nor does it secure safe water quality. Because of its scarcity, throughout the MENA water is often limited to either a few hours a day or a few days a week, and its quality is often unfit for human consumption (Zawahri et al., 2011). Rural areas are not as well served as urban centers. For example, in Yemen 47% are served (26% receive piped household water) and in Morocco 65% are served (23% receive piped household water) (Joint Monitoring Program Data for Water Supply and Sanitation, 2017). Along with insufficient quantities of water, rural and urban households confront poor water quality problems (Zawahri et al., 2011). Poor water quality presents health risks, especially for children, through waterborne diseases and threatens social welfare. According to the World Bank, the degradation of MENA's water supply is a drain on human welfare and ultimately the national economy (World Bank, 2007).

Food security

As populations across the MENA increase and economies develop, states confronted increasing demand for water and food. Socio-economic development also meant that the region's population began to experience a changing consumption pattern for higher value food products. Despite the disproportionate quantity of water allocated to the agricultural sector across the MENA, insufficient fertile land, an arid environment, and lack of water meant that the sector confronts significant limits to its productive ability to meet domestic self-sufficiency in food or grains. Whether in Egypt, Syria, Saudi Arabia or Jordan MENA states have tended to support the agricultural sector in an attempt to secure domestic self-sufficiency in grains despite the fact that these policies were inherently unsustainable. Leaders were concerned that dependence on the international market leaves them economically, politically and militarily vulnerable. This vulnerability increases exponentially at times of regional or international wars. During regional wars, a state must possess sufficient grain to feed its population and protect itself against an embargo and/or a disruption in the procurement of grain. Without sufficient reserves, a state's ability to fight a war is hampered by its inability to feed its soldiers and citizens (Morgenthau, 1948). The need for self-sufficiency grows exponentially in regions plagued by conflict due to the ever-present threat of wars or embargos (Ka'ddam, 2000). As a Middle Eastern government official noted, "We have grains distributed throughout the country in preparation for war".[4] If a drought or flood results in either domestic or international crop failure, a state must either enter the international market to purchase grains in case of domestic crop failure or pay premium prices in case of global food shortages. Alternatively, if the international system is preoccupied with a war or conflict, a state's ability to procure grains may be restricted and its domestic stability threatened.

In spite of its interests in food self-sufficiency, the MENA region faces structural limits on its ability to meet domestic food needs. Across the region, agricultural production is highly volatile because of poor irrigation techniques, high dependence on rainfall, ineffective management of existing supplies, insufficient research and development, and water shortages (*The Economist*, 2014; World Bank, 2009). Although there is some variance, with states such as Israel, Turkey, Morocco and pre-2011 Syria being food exporters, the majority of states in the MENA are heavily dependent on food imports. In fact, the MENA is the most food import-dependent area in the world. Every year, Arab states import over 50% of their caloric needs (World Bank, 2009). This high level of dependence leaves the region vulnerable to external shocks in agricultural commodity prices, which can threaten political stability, domestic economies, and the livelihoods of poor families and families near the poverty line. Because of population growth rates, increased urbanization and limits on domestic agricultural production, in the next 20 years the region's dependence on the international market for meeting domestic food needs is expected to increase by 64% (World Bank, 2009). Hence, regimes across the MENA are highly concerned about domestic food security (Larson et al., 2012).

The MENA's regimes experienced food insecurity and the threat a food shortage can generate in 2008 and 2011 when food prices in the international market increased substantially. The combination of extreme weather events in food exporting countries, high energy prices, depreciation of the US dollar, and protectionist trade policies in agricultural commodity exporting countries contributed to these price shocks. Because of the heavy subsidies regimes across the MENA provide for their populations, increases in import prices have a substantial impact on national budgets. Mineral resource (oil and natural gas) wealthy states in the region generally tend to have a better capacity to absorb these external price shocks. However, should energy prices fall in the international market this capacity to absorb price shocks will be threatened substantially. Mineral poor states in the MENA do not have the financial capacity to absorb food price shocks, which contributes to domestic inflation. During the recent shocks in food prices, mineral poor states attempted to increase their food subsidies but they were unprepared to fully absorb the increasing costs, which resulted in price hikes and inflation in their domestic food markets and added pressures on household budgets. For example, during the food price shocks of 2008 and 2010–11, prices increased more than 10% in Egypt, Iran and Yemen and about 5% in Lebanon, Kuwait, Oman, Qatar and Saudi Arabia (Larson et al., 2012). Moreover, while international agricultural commodity prices may fall, the decrease in cost does not automatically transfer to the domestic market because of inflation in prices (World Bank, 2009).

Due to a combination of structural forces, international food prices are expected to continue to rise and prices are expected to be increasingly volatile (World Bank, 2009). For example, climate change is expected to contribute to volatility in prices because of the increasing frequency of droughts and floods in agricultural producing countries along with the MENA's own agricultural sectors. As populations and consumption patterns increase throughout the world, pressure on limited international agricultural commodities is expected to increase along with competition for food from importing states.

Regimes in the MENA are concerned about food security because of its connection to political stability and domestic poverty. Approximately 25% of the region's population is poor and the majority of the poor live in rural areas in which the economy is highly dependent on farming (World Bank, 2009). The region's poor are highly vulnerable to shocks in food prices and crop failures because a significant portion of their income (between 35 and 65%) is spent on food (World Bank, 2009). For example, in the 2006 to 2008 period 35% more people in Yemen had inadequate food consumption – increasing from 24% to 59% (World Bank, 2009). Moreover, a high proportion of MENA's population lives near the poverty line and is highly sensitive to price shocks. Increases in food prices have the capacity to push those near the poverty line down into poverty. Inflation in food prices can have long-term impacts on the livelihoods and future productivity of poor families because they are likely to forgo spending on health care, food and education. As a result, they are likely to have more incidents of malnutrition and reduction in the family's future earning power (World Bank, 2009).

Water and food security in conflict-torn states

Civilians in conflict-torn and war-torn states, such as Syria, Iraq, Libya and Yemen, confront strong food insecurity because of soaring food prices, disruptions in food supplies, and consequently increasing reliance on international aid. In Syria, agricultural production has been disrupted by war and violence. Yemen confronts a challenge in feeding its population because of severe water shortages and depleting oil reserves that decrease fiscal earnings, along with an unstable political system. Civilians in states that confronted political instabilities after the 2011 Arab uprisings, such as Egypt and Tunisia, also confront increasing challenges in securing food because of high prices and insufficient supplies (*The Economist*, 2014).

Whether in Syria, Iraq, Libya or Yemen, people attempting to survive in war-torn states struggle to secure access to safe water and sanitation (Sowers et al., 2017). Due to the conflict, water and electricity is often cut off and sanitation systems fail to operate, contributing to water shortages. Over 80% of the population in Yemen lack access to safe water and struggle to find it, which has resulted in widespread waterborne diseases that have killed hundreds of people (Al-Mujahed and Naylor, 2015). A couple of years into the Syrian civil war, water supply decreased by 70% throughout the country, and it continues to decline due to breakdown in services, difficulties of maintaining pumping stations, and deliberate or unintentional bombing of environmental infrastructure (United Nations World Water Development Report, 2015; Sowers et al., 2017). In terms of safe water, because of the ongoing war access to it has decreased by 50% in Syria (Vidal, 2016). Because of destroyed water pipes, Syrians had to resort to unsafe sources of water such as using jerrycans to collect water from unsafe and untreated sources such as surface water (United Nations World Water Development Report, 2015). Residents with financial means can purchase water from the private sector, which often proved an unsafe and expensive source of water. After a power cut in the summer of 2015 in Aleppo, the price of water from the private sector increased by 3000%, which made it prohibitively expensive for most families (UNICEF, 2015). Purchasing water from private trucks is risky because oftentimes it comes from unprotected sources that are contaminated (Al-Dimashqi and Deeply, 2014). As civilians search for an alternative source of water to meet their needs, they often rely on unprotected wells that expose children and families to waterborne diseases such as diarrhea, typhoid and hepatitis (UNICEF, 2015).

Outbreak of conflict and turmoil in these states has had negative repercussions on neighboring states. It has impacted food and water security in neighboring states and overwhelmed their infrastructure, the domestic economy, health facilities, education and the labor market. Because Syria was a major food exporter to the region, its collapse into warfare deprived neighboring states, such as Jordan, of their major food supplier and hence resulted in national and individual food insecurity in the region as states became more dependent on the expensive and volatile international market for meeting food security needs. The increasing need to host registered and unregistered refugees from neighboring conflict-torn states has placed added pressure on domestic food and water supplies along with other resources. There are 657,000 registered Syrian refugees in Jordan and if unregistered refugees are added the number increases to 1.3 million, which represents about 20% of the domestic population (Ghazal, 2017). The influx of refugees has added tremendous pressure on the country's scarce water resources and caused domestic tension because local communities feel that refugees are not only over-consuming water but also failing to conserve the scarce resource. In fact, the government undertook the Disi aquifer project (costing USD 1.1 billion) to help meet the increasing demand of Jordan's urban centers through 2020. Due to the influx of refugees, the water is now being diverted to meet immediate need as opposed to helping the country meet future needs (Mercy Corps, 2014).

National security and political stability

Due to the absolute scarcity of water and the heavy dependence on transboundary water, water is viewed by leaders in the MENA as integral to national security and political stability (Zawahri, 2008b). As uprisings swept across the Arab world in 2011, demonstrators protested against their ineffective governments that failed to provide society with safe access to basic resources, food and jobs. Assuring sufficient domestic resources, such as water, food and energy, to meet the demands of various sectors of the economy and society is related to regime stability. It is important to note that water was (and is) not the one direct cause of the uprisings in the MENA, but it was (and is) certainly a "threat multiplier," that both directly and indirectly contributed to popular protests. As a recent report by the US intelligence community concluded, "when populations believe water shortages are the result of poor governance, hoarding, or control of water by elites", social protests that can destabilize states can occur (Intelligence Community Assessment, 2012: 3). This is especially likely to occur if the water shortage coincides with financial crisis, ineffective political institutions and an inability to provide immediate tangible relief to society. From 2006 through 2011, Syria experienced a severe drought that contributed to crop failure and threatened individual food security, which resulted in migration from rural to urban areas as people searched for food. It also represented an example of Bashar Al-Assad's failure to provide his people with basic essential goods. Throughout history regimes' response to natural disasters has been directly related to political stability. "Disasters pose significant threats to political stability and, hence, to those in positions of authority" (Drury and Olson, 1998: 153).

During the 2011 Arab uprising, Jordan also experienced waves of protests. Among the many reasons behind the protests was popular dissatisfaction with the government's failure to secure safe and sufficient household water (Zawahri, 2012; Mercy Corps, 2014). In these protests, people burned tires, blocked traffic and threatened government officials while shouting "You need to provide water to us!" (Mercy Corps, 2014). The tension between government officials and society continued after the 2011 uprisings and has reached the point where residents are threatening the lives of water officials and attacking their cars over their frustration with the lack of water (Mercy Corps, 2014: 31).

Just as the lack of sufficient domestic water resources can contribute to tension domestically, it can also contribute to regional tension between riparian states. The heavy dependence on transboundary water resources leaves riparian states vulnerable to their upstream riparian neighbor to meet domestic demands for water and hydropower. As the supply of water decreases in the transboundary basins throughout the region, tension between riparian states is expected to increase as they compete to secure access to this scarce resource (Intelligence Community Assessment, 2012; Zawahri, 2012). The protocols governing MENA's transboundary rivers discount the impact of climate change. As a result, riparian states with agreements regulating their use of transboundary basins can experience tension because climate change may challenge their ability to comply with allocation commitments, especially if those allocations are fixed numbers and not percentages. For those riparian states sharing transboundary basins without accords to regulate their development of the resource, they are likely to be susceptible to increasing interstate tension as they attempt to secure access to the resource (Zawahri, 2017). As states seek to secure sufficient water supplies to meet ever-growing demands, competition over transboundary resources may not lead to direct "water wars," but they can fuel existing conflicts between riparian states and contribute to bilateral or regional tension.

Water weapon

Transboundary rivers and hydrological infrastructure have also been a political lever in the game of regional and international politics (Zawahri, 2008b). In other words, they can be a weapon in the hands of riparian states. The water weapon is the purposeful manipulation of the complex relationships that rivers impose on riparian states to inflict direct losses on riparian neighbors. All states located along the river have at their disposal its potential use, irrespective of the balance of power. Moreover, the use of the weapon does not require the deterioration of bilateral relations and therefore, states may use, threaten to use, or play with it to signal their dissatisfaction with their neighbor.

The exact features of this weapon vary according to a state's location along the river and it is stronger in the hands of the upstream state. The downstream state, for example, depends on its upstream neighbor for delivering hydrological data; otherwise, it cannot prepare for floods and droughts or generate hydropower, which can lead to social, economic and political losses. To punish its downstream neighbor, the upstream state may withhold hydrological data, accidentally *forget* to provide data, or deliver poor quality data, which can result in substantial social, economic and political losses downstream. Given the construction of sufficient hydrological infrastructure, the upstream state can stop the river for a couple of hours, slow it down for a day, or open its spillway gates to submerge downstream territory. Due to the lack of hydrological data and the variability in the flow of the Euphrates River, Syria's ability to operate its dams decreased tremendously. Turkey has constructed the Karakamis dam 4.5 kilometers from the Turkish-Syrian border. This dam has the capacity to discharge 20,000 cubic meters per second once its spillway gates are opened (Zawahri, 2008b). If Turkey opens the Karakamis' spillway gates it can flood downstream lands because the topography along the Euphrates in Syria is flat.

Once the upstream state develops the river it becomes dependent on its downstream neighbor to dredge the shared river, maintain its drainage networks and manage minor floods; otherwise, it can incur losses. The downstream state can refuse to dredge the river or accept the upstream state's drainage, which can result in drainage congestion, waterlogging and salinization of soil in the upstream state. Alternatively, the downstream state may keep its barrages closed to minor floods, aggravating their impact on the upstream state. A stronger method available for the downstream state to signal its discontent with its upstream neighbor involves the manipulation of an alternatively shared river flowing in an opposite direction. For example, the Euphrates and Tigris Rivers are not the only rivers crossing this border; there is also the Asi (Orontes) River. While Syria is downstream and Turkey is upstream along the Euphrates, this relationship is reversed along the Asi – which flows from Syria into Turkish controlled Hatay (Iskandaron). When Turkey uses the Euphrates to flood its downstream neighbor, Syria reciprocates by releasing waters from the Asi (Zawahri, 2008b). As tension between riparian states increases over their shared water resources, we can expect states to increase their use of the water weapon.

Water, hydrological infrastructure and war

Regardless of whether a state is upstream or downstream, rivers and hydrological infrastructure become defensive and offensive weapons during wars (Gleick, 2008). Whether it is a dam, canal, desalination plant, sewage facility, or river, warring factions have a history of using hydrological infrastructure to flood oncoming enemies, cut off water supplies to enemy territory, or enable fighters a smoother access into enemy lands (Zawahri, 2008b). In the wars currently raging in the MENA, hydrological infrastructure has been targeted by warring factions in direct defiance of international law (Sowers et al., 2017). Given the MENA region's aridity, hydrological infrastructure and water have become a major strategic objective in the region's wars. Even the rebel groups and warring factions seeking to expand their territorial control recognize the importance of controlling water and hydrological infrastructure.

As it sought to conquer territory in its attempt to form a state, the Islamic State of Iraq and al-Sham (ISIS) took advantage of the Syrian uprising of 2011 to seize territory in the northeastern portion of the country to establish a base and work towards expanding control over Syria and Iraq (Cronin, 2015). To achieve its objective of statehood, ISIS sought to control two critical natural resources: water and oil. During its control of portions of the Euphrates and Tigris Rivers and the hydrological infrastructure along these basins, ISIS was able to generate wealth and use the infrastructure it captured as offensive and defensive weapons of war. From 2013 until May 2017, ISIS controlled the largest Syrian dam, which is an important source of hydropower and municipal water supply for major Syrian cities (Reuters, 2017). Control of the Tabaq Dam enabled ISIS to control and sell water and electricity to Aleppo and neighboring cities. ISIS also controlled the Samarra barrage west of Baghdad on the Tigris River along with areas surrounding the Mosul Dam. Using heavy bombing and air strikes, US, Kurdish and Iraqi forces managed to retake control of the Mosul Dam from ISIS in August 2014. ISIS also sought to control the Haditha Dam along the Euphrates River, which would allow it to control 30% of Iraq's electricity supply, critical water supply to the neighboring areas, and open its spillway gates to flood downstream towns and villages (Vidal, 2014). In April 2014, ISIS captured the Nuaimiyah Dam on the Euphrates and used the reservoir's waters to flood downstream land and cut off water to millions of people in Karbala, Najaf, Babylon and Nasiriyah (Vidal, 2014). Prior to its collapse, ISIS had a history of using water as a weapon in its conflict. ISIS has opened dikes to flood the oncoming Iraqi army. In return, the Iraq Government considered opening the floodgates to the Haditha dam to block ISIS advances (Karimi and Karadsheh, 2014).

Building adaptive capacity

Given the combination of these challenges and the multidimensional nature of water security, the MENA region must begin to build adaptive capacity to minimize the negative social, political and economic consequences of the impending water crisis. To meet the challenge of adapting to an ever decreasing supply of already scarce water, the MENA states will need to reform their water policy, build domestic capacity and invest in agricultural research. However, the nature of state–security relations, insufficient financial resources, and a fragmented donor community weaken the ability to build adaptive capacity.

Substantial savings of water can be made through policy reforms in the agricultural, municipal and energy sectors. For instance, the region can see substantial savings in water with more efficient agricultural practices, improved irrigations systems and improved resource management. However, shifting policies to improve the efficient use of existing water supplies – such as adopting progressive pricing for the municipal and agricultural sectors, providing incentives to farmers to shift to less water intensive and higher value crops, or using treated wastewater in irrigation – are generally perceived as upsetting delicate state–security relations (Zawahri, 2012). After the Arab uprising, regimes in the region became more anxious about upsetting the delicate state–security relations. Policies that would in effect increase prices on agricultural and municipal water users or compel farmers to change traditional inefficient farming practices are generally perceived as unacceptable by policy-makers because of the fear of upsetting important sectors of society. This fear explains the general preference for supply-driven or water augmenting projects, such as construction of large hydrological infrastructure, over implementing policies that increase the efficiency by which water is used.

What policy-makers neglect to consider is the fact that the impending water crisis means that focusing on the short-term goal of attempting to placate people to maintain a delicate state–security relationship is inherently unsustainable. Through the use of public relations campaigns and meetings with important powerful constitutions, such as elites, farmers and citizens, policy-makers can explain the desperate need to undertake more efficient policies for the future stability of the state and its residents. For example, during the Arab uprising, Jordan experienced substantial popular protests against regime ineffectiveness in improving livelihoods, insufficient jobs, lack of clean water and high food prices (Zawahri, 2012). One of many strategies used to placate society during these protests was to remind people of the instability that regime change can have on a state. With images of the violence and turmoil of Syria, Libya and Egypt in the media, the regime was successful in persuading the populace that maintaining the status quo is better than the turmoil inherent in regime change (Zawahri, 2012). Such a strategy can also be used to persuade society of the need for a new domestic water policy. Discussing the relevance of water security, explaining the impending crisis along with the need to improve the efficiency of water use can go a long way to empower policy-makers to implement policies to conserve water.

The nature of state–security relations in the region is not the only obstacle to the effective management of domestic water resources. Energy poor states lack the financial resources needed to undertake projects that can improve the domestic water situation, such as construction of wastewater treatment plants and transporting treated water to potential users, connecting households to water and sewer systems, updating an antiquated water distribution system that has many leaks, distributing new irrigation technology to farmers, and undertaking research to better understand the impact of climate change, drought and flash floods. In general, energy poor states lack the financial capacity to fund these activities. As a result, they tend to rely on international donors to provide financial assistance to undertake water projects. However, one may argue that donors represent an additional obstacle to the effective management of the region's water supply. International donors follow their individual national interest and foreign policy goals and many times these priorities may not match the needs of the recipient state. Donors also fail to coordinate their policies and their priorities can compete with one another. For example, a donor constructed a wastewater treatment plant in Beirut but there was no funding or other donor interest in building the necessary network to connect households to the new plant. The plant remained inoperative because of the lack of sewage. Cognizant of the negative consequences of the lack of coordination between themselves and sharing a similar interest in regime stability in countries such as Jordan, donors did attempt to remedy the problem through periodic donor meetings.[5] However, the diversity of national interests between donors complicates the ability to coordinate their activities and, as a result, these meetings became a means to notify and share information about their individual activities. Increased coordination and collaboration of the international donor community and more aggressive action by policy-makers will be essential to adopting effective water management strategies to mitigate water-related social and regional tensions that are only likely to increase in the near future.

Notes

1 The Faculty Scholarship Initiative Grant from Cleveland State University funded field research for this chapter.
2 In this study, the MENA consists of the Magrib, Mashreq and Gulf Cooperation Council States.
3 These are Algeria, Bahrain, Kuwait, Jordan, Libya, Oman, Palestine, Qatar, Saudia Arabia, Tunisia, the United Arab Emirates and Yemen.
4 Author's interview with Middle Eastern government official, 25 June 2001.
5 Author's interview with international donor, Amman, Jordan, 15 May 2012.

References

2030 Water Resources Group. 2009. *Charting Our Water Future: Economic Frameworks to Inform Decision-Making*. www.2030wrg.org/wp-content/uploads/2014/07/Charting-Our-Water-Future-Final.pdf (last accessed 17 March 2017).

Al-Dimashqi, Ahmad. 2014. Not a Drop to Drink: Syrian Shortages Feed Black Market for Water. *Christian Science Monitor* June 9. www.csmonitor.com/World/Middle-East/2014/0609/Not-a-drop-to-drink-Syrian-shortages-feed-black-market-for-water (last accessed 28 May 2017).

Al-Mujahed, Ali and Hugh Naylor. 2015. In Yemen's Grinding War, if the Bombs Don't Get You, the Water Shortages Will. *The Washington Post*. July 23. www.washingtonpost.com/world/middle_east/in-yemens-grinding-war-if-the-bombs-dont-get-you-the-water-shortages-will/2015/07/22/a0f60118-299e-11e5-960f-22c4ba982ed4_story.html?utm_term=.77a42fa29c0a (last accessed 28 May 2017).

Al-Otaibi, Ghanimah. 2015. By the Numbers: Facts about Water Crisis in the Arab World. *World Bank*, March 19. http://blogs.worldbank.org/arabvoices/numbers-facts-about-water-crisis-arab-world (last accessed 17 March 2017).

Cronin, Audrey Kurth. 2015. ISIS is Not a Terrorist Group, *Foreign Affairs*, March/April. www.foreignaffairs.com/articles/middle-east/isis-not-terrorist-group

Donat, M.G., T.C. Peterson, M. Brunet, A.D. King, M. Almazroui, R.K. Kolli, D. Boucherf, A.Y. Al-Mulla, A.Y. Nour, A.A. Aly and T.A.A. Nada, 2014. Changes in Extreme Temperature and Precipitation in the Arab Region. *International Journal of Climatology*, 34(3): 581–592.

Droogers, P., W.W. Immerzeel, W. Terink, J. Hoogeveen, M.F.P. Bierkens, L.P.H. Van Beek, and B. Debele. 2012. Water Resources Trends in Middle East and North Africa towards 2050. *Hydrology and Earth System Sciences*, 16: 3101–3114.

Drury, Cooper and Richard Olson. 1998. Disasters and Political Unrest: An Empirical Investigation. *Journal of Contingencies and Crisis Management* 6(3): 153–161.

Farber, E., A. Vengosh, I. Gavrieli, A. Marie, T.D. Bullen, B. Mayer, R. Holtzman, M. Segal and U. Shavit, 2004. The Origin and Mechanisms of Salinization of the Lower Jordan River. *Geochimica et Cosmochimica Acta* 68: 1989–2006.

Food and Agricultural Organization of the United Nations. 2015. *Towards a Regional Collaborative Strategy on Sustainable Agricultural Water Management and Food Security in the Near East and North Africa Region*. Main Report, second edition. www.fao.org/fileadmin/user_upload/rne/docs/LWD-Main-Report-2nd-Edition.pdf (last accessed 17 March 2017).

Ghazal, Mohammad. 2017. Jordan Hosts 657,000 Registered Syrian Refugees. *Jordan Times*, March 21. http://jordantimes.com/news/local/jordan-hosts-657000-registered-syrian-refugees (last accessed 22 May 2017).

Gleick, Peter. 2008. *Water Conflict Chronology*. Pacific Institute, Oakland. www.oneonta.edu/faculty/allenh/WaterResourcesTracyAllen/Water%20Conflict%20Chronology.pdf (last accessed 28 May 2017).

Immerzeel, Walter, Peter Droogers, Wilco Terink, Jippe Hoogeveen, Petra Hellegers, Mark Bierkens, Rens van Beek. 2011. *Middle-East and Northern Africa Water Outlook*. Future Water. http://siteresources.worldbank.org/INTMNAREGTOPWATRES/Resources/MNAWaterOutlook_to_2050.pdf (last accessed 17 March 2017).

Intergovernmental Panel on Climate Change (IPCC). 2007. *Climate Change 2007: Impacts, Adaptation and Vulnerability*. Cambridge University Press, New York.

Intelligence Community Assessment. 2012. *Global Water Security*. February. www.dni.gov/files/documents/Special%20Report_ICA%20Global%20Water%20Security.pdf (last accessed 17 March 2017).

Joint Monitoring Program Data for Water Supply and Sanitation. 2017. Country Reports. www.wssinfo. org/documents/?tx_displaycontroller[type]=country_files (last accessed 17 March 2017).

Ka'ddam, M. 2000. *Al-A'men al-Ma'e al-Suri*. Manshurat Wezarat al-Thaqafa, Dammashq.

Karimi, Faith and Jomana Karadsheh. 2014. US Airstrikes Target ISIS Fighters near 2nd-largest Dam in Iraq. CNN. September 9. www.cnn.com/2014/09/07/world/meast/us-isis-airstrikes/index.html (last accessed 28 May 2017).

Larson, Donald, Julian Lampiette, Christophe Gouel, Carlo Cafiero, and John Roberts. 2012. *Food Security and Storage in the Middle East and North Africa*. Policy Research Working Paper 6031. World Bank, Washington, DC. http://documents.worldbank.org/curated/en/293221468275336547/pdf/WPS6031.pdf

Mercy Corps, 2014. *Tapped Out: Water Scarcity and Refugee Pressures in Jordan*. March www.mercycorps. org/sites/default/files/MercyCorps_TappedOut_JordanWaterReport_March204.pdf (last accessed 22 May 2017).

Michel, David, Amit Pandya, Syed Iqbal Hasnain, Russell Sticklor, and Sreya Panuganti. 2012. *Water Challenges and Cooperative Response in the Middle East and North Africa*. The Brookings Project on US Relations with the Islamic World. US-Islamic World Forum Papers. www.brookings.edu/wp-content/uploads/2016/06/Water-web.pdf (last accessed 22 May 2017).

Morgenthau, Hans. 1948. *Politics Among Nations*. Knopf, New York.

Reuters, 2017. US-Backed Syrian Militias Say Tabqa Dam Captured From Islamic State. May 10, *New York Times*. www.yahoo.com/news/u-backed-syrian-militias-capture-tabqa-islamic-state-165345732.html (last accessed 26 November 2018).

Shetty, Shobha. 2006. *Water, Food Security and Agricultural Policy in the Middle East and North Africa Region*, Working Paper Series No. 47. July. http://web.worldbank.org/archive/website01418/WEB/IMAGES/WP47WEB.PDF (last accessed 22 May 2017).

Sowers, Jeannie, Erika Weinthal, and Neda A. Zawahri. 2017. Targeting Environmental Infrastructures, International Law, and Civilians in the New Middle Eastern Wars. *Security Dialogue* 48(5): 410–430.

The Economist. 2014. *Food Security in Focus: Middle East and North Africa 2014*.

United Nations Department of Economic and Social Affairs Population Division, 2016. *Data on Population Growth*. https://esa.un.org/unpd/wpp/DataQuery/ (last accessed 17 March 2017).

United Nations World Water Development Report. 2012. *Managing Water Under Uncertainty and Risk*. United Nations Education, Scientific, and Cultural Organization, France. http://unesdoc.unesco.org/images/0021/002156/215644e.pdf (last accessed 17 March 2017).

United Nations World Water Development Report. 2015. *Water for a Sustainable World*. United Nations Education, Scientific, and Cultural Organization, France. http://unesdoc.unesco.org/images/0023/002318/231823E.pdf (last accessed 17 March 2017).

UNICEF. 2015. *Press Release: Severe Water Shortages Compound the Misery of Millions in War-torn Syria-Says UNICEF*. August 25. www.unicef.org/media/media_82980.html (last accessed 27 May 2017).

Vidal, John. 2014. Water Supply Key to Outcome of Conflict in Iraq and Syria, Experts Warn. *The Guardian*. July 2. www.theguardian.com/environment/2014/jul/02/water-key-conflict-iraq-syria-isis (last accessed 28 May 2017).

Vidal, John. 2016. Water Supplies in Syria Deteriorating Fast Due to Conflict, Experts Warn. *The Guardian*. September 7. www.theguardian.com/environment/2016/sep/07/water-supplies-in-syria-deteriorating-fast-due-to-conflict-experts-warn (last accessed 27 May 2017).

World Bank. 2007. *Making the Most of Scarcity Accountability for Better Water Management in the Middle East and North Africa*. Washington DC.

World Bank. 2009. *Improving Food Security in Arab Countries*. Washington DC. http://siteresources. worldbank.org/INTMENA/Resources/FoodSecfinal.pdf (last accessed 27 May 2017).

Zawahri, Neda A. 2008a. Capturing the Nature of Cooperation, Unstable Cooperation, and Conflict over International Rivers: The Story of the Indus, Yarmouk, Euphrates, and Tigris Rivers, *International Journal of Global Environmental Issues*, 8(3): 286–310.

Zawahri, Neda A. 2008b. International Rivers and National Security. *Natural Resources Forum* 34(4): 280–289.

Zawahri, Neda A. 2012. Popular Protests and the Governance of Scarce Freshwater in Jordan, *Arab World Geographer* 15(4): 265–299.

Zawahri, Neda A. 2017. Adapting to Climatic Variability along International Basins in the Middle East. In Jean Axelrad Cahan (ed) *Water Security in the Middle East*. Anthem Water Diplomacy Series, pp. 145–166.

Zawahri, Neda A. and Sara Mitchell. 2011. Fragmented Governance of International Rivers, *International Studies Quarterly* 55(3): 835–858.

Zawahri, Neda A. and Erika Weinthal. 2014. The World Bank and Negotiating the Red Sea and Dead Sea Water Conveyance Project. *Global Environmental Politics* 14(4): 55–74.

Zawahri, Neda A., Jeannie Sowers, and Erika Weinthal. 2011. Assessing States' Progress towards Meeting the Millennium Development Goals for Water and Sanitation in the Middle East and North Africa, *Development and Change* 42(5): 1153–1177.

13
FOOD SECURITY IN THE MIDDLE EAST

Hussein A. Amery

Introduction and overview

The people of the Middle East have a long history of developing water resources and deploying them to meet the food and other needs of the population, which allowed local civilizations to grow and prosper. In ancient times, the precarious life of hunters and gatherers became more stable after they discovered the process of farming on the flood plains of the Tigris and Euphrates rivers. This meant that now a few farmers could predictably and consistently produce enough from the land to feed a large group. A few centuries later, residents of the Kingdom of Saba'a (Sheba) built the Great Dam of Marib between 750 and 700 BC. The kingdom, located in what is now northern Yemen, flourished during the first millennium BC, and was led by a legendary queen. The ancient Persians and Egyptians used water wheel technology whereby buckets were dropped into a river or stream, then filled with water only to be raised by the wheel and emptied into canals that were used to irrigate crops nearby. These masterful engineering feats allowed for effective control of water resources which helped residents produce sufficient food supplies to sustain the growing population of this semi-arid region.

Food security is a multi-dimensional concept that includes environmental, economic, political, policy and cultural considerations (Sen, 1981; FAO, 1985; Woertz, 2013). The World Food Summit 1996 declared that "Food security exists when all people, at all times have physical and economic access to sufficient safe and nutritious food that meets their dietary needs and food preferences for an active and healthy life" (FAO, 1996). Food security is then about the physical availability of food and access to it. It is also about the stability of supply as well as the utilization of nutritious and hygienic food to meet people's physiological needs.

Water and food security are closely intertwined in that some 70% of the world's fresh water supplies are used in the production of food stuffs. Tindall and Campbell (2012:1) define water security as "the protection of adequate water supplies for food, fiber, industrial, and residential needs for expanding populations, which requires maximizing water use efficiency, developing new supplies, and protecting water reserves in event of scarcity due to natural, [manmade], or technological hazards". At the regional and national scales, the more arid an area is, the more water is allocated for irrigation. Water scarcity can act as a risk multiplier, especially in politically and economically fragile countries. In addition to this, Quadrennial Defense Review (DOD, 2014: 8) of the American Department of Defense, observes that:

Food security in the Middle East

Climate change may exacerbate water scarcity and lead to sharp increases in food costs. The pressures caused by climate change will influence resource competition while placing additional burdens on economies, societies, and governance institutions around the world. These effects are threat multipliers that will aggravate stressors abroad such as poverty, environmental degradation, political instability, and social tensions – conditions that can enable terrorist activity and other forms of violence.

Climate variability and cumulative effects of mismanagement of water and land resources were important contributors to the popular uprising-cum-civil war in Syria that has continued unabated since 2011 (de Châtel, 2014; Gleick, 2014). Regionally, the possible impacts of climate change on the farming systems are summarized in Table 13.1.

Ecosystem degradation such as soil erosion and shrinkage of arable land due to the expansion of urban centers puts additional strain on food security. Wasteful irrigation practices and the general desire to consume more water-intensive protein are harder to change. Normative views of what constitutes development and modernity, consumption habits, diets and lifestyles can take a long time to change. In the early 1980s, Saudi Arabia embarked on a food self-sufficiency program. A decade later, the desert kingdom exceeded its own goals and became the sixth largest wheat exporter in the world. The heavily subsidized program was expensive both

Table 13.1 Climate change impacts on farming systems of the Middle East and North Africa region

Farming system	Exposure: What climate change-related events will occur	Sensitivity: Likely impacts on farming systems
Irrigated	Increased temperatures	More water stress
	Reduced supply of surface irrigation water	Increased demand for irrigation and water transfer
	Dwindling groundwater recharge	Reduced yields when temperatures are too high
		Salinization due to reduced leaching
		Reduction in cropping intensity
Highland mixed	Increase in aridity	Reduction in yields
	Greater risk of drought	Reduction in cropping intensity
	Possible lengthening of the growing period	Increased demand for irrigation
	Reduced supply of irrigation water	
Rainfed mixed	Increase in aridity	Reduction in yields
	Greater risk of drought	Reduction in cropping intensity
	Reduced supply of irrigation water	Increased demand for irrigation
Dryland mixed	Increase in aridity	A system very vulnerable to declining rainfall
	Greater risk of drought	
	Reduced supply of irrigation water	Some lands may revert to rangeland
		Increased demand for irrigation
Pastoral	Increase in aridity	A very vulnerable system, where desertification may reduce carrying capacity significantly
	Greater risk of drought	
	Reduced water for livestock and fodder	Nonfarm activities, exit from farming, migration

Source: World Bank (2013)

financially and ecologically as it sapped the country's mostly non-renewable aquifers. A United Nations (UN) report (UNDP 2006: 145) reveals the following stark facts about the costs of the wholly irrigated wheat program: "Production costs are estimated at four to six times the world price, discounting the costs of subsidies and groundwater depletion. Every tonne of wheat is produced with about 3,000 cubic meters of water – three times the global norm". Some three decades after the program was started, the Saudi Government reversed its course in 2008 by introducing a policy of phasing out wheat subsidy and cultivation at a rate of 12.5% per year, and in 2009 it introduced the King Abdullah Initiative for Saudi Agriculture Investment Abroad. That is to say the root causes of Saudi Arabia's water challenges are similar to those in many other parts of the world, namely poor water governance and overall mismanagement of limited natural resources, which exacerbate wasteful attitudes and behaviors (WWDR, 2003: 33).

The agricultural sector in hydrocarbon-rich Persian Iran has played a more prominent role in the economy than it did in the equally endowed Arab Gulf states. Farming in Iran continues to be an important economic sector as it employs some 19% of the labor force although its contribution to the gross domestic product (GDP) went from 12.5% in 1995 to 9.3% in 2014 (World Bank, n.d.). On the other hand, the weight of the agricultural sector in the Arab Gulf states has been shrinking since their hydrocarbon reserves were discovered, developed and exported starting in the middle of the 20th century. Their low population bases (except for Saudi Arabia) and geographic location in an arid to semi-arid peninsula where arable land is just as scarce as fresh water made it impossible to maintain a viable agricultural sector, thus making the dream of national food self-sufficiency fade away. In these countries, the share of agriculture to GDP has been always been low. Saudi Arabia has the "strongest" sector although its share of the GDP went from 5.9% in 1995 to 1.9% in 2014. In the other five GCC countries, the current share is under 1% (World Bank, n.d.).

For the three dominant religions of the Middle East, Islam, Christianity and Judaism, food and water carry a lot of religious symbolism. While on pilgrimage in Mecca, Muslims are required to sacrifice a sheep to commemorate Prophet Abraham's trial by God. The very practice of religion affects food demand and what is lawful to consume. For Muslims, demand for food usually peaks during the fasting month of Ramadan. In Saudi Arabia, demand skyrockets during the pilgrimage when around 2 million Muslims descend on Mecca. On the other hand, demand drops in the hot summer months when millions of Gulf Arabs and expatriate workers take extended vacations in cooler destinations.

In recent years, global food insecurity has been getting worse. People facing crisis-level food insecurity or worse increased from an estimated 80 million in 2015 to 108 million in 2016, which amounts to a 35% rise (EU, 2017). This significant worsening is partly a result of political instability and of cumulative mismanagement of natural resources. These circumstances weaken governments' ability to monitor and combat pests that threaten crops. Projections show that by 2050, food demand in the Arab World will increase threefold (Abdel-Gawad, 2015). This is related to the rapid population increase and to the continually improving quality of life in the region which translates to greater demand for all types of food, especially for the water-intensive, protein-based diets. This is a tough challenge when the requisite water resources are meager. The population growth over time (1980–2015) in Iran, Egypt and Turkey, the largest countries in the Middle East, gives a broad overview of the scale and complexity of this matter (Figure 13.1). Decades ago, theocratic Iran implemented family planning policies which resulted in its population size growing at a slower rate than secular Turkey and Egypt. (Relatedly, see also arable land per capita in each of these countries; Figure 13.2.) The globalization and interconnectedness of the food supply system is effective in meeting people's food needs, but trade flows can be interrupted by politics or natural phenomena such as droughts.

Food security in the Middle East

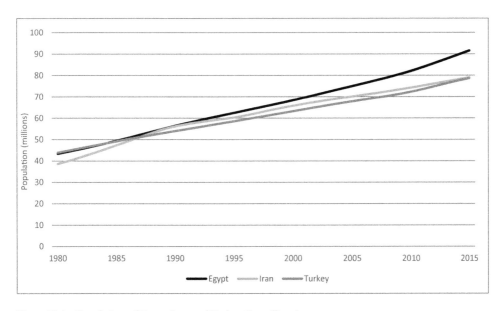

Figure 13.1 Population of Egypt, Iran and Turkey (in millions)

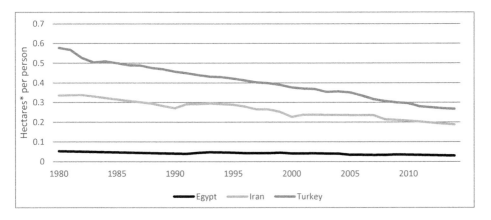

Figure 13.2 Arable land per capita in Egypt, Iran and Turkey
Note: 1 hectare = 0.01 km²

This chapter will analyze all the mentioned challenges and threats to food security in the Middle East, and then discuss two opportunities to enhance it: foreign agricultural investments and reducing food waste.

Eating more meat

Globally, the average food consumption went from 2194 calories per person per day in 1961 to 2870 in 2011. In the same period, food consumption in Kuwait rose from 2590 to 3470, and in Saudi Arabia from 1716 to 3121. Significantly, as Gulf Arabs were undergoing dramatic economic development and a significant improvement in their quality of life, their diet started to include a lot more protein. In Saudi Arabia, meat consumption per capita went from 67 calories per person per day in 1961 to 273 calories in 2011. While the current level of consumption is on par with the global average, its rate of growth has been much faster (National Geographic, n.d.). Consumers in Saudi Arabia pay around 3.50 per kg for locally produced frozen chicken and USD 15 per kg for fresh veal or lamb. This price differential and the understanding that white meat is healthier than red meat is boosting demand for chicken (USDA, 2016).

Some 70% of broiler production costs are feed. The hot climatic conditions for much of the year in the Arabian Peninsula necessitate temperature controlled chicken houses which increase production costs. In an effort to reduce the costs of local broiler meat producers, the Saudi Government provides numerous forms of support such as subsidies for animal feed, interest-free loans and the purchase of particular poultry equipment. However, about a year after oil prices plummeted, the Saudi Government reduced (summer 2015) its support of a wide spectrum of subsidies which increased the production costs of local broiler meat producers and "significantly reduced their ability to compete with lower priced imported products" (USDA, 2016).

In terms of beef consumption per capita (1993–2015) in the largest countries by population, one notices that consumption in Iran is lower than that in Egypt and Turkey (Figures 13.3, 13.4 and 13.5), and has been declining in recent years. Iran's trend-line could be due to the fact that the country has been under economic sanctions since 1979 and more comprehensive ones since 2006.

Political stability and food security

In the Arab World, food deficit is expected to climb to USD 63.5 billion in 2030 (Abdel-Gawad, 2015), where Egypt and the Arab Gulf countries are the most dependent on food imports. However, the interdependencies that trading systems create can backfire. Sternberg (2012) finds that the 2011 winter drought in eastern China's wheat-growing region led the government

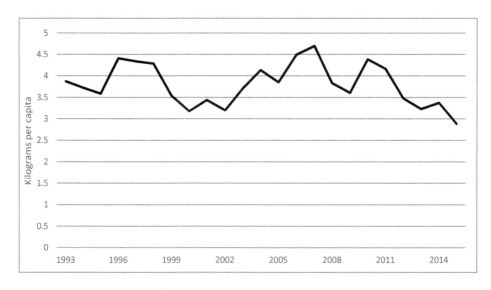

Figure 13.3 Beef consumption in Iran (kilograms per capita)

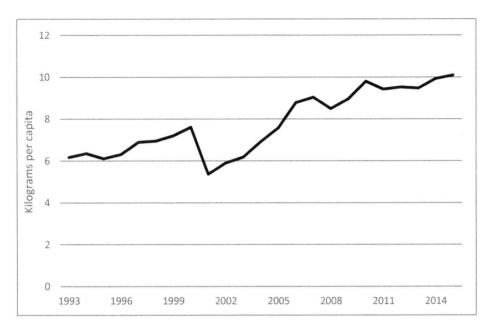

Figure 13.4 Beef consumption in Egypt (kilograms per capita)

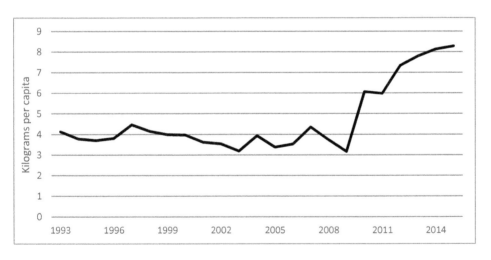

Figure 13.5 Beef consumption in Turkey (kilograms per capita)

to purchase the balance of its wheat needs from the international market. This in turn helped to double the global wheat prices which adversely affected many countries around the world including Egypt, impacting its political stability. Between 2008 and 2010, food prices went up by 37% in Egypt (*The Economist*, 2012). The self-immolation of a poor and frustrated Tunisian street vendor selling food became the spark for the Arab Spring that reached Egypt and toppled the regime of Hosni Mubarak. A study published by the IMF (Arezki and Brückner, 2011) finds "that increases in the international food prices lead to a significant deterioration of democratic institutions in the Low Income Countries" (Arezki and Brückner, 2011). Thus, there is a greater

Table 13.2 Percentage of consumer expenditures on food, alcoholic beverages and tobacco that were consumed at home, by selected countries, 2011

Country/Territory	Share of consumer expenditures	
	Food* (%)	Alcoholic beverages and tobacco
Qatar	12.3	0.3
Bahrain	13.7	0.4
United Arab Emirates	14.4	0.2
Israel	15.5	2.3
Kuwait	18.6	0.5
Turkey	22.1	4.4
Tunisia	23.1	3.3
Iran	26.0	0.5
Saudi Arabia	26.1	0.6
Jordan	36.0	5.4
Egypt	40.4	3.4
Algeria	42.7	2.3
USA	6.8	2.2
United Kingdom	8.9	4.3
Sweden	12.0	3.6

Note: The data were computed based on Euromonitor International data extracted August 2016.
* Includes nonalcoholic beverages.

Source: ERS, USDA calculations based on annual household expenditure data from Euromonitor International, available at: www.euromonitor.com/

likelihood that authorities will respond violently and suppress popular uprisings; this is what happened in Tunisia, Egypt, Syria and Yemen.

Bread consumption is so central to people's sustenance, especially for the poor, that one of the Arabic names for it is *A'yash* which literally means "to live". Because this segment of society spends a much higher percentage of its income on food than wealthier neighbors, price hikes can push them into malnutrition or starvation. The most recent data (from 2011) show that Jordanians and Egyptians spend, respectively, 36 and 40.4% of their expenditures on food, while Saudis and Iranians each spend 26% (USDA, 2016B; Table 13.2). In these countries, food price inflation or lifting of bread subsidies could push many poor over the edge, with all the human, social and political consequences that are associated with that.

A review of a composite, overall food security index (Table 13.3) reveals that between 2012 and 2017, there were various degrees of reversals in people's fortunes in all the Middle East countries that were included in the database, save for Israel which saw an improvement. The most severe negative change occurred in war-torn Syria and Yemen.

In an analysis of the relationship between food security and political stability, Sternberg (2012) notes that the top nine wheat-importing countries in the world are located in the Middle East, seven of which experienced popular protests during the Arab Spring period. To avoid the political backlash of high food prices, Gulf states adopted different mitigation methods. In 2010–2011, Oman invested USD 361 million to modernize its food production capability, introducing a subsidy system and local manufacturing fodder. It subsidized wheat

Food security in the Middle East

Table 13.3 Overall ranking of food security in the Middle East

2012			2016			Change in rank (2012–2016)
Rank	Country	*Score/100	Rank	Country	*Score/100	
22	Israel	77.7	17	Israel	78.9	+5
28	Saudi Arabia	68.7	20	Qatar	77.5	NA**
36	Turkey	63.7	26	Oman	73.6	NA
52	Egypt	51.6	27	Kuwait	73.5	NA
54	Jordan	50.6	30	United Arab Emirates	71.8	NA
70	Syria	42.0	32	Saudi Arabia	71.1	-4
83	Yemen	33.3	33	Bahrain	70.1	NA
			45	Turkey	63.6	-9
			57	Egypt	57.1	-5
			60	Jordan	56.9	-6
			96	Syria	36.3	-26
			100	Yemen	34.0	-17

*Score of 100 = most favorable.
**Not applicable because these countries were not included in the 2012 EIU report.
Source: EIU (2012, 2016)

sales by holding its price at levels similar to that of early 2008. As a response to street uprisings, the majority of Arab governments enlarged their subsidies which were deployed in different forms. The government of Kuwait sent its nationals a financial gift and provided them with food staples at no cost for a period of 14 months. To control rising food prices, the United Arab Emirates fixed prices of some 400 basic food and household items that are sold across the country, affecting local and multinational retailers like Carrefour and Spinneys (Alpen Capital, 2013; Amery, 2015; Zurayk, 2011).

The agricultural management system in Syria changed a great deal after Bashar al-Assad became President after his father died in 2000. Different ministries competed as opposed to cooperated with each other, bureaucracy was rife, and qualified human capital was in short supply. "The majority of staff in the ministries of Agriculture and Irrigation has barely finished secondary school and only a small minority had a university degree" (de Châtel, 2014: 11). The goal of food security has always been high on the Syrian Government's agenda which explains its subsidy of all inputs into the production of wheat, a food staple in the local diet, and its requirement for farmers to sell their produce though its outlets. The government also has food storage capacity for over ten months, which is the largest in the Arab world. Since the early years of his reign in the 1970s, Hafez Al-Assad sought to boost wheat productivity by investing in expanding and modernizing the irrigation infrastructure, investing in research and development, and in subsidizing inputs such as seeds, fuel and fertilizers. The government largely succeeded in meeting its economic and food security goals which were focused on self-sufficiency and food that is available at cheap prices (Ahmed, 2016).

The six year drought that started in 2006 turned Syria from an exporter of wheat into an importer, forcing hundreds of thousands of rural residents to migrate to already-strained urban centers. This nurtured social grievances against the government (Ahmed, 2016). By 2010, it is estimated that 17% of the Syrian population (or 3.7 million people) were food insecure (de

Châtel, 2014). This, as well as the drought, concomitant overgrazing, unsustainable management of groundwater supplies and weak governance structures coalesced to produce the civil war that continues to wreak havoc in the country. The violent turmoil and humanitarian crisis that ensued in 2011 "can be seen as the culmination of 50 years of sustained mismanagement of water and land resources, and the dead end of the Syrian government's water and agricultural policies" (de Châtel, 2014: 2). The Syrian civil war reduced domestic wheat production to its lowest levels in 30 years and inflicted extensive structural damage on homes as well as transportation and irrigation infrastructures, which makes post-conflict reconstruction that much harder to achieve. Despite this, a 2017 UN report finds that six years of wars has diminished the central role that agriculture plays in the Syrian economy. "The sector still accounts for an estimated 26% of gross domestic product (GDP) and represents a critical safety net for the 6.7 million Syrians – including those internally displaced – who still remain in rural areas" (FAO, 2017B: 1). Rehabilitation of the agricultural sector is critically important to poverty mitigation, economic development and to post-war construction and the eventual return of the refugees.

In the current Yemen war, Thornberry (2017) writes that even when residents were facing deep food insecurities, the Saudi-led armed forces targeted agricultural infrastructure thus destroying "cattle farms, food factories, water wells and marketplaces, along with the ports, airports, roads and bridges on which effective supplies of food aid depend". Saudis contest these claims, arguing that Houthi rebels in Yemen have destroyed seaport and other infrastructures which aggravate food insecurity (Ghobari, 2016). The reality is that Saudi-led forces are the ones who wanted to prevent the rebels from receiving weapons and munitions through their only outlet to the world, the port of Hodeidah. It is worth noting that in 2015, airstrikes by Saudi-led coalition forces against Houthi rebels damaged the somewhat preserved northern conduit of the Great Marib Dam (Romey, 2015).

Food refugees

Wars aggravate food insecurity and erode the resilience of both urban and rural communities. In times of political instability and war, the following factors limit the amounts of food and livestock available for residents: contraction of areas under cultivation (or accessible for harvesting), limits of farmers' mobility due to instability, damage or destruction of transportation infrastructure, making it harder to move produce to markets, and the collapse of disease control services for livestock. Also, sometimes fishing areas and seaports become inaccessible, reducing an area's ability to receive food aid. These factors, in turn, create spikes in food prices, leading to extreme food insecurity where people are forced to flee in pursuit of sustenance. "Food refugees" emerge when living conditions in afflicted areas deteriorate and people become unable to access sufficient quantities of food from the market place or from their fields; this forces them to abandon their residences for mere survival. The Syrian civil war started in 2011 yet the mass movement of humanity did not occur until 2015 and 2016. In Syria, for example, about 7 million people need help (EU, 2017). In the case of Yemen, more than half of the labor force in the country are employed in agriculture. An estimated 17 million residents are threatened with severe food insecurity in 2017 (FAO, 2017), and 2 million may become victims of famine unless emergency food aid is provided. Internally displaced people (e.g., to Aleppo) or refugees to nearby countries (e.g., to Lebanon or Turkey) consume their food stocks, spend their savings, try to adapt to life under conditions of uncertainty and tolerable threat. Eventually, they become worn down by the poor conditions (e.g., refugee camps), violence (e.g., Syria) and instability and lose hope of returning to their residences which drives them to seek alternative living arrangements.

Kassem Eid (2017), a Syrian survivor of the Assad government's gas attack in 2013, wrote about how the regime laid siege to a suburb of Damascus hoping to starve its residents into submission. Some people were forced into eating weeds, tree leaves and food remains in heaps of garbage. Under these conditions, the author witnessed children and infants starve to death. That same year, an imam in the Yarmouk Camp, a Palestinian refugee camp on the outskirts of Damascus, issued a rare and extraordinary fatwa (religious edict) making it permissible for besieged and beleaguered residents to eat dogs and cats to save their lives from a certain death (Al Arabiya, 2013). Islamic law (Sharia) considers such meats as being unfit for human consumption. Four years later, Tarakji (2017), a Syrian-American surgeon summarized the regime's policy in the besieged areas in a phrase: "starve or kneel". That is, Syrian forces will use food as a weapon to bring rebellious populations to their knees. He also states that about 1 million Syrians live under food sanctions, the vast majority are being besieged by Syrian Government forces. Food has been and continues to be used as weapon of warfare;[1] the United States of America, Israel and Russia have used it in recent history (Amery, 2015; Rothschild, 1976; Tarrant, 1981). In Islamic law, withholding water or food from domestic animals is unlawful, let alone from human beings (Amery, 2001; Taman, 2011).

Transnational threats to food security

Mismanagement of natural resources, corruption, and political instability converge to exacerbate occasional environmental "cruelties," thus undermining food security at the local or national levels. Transboundary pests and diseases affect the availability, stability, access and safety of supplies, and consequently pose a serious threat to food security in the Middle East and North Africa and beyond. The region, for example, is vulnerable to wheat rusts, a fungal-type pest that spreads by wind; hence, it moves long distances in a relatively short time. If it goes undetected and untreated in due time, it has the potential to decimate a healthy crop just before it is harvested. To protect famers at home and in nearby countries, authorities need to develop a system of continuous crop surveillance, share data, and to create emergency response protocols. This would help in the early detection and management which should limit the full impact of the pest. In Syria, the drought of 2009–2010 allowed for the yellow wheat fungal disease to spread more rapidly than normal which reduced wheat crop for that year from the predicted 4–5 million tonnes to 3.2 million tonnes (de Châtel, 2014).

As part of a global rust monitoring effort, scientists in Egypt collaborated with international rust laboratories and set up a system to track the spread of rust pathogens, especially the TTKSK (Ug99) race group of stem rust. In 2014, Egypt confirmed the detection of this pathogen race (BGRI, 2015) and mitigated its impacts. Egypt's success was facilitated by scientific collaborations with Western laboratories and by the general political stability in the country.

The quintessential and ancient threat to crops in the region is locusts. Each eats its bodyweight in food every day. The frequency of the pest's invasions and its destructiveness "earned" it reference in the Old Testament and the Quran. In 2013, locusts that originated in Sudan desert crossed into Egypt and Israel in thick swarms making it difficult for some drivers to see through their car windshields and destroying crops like cumin and potatoes along the way (Kershner, 2013). The governments of Israel and Egypt established locust monitoring stations, tracking and spraying the locusts with insecticide.

Encouraged by rabbis, some farmers in Israel cooked locusts as meals. In Jewish law, all flying insects that use four legs are not considered kosher except for members of the red, yellow, white and the "spotted gray" locust family (Kaplan, 1989). Islamic law has a similar position on eating locusts. During a 2004 invasion of locusts, the eminent al Azhar mosque issued a fatwa encouraging Egyptians to hunt, cook and eat locusts which would actively contribute to "wiping them out" (Al-Qaradawi, 2013). Although locusts are theologically sanctioned as a halal food (Al-Qaradawi, 2013), the wider society in Egypt and the Middle East do not find them to be appetizing. Consequently, the fatwa's relevance is more to promote a "good practice" than to legalize it.

Water mismanagement as a threat to food security

Globally, aquifers provide water for about 40% of irrigated areas, and for more than 33% of municipal and industrial water supply (World Bank, 2015). Junaid Ahmad of the World Bank argues that over the centuries, people have managed groundwater resources for the here and now without much consideration for their long-term sustainability. They, he argues, "have learned how to dig ever deeper, pump ever harder, and how to turn deserts into breadbaskets" without considering the rate at which groundwater is being recharged; hence, many wells have run dry (World Bank, 2015).

In Syria, hand-dug wells were shallow, and muscle-power was used to draw small amounts of groundwater for the people to meet their daily needs. The scale of consumption meant that precipitation routinely replenished the aquifers. All this changed with the unregulated introduction of diesel motor pumps in the 1960s. They spread across the country at a rapid pace so much so that between 1999 and 2010, the number of wells is believed to have gone from 135,089 to over 229,881. As recently as 2010, 57% of wells were unlicensed. Poor governance led to over-exploitation whereby groundwater levels in certain areas of the Damascus governorate dropped by more than 6 meters per year (de Châtel, 2014).

It is estimated that 20% of the world's aquifers are being over-pumped. In the Arabian Peninsula where the Gulf Cooperation Council (GCC) countries are located, fresh water "withdrawal, as a percentage of internally renewable water resources, was estimated at 505%" (WWDR, 2003, 13). The agricultural sector consumes up to 85% of fresh water supplies in the GCC. This water is drawn primarily from aquifers that are non-renewable, with the exception of a small number.

A World Bank report (2015) states that Iran and Saudi Arabia are the Middle Eastern countries where groundwater withdrawal intensity is among the highest in the world. It also reported that as groundwater abstraction accelerated at unprecedented rates, its governance "has been an area of policy neglect" causing degradation and depletion of this critical resource. Aquifers often suffer from pollution from farming and manufacturing runoff, and sometimes from leaky sanitation infrastructure. Coastal aquifers may become contaminated by salt-water intrusion due to over-abstraction or to sea level rise induced by climate change.

A new study published in *Nature* finds that the intensity of groundwater depletion for irrigation (GWD) varies greatly across regions and crop types. Some of the extreme variations from countries with GWD are the following: it takes 21,900 liters of GWD to produce 1 kilogram of wheat in Kuwait while the global average is 812 liters. And it takes 2,100 liters of GWD to produce 1 kilogram of rice in Iran compared with the global average of 199 liters, and 790 liters for 1 kilogram of maize in Saudi Arabia compared with the global average of 72 liters (Dalin et al., 2017). The authors

> find that large parts of the world's population live in countries that source 90% or more of their staple crops imports from partners depleting groundwater to produce these crops: 89% of the population for sunflower seed, three quarters for maize, and a third for wheat and rice.
>
> (Dalin et al., 2017: 702)

Food security in the Middle East

They also find that "a vast majority of the world's population lives in countries sourcing nearly all their staple crop imports from partners who deplete groundwater to produce these crops, highlighting risks for global food and water security". Iran, the USA and China are among these countries.

In the last few centuries, local and national food self-sufficiency have been giving way to the forces of globalization where producers can now meet the needs of consumers –even ones located in geographically distant places. Countries exporting GWD-based food are exposed to long-term risks because of their unsustainable management of their non-renewable resources. The top ten countries with the most GWD include Iran and Saudi Arabia which are also top importers of food produced through GWD. They import or export crops irrigated from highly over-pumped aquifers. Iran, for example, "mainly imports rice from Pakistan irrigated from the Upper Ganges and Lower Indus aquifers (overexploited by factors of 54.2 and 18.4, respectively) and exports perennial crops irrigated from the Persian aquifer (overexploitation factor 19.7) to neighboring Iraq" (Dalin et al., 2017). This GWD poses food security risks because if (when?) a stressed aquifer collapses, it would impact food supply locally and internationally. This interdependency highlights another vulnerability that the globalized trading system creates.

As the GCC countries were becoming increasingly dependent on food imports from the region and around the world, they experienced in 2008–2009 the ripple effects of tight food markets, trade restrictions imposed by some food-exporting countries, and a concomitant sharp increase in food prices. This global episode showed the Gulf countries are "highly vulnerable to external food price shocks" and are exposed to the risk of "embargoes by exporting countries" (Kotilaine, 2010).

In conclusion, the threats to food security are multifaceted and dynamic. Threats to trade route disruptions, for example, change over time. While the likelihood of Arab Gulf states losing food imports from Syria due to the ongoing war was very low, the threat to blockade the Strait of Hormuz by Iran is decades-old. In other words, not all threats can be predicted and mitigated. With this in mind, states in the Middle East have been responding to some of the food threats that they face. The following sections discuss only two of these possible responses.

Foreign agricultural investments

Countries that are heavily dependent on food imports like Egypt and the Gulf states are vulnerable to price risks and supply risks. Middle East governments, especially those in the Arab Gulf states, have become very concerned about the international price volatility of imported foods, the ever-present risk of supply disruption either by embargoes imposed by food-producing countries or by geopolitical events that would close the Hormuz or Bab El Mandab Straits. These concerns as well as the extensive natural constraints on food production in many Middle Eastern countries have led some to invest in farming abroad and to become more dependent on food imports (Woertz, 2013; Mohammed and Darwish, 2017; Amery, 2015).

For Arab governments, food security has always been an important issue, and the level of their concern ebbs and flows with fluctuations in international prices of basic staples like wheat and rice, and with threats to trade routes. Arab countries have long had an "obsession" with food security which was commonly expressed in the context of food "self-sufficiency" (Abdel-Gawad, 2015; Woertz, 2013). In the 1970s, this fixation was related to the idea of natural resource complementarities between Arab countries, and to the fervor of Arab nationalism that was sweeping much of the region then. The idea was that oil-rich Arab countries who are deprived of arable land and fresh water would invest their wealth in countries like Sudan, turning it into the breadbasket for the Arab World. This nationalist fervor was rather strong in the 1960s and 1970s; hence people's expectations were such that Arab leaders ought to collaborate and coordinate their policies; "strength in unity" was a common cry.

Sudan, today, is bearing the weight of 20 years of economic sanctions (they were lifted in January 2017) and the loss of an important revenue stream from oil fields that now belong to the new state of South Sudan. On the other hand, Sudan is a country with a lot of agricultural potential. The area of arable land is estimated to be 200 million acres, of which less than 45 million acres are being cultivated (Hussein, 2015).

In recent years, the President of Sudan, Omar al-Bashir, has become active in promoting his country as having ample under-utilized natural resources like water and arable land, and as being open for business – vowing to protect foreign investments. The Arab Gulf states have been particularly receptive to this allure. In 2016, the governments of Sudan and Saudi Arabia signed a massive agricultural agreement whereby the latter leases 1 million feddan (2,100 square kilometers) for a period of 99 years. It will invest USD 10 billion to develop the necessary infrastructure, and this will be followed by land restoration. The lands targeted by Saudi Arabia are located in the northeastern parts of the country, and will be irrigated by rainfall and by water from the Upper Atbarah and Setit rivers, each of which has a newly built dam (AlKhaleejOnline. net, 2016; BaBaker, 2016).

Saudi Arabia was particularly grateful for Sudan's support of its 2015 war in Yemen so it started encouraging investments in Sudan. Today, the vast majority of Saudi's foreign agricultural investments are in Sudan. For Sudan, Arab investments allow it to by-pass comprehensive economic sanctions that were imposed on it by US President Bill Clinton in 1997 and to find alternative sources of revenues to those that were lost to South Sudan. The current reality and trajectory of trade relations between Saudi Arabia and Sudan point to a significant intensification and to Sudan becoming a bigger contributor to the kingdom's food security. The political realities are such that Sudan is largely seen as a pariah state which is led by an authoritarian president who is wanted by the International Criminal Court on charges of genocide, war crimes and crimes against humanity. Consequently, by linking its food security to the political stability and resilience of Sudan, Saudi Arabia is accepting and underwriting a significant level of political risk.

Less food waste, fewer food imports

Globally, it is estimated that the quantity of food produced globally is about 4 billion metric tonnes per year, of which 30–50% is lost or wasted before consumption (The Institution of Mechanical Engineers, 2013). Reducing food waste boosts farmers' income, lowers food prices, conserves land, water, and energy used in producing and transporting food, and lowers emission of greenhouse gases. It is also an ethical practice because it improves the food security of others (Tielens and Candel, 2014). In Islamic law, food security is enhanced through the pillar of Zakah, Arabic for alms-giving. That is, wealthier Muslims are required to give to charity; providing the needy with food is explicitly mentioned in the Quran (2:267) where God instructs believers to "give to charity from the good things you earn, and from what we have produced for you from the earth". Zakah could be paid in money or "in the form of agricultural products, specifically in the form of food for the hungry" (Taman, 2011: 490). It is worth noting that this type of charitable giving must go to needy human beings, regardless of their religious, ethnic or racial backgrounds. Prophet Muhammad is reported to have said that one will not enter paradise ("heaven") if one has enough to eat while a neighbor goes hungry.

Food security is so important to Islamic theology that it allows consumption of otherwise unlawful foods all in the interest of preserving human life. This also explains why it is unlawful to cheat customers, sell spoiled goods, or to hoard food because a spike in prices may make it beyond the reach of certain economic classes. In the same token, the Quran (7:31) instructs Muslims to "eat and drink, but waste not by excess, for God loves not the wasters" (see also Amery, 2001). The reality of life often diverges from these normative theological guidelines.

In the Middle East, an estimated 1.3 billion tonnes of food worth more than 1 trillion dollars are wasted yearly (Malek, 2015). Dubai Municipality alone wastes some 1,850 tonnes of food per day, one-fifth of which is wasted during the month of Ramadan (Benham and Al-Jawahiry, 2011). A study by King Saud University estimates that 4,500 tonnes of food is wasted every day in Saudi Arabia, and some 30% of all prepared food in Ramadan is wasted (Tago, 2014). This is ironic on multiple levels. First, the Gulf States are top food importers and yet waste large amounts of it. Second, one of intended goals of fasting during the month of Ramadan is for Muslims to make an extra effort to abide by God's commandments (forbids wastefulness) and, third, to empathize with the hungry or otherwise less fortunate. The Arabian Peninsula is surrounded by refugee flows in the north (Iraq and Syria), the south (Yemen), and it is home to millions of low-skilled and low-paid expatriate workers. Governments and imams should undertake a public awareness campaign on specific strategies that individuals can take to reduce food waste.

Conclusion

There is no single answer to the food security question mostly because it is closely associated with natural resource endowments, good governance, political and climatic changes at the national and global levels. It is not a coincidence that the largest number of food-deficient people are located in war-torn countries in the Middle East. Turkey, Syria and Iran have relatively abundant amounts of fresh water and arable lands, while arid countries like those in the Arab Gulf lack them.

Food security is enhanced through improving resilience of farming communities, embracing sustainable farming methods and mobilizing investments in transportation, storage infrastructure, and in related science and technology. It would also be enhanced if food importers were to have a vision of "shared food security" where they work with producers to improve their economic and political resiliency. The tight relationship between water and food security require government officials to break the silos of their individual ministries and have an inter-sectoral dialogue which would help them develop seamless policies that reduce waste and protect the natural environment. Decision-makers need to work on improving groundwater governance, and on expanding the coverage of efficient irrigation infrastructure. Closing the yield gap in countries where land productivity is below its potential would go some way to boosting food security. Some countries in the region are also building or expanding strategic food reserves and diversifying foreign agricultural investments and trade relations.

A UN report found that between the years 2000 and 2014, cereals imports as well production experienced a sharp increase in the Middle East. The upward demand trend and the depletion of scarce water resources are forcing decision-makers to shed the long-held idea of food self-sufficiency. The report proposes the notion of "self-reliance" as a more appropriate policy conceptualization of food security in the Middle East. Self-reliance is "the ability to pay for one's own food bill". This would require a strategic shift in focus towards one of economic productivity of water and towards a country's comparative advantage (FAO, 2017c: 23–24). Starting in the mid-2000s, the Arab Gulf states began to gradually develop a long-term view of their groundwater supplies; they now consider them a strategic resource that could be of vital importance in times of emergencies. This explains why Saudi Arabia phased out (2008–2016) its heavily subsidized wheat cultivation program that had lasted decades. Despite the hydrological and financial wastefulness of this food self-sufficiency scheme, a large number of ordinary Saudis were concerned that their food security "survival" is now in the hands of "others" (producers).

While food security is ultimately about the "right" of people to food, the issue remains a foggy abstraction until we shift the discussion to who has an "obligation" and responsibility to provide food to needy residents. For reasons of culture, economics and governance, some Middle Eastern countries are well-positioned to take on the responsibility of providing (or enabling) food security.

Note

1 Food is also used to prop up and revive a political system that is battered by political or economic difficulties. Less than a year into the civil war in Syria, the *New York Times* reported that Russia's "steady supply of weapons, food, medical supplies and other aid" save the Assad regime from certain defeat (Herszenhorn, 2012).

References

Abdel-Gawad, Shaden (2015). Together towards a Secure Arab Water. *3rd Arab Water Forum, Final Report*. December 2014, Cairo, Egypt.

Ahmed, Ghada (2016). *Syria Wheat Value Chain and Food Security*. Duke MINERVA. Duke University Policy Brief. No. 08, March.

Amery, Hussein (2001). Islamic Water Management. *Water International* 26(4), 1–9.

Amery, Hussein (2015). *Water Security in the Arab World: Threats and Opportunities in the Gulf States*. Cambridge: Cambridge University Press.

Al Arabiya (2013). Syrian Clerics Plead for Help after Fatwa on Eating Dogs and Cats. 14 October. http://english.alarabiya.net/en/News/middle-east/2013/10/14/Syrian-imams-plead-for-help-after-permitting-people-to-eat-dogs-cats-.html

AlKhaleejOnline.net (2016). Al-Bashir Vows to Care for and Protect Saudi Investments in Sudan. 17 February (in Arabic).

Alpen Capital (2013). *GCC Food Industry*. May 01. Dubai, UAE.

al-Qaradawi, Yusuf (2013). *The Lawful and Prohibited in Islam*. Marawi, Philippines: Wisdom International School for Higher Education.

Arezki, Ranah and Markus Brückner (2011). *Food Prices and Political Instability*. IMF Working Paper. International Monetary Fund WP/11/62.

BaBaker, Saif Al-Yazal (2016). *Sudan Passes Law for Saudi Arabia to Cultivate 100 Million Feddans*. Asharq Al Awsat (London). July 18. https://eng-archive.aawsat.com/saif/business/sudan-passes-law-saudi-arabia-cultivate-100-million-feddans

Benham, Jason and Warda Al-Jawahiry (2011). Ramadan in Dubai: A Month of Soaring Food Waste? Reuters. 15 August.

BGRI (2015). Ug99 (TTKSK) Detected in Egypt. *BGRI Newsletter Special Edition*, 3 April 2015. BGRI (Borlaug Global Rust Initiative).

de Châtel, Francesca (2014). The Role of Drought and Climate Change in the Syrian Uprising: Untangling the Triggers of the Revolution, *Middle Eastern Studies* 50(4), pp. 1–15.

Dalin, Carole, Yoshihide Wada, Thomas Kastner and Michael J. Puma (2017). Groundwater Depletion Embedded in International Food Trade. *Nature* 543, 700–704 (30 March 2017).

DOD (2014). *Quadrennial Defense Review 2014*. Department of Defense.

The Economist (2012). Let Them Eat Baklava. *The Economist*, March 17.

Eid, Kassim (2017). I Survived a Sarin Gas Attack. *The New York Times*. April 7.

EIU (2012). *Global Food Security Index*. The Economist Intelligence Unit.

EIU (2016). *Global Food Security Index*. The Economist Intelligence Unit.

EU (2017). *Global Report on Food Crisis 2017*. European Union and FAO. March.

FAO (1985). *World Food Security: Selected Themes and Issues*. Papers and summaries of discussion at the Symposium on World Food Security convened by FAO: Food and Agriculture Organization of the United Nations. Rome, Italy.

FAO (1996). *Rome Declaration on World Food Security and World Food Summit Plan of Action*. Food and Agriculture Organization of the United Nations.

FAO (2017a). *Yemen*. Food and Agriculture Organization. Situation Report. April.

FAO (2017b). *Counting the Cost: Agriculture in Syria after Six Years of Crisis*. Food and Agriculture Organization of the United Nations.

FAO (2017c). *Near East and North Africa Regional Overview of Food Insecurity 2016*. Cairo, Egypt.

Ghobari, Mohammed (2016). Yemen's War-Damaged Hodeidah Port Struggles to Bring in Vital Supplies. Reuters. November 24.

Gleick, Peter H. (2014). Water, Drought, Climate Change, and Conflict in Syria. *Weather, Climate, and Society*. 6, pp. 331–340. DOI: http://dx.doi.org/10.1175/WCAS-D-13-00059.1

Herszenhorn, David M. (2012). For Syria, Reliant on Russia for Weapons and Food, Old Bonds Run Deep. *New York Times*. February 18.

Hussein, Walaa (2015). Egypt Plans to Raise Crops in sub-Saharan Africa. Al-Monitor. August 3. www.al-monitor.com/pulse/originals/2015/08/egypt-sudan-agriculture-irrigation-cooperation-blue-nile.html

Institution of Mechanical Engineers (2013). *Global Food: Waste Not, Want Not*. Institution of Mechanical Engineers, London.

Kaplan, Aryeh (1989). *The Torah Anthology: Yalkut Me'Am Lo'Ez - Vol. XI: The Divine Service*. New York: Moznaim Publishing Corp.

Kershner, Isabel (2013). A Locust Plague, Shy of Biblical Proportions, in Israel. *New York Times*. 6 March. www.nytimes.com/2013/03/07/world/middleeast/swarms-of-locusts-cross-into-israel-from-egypt.html

Kotilaine, Jarmo T. (2010). *GCC Agriculture*. NCB Capital, Riyadh, Saudi Arabia.

Malek, Caline (2015). More than One Trillion Dollars' Worth of Food Wasted by Middle East Each Year. *The National (UAE)*. 8 March. www.thenational.ae/uae/environment/more-than-one-trillion-dollars-worth-of-food-wasted-by-middle-east-each-year-1.19089

Mohammed, Sayeed and Mohamed Darwish (2017). Water Footprint and Virtual Water Trade in Qatar. *Desalination and Water Treatment* 66: 117–132 doi:10.5004/dwt.2017.20221

National Geographic (n.d.). What the World Eats. www.nationalgeographic.com/what-the-world-eats/

Romey, Kristin (2015). "Engineering Marvel of Queen of Sheba's City Damaged in Airstrike. The ancient Great Dam of Marib is one of several cultural casualties of Yemen" June 3. *National Geographic*.

Rothschild, Emma (1976). Food Politics. *Foreign Affairs*, pp. 285–307.

Sen, Amartya (1981). *Poverty and Famines*. Oxford: Clarendon Press.

Sternberg, Troy (2012). Chinese Drought, Bread and the Arab Spring. *Applied Geography* 34, pp. 519–524.

Tago, Abdul Hannan (2014). Food Wastage Remains a Serious Concern. *Arab News (Saudi Arabia)* 13 April. www.arabnews.com/news/554911

Taman, Salma (2011). The Concept of Corporate Social Responsibility in Islamic Law. *Indiana International & Comparative Law Review* 21(3).

Tarakji, Ahmad (2017). Syria: "Starve or Kneel" is Another Name for Mass Murder. *Fox News*. April 18, 2017.

Tarrant, J.R. (1981). Food as a Weapon? The Embargo on Grain Trade between USA and USSR. *Applied Geography*, 1, 273–286.

Thornberry, Emily (2017). Saudi Bombs are Decimating Yemen. Yet May's Glad-handing Goes On. *The Guardian* (UK), 5 April 2017.

Tielens, Joris and Jeroen Candel (2014). Reducing Food Wastage, Improving Food Security? The Hague, The Netherlands: Food & Business Knowledge Platform. July.

Tindall, James A. and Andrew A. Campbell (2012). *Water Security: Conflicts, Threats, Policies*. Denver, Colorado, DTP Publishing.

UNDP (2006). *Beyond Scarcity: Power, Poverty and the Global Water Crisis. The Human Development Report*. United Nations Development Programme. New York, USA.

USDA (2016a). *Saudi Arabia: Poultry and Products Annual*. GAIN Report SA1607. https://gain.fas.usda.gov/Recent%20GAIN%20Publications/Poultry%20and%20Products%20Annual_Riyadh_Saudi%20Arabia_8-31-2016.pdf

USDA (2016b). *Food Expenditure. Percent of Consumer Expenditures Spent on Food, Alcoholic Beverages, and Tobacco that were Consumed at Home, by Selected Countries, 2011*. Economic Research Series, US Department of Agriculture.

Woertz, Eckart (2013). *Oil for Food: The Global Food Crisis and the Middle East.* Oxford: Oxford University Press.

World Bank (2013). *Adaptation to a Changing Climate Change in the Arab Countries.* Washington, DC: World Bank.

World Bank (2015). *Global Agencies Call for Urgent Action to Avoid Irreversible Groundwater Depletion.* April 10. www.worldbank.org/en/news/press-release/2015/04/10/global-agencies-urgent-action-avoid-irreversible-groundwater-depletion

World Bank (n.d.). *Data.* https://data.worldbank.org/

WWDR (2003). *Water for People, Water for Life.* The United Nations World Water Development Report. World Water Assessment Program.

Zurayk, Rami (2011). *Food, Farming, and Freedom: Sowing the Arab Spring.* Charlottesville, VA: Just World Books.

14
CLIMATE-RELATED SECURITY RISKS IN THE MIDDLE EAST

Dan Smith and Florian Krampe

Introduction

One aspect that marks out the Middle East's special character is its climate and, with that, the arid natural environment of much of the region. It is not very revealing to think about the region without thinking about water. Its supply is deficient in most of the region yet comparatively abundant in parts. Regulating its use is a paramount requirement for human well-being, for agriculture, for the cities and for development. This is an old fact of the Middle East's life. In the contemporary context, thinking about climate and water means, *inter alia*, thinking about the changing global climate.

That much seems reasonably clear and we presume it commands general assent but it takes us quickly into areas of considerable controversy. From this uncontentious starting point, it is a logical step to posit an intrinsic connection between water and climate on the one hand, and a wide variety of important variables on the other, including development prospects, culture in the broad sense, social organization and stability, the organization of power and legitimacy of government, political stability, security and violent conflict.

There is, however, an academic debate about this connection and, in particular, the link between climate and water on the one hand and the last of the variables we listed on the other – violent conflict. At its core, this controversy revolves around causation and around competing but equally sweeping claims that climate change either does or does not cause violent conflict (Burke et al., 2009; Buhaug et al., 2014; Hsiang and Burke, 2013). The Middle East – where there are many violent conflicts and the importance of climate change and water is evident – has perhaps inevitably become a focal point in this controversy. It has generated a significant amount of literature but, for several reasons, we regard it as a distraction and agree with Gemenne et al. who argued that, for all its subtlety and complexity, much of this controversy is beside the point (Gemenne et al., 2014).

In our view, this is partly because it swings on the wrong question. In many academic studies – as well as in highly charged political discussions about climate change and its diverse impacts and effects (Randall, 2017; Selby et al., 2017b) – the question that is asked hinges on direct causality. The methodology of many such studies is a statistical inquiry spanning many years and many countries with a focus on verifying or refuting a presumed or hypothesized causal connection between one dependent and one independent variable. But armed conflicts do not have a single cause and attempting to isolate one implies chasing a phantasm. The most serious and useful research on the social, economic and political knock-on consequences of climate change accepts and, indeed, asserts that the influence of anthropogenic climate change and, *pari passu*, climate variability generated by other sources comes through its interaction with other features in the social, economic and political landscape. In other words, the focus on a possible single cause is to concentrate misleadingly on a detail; only the whole picture makes sense. This inevitably makes a high standard of proving causal effects very hard to attain. But for many in the policy world and in policy-oriented research, this does not matter because the issue has much more to do with risk – or probabilistic causal linkages. This is also acknowledged in a more balanced part of the academic debate (Hendrix, 2017). The focus is less on evidence that verifies (or dismisses) a hypothesis and more on evidence that supports (or challenges) the plausibility of a linkage, suggesting a degree of likelihood that the linkage may recur.

This is the approach we take in this chapter, exploring the background to conflict in three countries – Egypt, Syria and Yemen. We are not interested in *proving* that climate variability is a cause of events since 2011 in Egypt, Syria and Yemen, and even less interested in discussing whether it is the most important cause in the outbreak of violence. Instead, we are interested in showing that climate change and variability are a relevant part of the background to conflict in all three countries. Actors' motivations count as well as other contextual factors "like dependence on agriculture for livelihoods, patterns of exclusionary ethnic rule, and low levels of economic development" (Hendrix, 2017: 251).

There is also a more theoretical – possibly even philosophical – reason for opting away from simple determinism. It is relatively straightforward to reject the search for a mono-causal explanation of a phenomenon as complex as armed violence. It is perhaps more complex and elusive to acknowledge that multiple interacting causal factors produce multiple interacting consequences. Multi-causality meets multi-finality. In any one geographic location – a city, a country, a region – violent conflict might be but one among several consequences of the interaction of climate change with a range of social, political and economic variables. Others might be seasonal labor migration, adjustments of community relationships, changed crops, and other kinds of adaptation to climate change, existing in the same geographic space as famine, conflicts and other negative forms of adaptation. Research that stresses complexity and moves away from simple determinism has put climate in its place as one of the drivers of security concerns, functioning, like others, only when it interacts with others (among others Swain et al., 2011; Mobjörk et al., 2016). Ultimately, armed conflict is a choice by actors and climatic or other factors do not reduce responsibility and accountability of a government's or insurgency's choice to use violence.

In this chapter, we follow this line of argument through three cases in the contemporary Middle East – Egypt, Syria and Yemen.

The Middle East region

The Middle East is subject to a conflation of complex and compounding security risks. Conflictive identities, socio-economic livelihoods, as well as geopolitical interests are closely intertwined with the facts of geography, including climate and environmental change. Water is a fundamental issue. The rivers Euphrates, Tigris and Nile have been essential for the livelihood of millions of people for millennia. The flow of these rivers today is disrupted by dams and managed through dated water treaties. The issues are part and parcel of everyday politics in the region. Water is frequently the source of tensions and an element of the larger geopolitical struggle for power. Water is, moreover, an element of control and a tool of structural violence as seen over the last five decades in the Occupied Territories of Palestine.

The significance today of this long-lasting element of Middle Eastern politics and conflict is in part a product of how climate change impacts unfold. The supply of water is one of the main transmission mechanisms for the consequences of anthropogenic climate change. This supports the expectation that, as climate change progresses, there are rising risks of regional conflict escalation. A recent study by Lelieveld et al. (2016) stresses the prospect of increasing heat extremes in summertime: "the maximum temperature during the hottest days in the recent past was about 43 °C, which could increase to about 46 °C by the middle of the century and reach almost 50 °C by the end of the century" (Lelieveld et al., 2016). These temperature extremes interact with the drivers of political instability and conflict (Swain and Jägerskog, 2016) in a region in which every country, with the exception of Oman, has been affected by or actively involved in armed conflicts in the last ten years.

In the three cases in this chapter, we illustrate the approach whose broad outlines we have sketched above. Alongside the social and political factors, drought is a key issue in all of them, though in the case of Egypt the drought in question did not happen there. Our historical starting point is the surge of political unrest in the Middle East in 2011. It was primarily driven by widespread public grievance at failures in governance. Tracing the pathway to violent conflict, it is important to ask not only what the failures were, but why they mattered and, in particular, why they mattered *then*. Seen from one angle, they were about exclusion of most of the populations of most of the Middle East from a say in political decision-making, a lack of voice, an absence of democracy and, with that, infringement of basic freedoms of speech, assembly and organization. Seen from another angle, however, these deficiencies triggered upheaval at the time that they did because there were additional pressures, beyond the routine of marginalization, arbitrary power and repression. Our aim is not to ascribe one or the other case to climate change, but to illustrate how the impacts of climate and environmental change are different in each case, but still interacting with social, economic and political processes, creating unprecedented security challenges.

Egypt: The transnational dimensions of climate-related security risks

In Egypt, between the overthrow of King Farouk by the Free Officers movement led by Gamal Abdel Nasser in 1952 and the ouster of the country's third post-monarchy President, Hosni Mubarak, in 2011, much changed – and yet nothing changed. Six decades of economic development, including often impressive rates of economic growth, coincided with a population explosion. Yet the 1952 revolution and the huge popular mobilization that led to Mubarak's loss of power were about largely the same issues: revulsion at the misuse of power, the depth of inequality, the pervasiveness of corruption and the grip on power exerted by a small elite.

In view of this, it might be reasonable to ask why it is necessary to bring in climate change as a factor in explaining the Arab Spring in Egypt. We acknowledge it is *almost* possible to explain the popular uprising against Mubarak's rule in 2011 without any reference to nature. There had, after all, been a rising tide of grievance and activism over many years, focused on issues such as workers' and farmers' rights (Shenker, 2016). These movements formed a lasting and deeply rooted challenge to the legitimacy of the Egyptian state under President Mubarak. The effect was both slower and deeper than that which arose from the militant violence of *al-Jama'a al-Islamiyyah*, organized around what would now be referred to as a *jihadist* version of Islam, culminating in the group's massacre of 62 people, mostly foreign tourists, at Luxor in November 1997 (*The Economist*, 1997; Cowell and Jehl, 1997). A central development was the growth of the Muslim Brotherhood as a social, religious and political movement, providing welfare services for ordinary Egyptians that the state could not or did not offer, and gaining standing and credibility because of it. Deep though they went, nonetheless, these grievances and the localized movements that articulated them were in some ways marginal, because the political system provided no space for them. There was no room for maneuver. The actions of the security police were often draconian yet were also calibrated skillfully so as to avoid alienating middle class opinion too seriously or exciting mass opposition on an unmanageable scale. It was the combination of guile and determination that established what passed for political and social stability during the Mubarak presidency from 1981 to 2011, the whole of which was spent in a declared state of emergency that was only lifted in May 2012 after Mubarak had been driven from power (BBC, 2012).

What was it that broke this arrangement? As in Tunisia (Fraihat, 2016, 58), by 2011 rising food prices were an important source of grievance. It was the government's inability to keep Egyptian food prices down that was the final one in a combination of factors that meant the country's social and political contract broke. In Egypt state subsidies kept food prices in normal conditions to affordable levels for the mass of the population (Ahmed et al., 2001). Subsidies work effectively for much of the time but such a system is vulnerable to spikes in global food prices with knock-on consequences for social stability. The sharp rise in global food prices in 2008 generated hunger, protests and political instability in many countries (Hendrix and Haggard, 2015: 153). Egypt was among them. Prices rose because of the interaction of several factors. Among them were reduced farming output, irregularities in food markets and policy errors including export restrictions as the crisis unfolded (Wheeler and Braun, 2013). Only two and a half years later, with Egypt not having fully recovered from 2008, a second wave of food price volatility hit the country. As in 2008 and more dramatically, the government was unable to cushion the effect of the price increases in global markets. In the wake of increasing food insecurity, protest swelled, anger grew and the fundamentals of social stability came under threat.

The World Bank's 2014 report *Turn Down the Heat* cautiously surveys some of the research on the relationship between extreme climatic conditions, food prices and protests in Egypt (World Bank, 2014, 144–147). It suggests that the outbreak of violent protests in Egypt was linked both to global food price peaks and to drought in China's eastern wheat belt in late 2010 and early 2011 (Lagi et al., 2011; Sternberg, 2011, 2012). There was also the unfortunate coincidence of drought and wildfires in Russia and Ukraine in 2010, unusually cool, wet weather in Canada and heavy rainstorms in Australia's wheat growing regions (Femia and Werrell, 2013). As global wheat supply tightened, world prices doubled between June 2010 and February 2011.

As we track the reasons for the overthrow of Hosni Mubarak, it is important to understand why it occurred in 2011 and not before or later. What changed? The nature of the regime was unchanging but food security deteriorated because of the global effects of environmental change – drought in China and other grain producing countries, harsh climatic conditions elsewhere. As the World Bank survey concludes, the link between natural events and social and political events is not directly verifiable but it is plausible (World Bank 2014: 147). Whether this is climate variability or anthropogenic climate change at work is beside the point. Climate impacts cross huge distances and there are many pathways through which they affect livelihoods, grievances and the stability of societies. The case of Egypt provides a grim picture of the risks that will arise in a climate-changed world.

Still, this does not explain what happened next. The economic impact fed the grievances expressed through a two-decades long rising tide of social protests over both economic conditions and lack of political freedoms (see Shenker, 2016). The result was not only a mass mobilization, but a challenge to regime legitimacy. The army's self-separation from taking on any task of restoring public order during the days of mass protest in Cairo in early 2011 has indicated to many that there was some disillusionment in the army with Mubarak, perhaps because his favored successor appeared to be his son Gamal who had no military experience himself. When Mubarak demurred on stepping down, it appears senior army figures may have insisted; it also appears they did not see it as a matter of the army permanently retreating from power (Poletti, 2011; Spencer, 2014).

In short, it was not climate change alone or through direct cause-and-effect that brought masses of people to the streets of Cairo. But the pressures of nature in diverse countries are an essential part of explaining what happened. The consequent rise in the price of staple food added to several decades' worth of widespread grievances and helped trigger a mass movement. Internal strife at the top levels of the Egyptian Government rounds the explanation off. Other things being equal, if underlying grievances are not met and if affordable prices depend on government subsidies rather than a robust and growing economy, a future round of drought and other natural events driven by climate change may well produce similar results. The evidence is strong enough to be able to identify the risk and, therefore, to act on and, in principle, to mitigate it.

Syria: The politics of climate-related security risks

The Syrian civil war broke out in March 2011, after Syrian state authorities detained and tortured 15 boys who had written graffiti in the southern city of Daraa in support of the Arab Spring (Fahim and Saad, 2013). As the harsh response of the authorities was met by increasingly determined opposition, violence escalated. Groups began arming themselves. The democratically oriented opposition to the government of Bashir al-Assad was augmented by a *jihadist* opposition. Indeed, the Assad regime ensured this evolution in the conflict by releasing from prison "up to 1,500 of the most well-connected Salafist activists" (Yassin-Kassab and Al-Shami, 2016: 120), freeing them to join the battle. The war was also joined by external forces (SIPRI, 2017: 76–78) including Hezbollah fighters from Lebanon, advisors and fighters from Iran, and Saudi-funded fighters from various parts of the region. Foreign intervention has also come in the form of military advisors, trainers and special forces from the US, UK and France; the Russian, US, French, British, Turkish, Jordanian, Qatari, Saudi and UAE air forces; and fighters who joined the ex-al-Qaeda group that called itself the Islamic State.

The human consequences of the war have been devastating though the statistics are inevitably uncertain. The UN Special Envoy for Syria, Staffan de Mistura, stated in April 2016 that over 400,000 people had been killed (Johnson, 2016). Human Rights Watch, however, put the total by February 2016 at 470,000 (Human Rights Watch, 2017), a figure that has also gained some credence (Moore, 2017). In addition, by December 2017, there were 5.4 million Syrian refugees in other countries and 6.1 million who had fled their homes but remained inside Syria (UNHCR, 2017); that is, war has displaced over half the pre-war population (*The Economist*, 2015).

Both the complexity of events that have unfolded since the uprisings began and the scale of the human tragedy complicate analysis of how they came about. Many who write about the events are as interested in assigning responsibility for them as in explaining them. One starting point is an obvious element that has much in common with key elements of explaining other locales of the Arab Spring in the Middle East and North Africa. Dissatisfaction with the regime, repression, economic decline and marginalization are all key parts of the narrative.

However, it has also been widely noted that before the civil war in Syria, there was a multi-year drought from 2006 to 2010. It was far from Syria's first drought in recent times; indeed, over the half century from 1961 to 2009, the country experienced 25 drought years (De Châtel, 2014). Gleick was among the first to argue that the climate and water played a part in Syria's economic deterioration (Gleick, 2014: 331). He argued that global environmental change and mismanagement of water resources through outdated irrigation systems, for example, were factors leading to increased rural-urban migration, food insecurity and unemployment (Gleick, 2014: 338). A study by Kelley et al. (2015) went a step further, identifying the impact of anthropogenic climate change, mediated through "widespread crop failure," leading to "mass migration of farming families to urban centers" (Kelley et al., 2015: 3241). By contrast, another study could not see such a significant linkage between climate change and conflict onset in Syria (Selby et al., 2017b). These findings have been further contested (Kelley et al., 2017; Gleick, 2017) and on it goes (Selby et al., 2017a: 254).

One aspect of the critique of the argument that climate change is among the underlying causes is that it distracts from the Assad regime's actions and responsibilities (De Châtel, 2014). This may be true in the sense that claims can be made that a government is not responsible for something if nature played a part but it is hard to see how those claims can have much credibility; governments and individuals are always morally accountable for their actions, whatever the background.

Even those who contest the link between drought and war (e.g. Selby et al., 2017b) do not seem to contest that drought, its mismanagement by the Syrian Government, and a decrease in agricultural productivity, together with other misfiring policies, led to increased rural to urban migration in Syria (Swain and Jägerskog, 2016; De Châtel, 2014; Gleick, 2014). There are, however, disputes about the statistics of drought-driven displacement. Kelley et al. set the number at "1.5 million people" (Kelley et al. 2015: 3241). This number has also been used by the UN (UNHCR, 2016) although the UN's 2009–2010 Syria Drought Response Plan used lower – but still large – numbers; it identified 1.3 million people affected by drought, of whom 803,000 faced extreme hardship, of whom 300,000 were the most vulnerable and urgently in need of aid (UN Office for the Coordination of Humanitarian Affairs, 2009; UN Office for the Coordination of Humanitarian Affairs, 2010). Some current data records 433,000 internally displaced people in Syria in 2009, rising to 600,000 by the end of 2010 (International Displacement Monitoring Centre, 2017). In addition to drought-related migration and the Palestinian refugee population, there is also the impact of refugees arriving from Iraq to take into account, alongside an internal Syrian process of labor migration (Leenders and Heydemann, 2012; Leenders, 2008). Together different forms of migration from north-western Syria to urban centers increased the pressure on public services and stability (Erian et al., 2010). Kelley (2015) links rapid demographic changes in communities with the onset of conflict. The evidence for this claim in the peace and conflict literature is less clear (Hall, 2016). But it is notable that Daraa, the city where the mobilization against Assad began, was an area that had experienced the destabilizing influx of drought-driven migrants and neglect by central government (Yassin-Kassab and Al-Shami, 2016: 38).

Despite contested evidence and arguments, it is clear that the drought had a significant economic and social impact; it cannot be written out of the background to the Syrian uprising and war. There remains, however, the question of agency. It is necessary to balance global climatic dynamics and local environmental change with local actors, their interests and power. De Châtel's analysis of the effects of the drought in the Syrian civil war focuses on the Syrian Government's "long-term mismanagement of natural resources" and "failure to adapt to changing environmental, economic and social realities" (De Châtel, 2014: 522; also Swain and Jägerskog, 2016). In other words, human agency in the form of mismanagement of natural resources amplified the effects of the drought. Others broadly concur. Subsidizing crops like wheat and cotton that demand huge amounts of water, as well as outdated irrigation techniques, overgrazing and corruption are among the key failures of the government that made the effects of the drought on the population more severe and disruptive (Femia and Werrell, 2012; De Châtel, 2014; Swain and Jägerskog, 2016). Among other things, emphasizing these elements helps explain why Syria saw an outbreak of violence but its neighbors, Jordan and Lebanon, also affected by drought, did not (Hoerling et al., 2012).

Mismanagement of natural resources is, however, still only a part of the picture. It is not simply a question of drought and increased farming costs, nor of joblessness and rising poverty, nor of marginalization and deepening socio-economic inequalities; it is also an issue of politics. As Swain and Jägerskog remark, "(P)olitical oppression defined the relationship between rulers and the ruled" (Swain and Jägerskog, 2016: 26). The brutality of the Assad regime's response to the challenges it faced to its authority and legitimacy in spring 2011 was in keeping with the behavior of the Syrian State for the previous 40 years.

Overall, then, does climate change matter in Syria? Does it offer an alibi to Assad if we include the drought in the account of how the civil war came about? Or does it simply exclude an important factor if we leave nature out of it?

There is no worthwhile sense in which, on the basis of evidence available, it can be argued that climate change or the four-year drought directly *caused* the war in Syria. Nevertheless, it is also clear that climate variability and drought contributed significantly to the underlying situation in which the uprising unfolded. As in the example of Egypt, the narrative that includes the impact of drought is plausible.

It is important to understand agency in the onset of war because, ultimately, there is a choice in using violence or not. In Syria, the government's reaction to spreading instability reflected an already repressive and often brutal political system. Assad's way of handling it was wholly his decision. Neither climate change nor drought caused his forces to arrest and torture the group of teenagers who painted graffiti in March 2011 and many others before and after. They do not explain Assad's decision to let the Islamic radicals out of prison so they could overwhelm the secular democratic opposition. They neither explain nor excuse sending armed gangs into neighborhoods to cause terror and panic (Yassin-Kassab and Al-Shami, 2016: 48), and later using barrel bombs or nerve gas. But climate change and drought are part of the background explanation of how and why this tragedy unfolded.

Yemen: Tomorrow today?

Located in the far south of the Middle East, Yemen was known in antiquity for its comparative fertility, its pleasant climate and reputed riches in agricultural products and in spices. To the Romans, it was *Arabia Felix* (happy or flourishing Arabia), thus distinguished both from *Arabia Deserta*, in the center and north of the Arabian Peninsula, and from *Arabia Petraea* (stony Arabia) in the northwest (Encyclopedia Britannica, 2017). The days of Arabia Felix are long past. Today Yemen is known for war, poverty and extreme water scarcity. Some commentators see the "Future impact of climate change visible now in Yemen", as the World Bank headlined a blog in 2014 – published as part of the outreach effort for that year's report, *Turn Down the Heat* (World Bank, 2014a).

Yemen was united in its current borders only in 1990. Neither as North and South Yemen before unification nor as one country since has it known stability (Clark, 2010). A particularly intense period of instability started in 2011, the year of the Arab Spring, and in November of that year President Ali Abdullah Saleh stepped down. In March 2015, Saudi Arabia led a coalition of Arab governments into a major military intervention in the country, apparently intended to bring stability. It has done anything but. By the end of 2017, the UN estimated that, in a total population of some 27 million, 17.8 million people faced food insecurity, 16 million lacked access to safe water and sanitation, and 16.4 million lacked access to adequate health care, with 11.3 million people in acute need of humanitarian assistance in order to survive (UN Office for the Coordination of Humanitarian Affairs, 2017), including 8 million people at risk of famine (United Nations, 2017). The country had over 3 million refugees and displaced persons (UN Office for the Coordination of Humanitarian Affairs, 2017) a death toll from war of 10,000 since March 2015 (Sharp, 2017: 1), and a cholera epidemic of some 900,000 cases (WHO, 2017).

Three strands of instability weave together to form the backdrop to this tragedy. One is the influence of al-Qaeda, who first opened bases in the country in 1992. The second is the uprising by a small group of Zaydi Shi'a in 2004, now known as the Houthis after their leader, Hussein al-Houthi, who was killed in the early fighting. The third is widespread public discontent at decades of inadequate economic growth combined with distaste for the ruling regime's endemic corruption and a taste for more freedom and democracy. A combination of the mass mobilization of popular opposition and striking advances by the Houthi rebels in 2011, including an attack in June on the presidential compound in the capital, led to President Saleh stepping down after 33 years in power. In the background to all this stands the issue of water.

In the year that Saleh stepped down, the Maplecroft Water Stress Index ranked Yemen as the seventh most vulnerable country to water risk (Maplecroft, 2011). It was also the poorest of the ten countries with the highest water risk, meaning that compared with other high-risk countries such as the Gulf states, it could not opt for expensive alternatives like desalination as a way to secure fresh water supplies. The perception of Yemen's extreme water insecurity was widely shared. A report in 2010 foresaw the capital, Sana'a, potentially running dry by 2017 (IRIN, 2010). A 2013 study stretched the timeframe out to a little more than a decade; that is, approximately by the mid-2020s (Heffez, 2013). Though the extreme scenarios have not materialized, the cost of water in Sana'a tripled in 2009–2010 alone (IRIN, 2010).

The underlying problem is a combination of decreasing groundwater levels and an apparently almost total absence of planning to address the problem (Sowers et al., 2010). Groundwater levels have been falling sharply since the 1960s, with annual use averaging 200 million cubic meters, compared with input of 50 million cubic meters (IRIN, 2010). During these years, the population grew quickly and more and more land was absorbed into agricultural use, especially for the growth of qat, a chewable leaf narcotic that is highly popular and water intensive to grow (Sowers et al., 2010; Douglas, 2016). This increased use of water was unsustainable. The absence of replenishment and the lack of limitation on use must be put down to a failure of governance and of planning. A former Minister for Water and Environment said this explicitly in 2011 (Al-Eryani, 2011; see also Ward, 2014).

While, again, the conflict in Yemen is not to be explained purely or even primarily by Yemen's acute and long-standing water problems, nor even by the failure of Yemen's government to resolve or even manage the problem, their effect cannot be ignored. The World Bank saw migration from Yemen and urbanization within the country as driven by the long-term effects of failed harvests due to changing climate (World Bank, 2014: 143). Yet out-migration from rural areas had not eased the social situation. In 2013, it was reported that some 70–80% of conflicts in rural regions were water related, while the Yemen Ministry of Interior estimated there were 4000 deaths per year in land- and water-related disputes (Heffez, 2013). Against this arid background, numerous other factors, including the political decisions of key actors, have led violence in Yemen to unfold toward a humanitarian catastrophe of barely imaginable proportions.

The path to disaster has been stepped by many marching together. They include the long-lasting President Ali Abdullah Saleh and his successor, Abdrabbuh Mansur Hadi. The new leader had been Vice-President for the previous 18 years so the change of personnel implied no change in system. The background was the uprising, sporadic, but with increasing intensity since the turn of the 21st century, by the Houthis. Despite their determination and growing success, to the point that they could enter the capital in 2014 and, for a time, be the effective authority there, the Houthis' political program has not been clearly expounded. It is genuinely difficult to know what they stand for, apart from a militant opposition to both anti-Zaydi discrimination and corruption. Indeed, the Houthi takeover in 2014 initially received a quite widespread welcome in Sana'a, even from people who were suspicious of Zaydi motives, because the existing system of government was so corrupt and arbitrary that any alternative was worth trying. Whether the Houthis' goal ever was to run Yemen remains unclear. Much of the support for them from tribal leaders is tactical and opportunistic, and does not signify support for the Houthi cause as such, just like the alliance that was formed between the Houthis and Saleh, the President they rose up against in the first place (Fraihat, 2016: 45–57) and whom they killed in late 2017 when he turned against them (BBC News, 2017).

A part of the narrative of the route to catastrophe brings in al-Qaeda and the US. Al-Qaeda's attack on the USS *Cole* in Aden harbor in October was a significant step on al-Qaeda's road to 9/11. Likewise, the first use by the US of an armed drone for a targeted assassination was against an al-Qaeda leader and several suspects in Yemen in 2002 (Woods, 2015: xiv); since then, about 1500 Yemenis have been killed by US drone strikes (*New America*, 2018). Finally, of course, the decision by Saudi Arabia to launch an offensive against the Houthis in early 2015 has taken a situation of extreme peril for the Yemeni people into widespread destruction.

Yet if there is ever to be peace in Yemen, it will continue to be tenuous unless, as part of constructing the foundations for political stability, management of water resources is improved. Whatever the ruling system in Yemen, the government will have to solve the water problem or the country will know neither stability nor prosperity.

Conclusion

We set out in this chapter to illustrate that the impacts of climate and environmental change are spatially and temporally different in each case. We started with the basic approach that, when climate change is part of the picture in conflict escalation, it is not only climate change that is important in explaining what happened. Equally significant are its immediate impact on communities, the response to it and the decisions made by government, communities, individuals, the private sector, armed militias, regional organizations et al. To argue that the response is irrelevant defies facts and logic. But to argue that the response is key and the change in the climate is merely incidental, ignores the simple truth that if the climate were not changing, the response to it would not be an issue.

Our three cases show that the indirect impacts of climate change can have substantial interaction with social, economic and political processes. They can have that impact across great geographical distance and unfold over varying periods of time. And they can create severe security challenges in the Middle East. In each of our three cases, climate change has been a subtle driver of social and political instability, with water as the key transmission mechanism. Yet equally crucial in each case was the role of social and political marginalization, excluding segments of society from a say in political decision-making. The lack of voice, the absence of democracy and, with that, the long-lasting infringement of basic rights of organization, free speech and assembly restricted openings for a change in social and economic conditions. The grievance and resentment that ensued built up a potential for social and political explosion. The impacts of climate and environmental change were one of multiple factors feeding and finally igniting these social and political powder kegs.

For analysis of conflict escalation, we believe the lesson is simple: Don't leave nature out of it but don't overload it either. Climate change projections, given the power arrangements that exist, mean that what we have seen in the past decade in Egypt, Syria and Yemen and elsewhere may be gentle harbingers of the real storms to come.

The impacts of climate change are increasing in frequency and magnitude. Understanding how and why climatic factors contribute to instability is critical for strategies of prevention. Indeed, recognizing climate-related security risks in the Middle East offers the possibility to move toward more integrated and sustainable natural resource management in the region. Despite growing rivalries over identity and religion, all countries in the Middle East share vulnerability and risks in relation to climate change. Likewise, they share the need for water and food security as components of social and political stability. National approaches will be insufficient to deal with the growing impacts of climate change in the region; regional cooperation around climate action is necessary. It may be too optimistic to hope for climate change to bridge the rivalries among Middle Eastern nations, nevertheless, the need and opportunity are there.

References

Ahmed, Akhter U., Howarth E. Bouis, Tamar Gutner, and Hans Lofgren. 2001. *The Egyptian Food Subsidy System – Structure, Performance, and Options for Reform*. Washington, DC: International Food Policy Research Institute.

Al-Eryani, Mohammed. 2011. *Yemen's Water Crisis: Understanding the Causes and Designing the Solution*. Wilson Center. Washington, DC.

BBC News. 2012. "Egypt's State of Emergency Ends". *BBC News*, June 1.

BBC News. 2017. "Ali Abdullah Saleh, Yemen's former leader, killed in Sanaa". www.bbc.com/news/world-middle-east-42225574.

Buhaug, H., J. Nordkvelle, T. Bernauer, T. Böhmelt, M. Brzoska, J.W. Busby, A. Ciccone, H. Fjelde, E. Gartzke, N.P. Gleditsch, J.A. Goldstone, H. Hegre, H. Holtermann, V. Koubi, J.S.A. Link, P.M. Link, P. Lujala, J. O'Loughlin, C. Raleigh, J. Scheffran, J. Schilling, T.G. Smith, O.M. Theisen, R.S.J. Tol, H. Urdal, and N. von Uexkull. 2014. "One Effect to Rule Them All? A Comment on Climate and Conflict". *Climatic Change* 127 (3–4): 391–397. doi:10.1007/s10584-014-1266-1.

Burke, M.B., E. Miguel, S. Satyanath, J.A. Dykema, and D.B. Lobell. 2009. "Warming Increases the Risk of Civil War in Africa". *Proceedings of the National Academy of Sciences* 106 (49): 20670.

Clark, Victoria. 2010. *Yemen – Dancing on the Heads of Snakes*. New Haven: Yale University Press.

Cowell, Alan, and Douglas Jehl. 1997. "Luxor Survivors Say Killers Fired Methodically". *The New York Times*, November 24.

De Châtel, Francesca. 2014. "The Role of Drought and Climate Change in the Syrian Uprising: Untangling the Triggers of the Revolution". *Middle Eastern Studies* 50 (4): 521–535. doi:10.1080/00263206.2013.850076.

Douglas, Collin. 2016. "A Storm Without Rain: Yemen, Water, Climate Change, and Conflict". Washington DC. https://climateandsecurity.org/2016/08/03/a-storm-without-rain-yemen-water-climate-change-and-conflict/.

Encyclopedia Britannica. 2017. "Arabia Felix". Accessed December 21. www.britannica.com/place/Arabia-Felix.

Erian, Wadid, Bassem Katlan, and Ouldbdey Babah. 2010. *Drought Vulnerability in the Arab Region: Special Case Study: Syria*. Preventionweb.Net.

Fahim, Kareem, and Hwaida Saad. 2013. "A Faceless Teenage Refugee Who Helped Ignite Syria's War". *The New York Times*, February 8.

Femia, Francesco, and Caitlin E. Werrell. 2012. "Syria: Climate Change, Drought and Social Unrest". Climateandsecurity.org. https://climateandsecurity.org/2012/02/29/syria-climate-change-drought-and-social-unrest/.

Femia, Francesco, and Caitlin E. Werrell. 2013. "Climate Change Before and After the Arab Awakening: The Cases of Syria and Libya". In Caitlin E. Werrell and Francesco Femia (eds), *The Arab Spring and Climate Change*. Washington, DC: Center for American Progress, Simson Center, The Center for Climate and Security, pp. 23–32.

Fraihat, Ibrahim. 2016. *Unfinished Revolutions: Yemen, Libya, and Tunisia after the Arab Spring*. Yale University Press.

Gemenne, François, Jon Barnett, W. Neil Adger, and Geoffrey Dabelko. 2014. "Climate and Security: Evidence, Emerging Risks, and a New Agenda". *Climatic Change* 123 (1): 1–9. doi:10.1007/s10584-014-1074-7.

Gleick, Peter H. 2014. "Water, Drought, Climate Change, and Conflict in Syria". *Weather, Climate, and Society* 6 (3): 331–340. doi:10.1175/wcas-d-13-00059.1.

Gleick, Peter H. 2017. "Climate, Water, and Conflict: Commentary on Selby et al. 2017". *Political Geography* 60: 248–250. doi:10.1016/j.polgeo.2017.06.009.

Hall, J. 2016. "Are Migrants More Extreme Than Locals after War? Evidence from a Simultaneous Survey of Migrants in Sweden and Locals in Bosnia". *Journal of Conflict Resolution* 60 (1): 89–117. doi:10.1177/0022002714540471.

Heffez, Adam. 2013. "How Yemen Chewed Itself Dry". Farming Oat, Wasting Water. *Foreign Affairs*, www.foreignaffairs.com/articles/yemen/2013-07-23/how-yemen-chewed-itself-dry.

Hendrix, Cullen S. 2017. "A Comment on 'Climate Change and the Syrian Civil War Revisited'". *Political Geography* 60: 251–252. doi:10.1016/j.polgeo.2017.06.010.

Hendrix, Cullen S, and Stephan Haggard. 2015. "Global Food Prices, Regime Type, and Urban Unrest in the Developing World". *Journal of Peace Research* 52 (2): 143–157. doi:10.1177/0022343314561599.

Hoerling, Martin, Jon Eischeid, Judith Perlwitz, Xiaowei Quan, Tao Zhang, and Philip Pegion. 2012. "On the Increased Frequency of Mediterranean Drought". *Journal of Climate* 25 (6): 2146–2161. doi:10.1175/JCLI-D-11-00296.1.

Hsiang, Solomon M, and Marshall Burke. 2013. "Climate, Conflict, and Social Stability: What Does the Evidence Say?" *Climatic Change* 123 (1): 39–55. doi:10.1007/s10584-013-0868-3.

Human Rights Watch. 2017. *World Report 2017: Syria Events of 2016*. Human Rights Watch.

International Displacement Monitoring Centre. 2017. "Syria: Mid-Year Update 2017". Accessed December 21. www.internal-displacement.org/countries/syria.

IRIN. 2010. "Capital City Faces 2017 Water Crunch". www.irinnews.org/feature/2010/03/23/capital-city-faces-2017-water-crunch.

Johnson, Daniel. 2016. "Syria Envoy Claims 400,000 Have Died in Syria Conflict". *UN News*, April 22.

Kelley, Colin P., Shahrzad Mohtadi, Mark A. Cane, Richard Seager, and Yochanan Kushnir. 2015. "Climate Change in the Fertile Crescent and Implications of the Recent Syrian Drought". *Proceedings of the National Academy of Sciences* 112 (11): 3241–3246. doi:10.1073/pnas.1421533112.

Kelley, Colin P., Shahrzad Mohtadi, Mark Cane, Richard Seager, and Yochanan Kushnir. 2017. "Commentary on the Syria Case: Climate as a Contributing Factor". *Political Geography* 60: 245–247. doi:10.1016/j.polgeo.2017.06.013.

Lagi, Marco, Karla Z. Bertrand, and Yaneer Bar-Yam. 2011. "The Food Crises and Political Instability in North Africa and the Middle East". *SSRN Electronic Journal*. doi:10.2139/ssrn.1910031.

Leenders, Reinoud. 2008. "Iraqi Refugees in Syria: Causing a Spillover of the Iraqi Conflict?" *Third World Quarterly* 29 (8): 1563–1584.

Leenders, Reinoud, and Steven Heydemann. 2012. "Popular Mobilization in Syria: Opportunity and Threat, and the Social Networks of the Early Risers". *Mediterranean Politics* 17 (2): 139–159. doi:10.1080/13629395.2012.694041.

Lelieveld, J., Y. Proestos, P. Hadjinicolaou, M. Tanarhte, E. Tyrlis, and G. Zittis. 2016. "Strongly Increasing Heat Extremes in the Middle East and North Africa (MENA) in the 21st Century". *Climatic Change* 137(1–2): 245–260. doi:10.1007/s10584-016-1665-6.

Maplecroft. 2011. "Maplecroft Water Stress Index 2011". Verisk Maplecroft. https://maplecroft.com/about/news/water_stress_index.html.

Mobjörk, Malin, Maria-Therese Gustafsson, Hannes Sonnsjö, Sebastian van Baalen, Lisa Maria Dellmuth, and Niklas Bremberg. 2016. *Climate-Related Security Risks*. Solna: Stockholm International Peace Research Institute.

Moore, Jack. 2017. "Syria War Death Toll Hits 321,000 with 145,000 More Missing: Monitor". *Newsweek*, March 13.

New America. 2018. "Drone Strikes: Yemen". *New America*. www.newamerica.org/in-depth/americas-counterterrorism-wars/us-targeted-killing-program-yemen/.

Poletti, Matthew. 2011. "Mubarak Departs, Military Digs in". *Military Periscope*, February 24.

Randall, Alex. 2017. *Syria and Climate Change: Did the Media Get It Right?* Climate and Migration Coalition. Accessed November 14. https://climatemigration.atavist.com/syria-and-climate-change.

Selby, Jan, Omar Dahi, Christiane Fröhlich, and Mike Hulme. 2017a. "Climate Change and the Syrian Civil War Revisited: A Rejoinder". *Political Geography* 60: 253–255.

Selby, Jan, Omar S. Dahi, Christiane Fröhlich, and Mike Hulme. 2017b. "Climate Change and the Syrian Civil War Revisited". *Political Geography* 60: 232–244. doi:10.1016/j.polgeo.2017.05.007.

Sharp, Jeremy M. 2017. *Yemen: Civil War and Regional Intervention*. 7–5700. https://fas.org/sgp/crs/mideast/R43960.pdf.

Shenker, Jack. 2016. *The Egyptians*. London and New York: Penguin Random House.

SIPRI. 2017. *SIPRI Yearbook 2017*. Oxford: Oxford University Press.

Sowers, Jeannie, Avner Vengosh, and Erika Weinthal. 2010. "Climate Change, Water Resources, and the Politics of Adaptation in the Middle East and North Africa". *Climatic Change* 104 (3–4): 599–627. doi:10.1007/s10584-010-9835-4.

Spencer, Richard. 2014. "How Sisi Plotted to Save Army Rule Even While Hosni Mubarak Was in Power". *The Telegraph*, June 1.

Sternberg, Troy. 2011. "Regional Drought Has a Global Impact". *Nature* 472 (7342): 472169d–169. doi:10.1038/472169d.

Sternberg, Troy. 2012. "Chinese Drought, Bread and the Arab Spring". *Applied Geography* 34 (May): 519–524. doi:10.1016/j.apgeog.2012.02.004.

Swain, Ashok, and Anders Jägerskog. 2016. *Emerging Security Threats in the Middle East*. Lanham: Rowman and Littlefield Publishers.

Swain, Ashok, R.B. Swain, Anders Themnér, and Florian Krampe. 2011. *Climate Change and the Risk of Violent Conflicts in Southern Africa*. Global Crisis Solutions.

The Economist. 1997. "Bloodbath at Luxor". *The Economist*, November 20.

The Economist. 2015. "Syria's Drained Population". *The Economist*. www.economist.com/blogs/graphicdetail/2015/09/daily-chart-18.

UN Office for the Coordination of Humanitarian Affairs. 2009. *Syria Drought Response Plan*. United Nations.

UN Office for the Coordination of Humanitarian Affairs. 2010. *Syria Drought Response Plan 2009–2010 Mid-Term Review*. https://reliefweb.int/report/syrian-arab-republic/syria-drought-response-plan-2009-2010-mid-term-review.

UN Office for the Coordination of Humanitarian Affairs. 2017. *Yemen: 2018 Humanitarian Needs Overview*. https://reliefweb.int/report/yemen/yemen-2018-humanitarian-needs-overview-enar.

UNHCR. 2016. "Frequently Asked Questions on Climate Change and Disaster Displacement". *UNHCR*. www.unhcr.org/news/latest/2016/11/581f52dc4/frequently-asked-questions-climate-change-disaster-displacement.html.

UNHCR. 2017. "Syria Emergency". *UNHCR*. www.unhcr.org/syria-emergency.html.

United Nations. 2017. "Statement by the Humanitarian Coordinator for Yemen, Jamie McGoldrick, Calling on Parties to Facilitate Unimpeded Aid Delivery". *Sana'a*. https://reliefweb.int/report/yemen/statement-humanitarian-coordinator-yemen-jamie-mcgoldrick-calling-parties-facilitate.

Ward, Christopher. 2014. *The Water Crisis in Yemen*. London and New York: I.B. Tauris.

Wheeler, Tim, and Joachim von Braun. 2013. "Climate Change Impacts on Global Food Security". *Science* 341 (6145): 508–513. doi:10.1126/science.1239402.

WHO. 2017. "Epidemic and Pandemic-prone Diseases: Outbreak Update – Cholera in Yemen". Regional Office for the Eastern Mediterranean www.emro.who.int/pandemic-epidemic-diseases/cholera/outbreak-update-cholera-in-yemen-26-october-2017.html.

Woods, Chris. 2015. *Sudden Justice*. London: Hurst.

World Bank. 2014a. *Turn Down the Heat*. Washington, DC: World Bank.

World Bank. 2014b. "Future Impact of Climate Change Visible Now in Yemen". www.worldbank.org/en/news/feature/2014/11/24/future-impact-of-climate-change-visible-now-in-yemen.

Yassin-Kassab, Robin, and Leila Al-Shami. 2016. *Burning Country*. London: Pluto Press.

15

THE NILE AND THE MIDDLE EAST

Interlinkages between two regional security complexes and their hydropolitical dynamics

Ana Elisa Cascão, Rawia Tawfik and Mark Zeitoun

Introduction

The history of people and civilizations in the Middle East and the Nile regions has always been intertwined through multiple epochs/periods of time. It has included territorial expansions, trade routes, religious connections, political spheres of influence and numerous power struggles. The outcome of the historical interaction between these two regions has been strongly influenced by patterns of amity and enmity, involving a large constellation of actors – prior to and following the establishment of the borders and nation-states as we know them nowadays.

Water has played a key role in the social and political development of the regions. The Jordan, Nile and the Tigris-Euphrates rivers have been fundamental elements in the trajectories of national and regional political economies, including identity and political dynamics. Egypt is a central piece of the puzzle, not only because it is the only country that is common to both regions and thereby gives it geopolitical importance, but also because the Nile waters – as a natural resource and often as a mere political resource – have become a central piece in the relations between the two regions.

This chapter is divided into four interconnected sections. The first presents briefly the theoretical concepts informing our analysis – "security complexes", "power relations" and "proxy politics" are the three main components of the analysis. The second part describes the main hydropolitical dynamics within the Nile Basin region – which should be understood as a short account of the main sticking points in the interstate relations among the Nile riparians. The third (and main) section examines the role of non-traditional external partners – Middle East, in our case – in the ongoing hydropolitical dynamics in the Nile Basin, and how their involvement (often as result of "proxy politics") has impacted the power and security relations between Nile countries. The fourth part is the Conclusion that aims at providing some final observations/remarks on the implications of the external factors for the internal dynamics in the Nile Basin hydropolitical security complex.

211

Theoretical framework

This chapter will be informed by three sets of theoretical approaches – which combined will assist in the analysis of the features and dimensions of the interlinkages between the two regional settings (Middle East and Nile regions), and their implications in geopolitical and hydropolitical terms. Herein, the "Middle East" region is limited to the transcontinental region that includes Egypt, the countries of the Eastern Mediterranean, Turkey and the Persian/Arab Gulf countries. The Nile region is defined as comprising the 11 Nile riparian countries (Burundi, DR Congo, Egypt, Eritrea, Ethiopia, Kenya, Rwanda, South Sudan, The Sudan, Tanzania and Uganda). It is however important to clarify we will not treat these two regions as unified and monolithic blocks and, when relevant, we will be adopting different units of analysis to look at specific dynamics. In some cases, we provide an in-depth account of specific bilateral relations, for example, while in others the analytical focus crisscrosses these two regions, such as the sub-section focusing on the unique dynamics of the Red Sea.

Theoretical approaches

Our analysis relies on a suite of hydropolitical and geopolitical lenses. The first – "hydropolitical security complex" (Schulz, 1995; Turton, 2003) – is defined as a complex including actors (usually states) that geographically share and use water resources from the same transboundary basin, and wherein these resources have a strategic importance (namely being considered as a security issue) that drives and determines the interstate relations between those countries. A hydropolitical security complex (HSC) includes a set of political dynamics on their own, and where shared water resources play a central role in economic, political and diplomatic processes. Examining transboundary rivers as a HSC also takes into account the impact of tensions over water resources on the broader regional security. In addition to exploring hydropolitical relations between riparian states, scholars dealing with transboundary rivers as a HSC analyze how riparian states relate to international and regional powers, and how the HSC connects with other regional security complexes. Later in this chapter we provide a brief analysis of the current dynamics in the Nile Basin HSC, and how politicization and/or securitization processes are becoming the norm, particularly over the past decade. This chapter further examines how the political dynamics and actors of the Middle East regional security complex (see next paragraph) might be directly and/or indirectly contributing to a changing geopolitical and hydropolitical landscape in the Nile Basin region.

The work on HSC is a derivation of the "regional security complex (RSC) theory", as developed by Buzan (2003) and Buzan and Waever (2003). Regional security complex theory considers that security is clustered in geographically shaped regions, and that the security of actors interacts with security of other actors in the same region therefore creating security interdependence among them. In their own work (which was applied to the first decade of the post-Cold War era), these authors considered that there was a Middle East RSC, which in their case included North Africa, Gulf and Middle East countries, such as Egypt and Iran, but not Turkey for example (which we consider also as part). The authors also referred to a Horn of Africa pre-RSC, which included Sudan, Ethiopia, Eritrea, Djibouti and Somalia(s), which they considered as having many elements of strong security interdependence but at the time not yet linked in an integrated pattern (Buzan and Waever, 2003). Taking the Nile Basin as both an RSC and HSC, our focus remains on the manner and extent to which the Middle East RSC and the Nile RSC/HSC are increasingly interdependent.

A lens more active in the background than the foreground is the Framework of Hydro-Hegemony (Zeitoun and Warner, 2006; Cascão, 2008; Zeitoun and Allan, 2008; Cascão and

Zeitoun, 2010). Use of this framework obliges us to question the role that power relations play in the interaction of states over transboundary water, and how power asymmetries (and potential changes to these asymmetries) ultimately determine the outcome of that interaction. Based on Lukes (2005 [1974]), power is considered in its multiple dimensions – material, bargaining and ideational – which are understood to underpin hydropolitical configurations in transboundary basins. However, the fluidity of these power structures is a crucial point in the analysis – power relations and power balance are constantly being challenged and are constantly changing.

The third (and primary) lens is that of "proxy" politics, or proxy relationships and interventions, as a re-emergent characteristic of interstate relations and foreign policies of countries. This is where external parties get involved in the "internal" affairs of others (be they countries, other regions, other regional/hydropolitical security complexes). In extreme, proxy politics includes the external involvement in military conflicts and wars, siding with a certain faction/rival (or country) by providing political, technical and/or logistical support to achieve the patron's interests. While this assumes a convergence of interests between the patron and the proxy, it also entails an asymmetrical relation that enables the former to co-opt the latter to achieve its aims. It is also evident that the support extended to the proxy by the patron may not necessarily be material, but can be economic, political or diplomatic, contributing to a change in the balance of power in favor of the patron (Brewer, 2011; Duner, 1981). Although the focus in theorizing proxy politics has been on superpower rivalries during and after the Cold War (Duner, 1981; Mumford, 2011), a body of research literature explores the dynamics of proxy politics in regional power competition, with the Middle East and the Horn of Africa as major battlefields (Brewer, 2011; Abbink, 2003). Examples of the enduring conflict in Lebanon, and the more recent wars in Syria and Yemen are clear examples of how Middle East (and also Western) powers, in particular Saudi Arabia and Iran but also Turkey, play their political and military cards on stages outside of their own territories (Johnson, 2016). In the Nile Basin, the involvement of Ethiopia and Eritrea in the Somalia conflicts for example, has often been considered as a proxy war (Abbink, 2003; Sabala, 2011).

The lens is used in this chapter to explore how ongoing proxy wars primarily but not only between Iran and Saudi Arabia have been affecting the Horn of Africa and Nile Basin regions, through changing political alliances between Gulf countries and some Nile riparian countries, namely Sudan and Eritrea. As we shall see, these proxy politics (although often not related to water resources) have added complexity to hydropolitical relations in the Nile Hydropolitical Security Complex. The lens further also illustrates how Middle East power competitions play out in the Nile Basin (e.g. increasing presence of Turkey in the upstream Nile countries at a time of rising tensions between Egypt and Turkey).

In summary, the chapter explores the proxy relationships and interventions by actors from the Middle East regional security complex in the Nile hydropolitical security complex, and not the proxy interventions among Nile Basin countries. Among other topics, attention is given to how "foreign direct investment", in particular investments in water-intensive agriculture, by certain Middle East countries in the Nile Basin for the past decade can be analyzed. We question, for example, whether these "investments" are mainly an economic intervention, making use of the Nile upstream riparians as food-exporters/breadbaskets to the water-scarce countries of the Middle East, or part of a greater political game involving Egypt and the Middle East RSC countries, where the Nile waters are being used as a proxy element. The conclusions are necessarily speculative to a degree, limited by the data available, though the generalities hold: regardless of the overt and covert goals of the Middle East actors' involvement in the Nile, it is already contributing to influence, in a symbolic and tangible manner, over the internal power dynamics of the Nile Basin hydropolitical security complex.

Ana Elisa Cascão et al.

Recent hydropolitical developments in the Nile Basin

As mentioned in the previous section, in our analysis we consider that for the past decade the security (understood in the broad sense) dynamics in the Nile Basin region has evolved in a manner such that the region can now be defined as a regional hydropolitical security complex by itself, having water and hydropolitics as a central interlinkage element between the countries that comprise the region.

Historically speaking, the Nile has always been central in the political economy of Egypt, namely playing a fundamental role in state-building, in the economic growth and development for the past centuries, and a chief element in the country's social organization (spatial distribution, employment, culture, etc.). Not surprisingly, the management and allocation of the Nile water resources has always been treated as a political issue – both at national and basin/regional level. For the past century, interstate relations of Egypt with its upstream neighbors have been determined by politicization processes; i.e. processes in which governments proclaim water issues as a matter of top political priority (Zeitoun and Warner, 2006). This politicization of relations, agreements and collaboration/cooperation processes with the Nile neighbors was an essential part of the building and maintenance processes of a hegemonic position in the Nile Basin and a powerful mechanism to cement Egypt's bargaining and ideational power in the Basin. The securitization process can be considered as a step further; water issues are transformed into a national security issue, and as such jump the queue of other political priorities (Zeitoun and Warner, 2006).

All in all, Egypt's bilateral and multilateral relations with its southern neighbors are marked by a securitization discourse and agenda. This is particularly visible in its bilateral relations with both Ethiopia and Sudan, the first being the main contributor to the total Nile flows and the second being the second current main user of the waters and with the largest potential to increase withdrawals. Politicization and securitization trends can be found in all kinds of water, economic and political agreements signed between Egypt and these two neighbors. For example, directly or indirectly it transpires in almost all articles of the 1959 Agreement, which is still the main agreement (despite being bilateral) dictating the allocation regime of the Nile waters. The agreement was designed to ensure the water security of the two countries by formalizing their acquired rights and increasing their shares by implementing new projects for the "full utilization of the Nile waters" (Agreement 1959).

But securitization is also in the genesis of all the different stages of the process related to the Grand Ethiopian Renaissance Dam (GERD), since Ethiopia announced it as a national project in April 2011: throughout the negotiations and finally the signing of the Declaration of Principles in March 2015 by the three heads of state; the ongoing studies on the downstream impacts of the dam; and negotiations for the filling and long-term operations of the several existing infrastructures along the Nile River. For Ethiopia, the GERD is central to its plan to use water resources to increase energy security and promote the "developmental state" as preconized by the country's ruling party. For Egypt, the GERD project increases its vulnerability to Ethiopia's Nile policies, and to Sudan's policies and positionality. The flow of water arriving at Lake Nasser will ultimately depend on the filling approach of the dam in Ethiopia, but above all will depend on the withdrawals by Sudan which are likely to increase after the regulation of the flow (Tawfik, 2016). It is thus unsurprising that the trilateral talks on the implementation of the required studies on the downstream impacts of the dam (and parallel trilateral talks on different filling strategies) have faced several deadlocks over the past two years. This led the three negotiating countries to acquire additional means of influence through their bilateral and regional policies as our analysis will show.

Besides, the securitization process has also been affecting the multilateral relations between the Nile countries – both the technical and political tracks of cooperation (respectively the Nile Basin Initiative (NBI) and Cooperative Framework Agreement (CFA) processes). The technical track included the launching in 1999 of a multilateral river basin organization including all the Nile riparians – the NBI – a transitional arrangement to be replaced by a permanent river basin commission, once an agreement is achieved in the political track. The parallel political track was initiated in 1997, and included high-level negotiations for the CFA, which aimed at reaching agreement on the guiding legal principles for transboundary cooperation in the basin and also on the specifies of the would-be permanent institutional arrangement. It should not come as a surprise, for example, that the most controversial article during the negotiations of the CFA – and still nowadays the main source of controversy – covers the issue of "water security", upon which the Nile countries were not able to find a consensual definition as it brings all the historical grievances back to the surface. And the fact is that in recent years (since the end of the CFA negotiations in June 2007), but in particular since the decision of the upstream countries to go ahead with the signature of the agreement without Egypt and Sudan (in April 2010), this has dominated relations between the neighbors. And to a great extent it has contributed to a stalemate in the transboundary water cooperation process that generated so much optimism in the previous decade. At the time of writing, in mid-2017, the issue is being dealt with by political actors at the highest political level, namely ministries of foreign affairs and more recently even the intelligence agencies as far as the GERD talks are concerned (Egypt Independent, 2018). In June 2017, a Summit of Heads of State of the Nile Basin– the first ever – took place in Uganda, but the high expectations were not translated into any significant way forward to sort out the conundrum.

But perhaps more important than what has remained similar for the past two or three decades – the Nile issues being politicized and securitized by the different actors – is to understand what has actually been changing. In a nutshell, all Nile countries have been going through enormous social, economic, security and political transformations, which directly or indirectly have also affected their positionality in the Nile Basin, and somehow have been affecting the balance of power between countries, as analyzed in further sections.

For example, Ethiopia has moved from being a poor agriculture-based, highly populated country, with very little infrastructure development, and limited access to financial resources, toward being one of the fastest growing economies in the African continent since 2003, attracting different external investors and fund streams, and nurturing high ambitions of becoming a regional economic power wherein hydropower generation played a big role in both discourse and political agendas (Matthews et al., 2013). The GERD is an illustrative example combining changing internal political dynamics, regional ambitions and the expression of a new modus operandi in the relations with the Nile neighboring countries. In the case of Sudan, among many other changes there is a decisive one that came with the independence of South Sudan in 2011, and that has opened a completely new chapter in the political economy of Sudan: the end of the dependence on oil money, the required change in terms of economic diversification, the return to large-scale agriculture and consequently the increasing requirements for water, storage and electricity, which was progressively being developed with the assistance of external finance (Cascão and Nicol, 2016b). Finally, the significant changes in the Egyptian political and economic landscape in the aftermath of the revolution in January 2011 are not in any manner negligible – they came for example with several political internal transformations, negative impacts on economic stability, a transformation (in several periods since 2011, and in different directions) in the alliances of Egypt with regional and global actors, and consequently increased substantially the levels of political volatility.

The above changes, coupled with many others at the global and regional levels (which will partly be analyzed in this chapter), have contributed to challenge the hydro-hegemonic position that Egypt has held in the Nile Basin for some many decades or even centuries. Changes in the balance of power –in its material, bargaining and ideational dimensions – are becoming increasingly visible. The full consequences of it, and its magnitude, are yet difficult to analyze as we are talking about very rapid and simultaneous processes of change at many levels. But there is no doubt that the security interdependence of the Nile countries – in particular between the Eastern Nile countries – is much more manifest now than in the past, whereas the social changes, the economic trajectories and political (in)stability of one country has a great probability of affecting the other countries and the regional security dynamics.

Role of external partners in the Nile hydropolitical dynamics

The involvement and relevance of external actors in the hydropolitical dynamics in the Nile Basin is as old as the Nile itself – from immemorial times, the Nile region has attracted the attention of historians, travelers, explorers, missionaries, colonizers and superpowers. Some of these actors have been instrumental in the trajectories of the political economies of countries such as Egypt, Sudan, Ethiopia and the Equatorial Nile states. This has been particularly the case in two periods of recent history – the colonial and the post-colonial (Cold War) periods. It was during the colonial era that some of the most emblematic developments in the Nile Basin took place, such as the knowledge advancements about the complex hydrology of the Nile River, the development of comprehensive basin-wide plans, the construction of large-scale infrastructures, and the signing of key legal agreements (Waterbury, 2002; Tvedt, 2010).

The post-colonial period, in particular from the 1950/60s when the upstream riparians including Sudan got their independence, brought about new political and economic dynamics which were determinants for the new relations between Nile countries. But one factor remained similar to the colonial period: powerful external actors did not lose interest in the region, and kept a firm and continuous grip on the political developments in the region. Several authors have examined extensively how the Cold War power games (1950s–1990s) have influenced the Nile region, and how the involvement of the two main blocks in the regional and internal affairs of Nile countries has influenced the way that countries distribute, manage and negotiate the Nile water resources (Arsano, 2007; Erlich, 2002). Besides the vast geo-economic interests in the region (namely the availability of key natural resources), there have always been key geopolitical characteristics of the Nile region that justified the profound interest by external powers, such as: the proximity of the region to the Middle East regional complex, the strategic importance of the Red Sea/Gulf of Aden in trade, economic and political terms, and the Egyptian border (and respective peace agreement) with Israel, among others.

A brief analysis of the contemporary – post-Cold War – involvement of external actors in the region shows that they remain present and engaged in the Nile region. From the beginning of the 1990s, there has been an increasing involvement of Western development agencies and international financial institutions in supporting projects and programs in the Nile Basin countries, in a variety of economic fields and in terms of peace and security. In what concerns the Nile waters, these traditional development partners have been instrumental in providing technical and financial assistance to the two tracks of transboundary water cooperation – one more technical through the establishment of the NBI, and one more political through support to negotiations of a new legal and institutional CFA. The co-authors of this chapter have analyzed these dynamics and their effects extensively in previous works (Cascão, 2009; Nicol and Cascão, 2011; Tawfik, 2015; Zeitoun et al., 2017). However, for the purposes of this chapter we are

The Nile and the Middle East

particularly interested in the role of non-traditional external partners – in particular those actors from the Middle East region – and their increasing role in the Nile Basin, the political-economic origins and relevance of that involvement, and ultimately what are the linkages and implications for the transboundary water relations.

Since the early 2000s a lot has been written about the "arrival" of new external partners in the Nile region, such as China, India and other BRIC countries. These countries – the governments but also private companies and banks – brought with them to the Nile region different types of financial flows, compared with the traditional external partners: foreign direct investment (FDI), preferential trade agreements and favorable contracts instead of development aid, as well as funding for critical sectors of the economy such as infrastructure development (Swain and Jamali, 2011; Swain, 2011; Bossio et al., 2012). One major (at least apparent) difference is that these new external actors did not seem to have any political agenda beyond the economic/trade one – or at least one associated with geopolitical interests, such as the ones in the colonial and post-colonial/Cold War past. The same cannot be said about the external actors from the Middle East region that are also increasingly active in the Nile region, wherein the geo-economic and geopolitical agendas seem to come in tandem or have a proxy nature. This will be the main focus of our analysis in the next sections.

Because of geographical contiguity and proximity, the historical linkages, and a common cultural and religious past, the Middle East and the Nile Basin regions have been always intimately connected. Layers of common history can be traced back to the first migratory movements from the Rift Valley northwards, to the Greek and Roman Empires, the expansion of Christianity and Islam southwards and eastwards, the intercontinental trade routes, the terrestrial and maritime linkages between different geostrategic cities and ports, and ultimately the expansion of the Ottoman empire during the 19th century to part of the territory of the Nile Basin countries. The colonial and post-colonial period has apparently put a stop to these intimate cultural, social, economic and political relations, but as early as the 1980s there were clear signs that the history of the two regions was again to be intertwined. Some developments are of particular relevance in this regard: namely, the peace agreement between Egypt and Israel in 1979 and consequent negative reactions by other Middle East countries; the rapprochement in the 1980s of Saudi Arabia and other Gulf countries to Sudan as an investment (namely in agriculture) playground; the building and rebuilding of alliances between countries of the two regions during the two Gulf Wars; and the visible and invisible support to governments and/or oppositions, among others.

In most cases, as analyzed next, there is strong evidence of a proxy type of relations; that is, involvement in a certain country as a reaction/response to the relations with another third country. The next sub-sections provide an in-depth and original look at three different sets of relations that help us to understand the contemporary political and geopolitical linkages between the two regions, while at the same time analyzing its hydropolitical ramifications. The first sub-section looks at the most enduring relations between Saudi Arabia (and other Gulf countries) and the Nile region, but with a special focus on the last decade. The second looks at the recent Turkish-Nile region linkages. The third looks at the centrality of the Red Sea in these cross-regional dynamics.

The long involvement of the Gulf countries in the Nile Basin

The influence of the Gulf countries (in particular Saudi Arabia) in the internal and regional political dynamics in the Nile region is a long-standing one – in contemporary history, this involvement became particularly notorious in the 1970s with the growing prominence of Gulf economies on the global scene due to their rapid oil-related economic growth, and associated financial might and political aspirations. Egypt and Sudan have become part of this orbit of growing influence, in many different manners: on the one hand, by providing a large flow of skilled and non-skilled labor to the emerging economies on the other side of the Red Sea, and on the other hand by becoming major recipients of (and dependent on) economic support and investment from the Gulf countries (Verhoeven, 2016b). The 1970s and the 1980s can provide vivid examples of how the Gulf financial clout has turned into leverage in the internal political dynamics of Nile countries, in particular in Sudan where regimes have been supported and/ or undermined according to the Saudi religious-political agendas. The Saudi/Gulf relations with Egypt started on an equal footing, with both countries having leadership aspirations for the Arab region during the 1950/1970s, but ultimately this evolved to a rent-seeking type of relations with large implications for the Egyptian economy and political internal dynamics. This chapter is mainly interested in the period from 2007 onwards: the old/new configurations, the tipping points and ramifications of a growing involvement of Gulf countries in agricultural investments in the Nile Basin.

2007/2008: Gulf countries in search of new land

Water-scarce economies such as those in the Gulf (Saudi Arabia, United Arab Emirates, Kuwait, Qatar) have always faced challenges in terms of water and food security – in a nutshell, these countries are not endowed with enough natural resources to guarantee self-sufficiency in terms of food security. Importing virtual water through global food imports has been for many decades the best solution available – it has been a useful but invisible and silent process (Allan, 1997) that just recently is being discussed in the public domain. The 2007/2008 spike in global food prices was a tipping point. Countries that relied on food imports, such as the Gulf economies, considered that they needed to find alternatives in order to reduce their exposure to volatile prices, in particular those of cereals which they import in large quantities since they also decided to stop national production of wheat (Sandström et al., 2016; Swain and Jägerskog, 2016). As a follow-up, several regional strategies were approved by the GCC countries that eventually aimed at promoting international agricultural investments abroad in order to minimize their reliance on food imports, which became a cornerstone of the new Pan-Arab regional cooperation narratives (Hanna, 2016). Countries like Saudi Arabia and Qatar have even institutionalized their new approaches to overseas investments in agricultural land by establishing the King Abdullah Initiative for Saudi Agricultural Investment Abroad (KAISAIA) and Qatar National Food Security Programme (QNFSP), respectively. Both regional and national strategies have been instrumental in shaping public and private investments, including the land leases and contracts that have been signed with a lot of host countries. Not surprisingly, the Nile Basin countries (in particular Sudan and Ethiopia) have become preferential partners – not just because of their land and water availability and untapped potential for agricultural expansion (rainfed and irrigation), but also because of their geographical and cultural proximity (in the case of Sudan), the new favorable investment conditions, and ultimately also because of the political "advantages" that could come along (see several chapters in Sandström et al., 2016).

Gulf–Sudan

Nowhere more so than in Sudan are the abovementioned new dynamics so clear – since 2007 the strategic midstream Nile riparian countries have been experiencing a massive influx of credit and investment from the different Gulf countries for several different economic fields,

Table 15.1 Investors/shareholders in key Sudan projects

Merowe Dam (2009)	Heightened Roseires Dam (2013)	Kenana Sugar Company*
China Import-Export Bank	Arab Fund for Economic and Social Development	Kuwaiti Fund for Economic Development
Arab Fund for Economic and Social Development	Islamic Development Bank	Government of Saudi Arabia
Saudi Fund for Development	OPEC Fund for International Development	Arab Investment Company
Abu Dhabi Fund for Development	Abu Dhabi Fund for Development	Industrial Development Bank
Kuwaiti Fund for Economic Development	Saudi Fund for Development	Arab Authority for Agricultural Investments
Oman Fund for Development	Kuwaiti Fund for Economic Development	Consortium of Commercial Banks
State of Qatar		Gulf Fisheries Company

* Similar in White Nile Sugar Company and Dal Group Company

but in particular to launch the new hydro-agricultural mission, and related infrastructure development such as the construction of large-scale hydropower dams and agricultural expansion (Verhoeven, 2016b). It is not surprising that Sudan generates so much interest from agribusiness investors, taking into account that Sudan's arable land is estimated to be 105 million ha, of which only around 18 million ha are currently under cultivation. Table 15.1 provides a summary of the main investors and shareholders in emblematic hydraulic and agribusiness projects – Merowe Dam, Roseires Dam Heightening and Kenana Sugar Company (respectively located in the main, Blue and White Nile) – implemented in Sudan since the mid-2000s, which highlights the heavy reliance on Gulf money. It is worth noticing that these projects, because of their increased storage capacity, water withdrawals and/or evapotranspiration, have led Sudan to increase substantially its utilization of Nile waters. While a decade ago, the official figures indicated that Sudan was using "only" 14 billion cubic meters (bcm) of water, nowadays Sudan is rapidly approaching the 18.5 bcm allocation – but the potential water use in a scenario of development of the full potential is around 30–32 bcm of water (Cascão and Nicol, 2016a).

It is important to highlight that the involvement of Gulf countries in Sudan and the interest in its untapped water resources and fertile land is not new, and dates back the 1970s/1980s when Sudan was seen as the breadbasket of the Arab world because of its potential to grow the so-much wanted cereals. At that time there was investment in mechanized farming, some degree of infrastructure development, and economic and political support to elites in Sudan that favored the agreements. But the regional political upheavals at the beginning of the 1990s, with fuzzy alliances during the Gulf War, the differences over styles of political Islam, and the provocative positions of the outspoken Sudanese political leader Hassan Turabi, led to a boycott of economic assistance and investment from the Gulf countries. The boycott was lifted in 1999 leading to subsequent normalization of relations and return of investment (Verhoeven, 2016a).

In the 2000s, the regime of President of Sudan, Omar al-Bashir seems to have benefited from the rising competition in the region and his relations with Iran, Qatar, Saudi Arabia and the UAE were balanced (Verhoeven, 2016a). Nevertheless, this was a difficult balance to strike, taking into account the intense political changes in the Arab/Gulf region. Sudan's diplomatic relations with Iran started deteriorating in 2014. With the start of the Saudi-led military intervention in Yemen in 2015, Sudan took the Saudi's side contributing to the Arab forces fighting Iran-baked Houthi rebels. In January 2016, Sudan severed its diplomatic relations with Iran. The package of remunerations offered to Sudan in return was attractive. Saudi Arabia signed several agreements with Sudan to fund three new dams and cultivate more than 1 million acres near constructed dams (Ardemagni, 2016; Verhoeven, 2016a). Egypt has been closely watching the expanding Arab Gulf investments in Sudan and raising concerns, albeit not publicly, about its potential impact on Sudan's water withdrawals from the Nile waters (Tawfik, 2015). Lately, Sudan has also benefited greatly from Qatar's aid and investments that amounted to more than USD 1.5 billion in the fields of mining, real estate, banking and, of course, agriculture. This may explain why Sudan refrained from siding with Saudi Arabia, UAE and Egypt in their boycott campaign against Qatar, a decision that raised tensions between Sudan and the boycotting countries. In brief, the aspirations to tap into Sudan's huge agriculture potential are back in fashion, and so is the competition for the Nile waters and the challenges to Egypt's perceived water security.

Gulf–Ethiopia/Horn of Africa

Relations between the Gulf region and Ethiopia (and the Horn of Africa region) are weaker than with the downstream Nile countries – the social, cultural and religious bonds are not as strong – but in the last decade things have also been changing and economic cooperation has been intensifying rapidly. One of the underlining reasons is the referred new strategy of the GCC countries to invest in agriculture (and livestock as well) abroad, which has generated billions of dollars of foreign direct investment in African countries. For example, Saudi Arabia is among the four biggest investors in Ethiopia with a total of around USD 3 billion in 2017 (EIC in Nicolas, 2017), and it is one of the main export destinations of Ethiopian products. Saudi Arabia and Ethiopia have a large number of bilateral agreements and memorandums of understanding in place – some particular ones signed in 2009 between the Saudi and Ethiopian governments deal specifically with cooperation in agriculture investments and was facilitated by KAISAIA – King Abdullah's Initiative for Saudi Agricultural Investment Abroad (cf. Al-Obaid, 2010). Ethiopia also has similar agreements with Qatar signed after 2012 when the countries resumed diplomatic relations, which were severed in 2008 because of Qatar's political proximity to Eritrea, the arch-rival of Ethiopia. Since the visit of the Emir of Qatar to Ethiopia in 2013, a number of agreements in the infrastructure, tourism and energy sector have been signed (MFA of Ethiopia, 2016b; Ethiopian Investment Commission, 2017; Derso, 2017).

It is important to mention that this rapprochement to Ethiopia is not free of political connotations. First, it is part of a large strategic political game of the Middle East countries (the Gulf, but also Iran and Turkey) expanding their political clout and sphere of influence beyond their borders – and the new and changing alliances/enmities in the Horn of Africa region show how this region is becoming (again) a springboard for foreign interventions. The military presence and security agreements between the Gulf and Horn countries indicate there is also a parallel agenda on conflict prevention and mitigation, and control of migration routes. Second, it is intimately linked to the Saudi/Gulf enduring power play with Egypt. One the one hand, one could naively understand it as both competing for a regional leadership role in the Arab-Africa relations, but the asymmetries in economic power show that this is far from being an even competition. On the other hand, one can understand it as Gulf countries using their closeness to Sudan and Ethiopia as a way of provoking Egypt.

An example of this was the visit in December 2016 of a high-level Saudi delegation to Ethiopia by senior advisors to the Saudi Royal family, the Minister of Environment, Water and Agriculture and representatives from the Saudi Fund for Development (SFD), which also included a trip to the Grand Ethiopian Renaissance Dam and talks about Saudi's interest in developing and importing energy from Ethiopia (Ministry of Foreign Affairs of the Federal Democratic Republic of Ethiopia, 2016a). The visit sent shock waves through Cairo, and the Egyptian parliament called the Foreign Minister Sameh Shoukry to enquire about the Egyptian-Saudi relations in general, and the Egyptian position on the visit in particular (Ahram online, 21 December 2016). Not by chance, the Saudi visit also coincided with unsteady diplomatic relations between Cairo and Riyadh regarding the handling of conflicts in Syria and Yemen, as well as territorial disputes over two islands in the Red Sea, a token that has been on and off the bilateral agenda between the two countries (*The Economist*, 2016). In December 2016 there was a subsequent visit by a high-level Qatari delegation to Ethiopia to bolster investments in the areas of investment, financing and infrastructure (MFA of Ethiopia, 2016b) – and knowing about the ongoing hostility between Cairo and Doha, it is difficult not to speculate how this further visit to Ethiopia was politically extremely charged and which kind of reverberations this had in Cairo's political and popular circles. More notable was the visit by the Ethiopian Prime Minister to Qatar in November 2017 amid a new deadlock in GERD talks. The Ethiopian Premier signed new agreements of cooperation in the fields of agriculture, power, health and education and invited Qatar to support the development of the Omo-Gibe river basin (MFA of Ethiopia, 2017). Media circles in Egypt were so skeptical about the visit that the Ethiopian foreign ministry had to deny the claims that Ethiopia sought Qatari funding for the GERD.

Hydropolitical implications of Gulf presence in the Nile Basin

The difference between the planned and actual utilization of the Nile water resources by the new set of agricultural investments by Gulf countries is huge. As some analysts emphasize, a lot of these investments have not yet materialized and as such water is not yet being used or allocated (see several chapters in Allan et al., 2013) – but still the potential is there. However, there are evident signs of virtual water exports from the Sudan and Ethiopia to the Gulf countries, as part of an impressively growing livestock trade, but also on the ground investments in production of fodder crops, such as alfalfa, increasingly rapidly (Mordor Intelligence, 2017). Regardless of the speed and time of project implementation, it is obvious that the Gulf countries are already positioning themselves as potential users of the Nile waters. Though the bread-basket strategy failed in the 1980s, that might not be the case in the near future. One way or another, and regardless of the magnitude of investments and their water requirements, the fact is that the Gulf countries are back again as (in)direct hydropolitical players in the Nile Basin.

And if the impacts on water utilization/withdrawals are still indeterminate, the same cannot be said about the impacts of the newest involvement by Gulf actors in the Nile hydropolitical dynamics. This is visible in many ways. First, the Gulf's financial assistance/investment to Nile countries has partially contributed to the increased bargaining power of countries such as Ethiopia and Sudan in their positionalities regarding their discourses on potential future uses of the Nile waters. This can be understood as strong discursive and negotiating elements in the talks with Egypt and possibly contributing to erode Egypt's hydro-hegemonic bargaining position in the basin. Second, the Nile waters have become a political card in the regional power games between the Gulf countries and Egypt, with unpredictable consequences to regional power dynamics and stability. Third, increasing levels of politicization and securitization due to the involvement of additional external actors are likely to increase the tensions between Egypt and its neighbors and simultaneously do not seem to contribute to providing a conducive environment for reaching compromises in ongoing negotiations over the NBI/CFA and GERD.

Turkey as a strategic partner in the Nile Basin

The involvement of (modern) Turkey as a player in the Nile Basin is much more recent than the involvement of the Gulf countries analyzed above, and can be dated back to the beginning of the 2000s with the expansion of Turkish economic and political ambitions beyond its normal boundaries. What is worthy of note is that Turkey's role in the Nile has been increasing very rapidly and two major tipping points can be observed: the first was the "African Expansion" strategy approved by the Turkish Government in 2003 (currently Turkey is a major investor/trading partner with Ethiopia and Sudan); and the second is the diplomatic conflict between Egypt and Turkey's political leaders, ongoing since June 2013. How this plays out in hydropolitical terms will be analyzed next.

Turkey–Egypt

Egypt and Turkey share strong historical, cultural and religious ties, which were particularly cemented during the Ottoman Empire and Muhammad Ali's rule during which Egypt expanded widely its "hydraulic mission" in the Nile. In the contemporary era, both countries are among the most populated countries in the Middle East region, have strong economic, political and military powers, and capacity to project power beyond their national borders, influence the regional and global political spheres and, in a way, both have had aspirations of regional leadership in the broader Middle East region. Yet, since the 1990s the relations between the two countries have been often one of close and mutual cooperation. For example, in 2005 the two countries signed a Free Trade Agreement and in 2008 a Memorandum of Understanding on bilateral cooperation, including military relations, and investments (in particular in Egypt from public and private sources in Turkey) have been increasingly rapidly since then. The Egyptian revolution of January 2011, and in particular the rise to power of the Muslim Brotherhood, represented a watershed moment for Turkey's direct involvement in Egypt.

In political terms, the Turkish Government led by the then-Prime Minister Recep Tayyip Erdoğan supported President Mohamed Morsi and backed his regime, a support that was informed by Turkish "Green wave" aspirations that the Turkish model of political Islam could be emulated in Egypt and elsewhere in the Arab region, that was well captured in Erdoğan's tour to North Africa (Cairo, Tunis and Tripoli) in September 2011. In economic terms, for Egypt this was translated into dozens of bilateral agreements covering all kinds of fields of business, trade, science, banking, tourism, etc. during the one-year reign of President Morsi. The political honeymoon between two of the major Middle East regional powerhouses was expected to develop and thrive.

However, the removal of President Morsi and his Muslim Brotherhood government in July 2013 was followed by a significant and still ongoing political crisis between Egypt and Turkey. The consequences are enormous: strained diplomatic relations including downgrading of diplomatic representations, direct repercussions in the bilateral economic relations with several investments still on standby. Raw figures show that the strategic and political partnership crafted by Morsi and Erdoğan was worth around USD 5 billion of direct investment in the Egyptian economy – the vast majority of it is now "frozen" (Bakeer, 2013). The impacts of this stalemate in the Egyptian economy were significant, and in some way this has increased Egypt's dependence on the economic backing by other Middle East/Gulf countries, themselves also at odds with the ambitious Turkish leader. The following years (2014–2016) were populated with emblematic events increasing the diplomatic conflict: negative media campaigns on both sides, Turkey providing shelter to Muslim Brotherhood supporters, cancelation of the Ro-Ro Agreement that allowed Turkey's access to the Gulf via Egyptian ports, Saudi-Egyptian campaign against Turkey's seat in the UN Security Council, and finally in 2016 a series of personal attacks between Presidents Erdoğan and Sissi in the aftermath of the failed coup attempt in Turkey.

Although at the economic level, the two countries have been trying hard to resume bilateral relations, namely by promoting a bilateral Business Forum (that took place in Cairo in February 2017, the first since 2013), as a way to revive economic ties, restore trade and promote standby and future investments, the fact is that there is still a long way to go to re-establish the past good bilateral relations (Cook and Ibish, 2017; Hassan, 2017). In brief, it is expected that both will continue for some time as "frenemies", and their regional leadership ambitions might be limited due to the current internal and regional developments. But, as analyzed next, it might be that the political and economic chessboard is just moving elsewhere, namely to the upstream in the Nile Basin, where Turkey is exponentially increasing its presence.

Turkey–Ethiopia

Turkey's "African Expansion" strategy dates backs to 2003, and it reflected a growing interest by Turkey in fostering economic and strategic relations with a number of African countries. Interesting to observe is that the Horn of Africa countries have been the first entry point for the implementation of this strategy, and that currently Ethiopia is among the major partners of Turkey in the continent. The trajectory, events and figures speak for themselves. Although the first Ethio-Turkish Joint Economic Commission (including an agreement on reciprocal promotion and protection of investment) was established in 2000, the special ties between the two governments have increased after the visit of the Ethiopian PM Meles Zenawi to Turkey in 2004 and a second visit in 2007. This represented the beginning of a series of agreements, memorandums of understanding and high-level visits by public figures and private companies. Just to name a few: in 2005 both countries signed a military cooperation pact; in 2008 both countries co-chaired the Turkey-Africa Summit; between 2012 and 2014, as an outcome of a plethora of high-level economic and political consultations, the two countries signed numerous trade agreements in a series of economic fields (infrastructure, transport, industry, manufacturing, textile, renewable energies, etc.); in 2015, President Erdoğan himself and an entourage of large investors visited Ethiopia and organized a large business-to-business meeting followed by the Ethiopia-Turkey Business and Investment Forum at the end of 2016. In January 2017, the Ethiopian PM Hailemariam paid a visit to Turkey and later in April both countries organized a Summit on Agriculture and Agribusiness. The improvement of the bilateral relations in terms of both magnitude and scope is evident in three main trends:

- For Ethiopia, in the last decade Turkey became one of the three major trading partners for its fast-growing economy, side by side with China and India, and key in Ethiopia's Growth and Transformation Plans (GTP). Actually, since 2014 Turkey became Ethiopia's major partner in terms of total foreign direct investment inflows (above 40%), in particular in terms of capital layout, even overtaking China which is still in the lead only in terms of total number of companies (GIIN, 2015)
- For Turkey, Ethiopia is one of the major preferential African partners, side by side with strong economies such as South Africa and Nigeria, and around half of the Turkey's current

investment in the continent is actually directed to Ethiopia. In 2017, it is estimated that the Turkish public and private investment in Ethiopia was worth around USD 2.5 billion, but the recently stated goal is to quadruple this number by 2025 and reach the USD 10 billion target (MFA of Ethiopia, 2016c; The Ethiopian Herald, 2017a, 2017b)

- Although the main approach in terms of bilateral relations between Turkey and Ethiopia is a business-to-business one (FDI, preferential loans and trade agreements, support to both imports and exports, fast and less bureaucratic processes, etc.), it is possible to observe that the cooperation portfolio is also being extended to more political issues, such as military, peace and security issues (Shinn, 2015)

Finally, also relevant for the purposes of this chapter, a new trend in terms of Turkey's investment in Ethiopia is an increasing involvement in the agriculture sector, including large land leasing agreements. One of the most prominent is the one with the Omo Valley Farm Corporation, a commercial farm (10,000 ha), initiated in 2012–2013 and apparently later expanded in 2014 (Kamski, 2016). This investment is one of Ethiopia's largest cotton developments, and an essential part of Turkey's large joint venture working on cotton production and textile industry in Ethiopia. And if until recently Turkish investors seem to have refrained from investing in agricultural land along the Nile River, this seems to be rapidly changing. At the end of 2016, it was reported that a Turkish large-scale company – Bedisa, expert in irrigation schemes and dams construction – has acquired 75% of the Beles Sugar Project, a large-scale irrigation project (around 50,000 ha), in a total investment that could reach USD 1 billion (Ecofin News, 2016). This project located in the Ahmara region is expected to get its water requirements from the Beles River, one of the tributaries of the Blue Nile River, through a diversion weir (The Reporter, 2016). Finally, and also in relation to water resources, during a state visit to Ethiopia in February 2017, President Erdoğan encouraged Turkish business to invest in Ethiopia's hydropower (Presidency of the Republic of Turkey, 2017).

Turkey–Sudan

If involvement of Turkish investors in the Ethiopian agriculture/irrigation sector is a relatively recent trend, the same cannot be said about Sudan, the Nile riparian known for its large agricultural potential, namely along the fertile banks of the Blue Nile River. In April 2014, the Turkish and the Sudanese governments signed an Agreement on Bilateral Agricultural Cooperation and Partnership, which includes the establishment of a bilateral free trade zone for agricultural products and livestock, and mechanisms to support increased production, productivity and export-oriented processes. Talks by then were that TIGEM (Turkish General Directorate of Agriculture Enterprises), in a joint venture with the Sudanese Government, were leasing around 780,000 hectares of land for agricultural development (Şafak, 2017). Agriculture appeared as an important entry point for a Bilateral Investment Agreement that was signed soon after between the two governments by the end of April 2014 (MFA of Turkey, 2017). In 2016, the two countries would reinforce this relation with a new partnership agreement (Turkey-Sudan Strategic Dialogue Programme); the business portfolio now includes the construction sector, roads and railways, mining, and textile industry, etc. With a current USD 2 billion investment portfolio, Sudan is also among Turkey's largest five trading partners in the African continent. Last but not least, in June 2017 talks were of a USD 10 billion mix of public and private investment, in a bilateral partnership to move to implementation of agricultural projects, including irrigation – and an impending visit of President Erdoğan to Sudan is included in the package.

Hydropolitical implications of Turkey's presence in the Nile Basin

Similar to the previous analysis about the involvement of the Gulf states in the Nile regional hydropolitical dynamics, we can assume that there are two major kinds of hydropolitical implications of the involvement of Turkey in the Nile Basin. The first is at the (hydro-)political level, namely in terms of changes in power balance (material, bargaining and ideational); and the second is a potential direct impact on the utilization and allocation of the Nile water resources.

As analyzed already elsewhere, the heavy and increasing investment of non-traditional partners such as China, India and Turkey in economies such as Ethiopia and Sudan is directly and indirectly contributing to decrease the economic and power asymmetries in the Nile Basin (cf. several chapters in Allan et al., 2013; Sandström, 2016). In material terms, the upstream countries are not just experiencing unprecedented levels of economic growth and increasing demands for water, food and energy, but now also have access to financial resources for large-scale projects that were not available until recently. The current levels of Turkish investment – and the targets established for the next 10 years – indicate that there is a commitment that goes beyond notional promises and that includes much more than just economic cooperation. In bargaining terms, this new investment environment increases substantially the leverage power of countries such as Ethiopia, that are now less dependent on traditional donors and financial mechanisms and certain geopolitical agendas that come with it, but it also increases the bargaining power in the talks and negotiations with its neighboring riparians. Knowing that Turkey, the most upstream riparian in the Tigris-Euphrates Basin – the powerful hegemonic actor in that basin, main user of those transboundary waters, with decades of experience in dam building and expansion of large-scale irrigation – is now the main investor in Ethiopia, the most upstream Nile riparian and with ambitions to expand hydraulic infrastructure and water uses… makes it difficult not to establish some comparisons. This is particularly relevant if we take into account the fact that the diplomatic relations between Turkey and Egypt have soured exponentially since 2013. In ideational terms, as a result and/or in parallel with increasing material and bargaining power dimensions, one can observe that the ability and capacity of upstream riparians to influence the perceptions, narratives and discourses of both internal and external actors is increasing – this is already having an impact on the alliances and negotiations at the NBI/CFA and GERD tables – which is ultimately challenging the long-standing hegemonic position of Egypt in the Nile Basin.

Another possible hydropolitical impact of the arrival of newcomers as investors in the Nile Basin is that this is bound to increase dramatically the demands for land, energy and water. Because as investors, they might also want themselves to invest in the development of hydraulic infrastructure: storage capacity, hydroelectric connections and canals to bring water to their schemes. This is particularly relevant if the investments are in the irrigation sector –as we have been observing in both the Ethiopia and Sudan cases – which are expected to increase the demands for water dramatically. And although it is still unclear where most of these potential projects will be located, it is very possible they will be consumers of Nile waters, such as in the case of Turkish joint ventures in the Beles Sugar Project and the extension of Rahad Scheme, located along the Blue Nile banks in Ethiopia and Sudan, respectively.

Importance of Red Sea dynamics in the Nile hydropolitics

Both the Nile region and the Middle East are closely linked to the Red Sea as a strategic shipping lane that is increasingly becoming a center of international and regional competition. In spite of Arab claims in the 1970s that the Red Sea is an "Arab lake", Arab countries of the

Middle East have hardly cooperated to coordinate their Red Sea security policies and formulate a common position towards the role of other regional actors in maintaining its security (Ehteshami and Murphy, 2011: 11). At the same time, instability on the African side of the Red Sea, emanating from the collapse of the state in Somalia a couple of years after the rise of Islamists to power in Sudan, in addition to interstate conflicts in the region, increased regional security challenges. Somalia became a safe haven not only for home-grown terrorist movements, but also for organizations operating on the Arab side of the Red Sea, especially in Yemen. Flows of militants and weapons between Somalia and Yemen transformed the two sides of the Red Sea into a single security complex (Ulrichsen, 2011). It was against this background that Gulf countries started to get involved in East Africa motivated by protecting their national security.

The interest of Arab regional powers in maintaining a foothold in the African side of the Red Sea is also part of their effort to carve new spheres of influence (Ehteshami and Murphy, 2011; Ibish, 2017), against an expanding Iranian presence. Until recently, the Islamic Republic of Iran forged an alliance with the Islamist regime in Khartoum which was isolated from its Arab neighbors for most of its first decade in power. Similarly, in the past decade, international sanctions and tense relations with its direct neighbors pushed Eritrea towards Iran. Since November 2008, Iranian warships conducted anti-piracy operations using Eritrea's port of Assab, raising the concerns of not only Saudi Arabia but also Israel. Saudi Arabia and Yemen accused Iran of shipping weapons to the Shiite-Houthi rebels which have been fighting against the government in Sana'a and clashed with Saudi forces in north-western Yemen since 2004. Israel, in turn, accused Iran of providing weapons to Hamas, also using the Assab port. To ensure a closer surveillance of Iranian movements, Israel moved two warships from the Mediterranean to supplement its naval presence in the Red Sea (Lefebvre, 2012).

Since 2015, the military confrontation between Gulf countries and Iran in Yemen invited the former to promote their military presence on the African side of the Red Sea. According to UN reports, the UAE and Saudi Arabia approached Eritrea to allow the Saudi-led coalition forces in Yemen to use Eritrean land, airspace and territorial waters to fight the Iranian-backed Houthi rebels, a move that is considered as a violation of UN sanctions against Eritrea. During a state visit by the Eritrean President Isaias Afwerki to Saudi Arabia in April 2015, a security and military partnership agreement was sealed that reportedly granted the Arab coalition access to the port of Assab. In the same visit, Eritrea was asked to deny Houthi rebels access to its territory. In return, the Eritrean regime was promised Gulf financial compensation and fuel supplies (UN, 2015). More recently, the UN Monitoring Group on Somalia and Eritrea documented the construction of an Emirati military base with permanent structures at Assab international airport and a new port adjacent to it. Additionally, fighters from the UAE, Saudi Arabia, Sudan, Yemen and other member states of the Arab coalition were present in Assab for training and frequently deployed from Assab to the Gulf of Aden. The UN group warns that the development of the military base in Assab is a support for infrastructural development that could benefit the Eritrean military in violation of the international arms embargo on Eritrea (UN, 2016, see also Ibish, 2017).

In addition to Eritrea, Gulf countries are extending their presence into Ethiopia's spheres of influence in the Horn. In February 2017, the government of Somaliland accepted the application of the UAE to open an Emirati military base in Berbera, at the mouth of the Red Sea. Sources referred to concerns in Ethiopia, Somaliland's closest ally, which was not informed of the details of the deal (Copley, 2017). Less problematic was the multimillion dollar deal that granted the Dubai World Ports a 30-year control of the port of Berbera. The Ethiopian and Emirati sides reached a win–win arrangement later that gave Ethiopia 19% share in the port (Bloomberg, 2017). The DP World Chairman marketed this deal as an opportunity to boost economic growth not only in Somaliland, but in the region, especially landlocked Ethiopia as the region's largest economy (Dubai World, 2016). Ethiopian officials envisage benefits associated with the modern facilities that will be brought by DP investment and expect the port to provide a new outlet that would reduce Ethiopia's reliance on the congested Djibouti port (Addis Fortune, 2016).

Another Middle East regional power whose relations with Ethiopia (and the Horn of Africa) are much older is Israel. As pointed out earlier, the Horn of Africa has always been of strategic interest for Israel not only to secure its trade routes through the Red Sea, but also to reduce any threats emanating from shipping arms to its enemies through the region. Not surprisingly then, Israel is promoting its cooperation with Nile basin countries to "fight terrorism". During Netanyahu's visit to the region in July 2016, the first visit on that level in three decades, a regional summit that brought him together with the heads of state and government of Ethiopia, Kenya, Rwanda, South Sudan, Tanzania, Uganda and Zambia was convened in Entebbe. The communique of the Summit did not go beyond highlighting the states' agreement to strengthen cooperation on security and combatting all crimes that are associated with it, including cyber-crime (Israel Ministry of Foreign Affairs, 2016a). It, however, reflected the coordination that was already taking place for decades between Israel and some countries, especially Kenya, in this field (Butime, 2014).

Although the common Iranian enemy is drawing Arab Gulf countries (except Qatar) closer to Israel in a clear realignment of forces in the Middle East (Ulrichsen, 2016), Tel Aviv's policy in the Nile basin has always been seen by Arab scholars as aiming at threatening Egypt's water security and weakening the Arab influence in Africa (Al-Tawil, 2013; Muhareb, 2013). Water and agriculture are among the major fields of cooperation between Israel and Nile basin countries. During his last visit to Ethiopia, Uganda, Rwanda and Kenya, Netanyahu offered to transfer Israeli technology to these countries to allow them to make the best use of their water resources to boost their agricultural development (Israel Ministry of Foreign Affairs 2016b). Importantly, he portrayed this support as a means to implement the vision of the founding fathers of the Jewish state in helping African people achieve their freedom (from colonization in the past and from poverty presently) and his vision of contributing to Africa's economic rise, a narrative that resonates well with Ethiopia's claims of using Nile waters to alleviate poverty.

In light of the continuing tensions over the Nile water resources and the aspirations of the new regime to expose its regional preeminence, Egypt joined the race for Red Sea military dominance. In January 2017, the Egyptian President inaugurated the new USD 28-million headquarters of the Egyptian Navy's Southern Naval Fleet Command at Safaga, 64 km south of Hurghada. Although the specific tasks of the Command have not been defined, Egyptian military officials indicated that its purpose is to protect Egypt's maritime security that "extends from the Zagros Mountains in Iran to the Straits of Gibraltar in the Western Mediterranean and from the Horn of Africa to the sources of the Nile" (World Tribune, 2017). Besides, Egypt has been developing its military capabilities, signing new arms deals with France and Russia for acquiring helicopter carriers and fighter jets. In this sense, Egypt is building its deterrent capacities against threats emanating from a turbulent Middle East and developments in Nile upstream countries, especially Ethiopia, that may affect its water security.

Hydropolitical implications of Red Sea dynamics in the Nile Basin

While the Turkish economic relations with Ethiopia and Sudan may contribute to the changes in the balance of power in the Nile basin to the detriment of Egypt, the impact of the increasing Gulf presence in the Horn of Africa and the Nile basin is mixed. Although it does not reflect a common Arab geo-strategic policy towards Eritrea, the Gulf military build-up in Eritrean ports raised alarm bells in Ethiopia. Following a state visit to Saudi Arabia in November 2016, the Ethiopian PM Hailemariam Desalegn pointed out that he was assured that the operation in and around the Assab port will not be used to serve the Eritrean regime's "destabilizing agenda against Ethiopia" (Awramba Times, 2016). A hostile Eritrean regime emboldened by military coalitions with Gulf countries is seen as a threat to Addis Ababa. Given the continued Eritrean support to Ethiopian armed opposition (UN, 2015, UN, 2016; Berhanu, 2013) and the Ethiopian accusation against Egypt and Eritrea for inciting the late 2016 demonstrations in the Oromia and Amhara regions, the Saudi-UAE increasing engagement in Eritrea adds complexity to hydropolitics in the Nile basin. This has to be understood in light of the centuries-old Ethiopian fears of an Arab Middle East that might join forces with Arab-Islamic forces in the Horn of Africa to destroy the Christian state of Ethiopia and the historical Saudi and Egyptian support to Eritrean liberation movement (Erlich, 2002). More recently, the late Ethiopian Prime Minister Meles Zenawi voiced concerns that an Egypt infuriated by tensions with Ethiopia on the Nile waters after the construction of the GERD might join forces with Saudi Arabia to support "hostile forces in the Horn of Africa" (de Waal, 2015).

The rising Gulf economic interests in Ethiopia and the easing of tensions around the Nile waters with the rise of President Al-Sisi to power in Egypt may have only partly rested Ethiopian fears. As the unrest in Ethiopia in late 2016 shows, the Ethiopian regime would find it convenient to blame "anti-peace elements" supported by regional players, including Egypt and Eritrea, for its domestic failings (Lefort, 2016). Ethiopian and regional media reports circulate speculations about the potential of Egypt using the UAE base in Eritrea to destabilize Ethiopia, or the Egyptian move to establish a military base in Eritrea (Aiga Forum, 2016; Awate, 2016; Tekle, 2017).

More recently, other sources reported that Egyptian forces arrived at the Sawa military base on the Sudanese borders with Eritrea in coordination with the UAE, a move seen as a response to Erdoğan's visit to Sudan and his agreement with Khartoum to develop the Red Sea island of Suakin (Middle East Monitor, 2018). These new speculations, which were categorically denied by the Eritrean President Isaias Afwerki, were followed by a decision by Sudan to close its borders with Eritrea and deploy additional troops in the border state of Kassala. Khartoum justified these measures as emergency security arrangements to fight illicit arms trafficking (Sudan Tribune, 2018). However, the escalation of security tensions in the region amid a new deadlock in talks over the implementation of the required studies of GERD's downstream impacts and the close Sudanese-Ethiopian position in these talks indicated the tacit close interlinkages between hydropolitical developments in the eastern Nile and security dynamics in the Red Sea.

These developments also indicate that the Saudi-UAE incursion into Eritrea may not necessarily be translated into more bargaining power for Egypt vis-à-vis Ethiopia (and probably Sudan). However, it is seen by Addis Ababa (and occasionally by Khartoum whose relations with Gulf countries have been oscillating) as a source of material and bargaining power to Eritrea which is considered by Ethiopia (and sometimes by Sudan) as a proxy for Egypt to destabilize both countries and prevent them from using its Nile waters for their own development.

Although the interest of Israel in the Red Sea and the Nile HSC is not new, its revival amidst changing balance of power in the basin is a source of concern to Egypt, at least at the popular level. The Egyptian parliament discussed Netanyahu's visit to the Nile basin, calling upon the Egyptian Foreign Ministry to present its strategy to counter Israel's policy which it considers as a threat to Egypt's water and national security. Although this may not reflect the position of the current Egyptian government, for many observers in Cairo, Netanyahu's visit proved the Israeli support to the Ethiopian dam and indicated the two countries' alliance against Egypt as

The Nile and the Middle East

a common enemy (The Middle East Media Research Institute, 2016; Raslan, 2016; Abdullah, 2016). Similar to political and economic relations with Turkey and Gulf countries, the close diplomatic relations and technical cooperation (including in the water and agriculture sector) between Ethiopia and Israel to support Ethiopia's use of its natural resources to alleviate poverty is a source of material, bargaining and ideational power to Ethiopia as far as Nile hydropolitics is concerned.

Conclusion

At the broadest level, the analysis allows us to conclude that the interlinkages between the Middle East and Nile security complexes are going through a very dynamic process of change, including multiplicity of actors, renewed vested interests, changes in alliances, and different economic and political features from the past. In the background of the changes in the relations between the two regions are endogenous changes to each region and its countries, which are then being reflected in the foreign policies of all countries and the inter-regional relations. The Egyptian revolution, the split of Sudan into two countries, the Saudi- Iranian competition, and the Saudi-Qatar recent political fallout, are just a few examples of localized political developments that ended up having extensive regional repercussions, including implications for the hydropolitical relations.

Within the limits of the data available, we can also conclude that the Nile Basin region is nowadays not just a geopolitical sphere of influence, but it is also becoming a main stage of competition and conflict between powerful Middle East countries such as Saudi Arabia, UAE, Qatar, Turkey, Iran, Israel and Egypt. The situation is fluid and has several economic, political and security ramifications – in particular for the Nile HSC itself, adding several layers of complexity to already tense (hydro)political relations among riparian states in general, and Eastern Nile countries in particular. In economic terms, the Gulf and Turkish investments in Ethiopia and Sudan raise Egyptian concerns over future water abstractions upstream along the Nile Banks (especially from the Eastern Nile). In political and military terms, Sudan and Eritrea have been driven to proxy wars between Saudi Arabia and Iran, with Gulf military presence in Eritrea and the Horn of Africa, simultaneously raising Ethiopia's concerns regarding the increasing connection between Asmara and Cairo in the Nile hydropolitics. Simultaneously, in the period we have been analyzing we could observe that the Nile has often been used as a "card" by Middle East powers to project their influence in the regional power game between Qatar/ Turkey and Egypt, and in occasional disagreements between Egypt and Saudi Arabia.

All these new engagements are contributing to changes in the balance of power – namely in its material, bargaining and ideational dimensions – between the Nile Basin countries, and accordingly partially eroding Egypt's hydro-hegemonic control and leadership position in the Nile. The Nile HSC and the flows themselves are being increasingly politicized and securitized to an unprecedented extent, including by actors well outside of the Nile basin. Although Middle East states are interested in the land and water resources of the Nile Basin per se (as possible means to decrease their own water/food insecurity), the analysis also exposes how these new hydro-geopolitical dynamics have very little to do with the Nile water indeed. Much more significant is political power, influence, alliances and interventions. The Nile river, the Nile Basin, and the flows may thus be considered proxies themselves – for the regional geopolitical power plays.

Related to this observation – and within the limits of the data available – we can conclude that new engagements of Middle East powers in the Nile HSC are producing inter-dependencies between the two security complexes that are stronger than interdependencies within the Nile HSC itself. The Nile riparians remain definitely interconnected through their transboundary water resources and the focus remains on the impacts of ongoing upstream developments, such as the GERD or large-scale irrigation in Sudan, on downstream uses. The current negotiation between Eastern Nile countries on estimating the transboundary impacts of the GERD, and Ethiopia's hydropower exports to Sudan and other Equatorial Nile riparians, among other areas of increasing cooperation are cases in point. However, the size and level of economic (including trade), political and even military/security relations between these Nile riparians do not match their relations with the Middle East neighbors, a fact that is starting to feature clearly in the relations between the two regions and could have a significant impact on potential cross-regional alliances and conflicts in the future.

Finally, the increasing uncertainty about the impacts of the ongoing economic, military and political engagements of Middle East powers in the Nile hydropolitical security complex adds new sources of instability to an already turbulent Middle East. As long as much of these engagements (e.g. size of land investments and their estimated water withdrawals, mission and period of deployment of military forces, etc.) are not transparently revealed and openly discussed, they are strongly bound to represent additional causes for increasing uncertainty and enduring tensions between Nile riparians, especially those in the Eastern Nile Basin.

References

Abbink, J. 2003. Ethiopia-Eritrea: Proxy Wars and Prospects of Peace in the Horn of Africa. *Journal of Contemporary African Studies*. 21(3), pp. 407–426.

Abdullah, A. 2016. Israel's Africa Ambitions Highlight Egypt's Absence. *Al-Monitor*, July 12, www.al-monitor.com/pulse/originals/2016/07/egypt-israel-africa-shoukry-visit-role.html

Addis Fortune. 2016. Dubai Opens Door for Ethiopia in Somaliland, May 17, https://addisfortune.net/articles/dubai-opens-door-for-ethiopia-in-somaliland/

Ahram online. 2016. Egypt MPs to Meet with FM to Discuss Saudi Visit to Ethiopian dam, December 21, http://english.ahram.org.eg/NewsContent/1/64/253586/Egypt/Politics-/Egypt-MPs-to-meet-with-FM-to-discuss-Saudi-visit-t.aspx

Aiga Forum. 2016. US-Arab Cold War in the Horn of Africa, July 5, http://aigaforum.com/news2016/on-ethio-eritrea-070316.htm

Allan, T. 1997. Virtual Water: A Long-term Solution for Water Short Middle East Economies? Paper presented at the British Association Festival of Science, University of Leeds.

Allan, T., Keulertz, M., Sojamo, S. and Warner, J. (eds). 2013. *Handbook of Land and Water Grabs in Africa: Foreign Direct Investment and Food and Water Security*. Abingdon and New York: Routledge.

Al-Obaid, A. 2010. King Abdullah's Initiative for Saudi Agricultural Investment Abroad: A Way of Enhancing Saudi Food Security. Presentation to Expert Group Meeting on "Achieving Food Security in Member Countries in Post-crisis World", *Islamic Development Bank*, Jeddah, May 2–3, www.isdb.org/irj/go/km/docs/documents/IDBDevelopments/Internet/English/IDB/CM/Publications/IDB_AnnualSymposium/20thSymposium/8-AbdullaAlobaid.pdf

Al-Tawil, A. 2013. Israel and the Horn of Africa: The Determinants of the Relationship and Mechanisms of Implementation. In: Hamad, E., Al-basheer, A. and al-Qassab, A. (eds). *The Arabs and the Horn of Africa: Dialectics of Neighborhood and Identity*. Qatar: Arab Centre for Research and Policy Studies, pp. 319–350.

Ardemagni, E. 2016. *The Yemeni Factor in the Saudi Arabia-Sudan Realignment*, The Arab Gulf States Institute in Washington, www.agsiw.org/the-yemeni-factor-in-the-saudi-arabia-sudan-realignment/

Arsano, Y. 2007. *Ethiopia and the Nile: Dilemmas of National and Regional Hydro-politics*, Zurich: Swiss Federal Institute of Technology.

Awate. 2016. Nile Politics: Eritrea, Ethiopia, Sudan and Egypt, *Awate*, December 5, http://awate.com/nile-politics-eritrea-sudan-ethiopia-egypt/

Awramba Times. 2016. Hailemariam Warns Saudi Arabia and UAE over Military Moves in and around Eritrea's Assab Port, *Awramba Times*. December 2, www.awrambatimes.com/?p=14132

Bakeer, A.L. 2013. *Future of Turkish-Egyptian Ties After Military Coup*. Report to Al-Jazeera Center for Studies, http://studies.aljazeera.net/en/reports/2013/12/20131217113236236557.html

Berhanu, K. 2013. Conflicts in the Horn of Africa and Implications for Regional Security, in Bereketeab, R. (ed.) *Horn of Africa*. London: Pluto Press, pp. 71–94.

Bloomberg. 2017. Ethiopia Eyes Role in DP World-Managed Port in Somaliland, *Bloomberg*. June 9, www.bloomberg.com/news/articles/2017-06-08/landlocked-ethiopia-eyes-role-in-dp-world-managed-somali-port

Bossio, D., Erkossa, T. Dile, Y., McCartney, M. Killiches, F., and Hoff, F. 2012. Water Implications of Foreign Direct Investments in Ethiopia. *Water Alternatives*. 5(2), pp. 223–242.

Brewer, C. 2011. Peril by Proxy: Negotiating Conflicts in East Africa. *International Negotiation*. 16, pp. 137–167.

Butime, H. 2014. Shifts in Israel-Africa Relations. *Strategic Assessment*. 17(3), pp. 81–91.

Buzan, B. 2003. Regional Security Complex Theory in the post-Cold War world. In Soderbaum, F. and Shaw, T. (eds). *Theories of New Regionalism: A Palgrave Reader*. New York: Palgrave, pp. 140–159.

Buzan, B. and Waever, O. 2003. *Regions and Powers: The Structure of International Security*. Cambridge: Cambridge University Press.

Cascão, A. 2008. Ethiopia: Challenges to Egyptian Hegemony in the Nile Basin, *Water Policy*. 10, pp. 13–28.

Cascão, A. 2009. Changing Power Relations in the Nile River Basin: Unilateralism vs. Cooperation? *Water Alternatives*. 2(2), pp. 245–268.

Cascão, A. E., and Nicol, A., 2016a. Sudan, "Kingmaker" in a New Nile Hydropolitics: Negotiating Water and Hydraulic Infrastructure to expand Large-scale Irrigation, in Sandström, E., Jägerskog, A. and Oestigaard, T. (eds). *Land and Hydropolitics in the Nile River Basin: Challenges and New Investments*. Abingdon: Routledge-Earthscan.

Cascão, A. and Nicol, A. 2016b. "GERD: New Norms of Cooperation in the Nile Basin?". *Water International*, 41(4), pp. 550–573.

Cascão, A. and Zeitoun, M. 2010. Power, Hegemony and Critical Hydropolitics. In Earle, A., Anders J. and Joachim O. (eds.) *Transboundary Water Management: Principles and Practice*. London and New York: Routledge, pp. 27–42.

Cook, S.A. and Ibish, H. 2017. Turkey and the GCC: Cooperation amid Diverging Interests. The AGSIW *Gulf Rising* Series. Issue Paper 1. Washington DC: Arab Gulf States Institute in Washington.

Copley, G. 2017. *Geopolitical Time bomb: Chaos in Somaliland could Trigger Regional Conflict*, http://oilprice.com/Geopolitics/Africa/Geopolitical-Time-Bomb-Chaos-In-Somaliland-Could-Trigger-Regional-Conflict.html

Derso, B. 2017. Ethiopia, Qatar Vow to Take Multifaceted Relations to New Heights. *The Ethiopian Herald*, http://allafrica.com/stories/201704110341.html

De Waal, A. 2015. *The Real Politics of the Horn of Africa: Money, War and the Business of Power*. Cambridge: Polity.

Dubai World. 2016. *DP World Wins 30 Year Concession for Port of Berbera in Somaliland,* http://web.dpworld.com/wp-content/uploads/2016/09/2016-09-05-Somaliland-Concession_EN-Final.pdf

Duner, B. 1981. Proxy Interventions in Civil Wars. *Journal of Peace Research*. 4, pp. 353–361.

Ecofin News. 2016. *Turkish Firm Besida to Acquire 75% Stake in Beles Sugar Project*. November 24, www.ecofinagency.com/agriculture/2411-35931-ethiopia-turkish-firm-bedisa-to-acquire-75-stake-in-beles-sugar-project

Egypt Independent. 2018. *Egypt, Ethiopia, Sudan to hold meeting over GERD*. 13 March, https://egyptindependent.com/egypt-ethiopia-sudan-to-hold-meeting-over-gerd-on-april-4-5/

Ehteshami, A. and Murphy, E. 2011. *The International Politics of the Red Sea*. London and New York: Routledge.

Erlich, H. 2002. *The Cross and the River: Ethiopia, Egypt, and the Nile*. London: Lynne Rienner Publisher.

Ethiopian Herald. 2017a. *Ethiopia: Turkish Investments Roaring in Ethiopia*, March 31.

Ethiopian Herald. 2017b. *Ethiopia: Turkish Investment Rising in Ethiopia*, March 22.

Ethiopian Investment Commission. 2017. *Emir of the State of Qatar visits Ethiopia*, www.investethiopia.gov.et/fr/a-propos/nous-vous-assistons?id=434

Global Impact Investment Network (GIIN). 2015. *Ethiopia: East Africa's Rising Giant*. https://thegiin.org/assets/documents/pub/East%20Africa%20Landscape%20Study/09Ethiopia_GIIN_eastafrica_DIGITAL.pdf

Hanna, R.L. 2016. Transboundary Water Resources and the Political Economy of Large-scale Land Investments in the Nile: Sudan, Hydropolitics and Arab Food Security in Sandström, E., Jägerskog, A. and Oestigaard, T. (eds), *Land and Hydropolitics in the Nile River Basin: Challenges and New Investments*. Abingdon: Routledge-Earthscan.

Hassan, K. 2017. Can Economic Opportunity Bring Turkey, Egypt closer? *Al-Monitor*. February 17.

Ibish, H. 2017. *The UAE Evolving National Security Strategy*. Issue Paper 4: Washington: The Arab Gulf states Institute in Washington.

Israel Ministry of Foreign Affairs. 2016a. *Joint Declaration of the Regional Summit on Counter-terrorism*, www.mofa.go.ug/data/dnews/293/JOINT%20DECLARATION%20OF%20THE%20REGIONAL%20SUMMIT%20ON%20COUNTER-TERRORISM.html

Israel Ministry of Foreign Affairs. 2016b. *PM Netanyahu on Official Visit to Ethiopia*, http://mfa.gov.il/MFA/PressRoom/2016/Pages/PM-Netanyahu-on-official-visit-to-Ethiopia-7-July-2016.aspx

Johnson, H. 2016. *This Map Explains the Saudi-Iran Proxy War*, *Foreign Policy*, http://foreignpolicy.com/2016/01/06/this-map-explains-the-saudi-iran-proxy-war/

Kamski, B. 2016. The Kuraz Sugar Development Project (KSDP) in Ethiopia: between "Sweet Visions" and Mounting Challenges. *Journal of Eastern African Studies*. 10(3), pp. 568–580.

Lefebvre, J. 2012. Iran in the Horn of Africa: Outflanking US Allies. *Middle East Policy*. 19(2), pp. 117–133.

Lefort, R. 2016. The Ethiopian Spring: Killing is not an Answer to our Grievances. *Open Democracy*, www.opendemocracy.net/ren-lefort/ethiopian-spring-killing-is-not-answer-to-our-grievances.

Lukes, Steven. [1974] 2005. *Power: A Radical View* 2nd edition. Hampshire, UK, Palgrave Macmillan.

Matthews, N., Nicol, A. and Seide, W. 2013. Constructing a New Water Future? An Analysis of Ethiopia's Current Hydropower Development. In Allan, T., Keulertz, M., Sojamo, S. and Warner, J. (eds). *Handbook of Land and Water Grabs in Africa*. London: Routledge, pp. 774–800.

Middle East Media Research Institute. 2016. Reactions in Egypt to Israeli PM Netanyahu's Africa Visit – Egyptian MP: The Visit Threatens Egypt's National Security, July 12, www.memri.org/reports/reactions-egypt-Israeli-pm-netanyahus-africa-visit-egyptian-mp-visit-threatens-egypts

Middle East Monitor. 2018. UAE-backed Egyptian Forces Arrive in Eritrea. January 4, www.middleeastmonitor.com/20180104-uae-backed-egyptian-forces-arrive-in-eritrea/

Ministry of Foreign Affairs of the Federal Democratic Republic of Ethiopia. 2016a. Ethiopia, Saudi Arabia Vow to Strive for Major Breakthroughs in Priority Areas. *A Week in the Horn*, December 23. Addis Ababa: MFA.

Ministry of Foreign Affairs of the Federal Democratic Republic of Ethiopia. 2016b. Qatar's Foreign Minister on an Official Visit to Ethiopia. *A Week in the Horn*, December 23. Addis Ababa: MFA.

Ministry of Foreign Affairs of the Federal Democratic Republic of Ethiopia. 2016c. The 7th Ethio-Turkey Joint Economic Forum held in Addis Ababa this week. *A Week in the Horn*, December 30. Addis Ababa: MFA.

Ministry of Foreign Affairs of the Federal Democratic Republic of Ethiopia. 2017. Prime Minister Hailemariam Dessalegn's Visit to Qatar this Week. *A Week in the Horn*, November 17. Addis Ababa: MFA.

Ministry of Foreign Affairs of the Republic of Turkey. 2017. Relations between Turkey and Sudan, www.mfa.gov.tr/relations-between-turkey-and-sudan.en.mfa

Mordor Intelligence. 2017. *Sudan Alfalfa Market – Growth and Trends, Forecast to (2017–2022)*. Hyderabad, India: Mordor Intelligence.

Muhareb, M. 2013. Israel and the Horn of Africa: Repercussions and Interventions. In Hamad, E., Al-basheer, A. and al-Qassab, A. (eds). *The Arabs and the Horn of Africa: Dialectics of Neighborhood and Identity*. Qatar: Arab Centre for Research and Policy Studies, pp. 291–318.

Mumford, A. 2013. Proxy Warfare and the Future of Conflict. *The RUSI Journal*, 158(2), pp. 40–46.

Nicol, A. and Cascão, A. 2011. Against the Flow: New Power Dynamics and Upstream Mobilisation in the Nile Basin. *Review of African Political Economy*. 38, pp. 317–325.

Nicolas, F. 2017. "Chinese Investors in Ethiopia: The Perfect Match?", *Notes de l'Ifri*, Ifri, March 2017.

Presidency of the Republic of Turkey. 2017. *Ethiopia*, www.tccb.gov.tr/en/exclusive/africa/ethiopia/

Raslan, H. 2016. Egypt, Israel and the Nile Water. *Ahram Online*, 29 July, english.ahram.org.eg/NewsContentP/4/236135/Opinion/Egypt,-Israel-and-the-Nile-water.aspx

Sabala, K. 2011. Regional and Extra-regional Inputs in Promoting (in) Security in Somalia. In Sharamo, R. and Mesfin, B. (eds). *Regional Security in the post-Cold War Horn of Africa*, Monograph 178. Pretoria: Institute for Security Studies.

Şafak, Y. 2017. *Turkish Investors Eyeing Sudan*, www.yenisafak.com/en/economy/turkish-investors-eyeing-sudan-2725913

Sandström, E., Jägerskog, A. and Oestigaard, T. (eds). 2016. *Land and Hydropolitics in the Nile River Basin: Challenges and New Investments*. Abingdon: Routledge-Earthscan.

Schulz, M. 1995. Turkey, Syria and Iraq: A Hydro-political Security Complex. In Ohlsson, L. (ed). *Hydropolitics: Conflicts over Water as a Development Constraint*. London: Zed Books.

Shinn, D. 2015. *Turkey's Engagement in Sub-Saharan Africa Shifting Alliances and Strategic Diversification.* Research Paper to Africa Programme. London: Chatham House – The Royal Institute of International Affairs.

Sudan Tribune. 2018. Sudan Shut Down Border with Eritrea. January 8, www.sudantribune.com/spip. php?article64432

Swain, A. 2011. Challenges for Water Sharing in the Nile Basin: Changing Geo-politics and Climate Change. *Hydrological Sciences Journal.* 56(4), pp. 687–702.

Swain, A. and Jägerskog, A. 2016. *Emerging Security Threats in the Middle East: The Impact of Climate Change and Globalization.* Lanham, MD: Rowman & Littlefield Publishers.

Swain, A. and Jamali, Q. 2011. The China Factor: New Challenges for Nile Basin Cooperation. *New Routes.* 15(3), pp. 7–10.

Tawfik, R. 2015. *Revisiting Hydro-hegemony from a Benefit-sharing Perspective: The Case of the Grand Ethiopian Renaissance Dam,* Discussion Paper 5/2015. Bonn: German Development Institute.

Tawfik, R. 2016. The Grand Ethiopian Renaissance Dam: A Benefit-sharing Project in the Nile basin? *Water International,* 41(4), pp. 574–592.

Tekle, T. 2017. Egypt to Establish Military Base in Eritrea. *Sudan Tribune,* April 17, www.sudantribune.com/spip.php?article62221

The Economist. 2016. *As Egypt Quarrels with Saudi Arabia, it is Finding New Friends,* November 25.

The Reporter. 2016. *Turkish Giant to Invest USD One Billion in Beles Sugar Project.* November 5.

Turton, A. 2003. *The Political Aspects of Institutional Developments in the Water Sector: South Africa and its International River Basins.* D.Phil Thesis. University of Pretoria: Faculty of Humanities.

Tvedt, T. 2010. About the Importance of Studying the Modern History of the Countries of the Nile Basin in a Nile Perspective. In Tvedt, T. (ed.) *The River Nile in the Post-colonial Age.* London: I.B. Tauris.

Ulrichsen, K. 2011. The Geopolitics of Insecurity in the Horn of Africa and the Arabian Peninsula. *Middle East Policy,* 18(2), pp. 120–135.

Ulrichsen, K. 2016. *Israel and the Arab Gulf States: Drivers and Directions of Change.* Houston, TX: Centre for the Middle East, Rice University, Baker Institute for Public Policy.

United Nations Security Council. 2015. *Report of the Monitoring Group on Somalia and Eritrea Pursuant to Security Council Resolution 2182.* New York: UNSC.

United Nations Security Council. 2016. *Report of the Monitoring Group on Somalia and Eritrea Pursuant to Security Council Resolution 2244.* New York: UNSC.

Verhoeven, H. 2016a. Briefing: African Dam Building as Extraversion: The Case of Sudan's Dam Programme, Nubian Resistance, and the Saudi-Iranian Proxy War in Yemen. *African Affairs.* 115(460), pp. 562–573.

Verhoeven, H. 2016b. The Gulf States in the Political Economy of the Nile Basin: A Historical Overview. In Sandström, E., Jägerskog, A. and Oestigaard, T. (eds). *Land and Hydropolitics in the Nile River Basin: Challenges and New Investments.* London: Routledge, pp. 53–72.

Waterbury, J. 2002. *The Nile Basin National Determinants of Collective Action.* New Haven: Yale University Press.

World Tribune. 2017. Egypt Expands Navy with Formation of Southern Fleet Command, January 15, www.worldtribune.com/egypt-expands-navy-with-formation-of-southern-fleet-command/

Zeitoun, M. and Allan, J. 2008. Applying Hegemony and Power Theory to Transboundary Water Analysis. *Water Policy.* 10, pp. 3–12.

Zeitoun, M. and Warner, J. 2006. Hydro-hegemony: A Framework for Analysis of Transboundary Water Conflicts. *Water Policy.* 8, pp. 435–460.

Zeitoun, M., Cascão, A., Warner, J. Mirumachi, N., Mahhhews, N., Menga, F. and Farnum, R. 2017. Transboundary Water Interaction III: Contest and Compliance. *International Environmental Agreements.* 17(2), pp. 271–294.

16

WATER AND SECURITY IN THE MIDDLE EAST

Opportunities and challenges for water diplomacy

Martina Klimes and Elizabeth A. Yaari

Introduction

Water and in particular the governance of water resources has been part of the peace and security discourse in the Middle East since the early 1990s (Cook and Bakker, 2013). Multi-track water diplomacy efforts related to the joint management of shared water resources, including the Lower Jordan, have played an important role in negotiations between Israel and Palestine, and increasingly among actors in the Tigris-Euphrates. With the escalation of armed conflicts in Syria and parts of Iraq in 2011, and failure to resolve the ongoing conflict between Palestine and Israel, a renewed sense of urgency has been brought to theories and practices of water diplomacy processes as a potential entry point for broader transboundary cooperation in the Middle East. Water problems and challenges are often framed in the context of interstate and intrastate conflicts and are thus highly politicized. This politicization of water is re-enforced by the impacts of climate changes which exacerbate water scarcity and act as a "threat multiplier" to internal and regional political stability, migration and food insecurity (CNA, 2007; Chenoweth et al., 2011; Earle et al., 2015).

The term water security was first used in academic discourse in the 1990s in the context of Middle Eastern geopolitics but it became employed more widely in the following decade as linkages were made between water and other types of security, namely military and food (Cook and Bakker, 2013). Water is a vital and scarce resource in the Middle East and any interaction on the use of water resources in shared basins is thus politicized and securitized. This means that water decision-making is processed through a variety of perspectives – its importance to national security, scientific/technical viewpoints, as well as community generated outlooks (Leb and Wouters, 2013).

We define multi-track water diplomacy as a process of transboundary negotiation on water-related issues inclusive of formal actors and diplomats, technical water experts, representatives of affected communities (when applicable) and other riparian stakeholders. This multi-track approach enables a broad space for water-related dialogues, including opportunities for de-politicization.

This chapter presents the concept of multi-track water diplomacy and identifies specific entry points for formal and informal water diplomacy processes within two transboundary river basins in the Middle East: the Tigris-Euphrates and the Lower Jordan.[1] This chapter seeks to demonstrate how linkages within and between informal and formal water dialogue platforms increase shared understanding, both technical and psychological, to catalyse broader cooperation between riparian countries and proposes recommendations to increase water diplomacy impact through improvements in these linkages.

Water, security and water diplomacy

Water and security is no longer perceived, in the narrow traditional security perspective, as zero-sum competition over a strategic resource. Rather, increasingly as part of a broader security perspective encompassing people-centric approaches to peace and security. The latter, broader perspective is more apt a perspective to understand current water-related security challenges in the Middle East. Zeitoun (2013:15) places water security in the middle of six different security areas (human/community security, national security, water resource security, food security, energy security, and climate security) highlighting its interdependencies. Building on Zeitoun's conceptualization, water security, and the lack of it, can be regarded as a conflict indicator. We use the concept of water diplomacy to assess and generate opportunities for cooperation on water issues in shared basins.

In this chapter, water security is not only understood as securing sustainable access to water resources but as part of the broader context of the water and security nexus. Water scarcity can have implications both in terms of increased competition among inter and intra state actors for a strategic resource but also inadequate access to water as security implications on people's well-being – lost livelihoods and food insecurity, forced migration, and inability to mitigate impacts of climate change-induced natural disasters. Cook and Bakker (2011: 97) identify four interrelated themes in research on water security – water availability, human vulnerability to hazards, human needs, and sustainability. Understanding water and security in this wider context thus requires assessment of both traditional security challenges (state-to-state) and human security (well-being of individuals).

In the context of integrated water resource management, the perceptions of risks and benefits at basin level are subjected to having a shared knowledge of basin characterizations; i.e. countries sharing a water resource (transboundary river, lake, or aquifer) arrive at a shared understanding of the main water-related risks and benefits. Without creating shared understanding of technical characterizations and key water-related challenges, riparian countries are less likely to agree on what would be the mutually beneficial solutions and how to achieve a vision and management of their shared water resources. Shared understanding is highly influenced by the actor's interpretation of knowledge resources. Water negotiators are not immune to the functional and embedded prisms and socio-psychological barriers which influence how actors process information in biased manners leading to missed opportunities for assessing threats and benefits (Bar-Tal and Halperin, 2011; Ross and Ward, 1995). The challenge of overcoming socio-psychological barriers and their impact on information processes is particularly salient in basins located in areas of long-standing intractable conflicts (Bar-Tal, 2007).

Research on transboundary water cooperation suggests that states tend to collaborate rather than resort to armed conflicts over water resources (Wolf, 2006) but this is questioned amid increased water scarcity in regions with weak institutions (Mobjörk et al., 2016:7). Three issues are paramount for moving water cooperation forward, the presence of *political will* to support engagement/interaction with other riparian counterparts, the engaged actor's *ability to overcome socio-psychological barriers* to information processing, and the *ripe timing* of specific efforts (Zartman, 1995, 2003; Pruitt, 1997; Mitchell, 1995; Bar-Tal and Halperin, 2011).

Existing research shows that political will is instrumental for a sustainable cooperation on water issues in the Middle East (Kibaroglu, 2008). The wider region of Middle East and North Africa (MENA) is considered the most water scarce and water interdependent region in the world; with 80% of available water from resources shared by two or more countries (El Hajj et al., 2017). Political will is not only instrumental for reaching an agreement but requires longevity and broad stakeholder engagement to ensure ongoing cooperative problem solving is maintained in a dynamic context.

Theoretical and applied research in social and political psychology has demonstrated that societies involved in long-standing conflict are dominated by a rigid repertoire of embedded socio-psychological processes which greatly affects information processing. While the content of the conflict are real tangible issues, normative and functional psychological processes such as *motivated reasoning* i.e. unconscious motivation to assess new information to align with prevailing schema and reduce dissonance (Ross and Ward, 1995: 264; Bar-Tal and Halperin, 2011: 224); *divergent construal* i.e. "opposing partisans exposed to same objective information are apt to interpret those facts differently" (Ross and Ward, 1995: 268); or *confirmation bias* i.e. the tendency to reject information that disconfirms one's beliefs and search out information that confirms one's beliefs (Nickerson, 1998) – all act as barriers to conflict resolution in the context of long-term intractable conflicts. These barriers act to reinforce status quo beliefs and impede parties from accurately appraising situations and processing information (Bar-Tal and Halperin, 2011; Bar-Tal, 2007; Ross and Ward, 1995). Much like understanding the social, political and economic context of water diplomacy engagements, efforts to understand widely held embedded beliefs, values and narratives which act as barriers to enable openness to new information and acceptance of new ideas are a critical aspect of water diplomacy processes which take place in regions of long-standing conflict.

Political will and leadership can also play a decisive role in ripening situations for engagement in water cooperation. Zartman (1985, 2001) defines ripe moments stipulated by a mutually hurting stalemate (MHS), i.e. both parties reach the ripest moment for management when both arrive at a deadlock. In the context of water negotiations, the interpretation of when parties reach MHS can depend on the level of shared understanding of technical characterization of shared waters. The concept of ripeness (Zartman, 1995, 2003; Pruitt, 1997; Mitchell, 1995) can thus be used to identify opportune entry points for multi-track water diplomacy engagements.

Multi-track water diplomacy

Conventionally diplomacy is seen as high-level interaction and dialogue between nation-states (Morgenthau, 1946). Diplomacy can be defined according to various tracks (Diamond and McDonald, 1996; Mapendere, 2005). These different tracks vary in terms of formality, the actors involved, and purpose. Track One (T1) refers to official level formal engagements between state representatives with the authority and mandate to make decisions on behalf of their governments. Track Two (T2) refers to informal dialogue between non-officials to resolve conflicts or build trust and includes academics, non-governmental organization (NGO) representatives and community representatives, private sector actors, media or former officials (ibid.).

T1, formal diplomacy, represents meetings at a state-to-state level, between government representatives, most often diplomats. Mapendere (2005: 67) lists strengths of official diplomacy as "the ability to use political power to influence directions of negotiations and outcomes", "the capacity to access material and financial resources that give high leverage and flexibility in negotiations", in-depth knowledge about the parties' interests through intelligence, and finally, "states have the competence to use broad knowledge of their states' foreign policies". T1 processes and meetings adhere to strict protocol and agendas which often limit space for flexibility and exploring "out of the box solutions". This is particularly notable in low trust environments where issues deemed as sensitive/significant to national security are heavily politicized and where it may be challenging to explore different options for finding mutually acceptable solutions; particularly in water-scarce regions like the Middle East (Bakker, 2011, Kibaroglu, 2008) where water issues are perceived predominately through a national security lens. In the context of water diplomacy/water dialogues, this often means that government negotiators focus primarily on issues like water allocation and less on multiple use scenarios, no-regret actions and on exploring opportunities for mutual gains. As Trottier and Brooks (2013) noted, focus on quantitative water allocation contributes to the securitization of the water sector. Furthermore, water challenges or issues deemed interconnected to other sectors are considered outside the decision-making space of water ministers and water authorities requiring extensive engagement with other decision-makers and stakeholders on all sides.

T2, informal diplomacy, includes processes aimed to elevate a shared vision and understanding of the basin and explore and elaborate options and scenarios for cooperation in a non-binding environment. Informal diplomacy can include public awareness and educational activities, open source data-sharing exchange and integration, joint research and fact finding, policy dialogues, and other forms of grassroots stakeholder engagement activities. Informal water diplomacy approaches offer opportunities to enhance mutual understanding of shared risks and benefits generally or for specific stakeholder groups and offer a wealth of different entry points for engagement at various points in conflict escalating/ de-escalating phases. Moreover, T2 processes are often critical to complement T1 processes in that the informal environment is amenable to the participants' ability to explore issues beyond assumptions related to water allocation (Susskind and Islam, 2013) and foster awareness and engagement across diverse constituencies of impact.

Between T1 and T2 classifications, Track One and a Half (T1.5) engages former officials or government officials in informal roles. This process can sometimes be used as a substitute for dialogues between states that do not have established or otherwise utilized diplomatic channels and thus require informal opportunities for exchange, for example through side discussions at broader multilateral organizational meetings. T1.5 thus allows state representatives to use informal settings to discuss issues that cannot be raised in formal T1 platforms.

As opposed to T1 water diplomacy processes led by government representatives with decision-making authority, informal processes are driven by a range of unofficial actors. Government officials can participate as private individuals (T1.5) but many informal processes are led by well-connected concerned citizens including retired civil servants, independent experts, academics, NGO representatives, private sector actors, journalists, faith based leaders, celebrities and others. Informal diplomacy can play an important part in generating interest, knowledge and shared understanding of the basin, as well as in building ad hoc coalitions to advance a water diplomacy process. T1.5 meetings are often facilitated by non-state actors (NSAs) but can also be arranged by other types of third parties ranging from multilateral organizations, foreign states to NGOs.

The multi-track approach is complemented by new frameworks for understanding "transboundary" water management at both intra and interstate levels. Typically, "transboundary" activities refer to engagements that cross country borders. Today, "transboundary waters" have taken up a broader meaning to include not only surface and groundwater resources that traverse multiple countries but also water resources that cross municipal and state borders within a country, as well as unresolved borders, involve different sets of actors and users (for example industry, agriculture, domestic users), and between communities. This formulation recognizes that in a globalized world, disputes, and likewise water disputes, are no longer the purview of state actors alone, rather increasingly involve NSAs and take place within a country as well as between countries (Kaldor, 2006). As such, resolution and long-term approaches, processes and solutions are needed to address transboundary water management at multiple levels including globally, regionally, nationally and locally.

The multi-track approach to water diplomacy is further strengthened by the concept of a participatory approach to water management articulated in the 1992 Dublin Principles:

> Water development and management should be based on a participatory approach, involving users, planners and policy-makers at all levels. The participatory approach involves raising awareness of the importance of water among policy-makers and the general public. It means that decisions are taken at the lowest appropriate level, with full public consultation and involvement of users in the planning and implementation of water projects.
>
> *(The Dublin statement, 1992)*

When the relevant societies and communities of impact, including vulnerable groups, are directly engaged in decision-making forums around water resource management, decision-making processes can better address the needs and priorities of a broad range of stakeholders, resulting in decisions that provide benefits to more members of society, contributing to longer lasting solutions that can further mitigate conflict relapse (Collier et al., 2003: 12). Moreover, broad representative stakeholder engagement in water governance enhances forms of democratic participation, particularly when water negotiations are undertaken as part of post-conflict state building or to insulate against humanitarian crises, by providing a pathway to enact individual or community stakes in managing a shared water resource. Involvement of a broad range of stakeholders is thus key to mitigating security risks by mitigating and/or responding to challenges before they become overt problems. Strengthening linkages between tracks can further strengthen stakeholder engagement and the participatory approach to water management as envisioned in the Dublin Principles.

Processes categorized as T1 and T2 can independently have positive influences for water cooperation, but in the Middle East context given prevailing politicization of water, strengthening linkages between T1 and T2 processes is critical.

Linking the tracks

One of the main challenges of informal processes is to create sustainable and effective linkages to enhance or establish formal level processes while at the same time aligning expectations of what informal processes can achieve across process participants. Without linkages to official decision-making authorities, informal processes cannot reach their full efficacy. Islam and Susskind (2013: 12) frame water management and wider water issues in three different perspectives – political (political context), natural (ecosystem, water quality, water quantity), and societal (governance); multi-track water diplomacy can ensure that all three perspectives are addressed but the challenge is to establish effective linkages between the different tracks.

Adopting a multi-track water diplomacy approach aims to further broaden the diplomatic space to engage new actors, ways of thinking, ideas, and information that can better inform the official process. Multi-track water diplomacy's linkage of T1 and T2 engagements contributes to fostering an enabling environment for official engagement by creating a broad network of engaged stakeholders and constituents at multiple levels in the country or countries of concern lowering the risk of T1 cooperation in conflict sensitive basins. As such multi-track water diplomacy approaches offer more avenues to include influential individuals and representatives of stakeholder groups that would be likely be left out of formal meetings among designated government officials. In addition, multi-track processes can maintain different channels of communication amid deteriorating formal relations. When a T1 process reaches an impasse, T2 can maintain dialogue in an informal setting, develop political will and link back to T1 when political environment allows. T2 processes can maintain contacts and communications with states that do not have formal diplomatic relations – offering a unique advantage. In a different context, T2 can also set the stage for T1 meetings when the environment is not conducive for formal negotiations. Further, T2 processes can contribute to the erosion of socio-psychological barriers to formal conflict resolution by fostering trust, elaborating shared values and vision for the basin and finding common ground, potentially altering broadly held views or identifying alternative options.

The ability of actors to effectively undertake T2 water diplomacy related activities is predicated on key aspects of the political and social context. The right of actors to assemble and establish NGOs or other informal organizations, as well as access to and ability to share information, including information sourced from neighboring countries or internationally, is key to leverage T2 influence on T1. Broad variations on the ability to freely organize, assemble and establish organizations as well as freedom of speech, freedom of the press, and freedom of information access exist throughout the Middle East.

Freedom of information is critical to the ability of T2 water diplomacy actors to influence T1 actors, as well as the public at large, given the predominance of state generated data. Modern technologies, open source water data and social media platforms are enabling informal actors to more affordably and effectively access information or generate their own knowledge sources but state authorities remain the primary source for national water data. That some countries have established such freedom of information laws does not imply they are without limitations. The principles of these acts can be inhibited due to lack of alignment with other legal frameworks such as defamation, censorship and emergency laws, as well as restrictions on the type of person that can request information or the type of information that can be requested, and limited public knowledge or ability to use the legal platform. Furthermore, once legal avenues to access key information are established, fostering an embedding sense of transparency and partnership between officials and non-governmental stakeholders takes time to take hold given the widespread security focused context of water dialogues in the region. National and local authorities long operating without public engagement may take years to develop positive working relationships with informal level stakeholders.

Conventionally, state actors in the Middle East have conducted water dialogues on the formal level as water issues tend to be narrowed to urgent priority water allocation concerns. Generally multilateral processes are advanced in basins where there is greater symmetry of power relations and deeper understanding of interlinkages and benefits to cooperation. In the Middle East region, as elsewhere, power asymmetries on the political level contribute to the tendency of T1 processes to advance bilateral water agreements (Daoudy, 2007).

Water diplomacy entry points: Lower Jordan River and Euphrates and Tigris

This section will detail different multi-track water diplomacy processes in the Lower Jordan River and Euphrates and Tigris and specific water diplomacy entry points that were employed when developing and enhancing these platforms. Entry points in this chapter refers to an interaction or specific activity within either T1 or T2 that can be harnessed to advance cooperation on water issues among actors that share a water resource.

Most T1 and T2 water diplomacy entry points fall within the scope of the five pillars of environmental peacemaking developed by UNEP (2016):

1. **Conducts assessments** to identify rising tensions and conflicts over natural resources, opportunities for cooperation, and technical entry points for engagement
2. **Brokers meetings and provides a neutral platform** for dialogue, information-sharing and joint action in the management of natural resources and environmental threats
3. **Provides impartial expertise, scientific analysis and policy advice** over a contested natural resource or source of environmental degradation
4. **Builds capacity and catalyses resources** for the implementation of joint action plans and projects
5. **Monitors implementation of joint action plans and provides dispute resolution support**

These categories of entry points make space for various types of engagements accessible in diverse contexts given variants in relations between different parties in terms of political will, socio-psychological barriers, and the ripe timing of specific efforts.

Examples of formal water diplomacy entry points

There are 310 river basins that cross the border of two or more countries and 121 established River Basin Organizations (RBOs) in the world (OSU, 2018), none of the water dialogue processes in the Middle East has led to an establishment of a multilateral River Basin Organization (Schmeier et al., 2015). While there is an absence of institutionalized multilateral structures in transboundary basins in the Middle East, the governments in the region generally opt for bilateral negotiations focused on water allocation issues. As such political will to cooperate on water issues largely depends on the state of bilateral political relations. In the context of ongoing conflicts and the lack of final agreements in both the Euphrates and Tigris and Lower Jordan regions, government decision-makers have predominantly advanced bilateral processes rather than multilateral processes or institutional structures. The preference for bilateral water management is not unique to the Middle East, and can be seen elsewhere – notably in China's water agreements with its neighbors.

In the Euphrates-Tigris basin,[2] Syria and Turkey reached a number of water-related agreements, during the thaw in Syrian-Turkish relations between the late 1990s and 2011.[3] This included the 2008 agreement on the establishment of a Joint Water Institute (which also included Iraq)[4] and the 2009 Memorandum of Understanding on construction of a joint *Friendship* dam on the Orontes/Asi River. Further to this, the Syrian-Turkish rapprochement also contributed to reviving the Joint Technical Committee for Regional Waters (JTC) for the Euphrates and Tigris riparian countries (Syria, Turkey and Iraq) in 2007 (Kibaroglu and Scheumann, 2013). In this sense, the conducive political environment yielded cooperation on water issues, not vice versa. Following the escalation of conflict in Syria and the suspension of diplomatic relations between Turkey and Syria in November 2011, formal processes between the two countries on water issues diminished and Syria was left out of the Joint Technical Committee (JTC) for the Euphrates and Tigris riparian countries. Turkey ceased all formal cooperation with Syria's al Assad government on water issues but Turkish and Syrian technical water experts met in informal multilateral meetings in 2016 and 2017 (CPET Annual Report, 2017).

The Joint Technical Committee for Regional Waters was established by Turkey and Iraq in 1980 with Syria joining in 1983[5] as a platform to discuss regional water issues, but was paralyzed by long periods of conflict and instability in the region, particularly in Iraq (Kibaroglu and Scheumann, 2013). Following its revival in 2007, the JTC offered a platform for inter-governmental dialogue on water issues. Turkey and Iraq have continued to meet without the government of Syria but the meetings have not resulted in any specific arrangement for joint management of the Euphrates and Tigris rivers. In September 2016, joint fact finding and joint monitoring stations together with staff exchange visits were discussed during a JTC meeting between Turkey and Iraq. Joint capacity building and joint fact finding and monitoring, including exchange of information on climate change, have been on the JTC agenda since the resumption of the meetings in 2007.

The Euphrates and Tigris region faces rapidly increasing population, migration flows as a result of both armed conflicts and droughts, and other long-term climate change risks.[6] Inability of governments to deliver basic services such as water and electricity has led to public unrest in the Euphrates and Tigris region and elsewhere in the Middle East and globally. The region, and particularly Iraq's part of the basin, is heavily dependent on agriculture; around 80% of water from Euphrates and Tigris is used for agriculture (75–80% in Turkey, Syria and Iraq; Shamout and Lahn, 2015). Long periods of general negligence of the water and agriculture sector amid a long period of political and security instability prevented countries like Iraq from prioritizing investments in increasing the efficiency of irrigation systems. The Euphrates and Tigris riparians have not reached a formal consensus on baseline characterization of the basin such as water quality and hydrology and the countries have not reached an agreement on data sharing during the JTC meetings.

Water is only briefly mentioned in the 1993 Declaration of Principles between Israel and Palestine but the 1995 Agreement on the West Bank and the Gaza Strip, signed in 1995 as an interim agreement designed for five years, established a Joint Water Committee for the coordination of water and wastewater projects in the West Bank (Interim Agreement, 1995). The final status of shared waters was postponed to the final status negotiations alongside other core issues of the conflict that remain to be resolved to date. Criticized for built in asymmetry of power and mandate (Zeitoun, 2008; World Bank, 2009; Selby, 2013), the interim-turned-enduring Joint Water Committee continued meeting during periods of heightened conflict (Earle et al., 2015: 50), before reaching a deadlock in 2010. Efforts in 2016 to resume core functions and re-establish the Committee led to the endorsement of a 2016 agreement between the Palestinian Minister of Civil Affairs and the Israeli Coordinator of Government Activities in the Territories unlocking some joint functions. Subsequently, a July 2017 agreement endorsed by Palestine and Israel indicates the potential of further water to be sold by Israel to Palestine beyond the quantities identified in earlier agreements in an effort to relieve urgent water stress in Palestine. Despite these fragile formal level efforts, calls to establish a new comprehensive cooperative framework for shared waters either within the context of a final status agreement or as a separate agreement outside of final status negotiations persist.

The Joint Water Committee between Jordan and Israel, alternatively, stands out as a functional T1 bilateral water platform in that it has served as a water related negotiations platform between the two states since it was established as part of the 1994 peace treaty (Israeli-Jordanian Peace Treaty, 1994, Ann. II) which details water allocation, usage, storing and quality issues from both the Jordan and Yarmouk rivers. That said the Jordanian-Israeli Joint Water Committee's ability to employ water resource management approaches beyond allocation concerns, including multi-use and participatory approaches, is severely limited by the lack of regional engagement with the other basin riparians relevant to the shared water resources of Israel and Jordan.

Informal water diplomacy entry points

Existing or former T2 processes in the Lower Jordan include joint scientific research, data sharing, joint planning processes, policy dialogues, informal dialogue/trust building, joint project based activities, cross border small-scale water and wastewater infrastructure development, and educational and public awareness campaigns to develop shared understanding and vision (Earle et al., 2015). EcoPeace Middle East,[7] a regional environmental organization focused mainly on transboundary water cooperation processes in Jordan, Palestine and Israel, has hosted informal water cooperation activities in the Jordan for more than 20 years. In addition, several other well-established regional or bilateral T1.5 and T2 water cooperation projects or processes exist in the basin such as the EXACT process,[8] GLOWA Jordan River process,[9] the Arava Institute's academic programs and research projects,[10] and MEDRC's trilateral transboundary water cooperation process and regional capacity building programmes.[11] In many cases the actors or organizations engaged in informal processes leverage their knowledge of both the shared water resource in question and the national government interests and positions to identify entry points and linkages to advance T1 solutions. In other cases such as EcoPeace Middle East's Good Water Neighbors programs the process aims to establish and inform broader community-based transboundary constituencies through fostering of a shared vision and understanding of local neighboring communities' water challenges addressed through jointly identified shared solutions. Linking to formal processes, these "constituency of community residents" serve as organized pressure groups surrounding tangible solutions to shared water challenges (EcoPeace, 2016).

Existing science diplomacy processes are noteworthy among T2 entry points in the Euphrates and Tigris. Initiatives like the Euphrates-Tigris Initiative for Cooperation (ETIC), Blue Peace, and the Collaborative Programme Euphrates and Tigris (CPET) have contributed to water cooperation in the region through joint capacity building and joint fact finding.[12] Science diplomacy related to water diplomacy processes can both address the need for shared understanding of basin characteristics and foster regional connections and networks, potentially eroding psychological barriers to conflict resolution.

One of the first forms of informal science diplomacy in the Euphrates and Tigris region was the Euphrates-Tigris Initiative for Cooperation (ETIC) established by a group of academics and water professionals from Turkey, Syria and Iraq in May 2005. The main objective of this effort was to advance cooperation among Euphrates and Tigris riparian countries through creating shared knowledge on technical, social and economic development issues (Kibaroglu, 2008) through building an epistemic community.[13] Kibaroglu (2008: 195) asserts that epistemic communities like ETIC would thrive in a more favorable regional security environment. One of the main roles of the ETIC community was to raise awareness on the need of cooperation on shared waters in the region. With the deterioration of relations between Turkey and Syria the ETIC process was diminished. This reinforces the argument that adversary political developments can negatively affect informal processes.

In late 2013, the Collaborative Programme Euphrates and Tigris (CPET) was launched to provide another platform for building trust and shared knowledge on priority issues identified by participating government experts from Turkey, Iraq and Iran at that time. These included hydrology, water quality, hydropower, agriculture water productivity, marshlands and socio-economics (ICBA, 2017). Unlike the ETIC process, the CPET experts were formally nominated by participating governments who supported the engagement of national experts as an in-kind contribution to the program while maintaining the informal non-binding character of the program platform. Over the three years of the project's main phase, some level of trust and shared understanding has been established among the participating experts but a challenge remains in how to institutionalize and leverage trust and common ground in the formal processes. Aside from joint scientific studies and creating of shared knowledge products, the CPET platform also helped to enhance understanding among the riparian countries on what the others consider as the main water-related challenges and why. Political will was instrumental for launching the CPET initiative but once the program was established meetings continued amid increased tensions between the participating governments.

Another informal dialogue platform in the Euphrates and Tigris region was the Blue Peace project launched by the Strategic Foresight Group (SFG) in 2002. While the CPET project used science and joint fact finding as an entry point and did not focus on political dialogue on shared waters, the Blue Peace platform focused more on facilitating support for transboundary cooperation on the political level. One of the main results of the Blue Peace effort was the 2014 Geneva Consensus on Tigris River between Turkey and Iraq on joint capacity building, establishing a joint monitoring station, and sharing of technical data on the Tigris River (Strategic Foresight Group, 2017). As of July 2017, the agreement had not been fully implemented.

In both the Lower Jordan and Euphrates and Tigris, joint scientific research or science diplomacy processes involve independent or government nominated scientists working in parallel or cooperatively with counterparts from neighboring riparian states to publish knowledge products that often relate to the technical characterization (hydrological, socio-economic, water quality status) of a shared basin. These processes often focus on joint technical studies and fact finding and can bring together research teams from a particular discipline (e.g. environmental economists from all riparian countries) or complementary fields (e.g. botanists, hydrologists, planners, etc.) to explore transboundary water challenges. These endeavors often include international experts to facilitate knowledge sharing and harmonize results. Results from science diplomacy processes can subsequently be presented in each country by national experts or advocates increasing potential erosion of barriers to new information and acceptance of results and recommendations at the T1 level.

The impact of these T2 processes is not consistently apparent and further research, monitoring and evaluation to follow impacts and identify mechanisms to mitigate the effects of embedded power asymmetries within T2 efforts need to be undertaken. Moreover, not all T2 processes are successfully linked to the formal level. Intentional design of T2 processes focused on reducing risks to enable political will, eroding socio-psychological barriers and inducing ripeness through strengthening of inter-track linkages are all key components.

Linking the tracks: Prevailing challenges and emerging opportunities for water diplomacy

One of the main challenges of creating synergies between the tracks is how to ensure that the T1 and T2 processes are well-linked and that the knowledge generated in T2 processes can inform decisions made in the T1 decision-making arena. Gürkaynak (2006: 74) conducted research on perceptions of T2 diplomacy among Turkish and US diplomats. One of the observations was that many diplomats that were supportive or partly supportive of T2 processes agreed that a mechanism for providing exchange of information between the two tracks is needed.

Evidence indicates that depoliticizing water issues and other environmental risks is needed to create an enabling environment for cooperation and that increased politicization and securitization of shared waters contributes to negotiation deadlocks. The growing impact of climate change risks and increasing water scarcity in the Middle East can further narrow the focus of water dialogues to zero-sum water issues like water allocation. Water security will however be

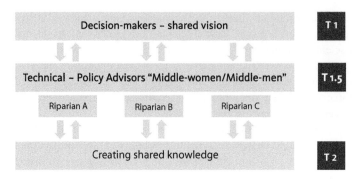

Figure 16.1 Linking the water diplomacy tracks

achieved by cooperation rather than securitization of water resources (Leb and Wouters, 2013). Traditional security and foreign policy mechanisms may lack entry points for water and climate change related dialogues as they tend to focus on main conflict issues and perceive the dialogue on scarce resources as a zero-sum game. As such, we conclude that a multi-track water diplomacy approach allows actors to explore cooperation on less politically charged issues with potential to influence core issues.

As elaborated throughout this chapter, both T1 and T2 processes can provide platforms and entry points to foster political will, create opportunities for actors to overcome sociopsychological barriers to conflict resolution, and instigate ripe timing – the presence of which is needed for creating a conducive environment for water cooperation. In the following subsections we have identified the prevailing challenges and opportunities to catalyze synergies between the different water diplomacy tracks. Identified solutions in this concluding section can contribute to eroding this overarching challenge in conflict-affected environments.

Figure 16.1 demonstrates the critical role of linkages between water diplomacy tracks. We postulate that in most cases that were described in this chapter, shared knowledge is generated from science diplomacy or epistemological community activities where scientists work together on reaching shared understanding of water-related challenges in the basin. Well-placed middle-women/middle-men who can access and broker knowledge generated by the scientific community can act as champions in conveying the knowledge results both "up" to decision-makers who have the mandate to support proposed processes leading to shared vision with political will as well as "down" to inform the broader public environment reducing risks of official level engagement.

1. Foster an enabling environment to empower multi-track water diplomacy processes to function effectively

Twenty-seven years have passed since the original Dublin statement on Water and Sustainable Development recognized that water management should be undertaken in a participatory approach engaging actors at multiple levels (The Dublin statement, 1992), but the challenge of providing space and opportunities to achieve effective multi-level water diplomacy processes remains. Improvements can be made from both the T1 perspective and the T2 perspective to increase mutual understanding of the value and benefits of multi-track water diplomacy processes. Formal platforms for water diplomacy are necessary and institutionalized basin structures such as RBOs can provide a set meeting platform as well as broader opportunities for exchange of technical data, verification and joint monitoring, and other types of knowledge exchange. T2 processes can both complement and inform T1 processes through engaging groups of stakeholders that are not conventionally part of T1 processes, elevating understanding of the needs and priorities of different basin stakeholders, fostering out of the box thinking, and building ad hoc coalitions of constituencies around key water cooperation issues.

Skepticism exists on both sides. T1 actors, cognizant of the risks of widening the sensitive dialogue space and not always fully aware of how T1 can benefit from T2 processes, can hesitate to engage informal actors. Likewise, T2 actors may oscillate with regards to if and how to engage T1, not necessarily fully understanding T1 priorities and processes, holding divergent viewpoints and assumptions, or adopting rigid or undeveloped strategies. This resulting skepticism can lead to inattention or insufficient attention to the costs of the status quo (i.e. the costs of non-cooperation or ineffective cooperation).

Creating an enabling environment for strong linkages between water diplomacy tracks requires both internal trust and coalition building, as well as legal frameworks and safeguards to enable access to information and freedoms of speech and public organizing. Increasing shared understanding of the mutual value of T1 and T2 water diplomacy processes can serve to move processes and agreements from the realm of government-to-government engagements to people-to-people processes with corresponding benefits for long-lasting regional water security.

This includes building relationships between complementary sectors (e.g., water/science–foreign affairs or non-governmental–government) but also between professional colleagues from riparian countries (science–science). For instance, the informal ETIC and CPET processes in the Euphrates and Tigris region focused on building relations among water experts from Turkey, Syria, Iraq and also Iran (CPET, 2017) that are not all included in the formal T1 meetings. This increases understanding of mutual challenges and as some of the experts are well-linked to decision-makers, these processes can also contribute to advancement of the formal dialogues. Discussing issues associated to water security in a broader framework with a more inclusive group of stakeholders fosters buy-in, a sense of shared ownership of process, and ensures easier entry for professional viewpoint beyond that of traditional T1 actors. Added to this, engaging a wider group of stakeholders can make the dialogue processes and their outcomes more sustainable. Sustained capacity building processes and the development of multi-level stakeholder platforms (MSPs) can contribute to increasing common ground, exchange of information, early warning for challenges, and understanding of the benefits of multi-track processes both within and between tracks.

2. Strengthen and institutionalize linkages within and between formal and informal water diplomacy tracks

One of multi-track water diplomacy's main challenges is establishing sustainable intra- and inter-track linkages among formal actors (e.g., ministry of water–ministry of foreign affairs), informal actors (e.g., NGO–NGO) and between informal and formal actors (T2–T1).

In the Middle East, interstate negotiations on water issues are predominantly bilateral and led by Ministries of Foreign Affairs representatives with limited knowledge and experience of water issues. Likewise, Ministries of Water have little regional transboundary experience and expertise. In addition, other ministries (agriculture, industry and regional cooperation), municipalities and cities as well as influential interest groups may have direct interests and priorities related to specific water-related policies. With transboundary water management challenges at the conflux of these various authorities and interests, cross ministerial committees and issue-based parliamentary caucuses are key to fostering intra-T1 exchange knowledge, prioritizing issues, and aligning positions. Inter-ministerial exchange can help to erode the securitization and over-politicization of water diplomacy efforts by ensuring that diverse perspectives and priorities are included. Likewise, actors and organizations involved in T2 water diplomacy processes would benefit from increased coordination and cooperation, as well as professional monitoring and evaluation in the interest of process coherency, knowledge management, inclusiveness, access to complementary capacities, agreement implementation and financial efficiency.

While trust can be built and knowledge shared among individuals or in small networks, such as within an informal science diplomacy processes, it remains a challenge how to gradually institutionalize linkages to ensure impact and sustainability. Participants of T1 processes should be well informed about the other tracks, and key individuals involved in designing national negotiation strategies on water issues as well as national water policies should be well-versed in outcomes and developments of informal water diplomacy processes. Likewise, T2 processes need to better understand driving priorities of T1 processes and possible entry points for joint engagements. To illustrate, science diplomacy actors are challenged to bridge this gap to both advance shared understanding of basin characteristics and provide evidence-based policy recommendations designed with diverse decision-maker readers in mind.

Strengthening and institutionalizing linkages within and between formal and informal water diplomacy tracks establishes diverse entry points and offers advantages to initiate, revive or enrich processes.

3. Establish shared technical knowledge platforms to inform formal and informal processes

Effective T1 and T2 water diplomacy processes, as well as national planning and policy-making, require shared understanding of basin characteristics as well as its social, political, environment and economic context. Actors at all levels require information, and developing an inclusive and transparent shared knowledge platform can contribute to increased understanding within and between actors. Science diplomacy in the field of water diplomacy can contribute to establishing shared technical basin baseline and increase understanding management options for transboundary waters.

MSPs have hosted this function elsewhere. Within an MSP structure or other similar information sharing platform, T2 processes can work in parallel with T1 processes to increase political will, erode socio-psychological barriers to conflict resolution and induce ripe-timing. Initial focus on scientific issues brings an opportunity to depoliticize and reach tangible results in an environment where political agreements are hard to reach. T2 water diplomacy processes provide opportunities to test cooperation in smaller settings, such as a designed group of experts, without the pressure to make binding decisions from the onset. Even relatively small-scale achievements such as a joint baseline report or a joint monitoring station can help to erode barriers to further cooperation.

Results and lessons learned from joint scientific finding as well as non-scientific but policy-relevant information shared during informal meetings can play an important role in identifying win-win opportunities when preparing national negotiation strategies. This knowledge is however not often shared effectively. This is partly due to the fact that information about informal processes is often scarcely disseminated and their purpose and mandate is often not clear/known to government officials. For example, diplomats involved in international negotiations on water issues may not trust informal information sources and/or find results of scientific studies fully accessible/understandable.

Emerging and already existing climate change trends and their transboundary character increase the need for cooperation among riparian states. The Middle East region is expected to be affected by negative impacts of climate change and increased water scarcity more than any other region in the world. To effectively tackle these transboundary issues, it is incumbent that the countries in the region will find ways to overcome hegemony of foreign and security politics in transboundary water dialogues. Understanding the costs and benefits of regional cooperation options based on evidence-based scientific diplomacy can not only lead to building of linkages in future vision but can also erode zero-sum framing among communities and decision-makers.

Conclusion

Available evidence from the Lower Jordan and Euphrates and Tigris indicates that water on its own does not usually serve as an entry point on the formal level when political relations between riparian countries have deteriorated. Political issues take precedence over water cooperation and national interests dominate (Kibaroglu and Scheumann, 2013; Kibaroglu, 2008). Desecuritization of water issues can however favor the promotion of cooperation (Daoudy, 2007). The humanitarian crisis in the region in the wake of armed conflicts in Syria and Iraq, growing populations which are heavily dependent on the agriculture sector for livelihoods, and already apparent impact of climate change in the region can contribute to increase the sense of urgency about the need for transboundary cooperation.

This chapter has demonstrated how traditional diplomatic approaches are not currently equipped to address the complexities of water security challenges in the Middle East. The dynamic and distinct political arenas of both the Tigris-Euphrates and the Lower Jordan, indeed diverse contexts globally, have much to benefit from access to a multitude of entry points able build a shared understanding across riparian communities. Well-linked, scientifically informed multi-track water diplomacy can foster political will and erode barriers to conflict resolution so that functional transboundary water platforms can be harnessed when ripe opportunities occur. These identified recommendations to leverage opportunities rooted in core challenges should be considered policy recommendations of relevance to both informal and formal water diplomacy processes.

Acknowledgments

The authors would like to thank Dr Marian J. Neal for reviewing earlier versions of this chapter and for her helpful comments as well as the UNESCO Category II International Center for Water Cooperation at the Stockholm International Water Institute (SIWI).

Notes

1 For the purpose of this chapter, the geopolitical context has been narrowed to the Lower Jordan and the Euphrates and Tigris regions, primarily, as we are cognizant of over-generalization in the diverse and distinct politically and socio-economic Middle East region. Further, focus is made on the specific regions in which we as authors have long-standing practical experience.
2 Syria and Iraq refers to the Euphrates and Tigris as two separate international rivers while Turkey regards Euphrates and Tigris as one transboundary river system. Turkey thus refers to the Euphrates and Tigris basin while Iraq and Syrian use Euphrates and Tigris basins.
3 The thaw started following the signing of the 1998 Adana Accord which ended the support of the Syrian Government to the Kurdistan Workers' Party (PKK).

4 Turkey, Syria and Iraq agreed to appoint 15 water engineers to work on designated goals of the joint water institute which included: to develop and share information on irrigation and potable water technology, to map water resources in the Middle East, and to release a report on effective water management in each country (Water for the Ages, 2008). The notion to establish the institute was never implemented.

5 Turkey, Iraq and Syria met under the Joint Technical Committee framework between 1983 and 1992 before the meetings were resumed again in 2007.

6 At the end of the century, expected temperature increase in the Euphrates and Tigris region is 3–4°C (Shamout and Lahn, 2015).

7 www.ecopeaceme.org

8 http://exact-me.org

9 www.glowa-jordan-river.de/ourProducts/HomePage

10 www.arava.org

11 www.medrc.org/

12 "Science for diplomacy – using science cooperation to improve international relations between countries" (The Royal Society, 2010 report).

13 "An epistemic community is a network of professionals with recognized expertise and competence in a particular domain and an authoritative claim to policy-relevant knowledge within that domain or issue" (Haas, 1992: 3).

References

Bakker, K. (2011). The Human Right to Water Revisited. In Sultana, F., Budds, J. and Loftus, A. (Eds). *The Right to Water*, pp. 19–44. London: Earthscan.

Bar-Tal, D. (2007). Socio-Psychological Foundations of Intractable Conflicts. *American Behavioral Scientist*, 50, 1430–1453. Accessed July 6, 2017 at www.tau.ac.il/~daniel/pdf/15.pdf

Bar-Tal, D., and Halperin, E. (2011). Socio-psychological Barriers to Conflict Resolution. In Bar-Tal, D. (Ed.) *Intergroup Conflicts and their Resolution: Social Psychological Perspective*, pp. 217–240. New York: Psychology Press.

Chenoweth J., Hadjinicolaou, P., Bruggeman, A., Lelieveld, J., Levin, Z., Lange, M., Xoplaki, E., and Hadjikakou, M. (2011). *Impact of Climate Change on the Water Resources of the Eastern Mediterranean and Middle East Region: Modeled 21st Century Changes and Implications*. Water Resources Research, June 2011.

CNA Corporation (2007). National Security and the Threat of Climate Change. Accessed July 6, 2017 at https://climateandsecurity.files.wordpress.com/2012/04/climate-change-as-threat-multiplier_understanding-the-broader-nature-of-the-risk_briefer-252.pdf

Collier, P., Elliot, L., Hegre, H., Hoeffler A., Reynal-Querol, M., and Sambanis, N. (2003). *Breaking the Conflict Trap: Civil War and Development Policy*. Oxford: Oxford University Press.

Cook, C. and Bakker, K. (2011). Water Security: Debating an Emerging Paradigm. *Global Environmental Change*, 22, pp. 94–102.

Cook, C. and Bakker, K. (2013). Debating the Concept of Water Security. In: Lankford, B., Bakker, K., Zeitoun, M. and Conway, D. (Eds). *Water Security: Principles, Perspectives, and Practices*. London: Earthscan.

CPET (2017). *CPET Annual Report, Year 4, November 2017*. Accessed November 20, 2018 at https://iati.openaid.se/docs/2174373_2_1.PDF

Daoudy, M. (2007). Benefit-sharing as a Tool of Conflict Transformation: Applying the Inter-SEDE Model to the Euphrates and Tigris River Basins. *The Economics of Peace and Security Journal*, 2/2, pp. 26–32.

Diamond, L. and McDonald, J. (1996). *Multi-track Diplomacy: A Systems Approach to Peace*. West Hartford, Conn.: Kumarian Press, p. 182.

Dublin Statement (1992). *The Dublin Statement and Report of the Conference: International Conference on Water and the Environment: Development Issues for the 21st Century: 26–31 January 1992*, Dublin, Ireland.

Earle, A., Cascão A., Hansson, S., Jägerskog, A., Swain, A., and Öjendal, J. (2015). *Transboundary Water Management and the Climate Change Debate*. New York: Earthscan Routledge, Stockholm International Water Institute.

EcoPeace Middle East (2016). *Community Based Problem Solving on Water Issues*. Accessed July 4, 2016 at http://ecopeaceme.org/wp-content/uploads/2017/03/Community_Based_Problem_Solving_Nov_2016_Final.pdf

El Hajj, R., Farajalla, N., Terpstra, T., and Jägerskog, A. (2017). *Enhancing Regional Cooperation in the Middle East and North Africa through the Water Energy-Food Security Nexus*. Planetary Security Initiative Policy

Brief. April 2017. Accessed July 6, 2017 at www.planetarysecurityinitiative.org/sites/default/files/2017-05/PB_PSI_MENA_WG_3_0.pdf

Gürkaynak, C.E. (2007). Track Two Diplomacy from a Track One Perspective: Comparing the Perceptions of Turkish and American Diplomats. *International Negotiation*, 12/1, pp. 57–82.

Haas, P.H. (1992). Introduction: Epistemic Communities and International Policy Coordination. *International Organization*, 46/1, pp. 1–35.

Interim Agreement (1995) *The Israel-Palestinian Interim Agreement on the West Bank and Gaza Strip*. Washington, DC. September 28, 1995.

International Center for Biosaline Agriculture (ICBA). 2017. Collaborative Programme Euphrates and Tigris (CPET), Research Poster. Accessed July 2, 2017 at www.biosaline.org/sites/default/files/project_brief_cpet_.pdf

Islam, S. and Susskind, L.E. (2013). *Water Diplomacy: A Negotiated Approach to Managing Complex Water Networks*. New York: Routledge.

Israeli-Jordanian Peace Treaty (1994). *Treaty of Peace between the State of Israel and the Hashemite Kingdom of Jordan*. October 26, 1994.

Kaldor, M. (2006). *New and Old Wars: Organized Violence in a Global Era*. 2nd edition. Cambridge: Polity Press, pp. 69–111.

Kibaroglu, A. (2008). The Role of Epistemic Communities in Offering New Cooperation Frameworks in the Euphrates-Tigris River System. *Journal of International Affairs*, 61/2.

Kibaroglu, A., and Scheumann, W. (2013). Evolution of Transboundary Politics in the Euphrates-Tigris River System: New Perspectives and Political Challenges. *Global Governance: A Review of Multilateralism and International Organizations*, 19/2, pp. 279–305.

Leb, C. and Wouters, P. (2013). The Water Security Paradox and International Law. In Lankford, B., Bakker, K., Zeitoun, M. and Conway, D. (Eds). *Water Security: Principles, Perspectives, and Practices*. London: Earthscan.

Mapendere, J. (2005). Track One and a Half Diplomacy and the Complementarity of Tracks. *Culture of Peace Online Journal*, 2/1, pp. 66–81.

Mitchell, C. (1995). The Right Moment: Notes on Four Models of "Ripeness". *Global Society*, 9/2, pp. 38–52.

Mobjörk, M., Gustafsson, M-T., Sonnsjö, H., van Baalen, S., Dellmuth, L-M., and Bremberg, N. (2016). *Climate-related Security Risks: Towards an Integrated Approach*. Solna: SIPRI, p. 72.

Morgenthau, H.J. (1946). Diplomacy. *The Yale Law Journal*, 55(5), pp. 1067–1080.

Nickerson, R.S. (1998). Confirmation Bias: A Ubiquitous Phenomenon in Many Guises. *Review of General Psychology*, 2, pp. 175–220.

Oregon State University (OSU) (2018). Transboundary Freshwater Dispute Database (TFDD). Accessed November 20, 2018 at: https://transboundarywaters.science.oregonstate.edu/content/transboundary-freshwater-dispute-database.

Pruitt, D. (1997). Ripeness Theory and the Oslo Talks. *International Negotiation*, 2/2, pp. 237–250.

Ross, L., and Ward, A. (1995). Psychological Barriers to Dispute Resolution. *Advances in Experimental Social Psychology*, 27, pp. 255–304.

Schmeier, S., Gerlak, K.A., and Blumstein, S. (2015). Clearing the Muddy Waters of Shared Watercourses Governance: Conceptualizing International River Basin Organizations. *International Environmental Agreements: Politics, Law and Economics*, 16/4, pp. 597–619.

Selby, J. (2013). Cooperation, Domination and Colonisation: The Israeli–Palestinian Joint Water Committee. *Water Alternatives*, 6/1, pp 1–24.

Shamout, N. and Lahn, G. (2015). *The Euphrates in Crisis: Channels of Cooperation for a Threatened River* London: Chatham House.

Strategic Foresight Group (2017). *The Blue Impact*, accessed on July 1, 2017 at www.strategicforesight.com/publication_pdf/78628The%20Blue%20Impact.pdf

The Royal Society (January 2010). *New Frontiers in Science Diplomacy: Navigating the Changing Balance of Power*. London: The Royal Society.

Trottier, J. and Brooks, D.B. (2013). Academic Tribes and Transboundary Water Management: Water in the Israeli–Palestinian Peace Process. *Science & Diplomacy*, 2/2. Accessed on July 1, 2017 at: www.sciencediplomacy.org/article/2013/academic-tribes-and-transboundary-water-management.

United Nations Environment Programme (UNEP) (2016). An Introduction to Environmental Cooperation for Peacebuilding. In *Environmental Cooperation for Peacebuilding Programme, Final Report 2016*. Nairobi: UNEP.

Water For the Ages (2008). Turkey, Iraq, and Syria to Form Collaborative Water Institute, March 13. Accessed July 1, 2017 at https://waterfortheages.org/2008/03/13/turkey-iraq-and-syria-to-form-collaborative-water-institute/

Wolf, A. (2006). *Conflict and Cooperation over Transboundary Water*. UNDP Human Development Report Office Occasional Paper 2006/19. New York: UNDP.

World Bank (2009). *West Bank and Gaza: Assessment of Restrictions on Palestinian Water Sector Development*, Sector Note, Middle East and North Africa Region – Sustainable Development, Report No. 47657-GZ. Washington, DC: The International Bank for Reconstruction and Development /World Bank. Accessed July 2, 2017 at http://documents.worldbank.org/curated/en/775491468139782240/pdf/476570SR0P11511nsReport18Apr2009111.pdf

Zartman, W.I. (1985). *Ripe for Resolution: Conflict and Intervention in Africa*. New York: Oxford University Press.

Zartman, W.I. (1995). *Elusive Peace: Negotiation an End to Civil Wars*. Washington, DC: The Brookings Institution.

Zartman, W.I. (2001). Preventive Diplomacy: Setting the Stage. In: Zartman, W.I. (ed.) *Preventive Negotiation: Avoiding Conflict Escalation*. Lanham, Maryland: Rowman & Littlefield Publishers.

Zartman, W.I. (2003). The Timing of Peace Initiatives: Hurting Stalemates and Ripe Moments. In: Darby, J. and Ginty, R. (eds). *Contemporary Peacemaking: Conflict, Peace Processes and Post-war Reconstruction*. New York: Palgrave Macmillan.

Zeitoun, M. (2008). *Power and Water in the Middle East: The Hidden Politics of the Palestinian-Israeli Water Conflict*. London: I.B. Tauris & Co Ltd.

Zeitoun, M. (2013). The Web of Sustainable Water Security. In Lankford, B., Bakker, K., Zeitoun, M. and Conway, D. (Eds). *Water Security: Principles, Perspectives, and Practices*. London: Earthscan.

PART III

Migration, political economy, democratization, identity and gender issues and security in the Middle East

17

LARGE-SCALE POPULATION MIGRATION AND INSECURITY IN THE MIDDLE EAST

Ashok Swain and Jonathan Hall

Population migration and the Middle East

The Middle East region has an interstate migratory history dating back to the collapse of the Ottoman Empire. However, voluntary migration at a major scale began in the 1970s only to the oil rich countries. After independence, suffering from a small and untrained local population but having some of the largest endowments of oil and gas, the Gulf countries depended upon their fellow Arab countries in the region for foreign workers. In 1971, Egypt even openly encouraged its nationals to migrate and linked the policy with the country's economic development (Baldwin-Edwards, 2005). Since the 1980s, though, the major labor source for the oil producing Gulf countries has switched to South Asia; still, the labor migration number from the Arab countries is high due to geographical proximity and cultural, religious and linguistic closeness.

The Middle East has also witnessed large-scale labor migration outside the region. Many migrants, particularly from the non-Gulf states, have also migrated permanently to other parts of the world, particularly from Lebanon. To compensate at home, Lebanon also attracts labor migrants from other neighboring countries. However, most of the countries in the region are primarily remittance receiving countries. Remittances represent an important source of income for many countries, particularly for Egypt, Lebanon and Jordan. In the case of Lebanon, remittances have helped to improve its creditworthiness and facilitate access to international capital markets. Thus, the economy of the region is very much connected to the vagaries of the global economy.

The region not only has voluntary migrants, it is also a source or host of a large number of forced migrants, refugees and internally displaced persons. Since 1948, the region has been hosting a large number of Palestinian refugees numbering more than 5 million in 2018. Besides the Palestinian conflict, the other long-standing issue affecting the Middle East region is the Kurdish issue. The Kurds, like the Palestinians, are a nation without a state. Besides Iraq and Syria, the other two neighboring regional powers, Turkey and Iran have substantial Kurdish minorities. The long-standing separatist struggle of the Kurds has also contributed to large-scale population displacement in the region. However, the number of refugees in the region has jumped significantly in recent years due to ongoing violent conflict in Iraq and Syria.

253

Middle East, labor migration and remittances

Nearly 13% of the total global remittances (inward and outward) comes from the Middle East. Saudi Arabia is second and UAE is sixth among the top ten remittance-sending countries in the world. A large share of remittance sent from these two countries also goes to other countries in the region. Around 70% of the total remittance sent and received in the Middle East is from Saudi Arabia and UAE. The Middle East is third largest hub of migration in the world and its oil rich Gulf countries have been hosting more than 15 million foreign workers. The six member states of the Gulf Cooperation Council (GCC), Bahrain, Kuwait, Oman, Qatar, Saudi Arabia and the UAE, pay out more than USD 100 billion in worker remittances to migrant workers living within their borders.

With increased oil production in the 1970s, demand increased for skilled and unskilled labor in the Gulf states. Once the oil producing countries in the region started raising oil prices, oil importing states began sending migrant workers there. Currently, Saudi Arabia is the largest recipient of migrant workers, with the UAE close behind with over two-thirds of its population classified as migrant workers. Remittance transfers from permanent migrants usually diminish over a period of time, as linkages between migrants and their country of origin weaken over time. The second-generation migrants might culturally and emotionally remain connected with their parental homeland, but they more or less distance themselves from any economic activities and obligations. The policies of the Gulf countries give priority in providing short-term work permits to the young migrant workforce and debar them from settling permanently. So, most of the foreign workforce in Gulf countries are temporary migrants and that encourages them to continue in sending most of their savings as remittances.

Remittances are extremely important for the economic development of the non-oil exporting countries of the Middle East region. More than 2.7 million Egyptian migrants are working abroad and approximately 70% of them are living in Arab countries. For a country like Egypt, remittances are three times more than the foreign exchange revenues from the Suez Canal or incomes from tourism or even the direct foreign investment in the country. Remittances represent the largest sources of foreign exchange after exports, and a critical source of household income in Egypt. According to the World Bank, in 2014 Egypt was the biggest recipient of remittances in the region, an estimated USD 19.6 billion, representing approximately 6.6% of national GDP. However, the remittance share used to be 10% of the country's GDP in 2008, before the advent of the global financial crisis and the "Arab Spring". The absence of favorable investment opportunities, high interest rates, and highly cumbersome exchange transactions also act as disincentives for migrant Egyptian workers to send home the remittances.

Besides Egypt, the economies of Lebanon, Jordan and Yemen are very much dependent on their received remittances. Jordan received USD 3.757 billion in remittances from its citizens working overseas in 2014. This figure represents only officially recorded remittances and it does not include remittances in kind and unrecorded remittances. Jordan is a small country with a very limited resource base. Remittances are the biggest source of foreign exchange for this oil importing country and a major pillar of the economic frame. Most of the remittance sending Jordanians are living in Gulf oil producing countries (Bel-Air, 2010). However, remittances are a double-edged sword for Jordan. No doubt, they make a very significant contribution to the country's income, but at the same time the outside money has brought high-inflation in the country, particularly in the real estate, and there is a serious domestic shortage of certain skills. Moreover, the country's economic health is highly dependent on the Arab economies.

In receiving remittances, Lebanon is second in the Middle East behind Egypt. Remittances constitute a major pillar of the Lebanese economy and play a critical role in poverty alleviation in this politically volatile country. However, Lebanon's over-dependence on foreign financial inflows tend to contribute to the increase in consumption, which has not led to productive industries and innovative activities needed for sustained, broad-based growth (Laureti and Postiglione, 2005). Moreover, Lebanon not only receives remittances, it has also been a source of remittances for some neighboring countries, particularly for Syria. There are nearly 300,000 Syrian workers in Lebanon (Seeberg and Eyadat, 2013).

Due to political unrest, civil wars and falling crude oil price, remittances to many countries in the region have declined since 2008. The future projection is not very promising, though the inflow of remittances is comparably much more reliable than other external resources available to the region. Saudi Arabia, the major provider of remittances to countries in the Middle East is gradually enforcing restrictive labor laws as the oil rich kingdom is seeking to increase the numbers of Saudi nationals working in the private sector through nationalization policies, the "Nitaqat" program. This has affected most of the remittance receiving countries in the region, particularly Egypt and Yemen. The ongoing crisis in Syria is highly problematic in terms of access to payment systems and remittances. Most of the remittances that used to be sent in to the country are now needed to be sent to Syrian refugees in their host countries. Moreover, the procedure of sending remittances to Syria has become exceedingly difficult as Syrian banks no longer allow transfers from some Gulf states.

With the oil boom of the 1970s, most of the Gulf countries, including Saudi Arabia, imported cheap labor from Asia, Africa and also from the neighboring countries in the Middle East. Saudi Arabia has continued to accept millions of these foreign workers, with most in lower-income jobs. In recent years, the practice has created serious problems for the country's economy. As the kingdom grappled with declining oil revenue, high unemployment among its nationals, and the lingering threat of domestic unrest, Saudi authorities started to streamline the process of recruiting foreign workers, through the "Nitaqat" policy, which aims at "Saudising" the workforce.

Since the 1970s the UAE has become a popular destination for temporary labor migrants, both low- and high-skilled, particularly from Asia and the Middle East. The country now hosts the fifth-largest international migrant stock in the world. To meet its labor demand, in 1971 UAE introduced the Kafala Sponsorship System, which allows nationals, expatriates and companies to hire migrant workers. This guest workers program has posed some challenges for the UAE authorities. There is a growing resentment within the country over the lack of job opportunities for UAE nationals.

In order to prevent social unrest at home the rich oil producing countries in the Middle East are imposing restrictions on receiving new migrant workers and are even deporting them; whether the policy will be successful or not, it could possibly create economic hardship and political uncertainties in the migrant-sending countries in the region. Remittances from the Gulf countries not only provide a major source of foreign direct investment to the fragile economies of Egypt, Jordan, Lebanon and Yemen but also supply aid and relief via family-to-family transfer in times of hardship. The large financial transfers play a significant role in preventing conflict in these vulnerable societies and also contribute to post-conflict reconstruction and economic recovery. The adverse impacts of restrictive migrant receiving policies in the oil rich Gulf states have started to be felt in the rest of the countries in the Middle East.

The Middle East: The region of and for refugees

International interventions and civil wars have created a serious refugee crisis in the region. The massive number of people being forced out of their homes in the region has created an unprecedented humanitarian crisis and has become a serious international concern. Most of the displaced people have remained inside the region and the host states for these "conflict migrants" are not the oil rich Gulf countries, but primarily their poorer neighbors, who are politically mostly not on the right side of the international powers. The refugee crisis is not new to the region as it has experience two large waves of forced migration in the 20th century and two more in the short time period of this century. The two long-term refugee crises involve Kurdish and Palestinians displacement and the new ones originate from Iraq and Syria.

After the fall of the Ottoman Empire, post-World War I treaties created Middle Eastern countries Syria and Iraq, but refused to create a Kurdish state. Even the Treaty of Lausanne, which recognized the formation of the Turkish Republic, did not keep any provision for allowing Kurdish autonomy. Turkey, Syria, Iraq and Iran joined hands to restrict Kurdish aspirations for a separate state that led the Kurds to rebel way back in the 1920s. In recent decades, violent actions by the Kurdistan Workers Party (PKK) in Turkey have led to the loss of over 30,000 lives and massive permanent and periodic forced migration. In the late 1980s, Saddam Hussein's Anfal Campaign against Kurds in Iran reportedly led to 100,000 deaths and forced displacement of 1.5 million people of which many fled to Turkey. However, when a major outflow of Kurds from northern Iraq took place in the Gulf War in 1991 fleeing after their rebellion was crushed by Iraqi troops, Turkey refused to admit them, so US-led coalition forces created a "safe haven" for them inside Iraqi territory in the north. However, only after the Second Gulf War in 2003, have the Kurds in Iraq received some autonomy. In Syria and Iraq, there have been several attempts to crush Kurdish ethnicity as well. Overall, the political conditions for the Kurdish minority had improved in Turkey and Iraq after the end of the Second Gulf War until the Arab Spring.

However, the recent ISIS crisis has exposed the Kurds in these two countries to greater uncertainties while a large number of Kurdish refugees are still living in various countries within and outside of the Middle East. The ongoing civil war in Syria has increased conflict among Kurdish groups within Turkey. As a by-product of the civil war, the autonomy given to Syria's Kurdish majority areas has provided some opportunity for Kurds in the region to come closer politically and militarily in their fight for separate statehood. Though it has fueled the rise of Kurdish nationalism across the northern Middle East, however, Kurds in Syria do not possess enough political or military muscle to determine the outcome of the conflict or their own future trajectory. The domestic politics within Syria, Iraq, Turkey and Iran and regional geopolitics will be crucial factor deciding future Kurdish aspirations. Thus, it is very hard to foresee the early resolution of this nearly 100-year-old separatist insurgency and the end of the hardship of the large Kurdish displaced population.

The other long-term refugee crisis, which is affecting this region and the rest of the world, is the case of Palestinian refugees. The refugee issue has been one of the most difficult and complex issues in Israeli–Arab relations (Tovy, 2003). Israelis and Palestinians do not even agree on the reasons for displacement in 1948. While Palestinians say that they were expelled by Israeli forces, Israelis argue that Palestinians fled as Arab commanders encouraged them to do so in a war that was foisted upon a newly born Israel by Arab neighbors. Similarly, Israel also blames the Arab host states for their failure to resettle the refugees while Palestinians blame the international community for failing to make Israel agree to refugee return. Moreover, both the parties even fail to agree on whom to consider a refugee: while Israel argues for the narrow definition covering only first generation refugees displaced by the 1948 and 1967 wars, Palestinians ask for a broad and inclusive definition covering family members (Remple, 2006).

The majority of displaced Palestinians are located in Jordan, hosting around 2.2 million refugees within its borders in ten refugee camps. Jordan sees the Palestinians as a "demographic

Population migration and insecurity

threat" and is regularly striving for a solution to this problem. Palestinian refugees face the discriminatory policies of the host state, particularly getting employment in government sectors and also play a very marginal role in the country's politics, but at the same time they constitute the major backbone of Jordan's economy. The perceived mistreatment of Palestinians inside Jordan is a ticking bomb waiting to explode (Zahran, 2012). The situation is quite similar for Palestinian refugees in neighboring Lebanon.

There are more than 450,000 Palestinian refugees living in Lebanon. The Lebanese Government brackets all the Palestinians arriving after 1948 as illegal residents and has prohibited them from entering the job market or even owning and inheriting properties. Palestinian refugees in Lebanon are thoroughly discriminated against and Lebanon has placed several legal restrictions, denying them political, social and civil rights. However, the situation of Palestinian refugees in Syria was relatively much better before the country plunged into the ongoing civil war, compared with their counterparts in Jordan and Lebanon. Syria had housed approximately 590,000 Palestinian refugees. Though they were not given citizenship and voting rights, they had the rights to employment, commerce and national service, and also access to a special travel document. However, the ongoing conflict has created an extremely difficult situation for Palestinians living in refugee camps in Syria.

Quite similar to the present situation in Syria, Palestinian refugees in Iraq had also suffered harsh treatment and dual displacement in the post-Saddam period (Goldenziel, 2010). Approximately 15,000 Palestinian refugees were living in Iraq. These Sunni refugees were receiving subsidies and other privileges under Saddam Hussein's regime. However, after the US invasion of 2003, the Palestinian refugees were subjected to anti-Sunni backlash, as Shias suspected them of supporting Sunni insurgency. Palestinians repeatedly received death threats and were attacked by insurgents. When these Palestinians wanted to move to Jordan or Syria, they were not allowed on legal grounds and were kept in the refugee camps at the border. The lingering predicament of Palestinian refugees, wherever they are in the region, seems to be continuing even after being displaced for seven decades.

Besides the long-running refugee situation concerning Kurdish and Palestinian displacements, the region has also been exposed to new waves of refugees. In the last decade, the major refugee crisis started with displaced Iraqis after the US launched its attack against Iraq in 2003. In the immediate aftermath of the fall of the Saddam regime, there were some Saddam loyalists who left the country, but the number was not that dramatic. However, the civil war in the country, which took a serious turn after the attack on Samarra Shrine in 2006, produced a serious humanitarian crisis by displacing large numbers of people. Many left the country and also a very substantial number of displaced persons moved to "safe" areas within Iraq.

Iraqi refugees prioritized countries to go to along sectarian lines. The large majority of Iraqi refugees in Jordan were Sunni, while Shiite Iraqis went to Jordan and Lebanon. In spite of this, by 2008, the host countries of Iraqi refugees in the region became extremely restrictive in accepting any more migration and wanted Iraqis to return as soon as possible to avoid political instability. Even the Iraqi Government wanted the neighboring countries to close their border in order to assert its control in the border areas. Growing poverty and lack of possibility to find work in the host countries also led many refugees to think of going back to their own country. There was also some improvement in the security situation in Iraq, which facilitated the process of refugees to return.

However, the return of refugees to Iraq has not been smooth. Although highly stressed host country capacities and the incentives offered by the Iraqi Government and the international community expedited the process of refugee returns, that also led to further tensions at the place of their resettlement. The formal end of conflict did not take away all of its manifestations and left behind intentionally created ethnically and religiously homogeneous societies. Sectarian control of neighborhoods due to civil war made it very unsafe for many returnees and they became internally displaced again. The situation became more volatile after the escalation of armed conflict in the central parts of Iraq after the rise of ISIS. This led to new displacements across central Iraq and also in northern Kurdistan region.

Syria has been the source of the latest refugee crisis in the region which has triggered the largest humanitarian challenge since World War II. The same Syria, which used to host the second largest refugee population in 2008 (after Pakistan), has turned out to be the largest refugee producer since 2012. A large number of Syrians have gone into Turkey, which has become the main destination country for refugees in the world. The humanitarian burden of the Syrian crisis was taken up mainly by Syria's neighbors, with Jordan, Lebanon and Turkey currently providing shelter to most of the displaced Syrians. The region has hosted millions of Palestinian and Iraqi refugees for some years and, with the vast majority of the fresh refugee flow out of Syria, is stretched to the limits of their economic and social resources (Berti, 2015).

Before the Syrian refugee crisis, for many decades, the world had not witnessed such a large refugee population originating from a single conflict. Neighboring countries hosting Syrian refugees have almost reached their saturation points, particularly Lebanon, Jordan and Turkey. With the growing influx of refugees, local communities are under growing pressure in terms of livelihood resources, such as food, water, education, health services and employment. The impact of these refugees challenges the already precarious stability of the host country in general and host communities in particular. Though the focus of the international community is on the displaced Syrian population reaching European borders, the plight of the more than 7.6 million internally displaced people does not receive much attention. In the Syrian civil war, the gross human rights violations by all the groups in the conflict are the foundational driver of this huge internal displacement.

The other ongoing violent conflict in the region, which has recently displaced a large number of people, is the civil war in Yemen. The total number of internally displaced people in Yemen is 1,439,100 (IDMC, 2015). Yemenis are being displaced as the result of growing socio-economic and humanitarian crisis in the country. However there are several conflicts in the country: the Shia al-Houthi movements in the north causing violent insurgency, the civil unrest in the central and southern parts of the country and the clashes between government forces and militants associated with the Southern Separatist Movement and Ansar al-Sharia, which is an offshoot of al-Qaeda in the Arabian Peninsula (IDMC, 2014). The increasing intervention of external forces, particularly Saudi Arabia, has made the conflict in Yemen increasingly difficult and people are being forced to flee more than once, which has been causing complex displacement patterns. According to an IDMC estimation, approximately 96% of the internally displaced people in Yemen are staying in urban settings and are not seeking shelter in relief camps due to cultural perceptions of the environment to be promiscuous (IDMC, 2015).

Besides the large number of refugees, the region has also produced internally displaced people (IDP) on a massive scale. The IDPs, though, have been displaced by the same causes as the refugees, but have stayed inside their home countries, under the protection of a regime that is mostly responsible for their plight and considers them as the enemy. Those who are unable to leave the country of the war zones of the Middle East due to fragmentation of society along sectarian lines and security threats, try to find safety and refuge in a very threatening environment. In most cases, the conditions of the IDPs can be worse than refugees as they are also generally ignored by the international community. The international community lacks any legal obligation to protect IDPs, help them to return home, or find them somewhere new to live. The absence of democratic governments, lack of free press and abundance of sectarian hatred make the situation of IDPs in the Middle East much more dangerous.

Migration contributing to further insecurity in the region

Large-scale forced migration has many facets for inducing conflict between host and home states in the region (Swain, 1996). In some cases, after settling in the host country, refugees indulge in anti-regime activities against their home government. Such activities by Iraqis after settling in Syria or in Iran have become a major source of tension in the region, creating more implications for regional security. Kurdish militants' frequent use of the host state's territory against homeland regimes is a very common security problematic in the region as well. There is no doubt that large population displacements because of the Israel–Palestinian conflict, Iraq War and Syrian Civil War have also posed structural threats to many refugee-receiving countries in the region. Competition with the local population over resources has become a serious law and order concern. In some cases, particularly in Jordan and Lebanon, the refugees have become serious threats to the host regimes. The region is increasingly worried about the threats posed by large-scale Syrian migration.

In today's globalized world, an increased mobility of people fueled by better transportation and communications systems has contributed to the erosion of state boundaries and promoted globalized migrant communities, who have become active and potentially crucial links between their countries of origin and the migrant receiving countries. As such, studies on the role of migrant communities in either contribution to development and peace or conflict escalation have been catapulted to the forefront. The complex nature of migrants is such that in some cases they promote peace while in others support conflicts, depending on the various opportunity costs (Hall and Swain, 2007). Migrant communities' involvement in homeland politics is not a new phenomenon. As a consequence of globalization, migrants have built vast transnational networks, with a potential to contribute to peace, reconciliation and development. In recent decades, remittances received from migrants have become an invaluable form of economic support for the homeland.

The Middle East region has been witnessing huge refugee movement at least since the Palestinian crisis of 1948. The ramifications of that exodus still continue and have even become more complex with violent conflicts in Iraq, Syria and Yemen. At present, the Syrian conflict and its spillover into Iraq have posed a serious challenge to the refugee situation in the region. Many of the poorer countries in the Middle East have been both home of and host to large numbers of displacedpersons. Oil rich countries in the region have actively worked to restrict their passage. Though these countries are still striving to recruit foreign workers, they are very reluctant to accept refugee populations. International legal obligations as well as sectarian divisions are the primary reasons for this policy. In neighboring Europe, developed countries are also trying to restrict refugees from getting to or staying within their borders.

Not only difficult economic conditions but also political instability in the Middle East have displaced a large population and forced them to move within and outside the region since the end of World War I. These migrant communities can potentially contribute to peace and development in their home countries by influencing the conflicting parties to engage in negotiations, targeting remittances and providing human capital at the time of negotiations and post-conflict reconstruction. Through lobbying foreign governments and international organizations and aiding processes of transition, these migrant groups may play an important role in achieving political compromise and nonviolent conflict resolution in their homelands. Unfortunately, the peacemaking and peacebuilding aptitudes of the migrants are rarely seen in the Middle East.

In addition to providing financial support and sending remittances recruitment as fighters to fight the struggle in the homeland is a regular phenomenon within the migrant groups originating from Middle Eastern countries (Swain, 2012). Many migrant communities have provided weapons, training or even personnel. The Kurdish groups based in Europe substantially contribute to conflicts in their homeland by providing financial and military support, as well as fighters to rebel groups. Middle Eastern migrant groups based in Europe and North America have played major roles in fomenting and supporting conflict in Israel, Palestine, Turkey, Iraq and Syria. The conflict in the homeland is often the yardstick of migrant groups' identity and therefore they have a tendency to keep homeland conflicts even more protracted (Lyons, 2004). In most of the conflict situations in the Middle East, migrants are seen as part of the problem not as part of the solution (Swain and Jägerskog, 2016).

References

Baldwin-Edwards, Martin, 2005. "Migration in the Middle East and Mediterranean", A paper prepared for the *Policy Analysis and Research Program of the Global Commission on International Migration*, September.

Bel-Air, Françoise De, 2010. *Highly-skilled Migration from Jordan: A Response to Socio-political Challenges*, European University Institute Robert Schuman Centre for Advanced Studies, CARIM-AS 2010 vol. 12.

Berti, Benedetta, 2015. "The Syrian Refugee Crisis: Regional and Human Security Implications", *Strategic Assessment*, vol. 17, no. 4, January, pp. 41–53.

Goldenziel, Jill, 2010. "Refugees and International Security", in Ellen Laipson and Amit Pandya, eds. *On the Move: Migration Challenges in the Indian Ocean Littoral*. Washington DC: The Henry L. Stimson Center, pp. 29–42.

Hall, Jonathan and Swain, Ashok, 2007. "Catapulting Conflicts or Propelling Peace: Diasporas and Civil War", in Ashok Swain, Ramses Amer and Joakim Öjendal, eds., *Globalization and Challenges to Building Peace*. London, New York & Delhi: Anthem Press.

IDMC, 2014. *Yemen: Resolving Displacement Essential for Long-term Peace and Stability*. Available at: https://reliefweb.int/sites/reliefweb.int/files/resources/201409-me-yemen-overview-en.pdf

IDMC, 2015. *Global Overview 2015: People Internally Displaced by Conflict and Violence*. Available at: www.internal-displacement.org/publications/global-overview-2015-people-internally-displaced-by-conflict-and-violence

Laureti, Lucio and Postiglione, Paolo, 2005. "The Effects of Capital Inflows on the Economic Growth in the Med Area", *Journal of Policy Modeling*, vol. 27, no. 7, pp. 839–851.

Lyons, Terrence, 2004. *Engaging Diasporas to Promote Conflict Resolution: Transforming Hawks into Doves*, Working Paper Presented at the Institute for Global Conflict and Cooperation Washington Policy Seminar, May.

Remple, Terry M., 2006. "Who are Palestinian Refugees", *Forced Migration Review*, no. 26, August, pp. 5–7.

Seeberg, Peter and Eyadat, Zaid, eds., 2013. *Migration, Security, and Citizenship in the Middle East: New Perspectives*. New York: Palgrave Macmillan.

Swain, Ashok, 1996. "Environmental Migration and Conflict Dynamics: Focus on Developing Regions", *Third World Quarterly,* vol. 17, no. 5, pp. 959–973.

Swain, Ashok, 2012. *Understanding Emerging Security Threats: Challenges and Opportunities*. London: Routledge.

Swain, Ashok and Jägerskog, Anders, 2016. *Emerging Security Threats in the Middle East: The Impact of Climate Change and Globalization*, Lanham: Rowman & Littlefield.

Tovy, Jacob, 2003. "Negotiating the Palestinian Refugees", *The Middle East Quarterly*, vol. 10, no. 2. Spring, pp. 39–50.

Zahran, Mudar, 2012. "Jordan is Palestinian", *The Middle East Quarterly*, vol. 19, no. 1, Winter, pp. 3–12.

18

SECURITY AND POLITICAL ECONOMY IN THE MIDDLE EAST

Raymond Hinnebusch

Introduction

This chapter examines how political economy issues affect the security of the Middle East and North Africa (MENA) area. Security issues are seen to be shaped by the interaction of the two main features of MENA political economy, namely, its position in the periphery of the global division of labor and the regional concentration of "global" hydrocarbons. State sovereignty is routinely securitized in the region, and economic independence has been widely seen as the deep foundation of sovereignty; the essay will first examine the region's resistance to its relegation to the global periphery through defensive modernization – a "securitization of sovereignty" – from the Ottomans to the Nasserist project and OPEC. The concentration of hydrocarbons in the region that makes it a focus of "energy security" of oil importers also has direct consequences for MENA security. The chapter will look at the consequences of hydrocarbons for regime security (defined as stability); for state security (defined as sufficient strength to ward off external threats and maintain territorial integrity); and for regional security (freedom from war and intervention).

Imperialism and resistance: Economic dependency as a security issue

Economic backwardness and dependency in the Middle East and North Africa (MENA) has been framed as a national security issue justifying extraordinary means – including attempted "revolution from above" in authoritarian nationalist regimes such as Ataturk's Turkey and Nasser's Egypt and widely imitated in other Arab republics. The perception was widespread in the region that political independence and military power were impossible without economic independence and that conversely dependence was the master mechanism by which the global great powers subordinated the region. However, each effort to overcome underdevelopment and dependency has failed or even exacerbated the problem.

The roots of regional underdevelopment, in the "structuralist" narrative widely accepted in the region, was the West's "peripheralization" of the Middle East economy, incorporating it into a global division of labor in which its role was mainly that of primary product (agricultural/mineral raw materials) exporter, dependent on the core for imports of technology and manufactured goods. This translated into underdevelopment: raw material terms of trade were poor or took a boom-bust character leading to debt and deepened dependency while human skills and value-added remained low. The consequent economic underdevelopment translated into military weakness.

Defensive modernization

Underdevelopment and dependency stimulated repeated attempts at "defensive modernization" – crash reforms meant to strengthen the region sufficiently to stand up to external threats. In the Ottoman case, the military decline of the empire, the increasing encroachment of Russia and the West on Ottoman territory, separatism in the Balkans and loss of control over the empire's Arab peripheries was preceded and accompanied by Western economic penetration that undermined the economic base of the empire. The West forced the empire to relinquish the state trade monopolies through which it had tried to ensure local processing of raw materials, while low tariffs frozen by Western-dictated commercial treaties offered no protection to local industry from the flood of Western manufactured imports. An agrarian commercial bourgeoisie came to dominate the economy which, enriched on the export of agricultural products to the West and, dominated by non-Muslim minorities exempted from local law and taxation by Western protection, had no interest in investment in local industry. The resulting combination of de-industrialization and the retardation of a national capitalist class forced the empire into the periphery of the emerging world capitalist system (Issawi, 1982: 138–155; Bromley, 1994: 46–85; Owen, 1981; Halliday, 2005: 261–324; Adelson, 1995).

These ills inspired the rise of reforming Sultans and Viziers who believed that to defend itself effectively the empire had to modernize – become like the West in order to be able to fight the West. Military modernization was the immediate priority but this required much broader bureaucratic modernization (to collect taxes and re-establish internal order); educational modernization (to staff the new army and state structures); Western style legal norms such as equality before the law and protection of private property to assure investors and get the growth that could support the modernizing state.

So what went wrong? The reforms did lead to the growth of a modern Westernized middle class (officers, bureaucrats, teachers). However, the costs of supporting the new state exceeded its ability to generate economic growth and tax extraction capacity. As a result, the reformers borrowed from European bankers: the resulting debt ended in the export of capital (repayment at exorbitant interest rates) and when repayment stopped, the European powers used gunboat diplomacy to grab control of state finances in both Egypt and the Ottoman domains, siphoning off local surplus to pay European bond holders (Brown, 1984: 21–81; Bromley, 1994: 53–55; Keyder, 1987: 25–69).

The post-World War I dismemberment of the Ottoman Empire and fragmentation of the region by an externally imposed states system under Western colonial tutelage deepened economic dependency. Colonial governments, viewing the Middle East as a source of raw materials and markets, discouraged industrial development and prioritized agricultural modernization that would turn regional states into plantations for export of raw materials to Western industries. The breakup of the big Ottoman market ended most inter-regional trade and investment, which was re-oriented from local states to the Western core. In the Gulf, the British established oil protectorates under tribal elites in city-states whose growing excess capital would be exported to Western banks, not invested regionally (Bromley, 1994: 62–85; Ayubi, 1995: 99–133; Owen, 1981: 8–23).

Along with economic dependence went corresponding security dependence. Western imposed arbitrary borders fostered border disputes and irredentism that made MENA states

Security and political economy

fear their neighbors. Israel's exceptional support by the West made it the dominant military power threatening to its neighbors. At the same time, no regional great power that could act as hegemon and enforce regional security independent of the Western powers was allowed to emerge, with each successive contender cut down by Western intervention or Israel (Lustik, 1997) – from Muhammad Ali to Nasser to Saddam Hussein. Regional insecurity translated into the security dependence of local states on the core great powers institutionalized through treaties and bases. Typical before World War II, most treaties lapsed in the age of Nasserism, only to return after the 1990 Gulf war, as a new wave of Western security treaties made the Arab Gulf states virtual Western protectorates. In parallel, high levels of regional insecurity also made arms access critical to states' security but dependency on external suppliers allowed the latter to use arms as instruments of influence in the region.

As such and despite formal political independence starting after World War II, the Middle East has remained more intensely penetrated by core powers than any other developing world region. Since this penetration generated popular resistance, the global hegemons (the UK, then the US) had to implant or co-opt local ruling client elites which they provided with resources to sustain themselves against rivals in return for defending the penetrated system (Brown, 1984). Dependent for their military and economic security on Western powers and enjoying only "semi-sovereignty", they bandwagoned with rather than balanced against Western domination.

The outcome in the Middle East closely resembled Galtung's (1971) "Structural Theory of Imperialism": a feudal-like hierarchy in which core states dominated the periphery by co-opting client elites/classes that shared greater interests with the core than their own populations; and owing to the debilitation of horizontal relations among regional states by imposed borders and their dependence on the core, which was thereby empowered to divide and rule the region.

The developmental logic of Nasserism: The economic bases of sovereignty

Imperialism provoked a nationalist response across the region that aimed to break out of the dependency system, with Egypt leading the way in the Arab world. Muhammad Ali had made an early abortive attempt at this: his main success, agricultural modernization (irrigated cotton cultivation) was meant to finance or supply local industrialization, needed, in turn to support the army and defend the county's security. However, Western inflicted military defeat (1841) forced him to cut his army, abolish state industries and open the Egyptian market to Western manufactures, thereby establishing Egypt's economic role as a purely agricultural exporter. This was reinforced under his successors who got Egypt deeply in debt, creating a crisis that ended in British occupation.

Egypt under Nasser made a second serious effort to create a national economy capable of sustaining political independence. This responded to Egypt's stalled development: stuck as primary product exporter (cotton) it was suffering from falling world agricultural terms of trade while the limits of agricultural modernization had been reached. Its land scarce, labor surplus economy suffered from rapid population growth, leading to land fragmentation, rural unemployment and a 50% decline in per capita income from 1900 to 1950. The only solution was seen as industrialization but the landed oligarchy that dominated agriculture and the foreigners that dominated trade invested little in industry. The perception grew that, in the absence of a nationalist capitalist class, the state had to take the lead in development (Berque, 1972).

In his first decade (1952–62), Nasser pursued a mixed economy, reflecting a search for a "middle way" between capitalism and communism. The three pillars of regime strategy were: land reform and co-operatization of agriculture (the latter to deliver inputs and allow economies of scale in use of equipment); a big investment push by the state in infrastructure, iron and steel factories; and the Aswan High Dam which would complete Egypt's hydraulic agriculture, spreading irrigation, flood control, and making vast new power resources available for industrialization. The private sector was considered a partner in light/medium industry and agriculture and foreign investment was welcomed (Mabro, 1974 140–343; Abdul Malek, 1968: 97–175).

However, a major national security crisis propelled a deepened turn to statism. Egypt's refusal of Western terms (seen to compromise sovereignty) to finance the High Dam and Nasser's attempt to fill the finance gap by nationalizing the Suez Canal provoked the 1956 Suez war – a "tripartite" invasion by Britain, France and Israel. In the aftermath, the confiscation of European assets in Egypt, a continuing failure of private investment in industry, and a perception that the Soviet Union would fill the funding gap without compromising national independence, stimulated a sharp lurch to the "Left". Under the banner of "Arab socialism" the heights of the economy were nationalized: banking, foreign trade, large and medium industry, even internal wholesale trade (Hinnebusch, 1985: 24–26).

The Nasserist project aimed to lay the foundations of a national economy. Investment in infrastructure – railroads, ports, electrification – stimulated industrial growth of 5.7%/year; increasing its share of GNP from 15 to 23%, diversifying from light to heavy industry and doubling the size of the industrial working class. Agricultural productivity was restored, with output growth 3%/year. GNP growth was restored to 4%/year, arresting the fall in GNP/capita since 1900. Skilled employment rose from 12% to 20% and educational expansion drove illiteracy down from 75 to 65% (Mabro, 1974: 56–106; Radwan 1977: 16–23, 56–106).

A wave of populist laws addressed the country's huge inequalities and won mass support for the regime. Land reform and nationalizations broke the socio-economic dominance of the oligarchy. The middle class was widened as opportunities for upward mobility opened up through free university education and state employment for graduates, hence careers in the military, bureaucracy and public sector. The lower classes were lifted up through rent and price controls, worker profit sharing in industry, and subsidization of basic foodstuffs: worker wages rose 43% while land reform reduced landless peasants from 60% to 40% of the total, which, plus tenancy laws, doubled the share of peasants in agricultural income. Thus, greater equality provide the needed basis of national citizenship (Issawi, 1982: 100; Mabro, 1974: 71–74; Radwan, 1977: 16–23).

Statist development had however been exhausted by 1970. Limits to capital accumulation through the public sector had been reached: use of public sector industry for populist policies, such as maximizing employment and keeping commodity prices affordable for the low income majority, plus flawed investment planning and inefficient management, as well as the siphoning off of profits for military spending or lost through corruption – all meant that there was no increase in domestic savings to cover the investment drive. The imbalances of import substitute industrialization (ISI) – imported machinery, parts, etc. for industry, but products sold domestically, not for export – resulted in endemic balance of payments deficits. The elite's political exhaustion after the 1967 defeat by Israel, public demoralization and loss of ideological faith in Nasserism debilitated the regime. As resources were transferred from development to war preparation (1967–70), economic stagnation set in. Nasser's successor, Sadat (1970–81), saw the solution to Egypt's problems in turning Nasserism upside down: realignment with the West and reopening (*infitah*) to the world capitalist market in order to attract US aid and investment, but most immediately to secure US diplomatic help in getting Israeli withdrawal from the Israeli-occupied Sinai. Again, economic policy was driven chiefly by security needs.

The Nasser to Sadat experience sharply exposed how far national security – defined as real sovereignty – requires a national economic base. Nasser's state-led industrialization reduced dependence on the Western core while diversifying markets and capital sources to the Eastern

Bloc enabled him to pursue an independent foreign policy. But once this project was exhausted and Egypt became dependent on American aid and Western investment, Egyptian foreign policy did a somersault: from being the main state resisting Western influence in MENA, it became, under Sadat, the bridge by which Western influence came back into the region (Hinnebusch, 1985).

Oil and regional security

The politics of OPEC

The Organization of the Petroleum Exporting Countries (OPEC) can be seen as a second attempt, following the failure of Nasserism, to reduce regional dependency on the West. At the time of the 1970s oil boom it was thought oil might become the basis of what was called Arab national security. Oil could replace dependence with inter-dependence vis-à-vis the core, provide collective Arab power that would force the US/West to attend to Arab interests in the Arab–Israeli conflict, and drive the regional economic integration needed to underpin a regional security order. Yet, oil proved more of a curse than a blessing as it ended up actually deepening dependence and invited devastating oil wars. Understanding why it turned out to be a curse exposes the hidden links between political economy and security.

Oil politics is intimately linked to security. Oil gives potential power to whoever controls it because it is a strategic commodity no state can do without, being vital to military power and energy intensive capitalism, especially in the US. Moreover, the industry has a natural tendency to oligopoly that can be used to access super-resources: because prices swing widely from lows below USD 10/barrel to heights of over USD 100, stable high prices depend on cartelization; moreover, the difference in the cost of production between high cost producers (US, Russia – up to USD 10/barrel) and low cost producers (USD 2/barrel in the Gulf) potentially enables the latter to capture the difference as rent, especially if a cartel can enforce limitations on supply. Because, with the formation of OPEC, Middle East oil producers controlled such a large proportion of "world" oil resources (78% of proven reserves and 41% of output in the 1990s), OPEC can control world oil supply in the interests of regional political economy, *if its members cooperate.*

Pre-OPEC, the "Seven Sisters" of mostly US/UK oil companies monopolized oil production and set up a cartel to stop price wars and to capture much of the economic rent at the expense of the producer states, with prices held quite low for decades. OPEC was founded in the 1960s to get some counter-leverage over the companies; but only in the 1970s was this realized when increasing demand for oil shifted market conditions in favor of the producer states. But a security crisis precipitated matters: the 1973 Arab–Israeli war led to an oil embargo on the sale of oil to the US by the Arab oil producers, leading to a supply drop of 15%, which quadrupled prices overnight (from USD 10 to 40/barrel). Even when the embargo ended, prices did not return to the old level since OPEC had the solidarity to keep them up and the oil market was still tight. Then, the 1979–80 Iranian Revolution and Iran–Iraq war reduced supply, creating another price boom (USD 76 in 1980). Because of the exceptional global dependence on oil for energy, OPEC was able to engineer stable and rising prices, which forced a big transfer of wealth and influence to the Middle East that the West had no choice but to accept. Nothing better shows the intimate connection between economics and security.

A rational OPEC strategy is to capture rent through limiting supply; thus, raising prices. Success depends on OPEC cooperation, notably acceptance of production quotas, but this cooperation fluctuates. It is easier when high prices keep revenues up; but with falling prices, maintaining revenue means producers need to increase output: members cheat on their quotas or compete among themselves for market share, thus further undermining prices. Also working against cooperation is the built-in divergences of interests between the high population, revenue-starved states (e.g. Iran, Iraq) that want high prices and the low-population ones (Kuwait, UAE) that want moderate prices since they have big foreign investments (that gain from low oil prices). Aggravating the problem is that OPEC producer states have conflicting *political* interests and some even represent military threats to each other. Such political conflicts destroyed OPECs 1970s solidarity: first revolutionary Iran, later Saddamist Iraq threatened the Gulf monarchies which became dependent on protection by external consumer powers (US) which, in turn, required they moderate prices. Moreover, Saudi Arabia and Kuwait practiced economic warfare by overproducing, driving down prices and revenues for Iran and Iraq in the two Gulf wars.

Pivotal to price stability is the role of Saudi Arabia as *swing producer*: the one oil producer in a position to rapidly increase (or restrain) its production, it is most able to influence other OPEC members and affect prices. The Saudis' long-term policy was to support prices in a weak oil market and moderate them in a strong one and in the 1970s the Saudis moderated the oil price boom; but after 1980, when oil demand fell, it sought to keep its market share, and increased production (also seeking to punish Iran), precipitating the 1986 oil bust. In the oil bust of 2014–15, rivalry with Iran again contributed to deterring the Saudis from supporting prices.

In reality, in spite of OPEC, the price of oil has continued to go through the boom-bust typical of primary products. After the 1970–86 period of price boom, there was an oil bust as recession, conservation and new discoveries (North Sea) reduced demand for OPEC oil, exacerbated by producer competition for market share. Another boom came in the 1990s with the Iraqi invasion of Kuwait; and in 1997–98 another bust as the East Asian crisis reduced demand (price falling to USD 12/barrel); OPEC cooperation only stabilized prices at USD 22–28 in 1999. In the 2000s another boom resulted from the 2003 US invasion of Iraq plus growing Asian demand. This is the context within which the regional security consequences of oil have to be understood (Alnasrawi, 1991; Parra, 2003; Noreng, 2005).

The failure of Oil Arabism as a basis of regional security

Oil-fueled economic integration seemed, during the 1970s, to be a potential force of cohesion among the Arab states, generating an economic undergirding for a political concert of Arab states. Inter-Arab economic ties proliferated from the post-war explosion in Arab oil wealth. The oil states transferred about 15% of their capital surpluses to the non-oil Arab states (in the form of development or defense aid). The oil-poor states started opening their economies to external Arab investment and free trade agreements were signed. A massive labor migration from poor to oil states took place, with worker remittances flowing back to stimulate home state economies. There was talk about a division of labor in a Pan-Arab market, e.g. the oil states had surplus capital, but little land and labor, while capital poor states such as Egypt had skilled labor and an industrial infrastructure. Joint ventures were proposed, the most successful of which was security-focused: the joint Egyptian-Saudi Arabia Military Industrial Organization meant to reduce dependence on foreign arms purchases (Kerr and Yassin, 1982).

In practice, however, oil did not fuel a new Arab order. Inter-Arab trade remained at less than 10% of total Arab trade, partly due to the similarity of their products (i.e. producers of either oil or competing agricultural/light industrial goods). Pan-Arab investment and joint ventures remained limited partly because of import substitute industrialization (non-competitive, not export-oriented economies) and partly because most Arab capital surpluses were recycled to the West: only 3% of oil revenues were invested in the region, filling only one-third of regional capital needs. Inter-Arab capital transfers declined after the oil bubble burst around 1986. By the 1990s, 98% of private Arab foreign investment was outside the region. Arab migrant workers acquired no rights in the Gulf and had to leave their host countries when the oil boom demand dropped. Oil linked the interests of the oil producers to the world economy rather than the Arab world. It accentuated the income gap between oil and non-oil countries, sharply differentiating their interests (Alnasrawi, 1991; Kubursi and Mansur, 1993).

In parallel it was initially thought in the Arab world that Arab oil would generate Arab power in the global arena. In 1973, the Arab oil producing states, led by Saudi Arabia, had sought to use the "oil weapon" – an embargo on oil sales to the US in order to force it to broker an "equitable" resolution of the Arab–Israeli conflict. However, even in the brief period of the oil boom, oil did not translate into global level power: the embargo did not force the US to pressure Israel into evacuating the occupied territories and America's pro-Israeli policies actually hardened in the Reagan period. Oil power failed for the same reason that Arab integration stalled, namely, the recycling of petrodollars earned by the oil states to the West – deposited in Western banks, US government bonds or spent on massive Western arms purchases that linked the interests of the oil producers to the West. Most important, Saudi Arabia, being dependent on the US for security and with its elites' economic interests invested in the US, was in no position to extract a change in US policy; despite an explosion of US arms and aid to Israel that kept it so strong it needed to make no concession to the Arabs in the peace process, Saudi Arabia continued to pump large amounts of oil to keep the price down at American behest. The brief moment of potential Arab oil power was lost, for the price boom was followed by a bust that was very damaging to MENA economies, and produced a new round of debt and submission by states such as Egypt to the Western dominated IMF (Aarts, 1994; Alnasrawi, 1991: 93–152; Kubursi and Mansur, 1993).

Finally, the oil explosion initiated the migration of power and influence in the Arab world from the core Arab republics (Egypt, Syria) which had prioritized national independence, to the periphery Gulf monarchies (which were invested in dependence), what Heikal (1975: 261–62) called a triumph of "*tharwa* (resources) over *thawra* (revolution)". The oil monarchies deployed their massive rent surpluses to buy influence in the Arab republics, a key factor in their deradicalization, exemplified in Sadat's de-Nasserization. Sadat's resulting separate peace with Israel put a decisive end to the brief Arab unity of the 1970s and opened the Arab world to security threats on both its western (Israel) and eastern (Iran) flanks.

Indeed, rather than becoming the basis of a new regional security order, oil exacerbated regional insecurity. Globally, petro-states are associated with high military spending and more militarized interstate disputes (Strüver and Wedenast, 2015). That MENA is the most militarized and conflictual global region is certainly partly a function of oil. To be sure, hydrocarbons, in themselves, do not explain its war proneness, which is rooted in the irredentism built into the region at its founding. But hydrocarbons have been issues provoking war and have fueled arms races, destabilizing the regional power balance. Indeed oil and regional conflict are linked in a chain of conflict events whose origins go back to the CIA's overthrow of Iranian Prime Minister, Muhammad Mossadegh, because of his nationalization of Iranian oil; this, in turn, was a major factor precipitating Iran's 1979 revolution after which oil helped fund Tehran's attempted export of Islamic revolution to its neighbors. This was an issue and oil an enabling factor in the Iran–Iraq war and the two Iraq wars for which it prepared the way. Oil translated into conflict in MENA via two kinds of agents/mechanisms, the creation of "war states", exemplified by Iraq, and the funding of militant trans-state movements, as exemplified by Saudi Arabia, both, in some ways, reactions to Iran's attempted export of its revolution. This dynamic will be treated in the following analysis of oil and state security.

The rentier state and security

The main development in MENA political economy in the post-Nasser period was the oil price explosion of the 1970s. The newly available rent had major consequences for regime stability, state strength and state conflict proneness. But these have not been straightforward. According to the resource curse thesis, oil undermines the long-term requisites of security, but in the short term the effects may be different.

Regime stability, state weakness?

The impact of hydrocarbons on domestic security has been ambiguous. It has tended to strengthen regimes but may weaken states. As regards regimes, is no accident that the 1970s oil boom separates a period of widespread instability (1940–70) in the Arab world from one of regime consolidation, with no regime overthrown between 1970 and 2010. Arab regimes' durability was partly down to the region's exceptional possession of hydrocarbon rent: it constituted an enormous patronage resource, especially in oil producers with small citizen populations, but non-oil states also received a share of the rent (indirect rentier states). Regimes' monopoly of hydrocarbon rent allowed the incorporation of constituents and, in fueling clientalism (in which individuals and groups competed for patronage), fostered divide and rule and deterred class mobilization against regimes. Rent also funded the expansion of the security apparatus, often made up of tribal levies, minorities, or foreign mercenaries who felt less compunction at using violence against populations. Also, in the monarchies, rent allowed a buildup of air forces which, piloted by royal princes or loyal minorities, did not pose the threats to ruling dynasties that standing armies had hitherto done and alleviated the need for the conscription that could fill armies with disloyal elements (Wright et al., 2015; Ross, 2001; Beblawi and Luciani, 1987; Herb, 2005; Lotz, 2008).

The main exception to the rule that oil consolidated regimes was Iran where rapid Westcentric oil-funded modernization actually destabilized the Shah's rule. Massive urbanization and social mobilization of Iran's very large population with high expectations exceeded the regime's oil-endowed co-optative capacity. However, Iran was also a special case because of a legitimacy deficit the Shah could never overcome that was linked directly to Iran's oil: the belief that he was a puppet of the US after he was restored to power by the CIA after Prime minister Muhammad Mossadegh's overthrow for nationalizing Iran's oil; added to this, was the perception that he was squandering Iran's oil wealth on expensive American arms by which Iran would police the Gulf on Washington's behalf (Cottam, 1979).

If rent usually strengthens regimes, it tends to keep *states* weak. States that need not extract taxes from populations do not develop the bureaucratic sinews to penetrate society (Chaudhry, 1997; Karl, 1997). Instead of relying on citizen armies, rentier regimes "buy" security from foreign patrons or mercenaries. Rent reinforces clientalism as the dominant political practice, at the expense of broader association, debilitating political parties and institutions. Unearned wealth combined with a lack of accountability leads to profligate corruption and waste of revenues e.g. on arms and white elephants. And, rent dependent modernization does not create national economies that are the true foundation of political and military strength.

The "resource curse" hypothesis claims that abundance in natural resources can also encourage internal conflict, from separatism to civil war (Ross, 2001; Klare, 2001). In high population states where the state is dispenser of economic benefits yet there is not enough revenue per capita to buy off citizens, the state can become a target of discontent by those unhappy with their share (Karl, 1997): thus, in Algeria, the shrinking of rental income produced civil war.

Moreover, where the state weakens, non-state or regional elites may contest central government control of resources and control over them allows funding of anti-regime militias; the conflict between Iraq's central government and the Kurds over control of Kirkuk became particularly virulent as the central government was demolished by the US invasion. And, where the state breaks down and civil war erupts, the struggle for control of oil resources will both incentivize its continuance and provide the means to prolong fighting, as in Libya after the Western intervention destroyed the Qaddafi regime.

Deterring democratization

Rent, it is widely argued, also deters the democratization and institution building that might strengthen the state. Rents give regimes autonomy from society, being dependent on it neither for taxes nor conscription. Material benefits substitute for political participation: rather than taxing society, a dynamic that elsewhere led to demands for representation, the state instead distributes benefits to society, diluting the urgency of calls for representation. Business, dependent on state contracts and insider connections, is in no position to push for rule of law or democratization and indeed may see authoritarian government as essential to discipline labor. Even if elections are introduced under limited political liberalization, they turn on candidates' ability to deliver material benefits through insider connections to the ruling regime. Regimes can selectively extend and withdraw benefits and political rights as part of a divide and rule strategy that sets elements of society against each other, enabling the ruler to stand above and broker such conflicts. More privileged groups – such as citizens entitled to benefits – have an interest in defending non-democratic regimes against demands by the less entitled, such as migrant labor, which, in any case, are readily expelled if they make political demands (Ross, 2004).

"Bonanza modernization"

Does oil promote or deter economic development? Oil provides the potential capital that can be used to import technology, diversify economies and reduce dependence on rent in the long term. Yet the oil industry tends to remains an export enclave, with little backward and forward linkages to stimulate other businesses; investment in petrochemicals downstream is a rational strategy, but such industries generate few skilled jobs and much are staffed by expatriates. Oil also discourages private investment in productive sectors, owing to import explosions, and an overdevelopment of tertiary sectors owing to high government spending (Aspergis and Payne, 2014). Petro city-states may create niche economies around off-shore banking, as transit depots (between East and West), and as tourism centers, but this inflates the tertiary sector. Investment in the Western economy (banks, property, stocks) i.e. sovereign wealth funds, is a rational strategy but merely reinforces rentierism. In principle, oil resources enable investment in "human capital", for example through mass education of citizens which has taken place in the Gulf monarchies; yet under bonanza modernization modern infrastructure was literally imported, not built by skilled indigenous work forces. The massive import of external labor (to do the work under a licensing system requiring a "citizen" as guarantor in return for a percentage of workers' wages), and the privileged access of "nationals" to generous welfare entitlements ruins the development "ethic" (to work, postpone consumption/save, invest). Excessive state intervention and rent-seeking activities are encouraged, notably corruption, which can undermine property rights and discourage long-term investments. Mineral export-based development leads to periods of rapid price booms followed by bust and, often, debt. There is the longer-term risk that once the minerals are exhausted, the economy returns to underdevelopment; but a more imminent security threat is the fact that massive demographic growth encouraged by oil welfare-ism is leading also to large increases in domestic hydrocarbon consumption which threatens export capacity, hence the revenue flows to the state in several oil producers. However, whether the potential blessings of hydrocarbons are realized or they become a curse, depends on the quality of governance. Not only democratic institutions but even strong non-democratic ones such as mass based ruling dominant parties can minimize the curse and maximize the blessings (DiJohn, 2010).

Oil and state belligerence

The presence of large oil deposits is associated with increased militarization, and resource wars (Struver and Wegenast, 2015; Klare, 2001). Does this mean the possession of oil resources encourages foreign policy belligerence? Or does it make states targets of external predators? In fact, oil can have quite different outcomes depending on state formation – whether states are constituted as revisionist or status quo will shape the foreign policy goals that oil resources serve. On the one hand Iraq exemplifies oil in the service of irredentism; on the other hand, Saudi Arabia, although a status quo regime, has, perhaps unintentionally, also fostered trans-state irredentist forces. The US wars on Iraq would not have happened had the country not been endowed with oil wealth.

Iraq as a war state?

War prone states result from a *combination* of the irredentism and border disputes built into the region at its founding, the rise of authoritarian republican nationalist governments whose legitimacy comes from rejection of this flawed order and the oil-funded capacity for arms build-ups. Iraq is the exemplary case: it has been involved in four wars and several more militarized disputes, recurrently with Iran, Kuwait and the US.

War proneness was embedded in state formation. The stabilization of the identity-fragmented Iraqi State under the Ba'ath party resulted from a combination of Saddam's hard authoritarianism, its legitimization by Arab nationalist ideology (whose credibility depended on being seen to defend Pan-Arab interests), and the oil boom revenues funneled into state formation – modernization, bureaucratic expansion and a big army – giving the capacity to follow a revisionist foreign policy (Mufti, 1996; Khafaji, 2000). How this could translate into war is exemplified by Iraq's 1990 invasion of Kuwait.

Iraq always had pretensions to be the Prussia (unifier) of the Arab world and Saddam Hussein was also ambitious to replace Nasser as Pan-Arab leader as Egypt withdrew from Arab leadership after 1980. To counter what he declared was the shift in the balance of power against the Arabs and to the benefit of Israel from the late 1980s decline of the Soviet Union and the tide of Soviet Jewish emigration to Israel, Saddam proposed reviving the oil weapon to force a change in US pro-Israel policy after Israel had rejected the latest bid for a negotiated settlement to the Arab–Israel conflict; he also warned he would use non-conventional weapons against Israel if it attacked any Arab country, winning wide acclaim in the Arab "street". Under his proposed new Pan-Arab order, Arab states would have to expel foreign bases and the rich states would have to share oil wealth with poorer ones. This was a threat to the US and all pro-US Arab regimes (Egypt, Saudi Arabia, the Gulf emirates) and they rebuffed Saddam: the invasion of Kuwait was in part an attempt to impose his will. Kuwait was the target because Iraq had never wholly accepted the legitimacy of its creation by Britain or of the borders that denied Iraq secure access to the Gulf – to secure which Iraq needed to incorporate or lease the Kuwait territories of Warba and Bubiyan (which Kuwait rejected).

At the same time, Iraq came out of the Iran–Iraq war dissatisfied. It had paid a high cost and seemed to win, but got no commensurate rewards. Rather, the war had bankrupted it and thousands of soldiers de-mobilized at a time of economic troubles were a domestic threat. Meanwhile, the Gulf monarchies were calling for debt repayment and Kuwait was engaging in over-pumping of oil, driving down its price when Iraq desperately needed income – what Saddam called economic warfare. Saddam calculated that the invasion of Kuwait would solve his economic problem and increase his domestic nationalist legitimacy, and that by dominating Kuwait's oil he could impose his leadership on the Arab world. Oil alone did not explain this war, but it raised the stakes (e.g. the border conflicts) inflated (Saddam's) ambitions, and provided the means to finance the war.

Saudi Arabia: From riyalpolitik to the export of Wahhabi jihadism

Although Saudi Arabia is a status quo state, usually on the defensive for its Western alignment, its use of oil in foreign policy has had quite varying consequences. From the 1960s, Saudi Arabia used its immense oil resources to promote an Islamic identity that could counter the threats from Pan-Arab republics and in the 1970s and1980s it deployed riyalpolitik to de-radicalize them. After the oil boom, Saudi wealth was also used to spread Wahhabi versions of Salafism regionally, through funding of mosques, schools, charities and, from the 2000s, the funding of militant preachers on satellite TV. While this Salafism was conservative, preaching submission to royal authority, its rigid worldview and rejection of the legitimacy of other versions of Islam, especially Sufism and Shiism, helped spread sectarian extremism that readily morphed into jihadism in conditions of conflict. Saudi financing of the Afghan Mujahedin was another key factor in the rise of jihadism, with the "Arab Afghans" who returned to their countries joining radical Islamist groups bent on de-stabilizing ruling regimes, notably in Egypt and Algeria where civil wars between secular republics and Islamist militants broke out. The rise of al-Qaida was similarly a product of Saudi private money (Bin Laden), turned against the US by the Saudi hosting of US forces attacking Iraq, whose destruction then provided a fertile field for al-Qaida to spread. After the Arab uprisings, GCC oil states such as Qatar, the UAE and Saudi Arabia financed rival actors, notably in Egypt where Qatari support for the Muslim Brotherhood was countered by Saudi support for Salafists and later the military regime of General al-Sissi who brutally repressed the Brotherhood; a similar dynamic happened in Libya and in Syria. Neither side in this competitive interference managed to buy lasting influence and only to prolong and intensify the costs for the target country; but excess oil wealth made such interference affordable. The destabilization of these countries became new incubators of trans-state jihadist terrorism, spilling over across North Africa and the Levant and giving rise, famously to ISIS. Without the combination of Saudi oil wealth and Wahhabi ideology, none of this would likely have happened.

Oil wars and global intervention

Oil and US global hegemony

Because oil is a strategic commodity, powerful states are unwilling to leave energy security of access to the market: rather, what is called *energy security* justifies exceptional measures, including war and intervention. This is the magnet that drove US intervention in the Persian Gulf and against Iraq: Iraq, Saudi Arabia and Kuwait control 40% of world oil reserves while that of the US, the world's biggest consumer of oil, had shrunk from 34 to 7% of global total in the 1990s; as such, US dependence on imports steadily rose to about 50%, 13% of the global total. Since the US is less energy efficient than its competitors (in Europe/Japan) and since its "motorization" profligately consumes gasoline, it also needs low oil prices. However, the US suffered from bad relations with many of the main MENA oil producers – Libya, Iran, Iraq – and an increasingly bad image among public opinion in the Middle East, largely because of its support for Israel (Noreng, 2005; Rutledge, 2006, Klare, 2001). As such, access to oil could not be left to normal commercial relations.

More than this, control of MENA oil was a key element in US global hegemony. Before OPEC, US oil companies controlled oil directly; afterwards, the alliance with Saudi Arabia and the US military presence in the Gulf substituted for that. Bromley (1990) argues that US dominance in the Gulf allowed it to exclude other powers from the region and gave it leverage over the many powers in Europe and Asia that were much more dependent on Middle East oil. Moreover, the US countered its loss of competitive industrial advantage by unleashing its finance capital globally to subordinate European and Asian productive capitals. Middle East oil was pivotal to this since the recycling of the oil producers' petrodollar windfall, not through the IMF, as Europe and Japan wished, but through US treasury bonds, private banks and US arms sales to the oil exporting states, gave US finance capital world dominance (Spiro, 1999; Terzian, 1985; Alnasrawi, 1991: 93–98). Michael Hudson (2003) shows that the fact that MENA oil producers dependent on US protection kept oil denominated in dollars gave the US a big economic advantage – it meant that all states had to earn dollars through access to the vast US market, which they kept in US banks, lowering the cost of capital for US firms and allowing them to buy up foreign assets while also permitting the US government to finance its global military reach, indeed, encouraging "imperial overstretch" (Burbach and Tarbell 2004). Doug Stokes (2007) argues that the US sought *both* to ensure stable energy supplies for world capitalism and to maintain US primacy over other core powers.

Resource wars: The US wars on Iraq

The 1990 Iraqi invasion of Kuwait became the occasion of a US oil war because were Iraq to have retained Kuwaiti oil fields and remained in a position to intimidate Saudi Arabia, the US feared it would be able to dictate the terms with which the West received oil, including price levels, and thereby threaten Western economies. To be sure, regardless of who controls the oil fields, they must sell the oil and Iraq was desperate for revenue (for reconstruction and debt repayment) and would have needed to maximize production (keeping prices moderate). But what Washington insisted on was oil in *safe hands*: regimes like the Saudi Arabia which, by virtue of their dependence on the US for security and their investments in the West, shared an interest in moderate prices and recycled proceeds on a massive scale through Western banks and the purchase of Western arms – thereby ensuring that the West did not experience a damaging hemorrhage of revenue to the Middle East. Iraq, by contrast, was not dependent and threatened to politicize the oil relation, making it conditional on a favorable Western policy in the Arab–Israeli conflict: to secure cheap gasoline needed to keep US consumers happy, Saddam would have to be appeased by leaning on Israel, but this would offend the powerful Israeli lobby – which was mobilizing to demonize Iraq. Thus, the Gulf war was a resource war not over Western access to oil but over the *terms* of that access.

For the US, the Iraqi invasion of Kuwait was not just a threat to energy security but also a unique *opportunity* to consolidate unchallengeable global hegemony, to shape a new liberal

Security and political economy

world order through military force. As the Cold War ended and the Soviet Union withdrew from the world power competition, the Soviet counter-balancing that had hitherto restrained US intervention in MENA collapsed, providing a window of opportunity to intervene on a massive scale. War against a salient representative of the main remaining enemies of the US-sponsored liberal world order, namely, militaristic developing world nationalist regimes, would send a deterrent warning to other potential troublemakers that, as President Bush put, it: "what we say goes". Iraq was the prime candidate owing to its effort to acquire non-conventional weapons and its growing challenge to the US and Israel. Rolling back Saddam would show that the enormous US military machine was usable (at a time when there were doubts about the utility of force in world politics). It would educate the US public that the US military-industrial complex had a new post-Cold War mission to justify continued military spending and, if the use of massive military power kept the war low cost, it would banish the Vietnam syndrome which had been constraining US intervention abroad. US planners also saw Gulf intervention as an opportunity to demonstrate the dependence of America's economic competitors, Europe and Japan, on its hegemonic role in securing oil supplies. Gulf petrodollars would continue to be cycled through US institutions and therefore serve US competitiveness. In addition, the US actually managed to make its economic competitors (Germany, Japan) and clients (Saudi Arabia, Kuwait) pay for the intervention (Bina, 1993; Kubursi and Mansur, 1993; Aarts, 1994; Hinnebusch, 2015: 225–243).

The First Iraq War (1991) was a great success for the US. Iraq was easily defeated at low cost; US military power was now so dominant in the region that all Arab states, even formerly hostile nationalist regimes such as Syria, starting bandwagoning with Washington. This allowed the US to broker the Madrid Arab–Israeli peace process which, it was hoped, would lay to rest the remaining issue that kept US–Arab relations tense. Yet, only 12 years later, the US thought it had to launch a second Iraq war aimed at heading off threats to the hegemony the first war had established. Iraq's continual defiance of the US, its ability to win Arab sympathy against the US-led economic sanctions, the move of Arab states to rehabilitate and restore Iraq as a member of the regional system, were alarming signs of slipping US hegemony. Seizing Iraq would put an end to this while capturing the Arab state with most power potential and revisionist history; turning it into a client regime and establishing permanent US bases in Iraq would demoralize nationalist and Islamic resistance to US hegemony and allow intimidation or elimination of any remaining recalcitrant regimes.

Oil was still at the center of US calculations in 2003: controlling Iraq would allow reduced reliance on Saudi Arabia since the Saudis were now seen as unreliable: Saudi society was generating opposition to the US presence/connection which had spawned the Bin Laden movement and Saudi nationals' participation in 9/11. As the US failed to deliver a Middle East peace that would accord the Palestinians national rights, the Saudis were gently warning that they would no longer use their swing position to serve US interests if the US did not become more even-handed in the Arab–Israel conflict. Seizing Iraq would give the US a new swing producer and secure access to Arab oil without having to accommodate Arab interests in regard to Israel (Klare, 2002; Duffield, 2005; Rutledge, 2006).

The second Iraq war had, of course, disastrous consequences for regional (and even US) security: leaving behind a failed state, which became a breeding ground for al-Qaida, unleashing sectarian conflict across the region, empowering Iran against the Gulf Arabs, and setting the stage for the rise of the Islamic State of Iraq and Syria (ISIS) and yet another US intervention in the region. Oil appeared to be a curse for many in the region even as its blessings were monopolized by a handful of ruling families in the Gulf.

Conclusion

Political economy factors constituted the deep structure that underlay both security threats and order in MENA. Western penetration and regional dependency stimulated nationalist states that saw sovereignty – ontological security – as contingent on breaking out of dependency; however, their efforts not only failed but were a factor in a chain of wars, beginning with Suez. The oil boom unleashed by the 1973 Arab–Israeli war was both a curse and a blessing for "Arab national security". Internally, the oil boom helped consolidate the Arab regimes (even though vulnerabilities persisted and only after having destabilized Iran), without much strengthening states or engendering the national economic base of sovereignty. Simultaneously, oil drove and also obstructed a nascent Pan-Arab economic order that had the potential to underpin a security system and empowered regional state rivalries and belligerence in the Gulf. Finally, in further tying the region into the Western dependency system, generating war states and trans-state terrorism, and inviting deeply destabilizing US interventions, oil proved, for regional security, to be less a blessing than a curse.

References

Aarts, Paul (1994), "The New Oil Order: Built on Sand?" *Arab Studies Quarterly*, 16:2, 1–12.

Abdel Malek, Anwar (1968), *Egypt: Military Society*, New York: Vintage Books.

Adelson, Roger (1995), *London and the Invention of the Middle East: Money, Power and War, 1902–1922*, New Haven, CT: Yale University Press.

Alnasrawi, Abbas (1991), *Arab Nationalism, Oil and the Political Economy of Dependency*, New York and London: Greenwood Press.

Aspergis, N. and Payne, J.E. (2014), "The Oil Curse, Institutional Quality and Growth in MENA Countries", *Energy Economics* 46, 1–9.

Ayubi, Nazih (1995), *Overstating the Arab State: Politics and Society in the Middle East*, London: I.B. Taurus.

Beblawi, Hazem and G. Luciani, eds. (1987), *The Rentier State*, Beckenham: Croom-Helm.

Berque, Jacques (1972), *Egypt: Imperialism and Revolution*, New York: Praeger.

Bina, Cyrus (1993), "The Rhetoric of Oil and the Dilemma of War and American Hegemony", *Arab Studies Quarterly*, 15:3, 1–20.

Bromley, Simon (1990), *American Hegemony and World Oil: The Industry, the State System and the World Economy*, Oxford, Polity Press.

Bromley, Simon (1994), *Rethinking Middle East Politics*, Oxford: Polity Press.

Brown, L. Carl (1984), *International Politics and the Middle East: Old Rules, Dangerous Game*, Princeton, NJ: Princeton University Press.

Burbach, Roger and Jim Tarbell (2004), *Imperial Overstretch: George W. Bush and the Hubris of Empire*, London: Zed Books.

Chaudhry, Kiren Aziz (1997), *The Price of Wealth: Economics and Institutions in the Middle East*, Ithaca, NY: Cornell University Press.

Cottam, Richard (1979), *Nationalism in Iran*, Pittsburgh: University of Pittsburgh Press.

DiJohn, Jonathan (2010), "The Resource Curse: Theory and Evidence", ARI, www.realinstitutoelcano.org/wps/wcm/connect/8719a780450e2d74a5dea7f55cb546a4/ARI172-2010_DiJohn_Resource_Course_Theory_Evidence_Africa_LatinAmerica.pdf?MOD=AJPERES&CACHEID=8719a780450e2d74a5dea7f55cb546a4

Duffield, John S. (2005), "Oil and the Iraq War: How the United States Could Have Expected to Benefit, and Might Still", *MERIA Journal*, 9:2, June 9.

Galtung, Johan (1971), "A Structural Theory of Imperialism", *Journal of Peace Research*, 8:2, 81–98.

Halliday, Fred (2005), *The Middle East in International Relations: Power, Politics and Ideology*, Cambridge: Cambridge University Press.

Heikal, Muhammad Hassanein (1975), *The Road to Ramadan*, New York: Reader's Digest Press.

Herb, Michael (2005), "No Representation without Taxation: Rents, Development, and Democracy", *Comparative Politics*, 37:3.

Hinnebusch, Raymond (1985), *Egyptian Politics under Sadat*, Cambridge: Cambridge University Press.

Hinnebusch, Raymond (2015), *The International Politics of the Middle East*, Manchester: Manchester University Press.

Hudson, Michael (2003), *Super Imperialism: The Origins and Fundamentals of US World Dominance*, London: Pluto Press.

Issawi, Charles (1982), *An Economic History of the Middle East and North Africa*, New York: Columbia University Press.

Karl, Terry L. (1997), *The Paradox of Plenty: Oil Booms and Petrol States*, Berkeley, CA: University of California Press.

Kerr, Malcolm and Sayyid Yassin, eds. (1982), *Rich and Poor in the Middle East: Egypt and the New Arab Order*, Cairo: American University in Cairo Press.

Keyder, Caglar (1987), *State and Class in Turkey*, London: Verso.

Khafaji, Isam (2000), "War as a Vehicle for the Rise and Demise of a State Controlled Society: The Case of Ba'thist Iraq", in S. Heydemann, *War, Institutions and Social Change in the Middle East*, Berkeley: University of California Press, 258–291.

Klare, Michael (2001), *Resource Wars: The New Landscape of Global Conflict*, New York: Metropolitan Books.

Klare, Michael (2002), "Washington's Oilpolitik", www.salon.com.

Kubursi, Atif and Salim Mansur (1993), "Oil & the Gulf War: An American Century or a 'New World Order'?" *Arab Studies Quarterly*, 15:4, 1–18.

Lotz, Christopher (2008), "Rentierism and Repression", *Journal of Politics and International Relations*, vol. 3, Spring.

Lustik, Ian (1997), "The Absence of Middle Eastern Great Powers: Political "Backwardness" in Historical Perspective", *International Organization*, 51:4, 653–683.

Mabro, Robert (1974), *The Egyptian Economy, 1952–92*, London: Oxford University Press.

Mufti, Malik (1996), *Sovereign Creations: Pan-Arabism and Political Order in Syria and Iraq*, Ithaca & London, Cornell University Press.

Noreng, Oystein (2005), *Crude Power: Politics and the Oil Market*, London: I.B. Taurus.

Owen, Roger (1981), *The Middle East in the World Economy, 1800–1914*, London and New York: Methuen.

Parra, Francesco (2003), *Oil Politics: A Modern History of Petroleum*, London: I.B. Taurus.

Radwan, Samir (1977), *Agrarian Reform and Rural Poverty, Egypt 1952–72*, Geneva: ILO.

Ross, Michael L. (2001), "Does Oil Hinder Democracy?" *World Politics*, 3:3, 325–361.

Ross, Michael L. (2004), "What Do We Know about Natural Resources and Civil War?" *Journal of Peace Research*, 41(3) May.

Rutledge, Ian (2006), Addicted to Oil: America's Drive for Energy Security, London: I.B. Tauris.

Spiro, David E. (1999), *The Hidden Hand of American Hegemony: Petrodollar Recycling and International Markets*, Ithaca, NY: Cornell University Press.

Stokes, Doug (2007), "Global Capital, Counter-Insurgency and US Energy Security", *Review of International Studies*, 33, 245–264.

Strüver, Georg and Tim Wegenast (2015), "The Hard Power of Natural Resources: Oil and the Outbreak of Militarized Interstate Disputes", *Foreign Policy Analysis*, 12, January.

Terzian, Pierre (1985), *OPEC: The Inside Story*, London: Zed Press.

Wright, J., E. Frantz and B. Geddes (2015), "Oil and Autocratic Regime Survival", *British Journal of Political Science*, 45:2, 287–306.

19

THE GOVERNANCE DEFICIT IN THE MIDDLE EAST[1] REGION

Michelle Pace

Introduction

What is governance? The study of governance, as practices of governing, organizing and managing political, economic and social matters, generally locates power in the Middle East at the state level. The state, as the basic unit of analysis, has the authority over its territorial sovereignty, a monopoly over the use of force, is a hierarchic bureaucracy with centralized decision-making, its pattern of rule is often authoritarian and corrupt and it is assumed as having a relatively coherent "national" identity (Bellin, 2004; Owen, 2004; Fish, 2002; Norris, 2011).

But, in a globalized world order – with a globalized economy, and technological leaps as well as the demographic explosion in the Middle East – this bureaucratic, authoritarian model in the Middle East began to weaken. The coercion, the clientelistic practices and the ideology on which these Arab states have relied to survive and stay in power has been challenged in such a context. Arab governments attempted to accommodate globalization's impact by further empowering selected elite groups (for example, they committed to reforms with the World Bank and the International Monetary Fund) – which intensified inequalities as these measures excluded the majority of their citizens who increasingly held grievances against their regimes. Thereafter, protests were stepped up and Middle Eastern regimes discovered that they could not keep people under their control so they turned back to coercion to suppress their populations. The Arab uprisings that kicked off in December 2010 were the epitome of the breakdown in the social contract between Middle Eastern governments and their populations – the rulers and those ruled.

This chapter focuses on two central concepts – human security and trust – as the core basis of a referential framework for assessing and re-imagining relations between MENA governments and their populations. The working hypothesis here is that one of the reasons why MENA countries have a governance deficit is precisely because of the embedded mistrust in Middle Eastern societies between rulers and those ruled. Trust is crucial as it avoids a "paralysing situation of ultimate uncertainty" and puts "social actors in the position to start a relationship" (Bachmann and Zaheer, 2006: 394).

The core proposition of this chapter is that trust is an essential element allowing social actors to make specific assumptions about each other's future behavior and hence reduce uncertainty and complexity which are so rife in relations between MENA governments and their populations.

Trust and the social contract in the Middle East and North Africa

While Nordic countries such as Denmark are highly developed societies based on social trust and on the assumption that citizens earn their entitlements by contributing (through taxation) over a lifetime of active work to the maintenance and growth of the national wealth (Kaspersen, 2005), Arab states have, for the last half-century, upheld a particular social contract: a patronage system in which citizens gave their consent to the regime, and in exchange the regime provided all kinds of economic and social goods to people, mainly in the form of state subsidies (Cofman Wittes, 2016). While high taxes have helped build effective welfare states in Northern Europe, the fact that in Middle Eastern countries (income) taxes are either low or non-existent tell us much about the governance deficit in this region. As Brian Whitaker (2010) puts it:

> Low taxes, and the erratic collection of them, are common features of life in most of the Middle East. Among the Arab oil producers, for example, taxation accounted for only 5% of gross domestic product in 2002, rising to 17% in the non-oil countries – which is still very low compared with Germany (39%), Italy (41%) and Britain (37%).
>
> The main reason, of course, is that many of them are rentier economies where the government has sources of income other than taxes. Oil is the classic example but there are others: Egypt benefits in a similar way from the Suez canal and several of the poorer Arab countries receive substantial rent in the form of foreign aid. Overall, slightly less than 20% of Arab governments' revenue comes from taxes.
>
> Taxation is an often-overlooked factor in the internal politics of the Middle East: it helps to explain why undemocratic regimes stay in power for so long. Governments that have substantial non-tax income can buy themselves out of trouble by showering largesse on the population, often keeping prices low through subsidies …
>
> As a rule of thumb, high taxes can act as a spur towards democracy and account-able government. Conversely, where taxes are low the pressure for democracy and accountability is usually less…
>
> The kind of tax system a country has tells us a lot about the relationship between the people and the state.

Whitaker continues to quote a World Bank report from 2009, which stipulates that:

- Raising taxes *efficiently* requires political effort to secure taxpayer consent (trust-building relations)
- Raising taxes *effectively* requires the development of a competent bureaucracy (citizens feeling secure in the belief that state institutions are effective)
- Raising taxes *equitably* requires political concern for the fair and equal treatment of citizens by the state (social justice)

The said report emphasizes that the three points above are, "at the center of good governance and state-building. The perceived fairness of the tax system is crucial to building an effective state based on citizens' consent. Willingness to pay taxes is a good indicator of the legitimacy of the state" (Whitaker, 2010).

The Arab uprisings of 2011 raised hopes for a completely new and revised social contract between Arab regimes and their populations (Hamzawy, 2016). They were in fact a call for social justice, citizen rights and state obligations toward their citizens. Across Tunisia, Egypt, Yemen, Libya, Syria, Bahrain, Saudi Arabia, Morocco, Algeria, Jordan, Oman and Kuwait, ordinary citizens unleashed a will for change and a resistance to existing power structures. "Our country's condition is getting worse and worse. There is corruption, torture, injustice, inequality and no freedom. Someone has to stand up and say 'enough is enough'" (protester, Tahrir square, July 2011, author interview). The debates in the major squares were about the new relationship that had to be built between citizens, employers/trade unions and governments. How could the persistent challenges of lack of development, sound governance and rule of law be transcended?

The widespread corruption and the complete absence of rule of law had created a huge chasm between the political, financial/economic elite and the marginalized, poor and low-income majorities. Good governance has been absent in the MENA region for other reasons than the use of oppressive state tactics against the people: the ruled – that is, the masses – have for a very long time been completely excluded from the public policy-making process, mechanisms and pathways; they simply have had no agency in this domain. Thus, the protests that the world witnessed across the MENA countries garnered among Arab citizens a thirst for a new beginning based on a core pillar of well-functioning democracies: trust. A key challenge that has been overlooked thus far in the literature on the governance deficit in the MENA region is that citizens of Arab states simply could not trust their ruling politicians and institutional structures and procedures to solve any of the serious problems of poverty, unemployment, corruption, huge inequalities and suppression. Nor could they trust external actors to enhance their daily lives (author's interviews with protestors, Tahrir Square, July 2011). At the very root of these so-called Arab uprisings lay a deeply seated lack of political, economic and social trust that is crucial in establishing sustainable, good governance structures that are accountable to the very people they represent.

Trust absorbs uncertainty, but at the same time it also produces risks. The relationship between cooperation and trust holds a predominant role in key interdisciplinary literature (cf. Hardin, 2004; Ostrom and Walker, 2003) which highlights the role of trust in facilitating cooperation and thus implicitly affecting the assorted behavioral outcomes (human security in the case of the MENA). Although trust is defined in many different ways, Farrell and Knight (2003:8) define trust as "a set of expectations held by one party that another party or parties will behave in an appropriate manner with regard to a specific issue". Substantial evidence acquired from research within the discipline of institutional economics, but also beyond, demonstrates that social norms prescribing cooperative or trustworthy behavior have a significant impact on whether societies can overcome obstacles to contracting and collective action that would otherwise hinder their development (Knack, 2001). From an economic perspective, trust enables real commitment and confidence among partners opening space for cooperation and allowing the development of a common vision for the long-run, as economic cooperation is explicitly impacted by trust (Vargas-Hernandez, 2008). While a lack of trust is capable of undermining cooperation, trust-based relationships can also result in direct economic gains of the involved parties. "What is needed is sufficient trust to initiate cooperation and a sufficiently successful outcome to reinforce trusting attitudes and underpin more substantial, and risky, collaborative behavior (...) Virtuous spirals of trust and effective collaboration need to be established" (Webb, 1991: 237). My argument here is that in the MENA region trusting attitudes need to be embedded at the political, economic and social levels. By no means an easy feat.

"Social trust in complex modern settings can arise from two related sources – norms of reciprocity and networks of civic engagement" (Putnam and Feldstein, 2003: 171). Putnam and Feldstein (2003:172) propose four key reasons why reciprocity characteristic of networks enhances cooperation: (1) it increases the costs of defection, (2) it fosters robust norms of reciprocity, (3) it facilitates communication and improves information flows, and (4) it embodies past success at collaboration and provides a blueprint for future cooperation. Furthermore, a positive relationship between trust and social capital, on the one hand, and political and economic success on the other has been further documented (Vargas-Hernandez, 2008). The notion of trust became even more relevant in contexts where social cooperation cannot be understood as simple institutional compliance.

> Cooperation through compliance with institutional rules in particular social settings affects an actor's beliefs about the propensity of others to cooperate (their level of trustworthiness) in similar settings, which affects that actor's willingness to cooperate at some subsequent point in time in that same social setting.
>
> *(Farrell and Knight, 2003: 10–11)*

Farrell and Knight (2003) argue that changes in trustworthiness and in trust between actors lead to changes in the extent and form of cooperation and further propose a model that specifies a set of causal relationships affecting trust and cooperation "to provide a good account both of cooperation between actors, and the evolution of this cooperation over time, in relations between economic [as well as political and social] actors" (Farrell and Knight, 2003:38; my additions in brackets).

Trust and human security

It is precisely the low levels of trustworthiness between social partners in the MENA region that can go a long way to explain the governance deficit in this region. Due to the failure of state structures, citizens in Arab MENA countries are often left to rely on their extended family for survival especially in terms of their basic needs. Kin ties enhance the security of the individual, in particular in the Arab Middle East culture. It is for this reason that this contribution moves away from traditional security articulations, and embeds its analysis regarding trust within the over-arching framework of human security, as a concept which expresses how best to both protect and empower people.

Here, human security operates as a primary analytical lens for understanding the political, economic and societal challenges with governance in the Middle East. The understanding of security here thus goes beyond the narrow definitions of state or resource security to include sectorial sustainability, resource allocation/distribution, economic development and political autonomy, affecting, directly or indirectly, human security.

Since it gained prominence in the 1990s, human security has in fact increasingly been adopted in the discourses about the MENA (Kaldor, 2007; Al-Rawashdeh, 2015; van Broekhoven et al., 2014). Human security expresses a holistic approach, the integration of security, development and good governance, and a normative concern based on cosmopolitan ethics. In prioritizing survival, livelihoods and the dignity of individuals, the concept of human security seeks to re-orientate policy-making toward context-specific, bottom-up and gender sensitive approaches, and mobilize actions which address the complex nature of everyday experience (GPPAC, 2014).

Human security acknowledges the agency of individuals and groups in the region (both beneficial and perverse) as well as the significant power of states and regional organizations, NGOs and the private sector as co-constructors of security and well-being.

A human security framework emphasizes the salience of the perspective of beneficiaries and targets of security and insecurity. Trust is also integral to the promotion of human security in its dimension as a component of social capital, while its affective nature – associated with perceptions and experiences of cooperation – is also consistent with the ambiguous quality which is noted in studies of human security in which individual experiences may produce unclear and sometimes perverse indications of security (Kostovicova et al., 2012).

Although it references individual security, human security is operationalized through a coalition of efforts, involving states, civil society, international organizations, and individuals and groups themselves. Various studies have recognized that it is necessary to take account not just of the multiplicity of actors, in addressing individual vulnerability, but to also focus on the relationships and cross-cutting roles of individuals/groups and states, civil society and external actors in governance, security and development reforms (Kostovicova et al., 2012). My argument here is that the governance deficit in the MENA region can be explained through the lack of a trusting relationship between MENA governments, their populations and surrounding actors such as NGOs, as well as the involvement of external actors – which only adds to the frustrations of the majority and their deep-seated human insecurity.

With the failure of the state in the MENA region to respond to the socio-economic and security needs of people, there is a heavy reliance of Southern societies upon informal networks that bring households together as communities, often at odds with formal political structures. A nuanced understanding of the interconnection between formal and informal institutional and political networks is important for understanding how the dynamics of power operate at the domestic political levels, and how they extend to cooperation with regional and international actors.

Informal social and cultural networks are defined as the codes of conduct, norms and values that arise or are articulated within society, and provide many of the rules that shape widespread behavior and expectations. Informal family networks in Arab countries are the most important source for social legitimacy and recognition (Cohen and Arato, 1993:345–346).

How do MENA individuals and groups react to insecurity, feelings of mistrust and vulnerability? Informal kin/family networks have two interlinked functional dimensions: one operates to enhance authoritarianism, corruption and patriarchy and contributes to stabilizing the status quo, whether monarchical or republican (Bayat, 1997, 1998); the other operates as a coping strategy, mostly by poor and vulnerable people, to generate sources of personal and familial livelihood security (Taraki, 2006, Muhanna-Matar, 2014, 2016). Informal networks are an effective means for legitimizing clientelism, patronage and corruption in most Arab countries. Clientelism and patronage in Arab countries extend vertically and horizontally to create a chain of corrupted people in society, who legitimize the corrupted regime and contribute to its continuity and stability (Freeman, 2015). Practices which result from and reflect people's security predicaments need to be taken into account to arrive at a dynamic picture of the challenges for effective governance in the Middle East.

The interweaving of formal and informal networks gives rise to greater potential for mistrust within all social segments of society, as vulnerable people create their own family and friends networks to survive, thus producing illegal and criminal actions such as human, weapon and goods smuggling, and recently smuggling of jihadists across the Mediterranean. Studying and analyzing such informal networks helps in generating more nuanced, analytical and critical knowledge of Middle Eastern societies' dynamics and governance problems.

What is the nature of mistrust in Middle East societies?

In his writings, Timur Kuran has reflected on the embedded mistrust that pervades Middle Eastern societies. Together with Jared Rubin, an economic historian, Kuran has investigated Istanbul's 17th and 18th century Islamic court records which the authors argue may hold some answers as to why we find such deeply embedded mistrust in this region. According to the authors,

... the legal system made it easier for Muslims to breach contracts with impunity, they were more often tempted to default on their debts and to renege on their obligations as business partners and sellers. Meanwhile, non-Muslims, whose obligations were enforced more vigorously, gained a reputation for trustworthiness...

So it seems that perceptions of trustworthiness in the Arab world are rooted, at least partly, in the uneven enforcement of commitments under Islamic law ...

... old impressions of Muslims being less trustworthy have endured, passed down through families and networks. Old habits of breaching contracts opportunistically have also survived in places, reinforcing the inherited stereotypes. The tendency to limit transactions to friends and acquaintances is a natural response in a low-trust environment.

(Kuran, 2016)

So how can the Middle East garner wide-ranging efforts to rebuild trust among and within communities and in private organizations and government so as to kick start progress in various areas, not least in effective governance, economic development and political reforms?

Consensus-building as a way forward to good governance? The case of Tunisia

The only case that has deemed to have been through any meaningful and positive political transition since the Arab uprisings is that of Tunisia.

From the fall of Ben Ali in 2011 to the elections in 2014, the democratic transition in Tunisia, specifically the process of writing the new Constitution,[2] was characterized by inclusiveness and pluralism.

In comparison with, for example, Egypt, Tunisia managed to uphold a certain degree of dialogue between secular and Islamist political parties, something that many would agree is crucial for the democratic development in the country. During 24–25 May 2012, a high level tripartite conference on social dialogue was organized in Tunis, Tunisia with the support of the Belgian Government and the International Labour Organization. The conference theme was "Tunisia: Social dialogue as a response to social and economic challenges of the day" and was attended by government representatives, employers and workers' organizations, as well as "experts" from regional and international organizations, who shared experiences and best practices on social pacts. The goal was precisely to examine what it takes to craft out and implement a new social contract for Tunisia for the period 2012–2020. The new social contract was aimed at ensuring the commitment of the three parties: the Tunisian Government, the powerful labor union UGTT (Union Générale Tunisienne du Travail, which played an important role in resolving the crisis in 2013) and the employers' organization UTICA (l'Union Tunisienne de l'Industrie, du Commerce et de l'Artisanat), to work together for peace and stability in the country through socio-economic reforms and the necessary political transformation.

What explains this, largely, positive process and continued inclusive democratic development in Tunisia? Are there constitutional mechanisms that can guarantee sustainable inclusive processes in the future? The basis of the newly forged constitution was precisely a redefinition of state–citizen relationships but has this materialized in practice?

In her analytical work Marie Kruse (2015) notes a wide diversity of assessments of the process and understandings of democracy within the political class in Tunisia. Through intensive interviews carried out among different groups in Tunisian society (in particular a diverse network of Tunisian politicians) Kruse notes that her interviewees viewed the open debates in the Assembly and with the public as one of the key democratic features of the process. However, while the government coalition, at the time led by the Islamist party Ennahda, practiced democracy by following agreed procedures and respecting election results, the secular opposition focused on the need for consensus. Kruse's analysis shows that the different understandings of democracy are not only based on ideological convictions, but are also (or mostly) linked to the quest to establish structures and procedures by which the actors could gain power. According to Kruse, this battle had its climax during a political crisis in the summer of 2013. However, mediation by four civil society organizations resulted in reconciliation between the two camps that allowed the constitutional process to continue. But the crisis also resulted in a deviation from the agreed procedures, which in turn diminished Ennahda's power considerably.

On the basis of this analysis, Kruse concluded that the constitutional process could well have a significant impact on the future political developments in Tunisia. On the one hand, she emphasizes that the process appeared to have built trust and to have created a common understanding of the basic principles of the "new Tunisia" within the political class, and thereby paved the way for a more constructive dialogue on Tunisia's future. The consensus building process and associated learned experiences also seem to have resulted in more professional and constructive negotiations and cooperative engagements within and between the political parties and civil society organizations. However, Kruse also notes that, on the other hand, the diminishing power of the National Constituent Assembly throughout the process may lead to Parliament losing power and respect, which is serious as the new Constitution states that the Parliament takes on an important role in counterbalancing the power of the President and the government. In addition, the procedures of consensus developed during the constitutional process may prevent Tunisian politicians from carrying out unpopular, but urgently needed reforms. Finally, the more radical Islamists and the disenfranchised youth were not part of the consensus and reconciliation between the Islamists and the seculars. On the contrary, they seem more and more marginalized and may be prone to radicalization. Kruse's key point is that a more nuanced understanding of the constitutional process and its implications can provide decision-makers with a better foundation for addressing challenges, but also utilizing the possibilities the process has created.

In its 2015 Tunisia report, Freedom House upgraded the country's overall status to "free" from "partly free" and gave it a political rights rating of 1, the highest possible rating.

One year later, writing on the great expectations that were created in Tunisia through the focus on a new constitution, Maha Yahya (2016) notes that the Tunisia Government still has a long way to go in winning the trust of its citizens, and, like Kruse, puts special emphasis on Tunisian youth who feel disengaged from the political processes and formal institutions and therefore cannot make any real differences in their own communities.

According to the Oxford Business Group (2016) structural economic reforms are underway in Tunisia including fiscal reforms such as changes to the country's energy subsidy regime, tax reforms, and new investment rules and incentives. Moreover, during a seminar entitled "Fighting Corruption: A Selective Campaign or Signs of a Genuine Political Will" held in Tunis, Tunisia on 12 July 2017, participants highlighted the importance of respect for state institutions and of the credibility of members of parliament, of strengthening the role of the Auditors branch in investigating any suspected infringements and of the need to cultivate a culture of the supremacy of the law: and of awareness campaigns to reach all actors so that all understand their responsibilities fully (CSID, 2017). The Tunisian National Anti-Corruption Commission's investigations have revealed that 90% of the files received by the said Commission concern corruption practices within the public administration, which benefits from public contracts and tenders. According to the Commission's President, Mr Shawqi Tbib, the Assembly of People's Representatives is responsible in part for taking far too long to adopt the legal framework on combatting corruption.[3]

Conclusion: Rethinking the governance deficit in the Middle East

Since the start of the Arab uprisings in December 2010, expectations were raised in terms of the possibility of positive democratic changes toward meaningful political reform in the MENA region. Almost seven years on, these aspirations have been dampened to a large extent.

In this chapter, emphasis was on the lack of trust in the relationship between the rulers and the ruled in the Middle East as one of the main reasons for the governance deficit in this region. Conceptually it has been argued that civic attitudes such as trust facilitate cooperation between social, economic and political actors in any democratic society, thus implicitly affecting citizens' sense of (human) security. Empirically it analyzed the case of Tunisia where, since the Arab uprisings, consensus building has been a key criterion for all parties involved in the writing of a new constitution. This process has resulted in more professional and constructive negotiations within and between the political parties and civil society organizations. However, even in what is deemed to be the success story of good governance thus far in the MENA region since the Arab uprisings, youth were left out of this consensus building process and as a result still feel disenfranchised and unable to make any difference within their communities.

This chapter has drawn attention to the convergence of trust, human security and good governance agendas necessary for a new dawn in a post-Arab uprising Middle East. It explored at some length the links between good governance, development, trust and human security. It argues that trust and human security lie at the core of good governance. Hence, the problems of social injustice, deepening inequality, corruption and authoritarianism are central concerns, and the unfolding of the Arab uprisings highlighted these problems to a great extent. The idea put forward in this chapter is that, for a thorough and critical examination of good governance in the Middle East, our focus has to be on the deeply embedded feelings of mistrust and human insecurity that the average citizen of this region has to live with on a day to day basis, which causes frustration not only about those who rule but also external actors whose neoliberal vision dominates their interventions in the MENA.

Notes

1 Although the term Middle East is subject to various definitions, here I use it to include the entire Arab world, Iran as well as Turkey.
2 Following the Arab uprisings, the constitutional process in Tunisia began with the election of a National Constituent Assembly on 23 October 2011 and ended with its adoption on 27 January 2014.
3 On 9 December 2012 the Tunisian National Constituent Assembly presented a proposal for a National Anti-Corruption Strategy which was ratified on 9 December 2016, four years later!

References

Al-Rawashdeh, M.S., 2015, "Human Security and Rights in the Middle East," *International Journal of Social Science and Humanities Research* 3(4), 227–238. Available at: www.researchpublish.com
Bachmann, R. and Zaheer, A., 2006, *Handbook of Trust Research*. Edward Elgar, Cheltenham.
Bayat, A., 1997, "Un-civil Society: The Politics of the 'Informal People'," *Third World Quarterly* 18(1), 53–72.

Bayat, A., 1998, "Revolution without Movement, Movement without Revolution. Comparing Islamic Activism in Iran and Egypt," *Comparative Studies in Society and History* 40(1), 136–169.

Bellin, E., 2004, "The Robustness of Authoritarianism in the Middle East: Exceptionalism in Comparative Perspective," *Comparative Politics* 36(2), 139–157.

van Broekhoven, L., Tiryaki, S. and van Tujil, P., 2014, *Human Security Perspectives on Developments in the Middle East*, GPoT Center.

Cofman Wittes, T., 2016, "Want to Stabilize the Middle East? Start with Governance", Brookings Institution blog. Last accessed 3 August 2017. Available at: www.brookings.edu/blog/markaz/2016/11/22/want-to-stabilize-the-middle-east-start-with-governance/

Cohen, J. and Arato, A., 1993, *Civil Society and Political Theory*. The MIT Press, Cambridge, MA.

CSID (Center for the Study of Islam and Democracy), 2017, "Fighting Corruption: A Selective Campaign or Signs of a Genuine Political Will." Last accessed on 1 March 2018. Available at: http://campaign.r20.constantcontact.com/render?m=1102084408196&ca=11882dc9-5a15-4911-88bf-a0eeed35a6ee

Farrell, H. and Knight, J. 2003, "Trust, Institutions, and Institutional Change: Industrial Districts and the Social Capital Hypothesis," *Politics and Society* 31(4), 537–566.

Fish, M.S., 2002, "Islam and Authoritarianism," *World Politics* 55(1), 4–37.

Freedom House, 2015, "Tunisia", *Freedom in the World*. Last accessed 1 March 2018. Available at: https://freedomhouse.org/report/freedom-world/2015/tunisia

Freeman, E., 2015, *The Political Salience of Corruption: The Politics of Corruption During the Arab Spring*, Department of Political Science, McGill University. Master's Thesis.

GPPAC (The Global Partnership for the Prevention of Armed Conflict), 2014. "Human Security". Available at: www.gppac.net/human-security

Hamzawy, A., 2016, "The Arab World Needs a New Social Contract," *Al Jazeera*, 22 September.

Hardin, R. (ed.), 2004, *Distrust*. Russell Sage Foundation, New York.

Kaldor, M., 2007, *Human Security: Reflections on Globalization and Intervention*. Polity Press, Cambridge.

Kaspersen, L.B., 2005, "The Origin, Development, Consolidation and Transformation of the Danish Welfare State," in N. Kildal and S. Kuhnle (eds), *Normative Foundations of the Welfare State: The Nordic Experience*. Routledge, Abingdon, 52–72.

Knack, S., 2001, "Trust, Associational Life and Economic Performance," in J.F. Helliwell (ed.) *The Contribution of Human and Social Capital to Sustained Economic Growth and Well-Being*. Proceedings of OECD/HRDC conference, HRDC, Quebec, Ottawa, March 19–21, 2000, 172–202.

Kostovicova, D., Martin, M., and Bojicic-Dzelilovic, V., 2012, "The Missing Link in Human Security Research: Dialogue and Insecurity in Kosovo," *Security Dialogue*, 43(6), 569–585.

Kruse, M., 2015, *Tunisia's Democratic Transition: An Analysis of the Constitutional Process*. Master of International Development Studies thesis, Roskilde University, Department of Society and Globalisation, Roskilde.

Kuran, T., 2016, "The Roots of Middle East Mistrust," *Project Syndicate* 8 July. Last accessed on 1 March 2018. Available at: www.project-syndicate.org/commentary/roots-of-middle-east-mistrust-by-timur-kuran-2016-07

Muhanna-Matar, A., 2014, *New Trends of Women's Activism after the Arab Uprisings: Redefining Women's Leadership*. LSE Middle East Centre paper series, 5. Middle East Centre, LSE, London.

Muhanna-Matar, A., 2016. *Agency and Gender in Gaza: Masculinity, Femininity and Family during the Second Intifada*. Routledge, Abingdon.

Norris, P., 2011, *Democratic Deficit: Critical Citizens Revisited*. Cambridge University Press, Cambridge.

Ostrom, E. and Walker, J. (eds.), 2003, *Trust and Reciprocity: Interdisciplinary Lessons from Experimental Research*. The Russell Sage Foundation, New York.

Owen, R., 2004, *State, Power and Politics in the Making of the Modern Middle East*. Routledge, London.

Oxford Business Group, 2016, "Tunisia's Economic Reforms Tackling Structural Issues". Last accessed 13 November 2018. Available at: https://oxfordbusinessgroup.com/overview/renewed-potential-reforms-are-under-way-tackle-structural-issues

Putnam, R.D. and Feldstein, L.D., 2003, *Better Together: Restoring the American Community*. Simon and Schuster, New York.

Taraki, L. (ed.), 2006, *Living Palestine: Family Survival, Resistance and Mobility under Occupation*. Syracuse University Press, Syracuse.

Vargas-Hernandez, J.G., 2008, "Relationships between Institutional Economics of Cooperation and the Political Economy of Trust," *Brazilian Political Science Review* (Online) 2(1). Last accessed 1 March 2018. Available at: http://socialsciences.scielo.org/scielo.php?script=sci_arttext&pid=S1981-38212008000100002

Webb, A., 1991, "Co-ordination: A Problem in Public Sector Management," *Policy and Politics* 19(4), 229–242.

Whitaker, B., 2010, "Why Taxes are Low in the Middle East," *The Guardian*, 23 August. Available at: www.theguardian.com/commentisfree/2010/aug/23/why-taxes-low-arab-world

Yahya, M., 2016, "Great Expectations in Tunisia" Carnegie Middle East Center March. Last accessed 13 November 2018. Available at: https://carnegieendowment.org/files/CMEC_60_Yahya_Tunisia_Final.pdf

20

THE HALTING PROCESS OF DEMOCRATIZATION IN THE ARAB WORLD

Current challenges and future prospects

Hamdy A. Hassan and Hassanein T. Ali

Introduction

The concept of an Arab democratic "deadlock" or "deficit" has become increasingly popular as a way to describe the lack of democratic governance in the Arab world. It is argued that the Arab states represent an exception to the democratic wave that has swept the rest of the world, from Eastern Europe to East Asia and Latin America and even sub-Saharan Africa. This situation naturally raises the question of why Arab countries have lagged in democratization. According to many scholars, political Islam is the main problem: the Arab mind cannot reconcile Islamic law (Sharia) with democracy or even secular government. Many writers have promoted a kind of Islamic dragon myth or adopted the dichotomy of tyranny or chaos as an intellectual instrument to justify the persistence of authoritarian Arab regimes.

Following the uprisings that began in 2010, a number of scholars leaped to hasty conclusions about the end of "Arab exceptionalism" in regard to democracy. More than half a decade later, however, the outcomes have generally been negative and disappointing, as some Arab countries have plunged into civil war and internal conflict that threaten their very existence as political entities. In other cases, the ruling elites have taken tentative steps on the path of political reform in an effort to divert the winds of change; alternatively, democratization has at times been considered a low priority in the face of perceived security and development challenges. All of these responses represent attempts by ruling regimes to modernize authoritarianism rather than to engage in genuine democratization (Elbadawi and Makdisi, 2007; Fish, 2002; Sadiki, 2004).

The aim of this chapter is to account for the most significant political and democratic trends in the Arab world in the wake of the Arab Spring and to analyze the current challenges facing the process of democratization. In what follows, we will present the main obstacles to democracy on the one hand and the positive indications on the other. Some of these obstacles are long-standing and others are new, and their effects vary from one state to another. The most pressing issues include the entrenched structures of domination, tyranny and corruption; establishing democratic foundations in the context of the aforementioned threat of state disintegration; the increasing role of Islamic organizations, which has involved a politicization of religion and a "religionization" of politics; frayed civil–military relations; the fragility of civil parties, whether nationalist, liberal or leftist; the weakness of non-governing organizations; worsening economic and social conditions; and changes in the interests of foreign powers with regard to the region's democratization. A further aim of this chapter is to analyze and anticipate the effects of democratization on regional security in the Arab world. Among the various factors that will receive emphasis are the new media revolution (i.e., social media), the new political culture brought about by developments in the Arab Spring, the mounting frustration among the youth in many countries, and the end of the rentier state. Given the challenges facing democracy, the region seems unlikely to witness a genuine democratic transformation, at least in the short or medium term, will probably waver between stability and instability with regard to the political and security environments, with anarchy and state failure occurring in the worst situations. At the same time, hybrid forms of political systems may arise that combine elements of democracy and authoritarianism in what scholars refer to as electoral or semi-authoritarianism or as electoral or semi-democracy. In this context, large-scale political, economic and social protests can be expected to become more common in many Arab countries over the coming years.

This chapter, then, will cover three broad issues: overall trends in political and democratic development after the Arab Spring, major challenges to and constraints on democratization in the Arab world, and democratization in the context of regional security. The conclusion will discuss the prospects for democratization and regional security.

Political and democratic developments after the Arab Spring: An overview

Political and democratic development has followed distinctive paths in the various Arab nations owing to the varying responses of regimes to the uprisings that began in Tunisia in late 2010. In general, these trends can be categorized as: (1) partial political reform intended to divert the winds of change within the framework of existing systems, resulting in the hybrid systems mentioned above, of which examples are Morocco, Oman, Algeria and Jordan; (2) the collapse of the nation-state and associated rise of armed non-state actors, as seen in Libya, Yemen, Syria and Iraq; or (3) the achievement of some form of democratic transition, although with challenges, as in Tunisia (Diamond and Plattner, 2014; Sarihan, 2014). In what follows, we will address each of these trends in turn.

Partial political reforms and hybrid political systems

Following the Arab Spring uprisings, many Arab regimes undertook political, economic and social reforms in order to accommodate popular demands without allowing for any fundamental changes. In Morocco, Algeria, the Sultanate of Oman, Jordan and elsewhere, constitutional and legislative amendments were adopted that strengthened legislative institutions and electoral systems, eased restrictions on political parties and civil society organizations, attempted to provide adequate funding to address acute economic and social problems, and provided ways to fight corruption (Mainuddin, 2016; Davis, 2016).

Some of these reform initiatives have managed to undermine the internal forces that supported the revolutions. The result has been a consolidation of the ruling regimes and the emergence of the aforementioned hybrid systems combining democratic and authoritarian elements, which were described in Freedom House's (2018) annual Freedom in the World report as "partly free" (as opposed to free or non-free) countries.

Among the various other hybrid political systems that emerged during the post-democratic transition in a number of Asian, Latin American, Eastern European and African nations since the 1970s, some have been assigned to a "gray political zone" or "foggy zone" thought to fall somewhere within the classic dichotomy between full democracy and non-democratic systems. It is now clear that such hybrid political systems do not necessarily represent a transition phase to full democracy, but instead have followed existing forms and patterns of existing systems, thereby maintaining a degree of continuity while acclimating to their various environments. As a consequence, hybrid political systems have become a priority on the policy research agenda. Several concepts have been introduced to classify these systems based on notions of democracy and authoritarianism, specifically electoral and defective democracy; the latter includes exclusive, domain and illiberal democracy and such other concepts as electoral, competitive and semi-authoritarianism (Zinecker, 2009; Bogaards, 2009; Wigell, 2008).

It therefore appears that hybrid political systems, or what Alfred Stepan and Juan J. Linz (2013) have identified as an "authoritarian-democratic hybrid", will remain one of the main features of political and democratic development of the Arab region. Thus the ruling regimes in many Arab countries have adopted multi-party systems in conjunction with political, administrative and security restrictions on opposition parties. These hybrid systems embed numerous other contradictions as well. They feature regular local, legislative and presidential elections but intervene in various ways to influence the outcomes; they allow for the establishment of civil society organizations but maintain control over them; they permit private and independent media channels and newspapers to function but impose restrictions on freedom of opinion and expression; and they emphasize human rights in constitutional and legal documents as part of official political discourse while regularly violating those rights. Moreover, the recognition of the impartiality and sanctity of the judiciary by the hybrid state fails to guarantee fair trials, as other branches of government may interfere with the judiciary in order to prevent implementation of judicial decisions.

Failed nation-states and the growing phenomenon of armed non-state actors

Many Arab states have suffered to varying degrees and in various ways with overlapping crises and problems in the wake of the Arab Spring. Some, such as Somalia, have disintegrated, while others have proved unable to function effectively or efficiently. The crisis of the nation-state in the Arab world is not a recent phenomenon, but the situation has generally deteriorated since 2010, and the risk that failed states may create political and security vacuums have allowed for the emergence and expanded roles of many armed non-state actors, such as ISIS. History shows that a state's failure to deliver public services to its citizens together with loss of legitimacy and control of its territory tend to result in two particularly significant outcomes, namely the emergence of tribal and religious identities as an alternative to national identity and the development of a political and security vacuum that armed non-state actors exploit in order to strengthen and expand their control of territory (Devlin-Foltz and Ozkececi-Taner, 2010; International Crisis Group, 2016; Ahram and Lust, 2016).

Thus, for example, Syria has failed to function as a state owing to the regime's brutal policies as a peaceful revolution transformed into armed action. Numerous local, regional and international powers have engaged in the Syrian conflict in order to further their own interests and agendas, while the country has become a battlefield among multiple stakeholders in which peaceful solutions have proved elusive for a variety of reasons. The collapse of the Syrian State's structures and institutions has further exacerbated its economic and social crises and has escalated the catastrophic problem of displaced persons and refugees. This situation has created an environment favorable for the expansion of ISIS and other jihadist terrorist groups. Although the recent military escalation has been driving back ISIS in Syria, as indicated by the liberation of Mosul in Iraq, such actions will not produce a solution to the crisis, for the compromises

Democratization in the Arab world

and arrangements for a post-ISIS era appear difficult to arrive at and complicated to implement (Khatib, 2015; Hassan, 2016).

In Iraq, the birthplace of ISIS, the situation has been no better. Following its occupation of Iraq in 2003 and overthrow of Saddam Hussein, the United States adopted chaotic policies toward Iraq and committed several key mistakes, in particular dismantling Iraqi State structures and institutions, including the army and security services, and thereby compromising central authority and state mechanisms that could have maintained security and enforced law and order. Additionally, multiple forms of marginalization, oppression and systematic violence are directed against Sunni Arabs in Iraq despite the major role played by the groups associated with the Sunni Tribal Awakening against the so-called "Islamic State of Iraq", which grew out of Al-Qaeda in Iraq in 2007 and 2008. The increasingly large political roles of Kurds and Shiites came at the expense of the marginalization of Sunni Arabs, which has been abetted by the emergence of Iranian-backed sectarian militias (International Crisis Group, 2013; Khatib, 2015: 8).

Compounding the failure of US policy in Iraq, successive Iraqi governments have proved unable to maintain national unity based on citizenship, the rule of law and state institutions. Instead, the country adopted a quota system with policies based on sectarianism, which has meant the exclusion of Sunnis and increased dependency on Iran. Iraq has thus descended into chaos, insecurity and ethnic violence, far from being the model of peaceful democracy and peace that the architects of the Iraq War envisioned. US political blundering, successive failed Iraqi governments, and the extension of Iranian influence have all contributed to the escalation of the sectarian crises and division within the country. It was under these conditions that ISIS and other militant groups arose and came to challenge the authority of the state and its institutions; thus ISIS succeeded in occupying about a third of Iraq in 2014, and holds about the same portion of Syria presently (Gerges, 2016; Cockburn, 2015). The military escalation against ISIS in Iraq in recent months, which has focused on the complete liberation of Mosul, does not spell the end of the Iraqi crisis. No agreement has been reached on the arrangements for the post-ISIS period, especially given the fact that numerous local, regional and international forces are arrayed against the group, each with its own political, economic, security and strategic interests and goals. Without a comprehensive settlement, the conditions that allowed the emergence of ISIS and its expansion will persist (Al-Obeidi, 2016).

Turning now to Libya, following the overthrow of the Gaddafi regime in 2011, governing institutions and central authority disintegrated and a large area of the country fell under the control of non-government armed forces, militias, religious tribes and various organizations. Ongoing internal political and military divisions have further complicated the Libyan situation, with the emergence of two competing parliaments and other divisions among interested regional and international powers (International Crisis Group, 2012). Regional and international efforts to solve the crisis have yielded no tangible results; thus the Skhirat agreement of December 2015 was never implemented. The result has been the creation of an environment that militant actors have exploited in order to expand their powers. ISIS, for example, was able to control the city of Sirte; and while the forces of the Government of National Accord, known as Al-Bunyan Al-Marsous, were able to liberate the city from ISIS after a nearly seven-month-long campaign, the Libyan crisis is nowhere near an end.

The neighboring Egyptian state, although cohesive, has endured mercurial transition periods following the revolution that began on 25 January 2011, owing to the conflicting agendas of political actors and an inability to reach a national consensus regarding democratization. Egypt has also suffered from deteriorating economic and security conditions and fragile institutions. Following the end of the Muslim Brotherhood regime in July 2013, terrorist attacks in Sinai increased from the Ansar Bait al-Maqdis ("supporters of the holy house", also known as Ansar

Jerusalem, "supporters of Jerusalem") group, which in November 2014 pledged loyalty to ISIS and changed its name to the Sinai Caliphate. In response, the Egyptian army and security forces have escalated military operations against attacks on members of the military and police as well as civilians within Sinai and without. Egypt's economic and social conditions are similarly compromised, further impeding the process of democratization and helping to define the current government as a hybrid system (Rezaei, 2015).

In Yemen, the state was further weakened and made vulnerable in the aftermath of the Arab Spring. Soon after the ouster of President Ali Abdullah Saleh under the Gulf Initiative, the Houthis, with Iranian support, intensified their military operations in the country, even occupying the capital of Sana'a in September 2014. A little over a year later, on 26 November 2015, an Arab coalition led by Saudi Arabia launched Operation Decisive Storm against the Houthis and allied forces at the request of Yemeni President Abed Rabbo Mansur Hadi and with the support of former President Saleh. Even as Operation Decisive Storm has been replaced by Operation Restoring Hope (on 21 April 2015), the military conflict in Yemen has continued amid failed attempts at a peaceful settlement. In this context, other armed groups, including ISIS, have reinforced their presence in Yemen, particularly in the provincial regions of Hadhramaut, Lahij, Abyan and Aden. Al-Qaeda has also continued to maintain a presence in Yemen, where it was active even before the Arab Spring (Schmitz, 2012). Clearly, one of the major challenges facing Yemen after the war will be the reconstruction and rebuilding of the state on new foundations that transcend regional, tribal and sectarian loyalties. Absent such a transformation, Yemen will remain a safe haven for ISIS, Al-Qaeda and other armed non-state actors (Al-Qadmi, 2017).

A democratic transition fraught with risks and challenges: The case of Tunisia

Following the "escape" of former President Ben Ali and the beginnings of the Arab Spring in Tunisia, the nation has witnessed a transition fraught with crises, as seen in particular in the sharp polarization between Islamists and secularists, an escalation in terrorist acts, and deteriorating economic and security conditions. Nevertheless, compared with other countries affected by the Arab Spring, Tunisia has been able to transcend the divisions among its political elite, at least to some extent. Thus in 2014 the country adopted, with majority consent, a new constitution that conforms to modern democratic standards. This constitution represents an important step toward completing the nation's transitional phase, as is evident in its ability to hold legislative and presidential elections. From the perspective of democratization, four factors have distinguished Tunisia from other countries that experienced the Arab Spring (Ali, 2013; Szmolka, 2015).

First, there is the nature of the Tunisian political elite. Despite frequent crises and polarization between secularists and Islamists, the moderates on both sides have exerted the strongest influence by consistently being able to open channels of dialogue and compromise, thereby restraining the influence of the extremists. Thus the coalition that governed following the elections of June 2011 (the so-called "Troika") included both Islamic and secular parties. Further, the government that was formed on the basis of legislative elections consisted of representatives of several parties – including the moderate Islamic Ennahda Party – as well as independent ministers.

Second, the relative flexibility shown by the Ennahda Party in agreeing to form a new government of independent national competencies earned the trust of the constituent national assembly in January 2014. The Ennahda Party was also accommodating when it gave up constitutional proposals that could have led to further polarization and disagreement between the parties and secular forces and disruption in the drafting of the constitution. Thus the party did not seek full power and attempt to seize control of the entirety of the nation-state as the Muslim Brotherhood did in Egypt. The Tunisian Islamists appear to have learned from the Egyptian experience and became more willing to offer compromises.

Third, civil society in Tunisia, unlike that in many other Arabic countries, is dynamic. So it was that, following the assassination of a leftist opposition leader and the worsening of political tensions between Islamists and secularists in 2013, a quartet of civil society organizations – the Tunisian General Labor Union (UGTT), the Tunisian Confederation of Industry, Trade and Handicrafts (UTICA), the Tunisian Human Rights League (LTDH), and the Tunisian Order of Lawyers – proposed a roadmap to peace. This roadmap called for the formation of a government of independent (nonpartisan) national competencies to lead the country through the transitional period, the adoption of the draft constitution, the formation of an independent body to supervise elections, and setting a date for elections. The four civilian organizations engaged in consultations with the political parties on the proposed roadmap, sponsored national dialogue, and at times applied pressure until they reached an agreement that has placed Tunisia on the path toward democratization.

Fourth, the Tunisian army has remained neutral with regard to the political process, unlike the armies in other Arab Spring countries, which played a decisive role in politics despite differences in the nature and degree of their professionalism, only to become major parts of the various political equations.

Despite these promising developments, however, democracy has not fully taken root in Tunisia, and the transformation process continues to involve risks and challenges. There is the continuing threat posed by terrorist groups and organizations (especially in light of the ongoing crisis in neighboring Libya), rampant corruption, poor economic and social conditions, and widespread social protests, especially since the root causes of the revolution that toppled Ben Ali's regime have yet to be confronted. Moreover, the regime must avoid a political setback of the type that occurred during the failed process of democratization in Algeria in the 1990s (Cristiani, 2016; Zoubir and White, 2016).

Significant challenges to democratization in the Arab world

The challenges and effects of democratization in the Arab world vary from one country to another. The future of the process in the Arab world largely depends on meeting these challenges. There are in addition economic and social problems plaguing the vast majority of Arab countries, which are manifest in weak growth rates, increasing unemployment, inflation and debt, growing economic and social disparities (especially in those that do not produce oil), and the declining stature of the middle class. A number of other major challenges are summarized in the following sub-sections.

Entrenched structures of domination, tyranny and corruption

Most Arab countries, far from experiencing true democracy, have been subjected to authoritarian control that has established structures and elements of tyranny through political, legal, security, economic, cultural and religious mechanisms. The most important of these structures in the post-independence era have included special laws restricting the rights and freedoms of citizens, the establishment of a large number of security organs and institutions, extravagant spending to protect the regimes in power, various forms of interference in the impartiality and independence of the judiciary, and control over civil society organizations through various legal, administrative and security measures. Additionally, authoritarian regimes often nurture power struggles within the ruling parties, pitting political forces against each other so that the ruler remains the sole locus of power within the entire political system.

Moreover, regimes have been known to use economic and political grants and rewards to ensure loyalty among political forces and social formations and to enable these systems to contain large segments of the intelligentsia by various means so that they depend upon the sole source of power and continually justify its policy. In most Arabic countries, all of this activity on the part of the regimes has been accompanied by the entrenchment of a pervasive culture of corruption. The forces of corruption are naturally keen to hinder any development of a true democracy, their goal being to continue to subvert state institutions, since their interests can only be achieved in the absence of the rule of law and accountability and they are abetted by official media outlets that serve to praise the leader and promote his achievements and attack opponents. For years, regimes have used the Islamic threat as a kind of "big bad wolf" in managing relations with Western powers, presenting themselves as preferable to religious extremism in defending Western interests in the region. Through the policies and methods just mentioned, these systems have been able to establish what are essentially "police states" that have succeeded in impairing their opponents in order to achieve a form of authoritarian political stability. It is for these reasons that the sudden wave of revolts and uprisings in several Arab countries beginning in late 2010 were driven neither by traditional political parties nor by the Islamic powers and currents. Rather, these revolts were sparked by the passion and energy of youth groups that effectively employed the Internet and social media to mobilize against the powers that be. The authoritarian rulers never anticipated such circumstances, much less made plans to confront them, and therefore were unable to adjust and regain control over their states (Bayat, 2013).

Based on the above considerations, tackling the heavy legacy of tyrannical and corrupt structures that were built and flourished in political, security, economic, social, cultural, religious and media contexts is one of the major challenges in the post-Arab Spring era (Al-Kuwari, 2006). Democratization accordingly cannot be achieved by the mere overthrow of an authoritarian system, since other processes, in particular the dismantling of structures of domination, tyranny and corruption, take time. What is important in this context is that the social forces, the main political parties and civil society organizations agree on the trends and on the policies that need to be pursued and the repairs that need to be effected in order to achieve this goal. Such policies must take into account the economy, education, media and culture, and religion, as well as the necessary reforms, so that the constitutional and legal structures may be consistent with the fundamentals and principles of democracy. Moreover, the security and justice sectors and local administrations are also in need of policy reform. With time, a nation can move steadily and progressively toward democratization. Only then will it be possible to question the nature of political actors in post-authoritarian regimes in order to determine whether their faith that democracy represents the best choice for their nations has been well-placed and whether their efforts to build national consensus can create solid foundations for democratization.

Coordinating state-building and the establishment of democracy

Comparison of the experiences of democratization internationally makes clear that the chances of establishing a democratic system improve in the context of established national states with legitimacy and control over their territories through a monopoly on the lawful use of force. In this context, one of the main impediments to democratization in the Arab world, before or after the Arab Spring, has been the difficult of coordinating the construction of a nation-state with the establishment of democracy. This challenge has become more complex since 2010, as internal wars have plagued several Arab countries and threatened their existence as political entities, as just discussed in regard to Libya, Syria and Yemen, while persistent conflicts and internal divisions afflict Iraq, Sudan, Lebanon and other countries (Mühlberger, 2015).

The greatest challenge in these latter countries is maintaining some form of central power while rebuilding the state on new foundations in the post-conflict period. Even if historical compromises in these countries should be reached so as to avoid a "Somali scenario", they would remain beset by weak institutions and therefore unable to carry out their core functions effectively and efficiently (Ayubi, 2009). All of these problems trace back to the history of corruption within these institutions that has been fostered by a lack of oversight and of coordination between governmental entities. This being the case, institutional reform is urgently needed to equip state institutions better, acknowledge the rule of law, and provide goods and services to citizens, with an emphasis on security. All of these issues must be taken into account in the course of the democratization process, since democracy cannot exist without security and cannot flourish without provisions that guarantee human, economic, social, civil and political rights.

Democracy and political Islamists: The politicization of religion and "religionization" of politics

It is a fact that none of the Islamist factions was involved in sparking the Arab Spring uprisings; and while some participated later on, others did not. Islamist factions were, however, the most successful on the political level. Thus Islamist parties took power in Egypt, Tunisia and Morocco, and several new Islamist parties or authorities emerged in the Arab world. Remarkably, this outcome in some cases extended the political role of traditional powers and Salafi parties, Egypt being the prime example. In light of these changes, several researchers have proceeded to analyze the "Islamists' moment", the transformation of the Arab Spring into an "Islamist Spring" and the "Islamist hijacking" of the Arab revolutions. In the post-revolution period as well, there has been a rise in the role of Salafist entities in several Arab countries (Dawisha, 2013; Bradley, 2012; Gerges, 2013; Ahmad, 2013; Knudsen and Ezbidi, 2014).

There is no contradiction between Islam as a religion and democracy as a political system, since Islam values freedom, justice, equality, human dignity, tolerance and respect for human rights, and a secular civil state. Indeed, Islam does not mandate any form of state or formula for governance that applies to all Muslims in every time and place; such considerations have been left to religious scholars. Yet while many consider modern democracy to be consistent with the principles of Islamic Sharia, the ascent of Islamist politicians, particularly in the wake of the Arab Spring, has posed and continues to pose real problems for democratization. The reasons for this state of affairs are several, and will now be considered in turn (Hamid, 2014).

To begin with, religious and political polarization between the Islamic movements on the one hand and the secular currents and parties on the other has been increasing, as is evident in both Egypt and Tunisia. The essential difference between these two cases in this regard was that the Ennahda party and Tunisia's main secular parties managed, despite the political and security crisis, to guide the nation through its transitional phase and to engage in a serious national dialogue brokered and sponsored by a number of civil society organizations that issued, in the aforementioned consensus, a clear roadmap (Kerrou, 2014). In Egypt, by contrast, the Islamic-secular divide was prominent in the country's three transitional stages after Mubarak stepped aside and, unsurprisingly, this divide had a negative impact on Egyptians' various political and constitutional rights. As a result, no genuine democratic transition took place, with political developments giving rise to the hybrid political system described above (Lust et al., 2012).

Second, the Islamists' recently discovered desire to exercise direct political power and to emerge as the sole authority highlights another key difference between the Muslim Brotherhood and its Freedom and Justice Party in Egypt on the one hand and Tunisia's Ennahda Party on the other. In Egypt, a form of estrangement occurred between the party and the community. In the narrow victory of Dr Mohamed Morsi in the presidential election over Ahmed Shafiq, the Brotherhood took control through the exclusion and marginalization of other political powers, attempting to control all state institutions and organizations and to employ them for its own benefit. President Morsi therefore clashed with the judiciary, media, police and armed forces, and his constitutional declaration in November 2012 granting himself nearly absolute powers further deepened the nation's social and political divide (El-Sherif, 2014).

In addition, President Morsi responded to strong opposition by taking steps to amend the disputed 2012 constitution and forming a government of national competencies to replace the short-lived government of Prime Minister Hisham Kandil, which was considered to have been as ineffective as the presidency had been in discharging its duties. Morsi also ignored the demands of millions of Egyptians who took to the streets in a revolutionary wave on 30 June 2013, to call for early presidential elections and thereby prompted the army to intervene decisively a few days later (on 3 July) and launch a new roadmap that isolated Morsi. In response, the Muslim Brotherhood and its supporters engaged in a "national coalition to support legality" that took the form of protests and acts of violence and terrorism calculated to demonstrate the military's ineffective authority and to hinder its role in the transition.

Conversely, following the October 2011 elections in Tunisia, the Ennahda Party alliance that claimed a majority in the founding National Council consisted of a troika involving the centrist and secular parties of the Congress for the Republic (CPR) and Ettakatol (also known as the Democratic Forum for Labor and Liberties). Following the 2013 political and security crises touched off by the assassinations of prominent opposition figures Shukri Belaid and Mohamed Brahman along with several army officials, the Ennahda Party was eventually compelled to make political concessions in order to work with the secular opposition and complete the transition phase, as discussed. The party then became eager to distinguish itself from Salafist groups that have engaged in violence against the state and society. Thus, for instance, an Ennahda leader in the government, Ali Al Areed, declared the Salafi group Ansar al-Sharia a terrorist organization and launched a vigorous security campaign against it. Ennahda, it appears, had learned from the Muslim Brotherhood's trials and tribulations in Egypt and were keen to avoid repeating its mistakes.

The third consideration is the expanded the role of the Salafis; for the political ascent of Islamist groups and traditional parties goes beyond groups like the Muslim Brotherhood in Egypt and Ennahda in Tunisia. Indeed, the rise of Salafist parties came as a surprise, particularly in those two countries, where it occurred in the context of the increasing role of Salafist groups that have committed acts of violence and terrorism against the state and society. Thus, as discussed, ISIS dominated, at least for a while, large swathes of both Syria and Iraq while maintaining branches and sleeper cells in many Arab and non-Arab countries. In addition, groups such as the aforementioned Ansar Bait al-Maqdis (now the Sinai Caliphate), Ajnad Misr in Egypt, Ansar al-Sharia in Tunisia, Al-Qaeda in the Arabian Peninsula in Yemen, and Ansar al-Sharia in Libya pledged loyalty to ISIS. In both contexts, the Salafist ascent represented an obstacle to democracy, as the Salafis who engaged in political action, forming political parties and participating in elections, did so without serious doctrinal revisions of well-known previous positions that rejected partisanship, democracy and elections on religious grounds. The perceptions and attitudes of these organizations and individuals toward such fundamental issues as the civil state, democracy, citizenship, and the rights of women and minorities are dubious and ambiguous at best, confirming that their involvement in politics reflects less acceptance of democracy and genuine commitment to its associated practices than political expediency and pragmatism with regard to their forces and parties, which do not act in the interest of a democratic transition (Aburman, 2013; Ali, 2013; Brown, 2011). On the other hand, jihadist organizations explicitly reject democracy as heresy, and their terrorist activities in countries such as Egypt, Tunisia, Yemen and Libya have adversely affected the democratization process, contributing to political and security instability. These policies inevitably give way to human rights violations of greater or lesser severity, thereby upsetting the balance between protecting human rights and combating terrorism, even as the terrorist acts themselves impact national economies, especially in the sectors of tourism and investment (Styszyński, 2015; International Crisis Group, 2013; Boukhars, 2014:12–15). This rise of Salafist currents has also helped to create and nurture religious and sectarian conflicts and tensions in many Arab countries, where religion and doctrine have been extensively employed for political purposes.

It is in these respects that the political ascent of various Islamist factions has led to the politicization of religion and what can be described as the "religionization of politics", complementary phenomena that highlight a major impediment to democratic change, namely the attempt by various religious currents and organizations to monopolize truth. In effect, those who refuse to conform to Islamist political and social visions will be labeled heretics or opponents of religion who are to be condemned and called to justice. Such is the outcome of employing religion to serve partisan political objectives and interests.

Nationalists, liberalists, leftists and the vulnerability and fragility of civilian political forces

The weakness and fragility of political forces described as civil, which include liberal (in favor of laissez-faire capitalism), leftist and nationalist parties, are among the main factors that explain the political ascension of Islamists in the post-revolution era and in the wake of the Arab Spring uprisings. This much is evident in the Egyptian and Tunisian election results during phase one of political change. Elections in other countries, such as Morocco, have reaffirmed this assessment, in that the concerned parties and forces failed to present themselves as viable political alternatives to the Muslim Brotherhood and the Salafist Al-Nour Party in Egypt, the Ennahda Party in Tunisia, or the Justice and Development Party in Morocco. Despite the declining influence of Islamists in many of these countries (as a result of numerous factors that are beyond the scope of the present discussion), the liberal, leftist and nationalist civil powers in Arab countries remain weak and fragile.

This weakness and fragility is due to many factors, some relating to security and administrative and political restrictions that the ruling regimes in many countries have imposed, and others relating to subjective problems experienced by these forces and parties, including fragmentation at the political level, as a consequence of which they have been unable to form strong political alliances and coalitions. At the same time, their social bases remain weak, since they have consistently concentrated their efforts on limited areas in capitals and major cities. The parties' elitist ideological and political disquisitions and frequent conflicts and splits have also contributed greatly to their weakness, since their commitment to intra-party democratic governance has been feeble and their approach to democracy generally has been opportunistic, most parties being inclined to support democracy if the results are in their favor and to oppose it when the opposite is the case (Wolf, 2014; Muasher, 2013; Ahmari, 2012). This situation is one of the main obstacles to democratization in the Arab world, for democracy requires parties that consider democratic principles to be the one true and right choice and are committed to fight peacefully for its attainment. The situations in Egypt and Tunisia are similar to those in many other Arabic countries.

The weakness of civil society organizations

Current democratization literature emphasizes that civil society organizations, which include civil and professional associations, trade unions, clubs, and other social movements, can play a number of influential roles during the transition to and consolidation of democracy (Ali, 2013). In the Arab world, it can be said that the weakness of civil society organizations is among the factors that explain the halting nature of the democratization process. Simply put, the thousands of private associations, trade unions, human rights organizations, and social movements in Arab countries have been unable to play active and influential roles in democratization. Their failure to do so can be attributed to, among other factors, the climate of religious and political polarization, in which the civil society sectors serve as tools for various political parties. Also significant in this context are legal, administrative and security constraints that reduce the effectiveness and independence of Arab civil societies. Consideration should also be given to the structural vulnerability of many civil society organizations in terms of limited membership, lack of funding, the absence or weakness of institutional transparency, and the predominance of religious and charitable organizations as opposed to juridical entities and broader associations. Similarly, foreign funding of many of these organizations has negative repercussions for civil society. In this context, the significance of internal divisions and conflicts among youth coalitions and revolutionaries, which has weakened the role of the youth in the political process in the countries affected by the winds of change of the Arab Spring, is unmistakable (Plaetzer, 2014).

The relative strength of Tunisia's civil society compared with those of other Arabic countries may explain why its democratization process has remained on track in the wake of the overthrow of Ben Ali, at which time divisions between Islamists and secularists would have destroyed any progress had it not been for the intervention of the four civil society organizations (UGTT, UTICA, LTDH, and the Tunisian Order of Lawyers) and their initiative for a roadmap leading to a national consensus among political parties through the transition stage, as discussed in detail earlier (Boose, 2012; Kerrou, 2014; Chayes, 2014).

The political role of the military and the complicated nature of civil–military relations

The revolutions and uprisings revealed the divergent positions of the various Arab national armies. The refusal of the Tunisian army, for instance, which is small and non-politicized, to fire on demonstrators precipitated the collapse of the political system. In the revolt against Gaddafi, on the other hand, the Libyan army disintegrated, with some battalions supporting the revolution and others supporting the regime. Thus there has been no official Libyan national army in the post-Gaddafi era, and the efforts of the transitional authorities to build a new one have been modest. In Yemen, the army also fractured internally, part of it siding with the revolutionaries; the country had certainly already been politicized, with former President Saleh filling leadership positions with loyalists, in particular his sons and members of his tribe. Therefore, one of the greatest challenges facing the new President Hadi was trying to restructure, unify and depoliticize the army.

In Egypt, the situation was vastly different. The army supported the 25 January Revolution, similar to the situation in Tunisia, thereby forcing Mubarak to give up power; the Supreme Council of the Armed Forces then took over the affairs of the country from 11 February 2011 to 30 June 2012. The lack of a clear direction and purpose on the part of the Morsi administration during the transitional period reduced the chances of establishing a new democratic order. In the aftermath, millions of Egyptians took to the streets on 30 June in a new wave of revolutionary protests, demanding early presidential elections. After President Morsi refused to respond to this demand, the army intervened decisively, on 3 July 2013, and proclaimed a new roadmap, under which President Morsi was removed from power (Taylor, 2014; Wehreyand Cole, 2013).

Regardless of the factors at play in the differing responses of the Arab armies to the revolutions and uprisings, relations between civilian and military authorities remain a major issue with regard to the future of political, and in particular democratic, development in the Arab world. Issues involving the military are rife with complexities and sensitivities, making them difficult to resolve in the absence of a genuine national consensus and effective constitutional and legal frameworks governing civil–military relations. There is thus a need for a well-defined foundation that is acceptable to authorities on both sides and that enhances the professionalism of the military. Such steps would enable the military to oversee civilian life within the context of a clear and detailed constitutional/legal framework in which non-military affairs and technical and operational strategies and plans are held accountable and subject to the oversight of the elected legislature. In such an environment, the military can commit itself to assuming a position of neutrality toward domestic policy processes, to being governed by the rules and fundamentals of democracy that safeguard its position as a professional national institution, and to fulfill its primary role of protecting and defending national borders. Achievement of these goals requires a genuine and complete democratic transition involving a legal constitution that represents the sole source of political legitimacy. Any such process requires a great deal of time and careful consideration of the many factors and variables involved. Crucial here will be the manifestation of a much-needed new social contract or national consensus characterized by clear and precise rules for a political process that are acceptable to and respected by the main political organizations and powers, thereby removing the justification for military interference in the political process, whether to support existing systems or to topple them.

The democratization process and regional security: Issues and challenges

The events of the Arab Spring have proved that the Arab alliances designed to ensure regional security are weak. The difficulty in providing a security umbrella for the Arab world can be traced back to the perpetual conflict of interests and divergent political agendas among the Arab countries. However deep its commitment to the notions of "one nation" and "Arab unity", every state remains focused on its own interests. Many of the Arab countries that are relatively well endowed with territory and competitive resources try to play leading roles in the region. Moreover, while Israel may have served as a unifying factor for Arabs in the past, this is not the case now, given the appearance of other players, including Iran and violent terrorist groups and of sectarian conflicts. There also seems to be the lack of a unified vision on the part of Arab states that could combine their efforts to achieve regional security goals, as was evident in the declining role of joint Arab action institutions, chiefly the Arab League (Dakhlallah, 2012: 393–412).

The strategic vacuum that is the result of the region's dramatic changes since 2011, then, has invited non-Arab regional players, such as Israel, Iran and Turkey, to attempt to expand their influence. Iran in particular has shown expansionist leanings, occupying islands claimed by the UAE and intensifying its presence in Arab Iraq, Syria, Lebanon and Yemen. Israel has also sought to exploit the presence of President Trump and the rise of European right-wing parties by taking unilateral measures in the occupied West Bank. It is possible that some of these transitions will spark unrest in parts of the Arab world and they may therefore involve serious regional and international security implications. Key features of the dialectical relationship between democratization and regional security in the post-Arab Spring period can be classified as follows.

- Although the Arab uprisings originated in local contexts, they soon took on regional and international dimensions. Since 2012, the Arab region has clearly become the scene of a new international and regional competition for power and influence, as exemplified by the cases of Syria, Libya and Yemen. While Iran, seeing itself as the main victor in the region, feels encouraged to adopt more expansionist policies, important Arab states like Saudi Arabia worry about losing ground to Iran and accordingly adopt defensive policies against it. These conflicting visions undoubtedly harm the prevailing regional security system
- The effects of the Arab Spring have transcended the social, political and economic issues that sparked the conflicts. The result has included the militarization of Syria and uprisings in Yemen and Libya and the ensuing negative regional and international complications, in particular the creation of enormous numbers of refugees and the rise of violent extremist ideologies in various forms. The argument has accordingly shifted away from democratic to regional transformation, thereby prolonging authoritarian rule, or reproducing it in new forms, and further impeding democratic transitions
- The dismantling of some Arab states and the militarization of uprisings in the region have nourished armed militias operating outside the control of any central authority, such as the Houthis in Yemen, the Kurdistan Democratic Union Party in Syria, and of course ISIS. It is noteworthy that these armed groups are sectarian or ideological in nature, for this orientation on their part increases the complexity of the region's security and political concerns. The effect of militarization and civil wars in some of the region's countries has been the creation of zones of influence and power struggles between regional and international powers, all of which affects the formation and reformation of the region's security systems
- The regional system has become dependent on the hegemony of the United States, particularly in terms of the region's security structure. It is not entirely clear whether other regional or international forces are capable of replacing the United States in this role. Obviously, the restoration of the region's geo-strategic influence, particularly regarding regional security, has put a damper on the democratization process. The US administration of Donald Trump has shown an inclination to ally with authoritarian and authoritarian-leaning regimes. Moreover, support for democratic values and policies in the Arab region is inconsistent with the political agendas of both Russia and China, while the European Union has played only a weak role in this regard

From the Israeli perspective, four trends link the Arab Spring to the region's balance of power and the very structure of the Arab region (Frisch, 2013: 33–50). First, there is the "Islamic Cold War"; for it seems clear that a strategic rivalry has developed between, on the one hand, the alliance of Egypt and Jordan and the Gulf states (except Qatar), with the tacit involvement of Israel and under the leadership of the United States, and, on the other, the Iranian-Syrian alliance with the participation of Lebanese Hezbollah party. Second, there is the conflict between the two regional blocs to recruit Egypt into their ranks. Third, there is the emergence of influential non-Arab powers, in particular Iran and Turkey. Fourth, there is the possibility of a potential alliance between Israel and the Arab countries in order to contain the growing expansion of Iran and Turkey. Such new alliances are certain to deepen the internal crisis of legitimacy among the ruling powers, as Arab systems yield to greater division and fragmentation.

Conclusion: Future prospects for democratization and security in the Arab world

Taking into consideration the relatively promising progress of democracy in Tunisia, the analysis of the consequences of the Arab Spring remains incomplete, as Arab countries continue to face numerous obstacles. Given the challenges that currently confront the democratization process across the Arab world, to varying degrees and in various forms, no Arab state is likely to achieve true democracy in the short or even medium term. The best that can be hoped for in this regard is the persistence of political "hybrid" systems that combine democratic and authoritarian elements in various proportions. In light of the conflicts and divisions in the region, both within and among states, and of the regional and international interventions in Arab affairs, the possibility that this region will enjoy a degree of peace, security and stability in the foreseeable future seems remote. This is especially true given the many impediments to achieving real political compromise, in particular the complexity of the internal conflicts that plague several Arab countries. This is the conclusion reached by the Global Peace Index Report (Institute for Economics and Peace 2017: 10–11) in which the Middle East and North Africa ranked poorly in terms of peace; 11 out of 20 Arab states were listed very low or low on the index, with Syria, Iraq, Yemen, Somalia, Libya and Sudan among the least peaceful countries.

It is apparent that, though the process of democratization may continue in the Arab world, in the absence of lasting peace and security for at least the short and medium term, environments conducive to the emergence of extremism, violence and terrorism will persist, particularly in Arab states threatened with disintegration as political entities.

Given the above considerations, several governing conditions need to be met in order to avoid the various pitfalls and to promote democratization and peace in the region. The first of these conditions is preservation of the nation-state and reform of its institutions; for a true democracy involves more than a nation's control over its territory and a monopoly on the legitimate use of force. These steps represent a fundamental challenge in the disintegrating states of Libya, Yemen, Syria, Iraq, Sudan, Somalia and Lebanon. In other cases, such as Tunisia and Jordan, the chances for democratization depend on the effectiveness of institutional reforms, which must be a priority for the security and justice sector as well as for local government.

Second, given that there can be no democracy without individuals committed to its establishment and maintenance, the future of the democratization process in Arab nations depends in part on the extent to which the invested parties are willing to develop and strengthen democratic mechanisms, to practice democratic values at the national level, and to coordinate among themselves during elections. The drafting of legislation that promotes democracy should accordingly take into account political parties and electoral laws so that it is consistent with the parties' initiatives for internal reform, whether in terms of political speeches, organizational structures or commitment to democracy.

Third, governance in Arab countries can be strengthened by establishing the values and practices of democracy, which include the rule of law, transparency, accountability, equal citizenship rights and duties, and curbing corruption. According to a recent World Bank study, the absence or weakness of economic and social policies that integrate various groups within a population has led to high unemployment, particularly among young people, and this has been a major factor in the dissemination of extremism and terrorism in the Middle East and North Africa. Putting an end to extremism will accordingly require the adoption of effective policies designed to achieve social justice and development, including jobs for young people and the psychological and social rehabilitation of children who have suffered the hardships of war and harbor feelings of bitterness towards their countries (Devarajan, 2016: 18–19).

Fourth, since the commingling of religion and politics is impeding democratization, the principle of absolute separation of the two must be observed in order to prevent the dominance of religious or sectarian political parties and, in accordance with constitutional and other legal texts, to criminalize the exploitation of religion for political objectives so as to confront and refute extremist thinking and renew religious discourse on solid foundations.

Lastly, the prominent role played by Western powers, particularly the United States, in consolidating authoritarianism in the post-independence Arab world deserves greater scrutiny. These powers could bolster the democratization process through, for example, economic assistance to the Arab countries, especially those without petroleum resources, thereby helping to reform state institutions and to support political parties and civil society organizations without prejudice to national laws. However, the Western role in promoting the process of democratization in the Arab world remains subject to internal factors, and if these factors are not favorable and there is no catalyst for democratic change, the West will remain an unreliable partner for Arab states.

References

Aburman, M. 2013. *Salafis and the Arab Spring: Question of Religion and Democracy in Arab Politics.* Beirut: Center for Arab Unity Studies.

Ahmad, T. 2013. *The Islamist Challenge in West Asia: Doctrinal and Political Competitions after the Arab Spring.* New Delhi: Pentagon Press.

Ahmari, S. 2012. The Failure of Arab Liberals: How a Celebrated Freedom Movement Fostered the Success of an Islamist Order. *Commentary*, www.commentarymagazine.com/articles/the-failure-of-arab-liberals. Accessed on 12 May 2017.

Ahram, A. and Lust, E. 2016. The Decline and Fall of the Arab State. *Survival*, 58(2): 7–34.

Ali, H. T. 2013. Democracy from an Arab Perspective, *Journal of Democracy* (in Arabic), 49.

Al-Kuwari, A. 2006. *Dominance in Contemporary Arab Governance*, Beirut: Center for Arab Unity Studies.

Al-Obeidi, M. 2016. *Mutual Pressures: The Dimensions of the Interplay between the Objectives of the Contestants in the Battle of Mosul and Aleppo. Analyses – Security Trends.* Center for the Future of Research and Advanced Studies.

Al-Qadmin, H. 2017. *Insights from the Inside: The Nine Reasons for the Failure of the Settlement of the Conflict in Yemen. Analyses, Political Changes,* Future Center for Research and Advanced Studies (in Arabic).

Ayubi, N. 2009. *Over-stating the Arab State: Politics and Society in the Middle East.* London, I.B. Tauris.

Bayat, A. 2013. The Arab Spring and its Surprises. *Development and Change*, 44: 587–601.

Bogaards, M. 2009. How to Classify Hybrid Regimes? Defective Democracy and Electoral Authoritarianism. *Democratization*, 16(2): 399–423.

Boose, J. 2012. Democratization and Civil Society: Libya, Tunisia and the Arab Spring. *International Journal of Social Science and Humanity*, 2(4): 310–315.

Boukhars, A. 2014. *In the Crossfire: Islamists' Travails in Tunisia.* Sada: Carnegie Endowment for International Peace.

Bradley, J.R. 2012. *After the Arab Spring: How Islamists Hijacked the Middle East Revolts.* New York: Palgrave Macmillan.

Brown, J. 2011. *Salafis and Sufis in Egypt. The Carnegie Papers, Middle East*, Carnegie Endowment for International Peace.

Chayes, S. 2014. *How a Leftist Labor Union Helped Tunisia's Political Settlement.* Carnegie Endowment for International Peace.

Cockburn, P. 2015. *The Rise of Islamic State. ISIS and the New Sunni Revolution.* London: Verso.

Cristiani, D. 2016. Consolidating Pluralism under the Terrorist Threat: The Tunisian Case and the Algerian Experience. *European View*, 15: 305–313.

Dakhlallah, F. 2012. The League of Arab States and Regional Security: Towards an Arab Security Community? *British Journal of Middle Eastern Studies*, 39(3): 393–412.

Davis, J. 2016. *The Arab Spring and Arab Thaw: Unfinished Revolutions and the Quest for Democracy.* London: Routledge.

Dawisha, A.I. 2013. *The Second Arab Awakening: Revolution, Democracy, and the Islamist Challenge from Tunis to Damascus.* New York: W.W. Norton & Company.

Devarajan, S. 2016. *Economic and Social Inclusion to Prevent Violent Extremism*. Washington DC: The World Bank: 18–19.

Devlin-Foltz, Z. and Ozkececi-Taner, B. 2010. State Collapse and Islamist Extremism: Re-evaluating the Link. *Contemporary Security Policy*, 31(1): 88–113.

Diamond, L.J. 2010. "Why Are There No Arab Democracies?" *Journal of Democracy*, 21(1): 93–104.

Diamond, L.J. and Plattner, M. 2014. *Democratization and Authoritarianism in the Arab World*. Baltimore, Johns Hopkins University Press.

Elbadawi, I. and Makdisi, S. 2007. "Explaining the Democratic Deficit in the Arab World", *Quarterly Review of Economics and Finance*, 46(5): 813–831.

El-Sherif, A. 2014. *Egypt's Post-Mubarak Predicament*. Carnegie Endowment for International Peace: 18–20.

Fish, M.S. 2002. "Islam and Authoritarianism". *World Politics*, 55(1): 4–37.

Freedom House. 2018. *Freedom in the World*, https://freedomhouse.org/sites/default/files/FH_FITW_Report_2018_Final_SinglePage.pdf

Frisch, H. 2013. "The Emerging Middle East Balance of Power". In: E. Inbar, ed., *The Arab Spring, Democracy and Security: Domestic and International Ramifications*. London: Routledge. pp. 33–50.

Gerges, F.A. 2013. The Islamist Moment: From Islamic State to Civil Islam? *Political Science Quarterly*, 128(3): 389–426.

Gerges, F.A. 2016. *Isis: A History*. Princeton: Princeton University Press.

Hamid, S. 2014. *Temptations of Power: Islamists and Illiberal Democracy in a New Middle East*. Oxford: Oxford University Press.

Hassan, H. 2016. Islamic State and the Transformation of Islamic Discourse in the Middle East. *Journal of Middle Eastern and Islamic Studies (in Asia)*, 10(4): 1–19.

Institute for Economics and Peace. 2017. *Global Peace Index 2017* St. Leonards, NSW, Institute for Economics & Peace: 10–11.

International Crisis Group. 2012. *Lost in Transition: The World According to Egypt's SCAF*. Middle East/North Africa Report, No. 121.

International Crisis Group. 2013. *Make or Break: Iraq's Sunni and the State*. Middle East Report, No. 144, 14 August 2013.

International Crisis Group. 2016. *Exploiting Disorder: Al-Qaeda and the Islamic State*. Crisis Group Special Report.

Kerrou, M. 2014. *Tunisia's Historic Step Toward Democracy*. Carnegie Middle East Center.

Khatib, L. 2015. *The Islamic State's Strategy: Lasting and Expanding*. Carnegie Middle East Center: Carnegie Endowment for International Peace.

Knudsen, A., and Ezbidi, B. 2014. *Popular Protest in the New Middle East: Islamism and Post-Islamism Politics*. London, UK: I.B. Tauris.

Lust, E., Soltan, G., and Wichmann, J. 2012. After the Arab Spring: Islamism, Secularism, and Democracy, *Current History,* 111(749): 362–364.

Mainuddin, R. 2016. Arab Spring and Democratic Transition in the GCC: Continuity amidst Change. *Asian Journal of Peacebuilding*, 4(2): 161–186.

Muasher, M. 2013. *The Path to Sustainable Political Parties in the Arab World*. Policy Outlook. Carnegie Endowment for International Peace.

Mühlberger, W. 2015. September. *The State of Arab Statehood. Reflections on Failure, Resilience and Collapse* (Paper IEMed, EuroMeSCo series, n.26).

Plaetzer, N. 2014. Civil Society as Domestication: Egyptian and Tunisian Uprisings beyond Liberal Transitology. *Journal of International Affairs*, 68(1): 255–265.

Rezaei, M. 2015. Egypt and "Democracy Dilemma". *African Journal of Political Science and International Relations*, 9(6): 217–224.

Sadiki, L. 2004. *The Search for Arab Democracy: Discourses and Counter-Discourses*. New York: Columbia University Press.

Sarihan, A. 2014. In Search of the Arab Uprisings: Social Movements, Revolution, or Democratization, *Turkish Journal of Politics* 3(1): 5–20.

Schmitz, C. 2012. *Building a Better Yemen*. The Carnegie Papers, Middle East, Carnegie Endowment for International Peace.

Stepan, A. and Linz, J. 2013. Democratization Theory and the "Arab Spring". *Journal of Democracy*, 24(2): 15–30.

Styszyński, M. 2015. Confrontation and the Reconciliation Process among Islamists after the Arab Spring. *Hemispheres Studies on Cultures and Societies*, 30: 89–100.

Szmolka, I. 2015. Exclusionary and Non-Consensual Transitions versus Inclusive and Consensual Democratizations: The Cases of Egypt and Tunisia. *Arab Studies Quarterly*, 37(1): 73–95.

Taylor, W. 2014. *Military Responses to the Arab Uprisings and the Future of Civil-Military Relations in the Middle East*. Palgrave Macmillan, New York.

Wehrey, F. and Cole, P. 2013. *Building Libya's Security Sector. Policy Outlook*. Carnegie Endowment for International Peace.

Wigell, M. 2008. Mapping "Hybrid Regimes": Regime Types and Concepts in Comparative Politics. *Democratization*, 15(2): 230–250.

Wolf, A. 2014. *Can Secular Parties Lead the New Tunisia?* Washington DC: Carnegie Endowment for International Peace.

Zinecker, H. 2009. Regime Hybridity in Developing Countries: Achievements and Limitations of New Research on Transitions, *International Studies Review*, 11(2): 302–331.

Zoubir, Y.H. and White, G. 2016. *North African Politics: Change and Continuity*. London and New York: Routledge.

21

DEMOCRACY AND SECURITY IN THE POST-ARAB SPRING MIDDLE EAST

Rex Brynen

Introduction

The "Arab Spring" of 2011 was, in many ways, a violent collision between two very different concepts of "security". On the one hand, citizens took to the streets en masse to demand greater *human security*: protesters called for improved employment opportunities, better public services, an end to corruption, and greater freedom or democracy. In response, the machinery of the state counter-mobilized to safeguard the *regime security* of political elites from these mounting challenges from below. Arab leaders variously offered the carrots of limited reform (notably in Morocco) or increased social spending (notably in the Gulf), and the stick of authoritarian repression (as in Bahrain, among many others). All this, in turn, has had substantial ramifications for the *regional security* environment in the Middle East – that is, the broader pattern of interstate and intrastate conflict.

The reverberations of the Arab Spring have been so significant precisely because the guardians of regime security failed in some cases. The Ben Ali regime in Tunisia was the first to fall in January 2011. Events there soon encouraged a cascade of unrest elsewhere. In Egypt, protests in Tahrir Square and across the country forced Hosni Mubarak from power a few weeks later. The brutally repressive Qaddafi regime in Libya faced protests, an uprising, and a bloody civil war that ultimately resulted in the dictator's ouster in August, and his death two months later. In Yemen, Ali Abdullah Saleh maneuvered adroitly for many months in an attempt to outlast the combined challenge posed by popular protests, military and tribal defections, and pressure from Saudi Arabia and others. Ultimately, he too was forced to resign, in February 2012.

For the most part, however, regional dictatorships were able to retain power. The most bloody and horrific example has been Syria, where Bashar al-Asad remains in office despite years of civil war, through a combination of brutal violence and outside support from Iran and Russia. The result has some 400,000 or more people killed, some 11 million or so forcibly displaced, and a country destroyed (al-Jazeera, 2016; UNHCR, 2017). In Bahrain, protests in 2011 brought widespread repression, leaving the monarchy intact but society more polarized along sectarian and political lines than ever.

Elsewhere the Arab Spring was characterized by a few months of limited protest and demands for reform before the status quo reasserted itself. However, the experience has heightened the apprehension of rulers and paranoia of state security officials alike.

Several years later, only one country – Tunisia – has emerged from the Arab Spring to make a largely successful transition to democracy. In Egypt, the military overthrew the elected Muslim Brotherhood government in 2013, and installed a new regime under Abdel Fattah el-Sisi. This has been even more intolerant of opposition than had been Mubarak's rule. In Libya, democratic transition was derailed by rival local militias and regional intrigue, resulting in the collapse of political order and continuing violence. In Yemen, the transitional government lost power to a coalition of Houthi rebels and supporters of the former Saleh regime. Saudi-led military intervention followed, resulting in continuing war and a desperate humanitarian crisis.

As noted, all of this has had profound ramifications for regional security. In a Middle East already afflicted by instability and violence associated with the long-standing Israeli–Palestinian conflict and more recent US intervention in Iraq, the post-Arab Spring era brought with it new challenges associated with the conflicts in Syria, Libya and Yemen. Such conflicts have provided an opening for, and have been exacerbated by, regional rivalries – most notably between Iran and Saudi Arabia, but also within the Gulf Cooperation Council. Political turmoil and failed states have also provided opportunities for non-state armed groups, especially jihadist groups, and most especially the so-styled "Islamic State" (also known as ISIS, ISIL or Daesh). Daesh declared itself to be the reborn Caliphate in 2014, and carved out for itself a genocidal sectarian regime amid the ruins of Syria and political dysfunction of Iraq. Such conflicts have also encouraged involvement and intervention by outside powers. Indeed, at no point in Middle Eastern history since the colonial era (or the Crusades) have quite so many local and foreign armies been fighting quite so many wars against quite so many opponents, all in a tangled web of alliances and rivalries.

This chapter will examine democracy and security in the post-Arab Spring Middle East, addressing each of the themes outlined above in greater detail. First, the issues of authoritarian persistence and democratic change will be explored. Second, attention will turn to the security dynamics of the post-Arab Spring regional order (and disorder). Finally, some thoughts will be offered as to both the possible trajectories of current trends and the theoretical implications of all this for the study of Middle Eastern security.

Authoritarian persistence and democratic change in the Middle East

Prior to 2011, the striking persistence of authoritarian regimes in the Middle East had been much noted, and discussed, in the scholarly literature. No other part of the world appeared to have been quite so resistant to the so-called "third-wave" of democratization which reshaped Latin American and East European politics in the 1980s and 1990s, and which had also left its mark on Asia and sub-Saharan Africa as well (Brynen et al., 2012: 3–8). A variety of causal factors were identified for this. These included, variously, legacies of colonialism and post-colonial state formation; political economy (and, in particular, the impact of oil rents); political culture; external intervention; and the adaptive strategies of regional autocrats. Indeed, so intense had been this debate that some scholars had begun to tire of what they saw as an excessive focus on democracy or its absence (Anderson, 2006).

The apparent persistence of authoritarian politics in the Middle East was fundamentally challenged by the Arab Spring. There is little doubt that the events of that period revealed the foundations of the *mukhabarat* (secret police) state to be far less solid than had previously seemed the case. As Lisa Wedeen (2015) has suggested, authoritarianism can be something of a performance art, wherein demonstrations of public loyalty are used to signal the futility of dissent. Viewed from another analytical paradigm, preference falsification had become rife, with citizens hiding their true political views for fear of the consequences of expressing opposition.

However, such rituals of intimidation and compliance are subject to sudden and catastrophic changes when a regime's aura of invincibility is threatened by openly rebellious acts. Thus, the surprising growth of anti-regime protests in Tunisia in December 2010, and even more so the toppling of President Ben Ali the following month, caused many in the region to imagine new political possibilities. Perhaps change *was* possible. The overthrow of the Mubarak regime in Egypt underscored this with even greater force. The result was the diffusion of revolt, an "informational cascade" whereby populations reassessed regime strengths and weaknesses, gained new insight into the views of their fellow citizens, and recognized new opportunities for political change through mass protest (Mekouar, 2014; Patel et al., 2014).

The role of the security forces

As Theda Skocpol (1979) has argued, an uprising by the ruled is insufficient to cause regime change on its own. It is also necessary that regimes are unable to continue ruling, whether by crushing protests or using other means of exerting social control. In the case of the Arab Spring, the stance of each regime's security forces proved to be a critical element in this (Sayigh et al., 2011; Lutterbeck, 2013; Mekouar, 2017).

In Tunisia, Ben Ali's primary coercive powerbase had been the Interior Ministry, where he had previously served as a general. The Tunisian military was relatively small, professional, and focused on defense against armed and external foes. As protests mounted and overwhelmed the capacity of the police, the Tunisian military made it clear to the beleaguered President that they would not turn their guns on fellow citizens to protect the regime. Ben Ali had little choice but to flee the country.

In Egypt, the leadership of the armed forces had little sympathy for the protesters. However, they were fearful that any orders to their conscript soldiers to use substantial violence could generate potentially fatal cracks in military discipline. They also recognized that, although one of their own, Mubarak had become an unredeemable political liability. They thus deposed their own President, and sought to guide the subsequent transition in a favorable way through the Supreme Council of the Armed Forces. Subsequent democratic elections saw the establishment of a Muslim Brotherhood-led government under Mohamed Morsi. When Morsi proved to be both increasingly unpopular and increasingly independent of the military, the latter took advantage of the public discontent to overthrow the elected government in a bloody coup in July 2013. More than a thousand people were killed (Human Rights Watch, 2014), and many thousands have been detained since.

In Libya, about a third of the Libyan military remained loyal to Qaddafi, about a third sided with the rebels, and the remainder went home – thus setting the stage for civil war. In Yemen, the defection of military units was an important element in President Saleh's agreeing to leave power. In Syria, many Sunni conscripts proved unreliable, thereby weakening the military power of the Asad regime. However, key praetorian units, disproportionately staffed from the same Alawi minority as the President, proved loyal enough to save the regime from total collapse in 2011–13. These were then supplemented by local thugs, imported militias (largely organized, trained and equipped by Iran), Hizbullah and, from 2015 onwards, Russian aircraft, artillery and advisors. The result has been that the regime has slowly pushed back rebel groups on all fronts, although its own military weaknesses makes it unlikely that it can secure full control over the country any time soon.

Elsewhere, military loyalties, often carefully cultivated over decades, held firm – and thus assured that threats from below could be contained. In Shiite-majority Bahrain, the security forces are – like the monarchy itself – overwhelmingly Sunni. They showed no reluctance to clear Shiite (and Sunni) protesters from Pearl Roundabout in March 2011 and launch a brutal crack-down across the small kingdom. Other Gulf Cooperation Council countries, alarmed at the threat to a fellow monarchy, contributed troops to back up the Bahraini authorities. Although protests took place in Jordan, Algeria, Morocco and elsewhere during this period, in none of these countries was regime control over the security forces ever seriously at risk.

Regime security through other means

This is not to say, of course, that regime coercion was the sole determinant of regime survival in this tumultuous period. As noted in the introduction to this chapter, some countries offered limited constitutional reforms to appease local demands for reform. Nowhere were these reforms particularly far reaching, although in Morocco King Mohammed VI agreed that a future Prime Minister must be chosen from the party holding the most seats in parliament, a change that might one day prove to be of importance. Wealthier Arab countries sought to head off or blunt protests by offering increases in public sector wages (especially to the military) or social welfare benefits. This was not universally successful, of course: in Libya oil rents were insufficient to save the Qaddafi government, while in Bahrain increases in state spending were hardly enough to defuse grievances rooted in decades of monarchical authoritarianism and sectarian discrimination.

In some cases, regimes were also able to play on social divisions or scapegoating to undermine calls for reform. Bahraini dependence on Sunni elites and security personnel – and, indeed, a proactive strategy of recruiting and naturalizing non-Bahraini Sunnis to reshape the demographic balance in the country – has been one example of this. Bahraini officials have also been quick to blame (Shiite) Iran for local instability, a charge that is certainly partly believed but also is used to discredit the opposition as tools of a foreign power. In Jordan, the Hashemite monarchy sometimes tried (with limited success) to rally its traditional East Bank supporters with veiled implications that reforms would benefit Jordanians of Palestinian origin. In Saudi Arabia, protests among the Shiite majority were sometimes used to rally Sunni support for the monarchy.

From Arab Spring to Arab winter?

Eight years (at time of writing) after the Arab Spring, the balance sheet for democracy is hardly an impressive one.

Tunisia has certainly made a democratic transition, with successful free and fair multi-party elections held in 2011 and 2014. It also agreed on a new constitution in a remarkably cooperative manner. Ennahda, the Islamist party that won the country's first free elections, and which has continued to be a major political actor since then, has enthusiastically embraced both the discourse and practice of democracy. However, Tunisia is hardly a model. Economic performance is unimpressive, in part because of the local uncertainties associated with the revolution. The population has seen few of the economic dividends it hoped for. Indeed, recent opinion polls (IRI, 2017) show that 83% of all Tunisians believe their country is headed in the "wrong direction", with 89% describing the situation as "bad" or "very bad". In this context, less than half the population is committed to the notion that democracy was always the preferable form of government. Given its small size and mixed results, the Tunisian revolution has failed to serve as the sort of standard-bearer of democratic change that would continue to inspire activists and reformers elsewhere in the region. Indeed, Tunisian politics now barely rates a mention in the Arab press.

Outside the Arab world, Turkey once proclaimed itself a model of Middle Eastern democratization. That claim has little credibility today. Instead, Turkey has slid back into growing authoritarianism under President Recep Tayyip Erdoğan, especially since the unsuccessful military coup of July 2016.

In Egypt, the Sisi regime has brutally repressed critics, and sought to project an aura of strength and stability in contrast with the political turmoil of the Morsi era. Islamists who were inspired by the Muslim Brotherhood's peaceful election victory in 2011–12 might be forgiven for concluding that the ballot box is a dead end. In this sense, the military coup of 2013 may have contributed to the rise of violent jihadism in the Sinai and elsewhere.

The onset of brutal violence in Libya, Syria and Yemen, as well as the violence in Iraq since 2003, might also suggest to populations more broadly that regime change is simply too bloody and violent to be worth the risk. Jordan has especially benefitted from this effect, with the status quo undoubtedly seeming preferable to many given the neighboring alternatives of civil war in Syria, violence in Iraq, Israeli occupation in Palestine, a coup in Egypt and monarchical absolutism in Saudi Arabia – a kind of "there but for the grace of the Hashemites go we" effect. Similarly, the anarchy of post-Qaddafi Libya likely discouraged many Algerians from pressing social and political demands too hard, even more so given Algeria's bloody experience with failed political and subsequent civil war in the 1990s. In turn, the Libyan and Algerian experiences probably contribute to political acquiescence in Morocco.

In short, just as the Arab Spring itself was driven by cascading changes in popular perceptions of political opportunity, alternatives and regime power, the "Arab winter" that has followed has been characterized by public perceptions that have shifted in such a way as to discourage activism or dramatic change. Thus, an authoritarian homeostasis (self-adjusting system) of sorts has returned, in which populations are intimidated or coopted, believing resistance is futile – or, perhaps, counter-productive. Simultaneously, the authoritarian "deep state" has reasserted itself, most notably in Egypt, while political elites have rallied around the current political order for fear of the alternatives.

Regional (in)security and (dis)order

The Middle East has long been one of the areas of the world most prone to violence and state warfare, as evidenced by more than seven decades of Arab–Israeli conflict, the bloody Iran–Iraq War (1980–88), Iraq's invasion of Kuwait (1991–92), and US intervention in Iraq (2003–). In relative terms, defense spending in the region dwarfs that of any other region of the world: 5.95% of GDP in 2016, compared with 1.47% in Asia, 1.25% in Africa, and a mere 1.12% in Latin America (IISS, 2017, Table 18). In absolute terms, Saudi Arabia – a country with a population and economy roughly equivalent to that of Florida – has the third largest defense budget in the world, outstripping that of Russia, the UK, India or France (IISS, 2017: 19). Of the estimated 2.2 million deaths worldwide from state and nonstate-based violence since 1989, almost one-quarter have taken place in the Middle East and North Africa – most notably in Syria, Iraq, Algeria (during the civil war), Yemen and Israel/Palestine (UCDP, 2017).

The region is also one of much broader strategic significance. It currently accounts for more than a third of world oil production (BP Global, 2017). Its proximity to Europe and presence of the Suez Canal increase its global geostrategic importance. Refugee and migrant flows to Europe, driven in part by conflict in Syria, Iraq and Libya, have heightened this connection still further. Some 2.5 million asylum claims were received in the EU in 2015–16, about four times the rate of a few years earlier (Eurostat, 2017). The Middle East is home to one nuclear-armed power (Israel), another with past – and possible future – nuclear ambitions (Iran), and has seen the use of chemical weapons during both the Iran–Iraq war and the Syrian civil war. It is the most important epicenter of global jihadist violence, most notably in the form of the self-styled "Islamic State" (Daesh) as well as the various violent franchises of al-Qaeda. Major American military facilities are located in Qatar and Bahrain. Russian, British, French, Turkish and now Chinese overseas military facilities can also be found in or around the region. In addition, troops, aircraft and advisors from several countries are involved in operations in Iraq (against Daesh) and Syria (on various sides against various opponents).

In the current era, by far the two most transformative regional security developments in the Middle East have been US intervention in Iraq and the Syrian civil war. These have accounted for most of the violent death and forced displacement in the region. Together, they have been critical in the rise of Daesh and the transformation of the jihadist challenge. Both have also exacerbated regional rivalries in a way that has contributed to a host of other tensions.

US intervention in Iraq in 2003, while toppling the dangerous and brutal dictatorship of Saddam Hussein, left in its wake a dysfunctional political system debilitated by corruption and cronyism, and torn by sectarian tensions. Moreover, despite the withdrawal of US combat forces from the country by 2011, the situation there proved difficult for Washington to disengage from. Under Prime Minister Nouri al-Maliki (2006–2014) in particular, political consolidation within the Shiite community took place at the cost of growing Sunni alienation. This set the stage for dramatic seizure of Mosul by Daesh in June 2014. The self-declared Caliphate embarked on a campaign of terrorism, genocidal mass killings and the enslavement of non-Sunni populations. It was this threat – to Iraq, the Middle East and beyond – that led to a return of US military forces to Iraq. Other Western countries also offered military assistance (Global Coalition, 2017), as did Iran. Tens of thousands of combatants and civilians subsequently died in the campaign to recapture the city.

Daesh would not have been able to project itself into Iraq in the way it did had it not been for the civil war in Syria. As the Iraqi state weakened and the conflict became polarized and radicalized along increasingly sectarian lines, the opening appeared for it to establish itself a foothold in eastern Syria and along the Iraqi border. In turn, the weakness or collapse of state authority elsewhere helped Daesh to spread still further, notably (but relatively briefly) to Libya.

The (in)security ramifications of the Syrian conflict are far, far broader than this, however. As noted earlier, the human toll has been horrific. Although the Asad government has slowly gained the upper hand, it is very far from being able to exert full control over all of the country. The reestablishment of control by one of the most brutal regimes on the planet, moreover, will come at a high cost: repression, torture, disappearances, summary executions, extending far into the future. Whenever the war might end, the task of reconstructing the country will be immense. Even if the war were to end tomorrow, therefore, Syria will take a generation or more to recover.

The impact of regional rivalry

The Syrian civil war has also sparked a fundamental escalation of long-standing tensions between Saudi Arabia (and fellow conservative Gulf allies) on the one hand and Iran on the other. As the Syrian civil war progressed, the Gulf states increasingly saw it as an opportunity to weaken Iranian strategic influence by deposing Tehran's most important international ally, namely the Syrian Government.

While these tensions have their roots in geopolitical rivalries in the Gulf – with both sides seeing themselves as the leading regional actor – they also contribute to, and are exacerbated by, religious differences. The dominant Wahhabi religious ideology of Saudi Arabia is deeply

Democracy and security post-Arab Spring

suspicious of Shiites, and the Kingdom's own Shiite minority is often marginalized. Riyadh was concerned by both the empowerment of the Shiite community in Iraq after the toppling of Saddam, and growing Iranian influence in that country. Increasingly the Syrian war was also seen by many in the Gulf as an existential struggle by the Syrian Sunni population against a (variously secular, Alawi or Iranian/Shiite-backed) regime.

For its part, Iran stepped up the provision of direct assistance, advisors and the deployment of proxies (Hizbullah, entering the fray from Lebanon) and mercenaries (Shiite militias recruited from Iraq, Afghanistan and elsewhere, trained and equipped by the Iranian Revolutionary Guard Corps). In Tehran's eyes, Riyadh's support for the Syrian opposition was both a subversive threat to the status quo and empowered dangerous, anti-Shiite Sunni Islamists.

Syria is not the only conflict to emerge from the Arab Spring that has exacerbated the strategic rivalry between the Riyadh and Tehran. Protests in Bahrain in 2011 were seen by Gulf hardliners (Saudi Arabia, the UAE and the Bahraini monarchy itself) as, in part, Iranian-sponsored. In Yemen, Iran provided some assistance to Houthi rebels. Although limited in scope, it was more than enough to set off alarm bells in Riyadh when the Houthis, backed by forces loyal to former President (and former US ally) Ali Abdullah Saleh, captured Sana'a in September 2014. In March 2015, Saudi Arabia intervened in the country in support of the deposed government, together with other GCC countries, a few forces from other Arab allies, and the reluctant support of the United States. More than two years later, and after more than 10,000 civilian casualties, the civil war there continues.

Saudi frustration at its inability to achieve a quick and decisive victory in Yemen, in turn, has only heightened the strategic rivalry between Riyadh and Tehran still further. For its part, Iran shows little willingness to curtail the sorts of activities that its neighbors find threatening.

Indeed, a degree of perceived friendliness between Qatar and Iran (or, perhaps more accurately, a lack of demonstrative unfriendliness between them) was one of the factors that led to the emergence of a major split in the GCC in mid-2017. Saudi Arabia, the UAE, Bahrain and others (notably Egypt) accused Doha of being too cozy with Tehran. However other factors contributed to the crisis too, highlighting how the events of the Arab Spring and its aftermath could have second and third order effects on regional politics. Gulf conservatives had long been highly critical of Qatar-based al-Jazeera television for its willingness to criticize regimes (other than its own) and host alternative voices. This concern grew still further in the aftermath of the cascading popular protest of 2011, which highlighted how dangerous the media could be. Qatar's friendliness to the Muslim Brotherhood – an alternative brand of Islamism beyond Riyadh's sway – has been another major irritant. In Egypt, Qatar had backed the Morsi government, while the Saudis and Emiratis endorsed the army coup. In Libya, Qatar and the UAE had found themselves backing rival sides in the post-Qaddafi conflict there. Emboldened by an erratic Trump Administration that seemed to receive Saudi and Emirati complains with a sympathetic Presidential ear, these countries and their allies severed diplomatic relations and launched an extensive array of sanctions and economic warfare against Qatar in June 2017, coupled with a chilling ultimatum to comply with Riyadh's wishes. The resulting rift threatened to severely weaken the Gulf Cooperation Council, with Oman and Kuwait refusing to support the Saudi/Emirati campaign, and Doha refusing to concede.

The foreign policy recklessness of Saudi Crown Prince Mohammad bin Salman has exacerbated all of this. Mohammad bin Salman was the prime architect of both Saudi intervention in Yemen and the dispute with Qatar. This and other rash actions – including the temporary kidnapping of Lebanese Prime Minister Saad Hariri and the murder of dissident Saudi journalist Jamal Khashoggi – all raise important questions as to whether Saudi Arabia has become a significant source of regional instability.

The death of the "Middle East Peace Process"

Over the past two decades, the post-2001 "global war on terror", US intervention in Iraq, the Arab Spring, the Syrian civil war, and the challenge of Daesh have all tended to overshadow the collapse of the Israeli–Palestinian peace process. Launched with much fanfare in 1991, years of negotiation did produce the Oslo Accords (1993) and a supposedly interim period of limited Palestinian autonomy, as well as a peace agreement between Israel and Jordan in 1994. However, successive rounds of Israeli–Palestinian talks – notably at Camp David (2000), Taba (2001), the Annapolis initiative (2007–08), and the Kerry initiative (2013–14) failed to produce agreement on a permanent peace deal between Israel and the Palestinians. On the Palestinian side, years of tension and conflict between Fateh (in control of the West Bank) and the Islamist Hamas movement (in control of Gaza) has severely weakened the Palestinian position. In Israel, increasingly right-wing governments have at best maintained a thin pretense of accepting a possible two state solution to the conflict, while at the same continuing illegal settlement activity in the occupied West Bank and East Jerusalem. The result has been that the occupation continues, supposedly "interim" arrangements have become interminable, and the stage is increasingly set for the conflict to become even more intractable. International pressure on the parties to reach agreement has been weak and ineffective (Thrall, 2017). Indeed, the Trump Administration's apparent support for maximalist Israeli positions appears to have hammered a final nail in the peace process coffin, with the Palestinians refusing to acquiesce in US dictates, and Washington imposing major cuts in humanitarian and development funding in response.

How much difference does all this make, however? For Palestinians – besieged in Gaza, occupied in the west Bank, and everywhere denied basic rights of national self-determination – the effects are obviously severe. Periodic violence threatens both sides. However, much of the rest of the Middle East is preoccupied with other issues, most notably the wars in Iraq and Syria, jihadist challenges and the Saudi–Iranian rivalry. The tumult of the Arab Spring and the insecurities of the post-Arab Spring Middle East have certainly made it easier for hardline Israeli politicians to argue against the risks inherent in peace and political compromise. In addition, an unspoken alignment of sorts has emerged between Israel and the conservative Gulf states, with both viewing Tehran as their primary foe.

This might be most likely to play out in Lebanon. The 2006 war between Israel and the Iranian-backed Lebanese Shiite movement Hizbullah was inconclusive, with both sides claiming victory. A future round would likely be even more destructive. Hizbullah has amassed up to 150,000 largely short and medium-ranged rockets in southern Lebanon, and its forces have gained impressive combat experience during the Syrian civil war. For its part, Israeli commanders have stated that "harming the population is the only means of restraining [Hizbullah]". This so-called "Dahiya Doctrine" (named after a pro-Hizbullah suburb of Beirut) would see Israel "wield disproportionate power against [them] and cause immense damage and destruction", forcing a million or more civilians from their homes (Harel, 2008l Lappin, 2015).

From the regional to the international

In 2003 the external factor of US intervention in Iraq profoundly changed, and destabilized, the regional security environment in the Middle East. Since the Arab Spring and in its aftermath, however, it might be argued that many of the key drivers of instability have been Middle Eastern in local origins: struggles for freedom, domestic repression, transnational violence, regional rivalries, civil war. Nonetheless, outside powers continue to play an important role in shaping these.

NATO military intervention in Libya in 2011, for example, certainly played a central role in the overthrow of Muammar Qaddafi. It should be noted, however, that NATO action followed a widespread revolt against the regime, a request from the Arab League for action, and a United Nations Security Council resolution explicitly authorizing the use of "all necessary means". While there has been suggested that a lack of vigorous external peacebuilding follow-up led to subsequent political conflict in the country, the Libyans themselves were reluctant to accept too much help, and local rivalries (exacerbated by regional meddling) were more important drivers of what subsequently happened.

In Syria, the US and other Western states lent considerable, if uneven, political and material support to the Syrian opposition. They did not, however, create the revolt. In practical terms, moreover, Gulf support was even more important. Moreover, external support for the opposition was fully offset by Iranian and Russian support for the regime. Given the deep political cleavages in the country, Syria would have suffered civil war even without outside actors, although its intensity, duration or outcome might have been different.

In addition to outside actors affecting regional security, events in the Middle East have also helped shaped broader global politics. Violent jihadism born in the area has become a worldwide threat. Russia has used power-projection in Syria to signal global power well beyond its limited economic capabilities. During the Obama Administration, willingness to negotiate with Tehran (ultimately resulting the Joint Comprehensive Plan of Action ending Iran's nuclear weapons program) and unwillingness to stand by regional dictatorships in the face of reformist protests (notably in Tunisia and Egypt) generated considerable concern in Riyadh and other conservative capitals, where it was viewed as abandonment at best and betrayal at worst. It also contributed to a broader narrative of a cautious Washington unwilling to rush into the sort of entanglements and quagmires that the Bush Administration stumbled into in Afghanistan and Iraq. The new Trump Administration has indicated a more forceful assertion of US power. This has only really been evident with regard to Iran, however, where it reneged on the Joint Comprehensive Plan of Action and reimposed sanctions in an attempt to force more compliant Iranian behaviour.

In assessing the impact of international actors on the Middle East, moreover, it is important to move beyond simplistic suggestions that more (or less) involvement is always better (or worse) for democracy or security. As one major simulation of a potential Iran–Saudi crisis concluded, *what* one does is more important than *how much* one does, and outside actors often overestimate their ability to determine local outcomes (Brynen, 2016).

Trends and trajectories

If there was one lesson to be learned from the tumultuous political events of 2011 it is that the authoritarian persistence of the Middle East is stable – but only until it is not. Few if any predicted that dramatic challenges would emerge so quickly and forcefully, and in so many places (Stimson Center, 2011). Certainly no one had Tunisia and Libya at the top of their list of regimes at risk. Partly this is because political prediction is hard (Tetlock, 2005; Tetlock and Gardner, 2015; Brynen, 2017). However, and of crucial importance, prediction is difficult because even participants in revolutionary change themselves often fail to perceive the possibilities of change until they are amidst them, a point that Charles Kurzman (2004) has made about the 1979 Iranian Revolution. The Arab Spring thus highlighted the need to recognize that an apparently stable status quo may be built on vulnerable fault lines, subject to sudden and dramatic tectonic shifts.

This chapter has also highlighted several acute security challenges that are almost certain to continue in the near and medium future: civil war in Syria, Yemen and Iraq; political instability in Iraq; the Saudi–Iranian rivalry; the entrenchment of an unresolved Israeli–Palestinian conflict. Despite military successes against Daesh in Iraq and Syria, the constantly metastasizing threat of regional global jihadism will not go away soon either. On the contrary, it will continue to gain sustenance from political dysfunction, state failure and social marginalization across the region. There are also other possible flashpoints that this chapter has not been able to address for reasons of limited space: efforts by Iraqi Kurds to gain political independence, for example. Finally, for the next few years at least, the potential effects of US policy under the Trump Administration. The potential unpredictability and unreliability of Washington means that US policy may, as has already happened in the Qatar–Saudi dispute, aggravate rather than diminish regional conflicts and instability.

Theoretical implications

If, as suggested above, the Middle East is likely to be affected by conflict and major security challenges for some time to come, it becomes all the more important to consider the analytical tools at our disposal for understanding and even anticipating such events. Here, and by way of conclusion, this chapter will briefly point to three areas where it would be useful to deepen or understanding of the forces at play in the region.

The politics of security

The events of the Arab Spring and its aftermath have highlighted the key role that security institutions play in regime survival. Indeed, as Gregory Gause (2011) has suggested, failure to appreciate the politics of security, and the potential unreliability of some security forces, was perhaps one of major shortcomings of earlier literatures on regional authoritarianism.

Today, we find somewhat greater attention to these issues. It is a difficult topic to research, however: authoritarian regimes hardly welcome outside scholars exploring the dynamics of civil–military relations or state repression, and local researchers are at even greater risk from the *mukhabarat*. Security officials are reluctant to talk, and none of them is likely to discuss – or even comprehend in advance – the conditions under which soldiers and police officers support or abandon their political leaders.

Fortunately, new information technologies and new analytic communities can offer insight into the politics of security in new ways. In Iraq and Syria in particular, and to a lesser extent in Libya and Yemen, social media and mobile phone videos have provided unique insight into the conduct of civil wars in those countries. The open source work done on Syrian chemical weapons use, for example, has been striking (Bellingcat, 2017). In some cases, defense journalists with extensive ties to the region and "mil geek" communities of amateur internet analysts have offered some of the best work available on, for example, the internal dynamics of the Syrian armed forces (Cooper, 2016). Traditional social scientists need to learn to utilize these open source tools more effectively, recognizing both their potential contributions and their limits.

Sectarianism and geopolitics

A second key aspect of regional politics worthy of greater attention is that of sectarianism, and its relationship to geopolitics (Hashemi and Postel, 2017). On the one hand, it is important to reject essentialist views of religion, ethnicity and politics that attribute an inevitability to conflict based on history and alleged ancient hatred (Salloukh, 2017a). At the same time, it is equally

Democracy and security post-Arab Spring

important to understand how sectarian appeals can be instrumentalized as a tool of influence and mobilization, how ideological views and biases may shape threat perception and behavior, and how all of this can become a self-fulfilling prophecy.

Again, there are challenges to doing this. It can be difficult to discern the causal impact of sectarianism precisely because political leaders deploy it in instrumental ways, possibly to rally support for actions taken for quite different reasons. Conversely, leaders also seek to obfuscate any bigotries that shape their behaviors, and try to cast sectarian motives in the more neutral language of rights or realpolitik. Here, qualitative interviews that probe the worldviews of foreign policy and security elites can be useful, if conducted in such a way as to probe beyond simple political rhetoric. Moreover, the gradual growth of methodically robust public opinion in the Middle East provides opportunities to assess the sort of popular perceptions that might help to sustain sectarian politics, and the correlates and possible determinants of such attitudes.

Finding a theoretical (and eclectic) synthesis

One key implication of this survey, and of the two areas for further research noted above, is that accounts of regional security that focus solely on interstate or intrastate dynamics are fundamentally flawed. As has been shown, many interactions between states have at their root concerns about regime security or other domestic political calculations. Similarly, domestic politics in Iraq, Syria, Libya, Yemen and elsewhere can hardly be understood without some reference to the alliances and other relations between local actors and regional or international patrons. Just as subversion remains a tool of statecraft, so too powerful outside friends can be a key resource in domestic political struggles, especially in the context of a failed or failing state. Finally, there is ample evidence that political and ideological differences between leaders can alter alliance patterns and other behaviors more than some solely structural accounts might suggest (Gause, 2017).

The region also remains highly permeable to transnational influences (Salloukh and Brynen, 2004). Ideas and ideologies can spill easily across state borders, whether underpinned by religious (Islam) or linguistic (Arabic) commonalities. Indeed, while the consolidation of Middle Eastern states in the post-colonial era has reduced some of the appeal of transnational influences by creating some sense of local citizenship, changes in information and communication technology have made it easier than ever for ideas to cross borders. The cascading protests of the Arab Spring are one very important case in point. The rise of Daesh, and the growth of its activities across multiple countries (primarily Syria and Iraq, but also the Egyptian Sinai, Libya and elsewhere) is another striking example.

The theoretical debates that followed the Arab Spring, and the complex dynamics of the post-Arab Spring security environment in the Middle East, together point to the need for cross-fertilization between comparative politics and the study of international relations, as well as between area specialists and generalists (Villebrun, 2017). Doing so is even more important in a context where sectarianism has become a potent resource in interstate competition, and where weak states provide opportunity for local actors and transnational political movements to exert considerable influence on their broader regional environment (Salloukh, 2017b).

References

al-Jazeera. 2016. "Syria Death Toll: UN Envoy Estimates 400,000 Killed". 23 April. Accessed at www. aljazeera.com/news/2016/04/staffan-de-mistura-400000-killed-syria-civil-war-160423055735629. html

Anderson, Lisa. 2006. "Searching Where the Light Shines: Studying Democratization in the Middle East". *Annual Review of Political Science* 9.

Bellingcat. 2017. *Bellingcat* (blog). Accessed at www.bellingcat.com

BP Global. 2017. "Oil Production". Accessed at www.bp.com/en/global/corporate/energy-economics/statistical-review-of-world-energy/oil/oil-production.html

Brynen, Rex. 2016. *Exploring US Engagement in the Middle East: A Crisis Simulation*. Atlantic Council Issue Brief, September. Accessed at www.atlanticcouncil.org/images/publications/Exploring_US_Engagement_Middle_East_web_0825.pdf

Brynen, Rex. 2017. "Here (Very Likely) Be Dragons: The Challenges of Strategic Forecasting". In Thomas Juneau, ed. *Strategic Analysis in Support of International Policy Making: Case Studies in Achieving Analytical Relevance*. Lanham, MD: Rowman & Littlefield.

Brynen, Rex, Moore, Pete, Salloukh, Bassel, and Zahar, Marie-Joëlle. 2012. *Beyond the Arab Spring: Authoritarianism and Democratization in the Arab World*. Boulder: Lynne Rienner Publishers.

Cooper, Tom. 2016. "What's Left of the Syrian Arab Army?" *War is Boring* (blog), 18 May. Accessed at: http://warisboring.com/whats-left-of-the-syrian-arab-army/

Eurostat. 2017. "Asylum Statistics". Accessed at http://ec.europa.eu/eurostat/statistics-explained/index.php/Asylum_statistics

Gause III, Gregory. 2011. "The Middle East Academic Community and the 'Winter of Arab Discontent': Why Did We Miss It?" In *Seismic Shift: Understanding Change in the Middle East*. Washington DC: Stimson Center.

Gause III, Gregory. 2017. "Ideologies, Alignments, and Underbalancing in the New Middle East Cold War". *PS: Political Science & Politics* 50(3).

Global Coalition Against Daesh. 2017. Website at http://theglobalcoalition.org/en/home/

Harel, Amos. 2008. "IDF Plans to Use Disproportionate Force in Next War". *Haaretz*, October 5. Accessed at www.haaretz.com/analysis-idf-plans-to-use-disproportionate-force-in-next-war-1.254954

Hashemi, Nader and Postel, Danny (eds.). 2017. *Sectarianization: Mapping the New Politics of the Middle East*. Oxford: Oxford University Press.

Human Rights Watch. 2014. "All According to Plan: The Rab'a Massacre and Mass Killings of Protesters in Egypt", August 12. Accessed at www.hrw.org/report/2014/08/12/all-according-plan/raba-massacre-and-mass-killings-protesters-egypt

International Institute for Strategic Studies. 2017. *The Military Balance 2017*. London: IISS.

International Republican Institute, 2017. *Public Opinion Survey of Tunisia, April 19- April 26, 2017*. Accessed at www.iri.org/sites/default/files/tunisia_poll_june_2017.pdf

Kurzman, Charles. 2004. *The Unthinkable Revolution in Iran*. Cambridge, MA: Harvard University Press.

Lappin, Yaakov. 2015. "IDF Source: We'd Evacuate a Million Lebanese if War Breaks Out with Hezbollah". *Jerusalem Post*, June 4. Accessed at www.jpost.com/Arab-Israeli-Conflict/IDF-source-Wed-evacuate-a-million-Lebanese-if-war-breaks-out-with-Hezbollah-404999

Lutterbeck, Derek. 2013. "Arab Uprisings, Armed Forces, and Civil-Military Relations". *Armed Forces & Society* 39(1).

Mekouar, Merouan. 2014. "No Political Agents, No Diffusion: Evidence from North Africa", *International Studies Review* 16(2).

Mekouar, Merouan. 2017. "Police Collapse in Authoritarian Regimes: Lessons from Tunisia". *Studies in Conflict & Terrorism* 40(10).

Patel, David Patel, Bunce, Valerie, and Wolchik, Sharon. 2014. "Diffusion and Demonstration". In Mark Lynch, ed., *The Arab Uprisings Explained: New Contentious Politics in the Middle East*. New York: Columbia University Press.

Salloukh, Bassel. 2017a. "The Sectarianization of Geopolitics in the Middle East". In N. Hashemi, and D. Postel, eds., *Sectarianization: Mapping the New Politics of the Middle East*. Oxford: Oxford University Press.

Salloukh, Bassel. 2017b. "Overlapping Contests and Middle East International Relations: The Return of the Weak Arab state". *PS: Political Science & Politics* 50, 3.

Salloukh, Bassel and Brynen, Rex (eds.). 2004. *Persistent Permeability? Regionalism, Localism, and Globalization in the Middle East*. London: Ashgate.

Sayigh, Yezid, Barak, Oren, Droz-Vincent, Philippe, Hertog, Steffen, Owen, Roger, and Springborg, Robert. 2011. "Roundtable: Rethinking the Study of Middle Eastern Militaries". *International Journal of Middle Eastern Studies*, 43(3).

Skocpol, Theda. 1979. *States and Social Revolutions*. Cambridge: Cambridge University Press.

Democracy and security post-Arab Spring

Stimson Center. 2011. *Seismic Shift: Understanding Change in the Middle East.* Washington DC: Stimson Center. Accessed at www.stimson.org/sites/default/files/Full_Pub-Seismic_Shift.pdf

Tetlock, Philip. 2005. *Expert Political Judgment: How Good Is It? How Can We Know?* Princeton: Princeton University Press.

Tetlock, Philip and Gardner, Dan. 2015. *Superforecasting: The Art and Science of Prediction.* Toronto: Signal Books.

Thrall, Nathan. 2017. *The Only Language They Understand: Forcing Compromise in Israel and Palestine.* New York: Macmillan.

United Nations High Commission for Refugees. 2017. "Syria Emergency". Accessed at www.unhcr.org/syria-emergency.html

Uppsala Conflict Data Program, 2017. "Database". Accessed at http://ucdp.uu.se

Valbjørn, Morten. 2017. "Strategies for Reviving the International Relations/Middle East Nexus after the Arab Uprisings". *PS: Political Science & Politics* 50(3).

Wedeen, Lisa. 2015. *Ambiguities of Domination: Politics, Rhetoric, and Symbols in Contemporary Syria.* Chicago: University of Chicago Press.

22

SUNNI–SHI'A RELATIONS AND THE IRAN–SAUDI SECURITY DYNAMIC

Simon Mabon and Nic Coombs

Introduction

In the years following the Arab uprisings, conflict across the Middle East has taken on an increasingly sectarian nature, seemingly pitting Sunni against Shi'a in a 21st century reworking of a primordial struggle. As history has shown us there is nothing inherently violent about sectarian difference, yet as such identities become bearers of political meaning, differences have the capacity to become increasingly violent (Mabon and Royle, 2017.) Speaking before the 9/11 attacks the then Saudi Ambassador to Washington, Prince Bandar bin Sultan Al Sa'ud, stated that "The time is not far off in the Middle East when it will be literally 'God help the Shi'a'! More than a billion Sunni have simply had enough of them"(Cockburn, 2016: 350).

This quote sharply illuminates a deep-seated thread in Saudi political thought which reveals much about themselves, and their relationships with others – principally the Shi'a – and how they – and others similarly – choose to use the sectarian as a tool for contemporary political ends. To understand the emergence of sectarian violence, we must then locate and separate meaning that is proscribed to these identities. But the labels mask huge regional and cultural variation in what it means to be Shi'a (and Sunni) and, also, what is perhaps actually happening. However, since we are considering Saudi Arabia and Iran, our focus is Wahhabism and Twelver Shi'ism, the belief systems that are dominant within the two states. Theology matters, without question; but a struggle for leadership, political pre-eminence is, we suggest, the principal driver for contest between Saudi Arabia and Iran and shapes contemporary Sunni–Shi'a "relations" in the Middle East, and also further east. Moreover, this position also frames a "Western" view of what is taking place which can confuse both our understanding of the issues from that perspective and also the nature of external relationships with regional players. As a consequence, it also shapes how Western actors engage with the region, on the basis of their (mis)perceptions.

Within the literature on Saudi–Iranian relations are three main approaches that seek to understand the rivalry. The first approach (Furtig, 2006; Chubin and Tripp, 1996) suggests that the best way to characterize the rivalry is to frame it within debates about the balance of power within the Persian Gulf. Regional security then plays a prominent role in shaping the rivalry, with a Manichaean view of regional order resulting in the emergence of serious tensions between the two. The second approach (Nasr, 2007) suggests that religion cannot be ignored and that to understand the nature of the rivalry across the Gulf, one must understand how religious identities emerge and how sectarian divisions are constructed. The third approach suggests that we must combine questions about the distribution of power across the Middle East with a consideration of the spread of religious identities and the construction of sectarian divisions (Mabon, 2013). We locate ourselves in this third camp, stressing that both religion and security are of paramount importance but that we must understand how the issues interact with one another and their local context.

Given this, the importance of political context should not be understated. Since the events of 1979 – the revolution in Iran, the seizure of the Grand Mosque in Mecca, the uprisings in the Eastern Province, the Soviet invasion of Afghanistan and the beginning of the Afghan wars, and the Camp David Egyptian–Israeli peace treaty – religion has become an increasingly important tool of the foreign policies of states across the Middle East. Religion plays a political role, serving to ensure the legitimacy of particular ruling élites, while also providing scope to interfere in the domestic events of other regional states. This chapter seeks to interrogate the role of religion within the rivalry between Saudi Arabia and Iran. In doing that, we must begin by providing a theological overview of the differences between Sunni and Shi'a and their role within the fabric of the Saudi Arabian and Iranian states. We then turn to a discussion of the theological tensions between the two before considering how religion is used as a tool of geopolitical interests. We end by considering how religion and geopolitics play out within the context of the Arab uprisings and the fragmentation of state sovereignty across the Middle East.

The religious and the political

Prince Bandar's sense of an approaching crisis was prescient, yet not quite as conveniently binary as he had suggested, nor even as balanced in favor of the Sunna as his rhetoric would imply. The battle lines are, of course, presently drawn as sharply between competing Sunni narratives, as the conflicting responses from Gulf states to the rise of Islamic State (IS) and the temporary rule of the Muslim Brotherhood in Egypt under President Morsi bear witness. But with Iran in mind as Saudi King Salman surveys the contemporary Middle East, the Saudis see a ranging of Shi'a influence in the region – if not direct control from – that emanates for them from Tehran.

Baghdad, Damascus, Beirut and Sana'a feature prominently within that perceived Saudi worldview of Shi'a encroachment although, as said, it is simplistic for them and us simply to refer to the Shi'a as if they were a neat homogeneous bloc, disregarding ethnicity, tribalism and ultimately politics.[1] They clearly are not, even aside from the obvious ethno-political distinctions of Arab and Persian, any more than Saudi Arabia's own population is a single coherent force; and the Al Sa'ud are torn between an internally attractive and comforting drive to try to make all Saudis unquestioningly adhere to the tenets of Wahhabism[2] on the one hand, and trying to navigate an external, more pluralist strategy that does acknowledge diversity. The implications of such issues are severe, not only for internal security but also for external factors contributing to the construction of regime security. Understanding the "Islamo-Liberal" (Lacroix, 2005) trend (an outward-facing line of thought opposing the hard-line conservative *salafi jihadis*) in modern Saudi Arabia is as relevant as unpicking that unhealthy support that Saudi Arabia has directly or indirectly[3] offered to the likes of IS, and examining its own emergence as a modern state delivered by Ibn Sa'ud's *ikhwan* in the early 20th century.

Similarly, in Iran, the tension between progressive social movement and political conservatism is a wider gap to manage than between the various conservatisms of Saudi Arabia; the Shi'a have kept alive better than the Sunna the concept of being able to adapt and change the message of the revelations to each generation. What is known as *ijtihad* – from the same Arabic word root as *jihad* – is the way in which the religious experts of a given generation may provide exegesis of the Qur'an. In the tradition of the Sunna this process was completed several centuries ago, where the "gates of *ijtihad* were closed" and the four schools of Sunni Islam were codified and handed down.[4] In the Shi'a tradition they were kept wide open. There is a theological and political dynamic in the Iranian Shi'a relationship with the world that is both advantageous (and challenging to the likes of Saudi Arabia and the "West") and self-threatening in that it allows for a greater and often constantly implicit test of the authority of the Council of Guardians within Iran. But Iranian identity is indeed wrapped tightly in the Shi'a cloth, albeit with Persian nationalist trim. In Arabia, there is a tension that drives deep into how Saudi Arabia identifies itself that is more challenging than the simple piety of being the Guardian of the Two Holy Places.

Geography plays its part, too. Most recently the Second Gulf War in 2003 resulted in a huge change in the local landscape of the Arab lands; for the first time the Shi'a are in government of an Arab country in Iraq. Saudi Arabia, already concerned at the charismatic attraction of Hizballah and Iran in the aftermath of the 2006 war in Lebanon and what it sees as a marginal-izing of Levantine Sunnism, is now trying to reassert a Sunni hegemony, to devastating effect in Syria. Across the region, alliances have been formed that have largely taken place along sectarian lines. In Lebanon, Iraq, Bahrain, Syria and Yemen, the importance of sectarian identity largely secures the support of sectarian kin in the Gulf. Yet the case of Hamas proves to be an outlier. As a member of the so-called "Axis of Resistance" (El-Husseini, 2010), a group comprising Iran, Syria and Hizballah, Hamas's rejection of Israel and the regional status quo sees geopolitical considerations trumping sectarian identities.

Theological reflections

It is politics rather than theology or dogma that is the struggle; the division in Islam between Sunna and Shi'a is far more to do with legitimacy of leadership of the community than profound religious differences. After the Prophet's death in 632 CE there was argument about who should succeed the Prophet Muhammad and have authority over the Islamic commu-nity (*umma*[5]), and whether this succession should be based on kinship to Muhammad or on the worthiness of the successor, *khalifah* (Caliph), in his knowledge of the life of the Prophet and his teachings. Those who favored Muhammad's descendants proposed his cousin and son-in-law, 'Ali; they were the "party of 'Ali" (*shi'at 'ali*). Others favored the Prophet's closest male companion, Abu Bakr who duly became the first *khalifah* (Caliph). 'Ali got his turn then only after 'Umar and 'Uthman[6] and while the Sunna regard all four Caliphs as legit-imate, the Shi'a begin their allegiance after Muhammad with 'Ali whom they style "Imam" (not Caliph).

The theological differences between the Sunna and Shi'a are actually negligible – but handily played upon by both sides and, frequently unwittingly, overplayed in turn by external observers. Both Sunni and Shi'a are orthodox, recognized parts of Islam. The Shi'a are not some off-shoot of Sunni Islam; the different paths have their origin in that argument about the succession following the death of the Prophet. The Qur'an and the hadith(s) are shared plinths, as are the Five Pillars of Islam: the *shahadah* (the professions of faith bearing witness to the one god, Allah and his Prophet, Muhammad); *salat* (prayer); *zakat* (the paying of alms); *sawm* (fasting in the month of Ramadhan); and *hajj* (pilgrimage to Makkah). Sunni myths about Shi'a belief in different texts, straying from the "true path" and general *takfiri* slanders about the Shi'a are manufactured. Doctrinal and religious self-definition and differentiation came after – were added to – an already well-understood social construct based on group loyalty (*'asabiya*).

The vehement resistance to difference, dissent (*fitna*) "otherness" that pervades so much apparently religious disagreement today in the Saudi–Iranian context taps into this ancient core sense of identity. "For posterity, history became overlaid with meta-history, so much so that the actual events were less important than the accretions of myth and sentiment surrounding them" (Ruthven, 1984:1). But it is identity less than sectarianism, power less than rightness that drives the struggle. Perhaps the most important feature distinguishing Shi'a from Sunna since the end of the 18th century is the separation of religious and political authority and the consequent autonomy of the religious institutions from the state.

We should not ignore the power of religion within the Middle East. Sectarian difference is an integral part of the construction of identity politics and such identities – and their histories – have strong contemporary relevance when understanding the behavior of a range of actors today. Take, for instance, the legacy of the Battle of Karbala, which occupies a central role within Shi'a thought. The battle saw the deaths – martyrdom – of Hussein and 'Ali, establishing feelings of guilt, shared martyrdom and sacrifice, which are central to the Shi'a identity today (see, for instance, Mabon, 2017 and Nasr, 2007).

It is temptingly easy to point to modern Saudi Arabia and Iran and to define their actions in polarizing, sectarian terms. Both, indeed, are "sectarian" in terms of their desire to mold their own population's identity – Wahhabism in Saudi Arabia, Twelver Shi'ism in Iran. So they duly both use sectarianism in their projection of regional power. Nevertheless, it is striking how careful both parties are themselves not to ascribe sectarian divisiveness as a reason for their contest for regional influence; it is other commentators who pin that badge on things. Saudi Arabia and Iran are playing to regional domestic audiences (Arab and Persian) whose ears are better attuned to getting along with each other than most external observers would credit, and has historically been the case for centuries; ethnicity, history, shared space and tribal hinterlands provide a deeper foundation for many of the relationships being tested currently. And those same foreign observers who try to make sense exclusively by seeing dichotomies find a recognizable Cold War paradigm in presenting the Saudi–Iran "contest" in sectarian terms whether that fits or not locally or chronologically.

Islamic narratives and political action

The power of Islamic narratives and the demographics of the region, where Sunni often lived side by side with Shi'a, meant that a number of Middle Eastern states were left open to external interference from states that were able to mobilize such narratives. Speaking to the *umma* involved transcending state borders, adding to security concerns.

The constitution of the newly formed Islamic Republic of Iran demonstrates this more universalist approach, stressing:

> the cultural, social, political, and economic institutions of Iranian society based on Islamic principles and norms, which represent an honest aspiration of the Islamic umma. This aspiration was exemplified by the nature of the great Islamic Revolution of Iran, and by the course of the Muslim people's struggle, from its beginning until victory, as reflected in the decisive and forceful calls raised by all segments of the populations.
>
> *(Constitute Project, 2018a)*

In contrast, the constitution of Saudi Arabia is more focused upon the exclusivity of a statehood with more tightly defined edges:

> The Kingdom of Saudi Arabia is a sovereign Arab Islamic state with Islam as its religion; God's Book and the Sunnah of His Prophet, God's prayers and peace be upon him, are its constitution.
>
> *(Constitute Project, 2018b)*

1979 proved to be a seismic year within the Middle East, witnessing an Islamic revolution in Iran, the seizure of the Grand Mosque in Saudi Arabia and the rise to power of Saddam Hussein in Iraq. These events would dramatically alter the balance of power across the Gulf region and had serious implications for the construction of Middle Eastern security calculations. The events brought Islam – and Islamic difference – to the forefront of political calculations that got to the very heart of regimes across the region. In Saudi Arabia, the Al Sa'ud faced existential threats to their legitimacy both internally and externally, stemming from the concept that religion serves as a "double-edged sword". For the Al Sa'ud, religion served as a means of ensuring their political vitality and the centuries-old alliance with the Wahhabis was instrumental in creating the third – and current – Kingdom of Saudi Arabia in 1932. This concept demonstrates how religion (and other concepts) can serve two different roles, both legitimizing a regime by demonstrating Islamic credentials while also providing other actors with fertile ground to criticize rulers for not being Islamic enough.

In the years following the 1979 revolution in Iran, the region witnessed an instrumental use of Islam for political ends. Religious rhetoric and symbolism became a prominent feature of foreign policy behavior, serving to speak to domestic and foreign audiences, opening up a new front for rivalry between states. The establishment of an explicitly Islamic state only 200 kilometers from the Eastern Province of Saudi Arabia would be a serious concern to many in Riyadh. Yet in the formative stages of the Islamic Republic, Ayatollah Ruhollah Khomeini would initially seek to demonstrate unity across the *umma*:

> There is no difference between Muslims who speak different languages, for instance the Arabs and the Persians. It is very probable that such problems have been created by those who do not wish the Muslim countries to be united [...] They create the issues of nationalism, of pan-Iranianism, pan-Turkism, and such isms, which are contrary to Islamic doctrines. Their plan is to destroy Islam and Islamic philosophy.
>
> *(Rubin, 2014: 2)*

Things quickly changed however:

> We will export our experiences to the whole world and present the outcome of our struggles against tyrants to those who are struggling along the path of God, without expecting the slightest reward. The result of this exportation will certainly result in the blooming of the buds of victory and independence and in the implementation of Islamic teachings among the enslaved Nations.
>
> *(Ibid.: 7)*

Such vitriolic rhetoric would become directed at the Al Sa'ud, which became a prime target for the regime in Iran.

> If we wanted to prove to the world that the Saudi Government, these vile and ungodly Saudis, are like daggers that have always pierced the heart of the Moslems from the

back, we would not have been able to do it as well as has been demonstrated by these
inept and spineless leaders of the Saudi Government.

(Ibid.: 5)

It was also the case that, after the 1979 overthrow of the Shah in Iran, the return of Ayatollah
Khomeini, the Soviet invasion of Afghanistan and the shared resistance to that invasion
between the US, UK and Saudi Arabia, the "West" paid scant attention to Saudi/Sunni support
for Sunni fundamentalism, being distracted by what appeared to be the more threatening
version of "Islamic fundamentalism" taking shape in Tehran and spawning proxies in the
likes of Hizballah in Lebanon. The Shi'a then were globally seen as anti-American, hostage-
taking and suicide bombing terrorists. Saudi Arabia was then seen – if it was considered in
this way at all – as wanting both to control its own Shi'a minority in the Eastern Province of
the country and to stem Khomeini's challenge to the Islamic legitimacy of the Al Sa'ud and
their Kingdom.

Despite the increasing prominence of Iran and its proxies in the years after the revolution,
it was Sunni militancy that began to grow to become the dominant concern globally from the
early 1990s onwards even if it took time for this to be recognized. In the decades that followed,
sectarian difference became co-opted by states and regimes seeking to perpetuate their national
interest, using religion as a tool through which to achieve this. Set against the centuries of relatively constructive cohabitation experienced by the wider Sunni and Shi'a communities, this
is far more challenging for the likes of a Prince Bandar. It truly is fundamental. While many
suggest that the Middle East is experiencing its own "30 years war", akin to that experienced
by Europe in the 17th century, such an approach is both Orientalist and suggestive of a linear
process of development that all states must go through. It is also factually inaccurate in so far as
parallels can be accurate.[7]

From this, it appears that it is Sunni militancy and Wahhabi activism, not Shi'a revolutionary
fervor, that remains the greatest danger to those inside and outside the region not wholly
devoted to the dogma of the likes of ISIS, because that Sunni militancy is an uncritical, self-
justifying, ideological (and cruelly violent) force that is not only anti-Shi'a but also explicitly
anti-anything other than itself (a hard part of the equation for conservative *Salafis* in Saudi
Arabia to swallow even if their *salafi jihadi* outliers welcome it). The use of an acerbic sectarian
discourse since the so-called Arab Spring is a striking aspect of Saudi rhetoric empowering the
takfiri jihadis.

But before examining the geopolitics and fragmentations in the region more (see below)
let us return to the question of identity. Saudi Arabia and Iran are modern names for places.
The degree to which their chosen ideological standpoint shapes their worldview has fueled the
aberration of bitter sectarian struggle. But from where did the two states emerge? And how has
that process shaped the position of the current stage?

In Persia, Twelver Shi'ism took form under the sixth Imam, Ja'far al-Sadeq (d.765 CE). Ja'far
specifically dissociated overarching religious authority from any political rule. Unlike the Sunni
mainstream, Twelver Shi'ism has always refrained from giving the ruling powers any religious
authority. The Safavids turned Persia from Sunni to Shi'a in the early 16th century by military
force. The Safavids were a millenarian Sufi warrior order. The extremist fervor of the fighters
for the early Safavid conquest was valuable in conquest but less so in subsequent state creation
when it became a threat. The Safavids used Arab Shi'a to inculcate "moderate" Twelver Shi'ism
and created an emergent priestly rule (hierocracy). The Safavid legacy remains important, with
the term used to negatively denote Iranian influence in Iraq.

In Arabia, in the Nejd desert of the 18th century, Muhammad ibn Sa'ud made his politico-religious pact with Muhammad ibn 'abd al-Wahhab, the ascetic revivalist, and propagated Wahhabism across the region. Subsequently defeated by forces from the Ottoman Empire in1818 the al Sa'ud lost power. Over the following century they struggled with a rival tribe until in 1902 'Abd al-'Aziz bin 'abd al-Rahman Al Sa'ud returned from British Kuwait and with a force of fanatically motivated Wahhabis (the *ikhwan*) conquered the Nejd, what is the modern day Eastern Province and took the Hejaz (and Makkah and Medinah). At which point, rather like the Persians, the Al Sa'ud then had to eliminate the *ikhwan* who had a too fundamental view of the overlap of politics and religion.

This tension about who controls which levers of power, and how, persists:

> Know that kingship and religion are twin brothers; there is no strength for one of them except through its companion, because religion is the foundation of kingship, and kingship the protector of religion. Kingship needs its foundation and religion its protector, as whatever lacks a protector perishes and whatever lacks a foundation is destroyed. What I fear most for you is the assault of the populace. Be attentive to the teaching of religion, and to its interpretation and understanding. You will be carried by the glory of kingship to disdain religion, its teaching, interpretation and comprehension. Then there will arise within religion leaders lying hidden among the lowly from the populace and the subjects and the bulk of the masses – those whom you have wronged, tyrannised, deprived and humiliated.
>
> *(Quoted by Arjomand, 1988: 76)*[8]

From this, it is clear that religion and politics are intertwined and that we cannot analyze one without the other. Moreover, although couched in religious terms, what we are dealing with is an attempt to shape the political environment within which ruling elites are located. This environment transcends the domestic and with the presence of sectarian kin across the Middle East also includes regional politics.

A geopolitical approach

To understand the nature of contemporary relations between Saudi Arabia and Iran one must return to the years before the Islamic revolution in Iran in 1979, to engage with factors that shaped the rivalry between the two. At this time, while there was a degree of mutual suspicion with occasionally fractious periods, the two were largely able to co-exist. The discovery of oil would play a transformative role within Middle Eastern states and also their foreign policies. In the case of the Saudi–Iranian rivalry, oil provided a new dimension for tensions, while also boosting domestic capabilities. Such rapid societal changes – both demographic and techno-logical – would have serious ramifications for the nature of domestic and foreign policy, pro-viding financial means for regimes to pursue their agendas. Realizing this, the Shah of Iran wrote a letter to King Faisal, urging him to modernize the Kingdom: "Please, my brother, modernize. Open up your country. Make the schools mixed women and men. Let women wear miniskirts. Have discos. Be modern. Otherwise I cannot guarantee you will stay on your throne" (Sciolino, 2001).

It would also lead to growing international focus upon the region and, ultimately, the pene-tration of the region by external powers. Such penetration can be traced to the turn of the cen-tury and the British presence in Persia, which was then furthered by the fallout from World War I and the establishment of the mandate system. This was largely centered on European states, however, and the rising importance of oil would solidify the importance of Gulf stability within international security calculations. Supporting this were US efforts to create an alliance between the Iranians and the Saudis as a means of ensuring the stability of the Gulf region. Of course, the revolution would prevent any chance of such an alliance gaining traction.

It was the establishment of a religious dimension that would prove to be the catalyst for the emergence of a deeply fractious rivalry across the Gulf. While one should not reduce the rivalry between Saudi Arabia and Iran to a religious competition – which overstresses the importance of religion and downplays the role of other factors – it is undeniable that religious competition added a new factor to the rivalry. It provided a new arena for competition and, given the importance of religion within the fabric of both states, religious rhetoric would take on existential importance.

In addition to such rhetoric, Khomeini created a new constitution which enshrined religion within the fabric of the state. This would be front and center of the Islamic Republic's foreign policy. Article 3.16 articles how: "the organization of the nation's foreign policy based on Islamic criteria, fraternal commitment to all Muslims, and unrestrained support for the impoverished people of the world".

Perhaps the most powerful example of this support to the downtrodden of the Muslim world can be seen in Lebanon, where the Shi'a community had long experienced marginalization and persecution. The establishment of Hizballah, the Party of God, in 1982 demonstrated that the newly emboldened regime in Tehran was serious about providing support to marginalized groups across the region. In the years that followed, one can trace this support to include groups such as Hamas, in the Occupied Palestinian Territories, and the Islamic Front for the Liberation of Bahrain, which orchestrated a (failed) *coup d'état* against the Al Khalifa regime in 1982 (Alhasan, 2011).

At this point, the Gulf region was in the throes of what appeared to be a war of attrition between Iran and Iraq, with the latter attempting to prevent the proliferation of revolutionary ideas across the region. The demographic constitution of both states led to concerns in both capitals as to the loyalty of minority groups – be it sectarian or ethnic – amidst the suggestion that these may be fifth columns. Broader concern among Sunni Arab states about Iranian expansionism ensured that Iraq had their support; however, only two years after the end of the war, their allegiance would move.

Amidst Iraq's expansionist aspirations, as seen in attempts to annex Kuwait, Sunni Arab states, smaller in terms of demographics and military security yet with great financial might, turned elsewhere to ensure their security. Despite the offer of protection from a wealthy Saudi millionaire who would later fund the attacks of 9/11, King Fahd preferred the military might of the United States, who would act as security guarantor, maintaining an "over the hill" presence.

In the following decade, a rapprochement with Iran shaped the nature of regional security, stemming in no small part from Saudi support to victims of a powerful earthquake in Iran that caused the deaths of 70,000 people. At this time, leaders of both states visited the other to build trust and facilitate this rapprochement, yet in 2001, world affairs shaped the regional security environment. Following the 9/11 attacks and the onset of the War on Terror, Saudi Arabia and Iran would find themselves on different sides, putting an end to this burgeoning friendship.

In his State of the Union speech in early 2002, US President George Bush posited Iran as a member of an "axis of evil", alongside Iraq and North Korea. A year later, Operation Iraqi Freedom would lead to the toppling of Saddam Hussein's Ba'athist regime and the installation of the Coalition Provisional Authority, a transitional government that would aim to facilitate the implementation of a democratic political system within Iraq. In the following years, Iraq would become a zone of proxy competition as Saudi Arabia sought to counter the increasing influence of Iran within Iraq. The ascendancy of Nouri Al Maliki and the Da'wa party would serve Iranian interests well, as a number of members of this Shi'a party had sought refuge in Iran during the Ba'ath era. Fearing this, Riyadh regularly sought to reduce Tehran's influence in Iraq while also urging the US to strike against the Iranian threat. One US diplomatic cable released by WikiLeaks recalls:

> the King's frequent exhortations to the US to attack Iran and so put an end to its nuclear weapons program. "He told you to cut off the head of the snake," he recalled to the Chargé, adding that working with the US to roll back Iranian influence in Iraq is a strategic priority for the King and his government.
>
> (WikiLeaks, 2008)

The Kingdom's long-standing security relationship with the US would continue in Iraq, despite the rising anti-American sentiment at this time. Such a reliance would remain a source of antagonism across the Gulf, with Iran considering itself to be "uniquely qualified" to ensure the security of the region. Tensions in Iraq would continue across the decade, as the struggle to preserve the sovereignty of the country would result in violence among a range of different actors.

The Arab uprisings and regional fragmentation

In December 2010, Mohammad Bouazzizi, a Tunisian street vendor, self-immolated. Frustrated at structural conditions across his country, coupled with a stagnating economy that provided few opportunities, Bouazzizi's act triggered a wave of protests across the Arab world that challenged regime–society relations, opening up a number of violent schisms. The fragmentation of regime–society relations provoked people to turn elsewhere to ensure their basic needs, facilitating a return to sub-state identities of religion and tribe and raising important questions about the construction of identity across the Middle East.

The Arab uprisings quickly spread across the region and a number of previously embedded autocratic rulers were deposed by popular veto. Other regimes managed to maintain control over their populations through a range of different strategies, including the manipulation of domestic populations. This fragmentation provided opportunities for a range of actors to improve their standing across the region, increasingly at the expense of the people of the Middle East as agency was marginalized by broader meta-narratives. Such meta-narratives around sectarian identities denied local agency and created artificial schisms within societies that perpetuated broader geopolitical agendas.

While there is nothing inherently violent in sectarian difference, when such identities take on a political dimension they have the capacity to become violent. Such political context provides a lens through which to engage with domestic affairs, and concepts get their meaning when placed within particular milieus (Wehrey, 2014; Potter, 2014; Matthiesen, 2013). As such, amidst increasingly hostile and political framing about the nature of sectarian difference, violence became an increasingly prominent part of difference.

We must, at this point, identify that there are a number of deeply problematic issues at play here. As noted at the start of our exploration, Western analysis of Middle Eastern affairs still suffers from the legacy of Orientalism, also is beset by a lack of nuance about theological difference and the nature of relationships between different groups. In particular, a great deal of analysis on the events of the Arab uprisings suggested that Iran was guilty of manipulating the behavior of Shi'a groups across the region. If one goes deeper, one sees that there are two serious problems with such a claim. First is a legacy of Arab–Persian tensions which has characterized the region for centuries and continues to do so.[9] Second, is that within the hierarchy of Shi'a Islam, clerics in Najaf are seen by many to possess much greater legitimacy than their Iranian counterparts in Qom. Moreover, there are serious political differences between clerics in Najaf and Qom, with the former suggesting that clerics should remain outside politics while the latter advocates clerical involvement.

Despite this, lazy analysis suggests that a malevolent Iranian hand is behind unrest across the region. If one considers events in Syria, Yemen and Bahrain, following events in Iraq, one can see that societies were characterized by sectarian difference. Within these contexts, regimes and external actors were able to frame events within particular ways as a means of ensuring their survival and the furthering of geopolitical interests. Such factors are also seen in the strategy that both apply to oil issues, particularly efforts by the Al Sa'ud to drive down prices in an attempt to detrimentally impact upon an Iranian economy less able to take the hit of low prices.

For reasons of brevity we are not able to offer an in-depth exploration of the nature of proxy competition between Saudi Arabia and Iran in all of these cases. Instead, we offer a brief overview that demonstrates how religion has been used as a political tool to engender support to presumed sectarian kin across the region. Historical precedent colored the views of many as to the extent of Iranian involvement with Shi'a groups across the region. Indeed, in the aftermath of the protests, many regimes sought to frame events as a consequence of Iranian manipulation.

In Bahrain, Syria and Yemen, Iran provided support for Shi'a groups, albeit in a range of different guises. In Bahrain, Iranian involvement in the protests is difficult to accurately ascertain, despite a number of allegations to the contrary (Matthiesen, 2013; Kasbarrian and Mabon, 2016). Protest movements took to the streets of the island in early 2011, calling for better democratic processes, comprising both Sunna and Shi'a. In the months that followed, the Al Khalifa regime framed events as part of a broader program of Iranian intervention in, and manipulation of internal affairs. In addition, a Saudi-led Gulf Cooperation Council Peninsular Shield Force was deployed to prevent the protesters from gaining too much ground. In the following years, the Shi'a threat was securitized and structural processes were created and modified to restrict the capacity of Shi'a agency to act. Similar issues arise in Yemen, where Houthi rebels directly challenge the government in Sana'a, which is supported by Saudi Arabia. Regular cross border incursions into the Kingdom forced Saudi Arabia to become directly involved in the conflict, participating in a bombing campaign to eradicate the Houthi threat, yet in doing so, contributing to a large-scale humanitarian disaster.

The most devastating case, however, is in Syria, which is widely accepted to be the worst humanitarian crisis since World War II. In the six years since the uprisings, around 500,000 people have been killed while 11 million people have been displaced from their homes. The uprisings in Syria provided Saudi Arabia with a strong opportunity to weaken Iranian influence across the region and to break the so-called "Axis of Resistance" between Iran, Syria, Hizballah and Hamas. Sensing this threat, members of the Iranian Revolutionary Guards Corps became increasingly involved in the conflict and in doing so, ensured the survival of the Assad regime.

Following the escalation of the Syrian conflict, the Saudi Foreign Minister, Adel Al Jubeir, set out perceptions of the Iranian regime, exposing:

> its true [character], as expressed by [its] support for terror, and continue the policy of undermining the security and stability of the region's countries… By defending the actions of terrorists and justifying them, the Iranian régime becomes a partner to their crimes, and it bears full responsibility for its policy of incitement and escalation.
>
> *(Varulkar and Ezrahi, 2016)*

While the rise of Daesh had occupied the minds of many, for Adel al Jubeir, Iran posed the most serious threat to regional stability. Indeed, for Jubeir, Iran was "the single-most-belligerent-actor in the region, and its actions display both a commitment to regional hegemony and a deeply held view that conciliatory gestures signal weakness either on Iran's part or on the part of its adversaries" (Al-Jubeir, 2016).

Concluding remarks

It is clear that religion matters, but we must not dismiss the importance of other aspects of identity that define both individuals and groups, but also feed back into religion. The construction – and performance – of identity is essential to understanding the rivalry, yet we should be careful not to frame identity in binary, zero-sum ways. Identity is a complex, malleable construct, which resides at the heart of contemporary politics and while not necessarily the driving factor of political action, it certainly underpins much of what occurs. Religion has a prominent role to play within such identities, along with the political behavior of actors who bear these identities.

Within these struggles for identity – and efforts to secure legitimacy within these struggles – we can locate broader regional struggles that harness religion as a means of achieving their political ends. Iran and Saudi Arabia are effectively engaged in a new Cold War; yet it is unlikely that either party would seek actually directly to engage militarily. This is largely "war" by proxy, soft-power projection but, in Yemen for example, the heat can rise sharply. Both Iran and Saudi Arabia have crossed the sectarian fault line in seeking regional allies, although we should be reminded that Iran has also allied itself with Hamas. Perhaps this is more of a strategic call for Iran than Saudi, as a "purely sectarian frame locks them into a minority position in most countries" (Gause, 2015: 6).

The ramifications of using religion as a means of securing legitimacy are felt across the region. Of course, religious tensions have political ramifications, and the onset of proxy conflicts across the Middle East is a consequence of the differences between Saudi Arabia and Iran, driven by the instrumentalized use of religion. We must not downplay the prominence of religion within the rivalry, yet we must not overstate it either. Instead, we must remember that religion plays a prominent role within political rivalries, but only as a contributing factor. To reduce tensions in the rivalry between Saudi Arabia and Iran, we must be conscious of the role that religion plays in escalating tensions, but we must also address other factors that have a much stronger impact across the region. Until we do this, we risk misplacing the focus of our analysis with potentially dangerous consequences.

Notes

1 What King 'Abdallah II of Jordan in 2016 called a "crescent of Shi'a", reflecting a changing balance of power and influence across the region, particularly stemming from the location of Shi'i communities.
2 The particularly conservative strain of Sunni Islam preached initially by Muhammad ibn 'Abd al-Wahhab following the *hanbali* school.
3 Through the provision of financial or ideological support.
4 *hanafi, maliki, shafi'i and hanbali.*
5 The *umma* – those people who are the objects of a divine plan for salvation.
6 The Rashidun – the "Rightly Guided" – Caliphs.
7 Stemming from the nature of political organization across the region and the extent to which states have been established. The 30 years war was an attempt to attain control and establish autonomous areas. Across the Middle East, this set of conflicts is about influence and, ultimately, geopolitics.

8 This is a pre-Islamic, Sasanian, tract preserved from an 8th century Arabic translation, attributed to Ardashir, son of Babak, the King of Kings to his successors among the Persian kings.
9 See, for example, the dispute about the name of the Persian Gulf, leading to the cancellation of the Islamic Solidarity Games in 2010.

References

Alhasan, Hasan T., 2011 "The Role of Iran in the failed coup of 1981: The IFLB in Bahrain", *Middle East Journal*, Vol. 65, No. 4.

Al-Jubeir, Adel Bin Ahmed, 2016 "Can Iran Change?" *New York Times*. Available at: www.nytimes.com/2016/01/19/opinion/saudi-arabia-can-iran-change.html?_r=2

Arjomand, Said Amir, 1988 *The Turban for the Crown: The Islamic Revolution in Iran* (New York: Oxford University Press).

Chubin, Shahram and Tripp, Charles, 1996 *Iran-Saudi Arabia Relations and Regional Order* (London: Oxford University Press for IISS).

Cockburn, Patrick, 2016 *The Age of Jihad: Islamic State and the Great War for the Middle East* (New York: Verso).

Constitute Project, 2018b *Iran (Islamic Republic of)'s Constitution of 1979 with Amendments through 1989*. Available at: www.constituteproject.org/constitution/Iran_1989.pdf?lang=en

Constitute Project, 2018b *Saudi Arabia's Constitution of 1992 with Amendments through 2005*. Available at: www.constituteproject.org/constitution/Saudi_Arabia_2005.pdf

El-Husseini, Rola, 2010 "Hezballah and the Axis of Refusal: Hamas, Iran and Syria", *Third World Quarterly*, Vol. 31, No. 5.

Furtig, Henner, 2006 *Iran's Rivalry with Saudi Arabia: Between the Gulf Wars* (Reading: Ithaca Press).

Gause, III, Gregory F., 2015 "Beyond Sectarianism: The New Middle East Cold War", *Brookings Doha Center Analysis Paper*, No. 11 (July).

Kasbarrian, Sossie and Mabon, Simon, 2016 "Restricting the Space, Responding to Protest: The Case of Bahrain", *Global Discourse*, Vol. 6, No. 4.

Lacroix, Stéphane, 2005 "Islamo-Liberal Politics in Saudi Arabia" in Paul Aarts and Gerd Nonneman (eds.), *Saudi Arabia in the Balance; Political Economy, Society, Foreign Affairs* (London: Hurst & Co), pp. 35–56.

Mabon, Simon, 2013 *Saudi Arabia and Iran: Soft Power Rivalry in the Middle East* (London: I.B. Tauris).

Mabon, Simon, 2017 "Hizballah, muqawimmah and the rejection of 'being thus'", *Religion, Politics and Ideology*, Vol. 18, No. 1.

Mabon, Simon and Royle, Stephen, 2017 *The Origins of ISIS: The Collapse of Order and Revolution in the Middle East* (London: I.B. Tauris).

Matthiesen, Toby, 2013 *Sectarian Gulf: Bahrain, Saudi Arabia and the Arab Spring that Wasn't* (Stanford: Stanford University Press).

Nasr, Vali, 2007 *The Shia Revival: How Conflicts within Islam will Shape the Future* (New York: W.W. Norton).

Potter, Lawrence (ed.), 2014 *Sectarian Politics in the Persian Gulf* (London: Hurst).

Rubin, Lawrence, 2014 *Islam in the Balance: Ideational Threats in Arab Politics* (Stanford: Stanford Security Studies), p. 2.

Ruthven, Malise, 1984 *Islam in the World* (Harmondsworth, UK: Pelican Books).

Sciolino, Elaine, 2001 "A Nation Challenged: Ally's Future; US Pondering Saudis' Vulnerability", *New York Times*. Available at: www.nytimes.com/2001/11/04/world/a-nation-challenged-ally-s-future-us-pondering-saudis-vulnerability.html

Varulkar, H. and Ezrahi, E., 2016 *Unprecedented Tension Between Saudi Arabia, Iran Following Execution of Shi'ite Cleric Nimr Al Nimr* (MEMRI, 04.01.16). Available at: www.memri.org/reports/unprecedented-tension-between-saudi-arabia-iran-following-execution-shiite-cleric-nimr-al

Wehrey, Frederic M., 2014 *Sectarian Politics in the Gulf: From the Iraq War to the Arab Uprisings* (Columbia: Columbia University Press).

WikiLeaks, 2008 *Saudi King Abdullah and Senior Princes on Saudi Policy towards Iraq* (20.04.08). Available at: https://wikileaks.org/plusd/cables/08RIYADH649_a.html

23

MUSLIM WOMEN AND (IN)SECURITY

A Palestinian paradox

Maria Holt

Introduction

Since the shocking events of the mid-1990s in Rwanda and former Yugoslavia, the "international community" has realized that "(s)exual violence in conflict needs to be treated as the war crime that it is; it can no longer be treated as an unfortunate collateral damage of war" (UN Special Representative on Sexual Violence in Conflict, Zainab Hawa Bangura, United Nations, 2014). While this development is of course to be welcomed, it raises several pertinent questions within the broader debate on violence against women. First of all, by focusing on rape and sexual assault, international attention disregards the many other forms of violence suffered by women in war. Second, rather than linking violence against women in insecure environments to issues of human rights or quality of life, it is conceptualized in terms of the predominant security concerns of the West. Third, the focus on wartime violence against women tends to be rather selective; quick to identify violations committed against "helpless" women in certain circumstances, the "international community" appears to be less concerned about other, less "worthwhile" victims. In other words, the response to violence against women in the context of conflict depends on the identity of the abused woman, the status of the violator and the impact of the conflict on global security.

When I interviewed Palestinian refugee women in Lebanon, a few years ago, one of the questions I asked them was what they thought about "the international community"; most were critical. For example, Nabila,[1] a married woman in her late 30s living in Bourj el-Barajne camp in Beirut, said that "the international community has been unfair towards Palestinians" (interview, June 2006). Midwife Khadijah shared her view; "the international community", she said, "discriminates against Palestinians"; she described it as "a kind of racism" (interview, June 2006). Layla, an 18-year old student, was equally dismissive; from her perspective, the international community is only interested in helping Israel (interview, June 2006). Abir, a mother of three, agreed; "the Palestinian position is distorted internationally", she said; "if a Palestinian does something bad, everyone is implicated as terrorists" (interview, June 2006). International "discrimination", as these women see it, results from the construction of an image of Palestinians as "uncivilized" people, Islamist extremists, and therefore not worth helping. Therefore, as they indicate, the international community prefers to take a hands-off approach and to leave a resolution of the conflict between Israelis and Palestinians to the parties concerned. This

Muslim women and (in)security

demonstrates inconsistency when compared with the treatment of conflicts elsewhere in the world. It suggests that conflict violence suffered by Palestinian women can be ignored. At the same time, many Palestinians continue to believe that the conflict with Israel "can only be resolved if the international community is actively engaged to fix the situation" (Kuttab, 2013).

The Palestinian–Israeli conflict, unresolved for almost 70 years, is a significant source of insecurity in the Middle East and North Africa (MENA) region. It highlights the inability of the international community to apply consistent standards of moral behavior when dealing with violent disputes. Worse, it indicates an international reluctance to engage constructively with political Islam. In the aftermath of the "Arab Spring" and with the emergence of the militant "Islamic State" group, the debate on "Islam and violent conflict" has become topical, in both academic and policy-making circles. In reality, it is a much older debate and encompasses the struggles of peoples against oppressive regimes, invaders and occupiers. Often articulated in terms of militarized masculinity, the debate has important gender dimensions and has implications for Palestinian women both in the Diaspora and in the territories occupied by Israel (the West Bank and Gaza Strip).

In order to gain a better understanding of violence against women in conflict, as well as its implications for international security, it is necessary to appreciate the macro level but also the smaller spaces where "ordinary" women such as Nabila, Abir and Layla struggle to make their voices heard. In this chapter, I will argue that global intervention, especially when applied to protect women from the violence of conflict, is a contested measure, unevenly applied. By focusing on the experiences of Palestinian women, I will discuss how, in the absence of external protection, they have had little option but to evolve their own strategies for survival. There are two strands to my argument, based on experience and response, and these will be contextualized within theoretical understandings of women, violence and conflict. In the first section, I will demonstrate how Palestinian women's lives unfold in an environment that offers relatively little security for vulnerable members of the community; women are forced to endure the everyday violence of exile and occupation, with violence coming both from outside and inside the home. They are represented as victims, but victims who are not deserving of international compassion. The second part of my discussion considers the coping mechanisms adopted by women to counter various forms of violence; in difficult circumstances, some women have turned to "Islam", in the shape of faith, tradition and activism, both as a form of protection and a tool of resistance. Others have evolved practical solutions in the form of "everyday tactics" to ameliorate the effects of violent conflict. The recourse to Islamic resistance paradoxically both empowers women but also renders them suspect in the eyes of international opinion.

Over the past few years, I have been conducting research in the West Bank and in the refugee camps of Lebanon, to assess the impact of violence against women in the context of conflict. I have interviewed dozens of women from a wide range of backgrounds.[2] Very often, the subjects of my research, as exemplified by the refugee women in Lebanon quoted at the start, have expressed incredulity at how very little concern the so-called "international community" appears to have for their plight. My chapter will reflect, first, the diverse stories told by these women and, second, the gap between their narratives of conflict and the security-dominated response of the international community. It will demonstrate some of the inconsistencies between international morality and the securitization of global conflict.

The particular question I will explore here relates to protection and empowerment. In the absence of global solidarity, how can Palestinian women be enabled to overcome, or at least endure, violence and persistent insecurity in order to play a full part in processes of survival? While it seems obvious that violence has a generally negative impact on women, I also want to make an argument that their coping abilities have been strengthened by the very absence of international concern; they have had little choice but to rely on their own resilience and ingenuity within an environment of communal solidarity, first, by a recourse to Islamic activism; second, by their willingness to engage in acts of resistance against what they consider to be oppressive systems or regimes; and, third, by their refusal to internalize an identity solely defined by victimization. In other words, they address insecurity by locating the secure sites of faith and community.

Double standards

Throughout this chapter, I will build on Martha Nussbaum's contention that "violence, and its ongoing threat, interferes with every major capability in a woman's life" (2005:167) and Judith Butler's question "When is life grievable?" (2010). Ungrievable lives, Butler argues, "are those that cannot be lost, and cannot be destroyed, because they already inhabit a lost and destroyed zone…which means that when they are destroyed in war, nothing is destroyed" (2010:xix). When a US-led coalition overthrew the Taliban regime in Afghanistan in 2001, the mistreatment of women was cited as one of the reasons for the invasion. In the post-9/11 era, as Corinne Mason argues, "American national security, including the threat of terrorism, is now casually connected to gender inequalities abroad" (2013:55). Muslim women "have inflamed the imagination not only of ordinary observers and feminists but also of Western activists and politicians, with a few claiming to want to save them from the alleged oppression of their culture and religion" (Al-Rasheed, 2013). The well-documented suffering of Palestinian women, in contrast, whether enduring enemy bombardment in the Gaza Strip or observing the withering of their national aspirations, has not led to calls for international intervention. This raises two question in the context of this chapter: first, do Muslim women, in Lila Abu-Lughod's words (2002), really "need saving"; and, second, why have Palestinian women, so far, been excluded from the international community's project of *protecting* Muslim women? Could it even be an advantage not to be imprisoned in "the international power context that allows Muslim women to remain that distant voiceless other, awaiting intervention" (Al-Rasheed, 2013)? Whether advantageous or not, the lack of international attention has heightened feelings of insecurity for Palestinian women and it is against this backdrop, the threat to "every capability in a woman's life", that my discussion will take place.

There is also a paradox here. In her discussion of "the centrality of narratives of gender to the production of a recognizable and legitimate narrative of war", Laura Shepherd seeks to understand "the ways in which the discursive construction of gender allowed for the US-led attack on Afghanistan to be considered a legitimate response to the attacks of 9/11" (2006:19). Soon after the invasion began, Laura Bush, wife of the American president, proclaimed that "our hearts break for the women and children in Afghanistan…because in Afghanistan we see the world the terrorists would like to impose on the rest of us". The fight against terrorism, she added, "is also a fight for the rights and dignity of women" (Bush, 2001). In her contribution to an otherwise masculinized debate, Mrs Bush was drawing attention to three key themes: the transformation of Islam into terrorism, the responsibility of the "civilized" world, and the powerlessness of women. Since then, the linkage between American military intervention and violence against women has been further reinforced. Colin Powell, at a reception for International Women's Day in 2002, declared that women's issues were central to American foreign policy, "and particularly to the war on terrorism". He added that the US is "a champion of the human rights and well being of women and minorities worldwide" (Hunt, 2004). During her tenure as Secretary of State, Hillary Clinton sought to promote women's rights internationally by introducing "state-based strategies to end violence against women as a means to eradicate national security threats" (Mason, 2013: 55).

The intervention of these two prominent American women focuses attention on the likelihood that, during times of conflict, "some types of masculinity come to be celebrated and actively promoted to a greater degree than others" (Pankhurst, 2010:154). While Western masculinity is represented as heroic and moral, "gendered and orientalist logics in…War on Terror discourses construct masculinities and femininities according to race, manipulating and deploying representations of the 'Other' to justify military involvement in Afghanistan and Iraq" (Khalid, 2011:15). In the Palestinian case, I would argue, "masculinity" has been constructed as backward and barbaric; Palestinians have been "sucked into the vortex of global terrorism by their implication in the massive justification of Orientalism represented by September 11" (Ashcroft, 2004:118–119). From this perspective, women are being failed both by international inaction and the weakness of their own society. However, the urge to "save" Muslim women disregards women's own agency. In contrast to the supposedly "helpless" women of Afghanistan, Palestinian women are often portrayed as complicit in their own fate. This somewhat convoluted understanding is dangerous; identifying Palestinian masculinity with weakness risks destabilizing Palestinian society still further.

In July 2006, members of the International Women's Commission for a Just and Sustainable Palestinian–Israeli Peace (IWC) convened an emergency meeting in Athens. They urged the international community to intervene; in their words: "Civilians, mainly women and children, are paying the price daily for this vicious cycle of retaliation and counter-retaliation. This is a time of great danger… If no action is taken today, tomorrow will be too late". As far as I can see, their call was not heeded, and Palestinian women and children continue to "pay the price". International protection, when it comes at all, takes the form of limited international activity, for example humanitarian assistance; occasional pronouncements by foreign governments about the need to restart the "peace process"; and the activities of non-governmental organizations working in the West Bank and Gaza Strip and in the refugee camps of Lebanon. But Palestinians have learned, over long years of bitter disappointment, that they are unlikely to see a more determined international response.

Theorizing gender and conflict

In June 2014, UK Foreign Secretary William Hague and Hollywood actor Angelina Jolie co-chaired a global summit in London, aimed at ending sexual violence in war zones.[3] Their initiative highlighted campaigns already underway to change attitudes towards violence against women in the context of conflict, including at the international level. As the Global Summit to End Sexual Violence in Conflict convincingly demonstrated, the everyday violence suffered by women is likely to intensify during periods of conflict. Cynthia Cockburn argues that a deeper understanding can be attained, first, by "conceptualizing gender as an enduring relation of power"; and, second, by "visualizing war as social, systemic and as a phased continuum" (2010:106). Violent conflict is understood as a continuum from the battlefield to the home, as can be seen in the Palestinian example where, in the West Bank, the Israeli military has invaded every corner of life. The "penetration of war into the private domain of the home…has become the most profound form of humiliation and trauma for the invaded communities" (Bleibleh, 2014:4); it depends most powerfully on the victimization of the female members of the household. This is the reality on the ground for many Palestinian women and it suggests that an exclusive focus on sexual violence in conflict is not realistic.

Violence against women occurs in every part of the world. It takes many forms, some of which are justified on the grounds of culture or religion. Muslim-majority states and areas are not exempt from the global propensity to harm and victimize women, in times of both war and peace. But, as elsewhere, the habit of violence by men against women during times of conflict and instability in the Muslim world needs to be placed in context and, in this respect, Cockburn's "continuum of violence" is a useful tool. In this chapter, I am trying to understand the propensity to harm and victimize women in terms of global security concerns and orientalism. The Palestinian case study, unlike the examples of Bosnia and Rwanda, does not solely involve the use of sexual violence against women but, rather, a broader range of violences, all of which "interfere" with "every major capability in a woman's life".

During the July 2014 war between Israel and Hamas, Palestinian president Mahmoud Abbas appealed to the UN to put the state of Palestine "under international protection" due to the worsening violence in the Gaza Strip (ABC News, 14 July 2014). Although women were not his primary concern, his plea highlighted the international refusal to "save Muslim women" if these women might be part of the Palestinian terrorist project. As always in such conflicts, Palestinian women were particularly hard hit as their homes were destroyed and their children terrorized. According to Qandil (2014), "if you ask Palestinian women in Gaza how they manage during times of conflict and what they view as their chief responsibility, most will speak of their children". Fear and anxiety has caused some Gazan women to develop severe mental health issues. But the "international community", despite the severity of the crisis, declined to intervene, and we need to understand, first, how the humiliation of Palestinian women is not recognized by agencies of international intervention tasked with responding to violence against women in conflict; and, second, how these women as a result of their own efforts within a community of solidarity have been represented in terms of international security not as victims but, on some level, as perpetrators.

The relationship between gender and war has been extensively theorized. In order to make sense of the paradoxical victimization of Palestinian women, I will build on three conceptual approaches. First, it is useful to remember that, following the atrocities in Rwanda and Bosnia, as well as the violent treatment of women in conflicts elsewhere, the international community embarked upon a series of gender-conscious measures. In 2000, the United Nations Security Council passed Resolution 1325, which urged the greater participation of women in conflict resolution and post-conflict reconstruction. Although this is a positive step forward, it has been criticized on the grounds that:

> rather than challenging or dismantling the dominant practices and discourses of international security, 1325 enables the "international community" to *harness* women's agency in the reproduction of racial-sexual hierarchies of power that are mobilized in the production of post-9/11 security discourses and practices.
>
> *(Pratt, 2013:773)*

Second, the events of 9/11 "destabilized the US sense of self" (Nayak, 2006:42). The urgent need to reassert state identity compelled the Americans to participate "in an orientalist project that institutionalizes gendered and racialized violence through the infantilization, demonization, dehumanization and sexual commodification of the 'Other'" (Nayak, 2006:42). As a result, the United States too has sought to address the problem of violence against women in war, building on Hillary Clinton's global promotion of women's rights and also proposing an International Violence Against Women Act. While apparently progressive, the US strategy of using violence against women as a cause for intervention, as we saw in Afghanistan, has raised concern that these measures are likely to "maintain systems of imperialist domination at the expense of more complex and nuanced strategies to end violence against women globally" (Mason, 2013:57).

Third, the association of Islam with terrorism since the events of 9/11 has led to normative constructions of the "civilized European" and the supposedly "dangerous Muslim man" (Razack, 2004). This "fear of Islam", as Thapar-Bjorkert and Shepherd argue, "is a discursive replay of the Orientalist representations" (2010:267). 9/11's "post-traumatic space" (Nayak, 2006:42) has contributed to the demonization of all Palestinians as "terrorists"; this perception is further enhanced by the apparent complicity of some Palestinian women in the execution of violent acts against Israelis.

Islam/Islamism: A contributor to conflict

A factor frequently cited to account for women's subordinate or disempowered status, especially in the Islamophobic post-9/11 era, is the dominance of Islamic cultural values in Arab societies. As Maryam Khalid argues, women's rights discourses have been co-opted into a broader discourse of gendered orientalism that marks "Other" women as voiceless victims of a barbaric (male) "Other" enemy, and positions the USA as enlightened, civilized and justified in its military interventions" (2011:16). However, "the colonial appropriation of women's voices" (Lazreg, 1994) has been challenged by the activism of women themselves. While some observers argue that "the Islamization of gender relations" (Mojab, 2001:124) has reinforced an oppressive patriarchal system, others claim that many women who identify as Islamist "are generally socially conscious and feel united in their mission to contribute towards the Islamization of 'modernity'" (Timmerman, 2000:15). Resistance, as Tuastad notes, "also involves resistance to the imaginaries produced by the hegemonic power" (2003:591).

The linkage of Palestinian resistance with Islam highlights another paradox. Islamism has been described in Western scholarly literature, on the one hand, as "a movement of rage, of marginal groups that have been excluded from the social and global orders lashing out at persons who are seen to oppress them"; or, on the other, as "movements bent on turning back the historical clock hundreds of years" (Robinson, 1997: 132). Following the events of 9/11, a "war on terror" discourse emerged, which emphasized a "dichotomy between the benevolent, civilized and moral masculinity of the West and the backward, barbaric, oppressive, deviant masculinity" (Khalid, 2011:20) of "the Muslim world". But this discourse tends to be both simplistic and self-serving; it disregards "the elaboration of a collective Islamic imaginary" (Gole, 2002:4).

Although some critics argue that the influence of Islam has restricted their mobility, many women claim that religion has in reality empowered their ability to resist. In the West Bank, some women described Islam as a motivation for political action and even violence. By "resisting the established order" (Crooke, 2009: 21) and "the imaginaries produced by the hegemonic power" (Tuastad, 2003:591), they are seeking to reinforce their own resilience. The link between Islam and violent conflict is here made explicit. There is an assumption that "Arabs are Oriental, therefore less human and valuable than Europeans and Zionists" (Said, 1980:28) Like the Taliban and al-Qaeda, the Palestinian Islamist group Hamas has been branded terrorist, by Israel, the US and some European states, and this has been used to justify the lackluster support for Palestinian self-determination.

In the camps of Lebanon, many women are disillusioned with politics and some are turning to Islam as a way of finding strength through enhanced religious knowledge. For example, according to Soraya, a 31-year-old woman in Bourj el-Barajne camp, women now have more awareness about religion; they understand more. She herself gives religious lessons to children and talks to other women about their Islamic and human rights (interview, June 2006). For women such as Soraya, a deeper understanding of Islam creates self-respect and resilience. But others are more cynical about the increase in religiosity. Maha, who works with an NGO in Beirut, explained that:

> when people are frustrated, they become more religious. There have been many changes in Palestinian society from 25 years ago; [for example] now many women wear the veil, whereas in the early 1990s, only a few women in the camps were wearing it, now almost all do. But this does not mean they are religious; it is a political statement, and it has been good for the Islamic groups.
>
> *(Interview, January 2007)*

Despite her skepticism, this more nuanced version of Islam cannot be ignored, whether symbolically or in reality. Many Palestinians in the West Bank, including women, have come to regard resistance that is sanctioned by religion as being one of the few options available to them. In the opinion of Zaynab, a student at Birzeit University, people voted for Hamas [in 2006] because they "needed to see changes in all aspects of life". Islamic movements, she added, "look at a woman in a different way to others; they look beyond her body to her mind and this is attractive to women" (interview, November 2007). Hanan, a 41-year-old mother of seven in Balata camp, Nablus, agreed: "the role of women in Hamas is very broad" she said. "They are seen as strong and important. Women helped Hamas to win the election" (interview, June 2007). Their words were supported by Jamila al-Shanti, an elected Hamas member of the Palestinian Legislative Council, who observed: "There are traditions here that say that a woman should take a secondary role – that she should be at the back… But that is not Islam" (Abunimah, 2008: 26).

There are more complex issues at work here and it is sometimes difficult to make sense of the somewhat contradictory strands of the "Islam and violent conflict" debate as they shape women's behavior and responses. On one side, we have Hamas representatives such as Jamila al-Shanti asserting the progressive character of Islamist politics. Her views are supported by Birzeit University student Zaynab and Balata resident Hanan. But they are disputed by the Western narrative of "barbaric, oppressive masculinity" and its subjugation of women, as evinced in Laura Bush's desire to save Afghan women. They are also thrown into question by incidents of violent conflict.

At the heart of the debate about the role of Islam in the Palestinian–Israeli conflict and its implications for international security lies the question of representation. Success for the Palestinian people, as Ashcroft notes, "will never come from armed struggle but from the control of representation" (2004:113). In his book *Orientalism*, Edward Said (1980) explored "the contest between an affirmation and a denial", a contest – in his view – "that sees the 'civilizing' forces of the Europeans pitted against the 'uncivilized' Arabs" (Ashcroft, 2004:116–117). This distinction, Said argued, "emerged out of the idea of the historic conflict between the West and Islam" (Ashcroft, 2004:118). Thus, "Arabs and Palestinians were not only prevented from representing themselves but deemed *incapable* of representing themselves" (ibid.:117). This resonates with the argument that equates international violence against women initiatives with racism.

Following 9/11, the representation of Islam, in Ashcroft's words, "has become even more brutally simplistic" (2004:118); it is represented as a religion of violence and all Muslims as potential terrorists. In the imaginaries produced by the dominant global powers, Palestinian resistance organizations, and indeed the whole Palestinian population, were labeled "terrorist" (Tuastad, 2003:591). The "new terrorism" refers to "the… 'irrational' violence that primarily targets Western civilians" (Goodwin, 2006). In the discourse of the "new terrorism", Muslim women are caught up in a paradox: on the one hand, they are denied agency and represented as in need of "saving" from their "barbaric" men; but, on the other, as in the case of Palestinian women, they too are implicated in the violence; they are portrayed as willing agents, encouraging their children to become "martyrs" and even ready to commit violence themselves. According to Palestinian Media Watch (2014): "Creating a supportive social environment for terrorists has been a critical factor in the Palestinian Authority's successful promotion of suicide terrorism" and, to this end, they "teach Palestinian mothers to celebrate when their children die as terrorist" martyrs. This sentiment both denies agency to women and, at the same time, holds them responsible for the violent acts of their children. It reinforces the notion of a cruel and irrational Islam, a terrorist religion that victimizes women, and provokes "militarized human rights interventions" (Zalewski and Runyan, 2013:293).

Palestinian women and (the lack of) international intervention

According to former UN Secretary-General Kofi Annan: "For generations, women have served as peace educators, both in their families and in their societies. They have proved instrumental in building bridges rather than walls". He is quite correct; women's peacebuilding efforts across enemy lines have enjoyed significant success in conflicts across the globe. But, while it is recognized that the participation of women is critical to processes of conflict resolution, they are rarely consulted or permitted to occupy decision-making positions. UN Security Council Resolution 1325 seeks to change this situation by mainstreaming "an official sensitivity to gender within UN institutions, as well as the decision-making processes of all governments, with regard to conflict resolution, peacekeeping, and peacebuilding" (Pratt, 2013:773). It is debatable how successful this measure has been; first of all, as Nicola Pratt argues, it uses women's agency to reproduce racial-sexual hierarchies of power (2013:773); and, second, it has been ineffectual when it comes to "less valued" women, such as Palestinians.

There is another space, neither part of the "axis of explosiveness" nor the "axis of vulnerability", in which Palestinian women are constructing their own narratives of resilience, in defiance of international censure. In response to their marginalized status, Palestinian women have resorted to "everyday tactics", which "reveal the ways in which people negotiate and reappropriate space and behavior within an environment that is constantly oppressed and confined, with limited or no freedom of movement or action" (Bleibleh, 2014:12). The everyday, as Chatterji and Mehta point out, provides an understanding of "ordinary" people's lives and deaths" (2007:17). In the words of Huda, an NGO worker in Beirut:

> Palestinian women, in general, become more active during difficult times, such as war; they become more involved in political and public life. For example, during the Israeli invasion of Lebanon in 1982 and afterwards, they played a very important role because the men were in prison or in exile and, therefore, women became responsible. They participated in the struggle against the invasion, and also in the camp wars; as the men could not go out of the camps, the women became responsible for defending the camps; women had to organize how to move because they were the only ones allowed to go outside.
>
> *(Interview, 2007)*

Some of the women told stories of how they rebuilt their homes and camps, for example Ain el-Hilwe camp following the Israeli invasion, and Shatila camp after the 1982 massacre; this is a source of immense pride. "The remaking of a social world", as Nina Gren observes, "was achieved through the endless repetition of small events in domestic, quotidian routines" (2015:11).

Conclusion

In this chapter, by focusing on the paradox of international intervention and efforts to "save" Muslim women, an endeavor based on ignorance and orientalist assumptions, I have argued that Palestinian women have been treated as an exception. Rather than benefitting from international measures to curb violence against women in conflict, they have suffered as a result of "the radical inequality that characterizes the difference between grievable and ungrievable lives" (Butler, 2010:xxii). These women have been forced to rely on their own "everyday tactics of survival", supported by faith and communal solidarity. The debate in the west on "Islam and violent conflict" continues to represent Muslim women principally as victims and men as barbaric and oppressive. This view fails to take into account that many women living in conflict-afflicted areas, with Palestinian women providing a good example, have evolved complex strategies of survival and resistance.

Notes

1 Not her real name; pseudonyms have been used throughout.
2 In 2006–07, I received funding from the Arts and Humanities Research Council to conduct a research project on Palestinian refugee women in Lebanon in terms of memory, identity and change. In 2007–08, I was funded by the United States Institute of Peace to undertake a project on women and Islamic resistance in Lebanon and the occupied Palestinian territories. In 2011 and 2015, I received funding from the Department of International Relations, University of Westminster to research violence against Palestinian refugee women in Lebanon (including Palestinian women who had fled from the conflict in Syria).
3 Global Summit to End Sexual Violence in Conflict, ExCel London, 10–13 June 2014.

References

ABC News (2014), "Palestinian President Mahmoud Abbas asks UN for International Protection in Gaza as Hostilities with Israel Continue", 14 July. www.abc.net.au/news/2014-07-14/palestinian-president-calls-for-international-protection-in-gaza/5593502
Abu-Lughod, Lila (2002), "Do Muslim Women Really Need Saving: Anthropological Reflections on Cultural Relativism", *American Anthropologist*, 104:3 (September), pp. 783–790.
Abunimah, Ali (2008), "Engaging Hamas and Hezbullah", *Al-Aqsa Journal*, 10:2, pp. 25–28.
Al-Rasheed, Madawi (2013), "Book Review of 'Do Muslim Women Need Saving?' by Lila Abu-Lughod", *Times Higher Education*, 7 November.
Ashcroft, Bill (2004), "Representation and its Discontents: Orientalism, Islam and the Palestinian Crisis", *Religion*, 34:2, pp. 113–121.
Bleibleh, Sahera (2014), "Walking Through Walls: The Invisible War", *Space and Culture*, pp. 1–15.
Bush, Laura (2001), "Radio Address by Laura Bush to the Nation", 17 November, www.freerepublic.com/focus/f-news/572960/posts
Butler, Judith (2010), *Frames of War: When Is Life Grievable?* London and New York: Verso.
Chatterji, Roma, and Deepak Mehta (2007), *Living with Violence: An Anthropology of Events and Everyday Life*, London and New York: Routledge.
Cockburn, Cynthia (2010), "Militarism and War", in Laura J Shepherd, editor, *Gender Matters in Global Politics: A Feminist Introduction to International Relations*, London and New York: Routledge, pp. 105–115.
Crooke, Alastair (2009), *Resistance: The Essence of the Islamist Revolution*, London: Pluto Press.
Gole, Nilufer (2002), "Close Encounters: Islam, Modernity and Violence, *Interdisciplines*, www.interdisciplines.org/terrorism/papers/2
Goodwin, Jeff (2006), "What Do We Really Know About (Suicide) Terrorism?" *Sociological Forum*, 21:2, pp. 315–330.
Gren, Nina (2015), *Occupied Lives: Maintaining Integrity in a Palestinian Refugee Camp in the West Bank*, Cairo: The American University in Cairo Press.

Hunt, Krista (2004), "The Fight against Terrorism is also a Fight for the Rights and Dignity of Women: The Ramifications of 'Embedded Feminism'", paper presented at annual meeting of International Studies Association, Montreal.

Khalid, Maryam (2011), "Gender, Orientalism and the Representations of the "Other" in the War on Terror", *Global Change, Peace and Security*, 23:1, pp. 15–29.

Kuttab, Daoud (2013), "Israel-Palestine Peace Depends on International Involvement", *Al-Monitor*, 26 August.

Lazreg, Marnia (1994), *The Eloquence of Silence: Algerian Women in Question*, New York and London: Routledge.

Mason, Corinne L (2013), "Global Violence Against Women as a National Security 'Emergency'", *Feminist Formations*, 25:2, Summer, pp. 55–80.

Mojab, Shahrzad (2001), "Theorizing the Politics of 'Islamic Feminism'", *Feminist Review*, 69:1, pp. 124–146.

Nayak, Meghana (2006), "Orientalism and 'Saving' US state Identity after 9/11", *International Feminist Journal of Politics*, 8:1, pp. 42–61.

Nussbaum, Martha (2005), "Women's Bodies: Violence, Security, Capabilities", *Journal of Human Development*, 6:2, pp. 167–183.

Palestinian Media Watch (2014), "Parents Celebrate Children's Death", http://palwatch.org/site/modules/print/news/preview.aspx?fi=479

Pankhurst, Donna (2010), "Sexual Violence in War", in Laura J Shepherd, editor, *Gender Matters in Global Politics: A Feminist Introduction to International Relations*, London and New York: Routledge, pp. 148–160.

Pratt, Nicola (2013), "Reconceptualizing Gender, Reinscribing Racial-Sexual Boundaries in International Security: The Case of UN Security Council Resolution 1325 on 'Women, Peace and Security'", *International Studies Quarterly*, 57, pp. 772–783.

Qandil, Ala (2014), "Women in Gaza Bear Psychological Scars of War", *Aljazeera America*, 28 July, http://america.aljazeera.com/articles/2014/7/28/women-in-gaza-bearpsychologicalscarsofwar.html

Razack, Sherene H (2004), "Imperilled Muslim Women, Dangerous Muslim Men and Civilised Europeans: Legal and Social Responses to Forced Marriages", *Feminist Legal Studies*, 12:2, pp. 129–174.

Robinson, Glenn E (1997), *Building a Palestinian State: The Incomplete Revolution*, Bloomington and Indianapolis: Indiana University Press.

Said, Edward (1980), *The Question of Palestine*, London: Vintage.

Shepherd, Laura J (2006), "Veiled References: Constructions of Gender in the Bush Administration Discourse on the Attacks on Afghanistan Post-9/11", *International Feminist Journal of Politics*, 8:1, pp. 19–41.

Thapar-Bjorkert, Suruchi, and Laura J Shepherd (2010), "Religion", in Laura J Shepherd, editor, *Gender Matters in Global Politics: A Feminist Introduction to International Relations*, London and New York: Routledge, pp. 265–279.

Timmerman, Christiane (2000), "Muslim Women and Nationalism: The Power of the Image", *Current Sociology*, 48:4, pp. 15–27.

Tuastad, Dag (2003), "Neo-Orientalism and the New Barbarism Thesis: Aspects of Symbolic Violence in the Middle East Conflict(s)", *Third World Quarterly*, 24:4, pp. 591–599.

United Nations (2014), "Background Information on Sexual Violence used as a Tool of War", www.un.org/en/preventgenocide/rwanda/about/bgsexualviolence.shtml

Zalewski, Marysia, and Anne Sisson Runyan (2013), "Taking Feminist Violence Seriously in Feminist International Relations", *International Feminist Journal of Politics*, 15:3, pp. 293–313.

INDEX

Note: Page numbers in **bold** denote tables.

al-'Abbadi, Haydar 98, 99
Abbas, Mahmoud 332
Abu-Lughod, Lila 330
Addis Ababa 228
Afghanistan 121, 128, 311, 332; Soviet invasion of
   39, 40, 68, 317, 321;
and US 56, 59, 63, 72; women and children of
   330–331, 334
Afwerki, Isaias 228
Agreement on Bilateral Agricultural Cooperation
   and Partnership (2014) 224
Agreement on the West Bank and the Gaza Strip
   (1995) 241
agriculture 161; foreign agricultural investments
   193–194, 220; *see also* water-energy-food
   (WEF) nexus
Ahmad, Junaid 192
Ahmadinejad, Mahmud 73, 76
Ain el-Hilwe camp 335
air bases 67–68
Ajnad Misr 294
AK Party (Justice and Development Party) 44, 295
Alawi minority 88, 116, 117, 119, 120, 122,
   124, 305
Algeria 9, 10, 36, 158, 268, 277; Arab Afghans'
   success in 40; civil war in 35, 268, 271, 307;
   hybrid political system 287
Ali, Muhammad 263
Ali, Zine El Abidine Ben 118, 145, 303, 305
Alwash, Azzam 107
ANERA 150
Anfal Campaign 256
Ankara 21, 22, 44, 124
Annan, Kofi 335
Ansar al-Sharia 258, 294

Ansar Bait al-Maqdis 294, 289–290
al-Aqsa *intifada* 7, 81, 82, 84, 114, 147
aquifers 147, 168, 183–184; contamination 192;
over-extraction of 170, 192–193
Arab Afghans 40, 271
Arab Authority for Agricultural Investment and
   Development (AAAID) 164
Arab civilian political forces 295–296
Arab countries 9, 91; civil–military relations
   296–297; coordinating state-building and
   democracy establishment 292–293; democracy
   and political Islamists 293–295; democratization
   challenges in 291–297; domination, tyranny
   and corruption in 291–292; governments, and
   food security 193–194; inter-Arab economic
   ties 266–267; leftism in 295; liberalism in
   295; nationalism in 295; oil-fueled economic
   integration 266; political hybrid systems
   287–288, 293, 299; political role of the military
   296–297; progress in human development
   19; rifts between 6; weakness of civil society
   organization 296
Arabian American Oil Company (ARAMCO) 67
Arab–Israeli conflict 73, 82, 85, 112, 265; Western
   policy in 272
Arab–Israeli–Palestinian conflicts 4
Arab-Kurdish tensions 96
Arab League 4, 6, 58, 123, 297
Arab Maghreb Union (AMU) 10, 91
Arab–Persian tensions 324–325
Arab Spring 5–6, 19, 21, 22, 86, 87, 92, 141, 145,
   146, 187, 203, 286, 297–298, 303, 311, 313, 321;
   and armed non-state actors, growth of 288; and
   climate change 201; and democracy transition
   287–291, 306–307; democratic transition, in

Index

Tunisia 290–291; failed nation-states 288–290; implications of 8; partial political reforms and hybrid political systems 287–288, 293, 299

Arab Sunnis 98, 99, 100, 101, 103; *see also* Sunni–Shi'a relations

Arab Union, collapse of 6

Arab uprisings 34, 37, 40–41, 45, 168, 174, 175, 177–178, 276, 277–278; and regional fragmentation 324–326

Arava Institute's programs and projects 242

Al Areed, Ali 294

armed conflict 3, 6, 10, 11, 33, 85, 149; typology of 31; *see also specific conflicts and wars*

Ashcroft, Bill 334

Assab port 226, 228

al-Assad, Bashar 40, 43, 44, 45, 47, 88, 115, 116, 118–119, 120–121, 175, 189, 203, 205, 303, 308

al-Assad, Hafez 88, 111, 113, 114, 116–117, 119, 189

Aswan High Dam 264

Australia, water-energy-good nexus 164–165

authoritarian-democratic hybrid system 287–288, 293, 299

authoritarianism and democratic change 304–305; regime security means 306; role of security forces 305–306

Awadallah, Bassem 165

Axis of Resistance 318, 325

al-'Aziz, King 'Abdullah bin 'Abd 72, 74, 76

al-'Aziz, King Fahd bin 'Abd 69, 323

Baathism 6, 35–38, 96

Ba'ath party 38, 88, 104, 106, 117, 270

Badr Organization 101, 102

Baghdad 42, 69–73, 98, 100, 103, 105, 107, 177, 317

Baghdad Pact 42, 112

Bahrain 10, 28, 40, 60, 66, 68, 73, 91, 303, 305–306, 309, 325; Iran's influence in 46, 59; sectarian identity 318; and United Kingdom 66; and United States 66–68, 74; water scarcity 158; *see also* Gulf Cooperation Council (GCC)

Baker, James 70

Bakker, K. 235

Balfour Declaration (1917) 34, 36, 112

Barak, Ehud 88

Barzani, Masoud 101

al-Bashir, Omar 194, 219

battle-related deaths 84–85

Bedisa 224

Beirut 89, 91, 114, 178, 317, 328, 334, 335

Beles Sugar Project 224

big water: challenges 158–159, 160–163; alternatives to management of 164; supply chain 160

big water/food-water, management by farmers 160

Black September war 83, 87, 88

Blue Nile River 224

Blue Peace 242, 243

bonanza modernization 269–270

Bouazzizi, Mohammad 324

Boutrous-Ghali, Boutrous 143

bread consumption 188

BRIC countries: as external partners in the Nile region 217

Bromley, Simon 272

Brooks, D. B. 237

Al-Bunyan Al-Marsous 289

Bush, George H. W. 69–70

Bush, George W. 56, 114, 323

Bush, Jr., administration 69, 71, 72–73, 311

Bush, Laura 330, 334

Butler, Judith 330

Buzan, Barry 9, 82–84, 212

Campbell, Andrew A. 182

Camp David Egyptian–Israeli peace treaty 7, 82, 90, 91, 310, 317

Carrefour 189

Carter, James E. 68

Carter Doctrine 54, 68

challenges, short- and long-term 19–21

Chatterji, Roma 335

chemical weapons 43, 114, 120, 148, 308, 312

Cheney, Richard 69

China *see* People's Republic of China

China National Petroleum Company 76

Christian Falangist militia 89

Christopher, Warren 71

civil–military relations 296–297

civil society organizations, weakness of 296

civil war(s) 49; in Algeria 35, 268, 271, 307; in Iraq 102, 103, 312; in Lebanon 6; between PLO and Jordan 90; in Syria (*see* Syrian civil war); in Yemen 59, 75, 258, 312

climate change 20, 169, 183; impact of 146–147, 169, **183**; impact on farming systems **183**; risks 243

climate-related security risks 199–201, 207–208; in Egypt 201–203; in Syria 203–205; in Yemen 205–207

climate sensitivity 20

Clinton, Bill 88, 194

Clinton, Hillary 74, 330, 332

Clinton administration 54, 71

Coates, Victoria 64

Cockburn, Cynthia 331, 332

Cold War 33–34, 38, 41–42, 53, 75, 84, 92; impact on MENA region 19; influence on Nile region 216

Collaborative Programme Euphrates and Tigris (CPET) 242–243, 245

Congress for the Republic (CPR) 294

Index

consensus-building, and good governance 281–283

continuum of violence 332

Cook, C. 235

Cooperative Framework Agreement (CFA) 215, 216, 222, 225

Copenhagen school framework 4

counter-insurgencies 49, 54, 57, 63, 118–119

Counter-Terrorism Force 98

cross border aid 131–135, 137, 147, 242

cross-border wars 49

Cuban Missile Crisis 6

Daesh/Da'esh *see* Islamic State (IS/ISIS/ISIL/ Daesh)

Dahiya Doctrine 310

Damascus 22, 43, 74, 89, 114–118, 120, 123, 131–135, 191, 192, 317

Daraa 203, 204

Da'wa party 324

De Châtel, Francesca 204

Declaration of Principles between Israel and Palestine (1993) *see* Oslo I Accord

de-escalation agreements 125

defensive modernization 261, 262–263

de Mistura, Staffan 203

democracy: and political Islamists 293–295

democracy and security in the post-Arab Spring 303–304; authoritarian persistence and 304–307; politics of security 312; regional insecurity and disorder 307–311; sectarianism and geopolitics 312–313; theoretical (and eclectic) synthesis 313; trends and trajectories 311–312

democratization 286–287; and Arab Spring 287–291, 306–307; challenges 291–297; future prospects for 299–300; and regional security 297–298

demographic development 20

demographic development challenges 20

Denmark 277

Desalegn, Hailemariam 223, 228

Dhahran air base 67

Diego Garcia 70, 74

displaced people 16–17; *see also* forced migration; internally displaced people (IDP); refugees

DP World 226–227

Droogers, Peter 169

dual containment policy 54, 71

Dubai World Ports 226

Dublin Statement on Water and Sustainable Development 238, 244

East Jerusalem 91, 310

economic dependency, as a security issue 261–262

economic integration 20–21, 44, 265, 266

economy, West's peripheralization of 261–262

Ecoparks 147

EcoPeace (former FOEME) 147, 242

Eco Warriors 150

Egypt 6, 7, 8, 47, 86, 91, 92, 135, 303; army 296–297; climate-related security risks 201–203; democracy in 304; democracy in, and security forces 305; democratic transition 307; Islamic-secular divide 293; and Israel, 1979 peace agreement between 217; migration in 253; military undermining Muslim Brotherhood 41; nation-state crisis 289–290; Navy's Southern Naval Fleet Command at Safaga 227; political economy 263–265; remittances 254; rust monitoring 191; and Turkey 222–223; water security 160

Egyptian Sinai Peninsula 6

Egypt–Israel–the Palestinians 90

Eid, Kassem 191

Eisenhower, Dwight 53

Eisenhower administration 67

Eisenhower doctrine 112

energy security 106–107, 214, 261, 271–272

Eng, B. 133

Ennahda Party 282, 290–291, 293, 294, 295, 306

environmental peacebuilding in Israel–Palestine 146–147

Erdoğan, Recep Tayyip 21, 44, 222, 223, 224

Eritrea 212, 213, 220, 226, 228–229

Ethiopia: and Gulf countries 220–221; and Israel 227; and Nile 214, 215; and Turkey 223–224

Ethio-Turkish Joint Economic Commission 223

ethnic cleansing 49, 142

Ettakatol 294

EU3+3 and Iran, nuclear deal between 44

Euphrates-Tigris Initiative for Cooperation (ETIC) 242, 245

Euphrates-Tigris river system 211, 225, 234; formal water diplomacy 240–241; hydropolitical security complex 9; Syria and Turkey, water-related agreements between 240

Europe 17, 24, 27, 272, 307, 332–333; and Arab–Israeli conflict 36; desalination of sea water 159; gunboat diplomacy 262; Iraqi Yezidis seeking asylum in 105; Kurdish groups based in 260; restriction of refugees in 259; Thirty Years' War 29

European Union (EU) 7, 44–45

EXACT process 242

farmers 170; and big water/food-water 160, 161–162, 163; and reduction of food waste 194

Farrell, H. 278, 279

Fatah party 62, 81, 90, 310

Feldstein, L.D. 278–279

food, as religious symbolism 184

food refugees 190–191

food security 182–185, 195–196; in conflict-torn states 174–175; enhancing methods 195;

food refugees 190–191; foreign agricultural investments 193–194, 218; Islamic theology 194–195; less food waste, fewer food imports 194; meat consumption 185–186; in MENA region 20; and political stability 186–190; self-reliance policy 195; transnational threats 191–192; water mismanagement as a threat to 192–193; and water security 172–174
food waste, reduction of 185, 194, 195
food–water scarcity 157, 160, 163–164, 165
forced migration 253, 256; security concerns 259; *see also* internally displaced people (IDP); refugees
foreign agricultural investments 184, 193–194, 195, 218, 220
Framework of Hydro-Hegemony 212–213
France 6, 35, 36, 42, 43, 59, 75, 89, 265; and Iraq nuclear power station building 91; and Libya 43, 45
Freedom and Justice Party 294
freedom of information, and water diplomacy 239
Free Syrian Army (FSA) 58, 119, 120
Friedman, David 64

Gaddafi, Muammar 289, 296
Galtung, Johan 83, 263
Gates, Robert 73, 74
Gause, Gregory 312
Gazan women, violence against 332
Gaza Strip 6, 62, 82, 85, **86**, 87, 91, 135, 169, 241, 330, 332; technical water projects in 147; *see also* Oslo Accords
GCC countries *see* Gulf Cooperation Council (GCC) countries
Gemenne, François 199
gender and conflict 331–333; *see also* Muslim women
genocide 49, 142, 194
geopolitics, and sectarianism 312–313
Germany 20, 45, 62, 73, 75, 105, 146
Glaspie, April 69
global economy and global trading patterns 17
global inequality 16
globalization: and migration 259
global powers: influence on regional development 19; shift and implications for the region 23–28; *see also specific countries*
Global Summit to End Sexual Violence in Conflict 331
global trends 16–18
global warming 135, 137; *see also* climate change
GLOWA Jordan River process 242
Golan Heights 88
Golden Division 98
Good Water Neighbors project 147
governance 276, 283; in Arab countries 299; and consensus-building 281–283; fragmented

governance 171; mistrust in societies 280–281; trust and human security 279–280; trust and the social contract 277
Gramsci, Antonio 48
Grand Bargain 136
Grand Ethiopian Renaissance Dam (GERD) 214, 215, 221, 228, 230
Grand Mosque in Mecca, 1979 siege 34, 39–40
The Great Game in Asia 66
Gren, Nina 335
groundwater: overexploitation 170, 192; unsustainable management 190, 192
groundwater depletion (GWD) 184, 192–193, 206
Gulen movement 21
Gulf Cooperation Council (GCC) countries 5, 10, 59, 74, 75, 77, 91, 168, 192, 271, 304; and crisis responses 10; democracy and security forces 306; food imports 193; investment in agriculture and livestock abroad 220; remittances 254
Gulf Cooperation Council Peninsular Shield Force 325
Gulf countries 9, 87, 99, 217, 323; farming in 184; food security and political stability 188
Gulf countries, involvement in Nile Basin 217–218; Gulf-Ethiopia/Horn of Africa 220–221; Gulf-Sudan 218–220; hydropolitical implications 221–222
Gulf War: first (1990–1991) 10, 54, 91, 104, 114, 217, 219, 256, 263, 277; second (2003) 217, 256, 318
Gürkaynak, C. E. 243

Haddad, Fanar 97
Haddad, Saad 89
Hadi, Abdrabbuh Mansur 59, 207, 290, 296
Haditha Dam 177
Hagel, Charles T. 74
Hague, William 331
Haig, Alexander 63
Hamas 10, 37, 81, 86, 89, 90, 92, 310, 318, 323, 333
al-Haq, Asa'ib Ahl 101, 102
Hariri, Saad 89, 309
al-Hashd al-Watani (National Mobilization Unit) 99
Hashemite Kingdom of Jordan 87, 88
Hassan II of Morocco, King 91
Heikal, Muhammad Hassanein 267
Hezbollah/Hizballah/Hizbullah 37, 43, 45–46, 63, 71, 89, 124, 135, 203, 305, 318, 323; and Israel, confrontations between 43, 82, 89, 92, 114, 310
Horn of Africa 212, 213, 223, 227–228; and Gulf countries 220–221
House of Saud 22, 30, 39
Houthis, 206, 207, 220, 226, 258, 290, 325; and Saudi Arabia 290; support in Yemen 46, 190, 226, 304, 309, 325; uprising 59
Hudson, Michael 272

Index

Hu Jintao 73
humanitarian assistance 106, 127–128, 148, 150; aid and conflict 128–129; aid and conflict, future of 135–137; by European Union 44–45; history, in the Middle East 129–130; Syria (*see* Syria, humanitarian crisis)
human security 276; Iraqi dilemmas 96, 97, 98, 102–108; Syrian 115–118; and trust 279–280; and water security 171–172
Hussein, Saddam 5, 7, 38, 69, 83, 256, 270, 272, 273, 308, 320
Hussein of Jordan, King 90
hybrid political systems 287–288, 293, 299
hydrocarbons 66–67, 76, 184, 261, 267, 268, 270
hydrological infrastructure 168, 170, 176–177, 178; *see also* water scarcity; water security
hydro-peacebuilding projects between Israelis and Palestinians 147
hydropolitical security complex (HSC) 9, 212, 221–222

Ibn Sa'ud, Muhammad 317, 322
Idlib 43, 116, 122, 125
ijtihad 317–318
ikhwan 317, 322
import substitute industrialization (ISI) 264, 266
India 17; as external partner in the Nile region 217; nuclear weapons programs 61
infitah policies 7, 264
informal social and cultural networks 280
Intergovernmental Panel on Climate Change (IPCC) 169
intermediate-range ballistic missile (IRBM) testing 69, 74
internally displaced people (IDP) 12, 96, 98, 102–103, 122, 130, 190, 204, 253, 258–259; *see also* forced migration; refugees
International Atomic Energy Agency (IAEA) 61, 72, 75
international law 55–56, 58, 177
International Monetary Fund (IMF) 187, 267, 272
international non-government organizations (INGOs), humanitarian assistance 128, 129–130, 131, 132, 134, 137
International Women's Commission for a Just and Sustainable Palestinian–Israeli Peace 331
intifada see al-Aqsa *intifada*
Iran 38, 43, 226, 297, 323; and China 76–77; and EU3+3, nuclear deal between 44; farming in 184; and foreign policy 22; groundwater abstraction 193–194; and Iraq, war between (*see* Iran–Iraq war); Islamic narratives and political action 319, 320; Islamic Revolution (*see* Iranian Revolution (1978–1979)); nuclear program 75; progressive social movement and political conservatism, tension between 317; and Saudi

Arabia 67, 311; and Syria 123; urbanization and social mobilization 268; and US 68–69
Iran-Contra scandal 63
Iranian Revolution (1978–1979) 5, 7, 10, 34–35, 38–39, 45, 67, 91, 265, 311, 322
Iranian Revolutionary Guards Corps 99, 325
Iran–Iraq war 6–7, 69, 265; US intervention 54
Iran–Libya Sanctions Act (ILSA) 71
Iraq 6, 38, 271; civil society organizations (CSO) 148; civil war in 102, 103, 312; community-based organizations (CBO) 148; dealing with ISIS remnants 100–102; electoral cycle 96–97; energy security 107; environmental security 107; expulsion of ISIS by military forces 96; future duopolies of violence 98; gender security 105–106; hard security dilemmas 96, 97–100; health security 106; honor crimes 105–106; human security dilemmas 97, 102–108; hydroelectric infrastructure 107; intermediate-range ballistic missile (IRBM) testing 69, 74; internally displaced peoples (IDPs) 98; invasion of Kuwait 69–70, 270–271; Kurdish minority in 256; military intervention in 7–8; militias issues 98–100; National Action Plan 148; nation-state crisis 289; need for human resources 108; oil resources security 107; Palestinian refugees in 257; political instability in 312; population displacement and refugees 102–103; reform of the regular military forces 98; removal of improvised explosive devices (IEDs) 103; security, conceptualization of 97; security, interrelated challenges 97; security complex 84; security for minorities 105; sexual slavery 106–107; soft security dilemmas 96, 102–106; and UNSCOM 70; and US 68, 69, 70–71; as a war state 270–271; water and food security in 107–108, 174; women and institution building in 148–149; youth security and education 104; *see also* Iran–Iraq war
Iraqi Christians 105
Iraqi Kurds 45
Iraqi Red Crescent 106
Iraqi refugees: in Jordan 257; resettlement of 257–258
Iraqi Security Forces (ISF) 98
Iraq Petroleum Company 67
Irbil 98, 100, 101, 105
ISIS *see* Islamic State (IS/ISIS/ISIL/Daesh)
Islam: linkage of Palestinian resistance with 333; role in Palestinian–Israeli conflict 334
Islam, S. 238
Islamic Jihad jihadism/jihadist groups
Islamic Republic 68, 71, 73; defusal of nuclear research crisis 75; foreign policy 323
Islamic Revolutionary Guards' Corps (IRGC) 73
Islamic Revolution in Iran *see* Iranian Revolution (1978–1979)

342

Index

Islamic State (IS/ISIS/ISIL/Daesh) 8, 22, 48, 57, 96, 120, 141, 177, 256, 273, 288–289, 294, 304, 308, 312, 313, 317

Islamic State of Iraq and al-Sham (ISIS) *see* Islamic State (IS/ISIS/ISIL/Daesh)

Islamic State of Iraq and Syria (ISIS) *see* Islamic State (IS/ISIS/ISIL/Daesh)

Islamic State (IS/ISIS/ISIL/Daesh) remnants, Iraq's dealing with 100–102; battle for smaller towns 101–102; battle over urban centers 100–101

Islam/Islamism 293; association with terrorism since 9/11 events 333; Five Pillars of 318; women's status under 333–335

Islamist extremism 62

Islamist opposition groups 5

Israel 6, 226, 297; and Arab 256; creation of state of 34, 36–38; and Ethiopia 227; and the Iranian-backed Lebanese Shiite movement Hizbullah, war between 310; and Lebanon, cease-fire agreement between 89; Lebanon wars 85, 90; military attacks 6; nuclear weapons 60–61; in Red Sea and Nile HSC 228–229; and United States 62–64; as Western foothold 37

Israeli–Palestinian conflict 10, 80, 141, 312; environmental peacebuilding in 146–147; and EU 44; historical overview of dynamics of 81–82; peace process, collapse of 310; preferred solution to **86**; security implications 82–84; US role in peace talks 62

Israeli–Palestinian security complex (IPSC) 83–84; Egypt–Israel–the Palestinians 90; global security implications 92–93; Israel–Syria–the Palestinians 88; Jordan–Israel–the Palestinians 87–88; Lebanon–Israel–the Palestinians 88–89; Palestinian diaspora 87; personal and state security implications of 84–86; security implications for sub-complexes of 86–90; security implications for the Middle East 90–91; UN's involvement 92–93

Israeli Peace Index 85

Israel–Syria–the Palestinians 88

Jägerskog, Anders 205

al-Jama'a al-Islamiyyah 201

Japan 17, 20, 67, 272, 273

Jasmine Revolution 145

Jerusalem 7, 37, 63, 81, 82, 85, 92

jihadism/jihadist groups 40, 48, 201, 295, 311, 312, 321; in Syria 121–122; *see also specific jihadist groups*

Joint Comprehensive Plan of Action (JCPOA) 62, 75, 77

Joint Technical Committee for Regional Waters (JTC) 240, 241

Joint Water Committee 147, 241

Jolie, Angelina 331

Jordan 6, 86, 87, 91, 169, 175; Hashemite monarchy in 306; Iraqi refugees in 257; Palestinian refugees in 256–257; Red-Dead water canal 170; remittances 254; water scarcity 157

Jordanian West Bank 6

Jordan–Israel–the Palestinians 87–88

Jordan river 88, 147, **163**, 170–171, 211, 239–240

al-Jubeir, Adel 325–326

Kakais 105

Kandil, Hisham 294

Karakamis dam 176

Karbala, Battle of 319

Kata'ib Ahrar al-Sham 121

Kata'ib Hizbullah 99

Kata'ib Imam Ali 99

Kelley, Colin 204

Kenya 212, 227

Kerry, John 7, 56, 57, 74

Khalid, Maryam 333

Al Khalifa, King Hamad 40, 323, 325

Khamene'i, 'Ali 75

Khartoum 34, 164, 226, 228

Khashoggi, Jamal 309

Khatami, Muhammad 71, 72

Khomeini, Ayatollah Ruhollah 7, 320–321, 323

Kibaroglu, A. 242

King Abdullah Initiative for Saudi Agricultural Investment Abroad (KAISAIA) 218, 220

King Khalid Military City 68

Kirkuk 269; and ISIS 101

Kissinger, Henry 63

Knight, J. 278, 279

Kruse, Marie 281–282

Kuran, Timur 280–281

Kurdistan Democratic Party (KDP) 98, 101

Kurdistan Regional Government (KRG) 98, 101, 103, 106

Kurdistan Workers Party (PKK) 44, 124, 256

Kurds 19, 21–22, 38, 47–48, 253, 269, 289; and Arabs 96, 117; demand for autonomy 91, 256; denial of state to 34–35; in Europe 260; in Iran 256; in Iraq 21, 42, 45, 70, 99, 101, 256, 312; militias 70, 72, 101–102, 104, 177, 259; People's Protection Units (YPG) 43, 98, 101, 120; in Syria 21, 22, 91, 124; in Turkey 113; *see also* Yezidis

Kurzman, Charles 311

Kuwait 69–70; Iraq's invasion 270–271; food security 189; meat consumption 185; and Saudi Arabia 266

labor migration 200, 204, 253, 266; and remittances 254–255

Lake, Anthony 54

law of return 85

Index

League of Arab States (LAS) 6, 90, 91
Lebanon 6, 42, 86, 87; civil war in 6; labor migration 253; Palestinian refugees in 257; remittances in 253, 254–255; Shi'a community in 323; US pressure on Israel to launch war on 63; women and Islamism 333–334; youth and peacebuilding in 149–150
Lebanon Agreement 149
Lebanon–Israel–the Palestinians 88–90
Lelieveld, J. 201
liberal peacebuilding 144
Libya 4, 8, 40, 43; democracy and security forces 305; democratic transition 304; national army 296; nation-state crisis 289; nuclear program 61; security complex 84; US role in the 2011 NATO intervention in 58; water and food security in 174
lineages and earthquakes 34
Linz, Juan J. 288
Liwa' Suqur al-Sham 121
locusts 191–192
Lower Jordan 234; informal water diplomacy 239, 242–243

Macmillan, Margaret 56
Madrid 7, 88, 273
Maghreb 9, 10
Malik, Adeel 165
al-Maliki, Nouri 98, 308, 324
Mapendere, J. 236
Martinez, J.C. 133
Mashreq 9, 168
Mason, Corinne 330
McKinsey consultants 157
Medvedev, Dmitry 76
Mehta, Deepak 335
migration: forced (*see* forced migration); and globalization 259; and lobbying 259; *see also* labor migration; population migration; refugees
Miliband, David 133
military modernization 262
modern history, of Middle East security 5
Mohammed VI, King 306
Morsi, Mohamed 222, 294, 297, 305, 317
Mossadegh, Mohammad 38, 42, 267, 268
Mosul 105, 308; and ISIS 101
Mosul Dam 96, 97, 107, 177
Mubarak, Hosni 28, 41, 90, 74, 118, 187, 201, 202, 203, 303
Muhammad, Prophet, succession of 318
mujahedin 40, 271
mukhabarat 116, 117, 304, 312
multidimensional water security: food security 172–174; human security 171–172; hydrological infrastructure and war 176–177; national security and political stability 175–176; water and food security in conflict-torn states 174–175; water weapon 176

multi-level stakeholder platforms (MSPs) 245, 246
Multinational Force (MNF) 42
multi-track water diplomacy 236–238; definition of 234; engaging former officials/government officials in informal roles 237; environment for effective functioning 224–225; formal diplomacy 236–237, 238–239; informal diplomacy 236, 237, 238–239; linkages between tracks 238–239
Mus'ab al-Zarqawi, Abu 100
Muslim Brotherhood 39, 41, 202, 222, 289, 294, 307, 317
Muslim women 328–329, 336; double standards 330–331; and Islamism 333–335; theorizing gender and conflict 331–333; violence against, in conflict 329

Najaf 70, 71, 100, 177, 325
Nasser, Gamal Abdel 42, 90, 203
Nasserism 37; developmental logic of 263–264
National Coordination for Syrian Revolution and Opposition Forces 120
National Council of Resistance of Iran 72
"neo-Ottomanism" 44
Netanyahu, Benjamin 227, 228
Newman, Edward 144
new terrorism 334
new Thirty Years' War 29–30
Nile Basin Initiative (NBI) 215, 216
Nile hydropolitics 229; and Red Sea 225–227; and Red Sea, implications 227–229
Nile/Nile Basin 211–213, 212, 227, 229–230; breadbaskets strategy 213, 221; Framework of Hydro-Hegemony 212–213; hydropolitical dynamics, role of external partners in 216–217; hydropolitical security complex (HSC) 212, 229–230; involvement of the Gulf countries in (*see* Gulf countries, involvement in Nile Basin); proxy politics 213; recent hydropolitical developments in 214–218; securitization of 214–215; Turkey's involvement (*see* Turkey, as a strategic partner in the Nile Basin)
Niles Water Agreement (1959) 214
9/11 attacks 7, 34, 56, 72, 207, 323, 332; representation of Islam after 334
Nixon, Richard 53
Nixon Doctrine 53, 67
Noble, Olam and Wilmar (the NOW companies) 164
"non-food water" supply chain 164
Non-Proliferation Treaty 72; Article VI 61
North Atlantic Treaty Organization (NATO), intervention in Libya 23, 43, 45, 58, 311
Nuaimiyah Dam 177
nuclear non-proliferation: United States 60–62
nuclear-weapons free zones (NWFZs) 60

344

Index

al-Nujaifi, Athil 100
Nussbaum, Martha 330

Obama, Barack 43, 56, 57–58, 61–62, 73
Obama administration 43, 57–58, 59, 63, 74, 75, 311
October War 91
Oil Arabism 266–267
oil embargo of 1973–1974 91
oil politics 265–267
Oman: food production capability modernization 188–189
Omo Valley Farm Corporation 224
Operation Decisive Storm 290
Operation Desert Storm 69
Operation Iraqi Freedom 323
Operation Litani 89
Operation Restoring Hope 290
Organization of the Petroleum Exporting Countries (OPEC) 265–266
Orientalism 324
Oslo I Accord 7, 81, 82, 86, 87, 88, 90, 91, 147, 241, 310
Oslo II Accord 81, 88, 147
Ottoman Empire 34–36, 262; Algeria, and instability 36; and Arab Springs (see Arab Springs); and Britain 35–36; challengers' ideological frameworks 36; and France 35–36; MENA conflicts and regime faltering, intertwined 35; Muslim Brotherhood 36; post-colonial secular regimes, and failures 35; religious opposition 35–36; resistance to new order 35; ruler-opposition dynamics 36
Oxford Business Group 282

Pakistan 74, 193; nuclear weapons programs 61
Palestine 6, 7, 36; and Israel, conflict between (see Israeli-Palestinian conflict); Israeli–Palestinian security complex (IPSC) (see Israeli–Palestinian security complex (IPSC)); and United States 63–64
Palestine Liberation Organization (PLO) 6, 46, 81, 82, 83–84, 86, 87, 89, 92
Palestinian Authority (PA) 83, 85, 86, 90, 92
Palestinian diaspora 87
Palestinian Media Watch 335
Palestinian refugees 256–257; humanitarian assistance to 129; in Iraq 257; in Jordon 256–257; in Lebanon 257; in Syria 257
Palestinians displacement 256
Palestinian women 328–329, 336; double standards 330–331; and international intervention 335; and Islamism 333–334; violence against 331–332
pan-Arabism 6, 37
Paris, Roland 144
partial political reforms 287–288

participatory approach to water management 238
The Party of God see Hezbollah/Hizballah/Hizbullah
Patriotic Union of Kurdistan (PUK) 98, 101
peacebuilding 141–142, 150–151; definition of 143; economic/social dimension 143; environmental peacebuilding in Israel–Palestine 146–147; military/security dimension 143; political/constitutional dimension 143; problems and challenges 144; psycho/social dimension 143; resilience in 145; in theory and practice 142–145; types 144; women and institution building in Iraq 148–149; and youth, in Lebanon 149–150
peacekeeping 92, 143, 335; security sector reform in Tunisia 145–146
People's Liberation Army Navy (PLAN) 77
People's Republic of China 21, 28–29, 193, 202; and economic progress 16; as external partner in the Nile region 217; foreign policy 24, 27; and global economy 17; and the Gulf 76–77; as Middle East's dominant trading partner 24–27; One Belt One Road (OBOR) initiative 24
Peres, Shimon 91
peri-urban agricultural parks 164
Persia: Twelver Shi'ism 321
Persian Gulf 27; US interests in 53, 59
Persian Iran 184
political economy 274; defensive modernization 261–262; developmental logic of Nasserism 263–265; failure of Oil Arabism 266–267; imperialism and resistance 261–265; oil and regional security 265–267; oil and state belligerence 270–271; oil and US global hegemony 271–272; politics of OPEC 265–266; rentier state 268–271; resource wars 272–273
political hybrid systems 287–288, 293, 299
political Islamists 293–295
political stability: and access to water 168, 234; and food insufficiency 173; and food security 186–190, 194, 208; and national security 175–176
political will 246; and cooperation on water issues 235–236; and CPET 243
politicization of water 234
politics of security 312
Popular Front for Liberation of Palestine (PFLP) 88
Popular Mobilization Units (PMU) 99
population displacement and refugees, in Iraq: effects of brain drain 102–103; future of 103; internal displacement 103
population growth: and big water challenge 158, 160–161; and food security 160–161, 173, 184; impacts of 263; and water crisis 169
population migration 253; forced migrants 253; security concerns 259–260
post-Arab Spring period 298

345

Index

post-Ottoman Empire period 5, 6
post-Ottoman order 34–35
Powell, Colin 72, 330
power struggle and competition 21–22
power vacuum in MENA region 21
Pratt, Nicola 335
proximate causes 34
proxy politics 211, 213
Putin, Vladimir 23, 43, 76, 164
Putnam, R.D. 278–279

Qaddafi, Muammar 40, 58, 311
al-Qaeda 22, 40, 41, 48, 59, 73, 120, 206, 207, 258, 271, 273, 289, 290, 294, 308
Qandil, Ala 332
Qatar 73; and Ethiopia 220; and Iran 309; and Muslim Brotherhood 309; overseas investments in agricultural land 218; and Syria 123
Qatar National Food Security Programme (QNFSP) 218
Qom 325
Quadrennial Defense Review of the American Department of Defense 182–183
quantitative water allocation 237

Rabin, Yitzhak 88
radical nationalism 62
Rafsanjani, Akbar Hashemi 71
Ramsbotham, Oliver 143
Rapid Deployment Force (RDF) 68
Rapid Deployment Joint Task Force (RDJTF) 68
Rathmell, Andrew 97
Reagan, Ronald 89, 267
Reagan administration 68, 114
realist peacebuilding 144
Red Sea dynamics in Nile hydropolitics 225–227
refugees 253, 255–259; Iraqi refugees 257–258; Palestinian refugees 256–257; restriction of, in European countries 259; Sabra refugee camp 89; Shatila refugee camp 89, 335; in Syria 190, 257, 258; and water and food security 174–175; in Yemen 190; *see also* displaced people; food refugees; forced migration; internally displaced people (IDP); population displacement and refugees, in Iraq
regional definition of Middle East 9
regional economic integration 20–21
regional hegemony 21, 22
regional order, disintegration of 30
regional security complex: definition of 9; Syria 113–115; theory 9, 212
religionization of politics 293–295
remittances 253, 254–255
rentier state: bonanza modernization 269–270; deterrence of democratization 269; regime stability and state weakness 268–269
research interests 4–6

resilient peacebuilding 145
resource curse hypothesis 268
resource wars 272–273; *see also* energy security; food security; water security
Rice, Condoleezza 73
ripeness concept 236, 240, 244, 246
River Basin Organizations (RBOs) 215, 240, 244
Riyadh 67, 74, 309; and Soviet Union 75–76
Roberson, B.A. 10
Rubin, Jared 280
Ruhani, Hasan 75
Russia 21, 23–24, 43; economy 24; foreign policy 23; and Iran 76; long-term challenges for 24; mediating Iraq-Kuwait war 69–70; military presence in Middle East 23; power gaps, US foreign policy ambiguity 23; power-projection in Syria 311; redistribution of power 23
Russian-Saudi Business Council 76

Sabra refugee camp 89
al-Sadat, Anwar 37, 91, 264, 267
al-Sadeq, Ja'far 321
al-Sadr, Muqtada: Mahdi Army of 102
Safavids 321
Said, Edward 334
Salafism 271, 293, 294–295
Saleh, Ali Abdullah 40, 59, 205, 206, 207, 290, 296, 303, 305, 309
Salman, Crown Prince Mohammad bin 309
Salman, Muhammad bin 76
Samarra Shrine, attack on 257
Al Sa'ud, King 'Abd al-'Aziz bin 'Abd al-Rahman 67, 74, 317, 320–321, 322, 325
Al Sa'ud, Prince Bandar bin Sultan 316, 317
Saudi Arabia 7, 8, 68, 99, 124, 169, 217, 226, 290, 309, 318; American oil interests in 53; demographic development of 20; and Ethiopia 220; financing of Afghan Mujahedin 271; food self-sufficiency scheme 183, 184, 196; groundwater abstraction 193–194; investment in agriculture abroad 218, 220; Islamic narratives and political action 319–320; and Kuwait 266; meat consumption 185–186; Nitaqat policy 255; political economy 271; remittances 254, 255; riyalpolitik 271; role in Middle East politics, and foreign policy 22; Al Sa'ud in 320; security complex 84; spreading of Wahhabi versions of Salafism 271; and United States 54, 267; and Yemen 205–206
Saudi–Iranian rivalry 39, 312, 316–317, 322
Saudi–UAE: engagement in Eritrea 228; military intervention in Yemen 46
Seale, Patrick 112
second *intifada see* al-Aqsa *intifada*
sectarianism 46, 97, 289, 319; and geopolitics 312–313
secularism 38

346

security-development nexus 8–9
security sector reform (SSR) 98, 100, 143;
  demilitarization, demobilization and
  reintegration (DDR) strategy 143, 145; in Iraq
  97; in Tunisia 145–146
September 2001 attacks *see* 9/11 attacks
"Seven Sisters" 265
sexual violence 328, 331–332
Shabak 105
Shabbiha 119
Shah of Iran 53–54, 322
al-Sham, Jabhat al-Nosra lil Ahl 121
al-Shanti, Jamila 334
Sharon, Ariel 114
Shatila refugee camp 89, 335
Shepherd, Laura 330, 333
Shia al-Houthi movements *see* Houthis
Shi'a militias 98–99
Shia Muslims 22, 309; and Sunni Muslims
  (*see* Sunni–Shi'a relations)
Shoukry, Sameh 221
Singapore, water security in 159
Sinjar, and ISIS 101
el-Sisi, Abdel Fattah 47, 90, 228, 304, 307
Sistani, Ali 99
Six-Day War 88
Skocpol, Theda 305
small water supply chain 159
social contracts 47; and trust 277–279
socio-psychological processes, for water issues 236
Somalia: nation-state crisis 288
Somaliland 226
Southern Separatist Movement 258
sovereignty, economic bases of 263–264
Soviet troops intervened in the civil war in
  Afghanistan 68
Spinneys 189
Sri Lanka: humanitarian aid 128–129; United
  Nations in 129
Standard Oil of California (SOCAL) 66–67
state-building processes 6, 90
state–security relationship 178
Stepan, Alfred 288
Sternberg, Troy 186–187, 188
Stokes, Doug 272
subsidies 20, 67, 116, 173, 183–184, 186, 188–189,
  202, 204–205, 277
Sudan 193–194, 217; and Gulf countries 218–220;
  investors/shareholders in key projects **219**; and
  Iran 220–221; and Nile 214, 215; and Saudi
  Arabia, agricultural agreement between 194;
  and Turkey 224
Suez crisis (1956) 42, 264; *see also* Arab–Israeli
  conflict
Sulaimani, Qasim 99
Sultan of Oman 54
Summit of Heads of State of the Nile Basin 215

Sundrop Farms 164, 165
Sunni Muslims: radicalization 39–40; and Shia
  Muslims (*see* Sunni–Shi'a relations)
Sunni–Shi'a relations 316–317; Arab uprisings and
  regional fragmentation 324–326; geopolitical
  approach 322–324; Islamic narratives and
  political action 319–322; politicization 39;
  religious and political 317–318; theological
  reflections 318–319
Sunnis Muslims: Arabs 98, 99, 100, 101, 103
Sunni Tribal Awakening 289
Susskind, L. E. 238
Swain, Ashok 205
Syria 4, 6, 8, 86, 87, 88, 92, 111, 303, 308; 2011
  uprising 118–123; agricultural management
  system in 189; 'Alawi networks 117; 'Alawis 119;
  alliance with Iran 115; alliance with the USSR
  112; as archetypical insecure state 112–118;
  brutalization of society of 122–123; civil society
  120; climate-related security risks 203–205; and
  Cold War 112; confessionalism and sectarian 124;
  counter-insurgency 118; crisis in 17, 43; cross
  border relief operations 132–133; Da'esh/the
  Islamic State 123; democracy and security forces
  305; droughts 191, 203–205; environmental
  sector 116; food aid 133; food refugees in 190;
  food security 189–190; humanitarian crisis
  127, 130–135, 325; human security 115–118;
  insecurity from above 118–119; and Iran–Iraq
  war 91; Islamist and Salafi jihadist extremist
  militants 121–122; Kurdish minority in 256;
  and Lebanon 115; mismanagement of natural
  resources 204–205; *mukhabarat* 116, 117, 304,
  312; nation-state crisis 288–289; new political
  actors 113; as new regional and international
  security problem 123–125; Palestinian refugees
  in 257; pan-Arab ideology 115; power resistance
  114; reactions to US policies 114; refugee crisis
  258; Regime's Ministry of Foreign Affairs
  132; regional security complex 113–115; rise
  of sectarianism/confessionalism 119; Russian
  intervention 124–125, 134; strategic parity 114;
  territorial fragmentation 120; unauthorized cross
  border aid response 132; underfunding 136; and
  United States 311; uprising 130; war of attrition
  121; waster mismanagement in 192; water and
  food security in 174; and Yemen 74
Syrian Arab Red Crescent (SARC) 131
Syrian civil war 21, 76, 88, 121, 123, 127, 146–147,
  174, 190, 203, 256, 307–308, 312; human rights
  violations in 258; and Turkey 21; and United
  States 58–59
Syrian Golan Heights 6
Syrian Kurdish groups 124
Syrian-Kurdish People's Protection Units 98
"Syrian Revolution 2011" (Facebook page)
  118, 120

Tabaq Dam 177
takfiri jihadis 321
Tal Afar, and ISIS 101
Tarakji, Ahmad 191
al-tawazon al-istrateji 114
taxes 277
Tbib, Shawqi 283
Tehran 22, 38, 42, 45–46, 67, 71–77, 267, 308, 309, 311, 321, 323, 324
Tel Aviv 227
Terminal High Altitude Area Defense (THAAD) systems 73
Thapar-Bjorkert, Suruchi 333
theorization of security 3–5
Thornberry, Emily 190
Tibi, Bassam 3
TIGEM (Turkish General Directorate of Agriculture Enterprises) 224
Tigris *see* Euphrates-Tigris river system
Tindall, James A. 182
transboundary river/waters 168, 170–171, 176, 237–238; cooperation on 20, 235; as hydropolitical security complex 212; *see also* Euphrates-Tigris river system
transformative peacebuilding 144
Trans World Airlines (TWA) 67
Treaty of Lausanne (1923) 34, 256
Treaty of Security and Cooperation (1980) 113
Trottier, J. 237
Trump, Donald 57, 59, 92, 297
Trump administration 47, 58, 63, 99, 310
trust 276; and human security 279–280; rebuilding of 280–281; and social contract 277–279
Tuastad, Dag 333
Tunisia 8, 142, 293, 303; civil society in 291, 296; consensus-building and good governance 281–283; democracy in 281–282, 299, 304; democracy and security forces 305; democratic transition in 290–291, 306; security sector reform in 145–146; Tunisian Confederation of Industry, Trade and Handicrafts (l'Union Tunisienne de l'Industrie, du Commerce et de l'Artisanat, UTICA) 281, 291; Tunisian General Labor Union (Union Générale Tunisienne du Travail, UGTT) 281, 291
Tunisian Confederation of Industry, Trade and Handicrafts (l'Union Tunisienne de l'Industrie, du Commerce et de l'Artisanat, UTICA) 281, 291
Tunisian General Labor Union (Union Générale Tunisienne du Travail, UGTT) 281, 291
Tunisian Human Rights League (LTDH) 291
Tunisian Institutional Reform (TIR) 146
Tunisian National Anti-Corruption Commission 282–283
Tunisian Order of Lawyers 291
Turabi, Hassan 219

Turkey 99, 256; African Expansion strategy 223; defensive aggressiveness 44; and democratic transition 307; and foreign policy 21–22; and Syria 124; and US diplomats, diplomacy among 243
Turkey, as a strategic partner in the Nile Basin 222; hydropolitical implications 225; Turkey-Egypt 222–223; Turkey-Ethiopia 223–224; Turkey-Sudan 224
Turkey-Africa Summit 223
Turn Down the Heat (World Bank report) 202, 205
Tuz Khurmato, and ISIS 101–102
Twelver Shi'ism 316, 319, 321

UGTT *see* Tunisian General Labor Union (Union Générale Tunisienne du Travail, UGTT)
uneven development, issues of 19–20
United Arab Emirates (UAE) 39, 69, 73, 226; food security 189; Kafala Sponsorship System 255; remittances 254; temporary labor migrants 255
United Kingdom (UK) 6, 42, 43, 53; dominance in the Gulf 66; and Israeli-Palestinian conflict 81
United Nations (UN): 2009–2010 Syria Drought Response Plan 204; codification of terms of post-war security in the Gulf 70; and confrontation between Hezbollah and Israel 89; Development Programme (UNDP) 150; effort to dismantle Iraq's weapons of mass destruction (WMD) programs 42; involvement in Israeli-Palestinian security complex 92–93; Iraqi disarmament 60; and Israeli-Palestinian conflict 82; Monitoring Group on Somalia and Eritrea 226; Office for the Coordination of Humanitarian Affairs (UNOCHA) 132, 137; Relief and Works Agency for Palestine Refugees in the Near East (UNRWA) 129; sanctions against Eritrea 226; Special Commission on Iraq (UNSCOM) 70, 72; in Sri Lanka 129; Supervision Mission in Syria 130; and Syria 130; "Whole of Syria (WoS) approach" 134
United States (US) 5, 6, 7, 28, 42–43, 48; 1991 Gulf War 54; and 2011 Egyptian revolution 59; addressing the problem of violence against women in war 332; and al-Qaeda 207; Army Corps of Engineers 68; attack on Yemen 207; Central Command (CENTCOM) 68, 69, 73; human rights in 330; International Violence Against Women Act 332; intervention in Iraq 304, 308; intervention in Syria's civil war 58–59; invasion of Iraq 38, 42, 56–57, 91, 272–273; and Israel 62–64; and Israeli-Palestinian conflict 84; -led no-fly zones 43; military training presence in Iraq 100; National Security Strategy (NSS) 56; nuclear non-proliferation 60–62; oil

and global hegemony 271–272; and Palestine 63–64; policy, evolution of 53–56; and popular uprisings in the Middle East 57–58; pro-Iraq War Democrats 56–57; -protected safe havens 43; relations with the GCC 74; role in the 2011 NATO intervention in Libya 58; and Saudi Arabia 67, 72; surrogate strategy 53–54; troops in the Middle East 59–60; US Air Force Airborne Warning and Control Systems (AWACS) aircraft 68; veto power in the UN Security Council 58; War Powers Act 54; weapons of mass destruction (WMDs) programs 56; and Yemen 59

United States (US), dominance in the Gulf: deterioration of 72–75; emergence of 66–68; during spring of 1987 68–69; zenith of 68–71

United States (US) policy: failure in Iraq 289; militarization of 57; priorities of 60; rogue state labeling 54–55; toward the Arabian Peninsula 73

USSR 58, 273; and the Gulf 75–76; and Israeli-Palestinian conflict 84

UTICA *see* Tunisian Confederation of Industry, Trade and Handicrafts (l'Union Tunisienne de l'Industrie, du Commerce et de l'Artisanat, UTICA)

Velayet-e Faqih doctrine 45
"Violence Free Schools Initiative" 150
violent insurgencies 49
violent internal repression 49
violent uprisings/revolutions 49; *see also specific uprisings*
virtual water 157, 164, 166, 218, 221

Waever, Ole 82–83, 212
al-Wahhab, Muhammad ibn 'abd 322
Wahhabism 39, 308–309, 316, 317, 319, 321, 322; weaponization of 39
War on Terror 310, 323, 330, 333
wars: of national liberation 49; over resources 49; *see also specific conflicts and wars*
water 200–201, 211; building adaptive capacity for 177–178; depoliticization of issues related to 243; desalination of sea water 159; governance of 238; integrated water resource management 235; mismanagement, as a threat to food security 192–193; politicization of 234; as religious symbolism 184; shared understanding 235; transboundary water cooperation 235–236
water diplomacy 235; entry points 239–243; formal diplomacy entry points 240–241; freedom of information 239; informal diplomacy entry points 242–243; linkage between tracks 243–247; linkages between tracks, strengthening and institutionalization of

245–246; shared technical knowledge platforms to formal and informal processes 246–247
water-energy-food (WEF) nexus 157, 165–166; agricultural potential 161; big water challenge 158–159; big water/food water security threats 161–163; big water supply chain 160; big water supply chain, alternatives to managing 164; farmers and big water/food–water 160; lessons from 164–165; population growth in the food bowls 160–161; small water supply chain 159; water security challenge 157–158
water scarcity 20, 146–147, 168–170, 235, 243
water security 234, 235, 243–244; in conflict-torn states 174–175; definition of 182; in energy poor states 178; international donors 178
water weapon 176
weapons of mass destruction (WMD) 42, 54, 56, 60, 70, 72, 122
Wedeen, Lisa 304
West Bank 6, 37, 62, 82, 84–85, **86**, 87, 90, 91, 298, 310, 329, 331, 333, 334; Israeli occupation of 63–64, 82, 129; Palestinian resistance campaign 82; technical water projects in 147; *see also* Oslo Accords
Westphalia security logics 4
wheat: exports 164, 183; imports 188; production 184, 186–187, 189–190, 192, 202, 218; subsidies 184, 188–189, 196, 204
Whitaker, Brian 277
"Whole of Syria (WoS) approach" 134
Wilson, Harold 53
Woertz, Eckart 97
Wolfers, Arnold 112
Women, Peace and Security (WPS) 148
World Bank 192, 202, 254, 277, 299
World Food Programme 131
World Food Summit 182
World Trade Organization (WTO), on intra-regional trade among the Arab states 20–21
World War I 5, 34, 322
World War II 53, 66

Xi Jinping 24, 77

Yahya, Maha 282
Yemen 4, 8, 169, 226; army 296; civil war in 59, 75, 258, 312; climate-related security risks in 205–207; democratic transition 304; food insecurities 190; food refugees in 190; Iran's assistance to Houthi rebels in 309; Iran's influence in 46; nation-state crisis 290; remittances 254; water and food security in 174; water scarcity 157
Yezidis 105; enslavement of women 105–106; *see also* Kurds
youth: and unemployment challenges 16–17
Youth Network for Civic Activism 150

Index

Zakah 194
Zartman, W.I. 236
al-Zawahiri, Ayman 40, 121
Zaydis 124
Zaydi Shi'a uprising 206

Zeitoun, M. 235
Zenawi, Meles 223, 228
Zionism 6
Zubair revolt 70
Zuesse, Eric 56